INVISIBLE MEN

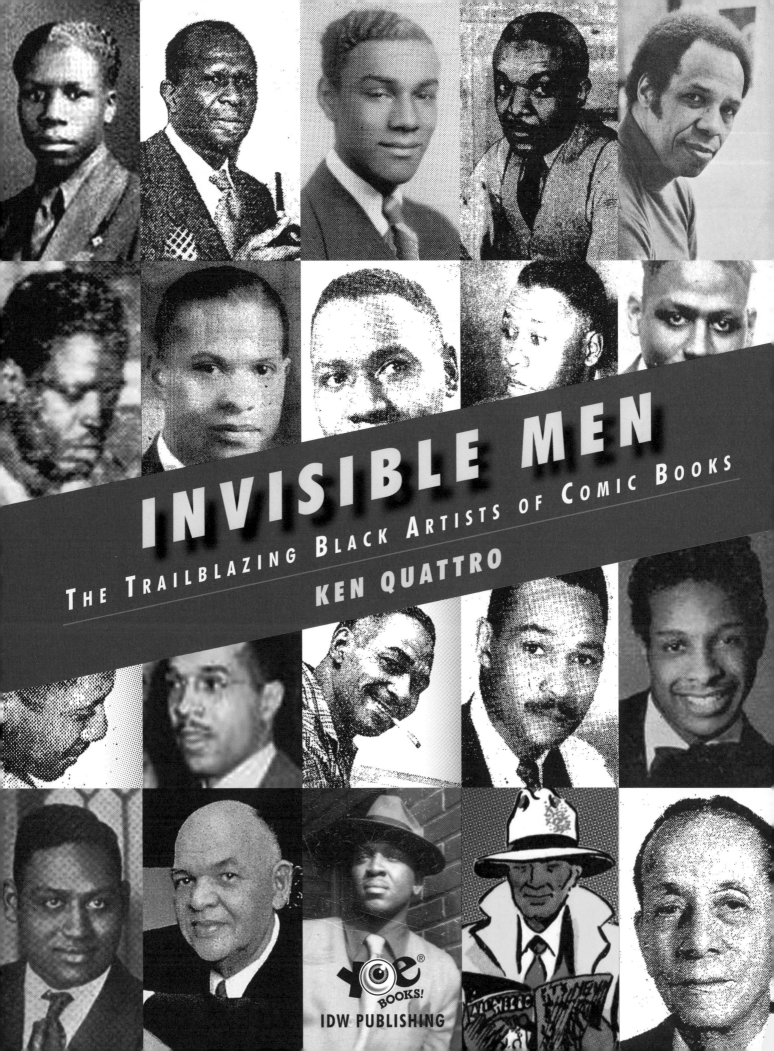

INVISIBLE MEN

THE TRAILBLAZING BLACK ARTISTS OF COMIC BOOKS

KEN QUATTRO

YOE BOOKS!

IDW PUBLISHING

DEDICATED TO PATTY.

SHE UNDERSTANDS.

ACKNOWLEDGMENTS

As with any undertaking of this scope, I couldn't have completed it without the invaluable help of many people.

First among those I wish to thank is Mr. Samuel Joyner. Mr. Joyner (and yes, I always refer to him with that honorific) started me on this project years ago when I wrote him in search of information regarding Elmer C. Stoner. Not only was Mr. Joyner's kind reply more than I expected, he supplied additional material that initiated my quest. I will forever be grateful to this wonderful man.

The groundbreaking historical research of Dr. Jerry Bails and Hames Ware, and their willingness to help me whenever needed, deserves recognition. Both men are now gone and I miss their friendship as well as their scholarship.

The rest of the people whom I want to acknowledge comprise a mind-boggling list of noted comics professionals, historians, and fans.

I wish to thank the late, great Al Feldstein for his remembrances about Matt Baker and the Iger shop. So too, Josef Rubenstein for his memories of Alvin Hollingsworth, Michael T. Gilbert for supplying Alex Toth's tribute to Alfonso Greene, and Will Murray for his interview with Walter Gibson.

At various points I was assisted by Allan Holtz with comic strip details, Rod Beck and Anthony Tollin for E.C. Stoner image scans, and Bill Schelly on multiple occasions.

Special thanks go to Wayne Smith of Warner Bros., who made it possible for me to use the Alfonso Greene story found in *Wonder Woman;* and to Jim Liubicich and the staff of the Cooper Union for the Advancement of Science and Art, who together searched for and found rare student information regarding Matt Baker.

Some who have gone above and beyond anything I could ever expect include: Dr. Michael Vassallo, for image scans and for being the source for anything related to Timely/Atlas comics; Ger Apeldoorn for Alvin Hollingsworth information and images; George Hagenauer for images of original artwork from his personal collection; Mikal Vollmer for the nearly impossible-to-find *Challenger* images; and Shaun Clancy, who supplied so many image scans and photos to me regarding Alvin Hollingsworth and Matt Baker. I cannot thank them all enough.

I especially want to thank Craig Yoe—publisher, editor, comics historian, and my friend. Without his guidance, encouragement, and occasional prodding, this book would never have seen print. His faith in this project made it all possible.

Finally, I want to thank my wife Patty. She is the one who puts up with my quirks and obsessiveness, and that is not an easy task.

The stories and art in this book are presented for historical purposes. Some aspects of this material are contemptible in regards to race, gender, and other issues, as we realize in our more enlightened times. The ignominious aspects of the content do not represent the views of Yoe Books or its associates.

Yoe Books thanks: Ho Che Anderson, Ger Apeldoorn, Cheryl Baker, Kyle Baker, Steve Banes, Stanford W. Carpenter, Gary Colombo, Sarah Feinsmith, William Foster III, Karen Green, George Hagenauer, Reginald Hudlin, Mike Howlett, John Jennings, Keith Knight, Peter Przysiezny, Calvin Read, Mark Seifert, Qiana Whitted, David Williams, and Joe Wos.

Yoe Books: Craig Yoe & Clizia Gussoni, Chief Executive Officers and Creative Directors • Jeff Trexler, Attorney • Mark Lerer, Peter Sanderson, and Steven Thompson, proofreaders

Randall Cyrenne, Copy Editor

Bill Stewart, Motion Graphics Artist

"I keep buying books from Yoe Books as gifts, then keeping them for myself! Check it out: YoeBooks.com!"
—Mark Hamill

To watch a video about *Invisible Men*, please go to bit.ly/3g1JawJ

IDW Publishing: Chris Ryall, President & Publisher/CCO • Cara Morrison, Chief Financial Officer • Matthew Ruzicka, Chief Accounting Officer • John Barber, Editor-in-Chief • Justin Eisinger, Editorial Director, Graphic Novels and Collections • Jerry Bennington, VP of New Product Development • Lorelei Bunjes, VP of Technology & Information Services • Jud Meyers, Sales Director • Anna Morrow, Marketing Director • Tara McCrillis, Director of Design & Production • Mike Ford, Director of Operations • Rebekah Cahalin, General Manager

Ted Adams and Robbie Robbins, IDW Founders

ISBN: 978-1-68405-586-9   23 22 21   2 3 4

CONTENTS

INTRODUCTION
Stanford W. Carpenter, PhD

This is a story about double lives and double consciousness.

It is the story of Black comic book creators. Men leading double lives, living on both sides of the color line, shifting between living in Black communities and working as cogs in a very White machine tasked with crafting fantastical stories. Black men working in an industry in which much of the work was unattributed, rendering their comings and goings all the more... invisible.

Ken Quattro's book provides an important context for addressing the relationships between Black and White people and Black and White cultural spaces. The term "color line" is often used to delineate the separation of Black and White spaces. These spaces are distinct with each space being associated primarily with Black or White culture. But these spaces are not absolute. They are not pure. They are not as separate as our collective imaginations would like to render them.

In the 1940s, comic books were in their infancy, an off-shoot of pulp magazines and newspaper strip anthologies circulating primarily among White readers. Comic books did not have the cultural cache that they have today. They were founded in large part by people who could not access more established publishing arenas. Back then, a *real cartoonist* created comic strips and editorial cartoons for newspa-pers and magazines. Still, comic books captured the national imagination with print runs in the hundreds of thousands containing a surreal mix of adventure, crime, horror, humor, and romance. And they were fantasies...about power, beauty, revenge, and desire...dominated by and created to center on White male protagonists and perspectives.

The color line is permeable. It is frequently crossed by people who bring with them aspects of the culture from which they previously occupied. And when they return or move on, they bring their skills and accumulated resources as well. So, what do we make of these invisible Black men leading double lives as unsung participants in the construction of White Power Fantasies, White Revenge Fantasies, White Beauty Standards, and White Desire?

W. E. B. Du Bois characterizes African-Americans as living in a state of double consciousness, "looking at one's self through the eyes of others, measuring one's soul by the tape of a world that looks on in amused contempt and pity." But what if we were to flip the script? What if we were to measure a White man's soul by the tape of a world of men and women whom he has rendered invisible?

The irony is that in comic books they have already done just that.

The Black men in this book were not the only comic creators living double lives as unsung participants in the construction of White Power Fantasies. Many comic creators were from immigrant groups who were not considered White at the time. These ethnic others who could not access more established publishing arenas found a creative outlet (and ready cash) in the burgeoning comic book industry. For example, Superman embodied an imagined Whiteness that Jerry Siegel and Joel Shuster, the two Jewish kids that created him, could not achieve in their lifetime. An imagined Whiteness with a Jewish sensibility that permeated the superhero genre as the character became the template for others.

Reconciling the Jewish influences on comic book images and narratives is still a relatively recent phenomenon. But taken alongside considerations of other ethnic and racial groups raises all kinds of questions about identity. Most importantly it highlights the processes and means by which all identity, including White identity with all of its allusions to purity, is ultimately a multicultural and multiethnic construction rooted in specific times…and places.

It is easy to get so caught up in the flashy colors and over the top narratives that we forget that comic books are artifacts that contain stories. Comic books are artifacts created by people engaged in creative processes…people with identities, lives, and stories that are at once separate from and intertwined with that which they create. Still, the enduring potential of an artifact is that once it is created it takes on an existence all its own. It moves through space and time, weaving in, out, and through the backgrounds and foregrounds of other stories that may or may not have anything to do with the stories that it contains.

Comic books offer stories of worlds with few limits. Yet, they are reined in by design, created with intent, and embedded in artifacts originally created with only White readers in mind. It didn't matter who created the comic books as long as the reader believed it was someone like them. After all, once the artifact was complete it could move on its own, rendering its creators invisible.

Space and time matter.

As the comic books move through space and time, they are less constrained by the original intent of their creation. We can look back at their artifactual journey and gain greater understanding.

Herein lies the contribution of Ken Quattro's book. His profiles of Black men who worked in what is an ostensibly White comic book industry lay bare the permeability of the color line. You see, once our notions of the separateness of spaces break down, we are confronted with a more dynamic world. One in which spaces dictate the terms of engagement as individuals move between and work within them. We get a framework to address a Black comic artist creating a comic strip for the Black Press who supplements his income by illustrating stories of a White male lord of the jungle that engage White power fantasies. Or a Black man making a living drawing idealized images of White women to satisfy the sexual desires of White men, some of whom would lynch a Black man for looking at an actual White woman.

Ultimately, this book exposes us to a hidden history that challenges readers to re-imagine both the origins of the images and stories that have shaped our world and the nature of our connections to them.

Enjoy!

—Stanford W. Carpenter, PhD is a Cultural Anthropologist, comics scholar, comics creator, and former archaeologist. He's on the advisory board and co-organizer of the Black & Brown Comix Art Festival. As a Pre-doctoral Fellow at the Smithsonian Institution, he conducted ethnographic research looking into identity in comics from the perspective of comic book creators. He has taught courses in anthropology, comics, journalism, and popular culture at University of Maryland, Johns Hopkins University, the Rhode Island School of Design, and the School of the Art Institute of Chicago. He has written on issues related to anthropology and identity in comics for Comics as Philosophy, *the* Greenwood Encyclopedia of Comics and Graphic Novels, Third Person: Authoring and Exploring Vast Narratives, What is a Superhero?, *and* Critical Approaches to Comics. *His recent comic work can be found in* Black Comix Returns *as well as* Cosmic Underground: A Grimoire of Black Speculative Fiction. *His comic art has been recently exhibited at Harvard University and Monmouth University. He is featured in an entry in the* Encyclopedia of Black Comics.

SEEING THE UNSEEN

Ken Quattro

I am an invisible man. No, I am not a spook like those who haunted Edgar Allan Poe; nor am I one of your Hollywood-movie ectoplasms. I am a man of substance, of flesh and bone, fiber and liquids—and I might even be said to possess a mind. I am invisible, understand, simply because people refuse to see me.

—Ralph Ellison,
prologue to Invisible Man *(1952)*

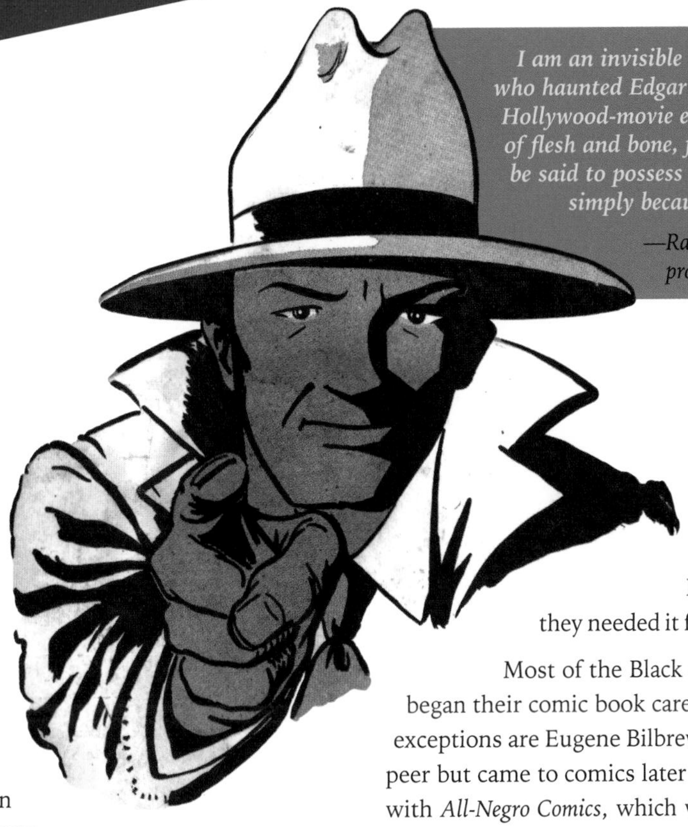

I came to this project by way of my interest in comic books, a seemingly trivial passion for an adult. I long ago realized that this medium, this industry, had a place in American culture as legitimate and rich as any other art form. It has imposed itself upon America, becoming as integral to its zeitgeist, and as much a part of its vocabulary as popular music, television, or film. Moreover, when viewed in its proper context, particularly in the early years during its so-called "Golden Age," the comic book "world" was a microcosm of the country at large.

Struggling out of the Great Depression, starving fine artists, under-employed illustrators, and cartoonists on the downside of their careers worked side-by-side with immigrants' kids just learning how to hold a pen. It was the ultimate level playing field that allowed even the most disenfranchised among the populace to participate.

Of course, being a business, this exhibition of egalitarianism wasn't just a product of benevolence. Necessity demanded it. By the end of the 1930s, comics had eclipsed the popularity of most other forms of printed entertainment. Publishers needed product, they needed it fast, and they wanted it cheap.

Most of the Black creators profiled in this book began their comic book careers during World War II. The exceptions are Eugene Bilbrew, who was their generational peer but came to comics later in life, and the ones involved with *All-Negro Comics*, which was unique unto itself. Some made it into the industry prior to America's entry into the war, such as Adolphus Barreaux, who entered the field before Superman came on the scene, but the numbers were small. The war provided an opportunity to Blacks that they may otherwise have been denied. It was an ironic development shared with women on the home front.

I didn't know how ignorant I was until I began this project. Much of what I learned came from Black publications, as contemporaneous White ones didn't carry the information I sought. I learned who Miss Ann and Mister Charley were, and what an ofay is. I was educated as to the source and significance of the Double "V" Campaign, and the repeated efforts—and repeated failures—to pass a federal anti-lynching law.

Another society existed outside the notice of the White majority, a separate culture they glimpsed in jazz clubs or stage shows. For the most part, the only daily interaction between the races came when porters retrieved baggage or cleared the dirty dishes off tables.

While Whites got along just fine without immersing themselves into the world of Blacks, Blacks didn't have that option. William Edward Burghardt "W. E. B." Du Bois described it as a "double-consciousness," which he explained in his classic 1903 essay, *The Souls of Black Folk*:

...the Negro is a sort of seventh son, born with a veil, and gifted with second-sight in this American world,—a world which yields him no true self-consciousness, but only lets him see himself through the revelation of the other world. It is a peculiar sensation, this double-consciousness, this sense of always looking at one's self through the eyes of others, of measuring one's soul by the tape of a world that looks on in amused contempt and pity. One ever feels his twoness,—an American, a Negro; two souls, two thoughts, two unreconciled strivings; two warring ideals in one dark body, whose dogged strength alone keeps it from being torn asunder. [Du Bois, W. E. B., *The Souls of Black Folk: Essays and Sketches*, 1903, p.3]

While Du Bois' words spoke to the struggle for reconciliation felt internally by Blacks, their external dual existence was evidenced in the lives covered by this book. There was little to no interaction between the Black comic book artists and their White peers. Other than Matt Baker, who had some White friends, there were only a few vague recollections by Whites of Black colleagues. Even then, they spoke of crossing paths incidentally. Research made apparent that even in the melting pot environment of the "sweat shop" comic book studios, Black artists and writers kept their distance, either choosing or required to work outside the studios' close confines at home or in studios of their own.

To give historical boundaries to the world these men knew places them in a period between Reconstruction and World War II. For Blacks, it was a time of ascension, to try and obtain an equal place in American society, to define themselves as both a group and as individuals. It was a time that witnessed the rise of the Ku Klux Klan, the emergence of the Lost Cause, forced segregation, and lynching as "justice." It was also the time that saw the formation of the NAACP, the Harlem Renaissance, Marcus Garvey's Pan-Africa movement, and the Great Migration of Blacks from the South.

The Black comic book artists were part of the "New Negro Movement" promoted by philosopher Dr. Alain LeRoy Locke and others. This called for the assertion of Black identity and culture and placed it on the Young Negro to carry out these goals in his poetry, his art, his education,

and his new outlook. [Locke, Alain, "Enter the New Negro," *Survey Graphic*, March 1925]

The first signs of this appeared in the 1920s and '30s. Black artists began exhibiting their artwork in coordinated shows, the Spingarn Medal and Harmon Award were created to honor their efforts, and cartoonist Elmer Simms Campbell made the leap into White media. Campbell was the direct inspiration and friend to several of the men in this volume, and the story of his beginnings contained much of their same experience.

Campbell did his art school training in Chicago, then returned to his hometown of St. Louis to begin his career; but like so many before and so many after, he would find it wasn't that easy.

St. Louis, as far as the Negro is concerned, is a southern city. The traditions of the South did not admit the Negro commercial artist. And failing to find employment in his field, Campbell sought and found a job on a dining car as a waiter.

It is generally known that Negro artists, particularly commercial artists, are barred from jobs in this field purely because of color. But young Mr. Campbell did not let that fact deter him. He deliberately went ahead and studied art at St. Louis and Chicago, and then tried his luck in New York. [Elmer, A. Carter, "E. Simms Campbell—Caricaturist," *Opportunity*, March 1932, pp.82-85]

...there was no precedent in New York for hiring a colored man to draw comic cartoons of white people and pay him handsomely for his work. Colored men have worked on daily newspapers in New York before, but not in the art department. Most colored artists are urged to draw their own people, and not just people. It seems not to be logical to a white man that a Negro can see humor in him and might then depict it and thereby amuse the white man just as a white artist could. [Floyd, J. Calvin, "Calvin's Digest," *Pittsburgh Courier*, April 2, 1932]

After struggling for about a year to get a job in his chosen profession, Campbell met a White cartoonist named Ed Graham. Impressed with Campbell's work, Graham began taking him around to various editors until he started making sales. Most of the later Black comic book artists would similarly use the agency of comic book art studios (aka "shops") to serve as a buffer between them and comics editors and publishers.

It must be noted, parenthetically, that Campbell wasn't the first, nor the most successful, Black cartoonist. Both categories he would have to concede to George Herriman, the creator of *Krazy Kat*. For comic strip aficionados, *Krazy Kat* needs no introduction. It was one of the greatest comic strips of all time, a deceptively simple, surrealist fantasy centered upon a bizarre love triangle: the Krazy of its title; Ignaz the brick-throwing mouse, whom Krazy loved without reason; and Offissa Pupp, who yearned for Krazy's love unrequitedly. A strange, but genius, creation.

Herriman was born in New Orleans and at the time of his 1880 birth, both he and the rest of his family bore the mixed-racial designation of "mulatto." It was an archaic term, rooted in colonial times, to describe a person with both Black and White ancestry. Many "mulattoes" were lumped with Blacks when it came to the perceptions of society, but those whose skin coloring was light enough to "pass" as White often did so. Herriman, throughout his life and on every legal document, identified himself as White. He not only wasn't held as an example to aspiring Black cartoonists, they probably never even knew he was part Black.

Comics are a Frankenstein's monster, forcing together both the most aesthetic and the most grotesque that humankind has to offer into one body, one product. This was even more so in the old days, during the so-called "Golden Age," the era spotlighted within this book. The disharmony was even more egregious then, when one considers that the finished product was marketed to children and the childlike, and sold for a dime.

Low requirements begat low expectations. Publishers and editors had more love for the fast and prolific than the artisan painstakingly crafting each panel, who slowed the production line and missed deadlines. As a result, the artists who came with fine art training often had difficulty converting their talent into comic book form. This applied across racial lines.

"Serious" artists, such as Elmer C. Stoner, Robert Pious, Elton Fax, and others, were revered and respected in the fine art world, but never revealed the full extent of their skills within the constraints of comics. It is my belief that some struggled to achieve the lowbrow look they assumed the comic book editors desired. "Dumbing down" their talent was harder than it seemed.

As the history of comic books has been mostly written by its fans, it has been a victim of fan preferences and genre prejudice. Matt Baker is acknowledged as one of the greatest art talents to ever work in the medium, not just as the greatest Black artist. But even his legacy is buoyed by the subjects he drew. He excelled at drawing the female form; "cheesecake" it was called, beautiful women displayed with little more purpose than to catch the eye of the male buyer.

That has maintained over time, as now the comics he drew fetch astronomical prices on the collector's market.

The other artists in this book were not Baker's inferiors, but it requires a step back to see that. I've tried hard to avoid the myopic view of a fan, something I hope is clear from my text.

My goal with each person profiled in this book is to provide context for their lives, the environment that formed them. There is a tendency to reduce a life to what a person does for money. One of the first questions asked when meeting a stranger is, "So, what do you do for a living?"—as if the entirety of a person's hopes and dreams, tragedies and triumphs, beliefs and experience, is contained in their answer. That is social reductio ad absurdum. We know the whole of ourselves to be greater than a part, yet it's a courtesy denied to others.

The lives I've chosen to outline herein are lives that for the most part have lingered unexamined. Each man, and it was only men I've found to this point, touched upon the comic book medium in his own way. For most, it was a paycheck—an additional income for a painter or a hungry artist out of work, often a brief stop along a career in commercial art or as a syndicated cartoonist. That was true, though, for most who worked in the comic book industry during its "Golden Age." For a few others, it was a career.

What set these men apart was that the pigmentation of their skin defined their opportunities. Circumstance, i.e. wartime, provided a crack in a wall that these men may never have hurdled otherwise. Inherent prejudices and institutional racism were lines that couldn't be previously crossed at all, and these continued to be impediments they faced and dealt with in many aspects of life, not just in their employment.

Certainly, that is the tie that binds, but each person's story is unique. They are all owed the respect to have their stories told factually. To tell their stories honestly, without rash speculation, without prejudice or agenda—I consider that my obligation.

Why does this all matter now? Why do these men matter today? After all, for most, their achievements in the comic book medium were relatively minor, even to them. Yet, they took that all-important first step, the one that everyone fears most. Quietly, they provided diversity to an industry before anybody was aware that was even a goal, let alone a possibility.

Without Elmer Stoner, there may not have been Matt

Baker. Without Matt Baker, there may never have been Keith Pollard, or Billy Graham, or Trevor Von Eeden. There surely wouldn't have been the sixteen Golden Legacy volumes (first published from 1966 to 1976, and still sold today), which told tales of Black history in comics form, and counted several Black Golden Age artists among their creators. And without all that preceded, that began with these few men, there would have been no Black-controlled Milestone Comics, nor a realization by the large comic book publishers that there were other voices to be heard, and diverse, underserved readerships to be served.

I don't consider myself to be a historian. I don't have post-nominal letters after my name or diplomas hanging on my walls, proclaiming I passed the classes to justify the title. I am a researcher, an armchair detective who hunted for factual information rather than relied upon apocryphal storytelling, conjecture, and fading memories. When any of that has crept into this book, I have tried to frame it so that you know its source.

I have striven to let the facts stand by themselves. That is why, in most cases, I've used primary sources—newspaper articles, contemporaneous publications, official documents, etc.—whenever possible. I've supplemented with autobiographies and interviews when no other means of obtaining information is available, but always with the caveat that the information has been filtered through another. If I am forced to make a guess, it is where the facts have taken me and, in those cases, I try to make my reasons clear.

The mountain of information I collected had to be pared down into digestible bites; therefore I made the tough choices: what to include, what to leave out. Subsequently, these biographies are intentional sketches, not finished portraits. My hope is that this book is not the final word, but an inspiration for more research.

A stylistic note: our language is as fickle as our constantly changing perspectives. What is accepted at one point in history, is shunned and reviled in another. African-American. Negro. Colored. All have been considered proper descriptions within living memory, within my lifetime. To avoid the dance of what is acceptable, I've settled on the inclusivity granted by the term "Blacks." Conversely, I've also chosen to use the term "Whites" when describing the dominant race of people of European descent, unless it comes in a quote or citation. I'm completely aware that many, if not most, Whites don't look at themselves in the aggregate. They—we—tend to separate into national or cultural identities. But that is not how they are generally viewed by Blacks. Whites are a monolithic presence to most Blacks, and to properly convey that perspective, I've gone with the term throughout this book.

There is one word that refers to Black people I find so offensive that when I need to quote it as part of a book title, I use asterisks.

This is a study of men with a common cultural and racial background whose lives met at the nexus of the comic book industry. Call it comic book history, call it Black history. Ultimately, it is a slice of human history, relatable on multiple levels.

ADOLPHUS BARREAUX GRIPON
[Adolphe Leslie Barreaux]
Visible Man, Invisible Pioneer

Color is a matter of perception. It depends upon how light falls upon a surface and upon how our brain processes the information it receives from our eyes. Color is subjective. Color is open to suggestion and to prejudice.

The word "mulatto" has an etymology rooted in antiquity and lost to history; it is a word with vague definitions, basically describing a biracial person; it is a term that birthed other such descriptive terms as quadroon and octoroon, each signifying increasingly indeterminate gradations of how much Black blood "tainted" the White blood of a person. Mulatto is a word reeking of racism and a word once given value by the United States census.

The Census Bureau began using the term "mulatto" with its 1850 head count, instructing the census-takers to apply it to people as they saw fit.

...censuses create the official language and taxonomy of race and imbue them with the authority of the state. Census racial policy defines the meaningful categories, locates boundaries between groups, assigns people to one category or another, and indicates which groups are subsets of or superordinate in relation to one another. [Hochschild, Jennifer & Powell, Brenna, "Racial Reorganization and the United States Census 1850-1930: Mulattoes, Half-Breeds, Mixed Parentage, Hindoos, and the Mexican Race," *Studies in American Political Development*, 2008; 22 (1) :59-96]

The institution of slavery in the Southern states led to the proliferation of mixed race children, often fathered through rape of Black women by White slave owners. In South Carolina alone, it was estimated that by 1860, fully three-quarters of the free Black residents of Charleston were classified as mulattoes.

The Gadsdens of Charleston were one family falling within this grayest of racial areas. The family head was James, a freedman even prior to the Civil War and a barber by trade, as was his father before him.

Howard University sociologist Elijah Horace Fitchett undertook a study of the Black freedmen in antebellum Charleston. His study, published in 1940, detailed the qualities that defined this group.

In the latter part of the eighteenth and during the first part of the nineteenth centuries there emerged in Charleston a relatively economically independent group of free Negroes. They were primarily the artisans of the system. [Fitchett, Horace *The Journal of Negro History*, 1940]

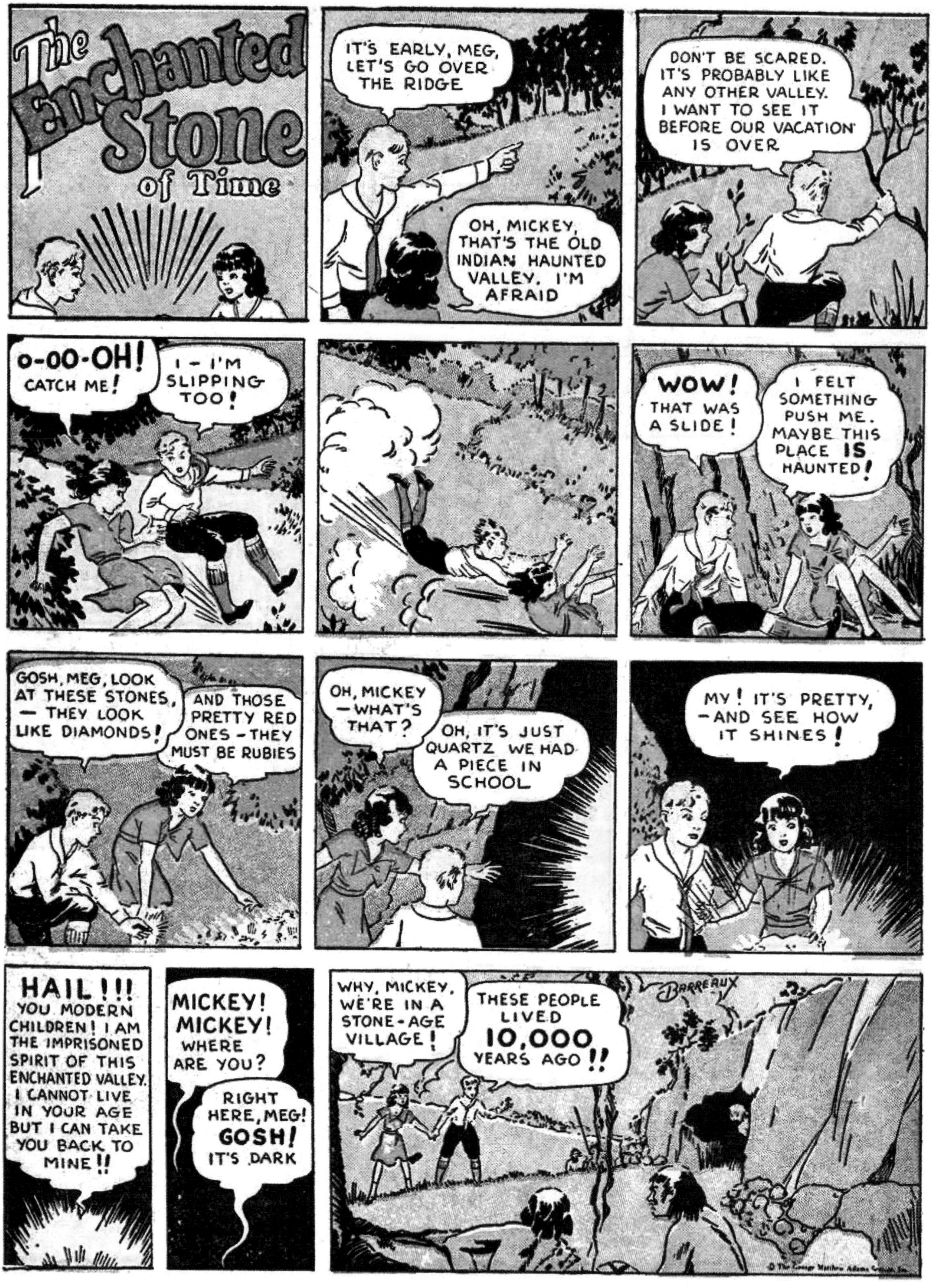
The Enchanted Stone of Time
IT'S EARLY, MEG, LET'S GO OVER THE RIDGE
OH, MICKEY, THAT'S THE OLD INDIAN HAUNTED VALLEY. I'M AFRAID
DON'T BE SCARED. IT'S PROBABLY LIKE ANY OTHER VALLEY. I WANT TO SEE IT BEFORE OUR VACATION IS OVER
O-OO-OH! CATCH ME!
I - I'M SLIPPING TOO!
WOW! THAT WAS A SLIDE!
I FELT SOMETHING PUSH ME. MAYBE THIS PLACE IS HAUNTED!
GOSH, MEG, LOOK AT THESE STONES, — THEY LOOK LIKE DIAMONDS!
AND THOSE PRETTY RED ONES - THEY MUST BE RUBIES
OH, MICKEY —WHAT'S THAT?
OH, IT'S JUST QUARTZ WE HAD A PIECE IN SCHOOL
MY! IT'S PRETTY, -AND SEE HOW IT SHINES!
HAIL!!! YOU MODERN CHILDREN! I AM THE IMPRISONED SPIRIT OF THIS ENCHANTED VALLEY. I CANNOT LIVE IN YOUR AGE BUT I CAN TAKE YOU BACK TO MINE!!
MICKEY! MICKEY! WHERE ARE YOU?
RIGHT HERE, MEG! GOSH! IT'S DARK
WHY, MICKEY, WE'RE IN A STONE-AGE VILLAGE!
THESE PEOPLE LIVED 10,000 YEARS AGO!!
BARREAUX

Among the most common occupations in this group were carpenter, tailor, shoemaker, seamstress, and the most common of all, barber. According to Fitchett, it was a class-conscious group.

Now the question may be asked, what were the attitudes of this class to other groups in the community? As I envisage it, their behavior was a replica of that class in white society which they aspired to be like. [Ibid.]

The Gadsdens indeed showed signs of prosperity. By 1880, along with James and his wife Charlotte, the household held their oldest daughter and her lawyer husband, another daughter who was a schoolteacher, a son who was apprenticing as a barber, and their own live-in domestic servant.

There was also the addition of an adopted girl named Georgiana Little, who, like the rest of the Gadsden family members, was listed as being a mulatto. A check of 1877 voting records reveals that the only families with the last name of "Little" found in Charleston were White. One of those was headed by a man named George Little, who owned the George Little & Co. clothing store down on King Street—a store that most likely employed seamstresses.

It is perhaps noteworthy that Charlotte Gadsden, James' wife, had the listed occupation of "mantua-maker" in the 1870 census. Charlotte had learned sewing from her mother, who also worked as a seamstress. A mantua-maker was a cut above the average seamstress, specializing in elegant gowns in a style popularized during Colonial times. Did Charlotte work for George Little? There is no documented proof, but it is a reasonable theory that Charlotte may have been Georgiana's mother and that George Little was her father. Regardless of whether the girl's mother was Charlotte or an unknown person, it seems evident that Little found himself in a quandary. He was a White man who, even though he gave the girl his last name, couldn't bear the social stigma that came with having her live in his home.

In another home in Charleston lived the Gripons. Perhaps not as prosperous as the Gadsdens, Clarence Gripon worked as a tailor, just as his father did. While he may have hoped his sons would follow him into that trade, at least one son, Adolphus, did not. He became a wheelwright.

In their early years, modern American comic books were generally comprised of reprinted comic strips, such as Barreaux's *The Enchanted Stone of Time*, which ran in newspapers in 1935–1936. It was later reprinted in *The Comics* #6, February 1938, Dell Publishing.

Born in 1870, Adolphus Barreaux Gripon married Georgiana Little in 1897 (some sources say 1895) and she gave birth to two children: daughter Helena and, on January 9, 1899, son Adolphus, named after his father.

The family didn't survive intact for long. On October 18, 1899, Adolphus Senior was killed by hemorrhagic typhoid fever. Faced with having to raise two young children, one an infant, Georgiana, aka "Georgie," took jobs as a seamstress, the same occupation as her mother and grandmother.

Georgie had to petition the court to gain control of her husband's estate. Even so, the next decade was difficult. She eventually had to move from the home the family was renting at 36 Alexander Street, and in 1909, the county seized a building they owned for non payment of taxes going back two years and sold it at auction. The hardships must have taken their toll on Georgie. It's not clear how it came about, but by his early teens, son Adolphus was living with his aunt Eugenia Gripon Steele, the married sister of his father. No further mention of his mother Georgie has been found until she reemerges in his life years later. In any case, neither she nor either of her children were buried near the elder Adolphus in Unity and Friendship Society Cemetery with the rest of the Gripon relatives.

Still, in later years, the younger Adolphus remembered this portion of his childhood fondly:

…so many simple pleasures of local interest: Washington Day parade; Friday Dress Parade on Citadel Green, easily accessible from everywhere; Metz Band concerts on South Battery on Wednesday evenings in the summer; September 'Gala Week,' a ballyhoo-shouting carnival on Calhoun Street from the Monument down to Anson, nightly lined with multicolored flares—a child's wonderland…and big, delicious groundnut-molasses cakes for a penny. [Barreaux, Adolphe, "Barreaux Reflects on Old Charleston," *Charleston News and Journal*, Dec. 13, 1973]

While living with his aunt, the boy developed typhoid, the same disease that felled his father. The family doctor advised he be moved to a less-humid climate, so when he was 15, newly-divorced Aunt Eugenia took Adolphus and moved in with her sister Marie in New York City. It would be a new life for them all. Not only had they left behind the humidity, they also left behind the mulatto designation. From then on, they would claim to be White.

There was one more change. Adolphus Barreaux Gripon began using the name Adolphe Leslie Barreaux. In many ways, he was reborn.

A name change was a simple matter in those days. There were as yet no Social Security numbers assigned to a person at birth, and immigrants with tongue-twisting names had for years been altering them to more easily pronounceable Anglo-Saxon versions in order not to draw attention to their ethnic origins. Changing your race was a bit more difficult, but not much. Many Blacks who were born with lighter complexions took advantage of it and "passed" for White. The benefits for being able to do so were undeniable, but there were risks as well.

Blacks who were able to "cross the color line" were rewarded with better jobs and economic opportunities. That was a given. It was a reality that Blacks during the Jim Crow era acknowledged, but not without resentment. It was a situation that some Whites feared, so much so that they employed "submarine Negroes" to spot those who were passing. One city so inclined to hire such racial monitors was Washington, D.C.

There are no less than five theatres, one hotel, and three exclusive stores which are now employing colored men and women to 'spot' colored customers and patrons who are fair enough to be mistaken for white. These "spotters" report to the management any person who is known to be colored and service is forthwith refused." ["Spotting 'Passers' is New Vocation in Nation's Capital," *Baltimore Afro-American*, June 7, 1930, p.2]

The consequences for a Black trying to pass went even beyond the refusal of service. One news story recounted the case of a light-skinned Black doctor in Baltimore who rented a home in an area of the city that was designated exclusively White. He lived there for months before it was found out he was Black when he tried to purchase the house. The city court ruled he had to forfeit the purchase and move. ["Would-be White Man Found to be a Negro," *Baltimore Afro-American*, Sept. 29, 1917, p.1]

Yet, the advantages outweighed the disadvantages in the minds of many Blacks—including, it's assumed, Barreaux.

In January 1916, Barreaux graduated from Public School 44 in the Bedford-Stuyvesant section of Brooklyn, and moved on to the all-boys DeWitt Clinton High School in Manhattan. By all accounts he was an exceptional student, resulting with his acceptance into Yale, providing the first step along the route that the rest of his life would take.

At Yale, Barreaux majored in fine art and Elizabethan English. He made the school's fencing team, wrote and sold his first piece of fiction, and reportedly worked for an advertising agency during school breaks. He was also a member of the university's Cosmopolitan Club, a private social club dedicated to fostering understanding and fraternity between foreign and American students in order to promote international cooperation and peace. Barreaux's involvement with the Cosmopolitan Club allowed him to develop friendships and make connections among his Eli classmates. Notably, he likely never would have experienced this valuable interaction if his cohorts knew he was Black.

Barreaux wasted no time launching his career. While his first professional writing was on a short story entitled "Hunch," appearing in the pulp magazine *Breezy Stories* vol. 11 #4 (Feb. 1921), his next sale wouldn't occur until after he left Yale, in a tale bearing the titillating title of "On the Trail of Dope," for *Mystery Magazine* vol. 7 #163 (Sept. 1, 1924). That same year he showed his more serious side with the publication of an essay for the highly influential fine art magazine, *International Studio* on "The Art of the Mayas," a result of the interest in archeology he developed while at Yale.

Though these sales may have indicated his interest in a writing career, Barreaux actually followed a different path. By 1925, he had opened the Leslie Barreaux Studio at 244 5th Avenue in Manhattan. It seems while at Yale, Barreaux added an additional layer of obfuscation to his past. He began using the name "Adolphe Leslie de Griponne Barreaux," providing an exotic, old-European flair to his given name. To his school chums he was simply known as "Leslie," leading to the name he gave to his art studio.

By the end of that year, the young artist had taken on a partner and, under the name of the Barreaux-Lippert Company, was running a classified ad seeking a solicitor for help selling advertising for a "new publication with wide field and no competition." ["Advertising Solicitors," *New York Times*, Nov. 17, 1925]

His personal illustration career was burgeoning as well. His work appeared in national weeklies such as *Collier's* and *Liberty Magazine,* and all the while he was still making the occasional story sale to the "girlie" pulp, *Snappy Stories*.

Pulp magazines derived their name from the cheap, rough-edged paper that they were printed upon. Their content varied, but among the most popular were those aimed at men, with heart-pounding stories of adventure and derring-do, starring merciless vigilantes and almost all featuring near-naked damsels in distress, obligingly reproduced on lurid covers that competed at pushing the limits of taste and censorial tolerance. Some pulps made no pretense of

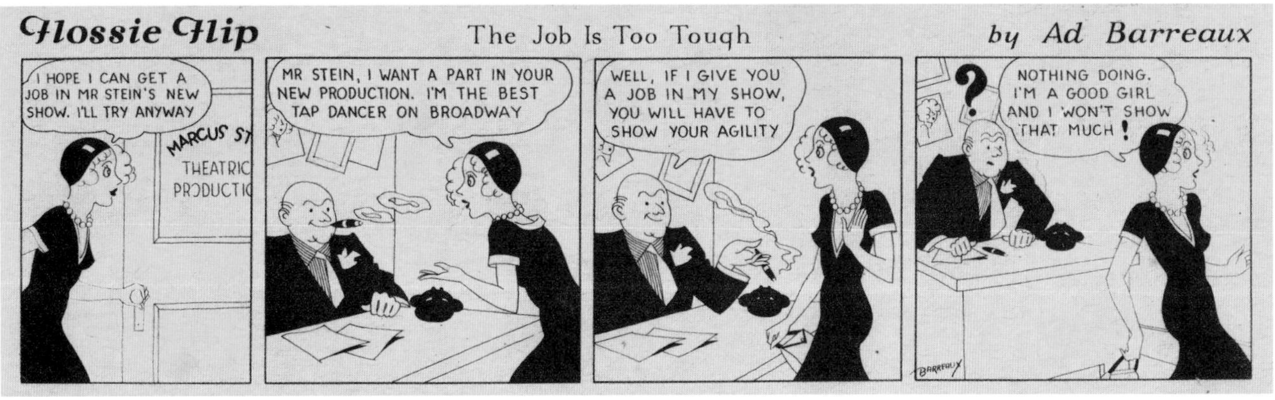
Flossie Flip
The Job Is Too Tough
by Ad Barreaux
I HOPE I CAN GET A JOB IN MR STEIN'S NEW SHOW. I'LL TRY ANYWAY
MARCUS ST
THEATRIC
PRODUCTI
MR STEIN, I WANT A PART IN YOUR NEW PRODUCTION. I'M THE BEST TAP DANCER ON BROADWAY
WELL, IF I GIVE YOU A JOB IN MY SHOW, YOU WILL HAVE TO SHOW YOUR AGILITY
?
NOTHING DOING. I'M A GOOD GIRL AND I WON'T SHOW THAT MUCH!
BARREAUX

their intentions, and blatantly displayed women in suggestive poses both on their covers and totally nude on their interior pages. These were the "girlie" pulps, the ones to which Barreaux contributed.

Toward the end of the 1920s, Barreaux seemed on track to great success. In an era that treated illustrators and cartoonists as celebrities, his name made regular appearances in gossip columns and on society pages. Sometimes it was as a groomsman at a Yale friend's wedding, or playing a tennis match at a Catskills' resort, but most often it was his funny yarns or witty bon mots that provided fodder for the columnists. One example reads:

Adolphe Barreaux, the illustrator, wants to know whether money stolen by absconding bookkeepers is charged to running expenses. ["Left at the Post," *New York Evening Post*, Nov. 18, 1929]

He was even one participant in a public feud with *Brooklyn Daily Eagle* columnist Rian James, supposedly over their disagreement about the treatment of women by artists. It had been precipitated by published comments from Barreaux stating that "women are created for petting and pettiness," "no man doing creative work should marry unless as an expensive luxury," and "these tales of wives being an artist's inspiration are just sentimental garbage." ["Women Called a Luxury by Noted Painter," *United Press*, Jan. 1, 1930]

James wrote:

Adolphe Barreaux, artist, illustrator, studio tyro and expert swordsman, takes exception to our recent column on the unfortunately large number of artists who demand sociability as well as adaptability from young ladies who are forced to model for a living."

Barreaux's response began:

In your choice bit today about the perils of girls in artists' studios you displayed all the sapience of a half-wit with a disordered imagination. You must have been reading Sloppy Stories. Speaking for myself and the rest of the illustrators, let me tell you that the girls who pose for us are safer than those in any other field of work. The public's idea of high jinks [sic] inside the studios is fed by just such journalistic pantaloons as you, who print such drivel." [Rian James, "Reverting to Type," *Brooklyn Daily Eagle*, April 25, 1930]

The outrage and response, whether real or faked, was based upon Barreaux's very public reputation with women. The year before, he set out on a personal quest to find the "ideal" female to pose for a painting he was planning. His trek around the nation was detailed in an article syndicated to small town newspapers everywhere and written by the artist himself.

Country girls have 'It.' The artificial life of the city girls make[s] them undesirable for the beautiful paintings which go to all parts of the country. Complexion is one of the model's greatest assets and we must go to the country for 'it,' and when I say 'It' I mean that intangible yet vital quality which makes one girl stand out above all others. ["Farm Girls Best Models Says Famous Illustrator," June 13, 1929]

It is unlikely that Barreaux's model search journeyed north of 110th Street into Harlem. Of all the quips and quotes attributed to Barreaux or the columns tracking his carefree lifestyle, none mentioned any involvement with Black writers or artists, peers of his who were participants in the ongoing Harlem Renaissance. In retrospect, his avoidance of all things related to Blacks and their culture comes close to total rejection of them.

On the face of it, Barreaux had made the correct career choice by determining to declare himself White. The color line even extended around the art community, as Black artists found that even they were subject to segregation and isolation.

From 1900 to 1925 Negroes generally had to make their own opportunities in the Fine Arts. They had to wrangle opportunities for study and travel and literally wheedle their way into the studios of white master artists under whom they wished to study. Later, to exhibit their work, they were forced to use the churches, the vestibules and reading rooms of public libraries and YMCA buildings, or the classrooms of public school buildings. [Porter, James, "Negro Artists Gain Recognition After Long Battle," *Pittsburgh Courier*, July 29, 1950]

Barreaux's *Flossie Flip* appeared in *Police Gazette* on September 5, 1933 (Police Gazette Corporation). This was the first issue of the revived scandalous pink-papered tabloid that had ended publication in 1932. The *Gazette* was bought by Harry Donenfeld, an unrepentant pornographer and the future publisher of *Superman*. He installed Merle Williams Hershey as editor. She was a pulp writer and editor, and the estranged wife of legendary writer/editor Harold Hershey, who figured prominently in the early days of pulp and comics publishing. Donenfeld's ownership didn't last long, however, as the *Gazette* was in receivership by November 1934.

A CARAVAN IS SOON DUE. BE SURE TO PLUNDER IT AND BRING ME THE PRISONERS.

YES, MASTER

"DRAGON'S TEETH"

BY BELLEM AND BARREAUX

DASH DOLAN, SOLDIER OF FORTUNE, WORKS WITH NALYA RANDOLPH, AMERICAN GIRL, TO FREE CHINA FROM AN OPPRESSING WARLORD. TWELVE STOLEN JEWELS KNOWN AS THE "DRAGON'S TEETH" MUST BE RECOVERED TO EQUIP A DEFENDING ARMY... TWO ARE RETRIEVED .... NOW DASH AND NALYA LEARN FROM DR. YING THAT A THIRD IS IN THE POSSESSION OF A MURDEROUS TIBETAN BANDIT-CHIEF CALLED "THE BLACK LAMA"

Barreaux had circumvented all of that, and the upward trajectory of his career reinforced his choice.

He dabbled in acting. Barreaux later claimed he appeared in several Broadway shows, specifically singling out *Dancing Mothers*, a vehicle for actress Helen Hayes, in 1925. ["New York City Resident's Heart Remains at Home in Charleston," *Charleston News and Journal*, April 1, 1971]

In 1930, he was chosen as the art director for the Green Roomers Revel, a private club for actors. He was also still getting attention for his outrageous comments regarding women, telling *Variety* that he only used chorus girls as models since they "not only pose better, but they also supply him material for his stories." ["Prefers Chorus Girls," *Variety*, June 1, 1930]

But by that time, his career may not have been going as well as it had previously. The 1930 census revealed that he had moved back in with his aunts Eugenia and Marie. With the advent of the Great Depression, Barreaux's illustration jobs began drying up, his commercial art partnership with fellow artist Raymond Thayer dissolved. He found himself facing the same realities as the rest of Americans—few job opportunities.

One field in which he had some experience was in the pulps. Although they were at the low-end of publishing, they were the one sector of publishing that was enjoying a booming business. They were cheap entertainment, a major selling point in a cash-strapped economy.

As both a writer and illustrator, Barreaux had employable talents that he utilized in securing jobs in the industry. His most successful relationship in pulps came out of his familiarity to Harry Donenfeld.

Donenfeld was a Manhattan printer who had built his empire through his shady connections to "The Mob," and

predatory business practices that manifested as he acquired ongoing publications when their publishers would default on printing costs. He was best known at the time for his own portfolio of risqué sex magazines that struggled to stay one step ahead of the law.

In 1933, Donenfeld teamed with Merle Williams Hersey, a longtime pulp writer and editor, and purchased the rights to the recently defunct, but venerable, *Police Gazette*. Barreaux was hired as an artist for the publication, creating a comic strip entitled, *Flossie Flip*. This revival did not last long, however, as the paper was in receivership by November 1934.

Nineteen thirty-four would be a pivotal year in Barreaux's life and career. On June 28th, he married Vera Marie Zirpolo, the daughter of Italian immigrants, born and raised in Brooklyn. For his wife, Barreaux would convert to Catholicism and become an active lay member of his church.

Later that year, a small, public notice ran in the *New York Times*, announcing the dissolution of yet another partnership, the advertising agency of Jaudon & Barreaux, taking effect on Nov. 9, 1934. At almost the same time, the Donenfeld-owned pulp, *Spicy Detective Stories*, ran the first of many appearances of "Sally the Sleuth," an adult-themed comic strip created by Barreaux that featured the adventures of a blond female detective who had trouble keeping her clothes on. Lastly, a retired Army major seeking to take a foray into the emerging comic book industry was preparing the publication of his first comic. The comic would contain contributions by numerous pulp and newspaper veterans, including Barreaux.

New Fun *is the title of a juvenile magazine that appeared today on the newsstands of the principal cities throughout the United States, according to an announcement by Malcolm Wheeler-Nicholson, president of National Allied Publications, Inc., 49 W. 45th St.* ["New Fun *Magazine for Juveniles Out," *Brooklyn Daily Eagle*, Jan. 11, 1935]

One of the most important comic books in history, *New Fun* stands not only as the first comic from the company

The splash panel for "Dragon's Teeth," from *Champion Comics* #6, August 1940, Worth Publishing.

that would become known as DC, it was also the first comic to present all-original features (as opposed to reprints). Unbeknownst to anyone but Barreaux himself, it would also contain the first published work by a Black artist in an American comic book.

One of Barreaux's contributions to the comic was a feature called "The Magic Crystal of History." The strip tells a story about two children who find in a cave a large glass crystal which is able to transport them through time. His artwork appeared on the strip through *New Fun #3* (April 1935). Not long after, a press release appeared from the George Matthew Adams Syndicate, announcing its production of a new color comic section insert being made available to subscribing newspapers. Among the new comic strips to debut in this section was one by Barreaux.

A graduate of Yale School of Fine Arts, Adolphe Barreaux is our sophisticated-artist—the one who draws THE ENCHANTED STONE OF TIME. Tho [sic] he started out to be a portrait painter, and studied in New York and Paris, his interests strangely enuf [sic] went into the field of archeology.

Tho [sic] he put in a 'trick' in Hollywood as a scenarist, did work for Liberty, Collier's, Smart Set *and others, he comes back to archeology by way of the cartoon strip!* ["Well-Known Cartoonists Create New Comic Pages for Weekly," June 21, 1935]

Curiously, the "Enchanted Stone" strip had almost the exact same plot line as "The Magic Crystal." Once again, two children stumble upon a stone with time-travelling properties. Although short-lived, "The Enchanted Stone of Time" lasted long enough to be reprinted in issues #6 through #9 of *The Comics*, comic book published by Dell in 1938.

By the time "Enchanted Stone" had ended, Barreaux had solidified his relationship with Donenfeld, who reportedly funded the operation of his art studio in order to have a dedicated staff of artists for his publishing ventures. Eventually named the Majestic Studio, this became the prototype for all comic book studios that would follow. Although their output generally appeared (anonymously) in various Donenfeld pulps, occasionally they would also provide material for the comics.

Barreaux's most notable personal contribution during this time was the aforementioned "Sally the Sleuth," which in itself spawned several other sexy heroines for Donenfeld pulps. One deserves particular mention, as "Olga Mesmer, the Girl with the X-Ray Eyes" displayed super-powers in her 1937 *Spicy Detective Stories* story, nearly a year before Superman debuted in *Action Comics #1* (June 1938). Though

likely not drawn by Barreaux (its artwork was signed using a pen name), he probably had a hand in her creation.

By the late 1930s, Barreaux had apparently reconnected with his mother, Georgiana. However, she too, had taken on another identity. She was now going by the name "Josephine Barreaux," claiming to be from Poughkeepsie, New York, and like her son, was listed as "White" in the 1940 census.

In addition to the work he was doing through Majestic Studio, Barreaux took on other work as well. In 1940, he took advantage of his theater background and taught acting at the Barbizon Modeling and Acting School.

In 1939, he drew the "Patty O'Day" feature that appeared in *Wonder Comics* and its successor, *Wonderworld Comics*. What made this unusual was that virtually all of the other material in the comic was produced by the Eisner and Iger Studio, one of Majestic's rivals. Then, in an odd turnabout, Worth Carnahan, a veteran pulp artist who usually worked for Barreaux through Majestic, started his own publishing company and employed Barreaux to work for him.

Champion Comics was a product of Worth Publishing Co., a one-title concern that began operations in late 1939. It was ostensibly co-owned by artist Worth Carnahan and Leo Greenwald, though there is a strong belief that Harry Donenfeld bankrolled the entire venture. For his part, Barreaux contributed several strips: the titular star "The Champ" and an episodic serial adventure titled, "The Dragon's Teeth," created with veteran pulp writer Robert Leslie Bellem. When Harvey Comics took over *Champion* and changed the title to *Champ Comics*, Barreaux and the rest of his Majestic Studio colleagues stayed on for several more issues into 1941.

While several standalone stories in early Ace Comics titles have been attributed to Barreaux, they are unsigned and possibly not his work. That would be the extent of Barreaux's comic book output until the very late 1940s. At that time, it was decided to bring back "Sally the Sleuth" and that her latest venue would be *Private Detective Stories*, with Barreaux as editor.

Published under yet another Donenfeld concern named Trojan Magazines, this version of "Sally," which debuted in the February 1949 issue, was a bit tamer, less prone to revealing stages of dishabille. She was to appear in *Private Detective* for about a year before she graduated to four color glory with the reprinting of her story from the June 1949 issue in the comic book, *Crime Smashers #1* (Oct. 1950).

Also published by Trojan Magazines, the comic *Crime Smashers* consisted of reprints from the pulp, with the addition of color and a toning down of the artwork in a few panels to placate any potential critics. *Crime Smashers* and *Crime Mysteries*, a companion title also edited by Barreaux, ended by 1954, effectively ending the Majestic Studio and his comic book career. Ironically, one of the artists to work on *Crime Mysteries*, in its final months was Black artist Alvin C. Hollingsworth.

With the demise of the pulps and the ending of the Majestic Studio, Barreaux spent the rest of his career writing and editing. He was employed by Fawcett Publications in their Special Interest Books Division, editing and contributing to their artsy photography magazines featuring nude models.

He also served as an editor and occasional writer for his local New Jersey newspaper. In his later years, Barreaux carried on a public correspondence with the staff of the Charleston, South Carolina *News and Courier* newspaper, contributing mostly nostalgia-filled remembrances of his youth in the city. These were also remarkably inconsistent with the truth and stories he told about himself previously.

One example can be found by comparing an article from the 1930s to his later recollections. Back in 1936, Barreaux had taken a trip to Charleston on a vacation to, "absorb the color of the old South."

"Of course, I haven't had much of a chance yet to take in all of Charleston," he told a reporter, *"but from what I've seen I'd say your women are certainly as lovely as any in the country and prettier than any in the South.* ["Girls Here South's Prettiest, Young Visiting Artist Says," *Charleston News and Journal,* Oct. 21, 1936]

Clearly, Barreaux was trying to give the impression it was his first visit to Charleston. In fact, he had been telling people since at least the 1920s that he was born in New Jersey. When writing his later letters and articles to the Charleston newspaper during the 1960s and 1970s, he either forgot his earlier falsehoods or he hoped people wouldn't notice.

At no point in these articles did Barreaux ever mention his multi-racial background. Based upon some of his writings in his hometown newspaper, his sympathies leaned in other directions.

While commenting upon the parts of "Old Charleston" that had disappeared in the years since his youth, **Barreaux** lamented the destruction of the "St. John's Hotel, the last antebellum hostelry, where I slept in Robert E. Lee's bed…"; and he cheered the news that "the old Market is being reactivated. The most important section is the Confederate Museum…" [Barreaux 1973, op. cit.]

Home means Charleston—always. My most esteemed friends are South Carolinians, both Strom and Nancy [Thurmond] for instance… ["Letters to the Editor," *Charleston News and Journal,* Dec. 6, 1969]

Reflecting the sorrow of all Charlestonians far from home, let me express my grief at the loss of my friend our faithful and dedicated representative in the United States Congress, L. Mendel Rivers, who with unflagging efforts on behalf of our beloved city will long live in our hearts and recollections amid the highest respect and warmest regard. ["Letters to the Editor," *Charleston News and Journal,* Dec. 30, 1970]

Senator Thurmond and Congressman Rivers were both well-known segregationists. Thurmond famously led the fight in the Senate against all civil rights legislation during his long tenure in office. He also fathered a child with his Black maid, which he publicly denied.

Adolphe Barreaux passed away on October 23, 1985. He was a talented, complicated man. He made the choices to deny his heritage, to alter facts to fit his purpose, to construct a new persona. He made choices that were pragmatically self-serving. Yet, it wasn't that Barreaux chose his color; society had chosen it for him. To succeed he felt he had to be White, to be visible. It was a choice not all Black artists got to make.

In her first appearances in pulp magazines, Barreaux drew Sally the Sleuth in various states of dishabille. These "spicy" publications brought pressure from censors. When she was revived in the pulp *Private Detective Stories,* the artist pictured her more modestly, as shown in the following story. Later, this story was reprinted in the comic book *Crime Smashers* #1 (Oct. 1950), altered to expose less of the murder victim's thigh on page 3. Still, that panel drew the attention of Dr. Fredric Wertham, infamous anti-comics crusader, who featured it in his notorious anti-comic book screed, *Seduction of The Innocent* (1954, Rinehart & Co.).

SALLY the SLEUTH

"DEATH BAIT"

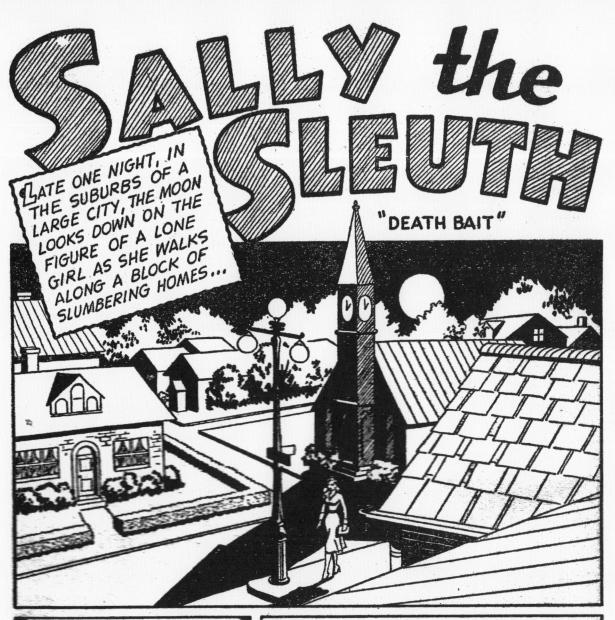

LATE ONE NIGHT, IN THE SUBURBS OF A LARGE CITY, THE MOON LOOKS DOWN ON THE FIGURE OF A LONE GIRL AS SHE WALKS ALONG A BLOCK OF SLUMBERING HOMES...

GOSH, IT'S DESERTED AROUND HERE -- ANYTHING CAN HAPPEN AT THIS HOUR!

PRESENTLY, AN OMINOUS FIGURE DETACHES ITSELF FROM THE SHADOWS...

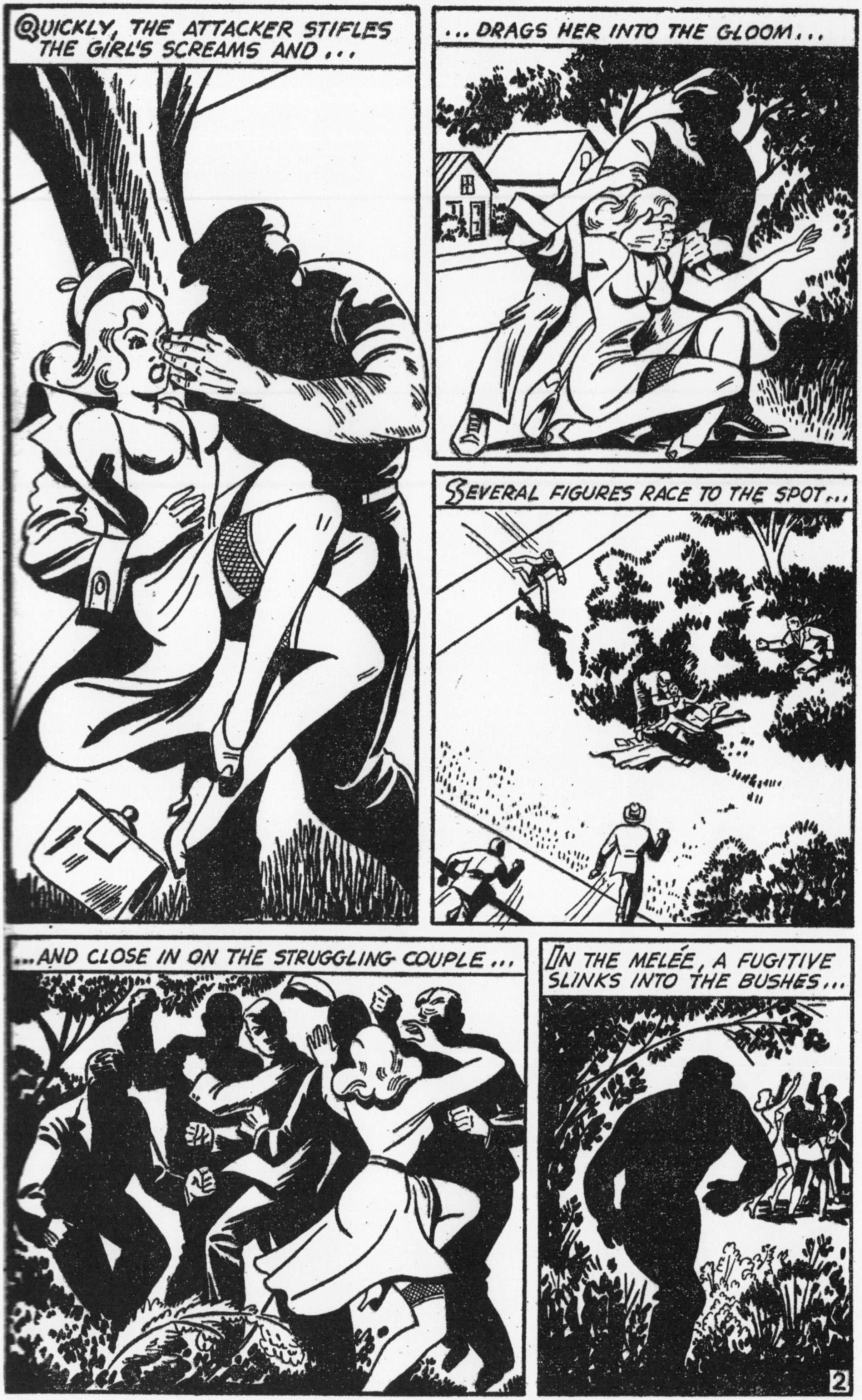
QUICKLY, THE ATTACKER STIFLES THE GIRL'S SCREAMS AND ...
... DRAGS HER INTO THE GLOOM ...
SEVERAL FIGURES RACE TO THE SPOT ...
... AND CLOSE IN ON THE STRUGGLING COUPLE ...
IN THE MELÉE, A FUGITIVE SLINKS INTO THE BUSHES ...
2

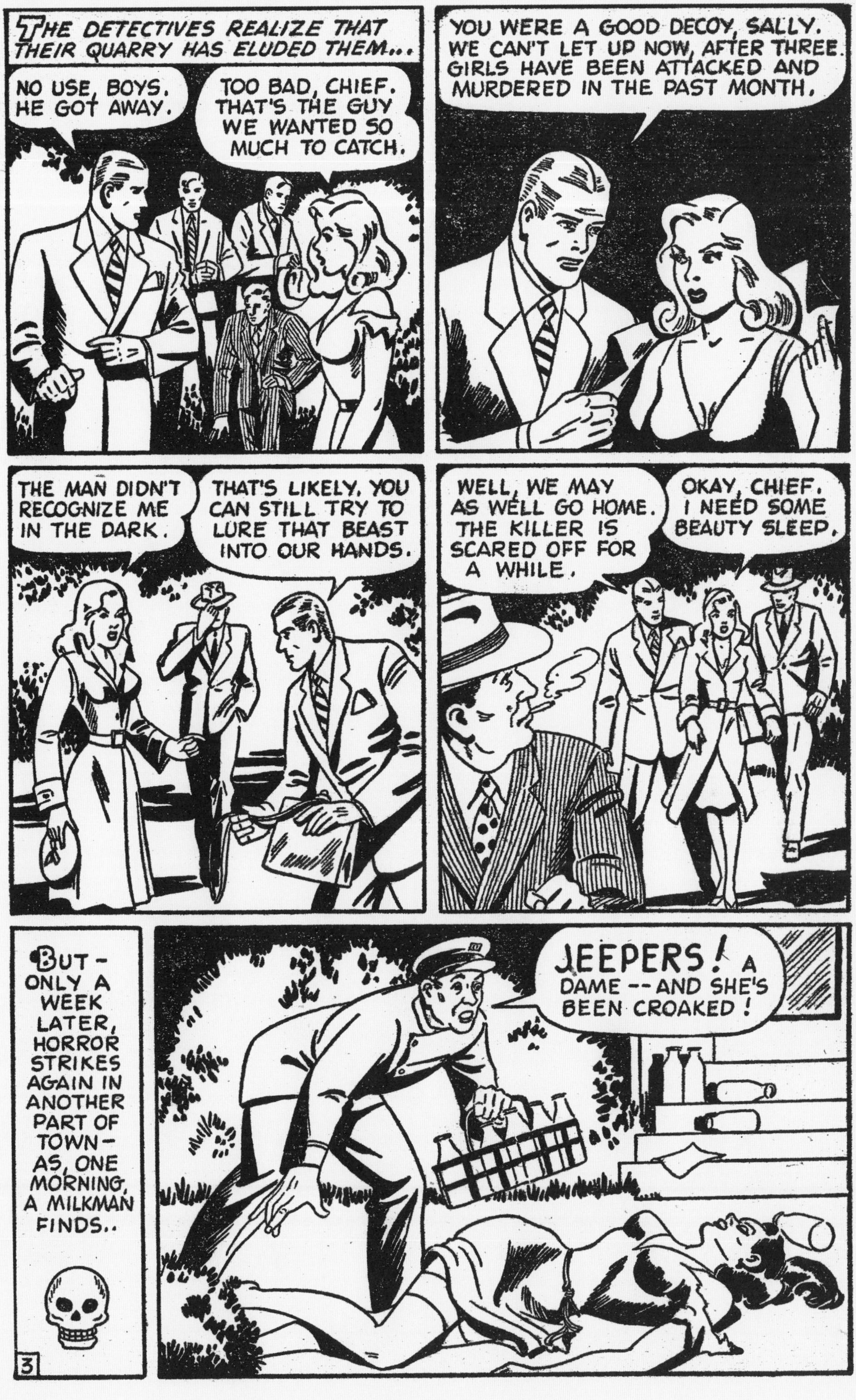

THE DETECTIVES REALIZE THAT THEIR QUARRY HAS ELUDED THEM...
NO USE, BOYS. HE GOT AWAY.
TOO BAD, CHIEF. THAT'S THE GUY WE WANTED SO MUCH TO CATCH.
YOU WERE A GOOD DECOY, SALLY. WE CAN'T LET UP NOW, AFTER THREE GIRLS HAVE BEEN ATTACKED AND MURDERED IN THE PAST MONTH.
THE MAN DIDN'T RECOGNIZE ME IN THE DARK.
THAT'S LIKELY. YOU CAN STILL TRY TO LURE THAT BEAST INTO OUR HANDS.
WELL, WE MAY AS WELL GO HOME. THE KILLER IS SCARED OFF FOR A WHILE.
OKAY, CHIEF. I NEED SOME BEAUTY SLEEP.
BUT-ONLY A WEEK LATER, HORROR STRIKES AGAIN IN ANOTHER PART OF TOWN-AS, ONE MORNING, A MILKMAN FINDS..
JEEPERS! A DAME--AND SHE'S BEEN CROAKED!
3

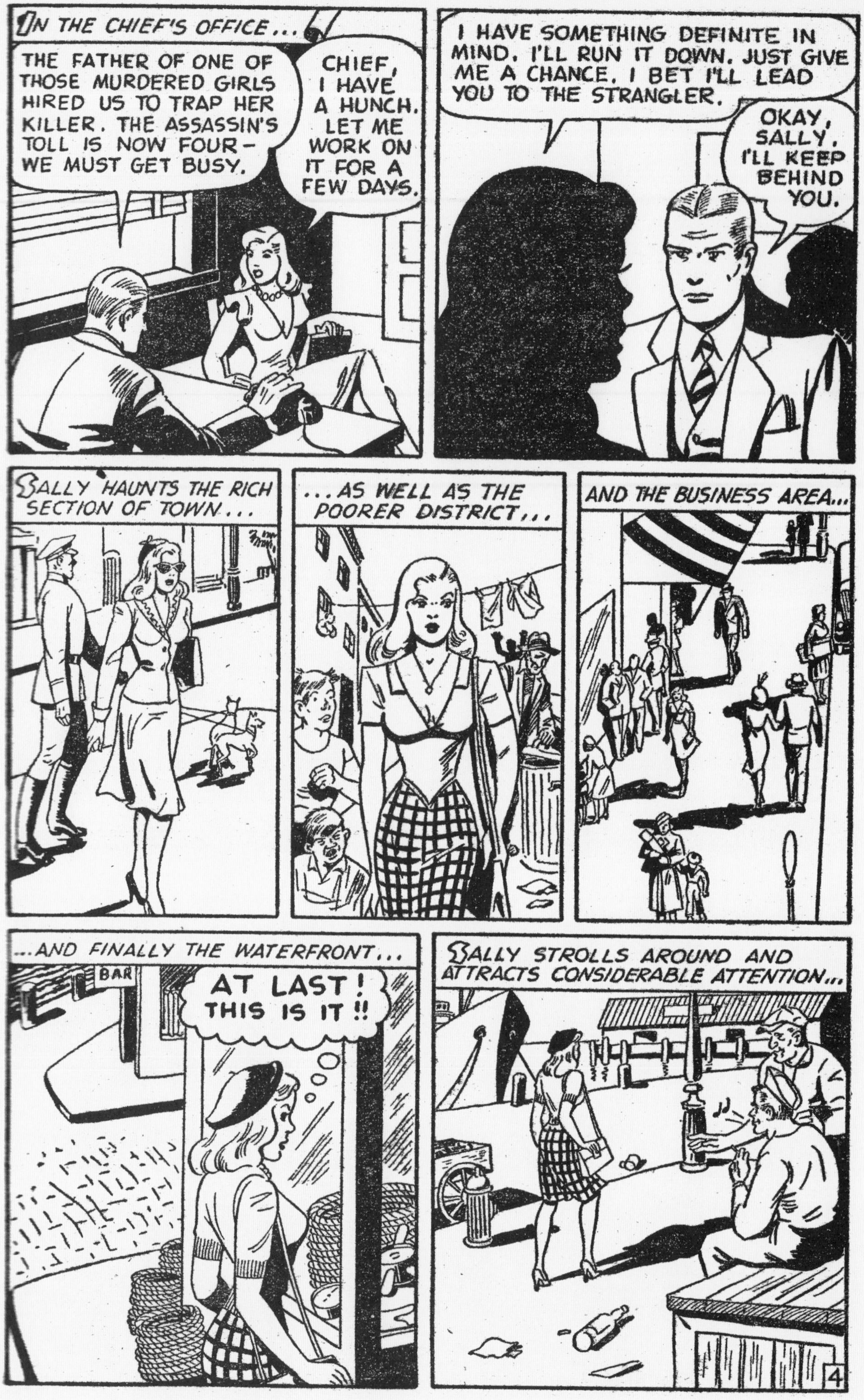
IN THE CHIEF'S OFFICE...
THE FATHER OF ONE OF THOSE MURDERED GIRLS HIRED US TO TRAP HER KILLER. THE ASSASSIN'S TOLL IS NOW FOUR-WE MUST GET BUSY.
CHIEF, I HAVE A HUNCH. LET ME WORK ON IT FOR A FEW DAYS.
I HAVE SOMETHING DEFINITE IN MIND. I'LL RUN IT DOWN. JUST GIVE ME A CHANCE. I BET I'LL LEAD YOU TO THE STRANGLER.
OKAY, SALLY. I'LL KEEP BEHIND YOU.
SALLY HAUNTS THE RICH SECTION OF TOWN...
...AS WELL AS THE POORER DISTRICT...
AND THE BUSINESS AREA...
...AND FINALLY THE WATERFRONT...
BAR
AT LAST! THIS IS IT!!
SALLY STROLLS AROUND AND ATTRACTS CONSIDERABLE ATTENTION...
4

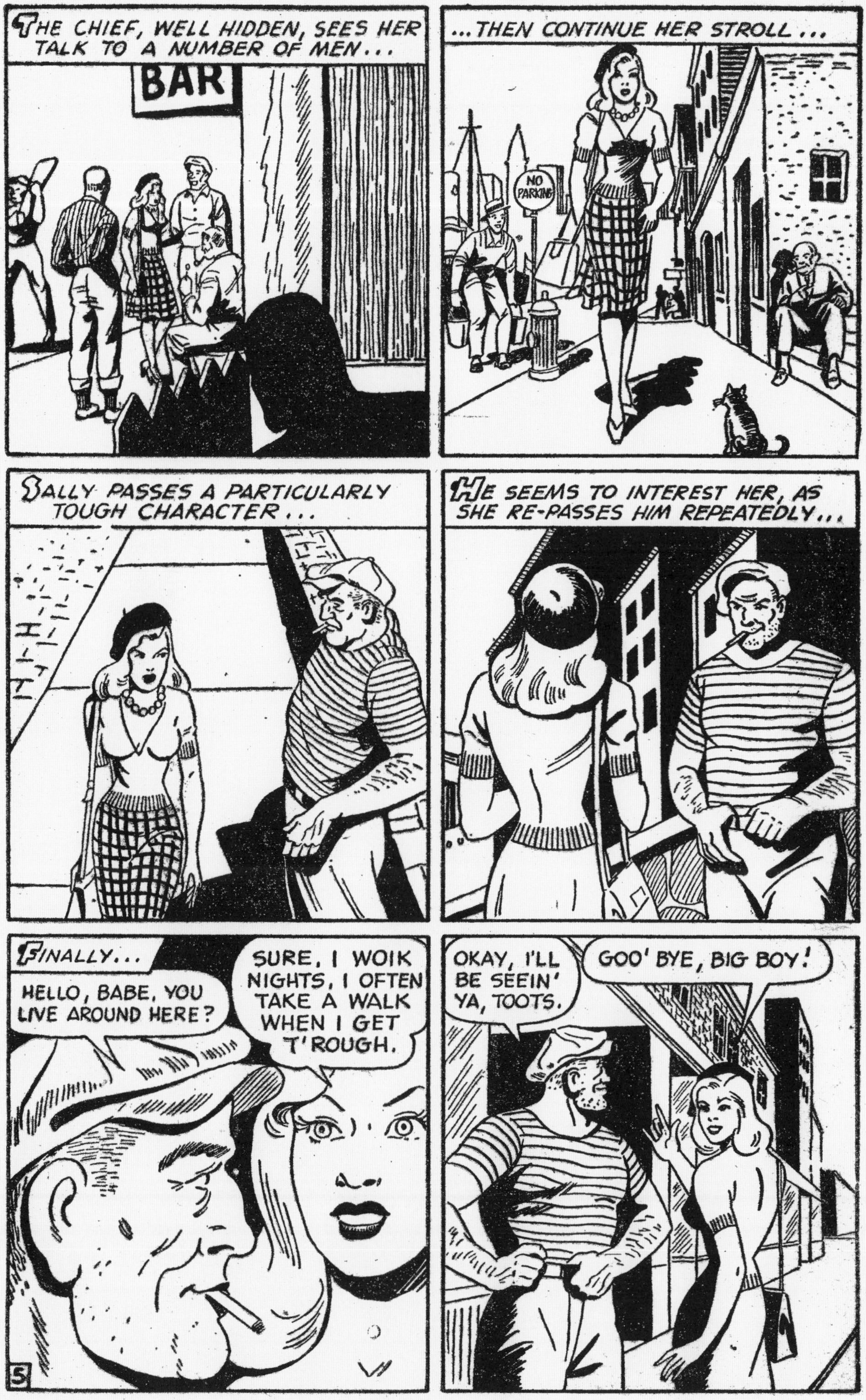
THE CHIEF, WELL HIDDEN, SEES HER TALK TO A NUMBER OF MEN...
BAR
...THEN CONTINUE HER STROLL...
NO PARKING
SALLY PASSES A PARTICULARLY TOUGH CHARACTER...
HE SEEMS TO INTEREST HER, AS SHE RE-PASSES HIM REPEATEDLY...
FINALLY...
HELLO, BABE, YOU LIVE AROUND HERE?
SURE, I WOIK NIGHTS, I OFTEN TAKE A WALK WHEN I GET T'ROUGH.
OKAY, I'LL BE SEEIN' YA, TOOTS.
GOO' BYE, BIG BOY!
5

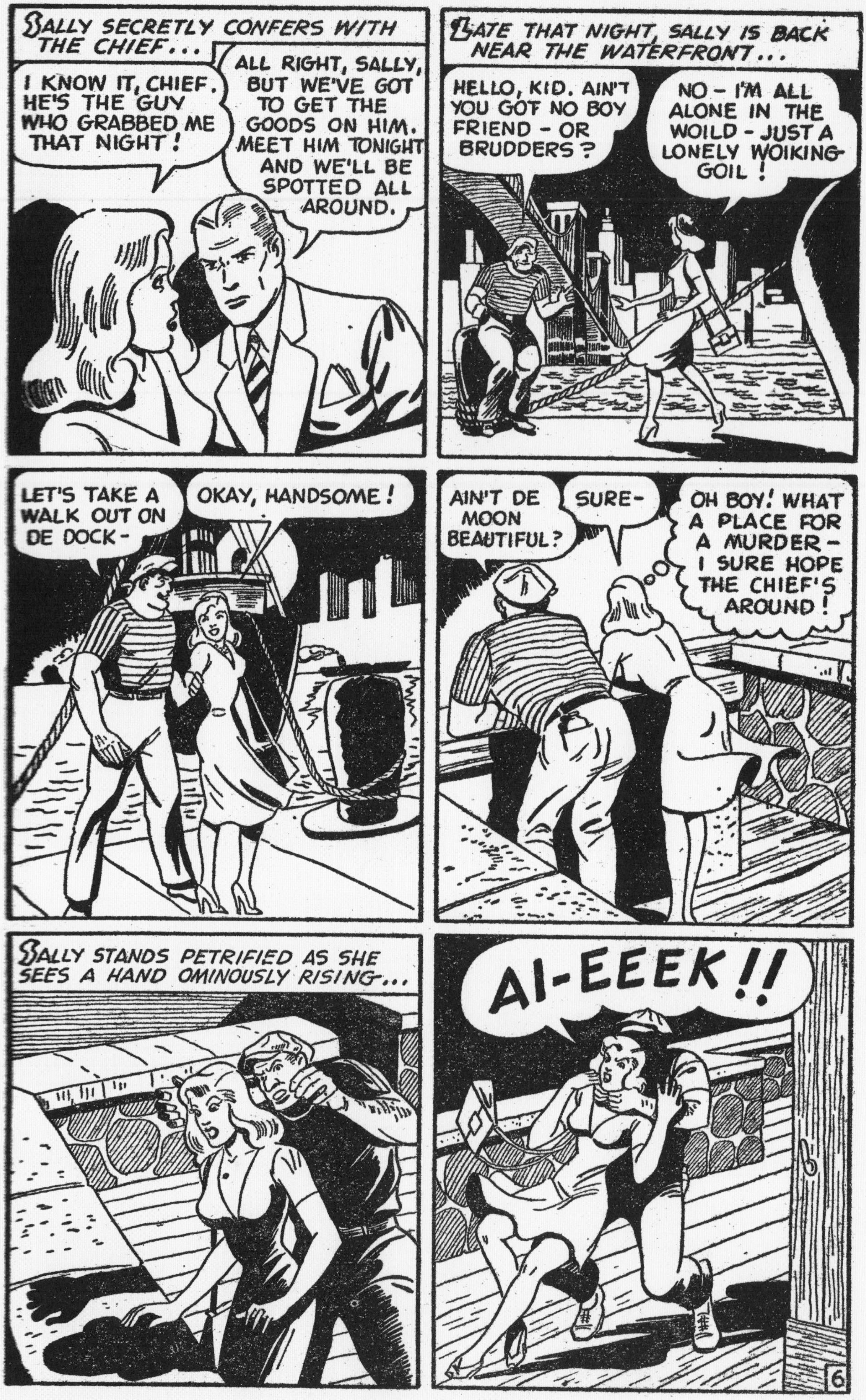
SALLY SECRETLY CONFERS WITH THE CHIEF...
I KNOW IT, CHIEF. HE'S THE GUY WHO GRABBED ME THAT NIGHT!
ALL RIGHT, SALLY, BUT WE'VE GOT TO GET THE GOODS ON HIM. MEET HIM TONIGHT AND WE'LL BE SPOTTED ALL AROUND.
LATE THAT NIGHT, SALLY IS BACK NEAR THE WATERFRONT...
HELLO, KID. AIN'T YOU GOT NO BOY FRIEND - OR BRUDDERS?
NO - I'M ALL ALONE IN THE WOILD - JUST A LONELY WOIKING GOIL!
LET'S TAKE A WALK OUT ON DE DOCK-
OKAY, HANDSOME!
AIN'T DE MOON BEAUTIFUL?
SURE-
OH BOY! WHAT A PLACE FOR A MURDER - I SURE HOPE THE CHIEF'S AROUND!
SALLY STANDS PETRIFIED AS SHE SEES A HAND OMINOUSLY RISING...
AI-EEEK!!
6

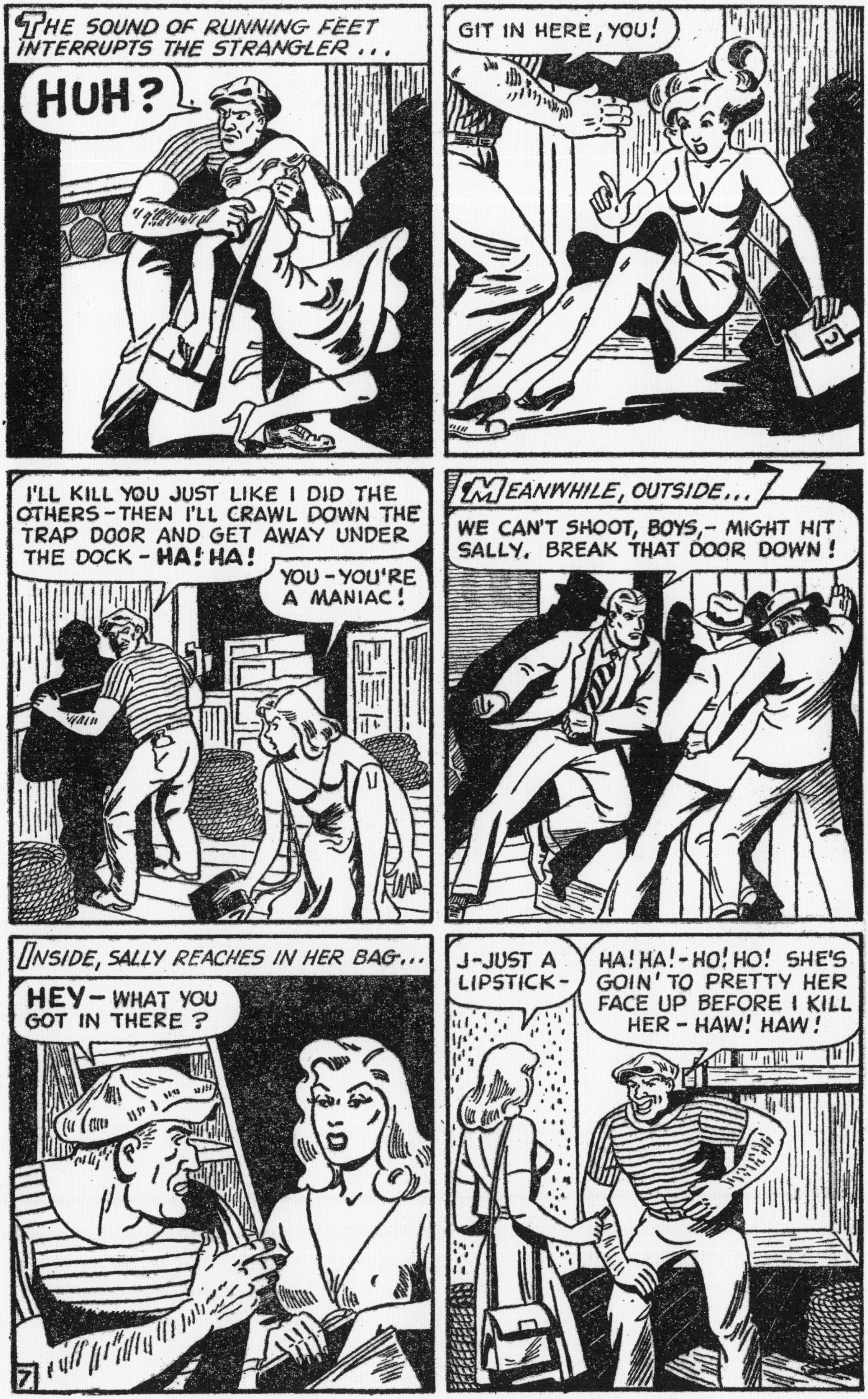
THE SOUND OF RUNNING FEET INTERRUPTS THE STRANGLER ...
HUH?
GIT IN HERE, YOU!
I'LL KILL YOU JUST LIKE I DID THE OTHERS - THEN I'LL CRAWL DOWN THE TRAP DOOR AND GET AWAY UNDER THE DOCK - HA! HA!
YOU - YOU'RE A MANIAC!
MEANWHILE, OUTSIDE...
WE CAN'T SHOOT, BOYS, - MIGHT HIT SALLY. BREAK THAT DOOR DOWN!
INSIDE, SALLY REACHES IN HER BAG...
HEY - WHAT YOU GOT IN THERE?
7
J-JUST A LIPSTICK-
HA! HA! - HO! HO! SHE'S GOIN' TO PRETTY HER FACE UP BEFORE I KILL HER - HAW! HAW!

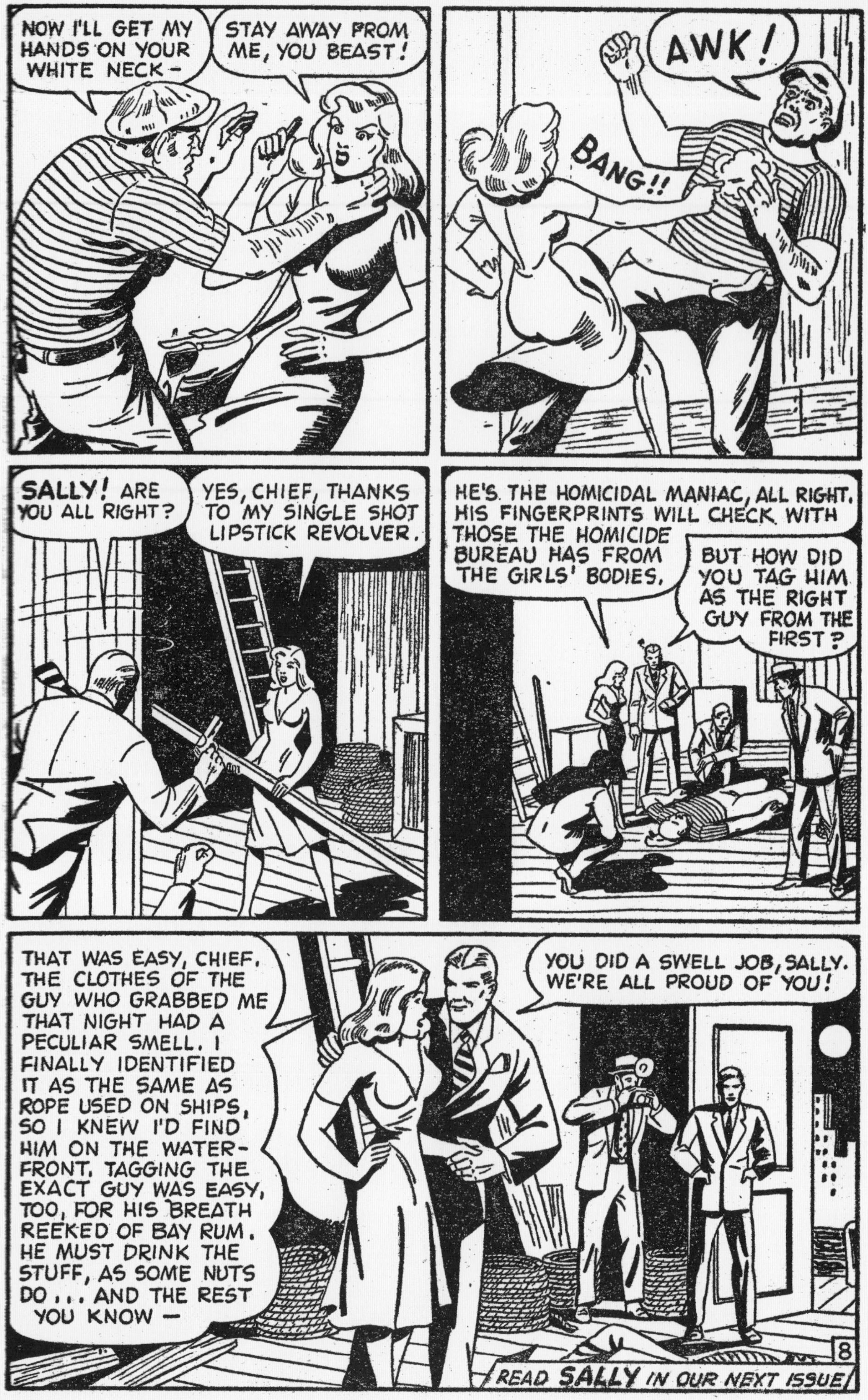
NOW I'LL GET MY HANDS ON YOUR WHITE NECK-
STAY AWAY FROM ME, YOU BEAST!
AWK!
BANG!!
SALLY! ARE YOU ALL RIGHT?
YES, CHIEF, THANKS TO MY SINGLE SHOT LIPSTICK REVOLVER.
HE'S THE HOMICIDAL MANIAC, ALL RIGHT. HIS FINGERPRINTS WILL CHECK WITH THOSE THE HOMICIDE BUREAU HAS FROM THE GIRLS' BODIES.
BUT HOW DID YOU TAG HIM AS THE RIGHT GUY FROM THE FIRST?
THAT WAS EASY, CHIEF. THE CLOTHES OF THE GUY WHO GRABBED ME THAT NIGHT HAD A PECULIAR SMELL. I FINALLY IDENTIFIED IT AS THE SAME AS ROPE USED ON SHIPS, SO I KNEW I'D FIND HIM ON THE WATER-FRONT. TAGGING THE EXACT GUY WAS EASY, TOO, FOR HIS BREATH REEKED OF BAY RUM. HE MUST DRINK THE STUFF, AS SOME NUTS DO... AND THE REST YOU KNOW -
YOU DID A SWELL JOB, SALLY. WE'RE ALL PROUD OF YOU!
8
READ SALLY IN OUR NEXT ISSUE

ELMER CECIL STONER
Harlem Renaissance Man

As the turn of the Twentieth Century approached, there were over 50,000 souls in Wilkes-Barre, Pennsylvania, fewer than 700 of whom were Black. One of those was a clerk, two worked for the post office, three were ministers. None of them were doctors. Most of the Black men worked manual labor jobs, including George Wainwright Stoner, who was employed as a porter.

Still, Elmer Cecil Stoner was proud of his heritage. The son of George and his wife Mary Alice, Elmer was quick to point out that he was a fifth generation Pennsylvanian. One grandfather was a drummer boy in the Civil War. A great-great-great grandmother was a former slave named Sally Ann Smith; she was freed by Martha Washington (for whom she served as a cook), then moved north to Pennsylvania and settled there in the early years of the nineteenth century. Smith joined other freed slaves who journeyed across the Mason-Dixon Line into the state, enjoyed its relative freedoms, and stayed.

A few years after Elmer's birth on October 20, 1897, his father became a sexton at the Bethel African Methodist Episcopal (A.M.E.) church. This is not to be confused with St. Stephen's Protestant Episcopal Church and its all-White congregation, many of whom were among the town's leadership. The Black A.M.E. denomination had been formed in nearby Philadelphia, when Blacks who wanted to worship in the White churches found out that there were boundaries they couldn't cross, even in the City of Brotherly Love.

The Stoner family was extraordinarily accomplished. In addition to his duties at his church, George Stoner was a poet and an inventor. In 1922, he was a founder of the Christian and Industrial Association for Colored Young Men, a local YMCA-affiliated club for the Black community. Mary Alice was a concert pianist, who passed along her talent and love of music to her children, including Elmer. His brother Charles did eventually become a professional musician, while his younger sister, Emily, went into costume design.

Elmer's artistic talent blossomed early, as he was painting at five years old. Even though he wouldn't be the most famous artist to come out of Wilkes-Barre High School (that distinction would likely go to Stoner's classmate, "Ham"

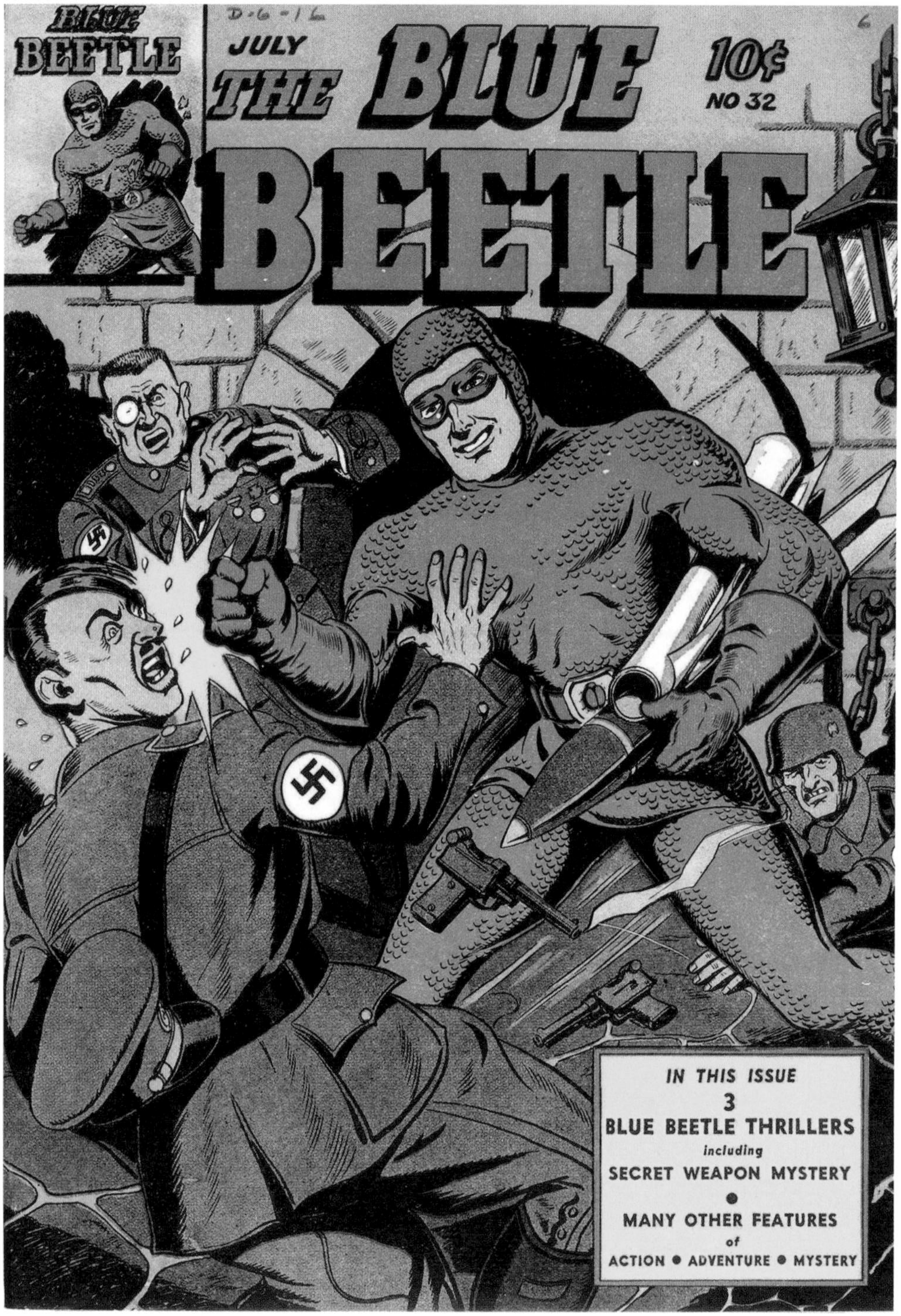
BLUE BEETLE
JULY
THE BLUE BEETLE
10¢
NO 32
IN THIS ISSUE
3
BLUE BEETLE THRILLERS
including
SECRET WEAPON MYSTERY
MANY OTHER FEATURES
of
ACTION • ADVENTURE • MYSTERY

Fisher, of "Joe Palooka" fame), Elmer came to the attention of wealthy philanthropist Fred Morgan Kirby.

Few, if any, men in Wilkes-Barre were more influential than Fred Kirby. As a 1930 history of the town would glowingly put it, his was, "a story of the romance of American business, and shows what determination, aided by genius and ability, can accomplish." [Harvey, Oscar Jewell & Smith, Ernest Gray, *A History of Wilkes-Barré, Luzerne County, Pennsylvania*, vol. 6, 1930, p.382]

Kirby had worked his way up from being a clerk in a dry goods store, to his partnership in forming a five-and-ten cent store with C. Sumner Woolworth. The first Woolworth and Kirby store opened in Wilkes-Barre in 1884, which eventually evolved into the huge F.W. Woolworth chain with stores throughout the country by the early 1900s. As Kirby's wealth grew, so did his participation in various local charitable organizations and his philanthropy. Along with being quite active in the aforementioned St. Stephen's Episcopal Church, he was a trustee of Presbyterian-affiliated Lafayette College, where he established the Kirby Chair of Civil Rights in 1920, with a contribution of $100,000.

On his draft registration card dated September 12, 1918, Stoner listed his occupation as "porter" and his employer as "F. W. Woolworth Co." It was likely here that Kirby became familiar with the talented young man, who impressed him to the point that he paid for Stoner's four years tuition at the Pennsylvania Academy of Fine Arts.

It should be noted that some sources claim that Stoner worked for a time for the local Planters Peanuts Company as an illustrator. Furthermore, the claims extend to include his creation of the company's famous mascot, "Mr. Peanut."

Founded in 1906, the Planters company was indeed from Wilkes-Barre, where Stoner was living at the time. In 1916, it sponsored a contest to find a company logo. As the story is recounted in the official history on the company's website:

Introduced in 1916, the debonair marketing image of Mr. Peanut derived from a crude drawing by a Virginia schoolboy.

[Above] In a profile of Stoner appearing in a contemporary issue of the *Daily Worker*, the writer commented, "Stoner is working right now on a 30-page volume of the Blue Beetle continuity. This renowned counter-spy is known to our troops on all battlefronts, and, being the practical anti-fascist that he is, Stoner sees to it that the Blue Beetle carries a practical lesson." The cover of *Blue Beetle* #32, July 1944, Fox Publications.

[Right] Released under the auspices of *Protestant Digest*, this comic was the first standalone effort to publish a comic book featuring minority characters in a positive light. Stoner drew the cover and three interior stories, all written by his wife, Henriette. *The Challenger* #1, January 1945, Interfaith Publications.

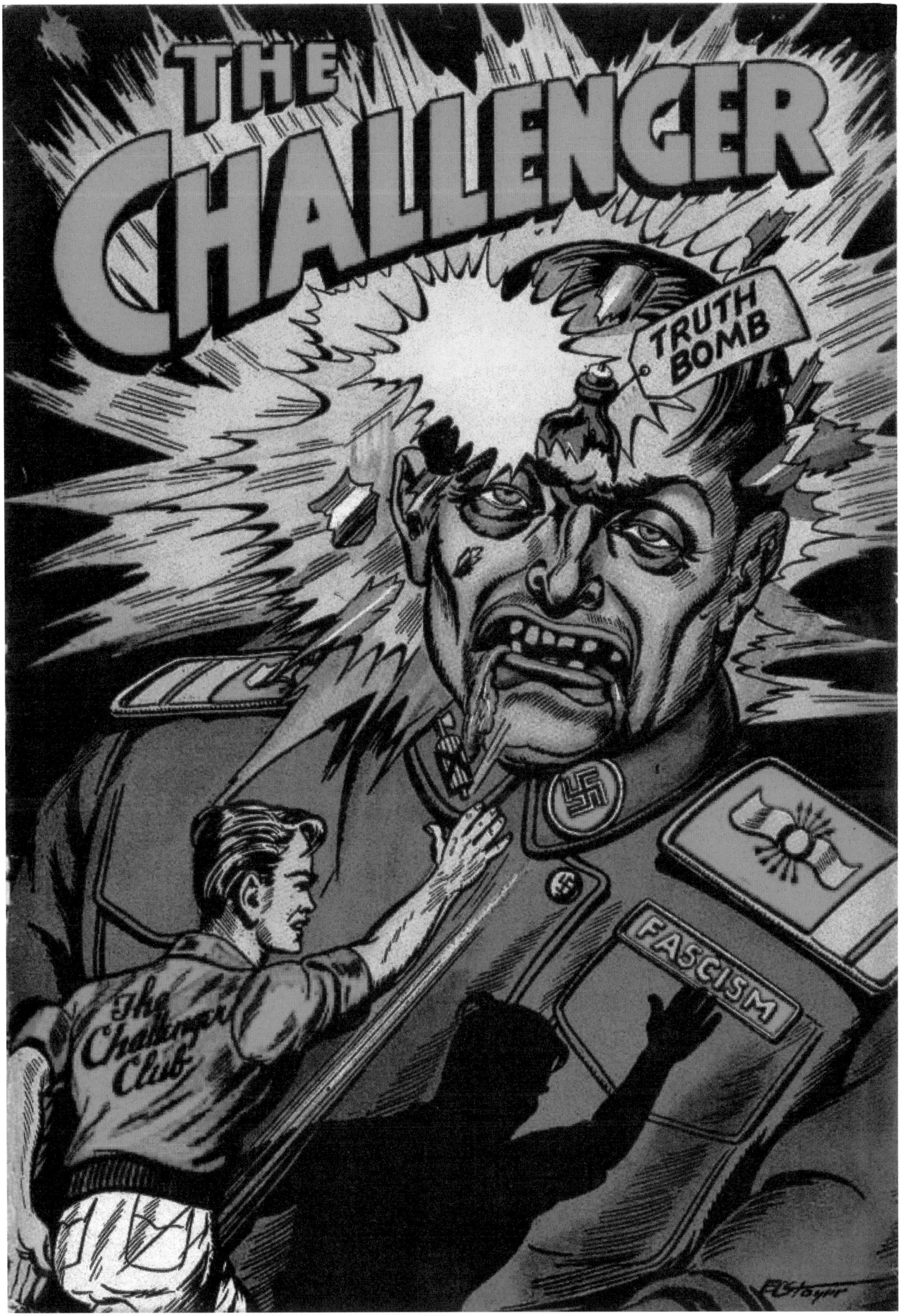
THE CHALLENGER
TRUTH BOMB
FASCISM
The Challenger Club

Prompted by a nation-wide logo contest sponsored by the Planters Company, (14-year-old) schoolboy Antonio Gentile won $5 for his design submission of Mr. Peanut. Then, a professional illustrator enhanced the youngster's drawing adding the top hat, monocle and cane. ["Planters History of the Planter Nut," Planters, http://www.planters.com:80/history.aspx (accessed Jan. 26, 2010)]

Various commercial artists have claimed this enhancement of Mr. Peanut, including Andrew S. Wallach. In 1916, the year of the character's creation, Stoner graduated from high school.

Stoner's widow, Henriette, listed the creation of this character among his accomplishments when she filled out the questionnaire for the online "Who's Who of American Comic Books" database; however, there have been no contemporary sources yet found to corroborate it. This is underscored by the fact that Stoner himself never mentioned Planters, nor Mr. Peanut, in any interviews conducted, or biographies written, during his lifetime.

Stoner was very active in his father's church, heading up various groups and serving as superintendent of the Sunday school program, for which he also served as a teacher. Elmer was studying at the Pennsylvania Academy in 1920, when he became the recipient of a John H. Packard Fund prize for second place in animal illustration. He was also named as the 1922 winner of a Cresson Travelling Scholarship, which paid for a summer of study in Europe. Upon his return from Europe, he participated in the groundbreaking "Exhibit by Negro Artists" beginning on August 1, 1922, in Harlem at the 135th Street branch of the New York Public Library.

The exhibition was organized by Ernestine Rose, the branch's White chief librarian. In recognition of the growing Black community served by the library, Rose integrated Blacks into staff positions and worked to make the branch a source of cultural pride.

Newspaper articles covering the exhibition singled out Stoner's work for commendation. One such lauded his "several excellent charcoal illustrations, including a spirited drawing of the Broad Street Station in the Quaker City." ["Masterpieces Displayed at N.Y. Exhibition," *Dallas Express*, Sept. 2, 1922]

It wasn't accidental that Stoner's involvement in this New York City-based event coincided with the advent of the Harlem Renaissance, the period of Black intellectual and artistic flowering that centered around that burgeoning community. This re-discovery and awakening of Black culture

attracted and nurtured a vast number of talents, with notables such as Langston Hughes, Zora Neale Hurston, and Duke Ellington among them. As a later writer described it:

Crime, dope and poverty were scarcely visible, protest and militancy were polite, the streets were clean and, above all, bourgeois aspiration prevailed. [Glueck, Grace, "Harlem's History Through a Camera," *New York Times*, Oct. 16, 1971]

The art exhibition at the Harlem library drew works from Black artists nationwide, but as with all such ambitious undertakings, it was an expensive project. A dance was organized at the Alpha Physical Club, a Black-run and Harlem-based athletic club, in conjunction with the exhibition for the purpose of raising additional funds to defray its costs. The person in charge of the entertainment committee that put on the dance was a dynamic young woman named Vivienne Anderson Ward.

Coming from a relatively small town, replete with its inherent limitations and prejudices, Stoner was understandably swept up into this intoxicating world. It's likely his indoctrination to the metropolitan multicultural, multiracial mix of Harlem came by way of Vivienne (known as "Vi" to her friends).

Vi, originally from Raleigh, North Carolina, had come to Harlem by way of the mostly White suburb of Lawrence, Long Island, where she attended high school. Early on, she worked as a stenographer at the *New York Amsterdam News*, but quickly moved on. She attended Columbia University for one year, worked at the newly formed National League on Urban Conditions (former name of the National Urban League), was appointed Assistant Superintendent of the New York State Bureau of Labor, and was head of women's housing for the Young Woman's Christian Association (YWCA), the first Black woman to ever hold that position. Along with all her accomplishments, Vi Ward still found time to involve herself with myriad social activities, including coordination of the dance fundraiser held at the Alpha Physical Club. She was also the wife of Anderson T. Stokes when she first met Elmer Stoner.

The circumstances involving the divorce of Vi and her husband aren't clear, but it was finalized in June 1922. One year later, on June 23, 1923, Vi married Elmer.

Although they first settled in Elmer's hometown of Wilkes-Barre, the Stoners soon relocated to a home on 124th Street in Harlem. By 1924, they moved once again, to racially integrated Greenwich Village, where Vi opened a gift shop on Christopher Street.

One of Vi's closest friends was author Nella Larsen, a librarian from the 135th Street branch library who would eventually be recognized as one of the most important writers of the Harlem Renaissance. Romare Bearden wrote:

Almost all creative people in the arts knew one another, as well as the leading ministers, physicians, lawyers, business leaders and national political leaders... [Bearden, Romare & Henderson, Harry, *A History of Blacks Artists: From 1792 to the Present*, 1993, p.234]

Larsen introduced the Stoners to her diverse group of friends, mostly Black literati, but also included noted White writer and photographer, Carl Van Vechten.

Van Vechten held a unique place in the story of the Harlem Renaissance. He was a wealthy Midwesterner who had bounced around for years in various writing jobs, particularly as a music and dance critic for the *New York Times*. He became enamored with the lively arts scene in Harlem and befriended many of its most prominent Black luminaries. They in turn courted his patronage and the exposure he had in the White media to promote their own agendas. His most lasting contribution, though, was his notorious novel entitled, *N****r Heaven*, Van Vechten's attempt to empathetically portray life in Harlem. While it became a best-selling sensation among White readers, it created divisions among Blacks, who either saw it as a celebration of their culture, or conversely, as "a blow in the face. It is an affront to the hospitality of black folk and to the intelligence of white." [Du Bois, W. E. B., "Books," *Crisis*, Dec. 1926]

This tight-knit circle would congregate at the Stoner home for intimate parties where they would sip drinks and discuss literature and the latest Broadway shows.

Elmer concentrated on his painting career during this period, a sought-after portraitist whose talent allowed him to work freely in both the Black and White communities. To augment his income, Stoner took on the occasional illustration job. In one case, he provided both the cover to the July 1924 issue of *The Messenger* and the drawings to the Mamie Elaine Francis' short story, "Raum-Sheba" in the April edition. His contributions to "The World's Greatest Negro Monthly" were a testament to his rising notoriety as an artist and his place in the emerging Black middle class. By 1925, he was successful enough to be part-owner of an apartment building at 203 W. 122nd Street in Harlem. The Stoners' marriage, however, wasn't nearly as successful.

In his Larsen biography, *In Search of Nella Larsen*, author George Hutchinson mentions that a few days after the Jack Dempsey-Jack Sharkey heavyweight championship bout (July 22, 1927), Vi Stoner—"whose marriage was in trouble"—showed up at Larsen's home with a new boyfriend. Society columns, which chronicled many of the Stoners' social activities, made note in May 1928, that Vi planned on spending the winter in New Mexico, with no mention of Elmer accompanying her. ["Society," *Baltimore Afro-American*, May 5, 1928]

"Even with the simplest water color, I strive for perfection. It's only through dedication that anything great is ever achieved."
"When I buy gin, I insist on the very best London Dry. Gordon's. It is ideally dry and crisp, makes a perfect martini. To me, Gordon's Gin is great gin."
Elmer C. Stoner, noted artist, author and editor, at home with his wife, Henriette.
Gordon's Gin, created in London, England in 1769. It's the biggest seller in England, America and the world.
PRODUCT OF U.S.A. 100% NEUTRAL SPIRITS DISTILLED FROM GRAIN. 90 PROOF. GORDON'S DRY GIN CO., LTD., LINDEN, N. J.

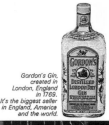

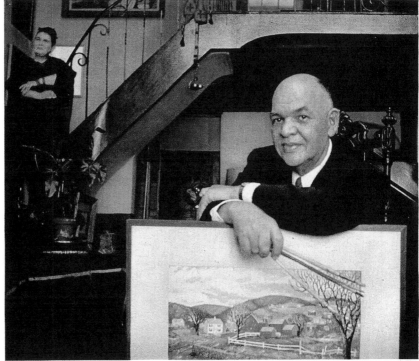

Stoner received probably his greatest prominence from this advertisement for Gordon's Gin, which ran in a number of Black publications throughout the mid-1960s. It depicts him and his wife Henriette posing in their Greenwich Village home.

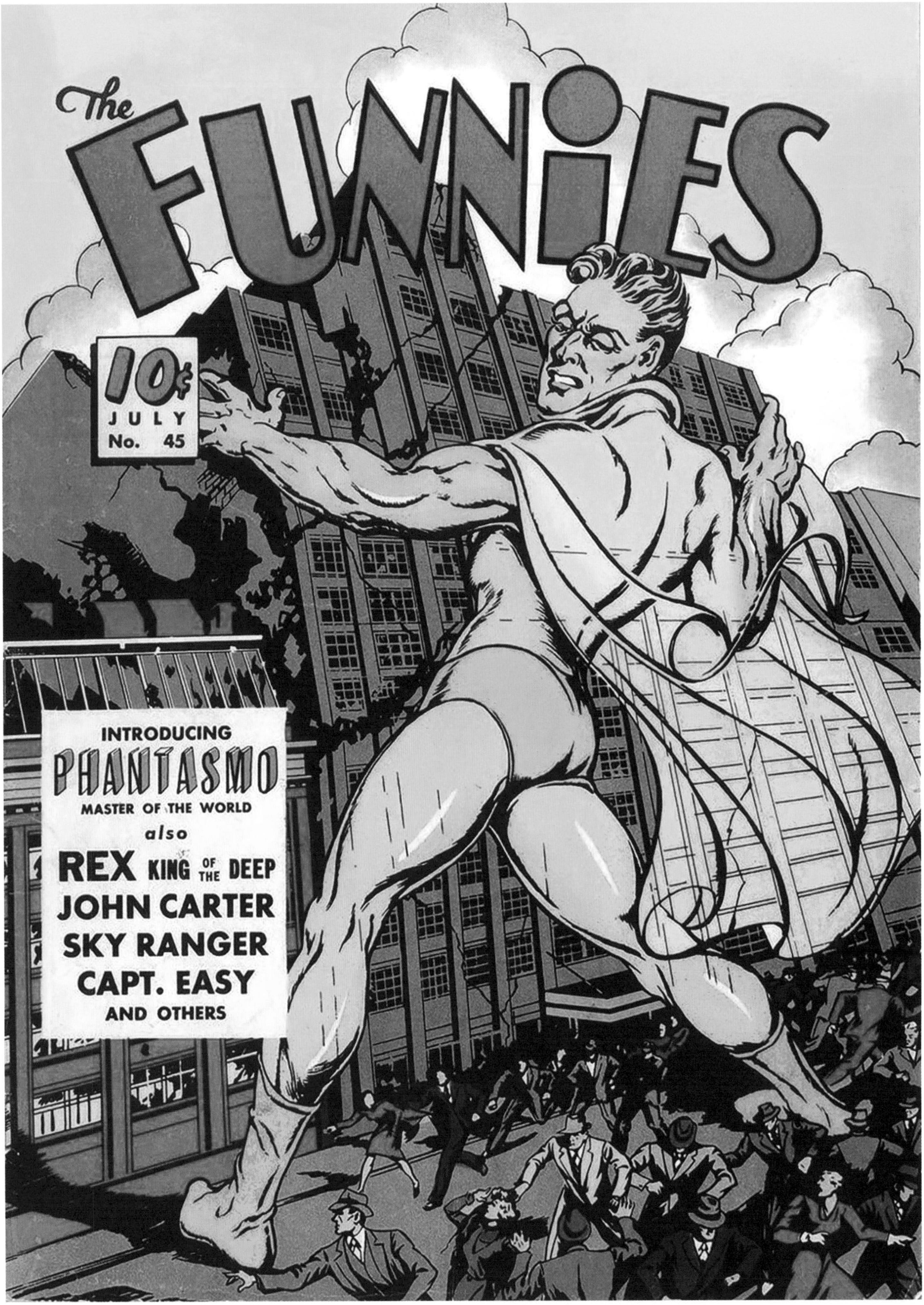
The FUNNIES
10¢
JULY
No. 45
INTRODUCING
PHANTASMO
MASTER OF THE WORLD
also
REX KING OF THE DEEP
JOHN CARTER
SKY RANGER
CAPT. EASY
AND OTHERS

By 1930, Vi was once again using her own last name. The Stoners had divorced. [Hutchinson, George, *In Search of Nella Larsen*, 2006, p.261]

Career-wise, that same year, Elmer was the illustrator of *Mic Mac on the Track*, a children's book about trains written by Zillah K. MacDonald. And starting in 1929, for several years Stoner was the artist of a series of national ads for Franklin Automobile Co., a luxury car brand. These full-color, full-page ads were rendered in the art deco style, and depicted a carefree lifestyle enjoyed by only a small segment of the car-buying public.

Curiously, while many Black cartoonists and illustrators found most of their work through Black newspapers and magazines, Stoner was an exception. Outside of *The Messenger* in the 1920s, Stoner did little for any of these publications. Most of his work appeared in White-owned media.

Stoner was employed for a time as the art director at Tower Magazines. This line of magazines, mainly oriented toward women and children, was to have exclusive distribution through the F. W. Woolworth's store chain. Initially, the sales of such titles as *Illustrated Love*, *Home*, and *Serenade* were brisk, but by 1935, printing costs drove the company to bankruptcy. A series of nasty court battles ensued, with several Tower executives indicted for mail fraud. There was also a lawsuit by the disgraced company president, Catherine McNellis, against its secret financial backer, Fred M. Kirby.

The connection of Kirby to Tower Magazines (which had its home office in Wilkes-Barre) may have accounted for his protégé's position with that publisher, but no matter the reason, it was a lofty position for a Black to achieve. Stoner was the rare Black artist, along with E. Simms Campbell, that found much of his success within the White art world. And unlike Adolphe Barreaux and George Herriman, he did so without denying his racial heritage.

The fact that Stoner not only continued to enjoy the patronage of Kirby, but thrive within his organization, was a stark anomaly within the F. W. Woolworth Company. In the late 1920s, the retailer had become the focus of a Black boycott in Chicago, for its adamant refusal to employ Blacks at the company's stores in their Southside neighborhood.

This issue featured the origin and first appearance of Phantasmo, a superhero created by Stoner. Subtitled "The Master of the World," Phantasmo's first story claimed he could "pick up a mountain and throw it into the sea...fly swift as thought around the Earth...bullets pass thru him harmlessly...fire, water and gravity are toys in his hands." *The Funnies* #45, July 1940, Dell Publishing.

The success of that boycott prompted its leader to utilize the same sort of protest at the 125th Street Woolworth's in Harlem.

...Woolworth's 5-and-10-cent store, whose management also vows that no colored individual will have any kind of reputable employment there. ["In My Travels: With the Pickets on 125th Street," "The Spectator," *Baltimore Afro-American*, June 30, 1934]

In particular, the protest centered around the lack of Black personnel at the store in anything other than a menial position. At the time, it employed two Black men: one a porter, one a stock man. There were no Blacks employed in the coveted position of sales clerk.

This business house thrives off the nickels and dimes of Harlemites day in and day out, but when approached in a reasonable manner as to whether they will hire a colored personnel,[sic] they shake their heads negatively. [Ibid.]

The initial boycott began in June 1932 and resulted in the arrest of the picketing protesters for disorderly conduct. Eventually, by 1934, the boycott grew, with the involvement of prominent Harlem clergyman-activist, Rev. Adam Clayton Powell, and the support of middle-class Blacks and celebrities. Finally, in September 1934, the store caved to the pressure, and the resulting decrease in business, and hired three Black women as sales clerks.

While the collapse of Tower in 1935 left Stoner unemployed, he certainly wasn't alone. The Great Depression had put many Americans of every race, creed, and job description out on the street, scrambling to find work. Given his skills, it was only natural that Stoner gravitated to pulp magazine illustration. Though he didn't have many credits in this area, among his pulp efforts were the covers to Carwood Publishing's, *The Witch's Tales* #1 and #2 (Nov. & Dec. 1936), as well as several interior illustrations.

Some sources have maintained that around this same time, Stoner drew a story for the first issue of *Detective Comics* (March 1937), which would likely make him the first openly Black artist to work in the comic book industry. However, despite some resemblance to Stoner's style, the "Speed Saunders" story in that comic often credited to him was not his work. Stoner's own recollection in a 1951 newspaper article stated, "I have been illustrating comic strips since 1939," which, if correct, clears up the frequent misattribution. [Holt, Nora, "Interracial Team Looks Into The Future: Negro Artist Plus White Writer 'Father' New Comic," *New York Amsterdam News*, Sept. 22, 1951]

Prior to entering the comic book industry, Stoner was hired as one of the artists at the upcoming 1939 New York World's Fair, on both the "Railroads at Work" diorama and assisting on an illustrated book for young fair-goers entitled *Seeing the World's Fair*. The World's Fair opening meant the end of Stoner's employment, but the comic book industry was booming, and he began picking up his first assignments. He emerged in 1939, as a member of the Harry "A" Chesler comic shop.

"Comic shops" were, by definition, art studios, but in practice they more closely resembled the production lines of Henry Ford. Usually these shops were located in lofts or large offices, with drawing tables lined up, cheek-by-jowl, and perhaps a desk or two inhabited by an editor or a writer. Artwork often was completed in stages, passing from a pencil artist, to a letterer, who would fill in the word balloons, to an inker. The market was ravenous, the pace was furious, and quality was a minor concern.

Although the pulp and comic markets were based in liberal-minded New York City, the decision to hire Stoner, or any Black artist, would have been born more out of necessity than an opportunity to make a social statement. Shop owners, editors, and publishers needing ever increasing amounts of material to fill their pages rarely considered its source.

Working through a shop offered a secondary bonus for Stoner, as it provided a buffer between him and an editor should they be reluctant to employ a Black man. This is an important point, as subsequent comic book Black artists, virtually without exception, worked through comic shops at some point in their careers.

Stoner most likely began as an uncredited inker in the Chesler shop. Some sources see his hand as the embellisher of Jack Binder's pencil work on "Breeze Barton" in early issues of *Daring Mystery Comics*, and he likely filled the same role on the "Flexo, the Rubber Man" and "Dynamic Man" features in that same publisher's *Mystic Comics*. It was far easier to discern Stoner's input in Dell comics. Much of the time he signed this work.

In 1940, Binder, who was also Chesler's art director, broke off to form his own shop. One of the artists to come along was Stoner, and his ascension to primary pencil artist status seems to have come with this move.

Stoner's unmistakably quirky style came to fruition at this time: the stiff, off-kilter figures, with knitted brows and toothy smiles, often incongruously at odds with the depicted situation. Considering his skill as a fine artist and illustrator, the awkwardness of Stoner's comic artwork comes as something of a surprise. Whether this was a stylistic choice, discomfort with the comic book medium, or the result of haste isn't known, but it was an awkwardness he shared with other comic book artists such as Henry C. Kiefer and Louis Ferstadt, who also came from fine art backgrounds.

In many cases, there was a "sameness" to Stoner's artwork that appears to indicate that he inked his own pencil drawings and lettered his own stories, signs that he apparently had an autonomy beyond the confines of the Englewood, New Jersey barn that housed the rest of the Binder shop. Stoner, indeed, maintained a studio in his Greenwich Village home.

Stoner was the main artist on "Phantasmo, Master of the World," which started its run in *The Funnies* #45 (July 1940). Phantasmo was one of the first Dell entries in the superhero genre, featuring an adventurer named Phil Anson, who spent 25 years in Tibet studying with the Grand High Lamas. He eventually returned to the United States, where he began using the powers he acquired during his apprenticeship. Even though he had a similar origin to Bill Everett's Amazing Man and the pulps' Green Lama, Phantasmo was far more powerful than his predecessors, being able to grow to incredible heights and exhibit unmatchable strength. These attributes would be shared with another character associated with Stoner, his version of the Blue Beetle, leading to the conclusion that he wrote the stories as well as drew them.

"Phantasmo" ran until *The Funnies* #63 (March 1942) and had the honor of having an entire issue devoted to him with *Large Feature Comics* #18 (1940). Adding to the presumption that Phantasmo was entirely Stoner's creation is the fact that nobody else ever drew the character.

Stoner was the main cover artist for a six-issue run of *Popular Comics*, which began with issue #54 (Aug. 1940) and ended with #59 (Jan. 1941). Additionally, he drew "Martan, the Marvel Man," a science fiction feature in *Popular*, starting with #66 (Aug. 1941) and ending with #71 (Jan. 1942).

Next to "Phantasmo," Stoner's biggest impact at Dell was seen in *War Heroes*, a reality-based anthology. From the second issue (Oct.-Dec. 1942) to issue #7 (Jan.-March 1944), Stoner provided many of the stories in this comic. In issue #5 (July-Sept. 1943) he not only drew the cover, but also contributed four interior stories. Perhaps significantly, this issue also features the only signed comic book artwork of Owen Middleton, another Black artist. There

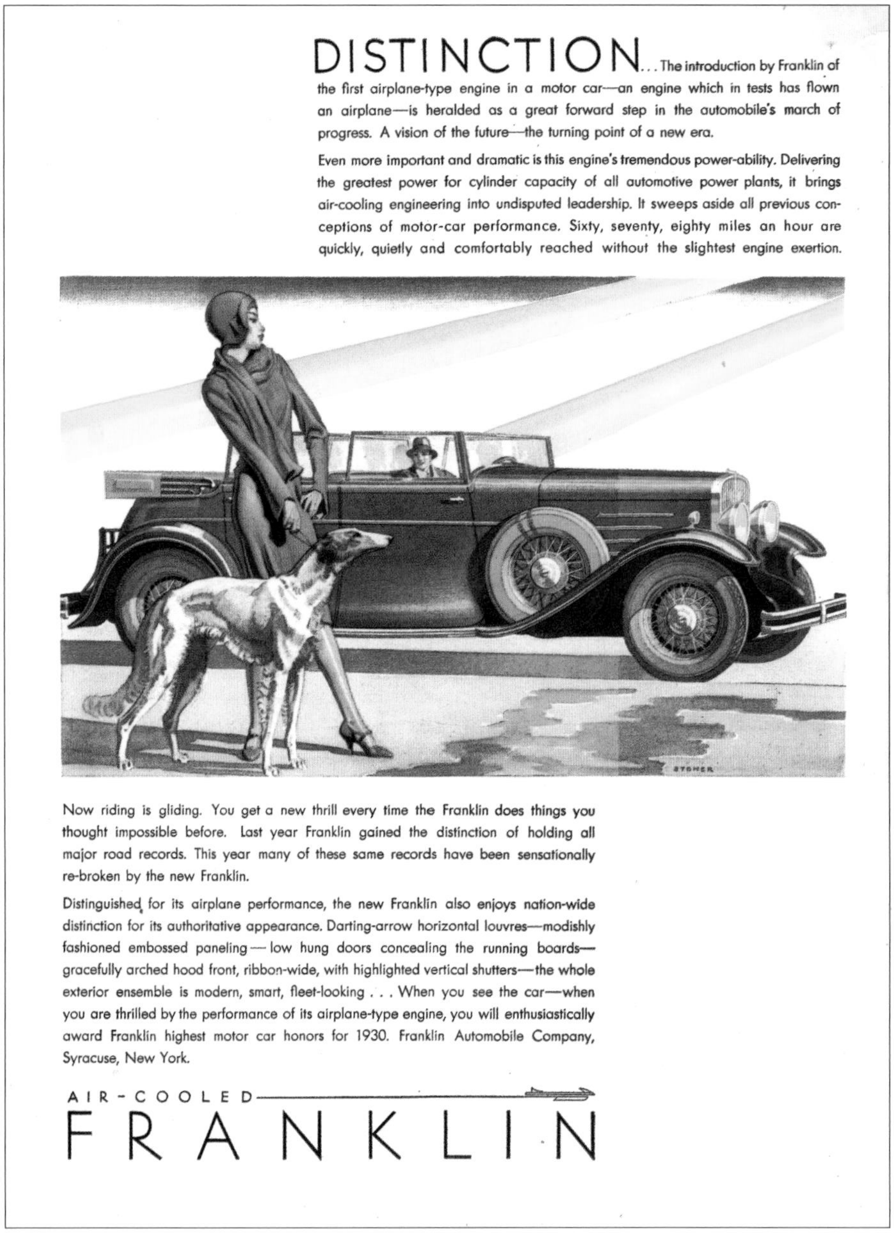
DISTINCTION... The introduction by Franklin of the first airplane-type engine in a motor car—an engine which in tests has flown an airplane—is heralded as a great forward step in the automobile's march of progress. A vision of the future—the turning point of a new era.
Even more important and dramatic is this engine's tremendous power-ability. Delivering the greatest power for cylinder capacity of all automotive power plants, it brings air-cooling engineering into undisputed leadership. It sweeps aside all previous conceptions of motor-car performance. Sixty, seventy, eighty miles an hour are quickly, quietly and comfortably reached without the slightest engine exertion.
Now riding is gliding. You get a new thrill every time the Franklin does things you thought impossible before. Last year Franklin gained the distinction of holding all major road records. This year many of these same records have been sensationally re-broken by the new Franklin.
Distinguished for its airplane performance, the new Franklin also enjoys nation-wide distinction for its authoritative appearance. Darting-arrow horizontal louvres—modishly fashioned embossed paneling—low hung doors concealing the running boards—gracefully arched hood front, ribbon-wide, with highlighted vertical shutters—the whole exterior ensemble is modern, smart, fleet-looking . . . When you see the car—when you are thrilled by the performance of its airplane-type engine, you will enthusiastically award Franklin highest motor car honors for 1930. Franklin Automobile Company, Syracuse, New York.
AIR-COOLED
FRANKLIN

For several years, Stoner was the artist on a series of national ads, like this one from 1929 for Franklin Automobile Co., a luxury car brand. These full-color, full-page ads ran in upscale magazines, and were rendered in the art deco style. They depicted a carefree lifestyle enjoyed by only a small, well-heeled segment of the car-buying public.

is the real possibility that Stoner served as a conduit for other Blacks looking for work in the comic book industry, a possibility alluded to in a biographical piece which proclaimed he "opened the way for many other Negro artists to be employed in this field." ["Artist-Author in Gordon's Ads," *Chicago Defender*, July 23, 1966]

Even his peers agreed.

E. Simms Campbell, with his cartoons, like Elmer Stoner in the pulps...helped to break hard ground on a path which many of us were to follow eagerly. [Shearer, Teddy, "Artists' Colony Lists Big Names," *New York Age*, Aug. 22, 1953]

By embracing the role as a trailblazer for subsequent Black comic artists, Stoner's career contrasted starkly against that of Adolphe Barreaux, who followed a similar path, but did so while benefiting mightily from his decision to pass for White and who never made any attempt to hire Blacks even though he was the head of an art studio. The light-skinned Stoner, too, had been designated by census takers as a "mulatto," but unlike Barreaux, he didn't use subterfuge to hide his multiracial background.

Stoner had a lesser impact on the comics Binder produced for pulp publisher Street and Smith. His most significant contributions came with Doc Savage, the company's bronze-skinned hero. Stoner had a hand in Savage's story in *Shadow Comics* vol. 1 #2 (1940) and took over the feature fully in issue #3 (May 1940). He also was one of the artists to work on the "Ajax, the Sun Man" backup feature in *Shadow* and "Iron Munro" over in *Doc Savage Comics*.

The dissolution of the Jack Binder shop circa 1943 didn't deter Stoner's comic career. If anything, he increased his workload. Late in 1943, Stoner's artwork began appearing through the Bernard Baily studio, yet another comic shop founded by an established artist. Stoner's work can be found in *Prize Comics*, beginning with issue #39 (Feb. 1944), wherein he illustrated "Ted O'Neil of the Commandos."

Stoner's most obvious presence, though, is seen on Fox comics of this period. Publisher Victor S. Fox had regained the rights to his various comic titles after a bankruptcy had led to the temporary loss of his characters and their respective comics to his printer. When Fox began publishing again in 1944, Stoner became his go-to cover artist.

Starting with *Blue Beetle* #31 (June 1944) and running into 1947, the vast majority of comics published by Fox (excluding the humor titles)—*Green Mask*, *Rocket Kelly*, *The Bouncer*, and early issues of *All Top*, *All Good*, and *All Great*—sported covers drawn by Stoner.

In addition to the dozens of covers, Stoner produced interior artwork for most of the same comics, but especially for *Blue Beetle*. Much of this work was unsigned or bearing the house name of "Otis." It was a common practice for publishers and shop owners to demand anonymity of their artists, who would change frequently, so that a false continuity could be presented to the readers. Upon occasion, though, Stoner was able to sneak his initials, "ECS," into a drawing, as he did on the cover of *Blue Beetle* #44 (Sept.-Oct. 1946), where they can be found in the headlight on the train.

Right now, in between doing his Blue Beetle continuities and painting portraits, he shows up regularly at USO centers to draw for servicemen and servicewomen. One of the USO centers is Harlem's, where, also, he teaches the soldiers to sketch. He occasionally gives art lectures as a means of improving Negro-white relations. [Gordon, Eugene, "Comics Go to War: This Negro Artist's Drawings Are Fighting Our Enemies." *Daily Worker*, May 21, 1944]

The fact that a feature article on Stoner's career would appear in America's leading Communist Party newspaper isn't as peculiar as it seems. Communism, in America as elsewhere, found its greatest support among the downtrodden, and Blacks found the ideology appealing. The Communists garnered even more support among Blacks in 1931, when they took up the cause of the Scottsboro Boys, nine Black youths arrested for the supposed rape of two White women. It was the International Labor Defense (ILD), legal arm of the Communist Party of the USA (CPUSA), that hired famed New York lawyer Samuel Liebowitz to defend the accused.

The *Daily Worker* routinely railed against the Jim Crow laws in the South, condemned lynchings, and covered the struggles of the burgeoning civil rights movement. While Stoner was a Democrat, his interview in the *Daily Worker* likely revealed that he was appreciative of their stands and receptive to their cause.

As with many American Blacks, Stoner was confronted with the challenge of fulfilling society's expectations of a "good American" in wartime, while also suffering the second-class citizenship that same society bestowed upon him. This conflict formed the basis of James G. Thompson's 1942 letter to the *Pittsburgh Courier*, and provided the impetus for the Double V campaign that called for victory over the Axis as well as victory against discrimination at home.

To that end, Stoner became involved with a comic entitled *The Challenger*. Published by Interfaith Publications under the auspices of *Protestant Digest*, this comic was conceived by the liberal theologian Kenneth Leslie in the waning months of WWII, as a challenge to the antisemitism and racism still prevalent in America. He assigned Gerald Richardson, associate editor of *Protestant Digest* and head of the Anti-Fascist Catholic Committee, to be the comic's editor. It would be the first standalone effort to publish a comic book featuring minority characters in a positive light.

The first issue of this short-run series was released in January 1945 and featured a striking Stoner cover of a "Challenger Club" member tossing a "truth bomb" into the face of a Nazi. On the inside, Stoner had two additional contributions, both tales written by his wife, Henriette: "Rev. Ben," the story of Black anti-fascist preacher Rev. Ben Richardson (who was also an associate editor at the *Protestant Digest*); and "Most Honorable Son Hara-Kiri," about Japanese-American airman Sgt. Ben Kuroki, the only Nisei to serve in the Pacific Theater.

Dr. Henriette Stoner, née Messinger, born Dec. 9, 1906, married Elmer on July 31, 1937. It was a bold union for the time, as she was a White Jew from The Bronx. As with his first wife, Vivienne, Henriette was also a highly accomplished woman. A trained psychiatrist, she studied in Vienna with renowned psychotherapist Dr. Alfred Adler. She was co-founder of the Mental Hygiene Clinics for the New York City school system and maintained her own Manhattan practice. Both she and Elmer were active in local Democratic Party politics and served in several community positions within their Greenwich Village neighborhood. Henriette would also collaborate with her husband as the writer on other comic book ventures.

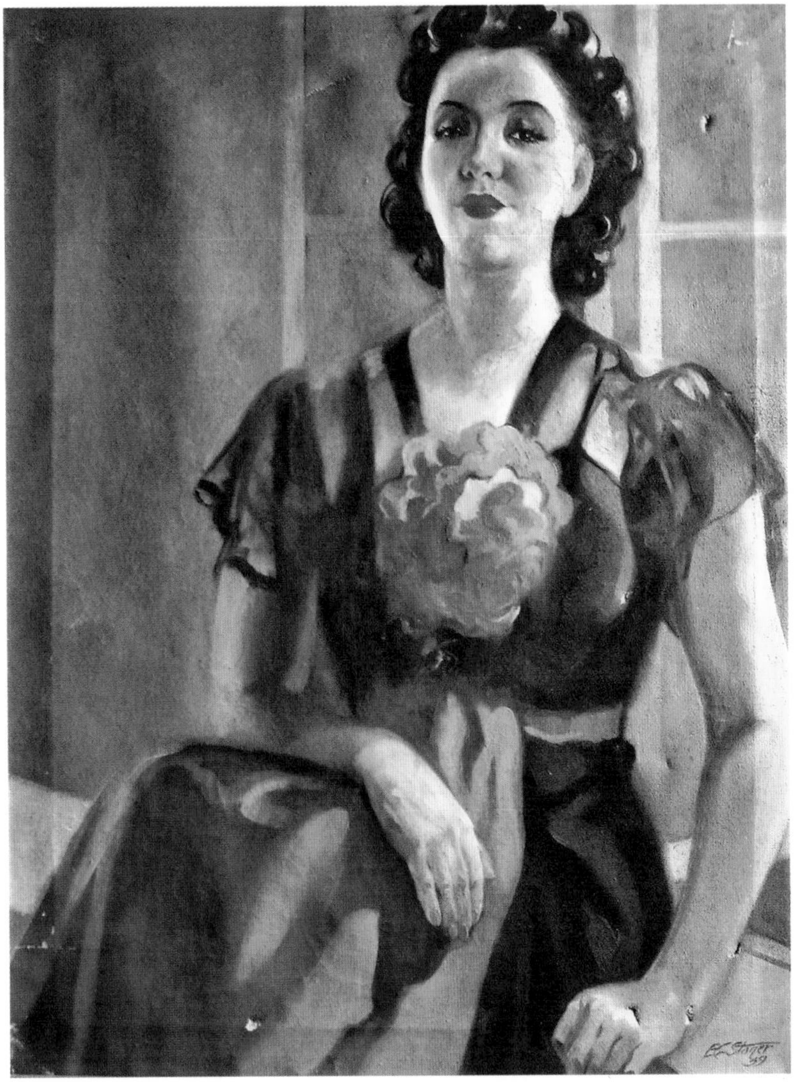

One such venture was Stoner's first as a publisher. In 1946, he and a partner with the last name of Gould (first name yet to be determined) established the Gould-Stoner Company. On October 8th of that year, they copyrighted their one and only publication, *Christmas Play Book*.

The concept was straightforward—a child's activity booklet, 16 pages in length, containing puzzles, games, and Stoner drawings throughout. It was distributed through department stores and by the 20th Century Fox movie studio. Fox bought the pamphlet from Gould-Stoner and was selling it to exhibitors, who would in turn distribute it to movie-goers. Reportedly, the comic had a print run of 1,000,000 copies. Any joy elicited by this comic's success was short-lived. It appears that in 1945, Fox had bought another publication with the same name of *Christmas Play Book*, and the publishers of that book were now suing both Fox and Gould-Stoner for copyright infringement and damages of $100,000. The outcome of the suit is unknown, but the fact that no other publication was forthcoming from Gould-Stoner seems to indicate that it effectively killed the company.

But Stoner wasn't without work. The first issue of *Blackstone, Master Magician* (March – April 1946), based on world-famous magician Harry Blackstone, featured both a Stoner cover and interior artwork. This comic was published by Vital Publications and was written by Walter Gibson, who had scripted Blackstone's manifestation as a comic character at each of his various publishers. Best remembered as the writer of the pulp and comic book versions of *The Shadow*, Gibson was the link to all parties involved. He was a friend of both the real-life Blackstone and Julien Proskauer, Vital's owner; and, like Stoner, he had a long association with publisher Street and Smith.

Vital's version of *Blackstone* ran only three issues (all with Stoner art) when it was then briefly published by M. C. Gaines' Educational Comics (EC). That one issue, again containing Stoner art, was cover dated Fall 1947, and bore the unwieldy title of *Blackstone the Magician Fights Crime*. Stoner also provided the covers to Blackstone's souvenir programs handed out at his performances in the late 1940s.

Despite his commercial work, Stoner's fine art career didn't suffer. He was commissioned to paint the portraits of three Black U.S. Army officers: Col. W. Woodruff Chisum, Col. Elmer Sawyer, and Col. Chauncey W. Hooper. These were done in commemoration of their service during WWII. The portraits were revealed to much praise from the gathered dignitaries at a tribute honoring the soldiers, which was held at the 369th Regiment Armory in Harlem on June 15, 1947.

Stoner eventually moved on from drawing newsstand comic books, a move likely precipitated by the influx of artists returning from military service. He didn't, however,

[Previous page] When the newspaper strip *Rick Kane* debuted, the *New York Amsterdam News* ran this photo with the caption, "[Walter] Gibson and [E.C.] Stoner collaborate on 'future' space strips, which means eight to ten weeks in advance, and average of 560 copies ready for distribution. The extraordinary feature of their partnership is great respect, complete confidence, and personal consultation in all matters of detail and purpose." [Holt, Nora, "Interracial Team Looks Into The Future: Negro Artist Plus White Writer 'Father' New Comic," *New York Amsterdam News*, September 22, 1951]

[Above] An untitled painting by Stoner from 1939 depicting his wife Henriette, whom he married in 1937. She was a trained psychiatrist and author of many of Stoner's comic stories. About Stoner's lifestyle, Nora Holt wrote in the *Amsterdam News*, "Living in a Greenwich Village penthouse, he finds diversion at a Steinway concert grand playing classical works by Bach, Beethoven, Brahms and Chopin, attended by his beautiful wife, Henriette and his champion boxer, 'Champ.'" [Ibid.]

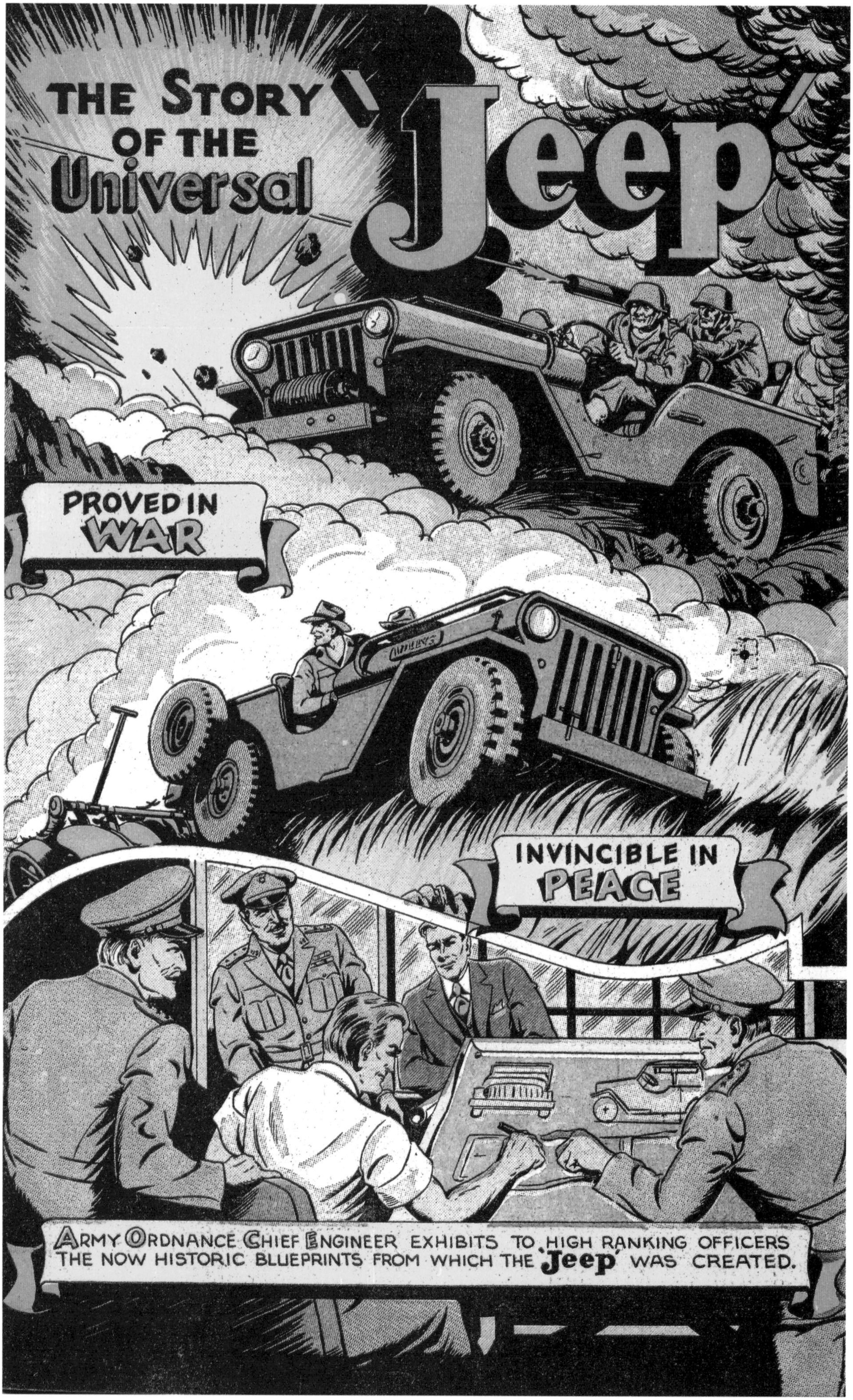
THE STORY OF THE Universal 'Jeep'
PROVED IN WAR
INVINCIBLE IN PEACE
ARMY ORDNANCE CHIEF ENGINEER EXHIBITS TO HIGH RANKING OFFICERS THE NOW HISTORIC BLUEPRINTS FROM WHICH THE 'Jeep' WAS CREATED.

leave the field entirely. Toward the end of the 1940s, Stoner began producing artwork for promotional comics.

Promotional comic books are exactly what their name suggests: comics produced with the intention to promote whatever product, propaganda, or image a client wishes to sell, convince, or convey. Most often, these comics were given away free to the general public, earning them the additional name of "giveaways." The comic book has been used for this purpose since its very beginnings back in the 1800s. This became a very lucrative part of the publishing industry, as publishers would be paid for the comics up front and not have to depend upon newsstand sales for their profits. By the 1930s, there were publishing companies formed expressly to create promotional comics. The companies producing these comics paid better than the newsstand comic book publishers, and Stoner made a wise decision turning to them for assignments.

Most of his assignments came from Vital Publications, the *Blackstone* publisher. Vital had actually started publishing promotional comics in 1944, as 16-page giveaways distributed through theaters. In 1948, they began producing a series of small, oblong-shaped comics to be used as premiums by such varied clients as Wisco 99 Service Stations and Carnation Malted Milk. Stoner was the artist of many of these titles, including *Johnny Starboard and the Undersea Pirates*, *Blaze Carson*, and *Jim Solar, Space Sheriff*. As with the *Blackstone* comics, his writing collaborator was Walter Gibson.

Stoner also found such work outside of Vital as illustrator of several historical giveaways. In his *George Washington's Railroad* (1948), produced for the Chesapeake and Ohio Lines, Stoner devoted a full page to John Henry, the legendary Black "steel-drivin' man," who died in his competition against a steam-powered drill building the railroad's Big Bend Tunnel. In 1949, Stoner drew *The Story of Salt*, for the Leslie Salt Company, and that same year, *The Amazing Story of Measurement* for Lufkin Rule Co., a maker of tape measures. Possibly his best promo comic work came on *The Story of the Universal Jeep* for Willys-Overland. This colorful 16-pager touted the utility vehicle's virtues with an enthusiasm that wouldn't have been out of place in a newsstand comic.

By 1950, Stoner was gaining more recognition for his fine art, but most of that came from the Black media. Evidence of this can be found in the coverage of a March 1951 exhibition of his paintings by the Wilkes-Barre YWCA in honor of World Fellowship Week. It received a long, laudatory article in one of the nation's leading Black newspapers:

The high point of his showing centered around scenes along the Lehigh Valley mainline, especially in the Wilkes-Barre area where he [Stoner] played as a boy and later recaptured the starkness of mining towns and "patches," the local country-side and moving trains, with startling fidelity, which besides its artistic charm has historical value. The exhibition included 28 watercolors and five oil portraits. [Holt, Nora, "Monday Morning in a Pennsylvania Mine Town," *New York Amsterdam News*, March 10, 1951]

Stoner's scenes of railroad trains and stark mining towns prompted James M. Rutter, writer for the *Wilkes-Barre Times Leader*, to comment:

I know of no American painter, exclusive of a few Post cover men, who could have captured this agglomeration of sheer ugliness with as much charm."

Holt also added:

Like Rembrandt, the man (Stoner) can take a banal, commonplace section of contemporary life, bathe it in the rare glow from his inner fire, and create a contribution to the very heart and soul of art. [Ibid.]

Later that same year, Stoner became one of the first, and one of the few, Black American artists to draw a nationally syndicated comic strip appearing in White newspapers. Debuting August 27, 1951, *Rick Kane, Space Marshal* would find Stoner once again collaborating with Walter Gibson.

The *New York Post* and the other 30 newspapers running the strip gave little-to-no background information about the strip's creators, but the *New York Amsterdam News* found the interracial duo worthy of a glowing, full-page article. Writer Nora Holt noted:

Walter Gibson (white) and Elmer Stoner (Negro) are far from novices in the professional field of journalism, fiction and commercial art, and have worked together on various assignments for the past eight years, hence when they were contracted by the company to do a 'space strip' on an interplanetary idea, they went into a huddle and Rick Kane *was born."* [Holt, Nora, "Interracial Team Looks Into The Future: Negro Artist Plus White Writer 'Father' New Comic," *New York Amsterdam News*, September 22, 1951]

In the *Amsterdam News*, Stoner also offered inspiration:

Mr. Stoner says his advice to young Negro artists is work, study, preparation and patience. "This break," he said, "is the culmination

Post World War II, most of Stoner's work appeared in commercial comics intended to promote products and industries. This colorful 16-pager touted the virtues of the famed utility vehicle. *The Story of the Universal Jeep*, c. late 1940s, Willys-Overland Motors.

of a long series of exacting experiences in the art field. I have worked as art director and delved into every field of illustration but fashion, and I find that today one must work harder than ever due to ever increasing competition." [Ibid.]

In an interview conducted years later, Walter Gibson expanded upon *Rick Kane*'s origins. The writer recounted to interviewer Will Murray:

We decided to do a comic called Rick Kane, Space Marshal, *Stoner did the first for me, and it was like* Star Wars, *taking off from the world on a trip to Mars. I treated Mars just as you would treat an airplane flight across the ocean.* [Murray, Will, "Walter Gibson's Secret Comics Career," *Comic Book Marketplace*, January 2005]

Despite a long-term contract with the Enterprising Feature Syndicate to produce the strip, it only ran from the summer of 1951 until early in 1952, with Stoner's work on it ending sometime sooner. Stoner sued the syndicate to restrain it from continuation of *Rick Kane* with another artist, as it violated the terms of his contract. A judge disagreed and on December 17, 1951, he denied Stoner's request. Gibson recalled:

Then there were some problems. Stoner quit, Higgins was handling it. He was one of these promoters, and he wanted to get more money out of it. So, he was bleeding him [Stoner] and trying to grab money from the people. And he wasn't paying Stoner. [Ibid.]

This experience was to be virtually Stoner's last in the commercial art field, except for one standalone venture in 1957. That year, he and Henriette collaborated on one final project: a promotional comic book entitled *Deadline*. Subtitled "The Story Behind the Headline," this was yet another historical comic, this time depicting the history of printing. The comic was the brainchild of Arizona publisher John R. Manning. Manning was a native New Yorker and a recent transplant to the state. He was once the publisher of the *Brooklyn Heights Press*, and just prior to his move to Arizona, worked for King Features Syndicate in New York, which was likely how he connected to Stoner. Manning's plan was to offer *Deadline* to newspaper publishers nationwide as a promotional tool, but it never was published. Only a few sample copies were distributed among a handful of Arizona papers.

In the Spring of 1952, Henriette Stoner opened Talents Unlimited at 61 Grove Street in Greenwich Village, a gallery, "specializing in the unusual." The ads for the gallery touted it as a "showcase for creative craftsmen," which included African wood carvings, ceramics, textiles, and, not surprisingly, paintings by her husband. Then, in 1961, he joined a cooperative of Bucks County artists and began exhibiting his work at the Upstairs Gallery in New Hope, Pennsylvania. New Hope was an upscale artists colony about 75 miles and a world away from the coal mine-scarred mountains surrounding Wilkes-Barre.

Late in life, Stoner was chosen as one of the in-print spokesmen for Gordon's Gin. Beginning in the mid-Sixties, ads began to appear in *Ebony* magazine and numerous Black newspapers around the country. They bore a photograph of Stoner posing with a painting and Henriette in the background, situated in their penthouse apartment. "Even with the simplest watercolor, I strive for perfection," Stoner was quoted in the ad, echoing his previous advice to young artists. "It's only through dedication that anything great is ever achieved." ["Gordon's Gin Ad," *Ebony*, June 1966]

On December 16, 1969, Elmer Cecil Stoner passed away at St. Vincent's Hospital in Greenwich Village. Per his request, he was cremated. Among his many accomplishments, Stoner's dual status as both a fine artist and a comics cartoonist established a unique template followed by other Blacks entering the comic industry in its early years.

First chapter in Stoner's classic "Threat From Saturn" serial that ran over six issues. Unfortunately, it ended without a conclusion in issue #41. *Blue Beetle* #34, September 1944, Fox Publications.

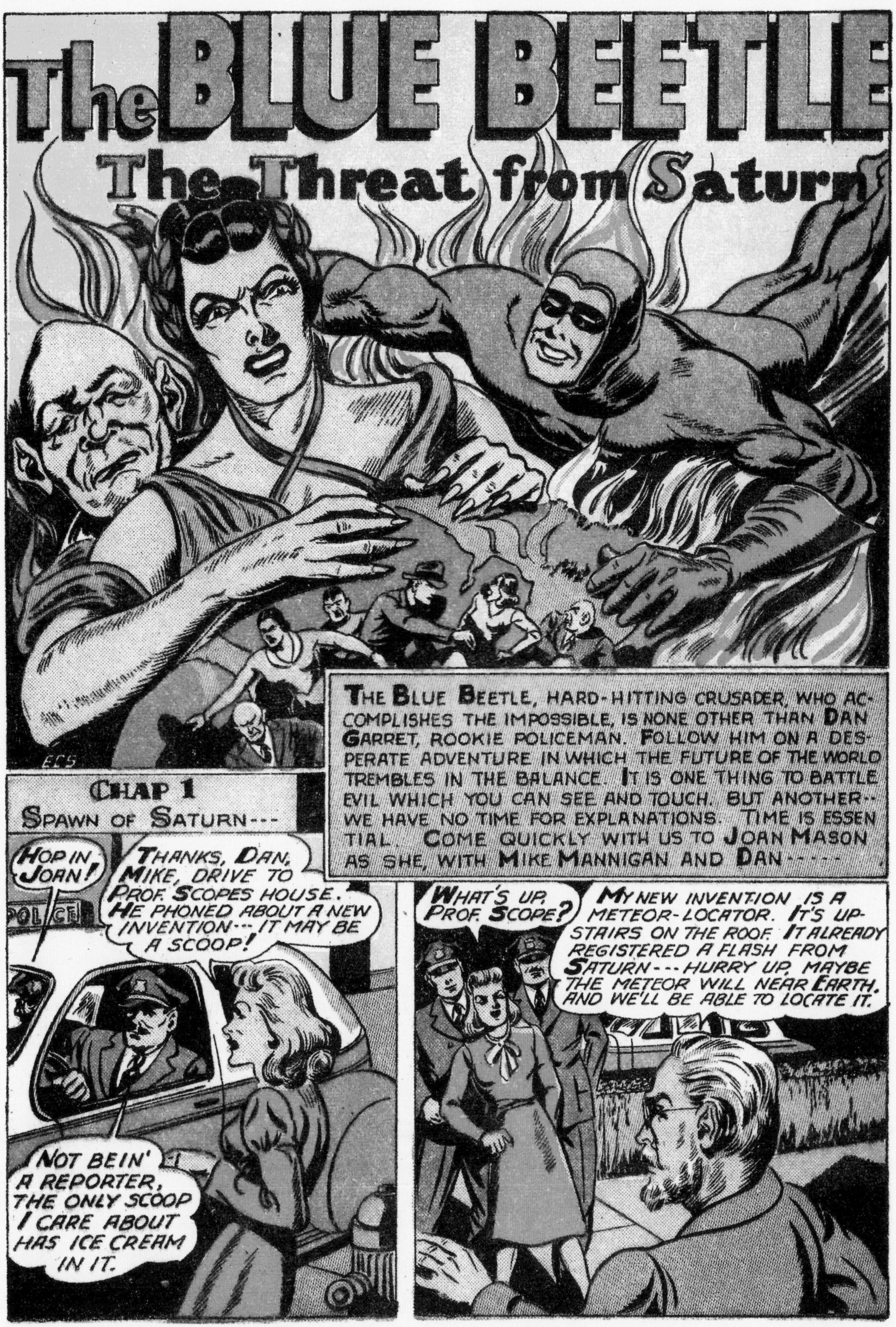
The BLUE BEETLE
The Threat from Saturn
THE BLUE BEETLE, HARD-HITTING CRUSADER, WHO ACCOMPLISHES THE IMPOSSIBLE, IS NONE OTHER THAN DAN GARRET, ROOKIE POLICEMAN. FOLLOW HIM ON A DESPERATE ADVENTURE IN WHICH THE FUTURE OF THE WORLD TREMBLES IN THE BALANCE. IT IS ONE THING TO BATTLE EVIL WHICH YOU CAN SEE AND TOUCH, BUT ANOTHER-- WE HAVE NO TIME FOR EXPLANATIONS. TIME IS ESSENTIAL. COME QUICKLY WITH US TO JOAN MASON AS SHE, WITH MIKE MANNIGAN AND DAN-----
CHAP 1
SPAWN OF SATURN---
HOP IN, JOAN!
THANKS, DAN. MIKE, DRIVE TO PROF. SCOPES HOUSE. HE PHONED ABOUT A NEW INVENTION--- IT MAY BE A SCOOP!
POLICE
NOT BEIN' A REPORTER, THE ONLY SCOOP I CARE ABOUT HAS ICE CREAM IN IT.
WHAT'S UP, PROF. SCOPE?
MY NEW INVENTION IS A METEOR-LOCATOR. IT'S UPSTAIRS ON THE ROOF. IT ALREADY REGISTERED A FLASH FROM SATURN--- HURRY UP, MAYBE THE METEOR WILL NEAR EARTH, AND WE'LL BE ABLE TO LOCATE IT.

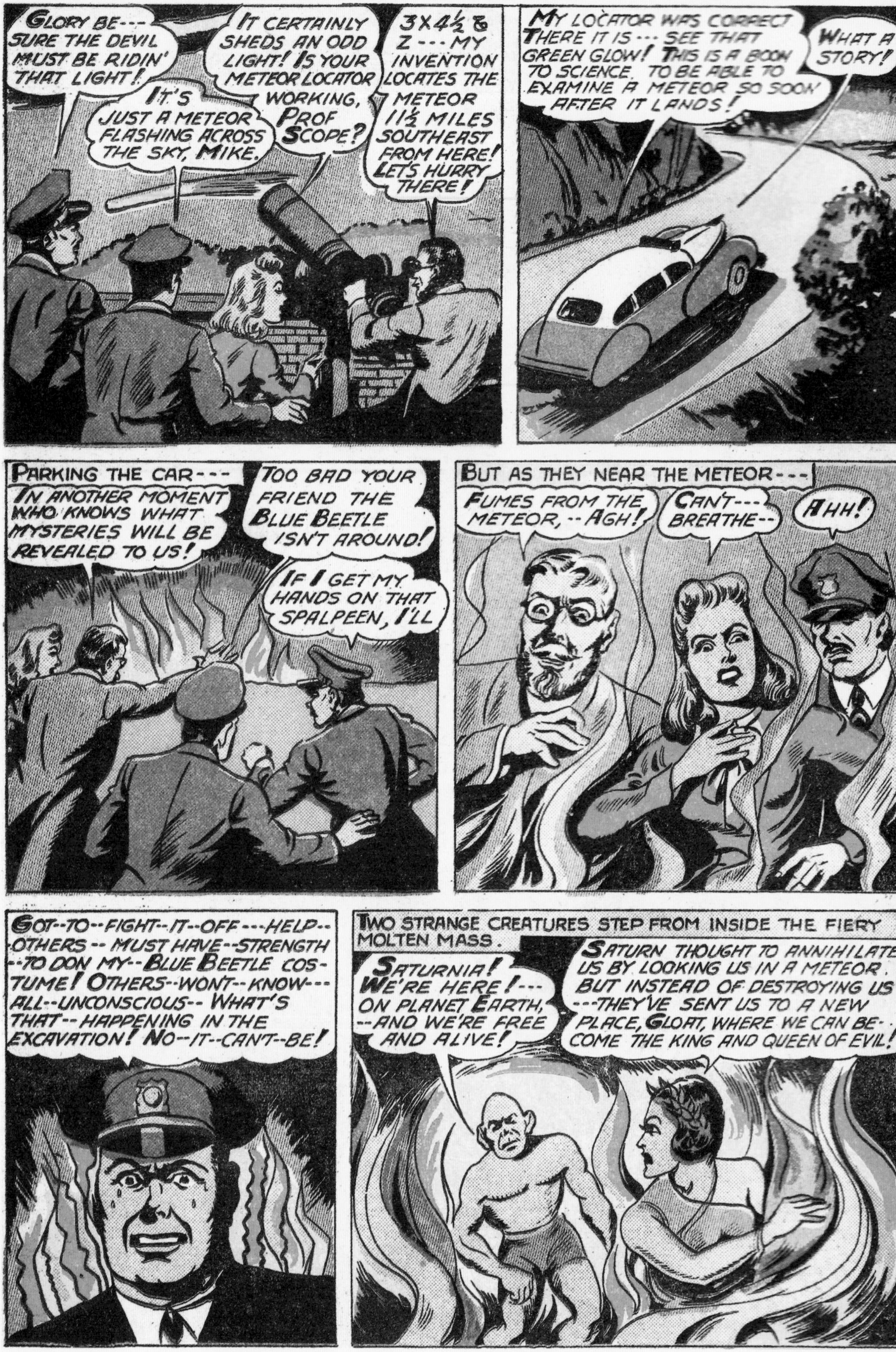
GLORY BE--- SURE THE DEVIL MUST BE RIDIN' THAT LIGHT!
IT'S JUST A METEOR FLASHING ACROSS THE SKY, MIKE.
IT CERTAINLY SHEDS AN ODD LIGHT! IS YOUR METEOR LOCATOR WORKING, PROF SCOPE?
3X4½ & Z --- MY INVENTION LOCATES THE METEOR 1½ MILES SOUTHEAST FROM HERE! LET'S HURRY THERE!
MY LOCATOR WAS CORRECT THERE IT IS --- SEE THAT GREEN GLOW! THIS IS A BOON TO SCIENCE. TO BE ABLE TO EXAMINE A METEOR SO SOON AFTER IT LANDS!
WHAT A STORY!
PARKING THE CAR---
IN ANOTHER MOMENT WHO KNOWS WHAT MYSTERIES WILL BE REVEALED TO US!
TOO BAD YOUR FRIEND THE BLUE BEETLE ISN'T AROUND!
IF I GET MY HANDS ON THAT SPALPEEN, I'LL
BUT AS THEY NEAR THE METEOR---
FUMES FROM THE METEOR, --AGH!
CAN'T--- BREATHE--
AHH!
GOT--TO--FIGHT--IT--OFF---HELP-- OTHERS-- MUST HAVE--STRENGTH --TO DON MY--BLUE BEETLE COSTUME! OTHERS--WON'T--KNOW--- ALL--UNCONSCIOUS-- WHAT'S THAT--HAPPENING IN THE EXCAVATION! NO--IT--CAN'T--BE!
TWO STRANGE CREATURES STEP FROM INSIDE THE FIERY MOLTEN MASS.
SATURNIA! WE'RE HERE!--- ON PLANET EARTH, --AND WE'RE FREE AND ALIVE!
SATURN THOUGHT TO ANNIHILATE US BY LOCKING US IN A METEOR. BUT INSTEAD OF DESTROYING US ---THEY'VE SENT US TO A NEW PLACE, GLORT, WHERE WE CAN BECOME THE KING AND QUEEN OF EVIL!

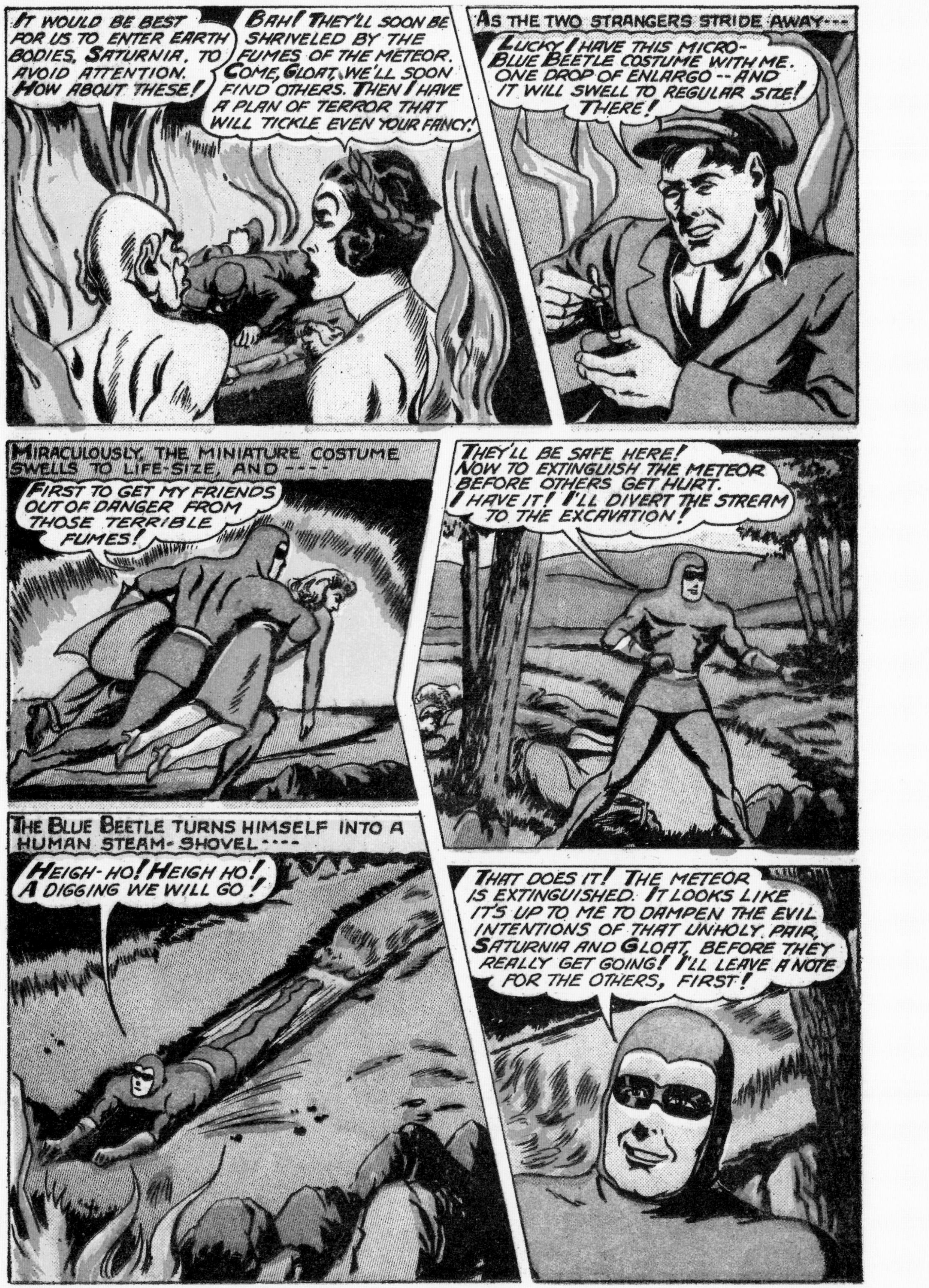
IT WOULD BE BEST FOR US TO ENTER EARTH BODIES, SATURNIA, TO AVOID ATTENTION. HOW ABOUT THESE!
BAH! THEY'LL SOON BE SHRIVELED BY THE FUMES OF THE METEOR. COME, GLOAT, WE'LL SOON FIND OTHERS. THEN I HAVE A PLAN OF TERROR THAT WILL TICKLE EVEN YOUR FANCY!
AS THE TWO STRANGERS STRIDE AWAY---
LUCKY I HAVE THIS MICRO-BLUE BEETLE COSTUME WITH ME. ONE DROP OF ENLARGO -- AND IT WILL SWELL TO REGULAR SIZE! THERE!
MIRACULOUSLY, THE MINIATURE COSTUME SWELLS TO LIFE-SIZE, AND----
FIRST TO GET MY FRIENDS OUT OF DANGER FROM THOSE TERRIBLE FUMES!
THEY'LL BE SAFE HERE! NOW TO EXTINGUISH THE METEOR BEFORE OTHERS GET HURT. I HAVE IT! I'LL DIVERT THE STREAM TO THE EXCAVATION!
THE BLUE BEETLE TURNS HIMSELF INTO A HUMAN STEAM-SHOVEL----
HEIGH-HO! HEIGH HO! A DIGGING WE WILL GO!
THAT DOES IT! THE METEOR IS EXTINGUISHED. IT LOOKS LIKE IT'S UP TO ME TO DAMPEN THE EVIL INTENTIONS OF THAT UNHOLY PAIR, SATURNIA AND GLOAT, BEFORE THEY REALLY GET GOING! I'LL LEAVE A NOTE FOR THE OTHERS, FIRST!

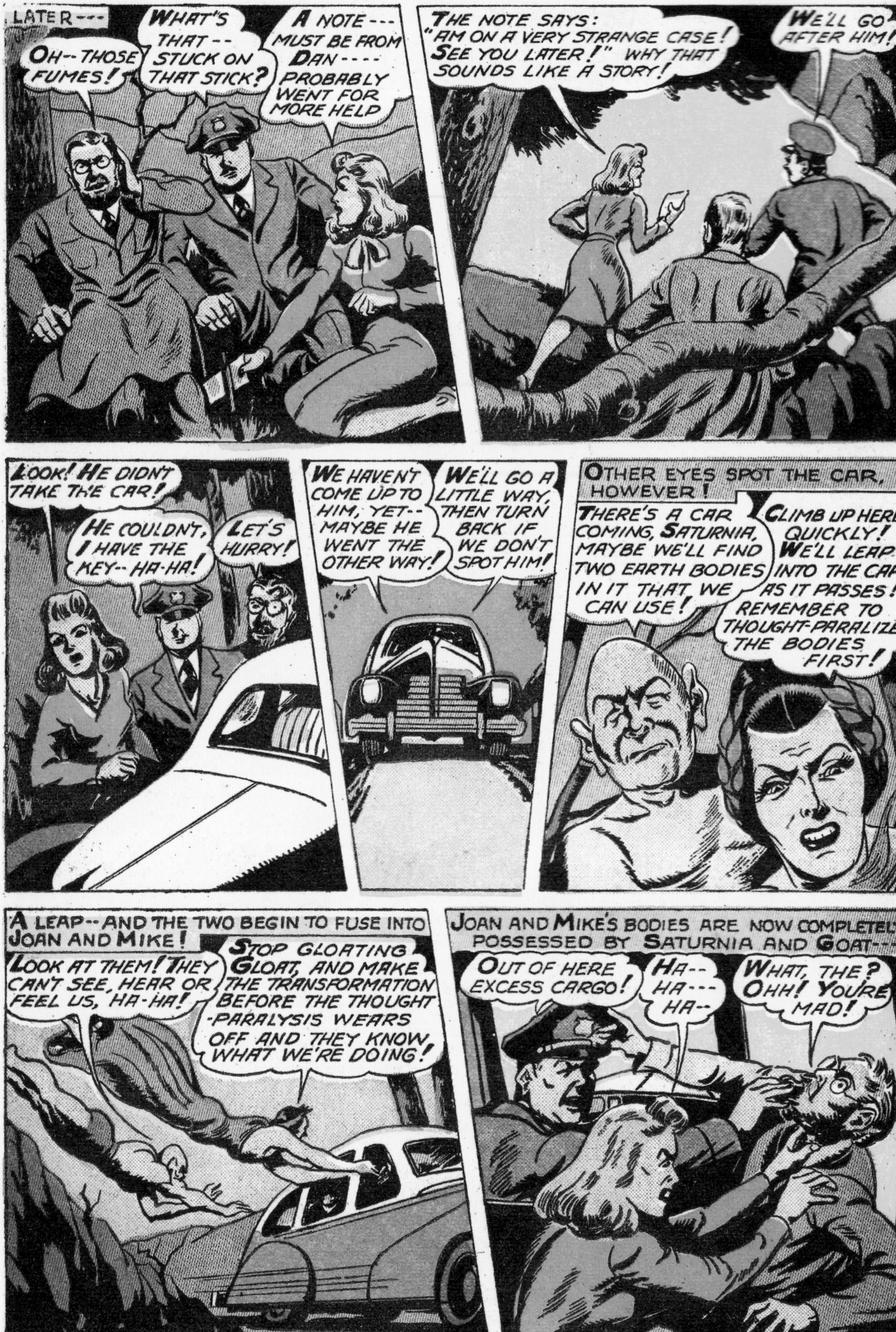
LATER---
OH--THOSE FUMES!
WHAT'S THAT-- STUCK ON THAT STICK?
A NOTE--- MUST BE FROM DAN---- PROBABLY WENT FOR MORE HELP
THE NOTE SAYS: "AM ON A VERY STRANGE CASE! SEE YOU LATER!" WHY THAT SOUNDS LIKE A STORY!
WE'LL GO AFTER HIM!
LOOK! HE DIDN'T TAKE THE CAR!
HE COULDN'T, I HAVE THE KEY-- HA-HA!
LET'S HURRY!
WE HAVEN'T COME UP TO HIM, YET-- MAYBE HE WENT THE OTHER WAY!
WE'LL GO A LITTLE WAY, THEN TURN BACK IF WE DON'T SPOT HIM!
OTHER EYES SPOT THE CAR, HOWEVER!
THERE'S A CAR COMING, SATURNIA, MAYBE WE'LL FIND TWO EARTH BODIES IN IT THAT WE CAN USE!
CLIMB UP HERE QUICKLY! WE'LL LEAP INTO THE CAR AS IT PASSES! REMEMBER TO THOUGHT-PARALIZE THE BODIES FIRST!
A LEAP-- AND THE TWO BEGIN TO FUSE INTO JOAN AND MIKE!
LOOK AT THEM! THEY CAN'T SEE, HEAR OR FEEL US, HA-HA!
STOP GLOATING GLOAT, AND MAKE THE TRANSFORMATION BEFORE THE THOUGHT -PARALYSIS WEARS OFF AND THEY KNOW WHAT WE'RE DOING!
JOAN AND MIKE'S BODIES ARE NOW COMPLETELY POSSESSED BY SATURNIA AND GOAT----
OUT OF HERE EXCESS CARGO!
HA-- HA--- HA--
WHAT, THE? OHH! YOU'RE MAD!

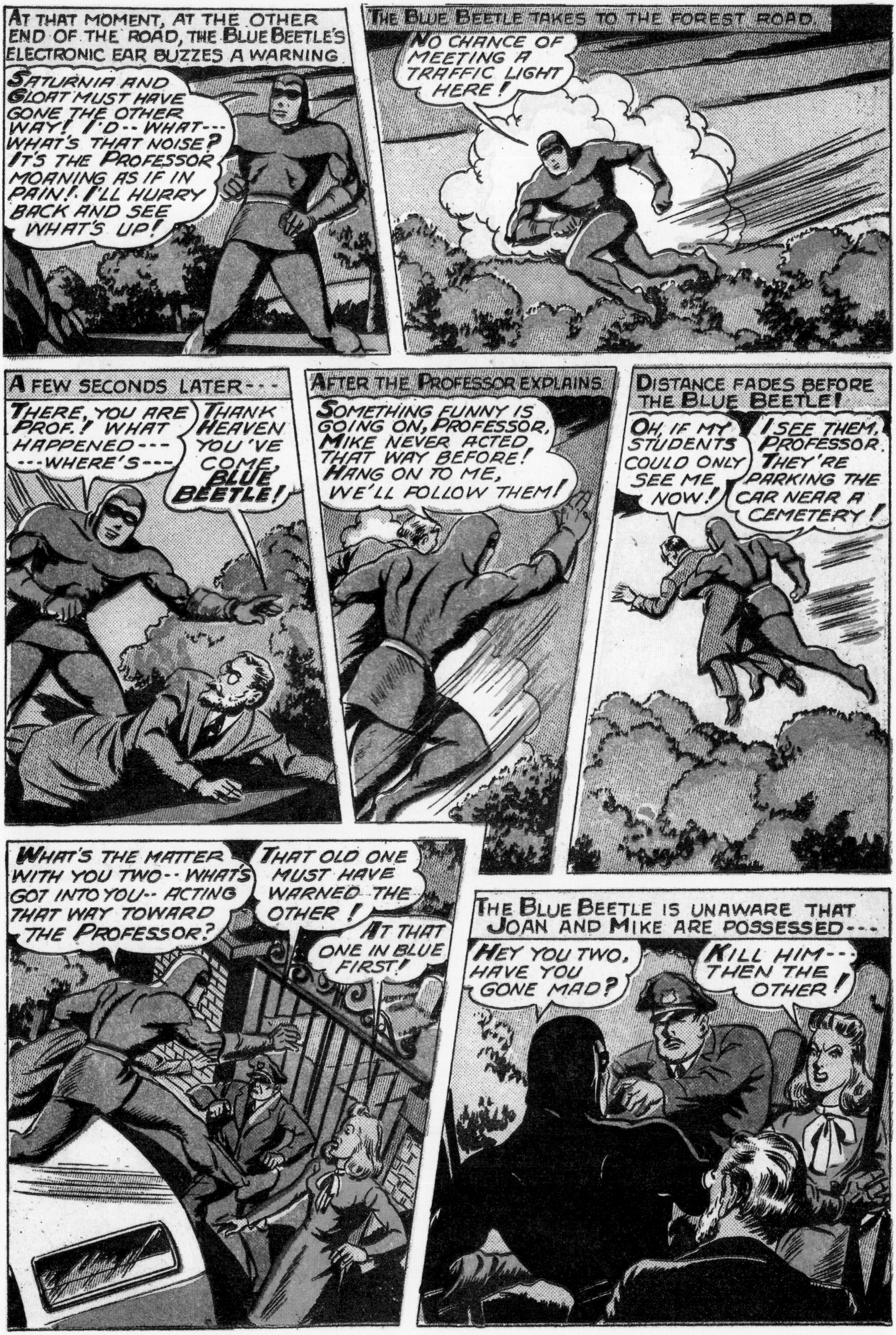

AT THAT MOMENT, AT THE OTHER END OF THE ROAD, THE BLUE BEETLE'S ELECTRONIC EAR BUZZES A WARNING
SATURNIA AND GLOAT MUST HAVE GONE THE OTHER WAY! I'D-- WHAT--- WHAT'S THAT NOISE? IT'S THE PROFESSOR MOANING AS IF IN PAIN! I'LL HURRY BACK AND SEE WHAT'S UP!
THE BLUE BEETLE TAKES TO THE FOREST ROAD
NO CHANCE OF MEETING A TRAFFIC LIGHT HERE!
A FEW SECONDS LATER---
THERE, YOU ARE PROF.! WHAT HAPPENED--- ---WHERE'S---
THANK HEAVEN YOU'VE COME, BLUE BEETLE!
AFTER THE PROFESSOR EXPLAINS
SOMETHING FUNNY IS GOING ON, PROFESSOR, MIKE NEVER ACTED THAT WAY BEFORE! HANG ON TO ME, WE'LL FOLLOW THEM!
DISTANCE FADES BEFORE THE BLUE BEETLE!
OH, IF MY STUDENTS COULD ONLY SEE ME NOW!
I SEE THEM, PROFESSOR. THEY'RE PARKING THE CAR NEAR A CEMETERY!
WHAT'S THE MATTER WITH YOU TWO-- WHAT'S GOT INTO YOU-- ACTING THAT WAY TOWARD THE PROFESSOR?
THAT OLD ONE MUST HAVE WARNED THE OTHER!
AT THAT ONE IN BLUE FIRST!
THE BLUE BEETLE IS UNAWARE THAT JOAN AND MIKE ARE POSSESSED---
HEY YOU TWO, HAVE YOU GONE MAD?
KILL HIM--- THEN THE OTHER!

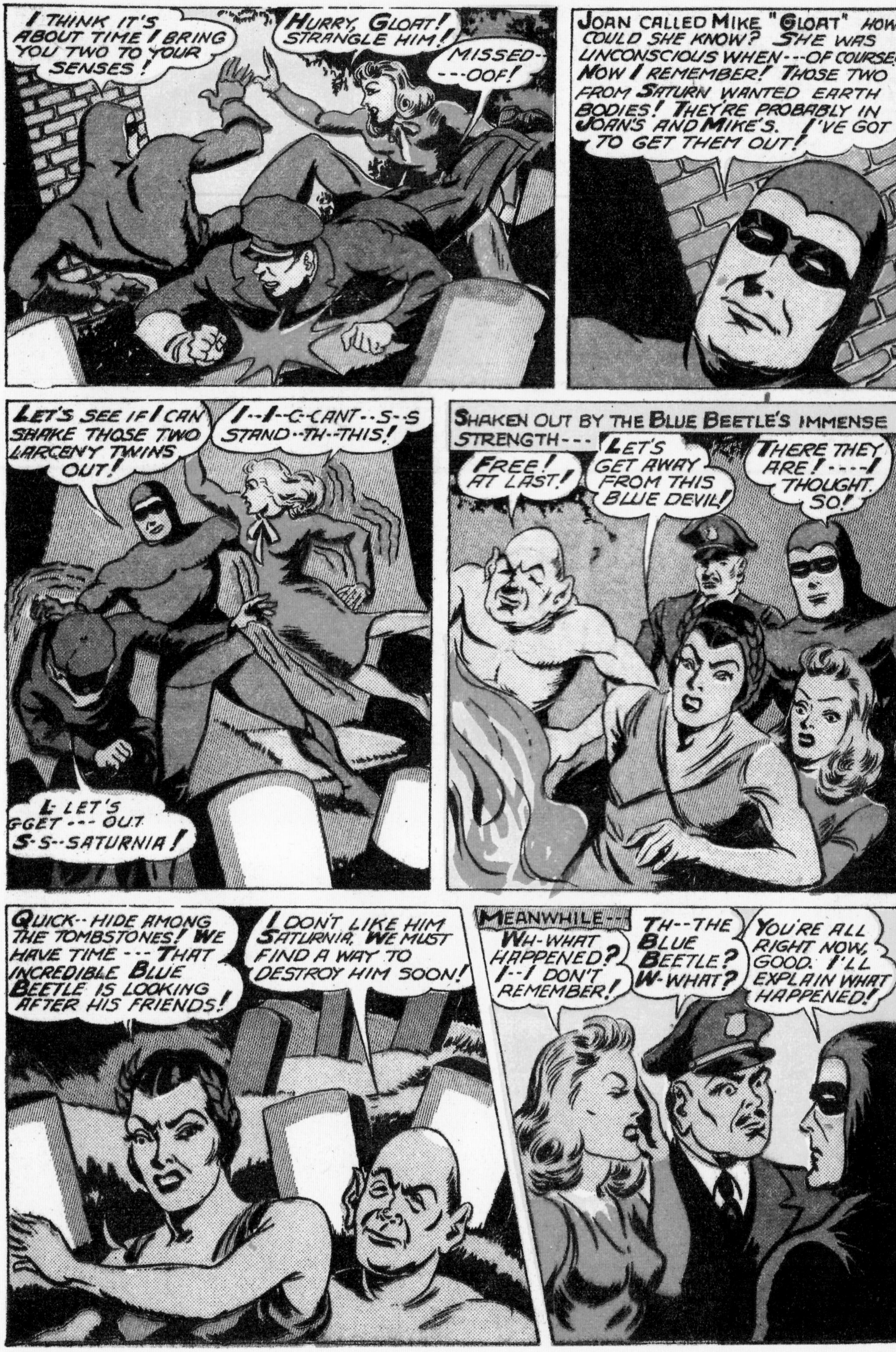

I THINK IT'S ABOUT TIME I BRING YOU TWO TO YOUR SENSES!
HURRY, GLOAT! STRANGLE HIM!
MISSED-- ---OOF!
JOAN CALLED MIKE "GLOAT" HOW COULD SHE KNOW? SHE WAS UNCONSCIOUS WHEN---OF COURSE! NOW I REMEMBER! THOSE TWO FROM SATURN WANTED EARTH BODIES! THEY'RE PROBABLY IN JOAN'S AND MIKE'S. I'VE GOT TO GET THEM OUT!
LET'S SEE IF I CAN SHAKE THOSE TWO LARCENY TWINS OUT!
I--I--C-CANT--S--S STAND--TH--THIS!
L-LET'S G-GET --- OUT S-S--SATURNIA!
SHAKEN OUT BY THE BLUE BEETLE'S IMMENSE STRENGTH---
FREE! AT LAST!
LET'S GET AWAY FROM THIS BLUE DEVIL!
THERE THEY ARE!----I THOUGHT SO!
QUICK--HIDE AMONG THE TOMBSTONES! WE HAVE TIME---THAT INCREDIBLE BLUE BEETLE IS LOOKING AFTER HIS FRIENDS!
I DON'T LIKE HIM SATURNIA. WE MUST FIND A WAY TO DESTROY HIM SOON!
MEANWHILE--
WH-WHAT HAPPENED? I--I DON'T REMEMBER!
TH--THE BLUE BEETLE? W-WHAT?
YOU'RE ALL RIGHT NOW, GOOD. I'LL EXPLAIN WHAT HAPPENED!

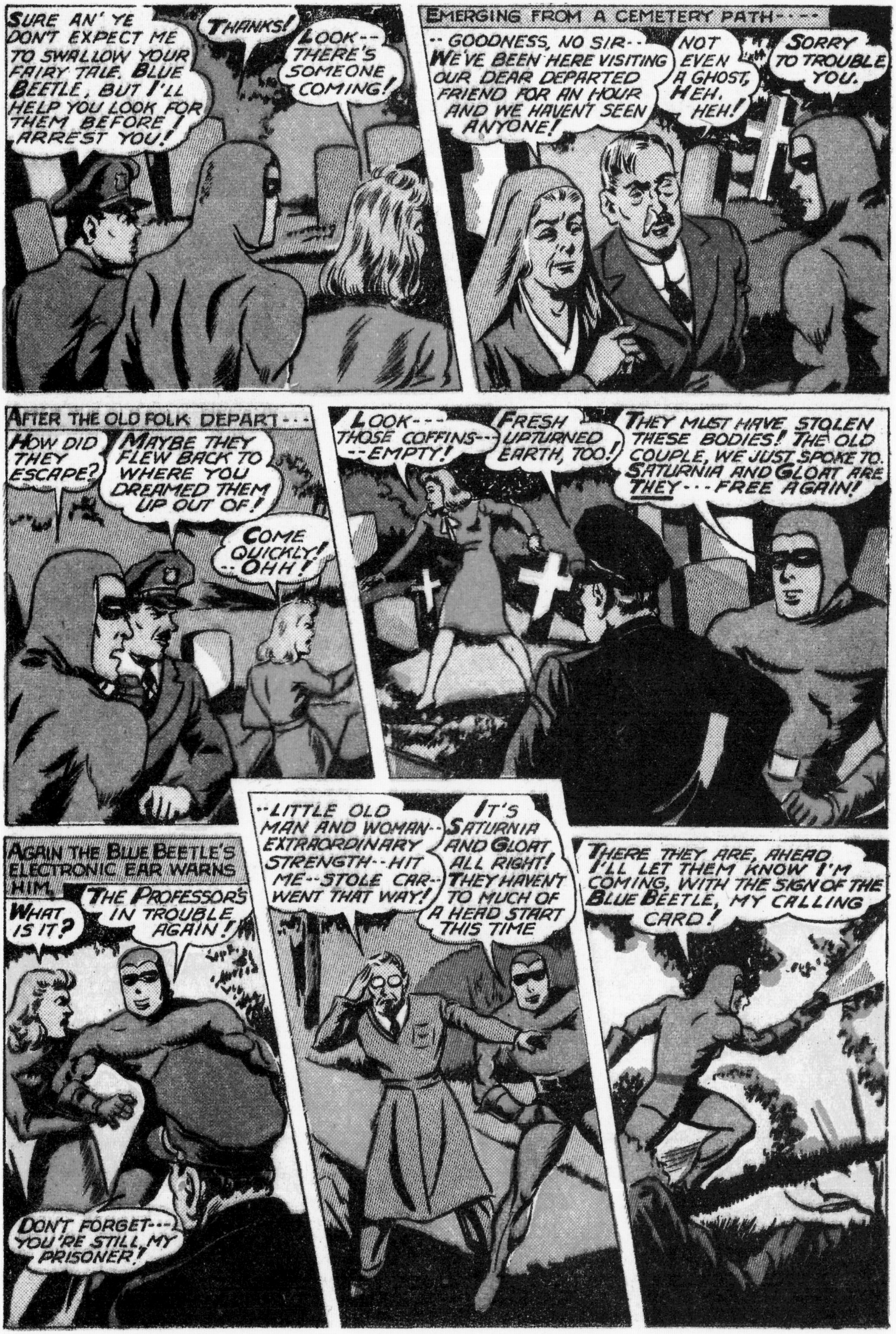
SURE AN' YE DON'T EXPECT ME TO SWALLOW YOUR FAIRY TALE, BLUE BEETLE, BUT I'LL HELP YOU LOOK FOR THEM BEFORE I ARREST YOU!
THANKS!
LOOK-- THERE'S SOMEONE COMING!
EMERGING FROM A CEMETERY PATH---
--GOODNESS, NO SIR-- WE'VE BEEN HERE VISITING OUR DEAR DEPARTED FRIEND FOR AN HOUR AND WE HAVEN'T SEEN ANYONE!
NOT EVEN A GHOST, HEH, HEH!
SORRY TO TROUBLE YOU.
AFTER THE OLD FOLK DEPART---
HOW DID THEY ESCAPE?
MAYBE THEY FLEW BACK TO WHERE YOU DREAMED THEM UP OUT OF!
COME QUICKLY! --OHH!
LOOK--- THOSE COFFINS--- --EMPTY!
FRESH UPTURNED EARTH, TOO!
THEY MUST HAVE STOLEN THESE BODIES! THE OLD COUPLE, WE JUST SPOKE TO, SATURNIA AND GLOAT ARE THEY---FREE AGAIN!
AGAIN THE BLUE BEETLE'S ELECTRONIC EAR WARNS HIM.
WHAT IS IT?
THE PROFESSOR'S IN TROUBLE AGAIN!
DON'T FORGET--- YOU'RE STILL MY PRISONER!
--LITTLE OLD MAN AND WOMAN-- EXTRAORDINARY STRENGTH--HIT ME--STOLE CAR-- WENT THAT WAY!
IT'S SATURNIA AND GLOAT ALL RIGHT! THEY HAVEN'T TO MUCH OF A HEAD START THIS TIME
THERE THEY ARE, AHEAD I'LL LET THEM KNOW I'M COMING, WITH THE SIGN OF THE BLUE BEETLE, MY CALLING CARD!

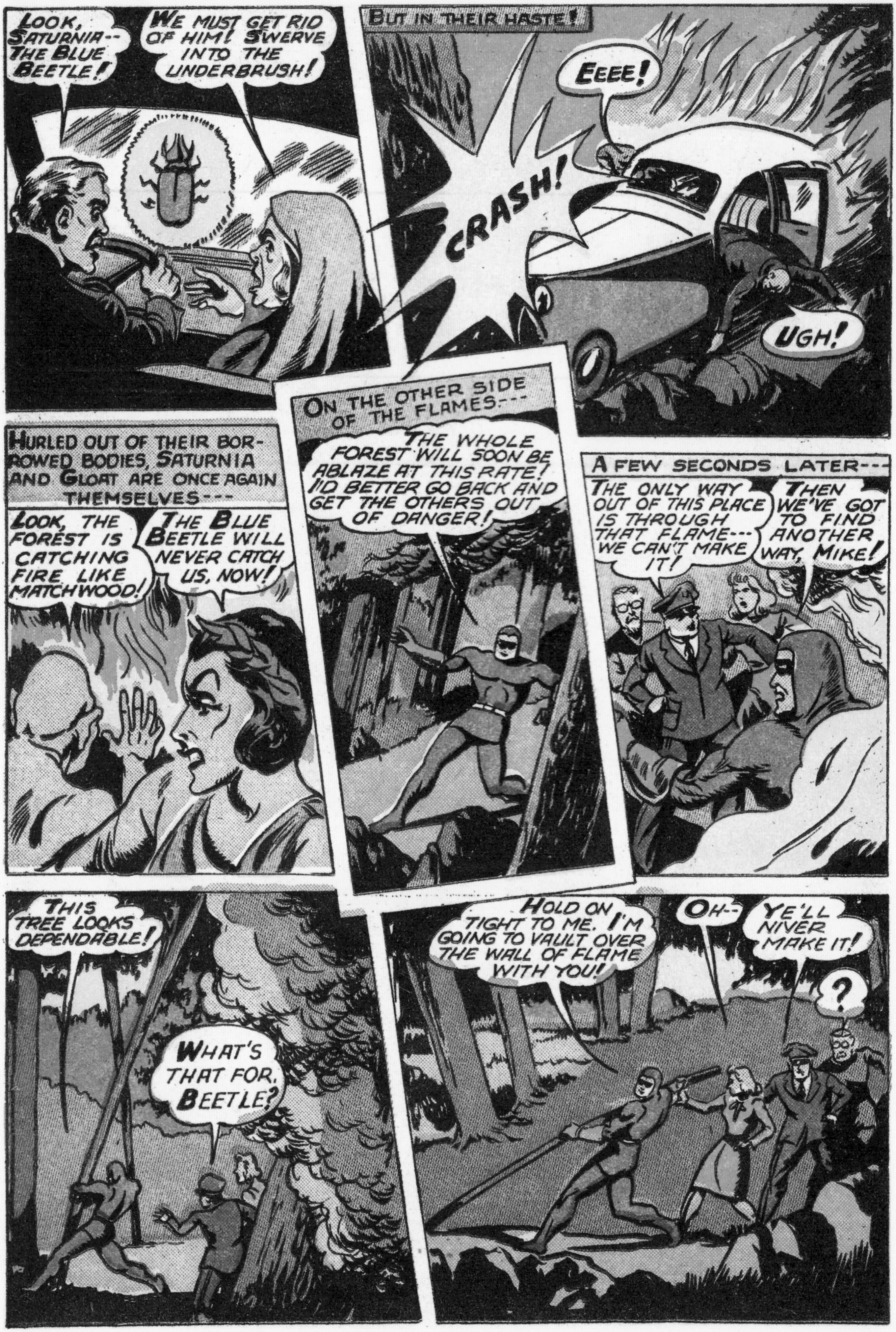
LOOK, SATURNIA-- THE BLUE BEETLE!
WE MUST GET RID OF HIM! SWERVE INTO THE UNDERBRUSH!
BUT IN THEIR HASTE!
EEEE!
CRASH!
UGH!
HURLED OUT OF THEIR BORROWED BODIES, SATURNIA AND GLOAT ARE ONCE AGAIN THEMSELVES---
LOOK, THE FOREST IS CATCHING FIRE LIKE MATCHWOOD!
THE BLUE BEETLE WILL NEVER CATCH US, NOW!
ON THE OTHER SIDE OF THE FLAMES---
THE WHOLE FOREST WILL SOON BE ABLAZE AT THIS RATE! I'D BETTER GO BACK AND GET THE OTHERS OUT OF DANGER!
A FEW SECONDS LATER---
THE ONLY WAY OUT OF THIS PLACE IS THROUGH THAT FLAME--- WE CAN'T MAKE IT!
THEN WE'VE GOT TO FIND ANOTHER WAY, MIKE!
THIS TREE LOOKS DEPENDABLE!
WHAT'S THAT FOR, BEETLE?
HOLD ON TIGHT TO ME. I'M GOING TO VAULT OVER THE WALL OF FLAME WITH YOU!
OH--
YE'LL NIVER MAKE IT!
?

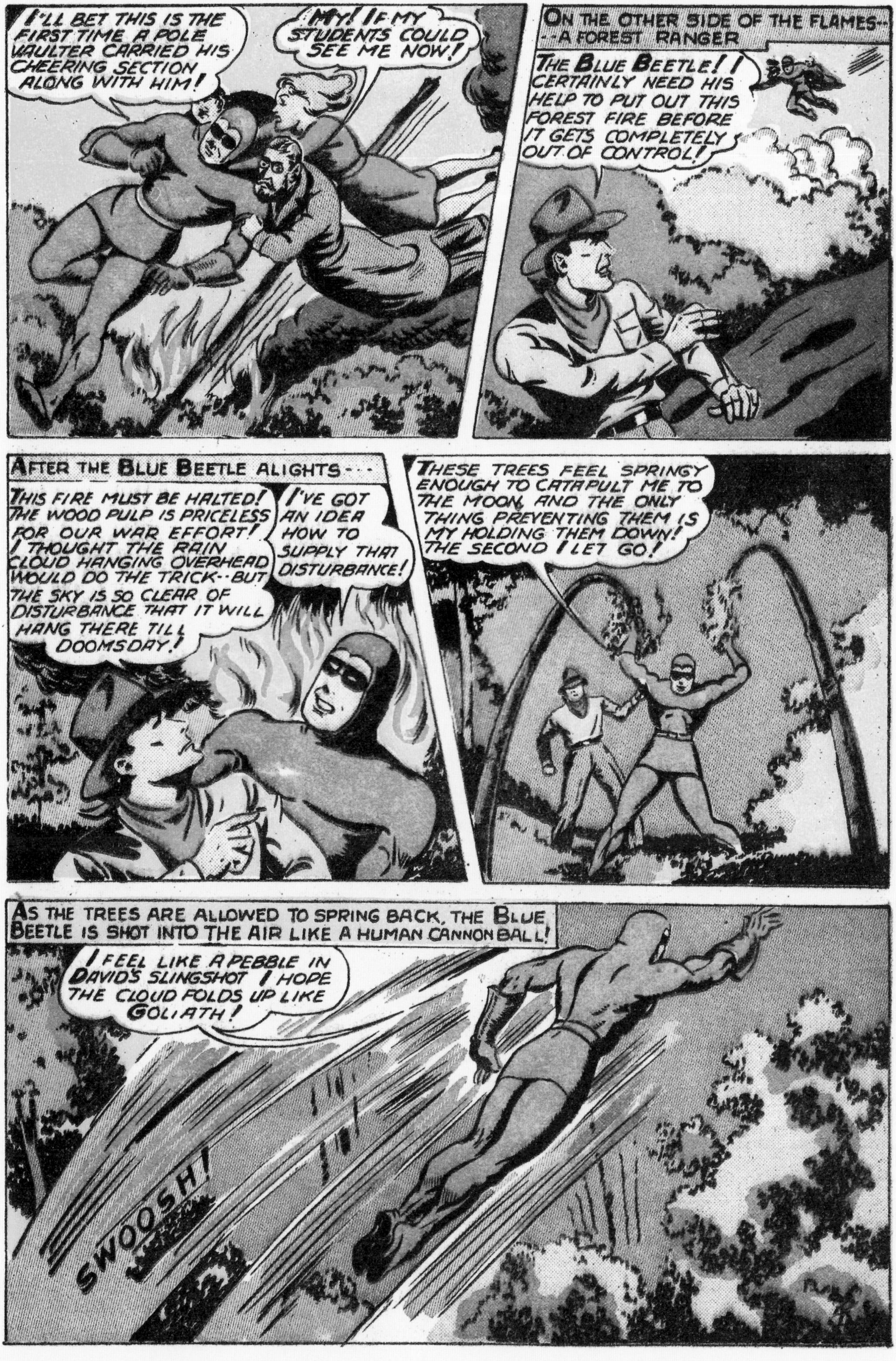
I'LL BET THIS IS THE FIRST TIME A POLE VAULTER CARRIED HIS CHEERING SECTION ALONG WITH HIM!
MY! IF MY STUDENTS COULD SEE ME NOW!
ON THE OTHER SIDE OF THE FLAMES-- --A FOREST RANGER
THE BLUE BEETLE! I CERTAINLY NEED HIS HELP TO PUT OUT THIS FOREST FIRE BEFORE IT GETS COMPLETELY OUT OF CONTROL!
AFTER THE BLUE BEETLE ALIGHTS---
THIS FIRE MUST BE HALTED! THE WOOD PULP IS PRICELESS FOR OUR WAR EFFORT! I THOUGHT THE RAIN CLOUD HANGING OVERHEAD WOULD DO THE TRICK--BUT THE SKY IS SO CLEAR OF DISTURBANCE THAT IT WILL HANG THERE TILL DOOMSDAY!
I'VE GOT AN IDEA HOW TO SUPPLY THAT DISTURBANCE!
THESE TREES FEEL SPRINGY ENOUGH TO CATAPULT ME TO THE MOON, AND THE ONLY THING PREVENTING THEM IS MY HOLDING THEM DOWN! THE SECOND I LET GO!
AS THE TREES ARE ALLOWED TO SPRING BACK, THE BLUE BEETLE IS SHOT INTO THE AIR LIKE A HUMAN CANNONBALL!
I FEEL LIKE A PEBBLE IN DAVID'S SLINGSHOT I HOPE THE CLOUD FOLDS UP LIKE GOLIATH!
SWOOSH!

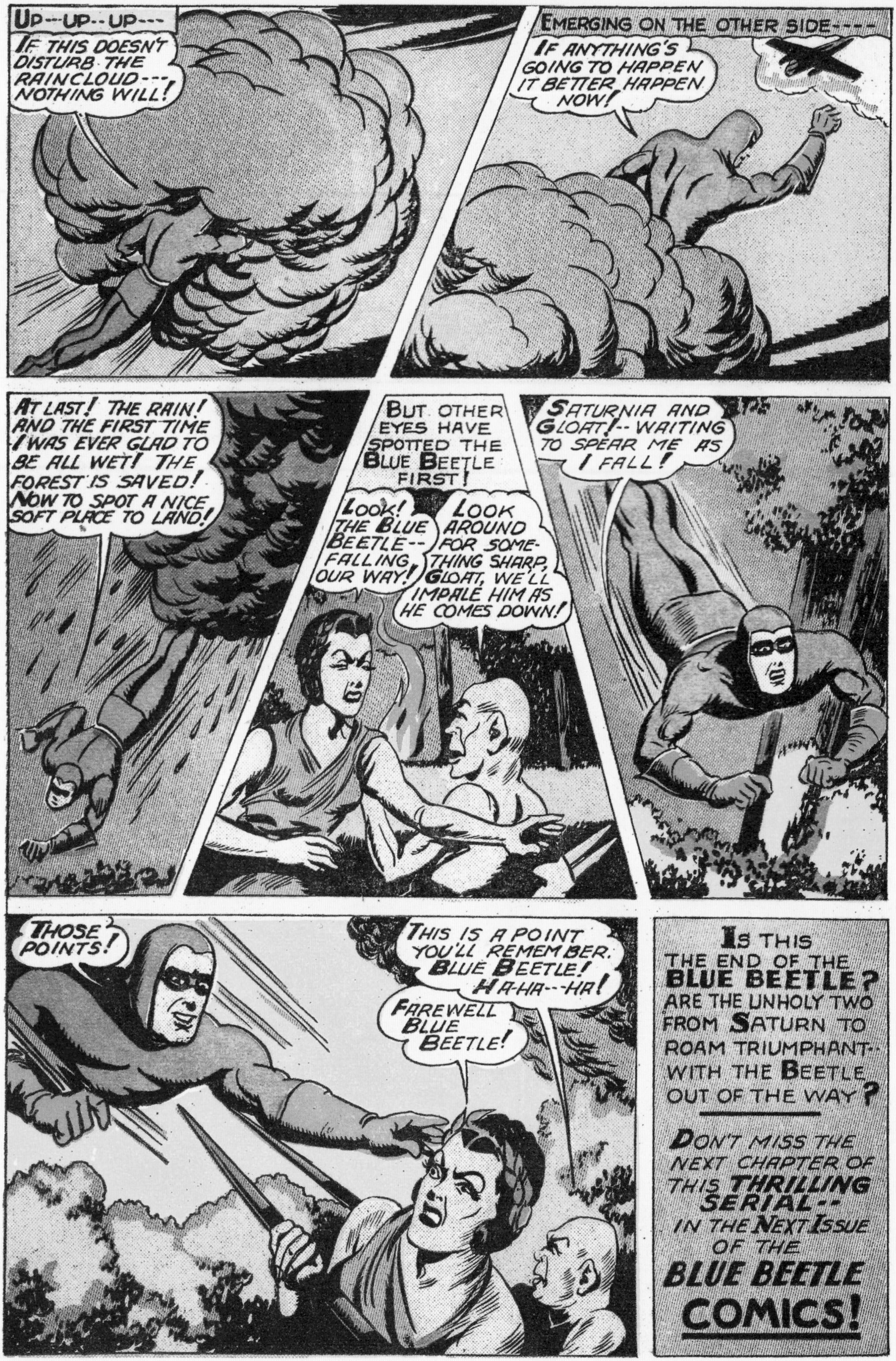
UP--UP--UP---
IF THIS DOESN'T DISTURB THE RAINCLOUD--- NOTHING WILL!
EMERGING ON THE OTHER SIDE----
IF ANYTHING'S GOING TO HAPPEN IT BETTER HAPPEN NOW!
AT LAST! THE RAIN! AND THE FIRST TIME I WAS EVER GLAD TO BE ALL WET! THE FOREST IS SAVED! NOW TO SPOT A NICE SOFT PLACE TO LAND!
BUT OTHER EYES HAVE SPOTTED THE BLUE BEETLE FIRST!
LOOK! THE BLUE BEETLE-- FALLING OUR WAY!
LOOK AROUND FOR SOMETHING SHARP, GLOAT, WE'LL IMPALE HIM AS HE COMES DOWN!
SATURNIA AND GLOAT!-- WAITING TO SPEAR ME AS I FALL!
THOSE POINTS!
THIS IS A POINT YOU'LL REMEMBER. BLUE BEETLE! HA-HA--HA!
FAREWELL BLUE BEETLE!
IS THIS THE END OF THE BLUE BEETLE? ARE THE UNHOLY TWO FROM SATURN TO ROAM TRIUMPHANT-- WITH THE BEETLE OUT OF THE WAY?
DON'T MISS THE NEXT CHAPTER OF THIS THRILLING SERIAL-- IN THE NEXT ISSUE OF THE BLUE BEETLE COMICS!

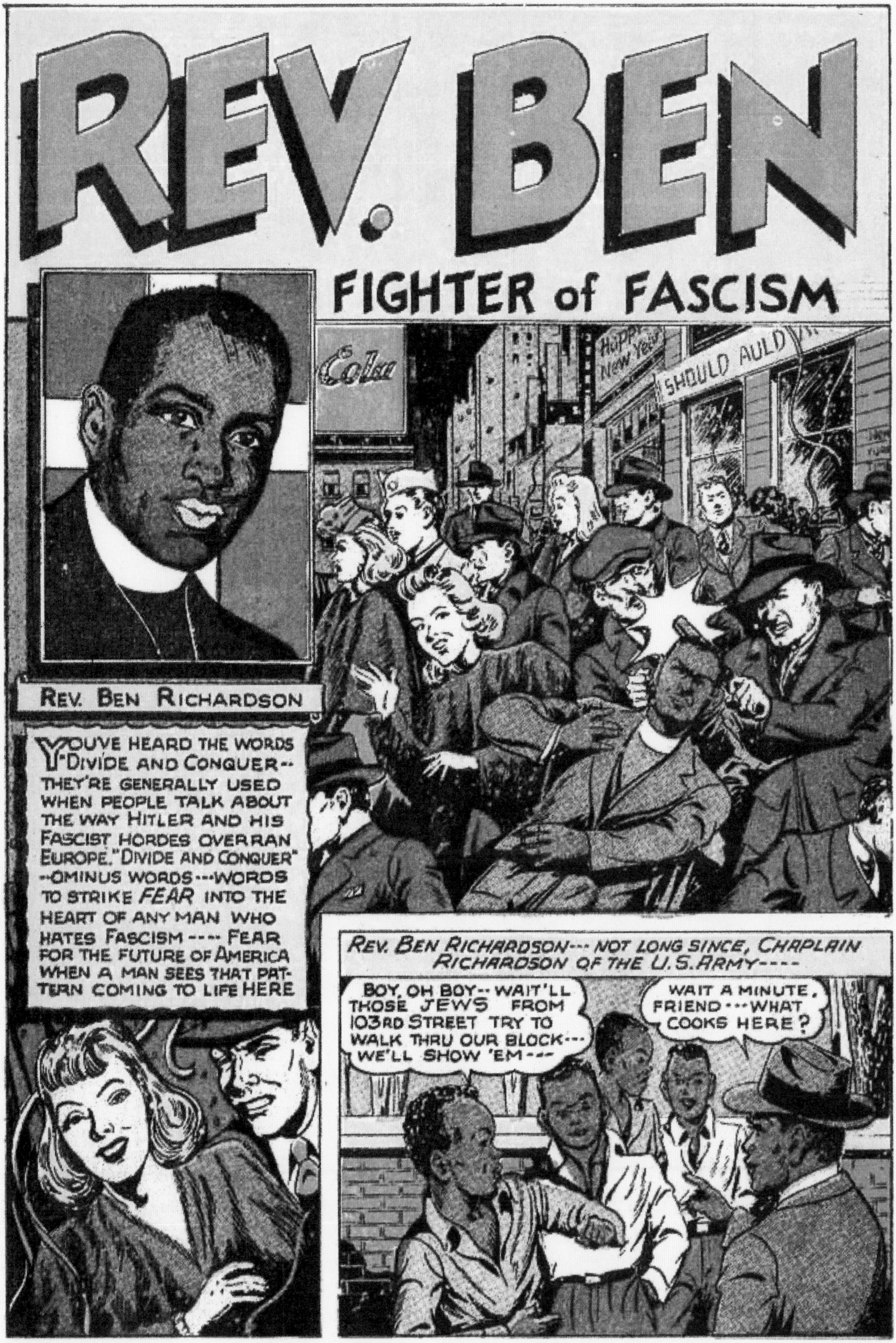
REV. BEN
FIGHTER of FASCISM
REV. BEN RICHARDSON
YOU'VE HEARD THE WORDS "DIVIDE AND CONQUER"-- THEY'RE GENERALLY USED WHEN PEOPLE TALK ABOUT THE WAY HITLER AND HIS FASCIST HORDES OVERRAN EUROPE. "DIVIDE AND CONQUER" --OMINUS WORDS---WORDS TO STRIKE FEAR INTO THE HEART OF ANY MAN WHO HATES FASCISM ---- FEAR FOR THE FUTURE OF AMERICA WHEN A MAN SEES THAT PATTERN COMING TO LIFE HERE
Happy New Year
SHOULD AULD
REV. BEN RICHARDSON--- NOT LONG SINCE, CHAPLAIN RICHARDSON OF THE U.S. ARMY----
BOY, OH BOY-- WAIT'LL THOSE JEWS FROM 103RD STREET TRY TO WALK THRU OUR BLOCK--- WE'LL SHOW 'EM---
WAIT A MINUTE, FRIEND---WHAT COOKS HERE?

Biographical story about Rev. Ben Richardson, a Black anti-fascist preacher and associate editor at the *Protestant Digest*, publishers of this comic. *The Challenger* #1, 1945.

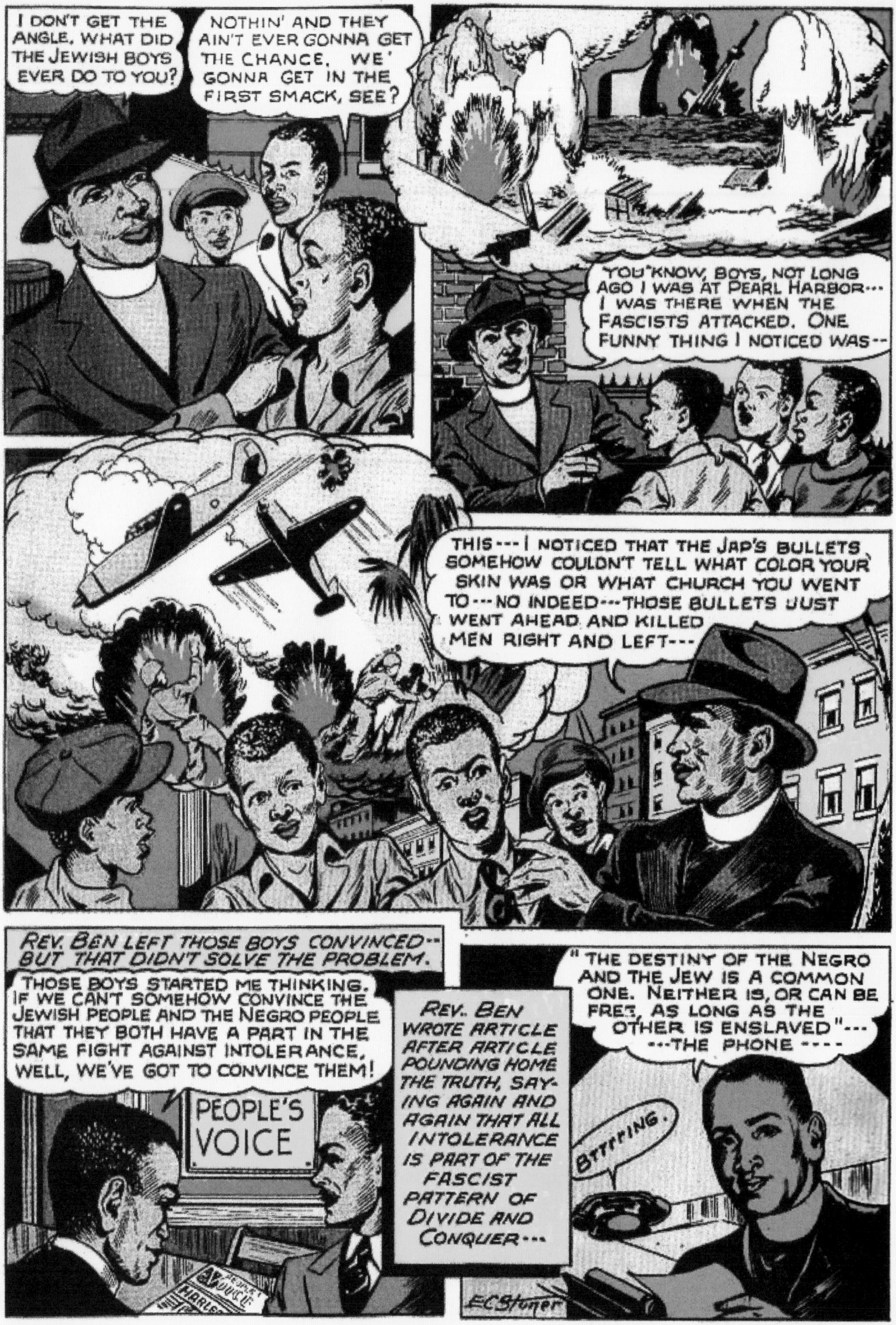
I DON'T GET THE ANGLE. WHAT DID THE JEWISH BOYS EVER DO TO YOU?
NOTHIN' AND THEY AIN'T EVER GONNA GET THE CHANCE. WE' GONNA GET IN THE FIRST SMACK, SEE?
YOU KNOW, BOYS, NOT LONG AGO I WAS AT PEARL HARBOR--- I WAS THERE WHEN THE FASCISTS ATTACKED. ONE FUNNY THING I NOTICED WAS--
THIS---I NOTICED THAT THE JAP'S BULLETS SOMEHOW COULDN'T TELL WHAT COLOR YOUR SKIN WAS OR WHAT CHURCH YOU WENT TO---NO INDEED---THOSE BULLETS JUST WENT AHEAD AND KILLED MEN RIGHT AND LEFT---
REV. BEN LEFT THOSE BOYS CONVINCED-- BUT THAT DIDN'T SOLVE THE PROBLEM.
THOSE BOYS STARTED ME THINKING. IF WE CAN'T SOMEHOW CONVINCE THE JEWISH PEOPLE AND THE NEGRO PEOPLE THAT THEY BOTH HAVE A PART IN THE SAME FIGHT AGAINST INTOLERANCE, WELL, WE'VE GOT TO CONVINCE THEM!
PEOPLE'S VOICE
REV. BEN WROTE ARTICLE AFTER ARTICLE POUNDING HOME THE TRUTH, SAYING AGAIN AND AGAIN THAT ALL INTOLERANCE IS PART OF THE FASCIST PATTERN OF DIVIDE AND CONQUER---
"THE DESTINY OF THE NEGRO AND THE JEW IS A COMMON ONE. NEITHER IS, OR CAN BE FREE, AS LONG AS THE OTHER IS ENSLAVED"--- ---THE PHONE ----
Brrrring.
EC Stoner

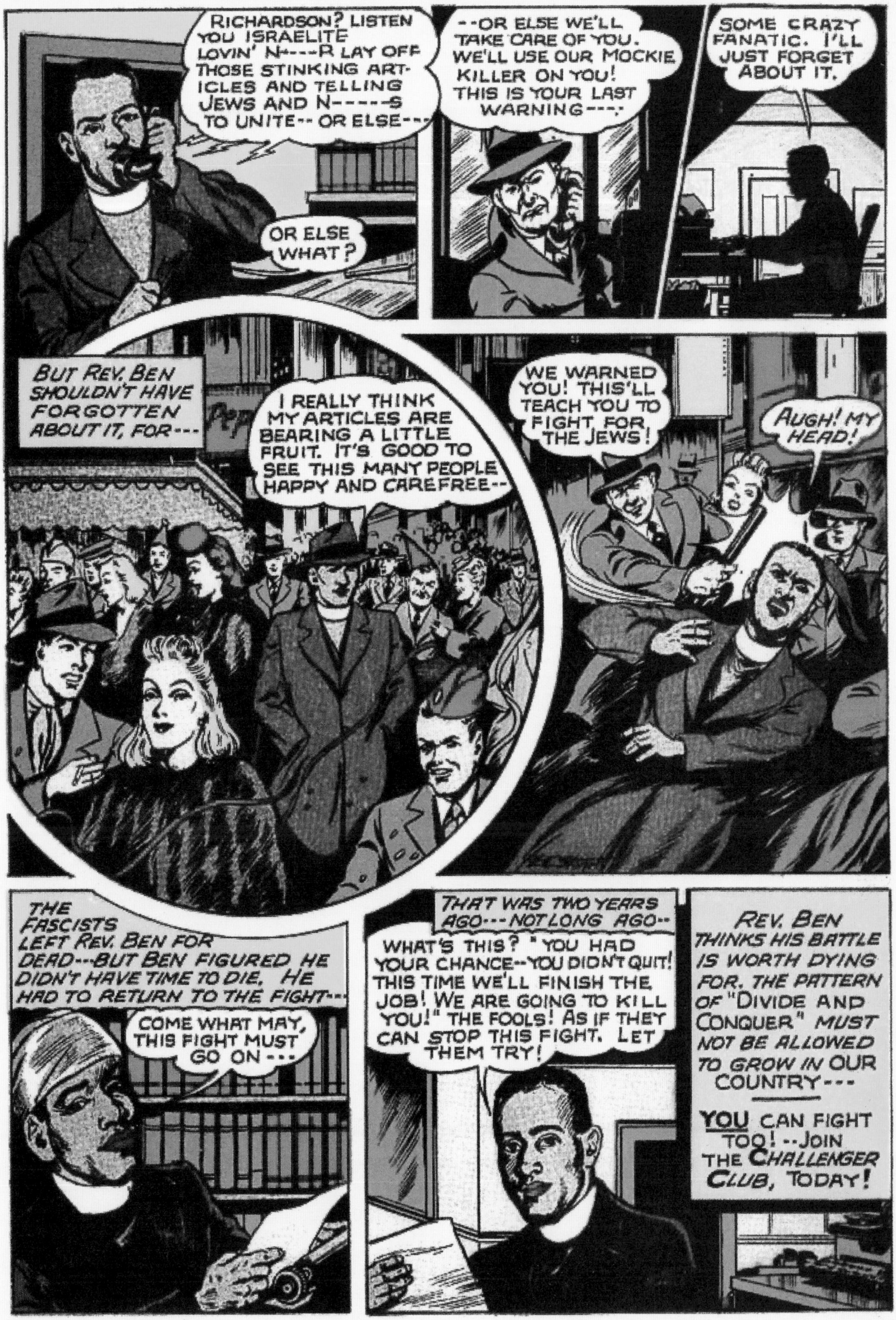
RICHARDSON? LISTEN YOU ISRAELITE LOVIN' N----R LAY OFF THOSE STINKING ARTICLES AND TELLING JEWS AND N-----S TO UNITE-- OR ELSE---
OR ELSE WHAT?
--OR ELSE WE'LL TAKE CARE OF YOU. WE'LL USE OUR MOCKIE KILLER ON YOU! THIS IS YOUR LAST WARNING---.
SOME CRAZY FANATIC. I'LL JUST FORGET ABOUT IT.
BUT REV. BEN SHOULDN'T HAVE FORGOTTEN ABOUT IT, FOR---
I REALLY THINK MY ARTICLES ARE BEARING A LITTLE FRUIT. IT'S GOOD TO SEE THIS MANY PEOPLE HAPPY AND CAREFREE--
WE WARNED YOU! THIS'LL TEACH YOU TO FIGHT FOR THE JEWS!
AUGH! MY HEAD!
THE FASCISTS LEFT REV. BEN FOR DEAD---BUT BEN FIGURED HE DIDN'T HAVE TIME TO DIE. HE HAD TO RETURN TO THE FIGHT---
COME WHAT MAY, THIS FIGHT MUST GO ON ---
THAT WAS TWO YEARS AGO--- NOT LONG AGO--
WHAT'S THIS? "YOU HAD YOUR CHANCE--YOU DIDN'T QUIT! THIS TIME WE'LL FINISH THE JOB! WE ARE GOING TO KILL YOU!" THE FOOLS! AS IF THEY CAN STOP THIS FIGHT. LET THEM TRY!
REV. BEN THINKS HIS BATTLE IS WORTH DYING FOR. THE PATTERN OF "DIVIDE AND CONQUER" MUST NOT BE ALLOWED TO GROW IN OUR COUNTRY---
YOU CAN FIGHT TOO! --JOIN THE CHALLENGER CLUB, TODAY!

ROBERT SAVON PIOUS
The Afrocentric Historian

Imagine an artist in two worlds: in one, he is an eminent editorial cartoonist known for unapologetic social commentary and a highly respected painter of Black historical figures and themes—a virtual icon. In the other, he toils as an illustrator of cheap paper pulps and low-paying, ill-reputed comic books—perceived as a nondescript hack working in the lowest end of publishing.

This was Robert Pious' reality.

Robert was born in Meridian, Mississippi, on March 7, 1908, to Nathaniel ("Nattie") and Loula ("Lou") Pious. The city was enjoying its boomtown status, owed to it being the convergence point for several major railways. Despite its apparent prosperity, Meridian was still scarred by the race riot of 1871. The shadow of this difficult incident would long affect the lives of those who would be born and live there.

Long-simmering resentment from Whites, angered by the changes brought on by Reconstruction, culminated with the installation of a Republican mayor. This led to an exchange of hostilities between the Whites, who were en-

couraged by the Ku Klux Klan, and the majority Black population. A mysterious fire destroyed much of the town's business district, which led to conflicting rumors and growing anger from both sides. Three Blacks—Warren Tyler, William Clopton, and Aaron Moore—were charged with incitement of riot and were put on trial. During the trial, one of the White witnesses attacked one of the Black defendants with a cane and, during the ensuing confusion, someone shot the judge.

A general melee ensued. [Defendants] Tyler and Loften [sic] were killed instantly. J. Aaron Moore, negro, a prominent politician, and member of the Mississippi Legislature, was also a prisoner as an accessory to the burning. He was shot; it is supposed mortally. ["A Judge Killed in Court," *Charleston Daily News*, March 8, 1871]

The violence spilled over from the courthouse and throughout the city, with estimates of 25 to 30 Blacks killed in the resulting violence. The news dispatch goes on to report that the Connecticut-born Republican mayor, "a

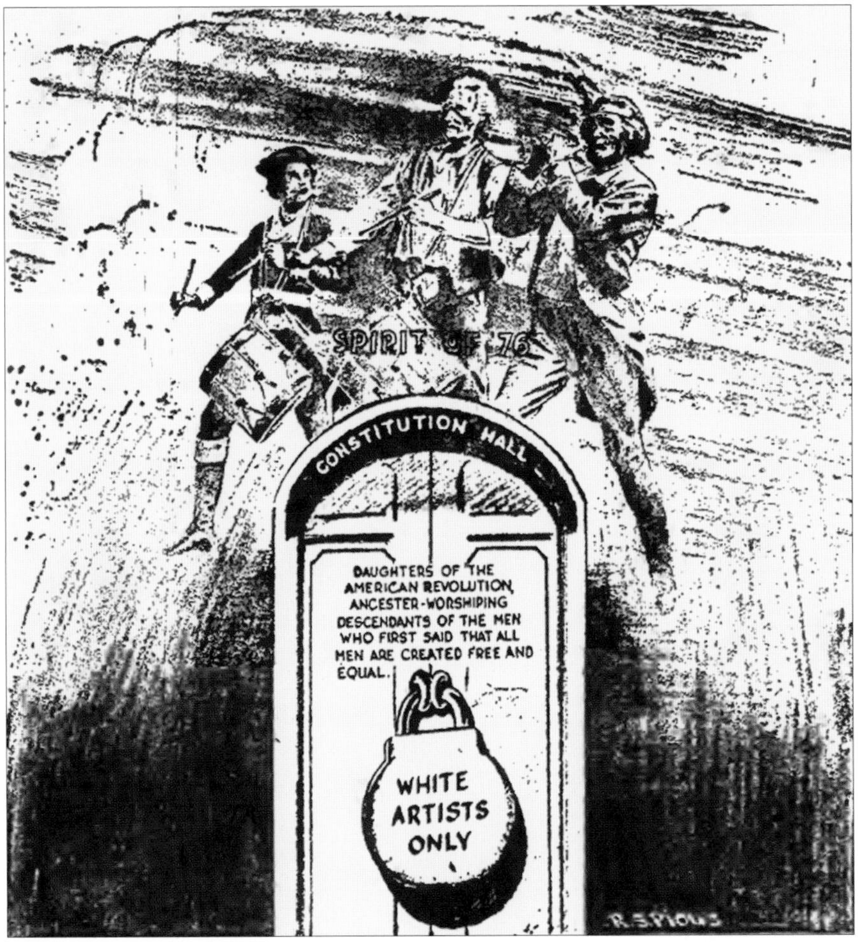
SPIRIT OF '76
CONSTITUTION HALL
DAUGHTERS OF THE AMERICAN REVOLUTION, ANCESTER-WORSHIPING DESCENDANTS OF THE MEN WHO FIRST SAID THAT ALL MEN ARE CREATED FREE AND EQUAL.
WHITE ARTISTS ONLY
R.S.PIOUS

teachers, who thought of innumerable ways to curb his genius which was still in the embryo stage. These obstacles only made the little Mississippian's desire to master the paint brush more acute.

"My mother threatened many times to deprive me of room and board," Pious recalled. "At night I used oil lamps to draw in order not to attract her attention and my teachers were forever communicating with mother, due to the lack of interest I showed in my assigned subjects." [Finger, Mary, "Robert S. Pious Had a Yen for Drawing at the Age of 7, Is Now Painter of Fine Portraits," *New York Age*, Jan. 13, 1940]

Eventually, his family moved to Chicago, where Pious attended the School of the Art Institute of Chicago for two years in the late 1920s, eventually leaving to find full-time work. During this period, he produced artwork for the *Bronzeman* (a locally based magazine), the National Urban League's *Opportunity: Journal of Negro Life*, and for Murray's Superior Hair Care Product Company.

A four-year scholarship to the National Academy of Design prompted Robert's relocation to New York City. It was just in time for him to become part of the ongoing Harlem Renaissance.

Harlem had become the center for Blacks migrating to the North, looking for jobs and getting away from the Jim Crow discrimination of the South. A growing Black middle-class and the proximity of New York's cultural assets drew an influx of Black writers, artists, and musicians looking for opportunities and freedom of expression. Pious' arrival in the early 1930s put him in the midst of this welcoming community, where he became an enthusiastic participant in the "New Negro Movement." Artist Romare Bearden wrote:

Harlem then resembled a small town. Almost all creative people knew one another, as well as the leading ministers, physicians, lawyers, business leaders and national political leaders." [Bearden, Romare & Henderson, Harry, *A History of Blacks Artists: From 1792 to the Present*, 1993, p.234]

As the protégé of Dr. Gertrude Curtis (the first Black dentist in New York State), who financed the artist's early career, Pious' work was shown in the Harmon exhibitions of Blacks artists in 1930 and 1931. As a result, his portrait of renowned classical tenor Roland Hayes earned

tormentor of strife in this town," was put on a train and run out of town. Nobody was ever prosecuted for any of these killings. The Klan was emboldened by this outcome. They increased their intimidation of Blacks and helped to drive Republican politicians from office, in favor of installing Democrats. The Democrats in turn passed the first Jim Crow laws, which disenfranchised Blacks in the South for nearly a century.

As were many others in Meridian, Nattie Pious was employed as a railroad laborer, providing a meager existence for his wife and seven children. When Nattie died in 1915 at the age of 40, Lou took her children and left Mississippi, moving north to St. Louis. She remarried there in 1917. Son Robert's talent emerged early, but wasn't met with much encouragement, by either his mother or his teachers. Feature writer Mary E. Finger wrote:

Mr. Pious' gift for drawing was revealed to him at the age of seven. His constant figure drawing was frowned upon by his mother and

In 1939, Black classical music singer Marion Anderson was refused permission to perform at Constitution Hall, owned by the Daughters of the American Revolution (DAR). The incident was one of the first milestones in the struggle for civil rights in America. Washington, D.C. was a segregated city at that time, and the DAR banned Black entertainers from their hall. Outraged, Eleanor Roosevelt quit the DAR, and Anderson finally performed an open-air concert from the steps of the Lincoln Memorial. It would not, however, be the last such incident.
"The Reality of 1945" (October 25, 1945) is representative of the editorial cartoons Pious created after World War II. It specifically references the DAR's similar discrimination against Black jazz pianist Hazel Scott, barring her from performing at Constitution Hall in 1945.

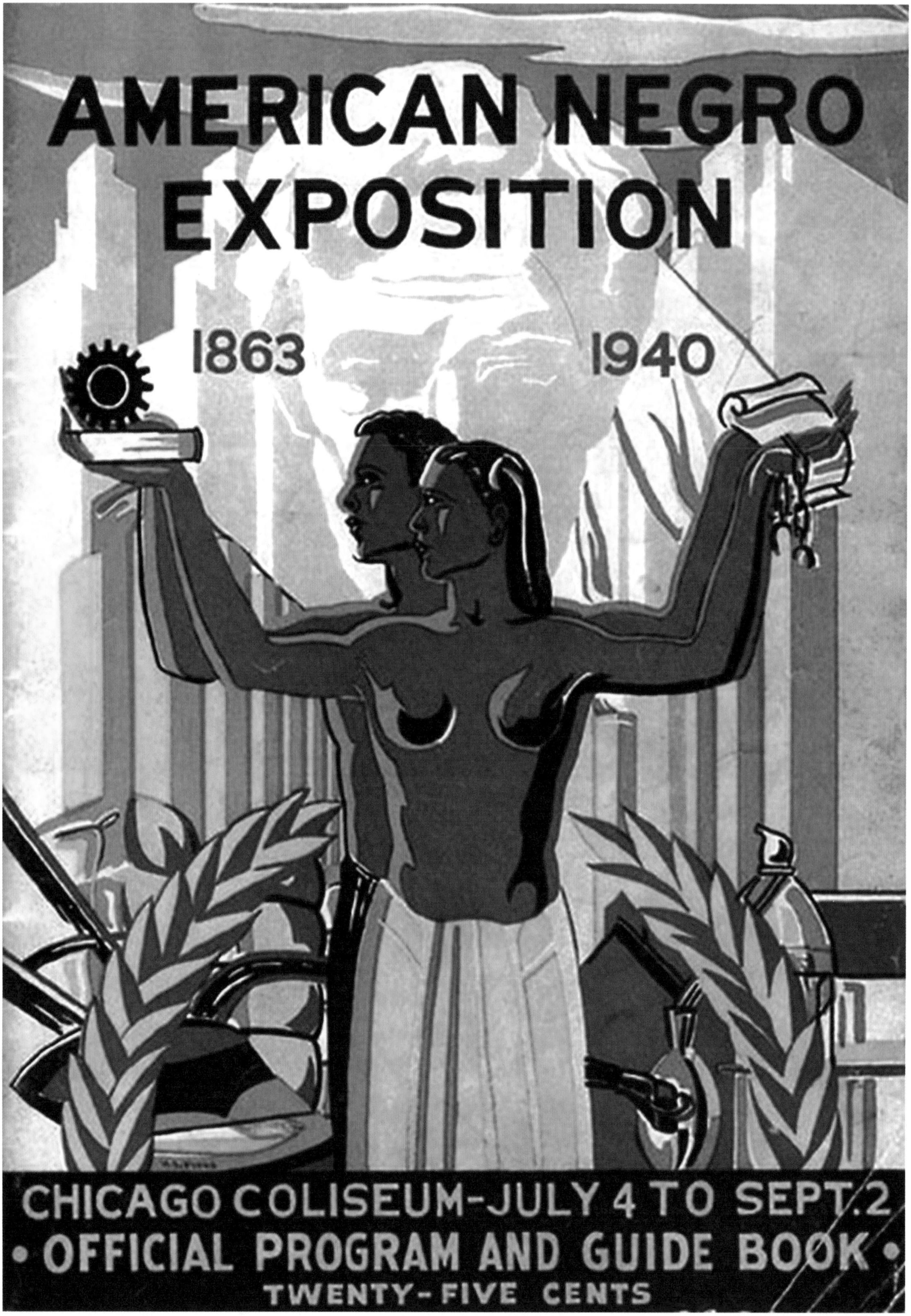
AMERICAN NEGRO
EXPOSITION
1863
1940
CHICAGO COLISEUM-JULY 4 TO SEPT. 2
• OFFICIAL PROGRAM AND GUIDE BOOK •
TWENTY-FIVE CENTS

him the highly coveted Spingarn Medal for drawing by the National Association for the Advancement of Colored People (NAACP). Pious also worked with, and provided illustrations for, the seminal Black historian Charles C. Seifert. Among this work was an Afrocentric rendition of the carvings on Egypt's Hall of Karnak. Seifert's influence had a profound effect upon Pious, spurring his lifelong interest in Black history.

The busy young artist, working under the friendlier byline of "Bob Pious," also found time to create a Saturday-only comic strip for the Stanton Feature Syndicate in early 1933, which ran in such Black newspapers as the *Pittsburgh Courier* and the *Atlanta Daily World*. Titled *The Dopes* in its earliest incarnation, the strip quickly changed its name to *The Dupes*, and was basically a Black take on *Bringing Up Father*.

The strip centered around a middle-class Black family, headed by Henry, the hapless, but college-educated father, who dispensed wisdom to his college-going son, Billy. This humorous depiction of Black domesticity was in stark contrast to mainstream White comic strips, which rarely showed Blacks in "realistic" form or afforded them such dignity. Pious' art on *The Dupes* was relatively crude, particularly in comparison to some of its companions on the comic page drawn by Ollie Harrington and Wilbert Holloway, but it was his first attempt in the comic medium. It wouldn't be his last.

Pious' reputation grew throughout the 1930s, as he regularly participated in various art exhibitions, which included the one held at the Harlem YWCA auditorium in March 1935. This showing was sponsored by the newly-formed Harlem Art Committee. The exhibition featured some 200 works of Black art, "ranging from the grotesqueries of early African sculpture to the academic perfection of Henry O. Tanner and W. Edouard Scott, from a primitive simplic-

ity of the Congolats to the modern naivete of Georgette Seabrook..." [Bennett, Gwendolyn, "Toward an Art Center," *New York Amsterdam News*, March 23, 1935]

The exhibition was put together and juried by a group formed of prominent Black artists and collectors, including E. Simms Campbell, Arthur Schomburg, Augusta Savage, and Richmond Barthé. Since its opening, the still-segregated YWCA (integration was introduced in 1946) was the center for culture within the community, being dubbed "the living room of the Harlem Renaissance." This showing was so significant that even the *New York Times* dedicated four paragraphs to it, mostly devoted to words spoken by the exhibition's guest speaker, Dr. Alain Locke, philosopher and the unofficial "dean" of the Harlem Renaissance.

"Negro art does not restrict the Negro artist to the use of the racial theme in art exclusively," Dr. Locke was quoted, *"but it is important in him, as in every artist, to come to grips with the life material nearest to him and into which he has the deepest insight."* ["Negro Art Put on Display," *New York Times*, March 18, 1935]

Along with Romare Bearden, Charles Alston, and several others, Pious was singled out in the *New York Amsterdam News* article for his artwork. It held up his art as "indicative of the admirable work being done by the younger painters of the race," while his "Slave Ship" painting was used to illustrate the text.

[Left] Pious' poster for the American Negro Exposition in Chicago, May 1940. Pious won first prize in the national contest to design the official poster and was awarded $100 by New York City mayor Fiorello La Guardia [above].

[Right] Pious 1951 painting of civil rights pioneer Harriett Tubman, donated by the Harmon Foundation to the National Portrait Gallery in Washington, D.C.

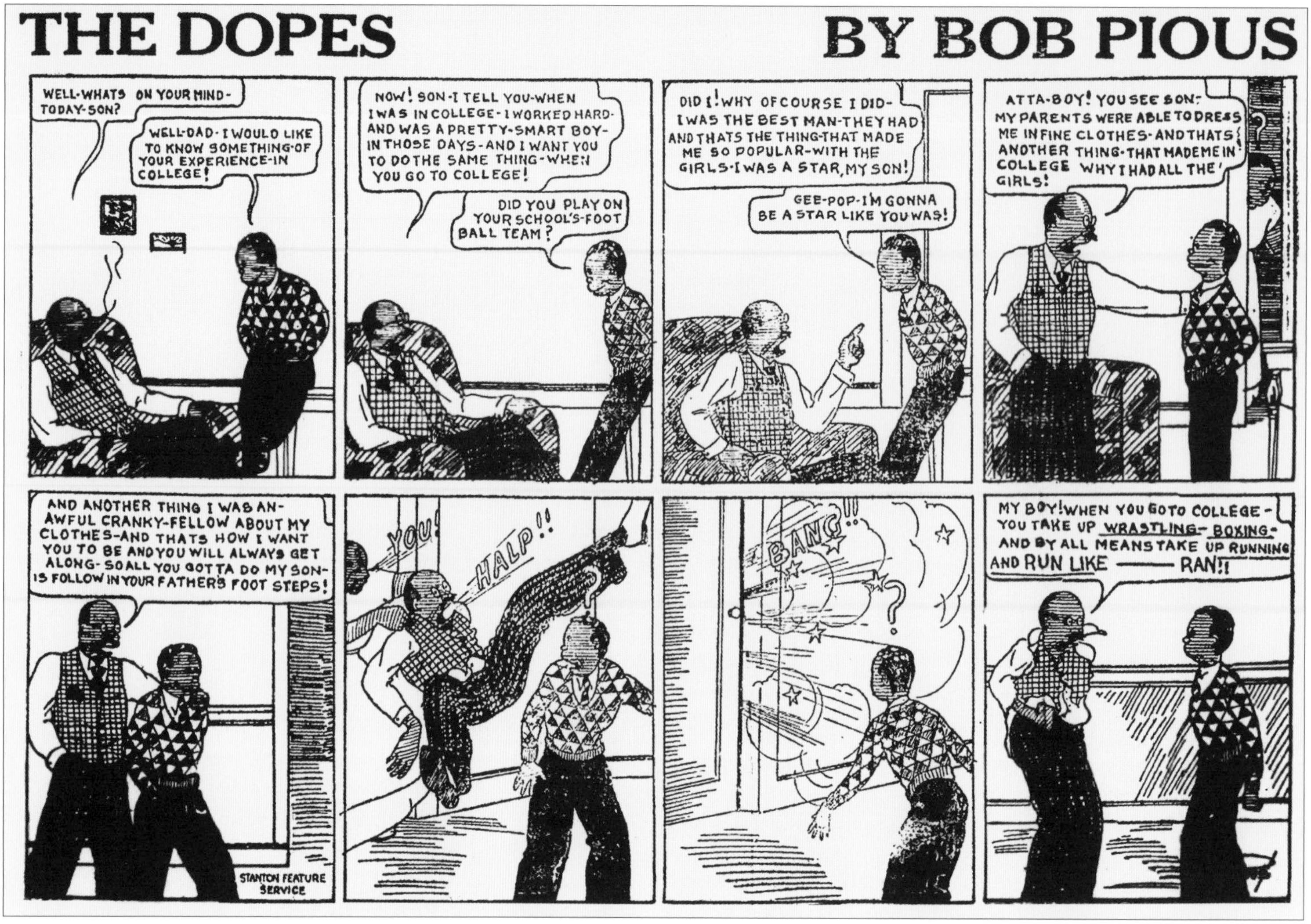
THE DOPES
BY BOB PIOUS
WELL-WHATS ON YOUR MIND-TODAY-SON?
WELL-DAD-I WOULD LIKE TO KNOW SOMETHING-OF YOUR EXPERIENCE-IN COLLEGE!
NOW! SON-I TELL YOU-WHEN I WAS IN COLLEGE-I WORKED HARD-AND WAS A PRETTY-SMART BOY-IN THOSE DAYS-AND I WANT YOU TO DO THE SAME THING-WHEN YOU GO TO COLLEGE!
DID YOU PLAY ON YOUR SCHOOL'S-FOOT BALL TEAM?
DID I! WHY OF COURSE I DID-I WAS THE BEST MAN-THEY HAD AND THATS THE THING-THAT MADE ME SO POPULAR-WITH THE GIRLS-I WAS A STAR, MY SON!
GEE-POP-I'M GONNA BE A STAR LIKE YOU WAS!
ATTA-BOY! YOU SEE SON: MY PARENTS WERE ABLE TO DRESS ME IN FINE CLOTHES-AND THATS ANOTHER THING-THAT MADE ME IN COLLEGE WHY I HAD ALL THE GIRLS!
AND ANOTHER THING I WAS AN-AWFUL CRANKY-FELLOW ABOUT MY CLOTHES-AND THATS HOW I WANT YOU TO BE AND YOU WILL ALWAYS GET ALONG-SO ALL YOU GOTTA DO MY SON-IS FOLLOW IN YOUR FATHERS FOOT STEPS!
STANTON FEATURE SERVICE
YOU!
HALP!!
BANG!!
?
MY BOY! WHEN YOU GO TO COLLEGE-YOU TAKE UP WRASTLING-BOXING-AND BY ALL MEANS TAKE UP RUNNING AND RUN LIKE ——— RAN!!

Pious was teaching art part-time at the Harlem YMCA. Also, like other underemployed artists during the Great Depression, he found additional work through the Work Projects Administration (WPA) as a muralist. Pious and many other artists and writers congregated at 306 West 101st Street; this was a converted horse stable, owned by Charles Alston and reconfigured as studio space.

Alston began inviting people he knew from the WPA to social parties. These turned into intellectual discussions, and 306 rapidly became a unique community institution. [Bearden & Henderson 1993, op. cit. p.235]

Here, Pious could rub elbows with Ralph Ellison, Richard Wright, Langston Hughes, and "too many artists to count." Bearden goes on to note, though, that Pious in particular had a problem fitting in.

The emphasis on fine-art painting and socially conscious art made Robert Pious, who wanted to be a commercial illustrator, so uncomfortable that he stopped coming. [Ibid.]

In 1940, Pious attained his first high-profile recognition, when he beat out over 100 entrants and won the $100 first prize for the artwork used for the program booklet and official poster of the American Negro Exhibition in Chicago. Focused entirely upon Black achievement and culture generally overlooked by White America, this expo was the Black answer to the ongoing New York World's Fair. Photos of Pious being awarded the prize by New York City mayor Fiorello La Guardia appeared nationwide.

His celebrity grew within the Black community as the portraitist of such notables as pastor and future congressman Adam Clayton Powell, opera singer Marian Anderson, and sculptor Richmond Barthé. However, despite his success, Pious apparently needed additional paying work. To that end, he followed the path of fellow Harlem Renaissance artist Elmer C. Stoner and began producing work for comic books.

The earliest comic book work attributable to Pious seems to have been on the back-up feature "Kalthar," which ran in 1940 issues of *Zip Comics*. In a cruel irony certainly not lost on Pious, "Kalthar, the Giant Man King of the Jungle" was a typical story of the blond, White savior (giant-sized, at that) among the dark-skinned African savages.

[Above] *The Dopes* was an early, short-lived Pious comic strip that ran in various Black newspapers. Soon after this cartoon appeared, its name was changed to the less offensive *The Dupes*. March 10, 1933; Stanton Feature Syndicate.

[Right] Pious' portrait of civil rights activist Rosa Parks for the cover of the *National Scene*. From the 1960s to nearly the end of his career in the early '80s, Pious was a frequent contributor to the revival of L. H. Stanton's monthly Black newspaper supplement. October 14, 1965; *Pittsburgh Courier*.

National **Scene**
FAMILY NEWS SUPPLEMENT

Pittsburgh Courier

• PERSONALITIES • MUSIC • ART
• DRAMA • DANCE • FASHIONS
• THEATRE • BOOKS • HOME
• TRAVEL

Kalthar's origin was explained on the first page of his debut story (which was drawn by Lin Streeter and not Pious) in *Zip Comics* #1 (Feb. 1940). He had "been reared from infancy by savage blacks, the Ugarnas, who were rescued from Arab slavers by Kalthar's father." The grateful Ugarnas raise Kalthar after his father's death, eventually make him their chief. He is given some magic grains by their witch doctor, which allow him to grow to fifteen feet tall. The fact that the inappropriateness of this origin didn't occur to its writer speaks volumes about the prevailing White mindset of the pre-World War II era. The fact that Pious was assigned to draw this feature beginning with the next issue of *Zip Comics* is even more evidence.

Pious' fine art training is evident from the first panel on. The musculature of his people was well-defined and accurate; and even at full-giant size, Kalthar is proportionate with his surroundings. So, too, was the noticeable difference of Pious' depictions of the Black natives, who actually looked like humans and not the bug-eyed, boot-lipped caricatures that were common in other comics of the time. Pious' run on Kalthar began with *Zip Comics* #2 (March 1940) and continued over several more issues.

Although the online "Who's Who of American Comic Books" has Pious working for the Harry "A" Chesler studio uninterrupted from 1940 on, that timeline has yet to be corroborated. In fact, there is no discernible Pious comic book work after "Kalthar" until 1943 at the earliest. Assuming that the embarrassment of drawing "Kalthar" didn't drive him away, then there are several possible reasons why.

For at least part of that time, Pious was teaching at the Harlem Community Art Center. Established in 1937 by sculptor Augusta Savage, the center provided art instruction to the community's residents free of charge.

Significantly, working there also was Elton Fax, another artist whose career would intersect with Pious' in the near future.

And part of the reason was the advent of WWII.

At the time of the Japanese attack on Pearl Harbor, December 7, 1941, Pious was nearly 34 years old and married, giving him a low priority draft status. More to the point, being Black meant that he probably wouldn't have been drafted anyway, as in the early months of the war, White draft boards frequently passed over Blacks otherwise eligible to serve. It was only later, after pressure from the NAACP, that Blacks were drafted in larger numbers. In any case, Pious didn't enter the military. He did, however, volunteer to work for the Office of War Information (OWI).

The OWI was formed in June 1942 to coordinate the government's wartime message through oversight of all forms of media—newspapers, film, radio, etc. In other words, it was the United States government's propaganda department. It was deemed essential that all information presented to the public was all positive and directed to the shared goal of winning the war, and that included the Black American population.

Pious was hired to draw single-panel editorial cartoons that often contained clips of news articles pertaining to Black Americans' participation in the war effort. These cartoons contained the same pleas to patriotism, self-sacrifice, and support on the home front that were being asked of White Americans, except they featured a Black cast. Pious' cartoons were widely distributed to major Black newspapers such as the *New York Age* and appeared from about late 1943 to 1945.

With the war's end, the OWI was dissolved and Pious continued as an editorial cartoonist, but now he was free to speak to issues important to his Black readership. He had much to talk about.

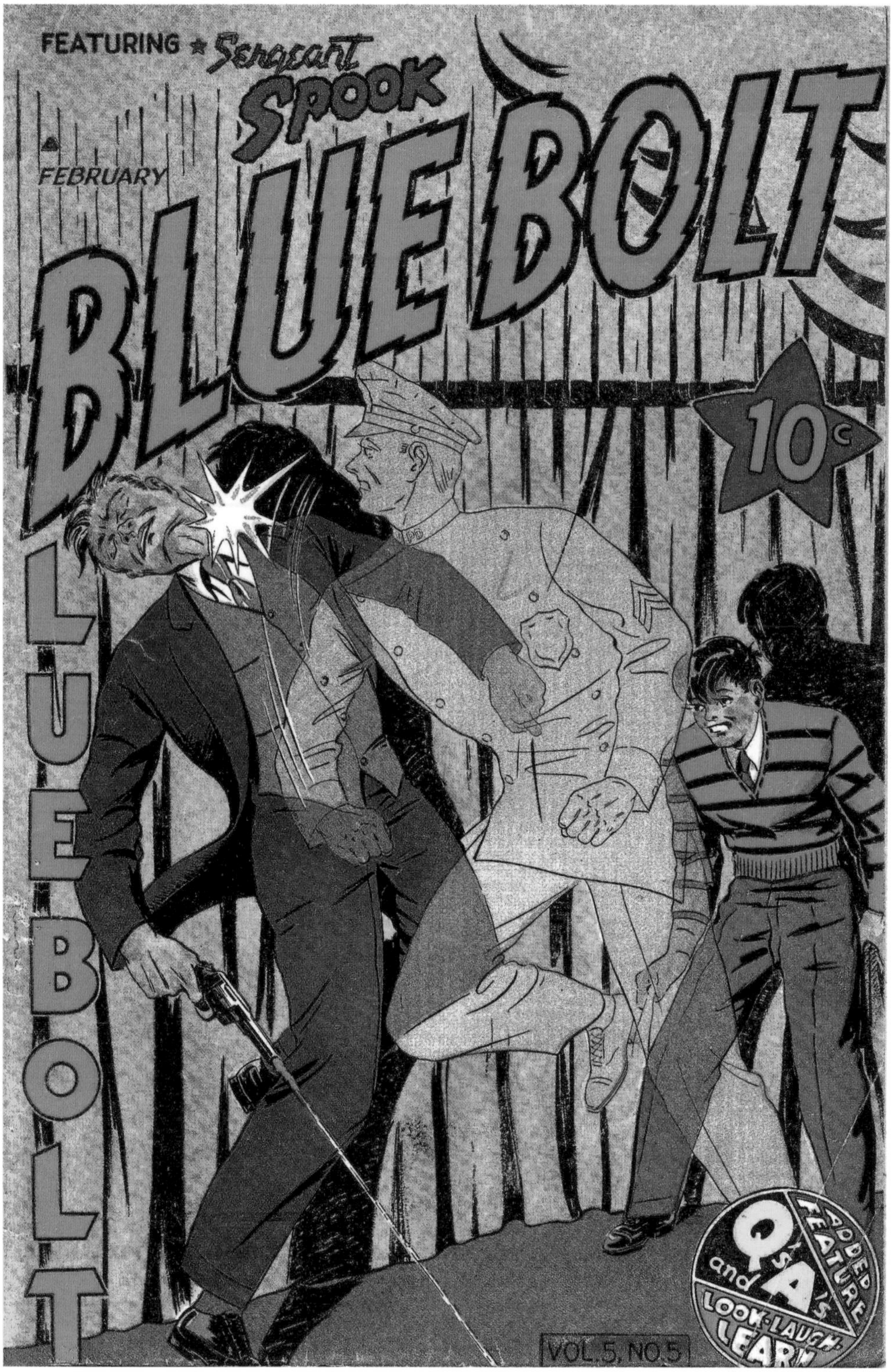
FEATURING ★ Sergeant
SPOOK
FEBRUARY
BLUE BOLT
10¢
ADDED FEATURE
Q and A is
LOOK-LAUGH-LEARN
VOL.5, NO.5

In 1942, the *Pittsburgh Courier* had created the "Double V" campaign, which called for victory not only in the war against the Axis, but also at home against racism. Pious wasn't able to address that effort or any other discordant subjects in his OWI-sponsored cartoons.

Pious' editorial cartoons confronted the denial of freedoms at home that Blacks had fought for in defense of other nations, the jobs they were losing to White servicemen returning from the war, and the shameful fact that Jim Crow laws still prevailed in the South.

At about the same time, Pious returned to drawing comic books. It was still an industry in need of artists, and while it didn't pay well, it was better than nothing.

Reportedly, according to the online Grand Comics Database, Pious drew one story, "General Tom—Fighting Anzac," for Street and Smith's *Super-Magician Comics* vol. 2 #7 (Nov. 1943). Curiously, this story seems to be the only one he drew for this publisher. However, Pious was also doing some illustration work for the pulps at this time, and it's possible he picked up this single comic book gig as a side job from that prominent pulp publisher.

He began drawing comics in earnest in 1944, particularly for *Blue Bolt*, in which he drew both the "Old Cap Hawkins Tales" and "Sergeant Spook" features, along with other random titles connected to the Lloyd Jacquet's Funnies Inc. comic shop. The published evidence seems to indicate that he worked through Funnies Inc. for a while. In addition to *Blue Bolt*, there was also Pious art in *Catholic Comics* and *Marvels of Science*, for which he contributed the covers to issues #1 and #2.

There was always a dour, serious look to Pious' depiction of people—a probable reason why he was generally assigned serious-minded comics to draw.

Unlike most other Black comic book artists, Pious continued working in the industry after WWII ended. Circa 1946-1947, he apparently freelanced, with work appearing in several issues of Holyoke's *Sparkling Stars* and the second issue (Nov. 1947) of the short-lived title *X-Venture*, for which he drew the "Tamor" cover and interior story of yet another White jungle hero freeing Nazi slaves.

Beginning in 1948, Pious collaborated with John M. Lee, editorial writer for the *California Eagle*, in the creation of a historical panel titled "Facts on the Negro in World War Two." The cartoon, which ran at least until 1949, was sold to Black newspapers through the Continental Features syndicate owned by L. H. Stanton.

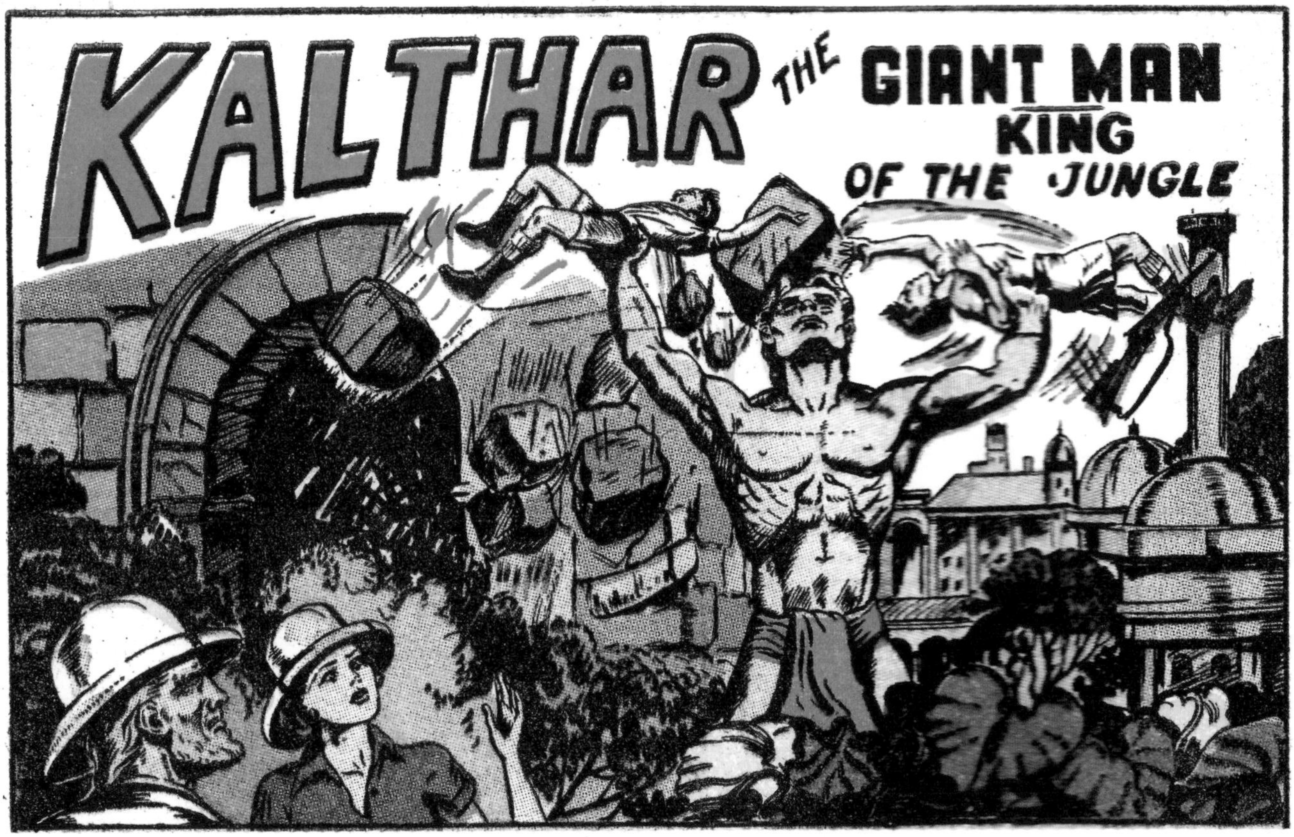
KALTHAR THE GIANT MAN KING OF THE JUNGLE

From 1949 on into 1951, Pious drew stories for issues of American Comics Group's *Adventures Into the Unknown* #6 through #9, and several issues of *Spy-Hunters* from that same publisher. Although he has been credited as the artist on other comics from Fawcett, Charlton, and others, many of those attributions are doubtful.

Outside of comics, Pious' reputation as an illustrator and painter continued to grow. His 1951 portrait of Harriet Tubman, originally painted for the Harmon Foundation, was eventually donated to the National Portrait Gallery, where it still resides. By the late 1950s, he was providing illustrations for a wide variety of books, including Addison B.C. Whipple's *Famous Pirates of the New World*; the Inspirational *Paths That Cross*, by former missionary Esther D. Horner; and the juvenile novel *Kalena and Sana*, the story of a young girl from the Congo, by Emsa Rideout Booth.

Pious' fame had risen to the point that he was chosen by the giant advertising firm Batten, Barton, Durstine & Osborn (BBD&O) to appear in their 1958 print ads, running in such Black publications as *Ebony* and the *Baltimore Afro-American*. In these ads, he was a spokesman for Lucky Strike cigarettes, foreshadowing the Gordon's Gin ads Elmer C. Stoner would appear in a decade later.

From the 1960s to nearly the end of his career in the early 1980s, Pious was a frequent contributor to the revival of Stanton's *National Scene*, a monthly Black newspaper supplement. True to his lifelong devotion to Black history, his cover illustrations and paintings depicted Black historical figures and civil rights pioneers. Of particular note was his portrait of Rosa Parks, which served as the cover to the October 14, 1965, issue.

All the while, Pious continued drawing editorial cartoons until 1966, at least. This was long enough to have seen and been able to comment on much of the civil rights movement. A powerful voice for Black America, unheralded and mostly unknown to White America, Robert S. Pious died on February 1, 1983.

[Left] Pious' cover featuring Sgt. Spook, a crime-fighting ghost policeman. Pious drew this along with "Old Cap Hawkins Tales" for *Blue Bolt* while working through the Funnies, Inc. comics studio. *Blue Bolt* vol. 3 #5, February 1945, Novelty Press.

[Above] Another Tarzan-inspired, White jungle lord, Kalthar was nicknamed The Giant Man by the "Urgana" tribe who raised him. Their medicine man shared the secret of red grains with Kalthar, which allowed the hero to turn into a 15-foot giant to better fight their foes. *Zip Comics* #3, April 1940, MLJ (later called Archie Publications).

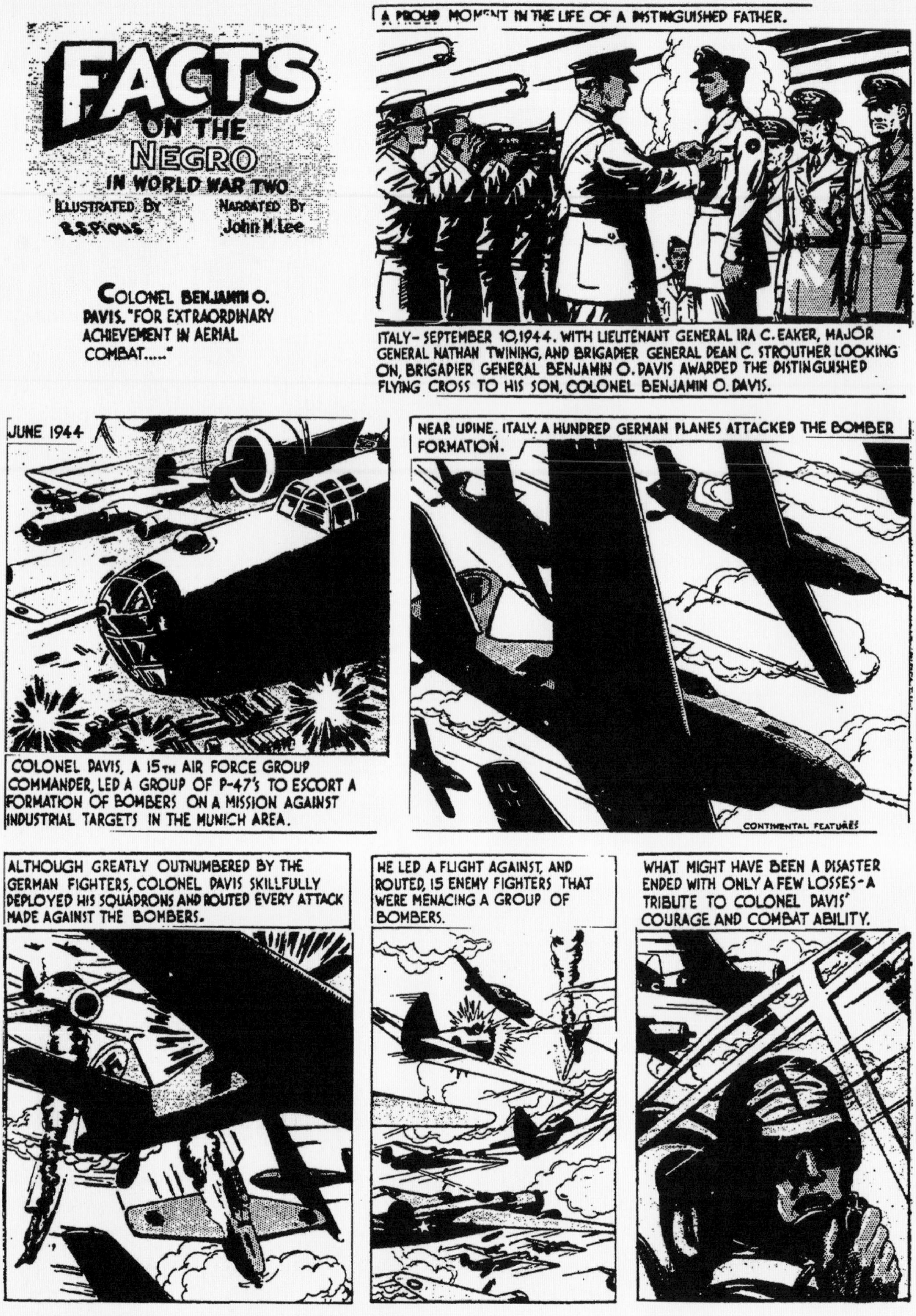
FACTS ON THE NEGRO IN WORLD WAR TWO
ILLUSTRATED BY R.S. PIOUS
NARRATED BY John M. Lee
COLONEL BENJAMIN O. DAVIS. "FOR EXTRAORDINARY ACHIEVEMENT IN AERIAL COMBAT....."
A PROUD MOMENT IN THE LIFE OF A DISTINGUISHED FATHER.
ITALY - SEPTEMBER 10,1944. WITH LIEUTENANT GENERAL IRA C. EAKER, MAJOR GENERAL NATHAN TWINING, AND BRIGADIER GENERAL DEAN C. STROUTHER LOOKING ON, BRIGADIER GENERAL BENJAMIN O. DAVIS AWARDED THE DISTINGUISHED FLYING CROSS TO HIS SON, COLONEL BENJAMIN O. DAVIS.
JUNE 1944
COLONEL DAVIS, A 15TH AIR FORCE GROUP COMMANDER, LED A GROUP OF P-47'S TO ESCORT A FORMATION OF BOMBERS ON A MISSION AGAINST INDUSTRIAL TARGETS IN THE MUNICH AREA.
NEAR UDINE, ITALY, A HUNDRED GERMAN PLANES ATTACKED THE BOMBER FORMATION.
CONTINENTAL FEATURES
ALTHOUGH GREATLY OUTNUMBERED BY THE GERMAN FIGHTERS, COLONEL DAVIS SKILLFULLY DEPLOYED HIS SQUADRONS AND ROUTED EVERY ATTACK MADE AGAINST THE BOMBERS.
HE LED A FLIGHT AGAINST, AND ROUTED, 15 ENEMY FIGHTERS THAT WERE MENACING A GROUP OF BOMBERS.
WHAT MIGHT HAVE BEEN A DISASTER ENDED WITH ONLY A FEW LOSSES - A TRIBUTE TO COLONEL DAVIS' COURAGE AND COMBAT ABILITY.

Pious collaborated with John M. Lee, editorial writer for the *California Eagle*, in the creation of a historical feature titled "Facts on the Negro in World War Two." The series, which ran at least until 1949, was sold to Black newspapers through the Continental Features Syndicate.

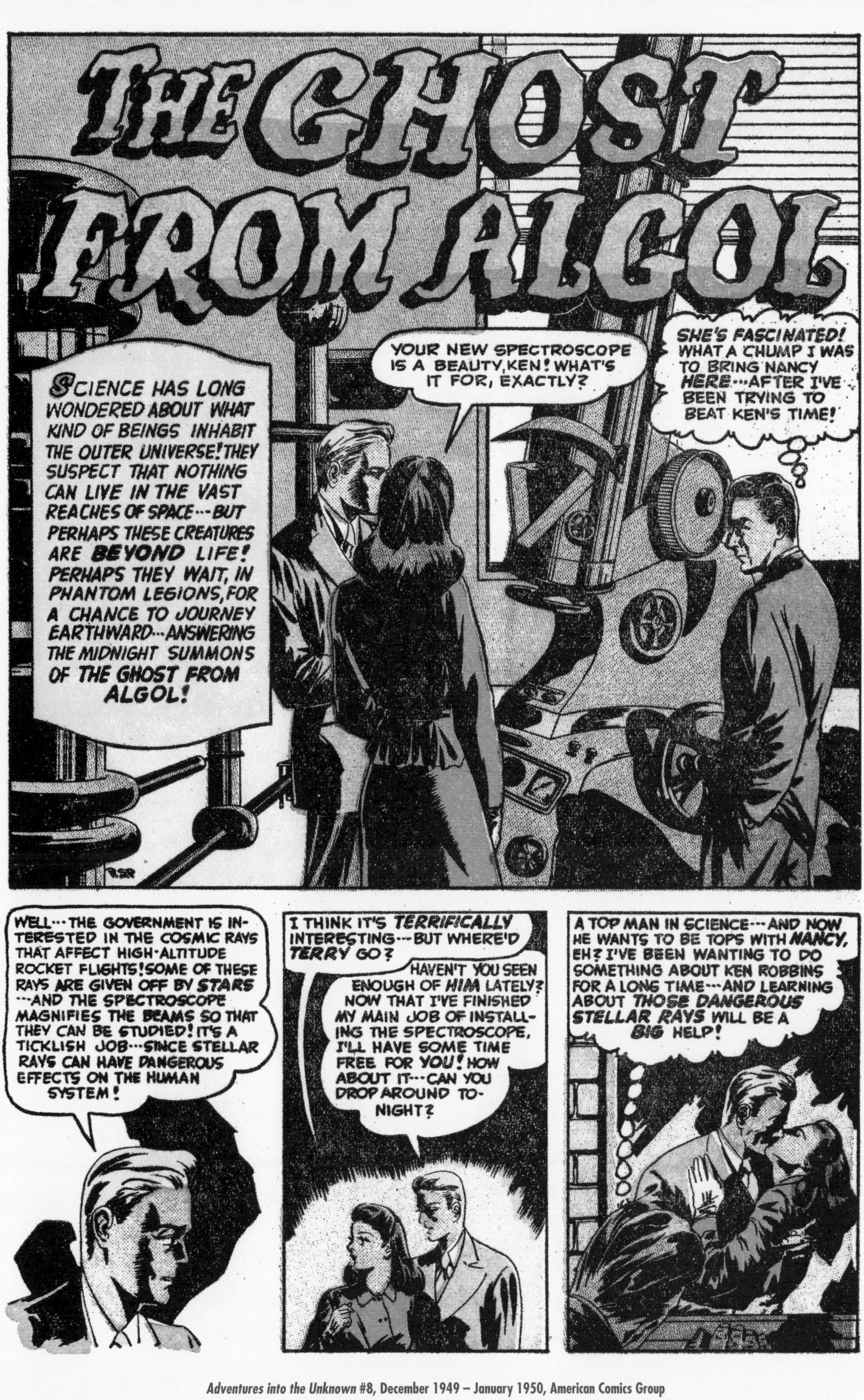
THE GHOST FROM ALGOL
SCIENCE HAS LONG WONDERED ABOUT WHAT KIND OF BEINGS INHABIT THE OUTER UNIVERSE! THEY SUSPECT THAT NOTHING CAN LIVE IN THE VAST REACHES OF SPACE--- BUT PERHAPS THESE CREATURES ARE BEYOND LIFE! PERHAPS THEY WAIT, IN PHANTOM LEGIONS, FOR A CHANCE TO JOURNEY EARTHWARD--- ANSWERING THE MIDNIGHT SUMMONS OF THE GHOST FROM ALGOL!
YOUR NEW SPECTROSCOPE IS A BEAUTY, KEN! WHAT'S IT FOR, EXACTLY?
SHE'S FASCINATED! WHAT A CHUMP I WAS TO BRING NANCY HERE--- AFTER I'VE BEEN TRYING TO BEAT KEN'S TIME!
WELL--- THE GOVERNMENT IS INTERESTED IN THE COSMIC RAYS THAT AFFECT HIGH-ALTITUDE ROCKET FLIGHTS! SOME OF THESE RAYS ARE GIVEN OFF BY STARS ---AND THE SPECTROSCOPE MAGNIFIES THE BEAMS SO THAT THEY CAN BE STUDIED! IT'S A TICKLISH JOB--- SINCE STELLAR RAYS CAN HAVE DANGEROUS EFFECTS ON THE HUMAN SYSTEM!
I THINK IT'S TERRIFICALLY INTERESTING--- BUT WHERE'D TERRY GO?
HAVEN'T YOU SEEN ENOUGH OF HIM LATELY? NOW THAT I'VE FINISHED MY MAIN JOB OF INSTALLING THE SPECTROSCOPE, I'LL HAVE SOME TIME FREE FOR YOU! HOW ABOUT IT--- CAN YOU DROP AROUND TONIGHT?
A TOP MAN IN SCIENCE--- AND NOW HE WANTS TO BE TOPS WITH NANCY, EH? I'VE BEEN WANTING TO DO SOMETHING ABOUT KEN ROBBINS FOR A LONG TIME--- AND LEARNING ABOUT THOSE DANGEROUS STELLAR RAYS WILL BE A BIG HELP!

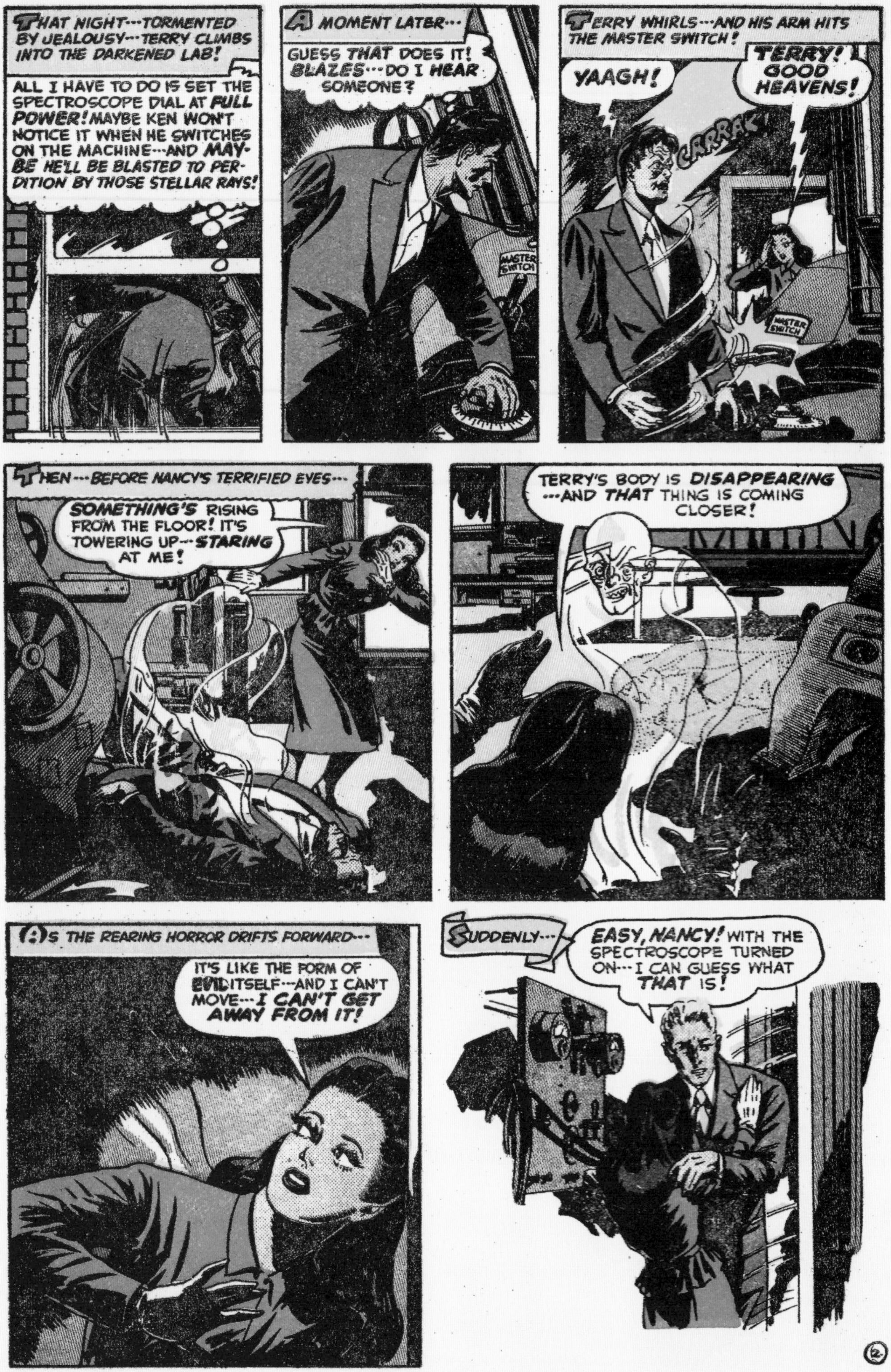
THAT NIGHT---TORMENTED BY JEALOUSY---TERRY CLIMBS INTO THE DARKENED LAB!
ALL I HAVE TO DO IS SET THE SPECTROSCOPE DIAL AT FULL POWER! MAYBE KEN WON'T NOTICE IT WHEN HE SWITCHES ON THE MACHINE---AND MAYBE HE'LL BE BLASTED TO PERDITION BY THOSE STELLAR RAYS!
A MOMENT LATER---
GUESS THAT DOES IT! BLAZES---DO I HEAR SOMEONE?
MASTER SWITCH
TERRY WHIRLS---AND HIS ARM HITS THE MASTER SWITCH!
YAAGH!
TERRY! GOOD HEAVENS!
CRRRAK
MASTER SWITCH
THEN---BEFORE NANCY'S TERRIFIED EYES---
SOMETHING'S RISING FROM THE FLOOR! IT'S TOWERING UP---STARING AT ME!
TERRY'S BODY IS DISAPPEARING ---AND THAT THING IS COMING CLOSER!
AS THE REARING HORROR DRIFTS FORWARD---
IT'S LIKE THE FORM OF EVIL ITSELF---AND I CAN'T MOVE---I CAN'T GET AWAY FROM IT!
SUDDENLY---
EASY, NANCY! WITH THE SPECTROSCOPE TURNED ON---I CAN GUESS WHAT THAT IS!
2

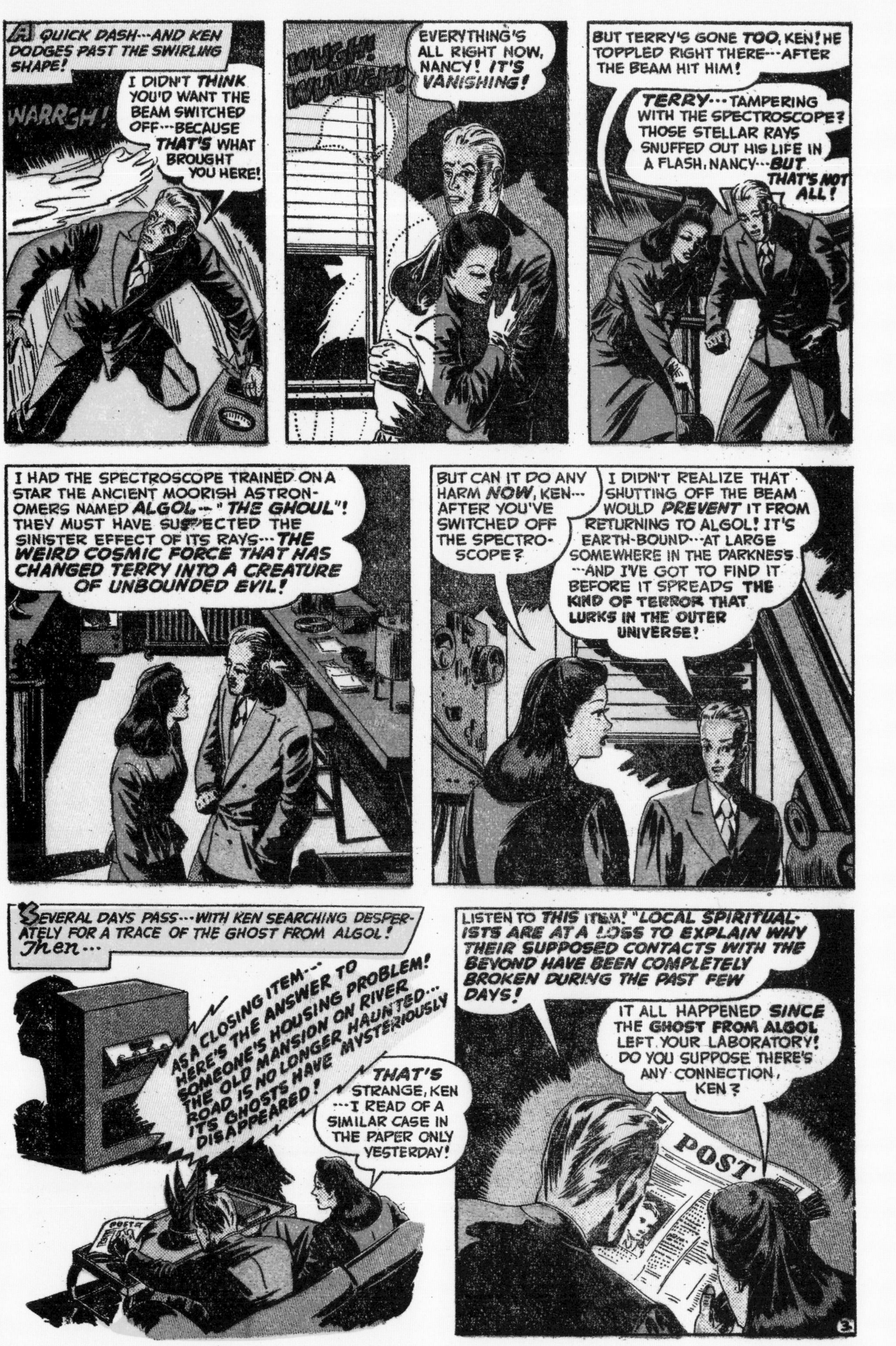

A QUICK DASH---AND KEN DODGES PAST THE SWIRLING SHAPE!
WARRGH!
I DIDN'T THINK YOU'D WANT THE BEAM SWITCHED OFF---BECAUSE THAT'S WHAT BROUGHT YOU HERE!
EVERYTHING'S ALL RIGHT NOW, NANCY! IT'S VANISHING!
BUT TERRY'S GONE TOO, KEN! HE TOPPLED RIGHT THERE---AFTER THE BEAM HIT HIM!
TERRY---TAMPERING WITH THE SPECTROSCOPE? THOSE STELLAR RAYS SNUFFED OUT HIS LIFE IN A FLASH, NANCY---BUT THAT'S NOT ALL!
I HAD THE SPECTROSCOPE TRAINED ON A STAR THE ANCIENT MOORISH ASTRONOMERS NAMED ALGOL--"THE GHOUL"! THEY MUST HAVE SUSPECTED THE SINISTER EFFECT OF ITS RAYS---THE WEIRD COSMIC FORCE THAT HAS CHANGED TERRY INTO A CREATURE OF UNBOUNDED EVIL!
BUT CAN IT DO ANY HARM NOW, KEN---AFTER YOU'VE SWITCHED OFF THE SPECTROSCOPE?
I DIDN'T REALIZE THAT SHUTTING OFF THE BEAM WOULD PREVENT IT FROM RETURNING TO ALGOL! IT'S EARTH-BOUND---AT LARGE SOMEWHERE IN THE DARKNESS---AND I'VE GOT TO FIND IT BEFORE IT SPREADS THE KIND OF TERROR THAT LURKS IN THE OUTER UNIVERSE!
SEVERAL DAYS PASS---WITH KEN SEARCHING DESPERATELY FOR A TRACE OF THE GHOST FROM ALGOL! Then---
AS A CLOSING ITEM---HERE'S THE ANSWER TO SOMEONE'S HOUSING PROBLEM! THE OLD MANSION ON RIVER ROAD IS NO LONGER HAUNTED...ITS GHOSTS HAVE MYSTERIOUSLY DISAPPEARED!
THAT'S STRANGE, KEN---I READ OF A SIMILAR CASE IN THE PAPER ONLY YESTERDAY!
LISTEN TO THIS ITEM! "LOCAL SPIRITUALISTS ARE AT A LOSS TO EXPLAIN WHY THEIR SUPPOSED CONTACTS WITH THE BEYOND HAVE BEEN COMPLETELY BROKEN DURING THE PAST FEW DAYS!
IT ALL HAPPENED SINCE THE GHOST FROM ALGOL LEFT YOUR LABORATORY! DO YOU SUPPOSE THERE'S ANY CONNECTION, KEN?
POST
3.

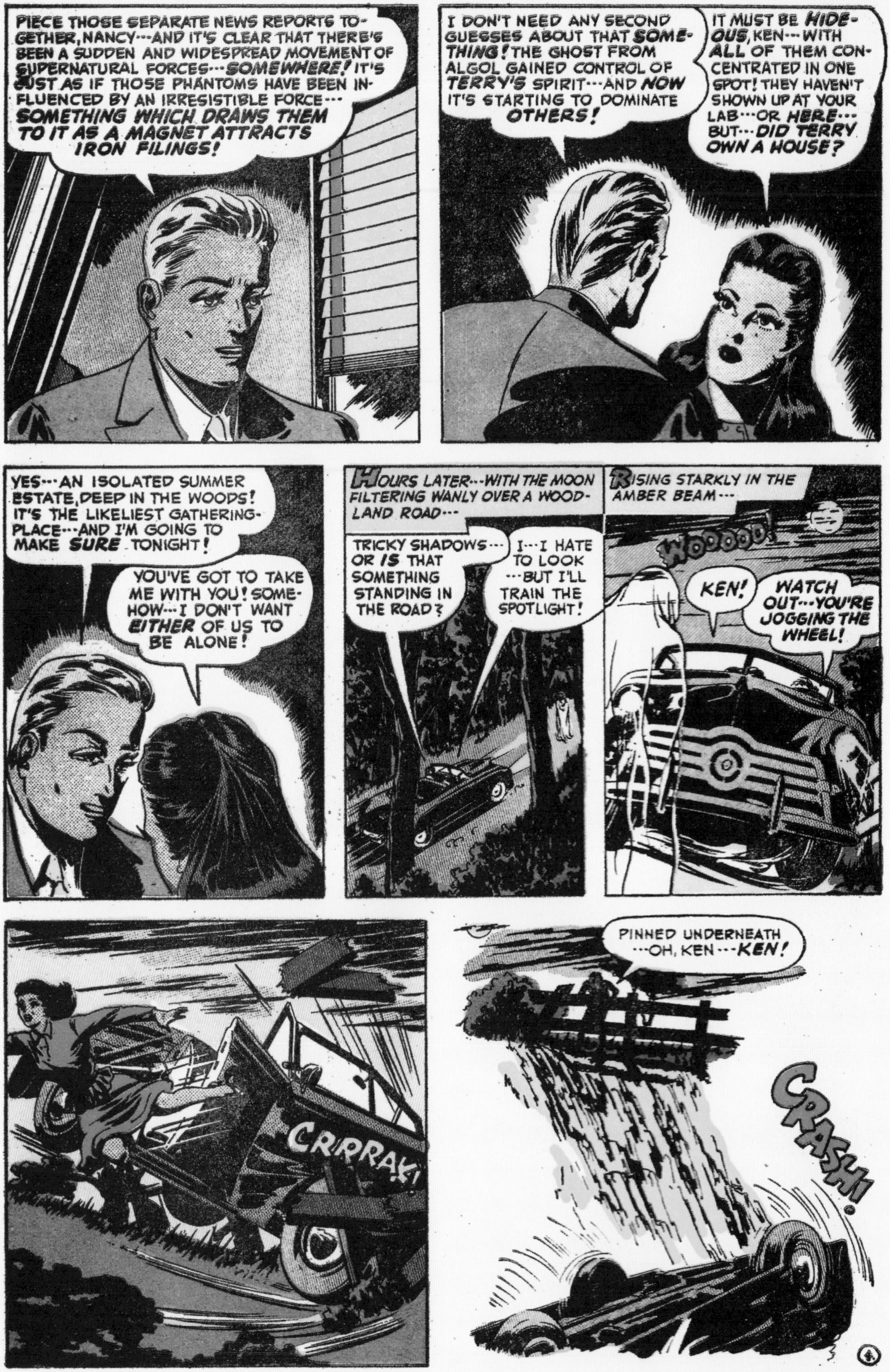
PIECE THOSE SEPARATE NEWS REPORTS TOGETHER, NANCY---AND IT'S CLEAR THAT THERE'S BEEN A SUDDEN AND WIDESPREAD MOVEMENT OF SUPERNATURAL FORCES---SOMEWHERE! IT'S JUST AS IF THOSE PHANTOMS HAVE BEEN INFLUENCED BY AN IRRESISTIBLE FORCE---SOMETHING WHICH DRAWS THEM TO IT AS A MAGNET ATTRACTS IRON FILINGS!
I DON'T NEED ANY SECOND GUESSES ABOUT THAT SOMETHING! THE GHOST FROM ALGOL GAINED CONTROL OF TERRY'S SPIRIT---AND NOW IT'S STARTING TO DOMINATE OTHERS!
IT MUST BE HIDEOUS, KEN---WITH ALL OF THEM CONCENTRATED IN ONE SPOT! THEY HAVEN'T SHOWN UP AT YOUR LAB---OR HERE---BUT---DID TERRY OWN A HOUSE?
YES---AN ISOLATED SUMMER ESTATE, DEEP IN THE WOODS! IT'S THE LIKELIEST GATHERING-PLACE---AND I'M GOING TO MAKE SURE TONIGHT!
YOU'VE GOT TO TAKE ME WITH YOU! SOMEHOW---I DON'T WANT EITHER OF US TO BE ALONE!
HOURS LATER---WITH THE MOON FILTERING WANLY OVER A WOODLAND ROAD---
TRICKY SHADOWS---OR IS THAT SOMETHING STANDING IN THE ROAD?
I---I HATE TO LOOK---BUT I'LL TRAIN THE SPOTLIGHT!
RISING STARKLY IN THE AMBER BEAM---
WOOOOO!
KEN!
WATCH OUT---YOU'RE JOGGING THE WHEEL!
CRRRAK!
PINNED UNDERNEATH---OH, KEN---KEN!
CRASH!
4

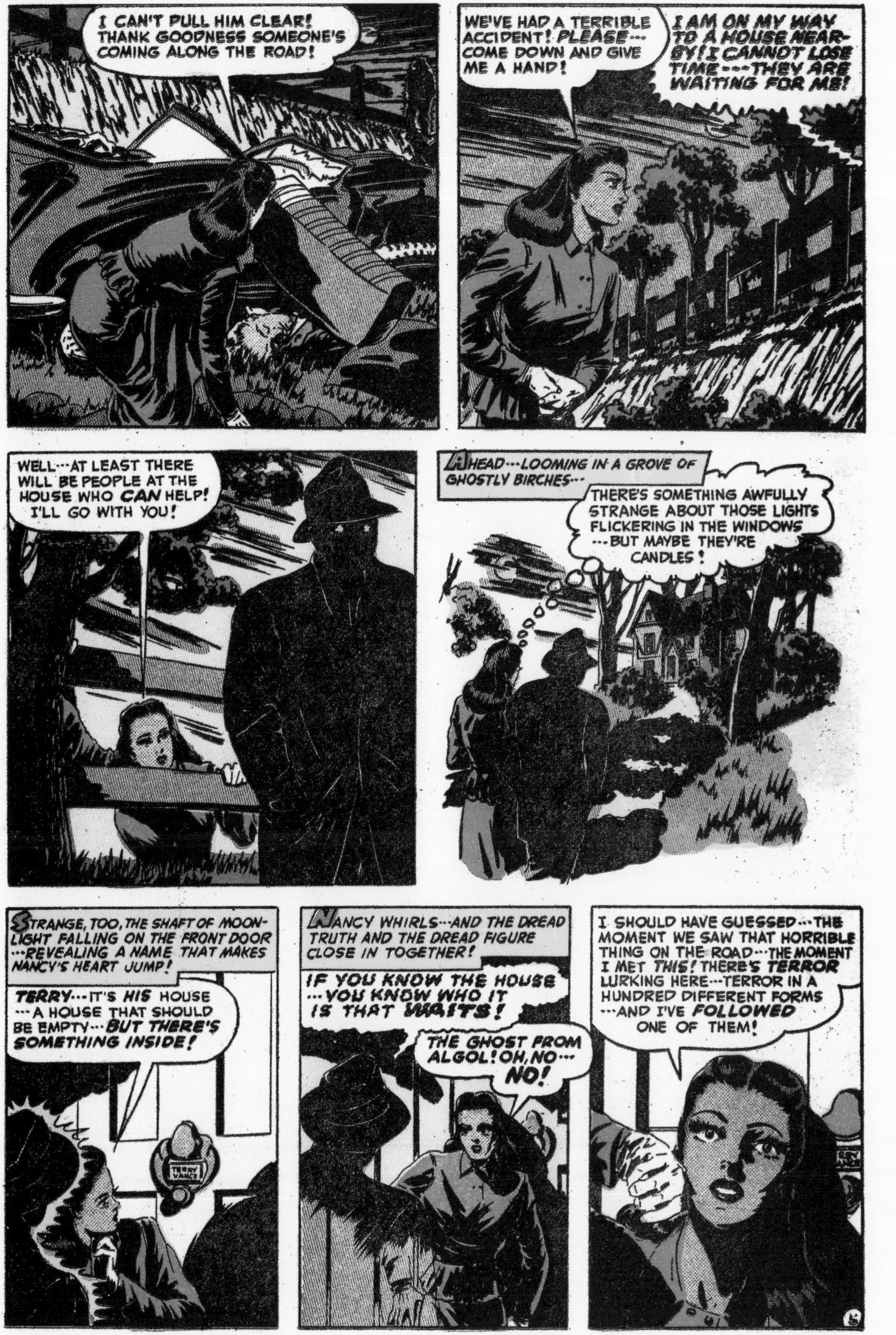
I CAN'T PULL HIM CLEAR! THANK GOODNESS SOMEONE'S COMING ALONG THE ROAD!
WE'VE HAD A TERRIBLE ACCIDENT! PLEASE--- COME DOWN AND GIVE ME A HAND!
I AM ON MY WAY TO A HOUSE NEAR-BY! I CANNOT LOSE TIME--- THEY ARE WAITING FOR ME!
WELL--- AT LEAST THERE WILL BE PEOPLE AT THE HOUSE WHO CAN HELP! I'LL GO WITH YOU!
AHEAD---LOOMING IN A GROVE OF GHOSTLY BIRCHES---
THERE'S SOMETHING AWFULLY STRANGE ABOUT THOSE LIGHTS FLICKERING IN THE WINDOWS ---BUT MAYBE THEY'RE CANDLES!
STRANGE, TOO, THE SHAFT OF MOON-LIGHT FALLING ON THE FRONT DOOR ---REVEALING A NAME THAT MAKES NANCY'S HEART JUMP!
TERRY---IT'S HIS HOUSE ---A HOUSE THAT SHOULD BE EMPTY--- BUT THERE'S SOMETHING INSIDE!
TERRY VANCE
NANCY WHIRLS---AND THE DREAD TRUTH AND THE DREAD FIGURE CLOSE IN TOGETHER!
IF YOU KNOW THE HOUSE ...YOU KNOW WHO IT IS THAT WAITS!
THE GHOST FROM ALGOL! OH, NO--- NO!
I SHOULD HAVE GUESSED--- THE MOMENT WE SAW THAT HORRIBLE THING ON THE ROAD--- THE MOMENT I MET THIS! THERE'S TERROR LURKING HERE---TERROR IN A HUNDRED DIFFERENT FORMS ---AND I'VE FOLLOWED ONE OF THEM!

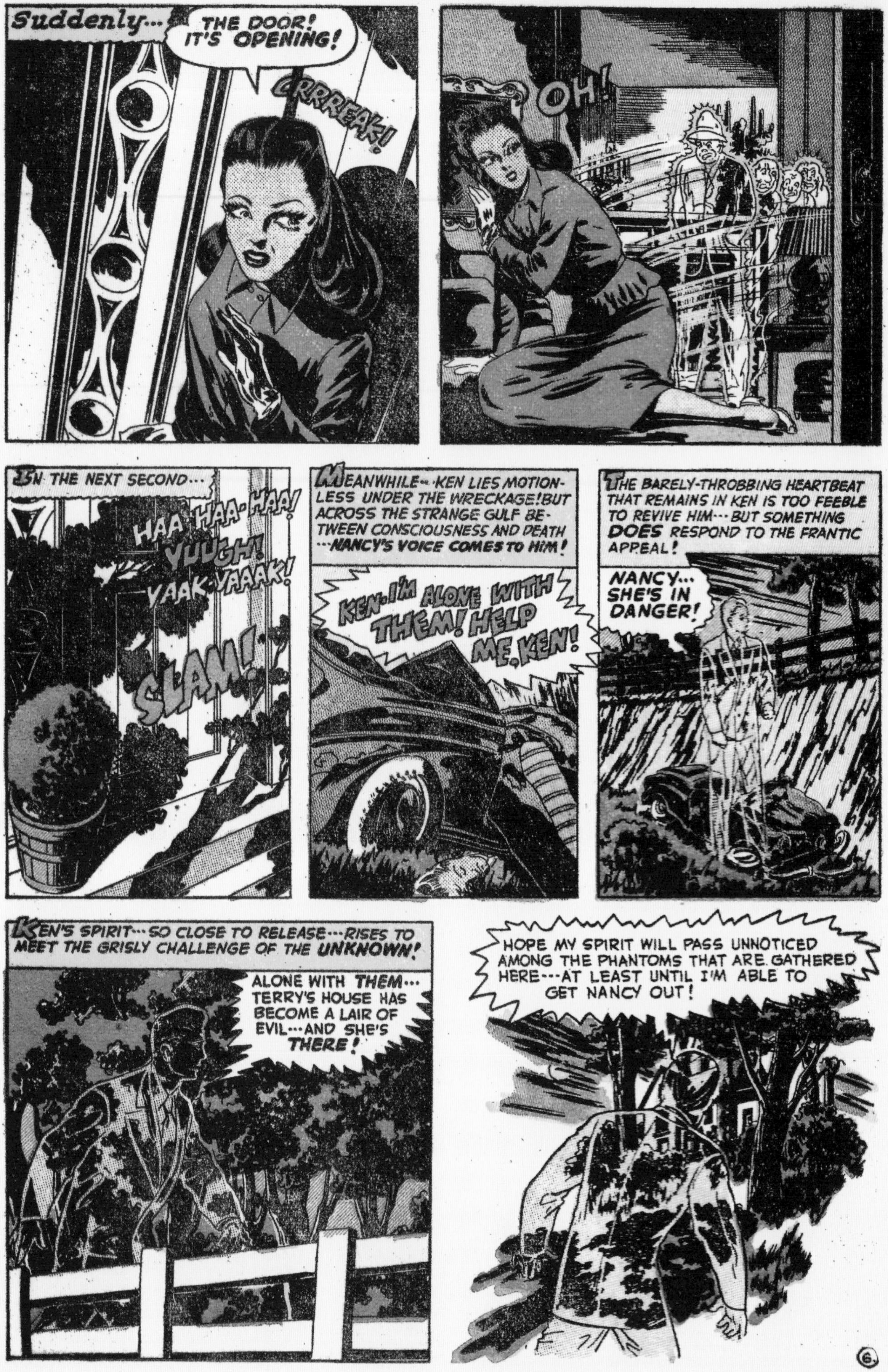
Suddenly...
THE DOOR! IT'S OPENING!
CRRREAK!
OH!
IN THE NEXT SECOND...
HAA HAA-HAA!
YUUGH!
YAAK-YAAAK!
SLAM!
MEANWHILE--KEN LIES MOTIONLESS UNDER THE WRECKAGE! BUT ACROSS THE STRANGE GULF BETWEEN CONSCIOUSNESS AND DEATH ...NANCY'S VOICE COMES TO HIM!
KEN-I'M ALONE WITH THEM! HELP ME, KEN!
THE BARELY-THROBBING HEARTBEAT THAT REMAINS IN KEN IS TOO FEEBLE TO REVIVE HIM... BUT SOMETHING DOES RESPOND TO THE FRANTIC APPEAL!
NANCY... SHE'S IN DANGER!
KEN'S SPIRIT... SO CLOSE TO RELEASE... RISES TO MEET THE GRISLY CHALLENGE OF THE UNKNOWN!
ALONE WITH THEM... TERRY'S HOUSE HAS BECOME A LAIR OF EVIL... AND SHE'S THERE!
HOPE MY SPIRIT WILL PASS UNNOTICED AMONG THE PHANTOMS THAT ARE GATHERED HERE... AT LEAST UNTIL I'M ABLE TO GET NANCY OUT!
6.

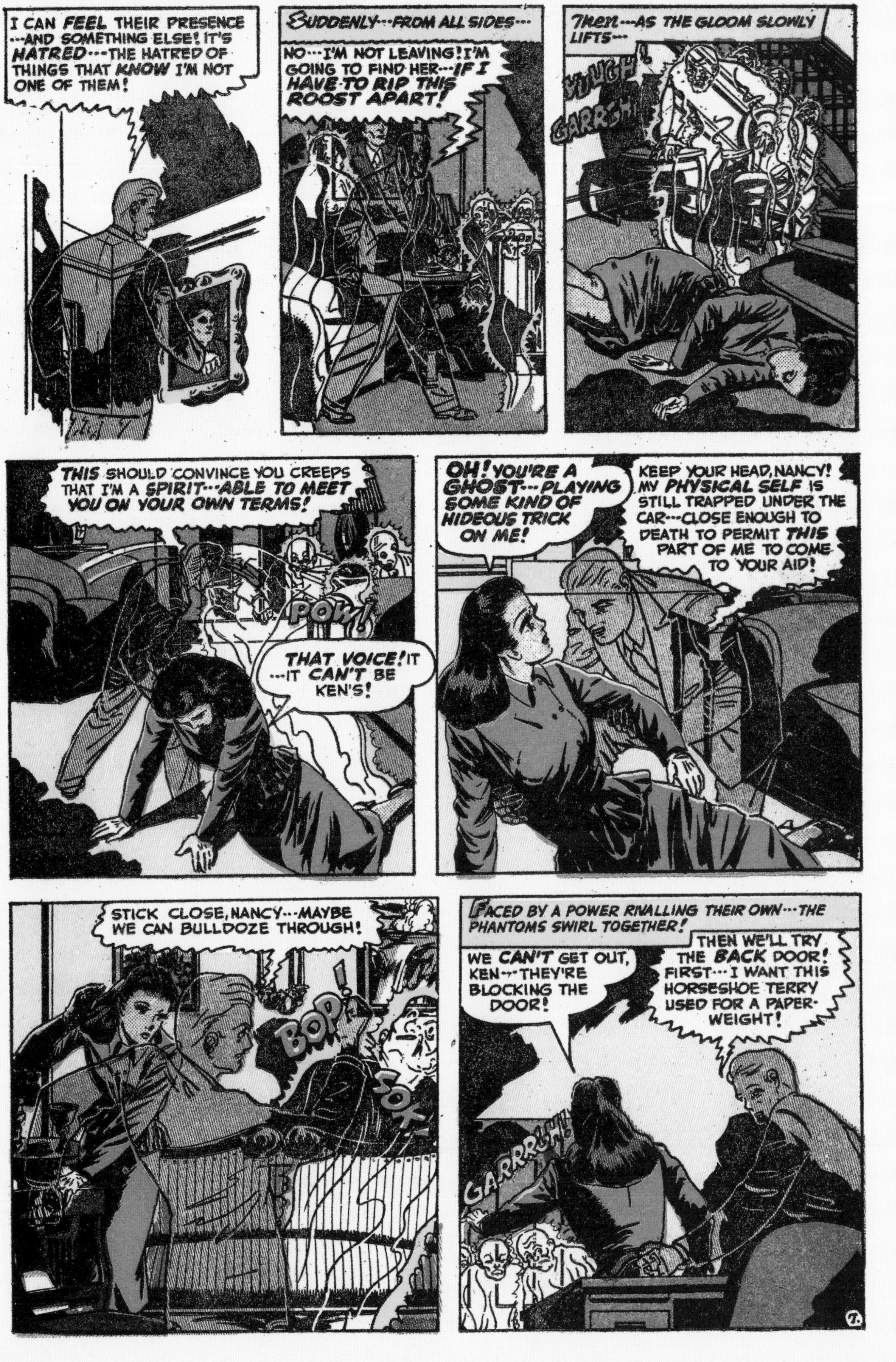

I CAN FEEL THEIR PRESENCE ---AND SOMETHING ELSE! IT'S HATRED---THE HATRED OF THINGS THAT KNOW I'M NOT ONE OF THEM!
SUDDENLY---FROM ALL SIDES---
NO---I'M NOT LEAVING! I'M GOING TO FIND HER---IF I HAVE TO RIP THIS ROOST APART!
THEN---AS THE GLOOM SLOWLY LIFTS---
YUUGH!
GARRSH!
THIS SHOULD CONVINCE YOU CREEPS THAT I'M A SPIRIT---ABLE TO MEET YOU ON YOUR OWN TERMS!
POW!
THAT VOICE! IT ---IT CAN'T BE KEN'S!
OH! YOU'RE A GHOST---PLAYING SOME KIND OF HIDEOUS TRICK ON ME!
KEEP YOUR HEAD, NANCY! MY PHYSICAL SELF IS STILL TRAPPED UNDER THE CAR---CLOSE ENOUGH TO DEATH TO PERMIT THIS PART OF ME TO COME TO YOUR AID!
STICK CLOSE, NANCY---MAYBE WE CAN BULLDOZE THROUGH!
BOP!
SOK
FACED BY A POWER RIVALLING THEIR OWN---THE PHANTOMS SWIRL TOGETHER!
WE CAN'T GET OUT, KEN---THEY'RE BLOCKING THE DOOR!
THEN WE'LL TRY THE BACK DOOR! FIRST---I WANT THIS HORSESHOE TERRY USED FOR A PAPER-WEIGHT!
GARRRGH!
7.

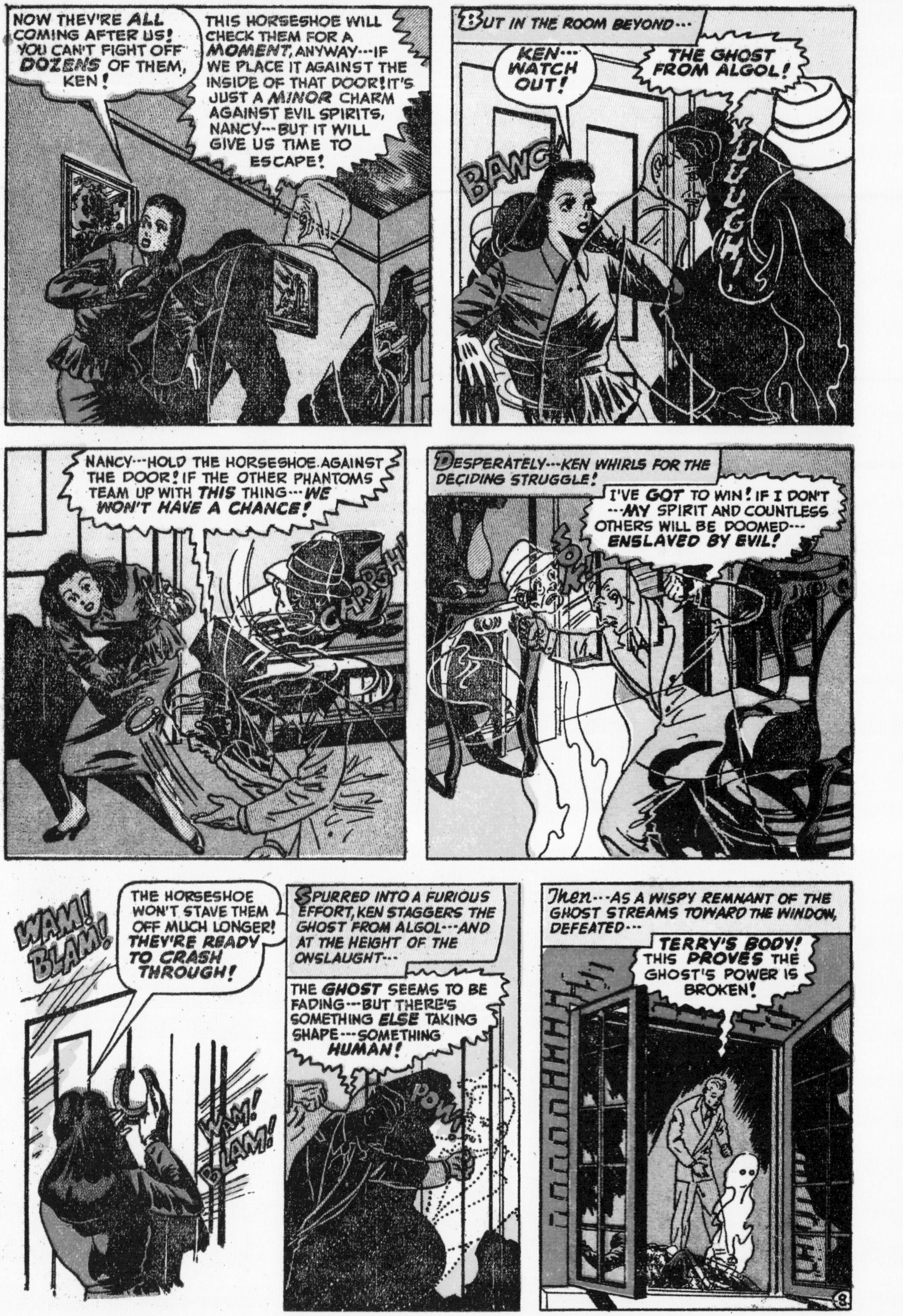
NOW THEY'RE ALL COMING AFTER US! YOU CAN'T FIGHT OFF DOZENS OF THEM, KEN!
THIS HORSESHOE WILL CHECK THEM FOR A MOMENT, ANYWAY---IF WE PLACE IT AGAINST THE INSIDE OF THAT DOOR! IT'S JUST A MINOR CHARM AGAINST EVIL SPIRITS, NANCY---BUT IT WILL GIVE US TIME TO ESCAPE!
BUT IN THE ROOM BEYOND...
KEN--- WATCH OUT!
THE GHOST FROM ALGOL!
BANG
UUUGH
NANCY---HOLD THE HORSESHOE AGAINST THE DOOR! IF THE OTHER PHANTOMS TEAM UP WITH THIS THING---WE WON'T HAVE A CHANCE!
CHRRSH!
DESPERATELY---KEN WHIRLS FOR THE DECIDING STRUGGLE!
I'VE GOT TO WIN! IF I DON'T ---MY SPIRIT AND COUNTLESS OTHERS WILL BE DOOMED--- ENSLAVED BY EVIL!
SOK!
WAM! BLAM!
THE HORSESHOE WON'T STAVE THEM OFF MUCH LONGER! THEY'RE READY TO CRASH THROUGH!
WAM! BLAM!
SPURRED INTO A FURIOUS EFFORT, KEN STAGGERS THE GHOST FROM ALGOL---AND AT THE HEIGHT OF THE ONSLAUGHT---
THE GHOST SEEMS TO BE FADING---BUT THERE'S SOMETHING ELSE TAKING SHAPE---SOMETHING HUMAN!
POW
Then---AS A WISPY REMNANT OF THE GHOST STREAMS TOWARD THE WINDOW, DEFEATED---
TERRY'S BODY! THIS PROVES THE GHOST'S POWER IS BROKEN!
8

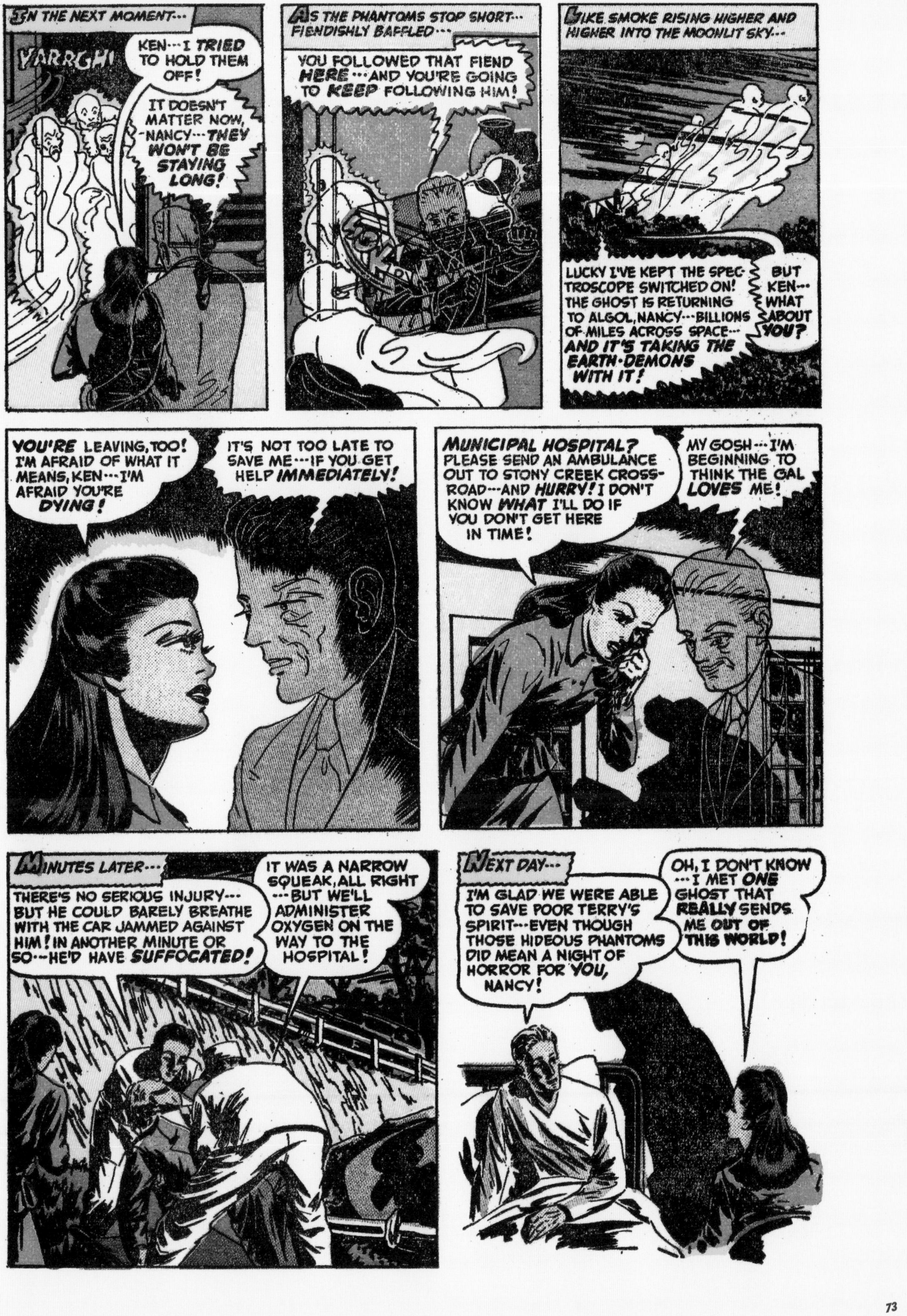
IN THE NEXT MOMENT...
YARRGH!
KEN... I TRIED TO HOLD THEM OFF!
IT DOESN'T MATTER NOW, NANCY... THEY WON'T BE STAYING LONG!
AS THE PHANTOMS STOP SHORT... FIENDISHLY BAFFLED...
YOU FOLLOWED THAT FIEND HERE... AND YOU'RE GOING TO KEEP FOLLOWING HIM!
LIKE SMOKE RISING HIGHER AND HIGHER INTO THE MOONLIT SKY...
LUCKY I'VE KEPT THE SPECTROSCOPE SWITCHED ON! THE GHOST IS RETURNING TO ALGOL, NANCY... BILLIONS OF MILES ACROSS SPACE... AND IT'S TAKING THE EARTH-DEMONS WITH IT!
BUT KEN... WHAT ABOUT YOU?
YOU'RE LEAVING, TOO! I'M AFRAID OF WHAT IT MEANS, KEN... I'M AFRAID YOU'RE DYING!
IT'S NOT TOO LATE TO SAVE ME... IF YOU GET HELP IMMEDIATELY!
MUNICIPAL HOSPITAL? PLEASE SEND AN AMBULANCE OUT TO STONY CREEK CROSS-ROAD... AND HURRY! I DON'T KNOW WHAT I'LL DO IF YOU DON'T GET HERE IN TIME!
MY GOSH... I'M BEGINNING TO THINK THE GAL LOVES ME!
MINUTES LATER...
THERE'S NO SERIOUS INJURY... BUT HE COULD BARELY BREATHE WITH THE CAR JAMMED AGAINST HIM! IN ANOTHER MINUTE OR SO... HE'D HAVE SUFFOCATED!
IT WAS A NARROW SQUEAK, ALL RIGHT... BUT WE'LL ADMINISTER OXYGEN ON THE WAY TO THE HOSPITAL!
NEXT DAY...
I'M GLAD WE WERE ABLE TO SAVE POOR TERRY'S SPIRIT... EVEN THOUGH THOSE HIDEOUS PHANTOMS DID MEAN A NIGHT OF HORROR FOR YOU, NANCY!
OH, I DON'T KNOW... I MET ONE GHOST THAT REALLY SENDS ME OUT OF THIS WORLD!

JAY PAUL JACKSON
An Artist Apart

It was a cold reality that for many comic book creators—of all skin colors—it was a fleeting occupation, a way to pay the bills, a stopover on the way to something better. It was simply the nature of the business. It was just a job, not a career of any permanence. One artist among them, Jay Paul Jackson, certainly understood the impermanence of jobs, and of life.

He was born in Oberlin, Ohio on September 10, 1905, even if that detail wasn't totally clear to his father. Frank Jackson said:

"What the Hell! Who cares whether the kid was born on the tenth or eleventh of September. It's here! It's a boy, and everything is fine. Hot damn!" [Jackson, Jay Paul, "Introducing the Author," *Fantastic Adventures*, Oct. 1941, p.139]

The family, which included mother Nellie and Jay's three sisters, lived in Oberlin, a town with an integrated Black and White population and a history of abolitionist activism. In 1858, a fugitive slave from Kentucky named John Price sought refuge in Oberlin, but according to the prevailing federal Fugitive Slave Law of 1850, federal officials in every state, free as well as slave, must comply by arresting the runaway slave. The federal marshal in the town did just that and moved Price to a nearby town surreptitiously to avoid any trouble. But the townspeople of Oberlin still found out that Price was in custody, so a large group of them went to the neighboring town, found Price, took him back to Oberlin, and hid him. They then managed to smuggle him across Lake Erie, into Canada, and to freedom.

The welcoming nature of Oberlin probably explains how Frank Jackson was able to follow a career as a gallery photographer, when the best most other Blacks of the time could hope for was a job as a Pullman porter. His relative prosperity, though, didn't allow son Jay to dodge labor. At the age of thirteen, he took a job driving spikes on a railroad near Columbus, Ohio. A few years later, he was employed in a Pittsburgh steel mill, "with a pair of steel tongs in his

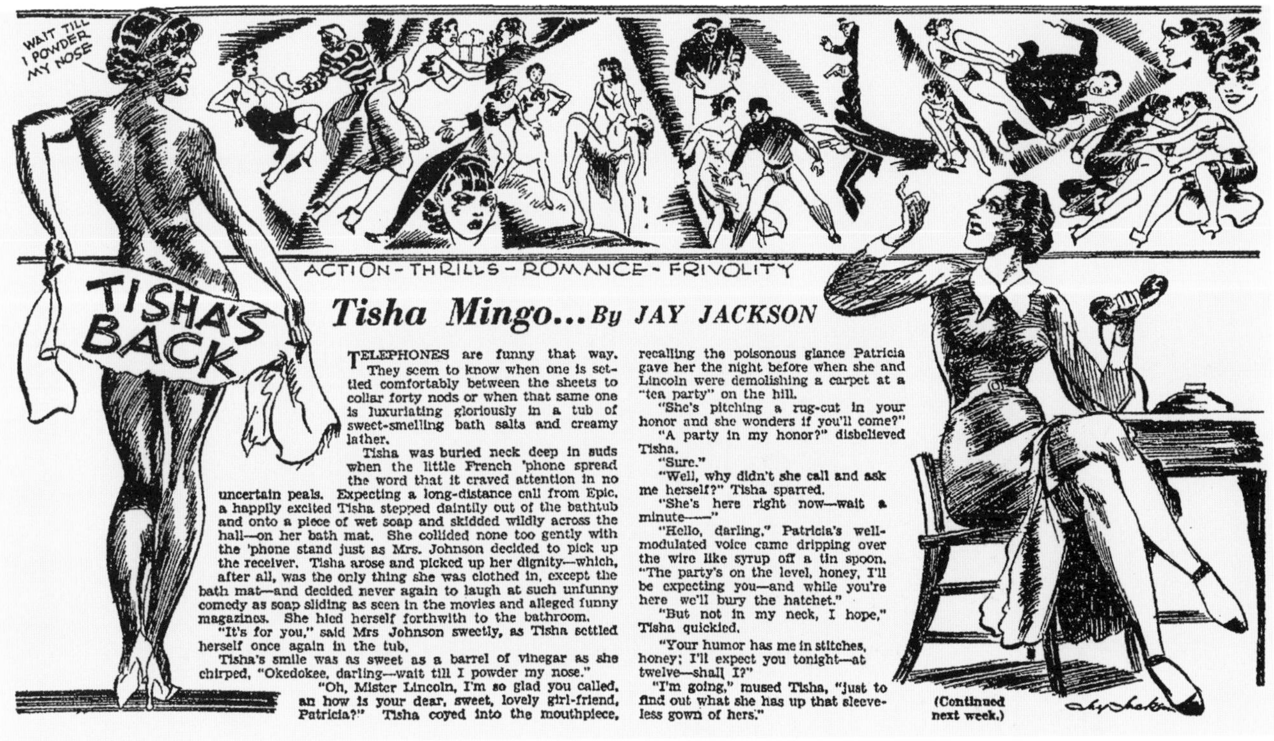

WAIT TILL I POWDER MY NOSE

TISHA'S BACK

ACTION - THRILLS - ROMANCE - FRIVOLITY

Tisha Mingo... By JAY JACKSON

TELEPHONES are funny that way. They seem to know when one is settled comfortably between the sheets to collar forty nods or when that same one is luxuriating gloriously in a tub of sweet-smelling bath salts and creamy lather.

Tisha was buried neck deep in suds when the little French 'phone spread the word that it craved attention in no uncertain peals. Expecting a long-distance call from Epic, a happily excited Tisha stepped daintily out of the bathtub and onto a piece of wet soap and skidded wildly across the hall—on her bath mat. She collided none too gently with the 'phone stand just as Mrs. Johnson decided to pick up the receiver. Tisha arose and picked up her dignity—which, after all, was the only thing she was clothed in, except the bath mat—and decided never again to laugh at such unfunny comedy as soap sliding as seen in the movies and alleged funny magazines. She hied herself forthwith to the bathroom.

"It's for you," said Mrs Johnson sweetly, as Tisha settled herself once again in the tub.

Tisha's smile was as sweet as a barrel of vinegar as she chirped, "Okedokee, darling—wait till I powder my nose."

"Oh, Mister Lincoln, I'm so glad you called, an how is your dear, sweet, lovely girl-friend, Patricia?" Tisha coyed into the mouthpiece, recalling the poisonous glance Patricia gave her the night before when she and Lincoln were demolishing a carpet at a "tea party" on the hill.

"She's pitching a rug-cut in your honor and she wonders if you'll come?"

"A party in my honor?" disbelieved Tisha.

"Sure."

"Well, why didn't she call and ask me herself?" Tisha sparred.

"She's here right now—wait a minute——"

"Hello, darling," Patricia's well-modulated voice came dripping over the wire like syrup off a tin spoon. "The party's on the level, honey, I'll be expecting you—and while you're here we'll bury the hatchet."

"But not in my neck, I hope," Tisha quickied.

"Your humor has me in stitches, honey; I'll expect you tonight—at twelve—shall I?"

"I'm going," mused Tisha, "just to find out what she has up that sleeveless gown of hers."

(Continued next week.)

leather-encrusted hands, grabbing at a hunk of white-hot steel as it jumps out of the rollers." [Ibid, p.139]

Jackson attended Ohio Wesleyan University in Delaware, Ohio. Along with his art studies, he drove a mail truck and found time to box. He also married his college sweetheart, Adaline Smith, on July 14, 1925. Jackson started upon a successful business as a sign painter, until he contracted lead poisoning from the paint. This led him to move to Chicago, where he spent some time painting posters. He soon made a side-step and worked as a shop foreman for the Warner Bros. theater chain. Then tragedy struck Jackson. Repeatedly.

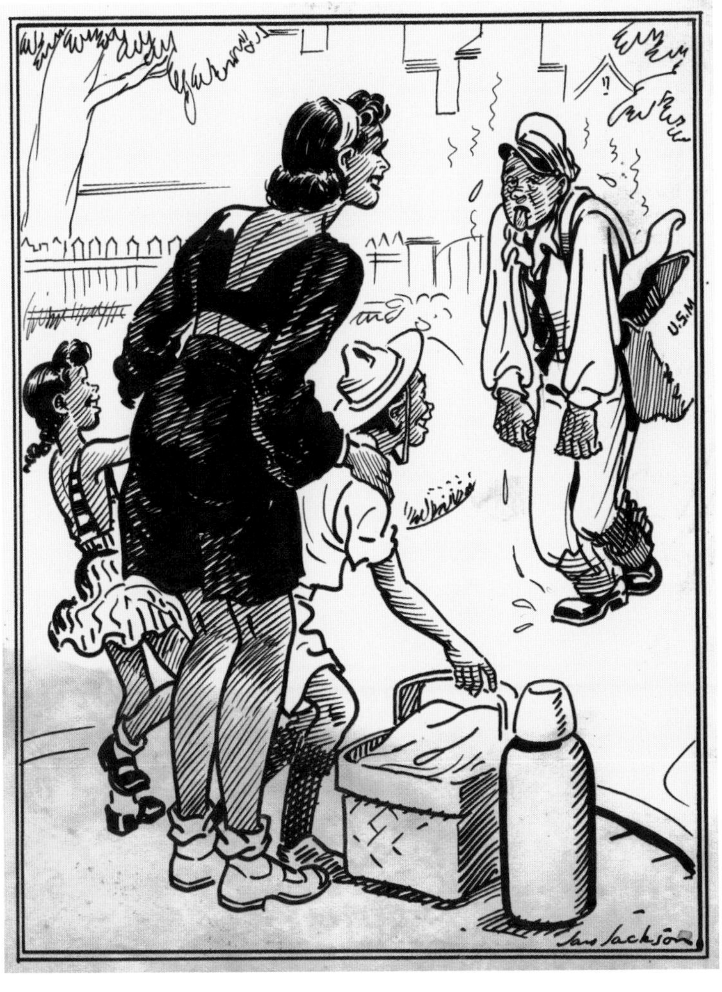
U.S.M
Jay Jackson

In quick succession, his father, first child, and wife all died. Devastated and reeling, Jackson was also left with the responsibility of raising his infant daughter, Carrie Lou. All this occurred by the time he was 22 years old. Jay wrote:

The next scene comes on like an Orson Welles film set, crazy pictures at crazy angles...loneliness, bitterness, sullenness, strange hotels and soulless rooms, moonshine whiskey, bathtub gin, despair.

Life had done me dirt and I resented it, so I drew and wrote about people on the down beat—my inborn humor turned sour and came out on paper with a sardonic grin. [Ibid, p.142]

Despite his despair, Jackson was making good money painting signs for the theaters—for a while. Along came the Great Depression, and by 1933, he was unemployed. Jackson gave up his nice apartment in the classy Bronzeville neighborhood and took up residence in the first-class Southway Hotel on Chicago's South Side. It was

[Above] Printed in a leading Black newspaper, Jackson's *Tisha Mingo* was originally an illustrated serialized text story of a woman's adventures trying to make it as an actress in New York City. Tisha often found herself working menial jobs, most notably as the maid to a vain, White movie star. The storylines were far edgier and more risqué than White newspapers would have allowed. Over time *Tisha* became a more traditional comic strip, similar to Gladys Parker's *Flapper Fanny*. (*New York Amsterdam News*, February 6, 1936).

[Left] Original Jackson cartoon captioned, "Here comes daddy leaping with enthusiasm for our hike in the country" (c. 1940s) Original artwork from the collection of George Hagenauer.

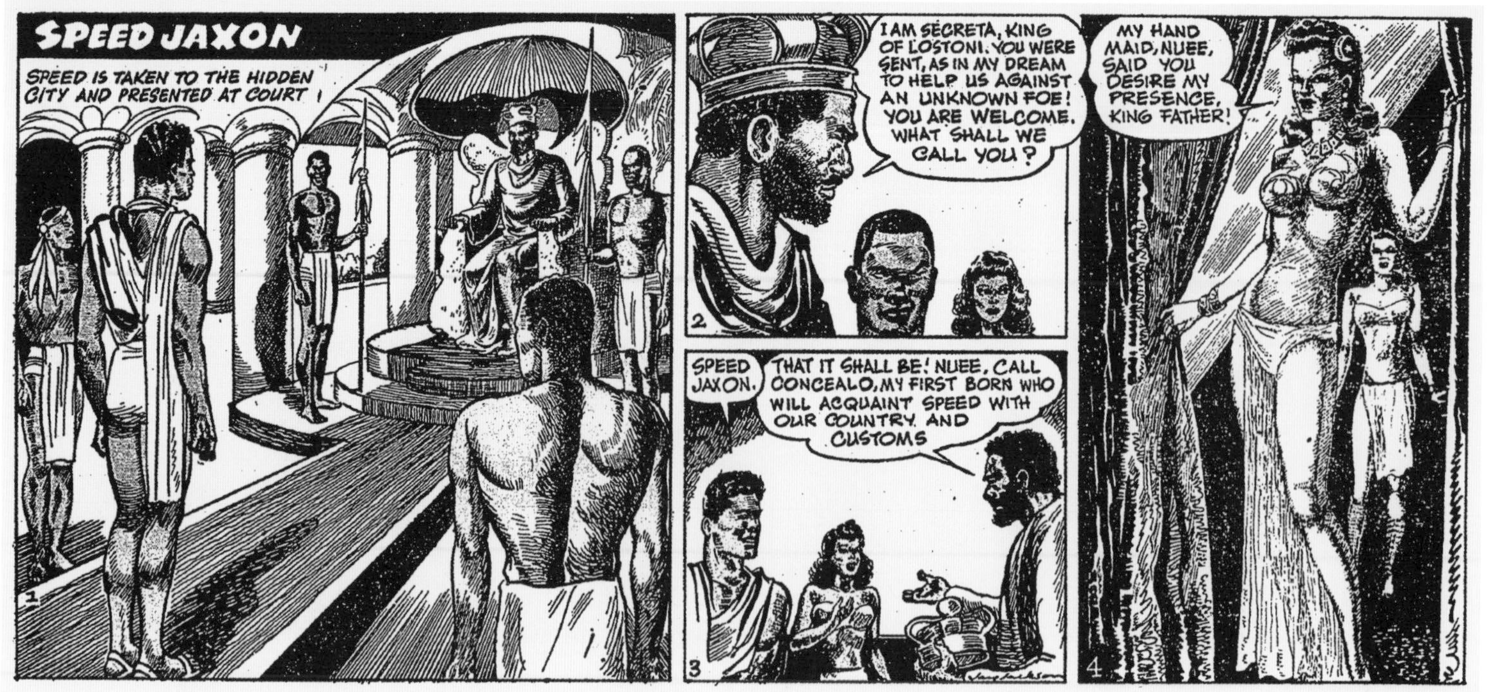
SPEED JAXON
SPEED IS TAKEN TO THE HIDDEN CITY AND PRESENTED AT COURT !
I AM SECRETA, KING OF LOSTONI. YOU WERE SENT, AS IN MY DREAM TO HELP US AGAINST AN UNKNOWN FOE! YOU ARE WELCOME. WHAT SHALL WE CALL YOU ?
SPEED JAXON.
THAT IT SHALL BE! NUEE, CALL CONCEALO, MY FIRST BORN WHO WILL ACQUAINT SPEED WITH OUR COUNTRY. AND CUSTOMS
MY HAND MAID, NUEE, SAID YOU DESIRE MY PRESENCE, KING FATHER!

a financial stretch, but he made it work to keep from sinking back into the gloom.

Jackson got a temporary job painting murals for the Old Mexico exhibit at the Century of Progress International Exposition, but he needed something more secure. He began submitting drawings he had made back in high school to publications around the nation. Some of his first submissions were to *Abbott's Monthly*, a high-class Black magazine published by Robert S. Abbott, owner of the *Chicago Defender*. This directly led to Jackson's staff job on that newspaper, a position he would hold for almost 20 years.

At the *Defender*, Jackson met a young woman named Eleanor Poston, who worked as a secretary in the circulation department. His playful teasing about her "hayseed" upbringing back in Nebraska gradually warmed into a romantic relationship, and led to their eventual marriage on September 7, 1935.

Jackson took over the production of the *Bungleton Green* comic strip from its former artist, Henry Brown, at the beginning of 1935. Immediately, it was an improvement. What had been a visually dull, wordy, unfunny cartoon developed into a weekly showcase of both Jackson's wit and artistic skill. His barbed observational commentary became a hallmark of his work.

He didn't stop there. Jackson created *Tisha Mingo* in mid-1935 for the *New York Amsterdam News*. It told the serialized story of a young Black woman trying to make it as an actress in New York City. Her dreams didn't always come true, so she frequently worked other jobs, most notably as the maid to a vain, White movie star. It was basically a text story accompanied by illustrations, and was definitely aimed at a mature audience, with edgy plotlines and its many depictions of a semi-clad Tisha. However, it ended its run three years later in a traditional sequential panel strip format on the newspaper's comics page, devoid of adult themes and risqué art.

While Jackson's star was rising rapidly in the Black newspapers, his next move was into White media, along the same route followed by Stoner, Pious, and Fax. Editor Ray Palmer wrote:

Perhaps the finest interior artist of them all, in not only our opinion, is the man who was slugged from all angles with his first efforts—but who didn't give up. He is Jay Jackson, whom today we are lucky to retain for our pages. Frankly, he is (with the exception of J. Allen St. John), the only "real" artist who can present his talent in the pulp style without losing his individuality. We advise you to watch for him in big letters in the art world before too long. [Palmer, Raymond, "The Observatory by the Editor," *Amazing Stories*, Sept. 1941, p.60]

Jackson had been drawing illustrations for various pulps for about two years when Palmer, managing editor of Ziff-Davis' *Amazing Stories* magazine, wrote his comments. He was referring to the reception Jackson's earliest efforts had been given by the very judgmental pulp readership, which complained about the "unrealistic" anatomy of the people in his drawings. In time, Jackson's work took on a more

[Above] Speed Jaxon was Jackson's eponymous Black secret agent for the United Nations. Speed crash-lands in the hidden African city of Lostona. This advanced Black-ruled civilization, unknown to the rest of the world, predates by two decades the similar nation of Wakanda, first appearing in Marvel comics in the 1960s and, later, in the highest-grossing superhero movie to date, *Black Panther*. *Chicago Defender*, April 24, 1945.

[Right] *Home Folks*, c. 1951, was a Black take on Dudley Fisher's *Right Around Home* newspaper feature, with its crowded bird's-eye views. In the early 1950s, Jackson attempted to sell several comic strip proposals for syndication. Unsuccessful in that attempt, he re-sold the strips to the *Chicago Defender*, which published them circa 1954. Original artwork from the collection of Craig Yoe.

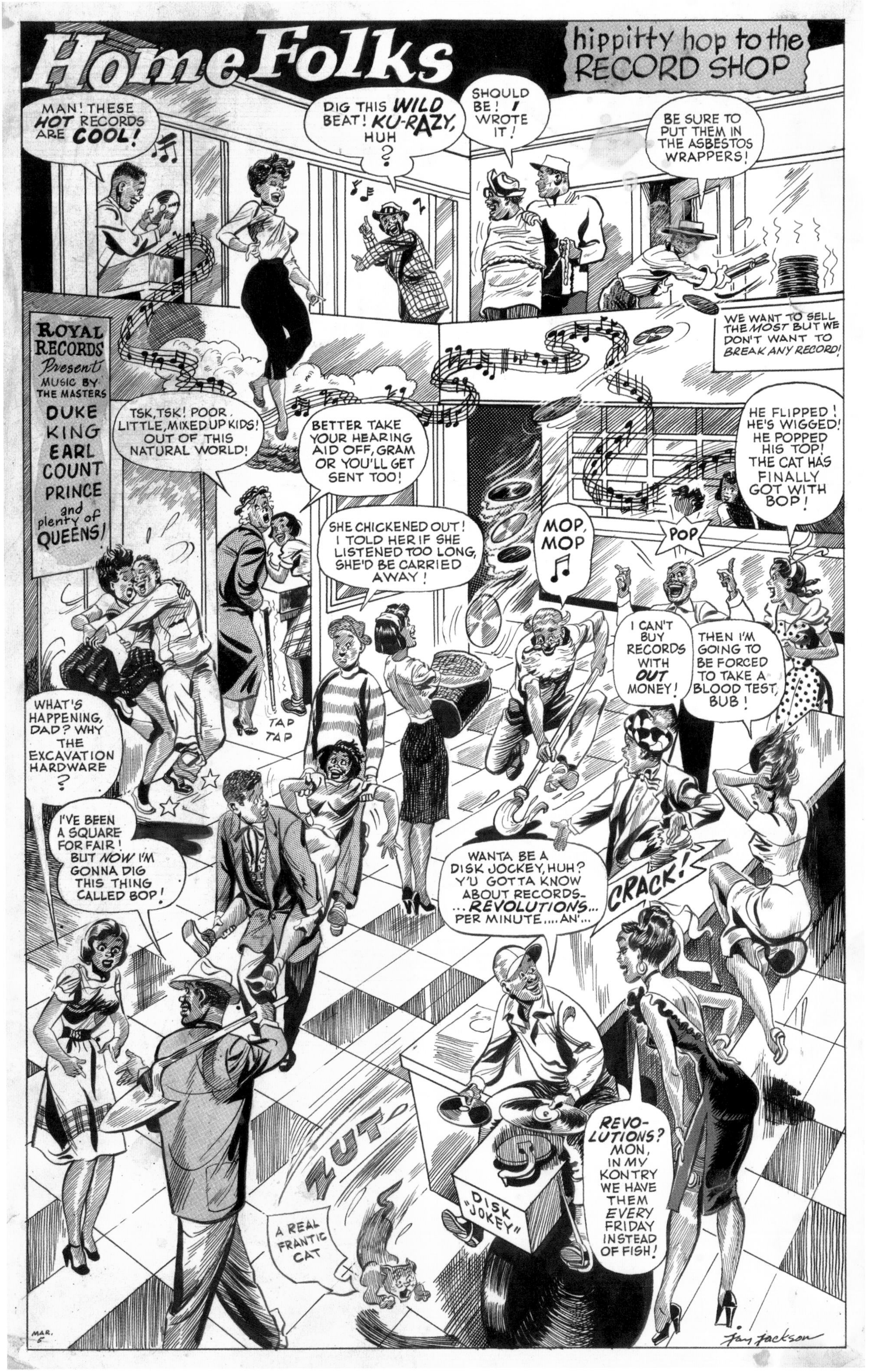
Home Folks
hippitty hop to the RECORD SHOP
MAN! THESE HOT RECORDS ARE COOL!
DIG THIS WILD BEAT! KU-RAZY, HUH ?
SHOULD BE! I WROTE IT!
BE SURE TO PUT THEM IN THE ASBESTOS WRAPPERS!
WE WANT TO SELL THE MOST BUT WE DON'T WANT TO BREAK ANY RECORD!
ROYAL RECORDS Present MUSIC BY THE MASTERS DUKE KING EARL COUNT PRINCE and plenty of QUEENS!
TSK, TSK! POOR. LITTLE, MIXED UP KIDS! OUT OF THIS NATURAL WORLD!
BETTER TAKE YOUR HEARING AID OFF, GRAM OR YOU'LL GET SENT TOO!
HE FLIPPED! HE'S WIGGED! HE POPPED HIS TOP! THE CAT HAS FINALLY GOT WITH BOP!
POP
SHE CHICKENED OUT! I TOLD HER IF SHE LISTENED TOO LONG, SHE'D BE CARRIED AWAY!
MOP, MOP
TAP TAP
I CAN'T BUY RECORDS WITH OUT MONEY!
THEN I'M GOING TO BE FORCED TO TAKE A BLOOD TEST, BUB!
WHAT'S HAPPENING, DAD? WHY THE EXCAVATION HARDWARE ?
I'VE BEEN A SQUARE FOR FAIR! BUT NOW I'M GONNA DIG THIS THING CALLED BOP!
WANTA BE A DISK JOCKEY, HUH? Y'U GOTTA KNOW ABOUT RECORDS... REVOLUTIONS... PER MINUTE.... AN'...
CRACK!
ZUT
REVO-LUTIONS? MON, IN MY KONTRY WE HAVE THEM EVERY FRIDAY INSTEAD OF FISH!
DISK "JOKEY"
A REAL FRANTIC CAT
MAR. 5
Jay Jackson

Chicago Defender
WORLD'S GREATEST WEEKLY
This Magazine Section Is A Part Of Your Chicago Defender ---Not To Be Sold Separately
MAGAZINE SECTION
COMICS and FEATURES
WEEK OF OCTOBER 16, 1948
3RD SECTION
Summer's gone-
Now fall is here,
And Jackie Frost
Is lurking near...
This skimpy suit
Will too be gone
At his decree-
'Winter draws
On.'
Jay Jackson

"pulpish" look, garnering Palmer's plaudits and leading him to make the comparison to the legendary artist J. Allen St. John. Heady praise indeed.

It was Jackson's work for one Chicago-based pulp publisher that led to his one and only comic book assignment.

Sun Publications was known for publishing the "spicy" humor magazine *Lulu*, and some of the more scandalous "nudie" pulps, such as *Girl Parade* and *10-Story Book*, which were generally kept under the counter by newsdealers, away from the eyes of women and children. In May 1938, police raided their operation on Clark Street, seized three truckloads of these magazines, and arrested publisher Arthur J. Gontier and his son, Robert. Sun Publications subsequently made the decision to begin publishing different types of material.

Their first step in a different direction came with the publication of *Golden Fleece* in October 1938. Termed a "historical adventure magazine," this was a radical departure from their previous output. While stalwart illustrator Harold Delay was the magazine's primary artist, joining him on the interior artwork, and one cover, was Jackson. This was likely his first pulp experience, albeit short-lived, as the magazine ended with its June 1939 issue.

That same year, Sun made an even more drastic detour, by taking the plunge into comic book publishing. The result was *Sun Fun Komiks*, a humorous commentary on the effect of comic books on their readers, which included a very early parody of Superman. While a house ad within the comic indicated that it was intended as an ongoing venture, this was its one and only issue.

In late 1939, Sun took one more foray into comic book publishing. Debuting with a cover date of March 1940, *Colossus Comics* #1 contained work by some of the same creators who had produced *Sun Fun Komiks*, with Jackson along this time as one of its artists. The curiosity is the assignment he drew.

HERE IT IS !!
IN BLACK AND WHITE
355
Jay Jackson

The editor of *Colossus*, Bill O'Donnell, cobbled together a group of artists and writers culled from various Chicago area media: Guy Murchie Jr. was a globe-trotting reporter and staff artist for the *Chicago Tribune*; Gene Rowls, a freelancing cartoonist; and Norman Modell, a local radio scriptwriter and columnist who covered the city for *Billboard* magazine. Jackson was an easy choice, a known quantity, having worked for Sun previously on *Golden Fleece*. O'Donnell may not have even been aware of Jackson's prestige in the Black newspapers.

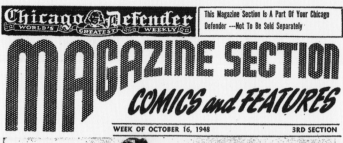

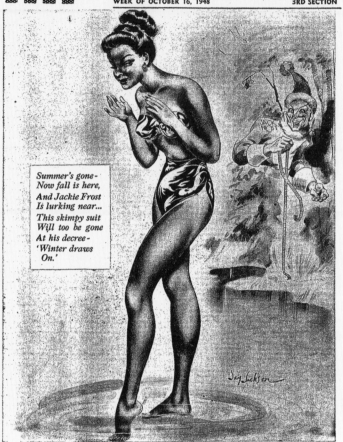

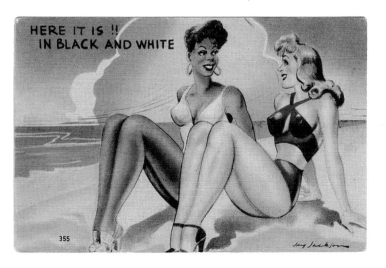

[Left] Jackson was known for drawing pin-up-style art on popular postcards of the period. These usually featured White women, but on this rare and interesting example, a Black woman gets equal time. "Here it is!! In Black and White," c. 1940s, Colourpicture Publication.

[Above] Cover for the *Chicago Defender Magazine Section* (October 16, 1948).

[Right] "Keep Faith" (c. 1940s) is an original watercolor illustration for a War Bonds poster. It encouraged women to stay faithful while their loved ones served in WWII.

Jackson's contribution to the comic was titled, "Blond Garth, King of the Isles." The writing was credited to "Ramond Mellon," an anagram of Norman Modell's name, apparently to give the impression that a larger staff worked on this comic.

The tale of Blond Garth begins like a mash-up of the Biblical story of Moses and Tarzan. As a baby, he was found clinging to a water cask that had washed ashore from a shipwreck. He was raised by the medicine man from a tribe of slightly darker-skinned natives. Of course, Garth grows to be the biggest and strongest among them. The writer probably gave Garth the descriptor of "Blond" to denote his accepted superiority. It's unlikely Modell, himself a Jew, ever stopped to consider the Nordic Aryan claims being made by the mad führer across the ocean, or the insensitivity of his story being drawn by a Black man.

The rest of his story concerns the evil machinations of a duplicitous priestess, who convinces the tribe to blame Garth for the attacks they were suffering from a killer shark. As such stories generally go, Garth vanquishes the shark, he settles down with the daughter of the king and is crowned king himself. A final panel promised that in the next issue of *Colossus Comics*, Garth would get revenge. Alas, a second issue was never published.

Jackson's artwork on this nine-page story is solid, comparable to the artwork coming from any of the large comic publishers, and better than many. He had already shown he could handle these types of sequential adventures with his work on *Tisha Mingo* and *Bungleton Green*. He seemed primed to continue in the booming comic book field, but the failure of *Colossus Comics* ended any chance of that. Apparently, if Jackson was to make a career as a comic book artist, he would have to relocate to New York City. It was a move he never made.

It's not that he lacked for work, though. He was still getting work from Ziff-Davis on their pulps at the time of *Colossus'* demise. And he never stopped his prodigious output for the Black newspapers.

He applied his pen to searing editorial cartoons, a panel under the title of *So What?*, commenting upon the state of Black America. In addition to the ongoing *Bungleton Green*, Jackson rolled out a number of other comic strips, such as *Billy Ken*, a typical mischievous kid strip; and *Cream Puff*, for which Jackson drew upon his own pugilistic experience to tell the story of a boxer, which read like a more realistic, Black version of *Joe Palooka*.

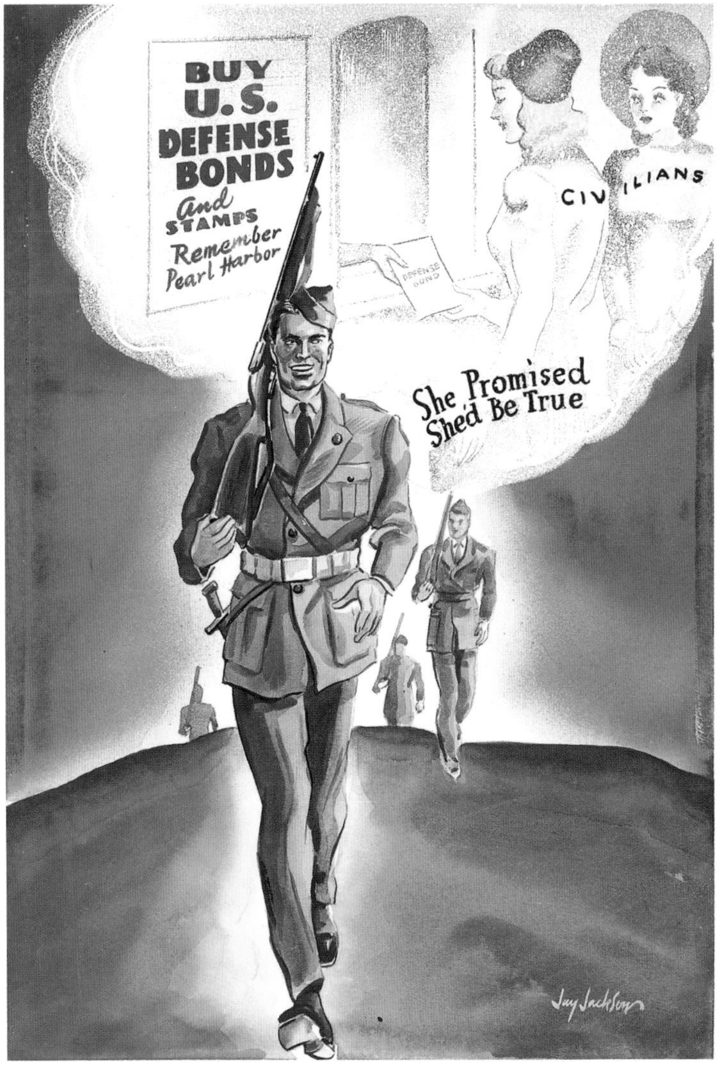
BUY
U.S.
DEFENSE
BONDS
And
STAMPS
Remember
Pearl Harbor
CIVILIANS
She Promised
She'd Be True
Jay Jackson

If that wasn't enough, there were also his contributions to the war effort.

For the second time in as many years, Jay Jackson, nationally known illustrator for the Chicago Defender, *has been cited by the U.S. Treasury Department for his poster contributions in the war savings bond campaign.*

Jackson's latest poster to win official recognition is one entitled "Prospect Your Tomorrows Today" that depicts the Negro's efforts in the war. ["Jay Jackson Wins New War Bond Poster Honors," *Chicago Defender*, Aug. 14, 1943]

Still, Jackson stayed at the *Defender*, eventually retiring some strips and starting others. One of them was *Ravings of Prof. Doodle*, a two-panel cartoon that featured the curmudgeonly old man of its title. Then, on October 16, 1948, the *Defender Magazine Section* premiered, with a Jackson-drawn cover of a Black bathing beauty. Inside, he debuted yet another comic strip, one which reflected a major change in his personal life. The strip was *Glamour Town*, a full-page panel about life in Hollywood, California. Jackson and family had left their hometown of Chicago for life on the West Coast. If the acerbic commentary in this strip had any truth to it, it would seem to indicate that the transplanted Midwesterner was having some problems adapting to his new lifestyle.

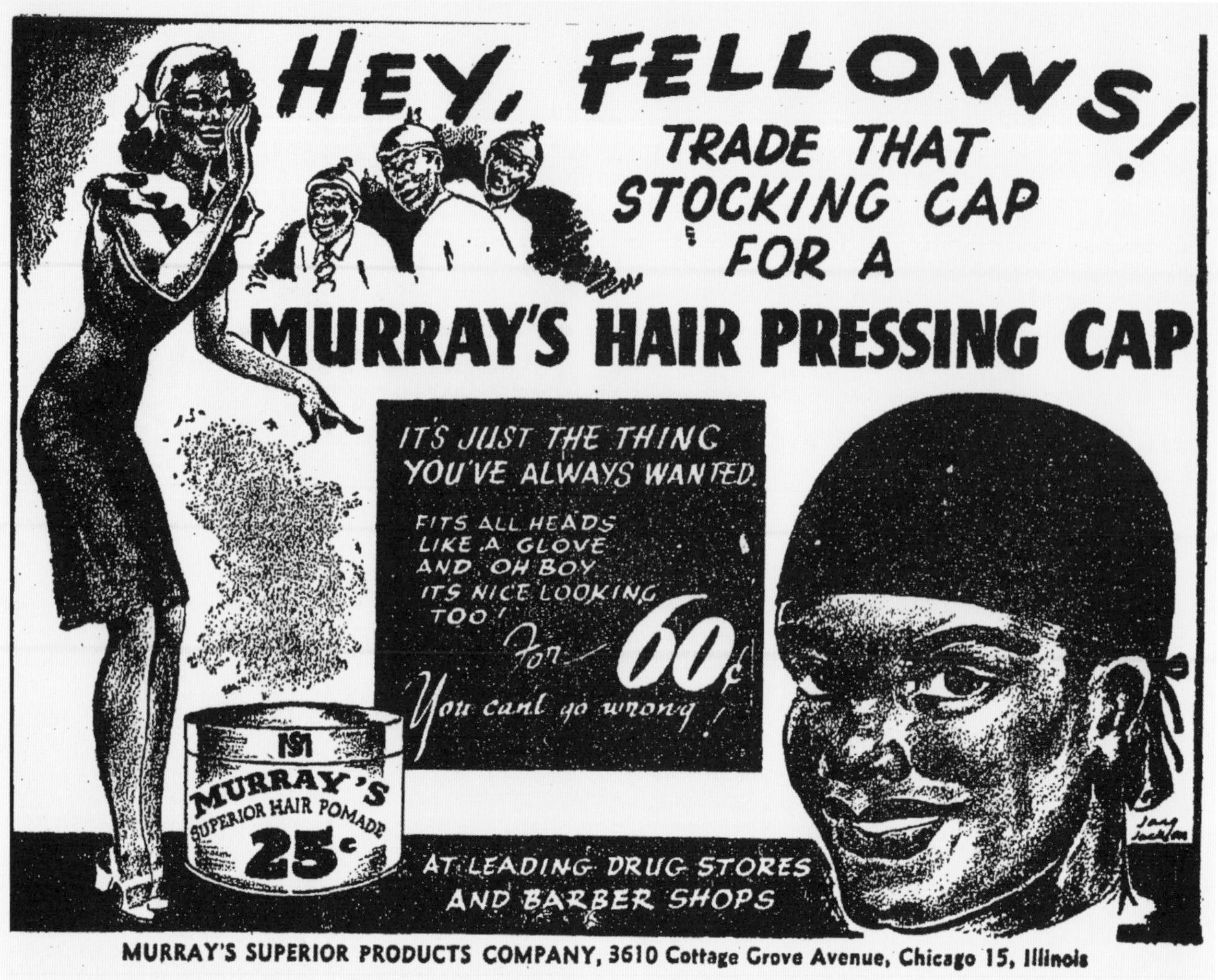
HEY, FELLOWS!
TRADE THAT STOCKING CAP FOR A
MURRAY'S HAIR PRESSING CAP
IT'S JUST THE THING YOU'VE ALWAYS WANTED.
FITS ALL HEADS LIKE A GLOVE AND OH BOY ITS NICE LOOKING TOO!
For 60¢
You can't go wrong!
MURRAY'S SUPERIOR HAIR POMADE 25¢
AT LEADING DRUG STORES AND BARBER SHOPS
MURRAY'S SUPERIOR PRODUCTS COMPANY, 3610 Cottage Grove Avenue, Chicago 15, Illinois

Even as he continued with his obligations to the *Defender*, Jackson took on other jobs. In 1950, he completed the prestigious assignment of drawing the montage endpapers for *Who's Who in Colored America*. And in 1951, he joined the *California Eagle* as one of its staff. At the same time, Jackson was creating a couple of comic strips that he hoped to sell for national syndication. *Girli Gags* was a single-panel cartoon featuring attractive young Black women, similar in theme and style to Don Flowers *Glamor Girls*.

The other strip was *Home Folks*, a very well-drawn large panel cartoon that depicted the hectic goings-on of a suburban Black family. Neither strip sold, however, but were repurposed by Jackson in early 1954 and run in issues of the *Defender*.

At some point, Jackson fully embraced the environment he had moved into and took a job at Telecomics, an animation company that developed a method of turning comic strips into cartoons for television. It was owned by Steven Slesinger, a literary agent turned merchandising mogul, who made a fortune off the rights he owned to *Red Ryder* and other properties. The headquarters for Telecomics was in New York City, but Jackson was hired at their Pasadena office. One of his major projects while at the company (now renamed Illustrate, Inc.) was on *The Search for Christ*, a 13-part film series made for television that debuted in late 1952.

On May 15, 1954, Jackson suffered a heart attack at his home on West 23rd Street in Los Angeles. With help, he was able to walk to a car and was taken to a nearby hospital, but at 2:30 a.m. early the next day, he passed away. He was only 49 years old.

Jackson had left behind a number of unpublished *Girli Gags* and *Home Life* strips. Due to his popularity, the *Defender* ran them for nearly a year after his death. One article mourning his passing read:

> *Jay was a quiet, easy-going sort of chap who had no axes to grind, no great mission to perform. He used his great talent to provide the seasoning that made life more palatable for millions. He will long be remembered for that.* ["Jay Jackson's Art Work Was Seasoning for Life," *Chicago Defender*, June 5, 1954]

[Above] Beginning in 1943, Jackson illustrated a number of ads promoting Black hair products. This one dated June 9, 1945 concerns Murray's Hair Pressing Cap, Murray's Superior Hair Products.

[Right] "Blond Garth" was Jackson's only known comic book work, created for Chicago-based Sun Publications. It told the story of a white baby named Garth, found by a South Seas medicine man. Garth grows to be the biggest and strongest member of the tribe. *Colossus Comics* #1, March 1940, Sun Publications.

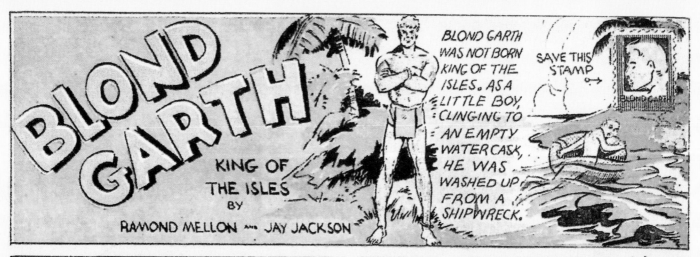

BLOND GARTH
KING OF THE ISLES
BY RAMOND MELLON AND JAY JACKSON

BLOND GARTH WAS NOT BORN KING OF THE ISLES. AS A LITTLE BOY, CLINGING TO AN EMPTY WATER CASK, HE WAS WASHED UP FROM A SHIPWRECK.

SAVE THIS STAMP →

HE WAS RAISED BY BUBU THE MEDICINE MAN WHO TAUGHT HIM THE SECRET OF GROWING STRONG.

DON'T WASTE YOUR STRENGTH THROWING SPEARS AT THE SEA. THE MAN WITH THE GREATEST POWER IS HE WHOSE BRAINS ARE BEHIND HIS BRAWN.

UNDER THE WISE TUTELAGE OF BUBU, BOY GARTH GREW TO BE —

A MIGHTIER HUNTER THAN TARANTHA

A KEENER FISH SPEARER THAN NEHOA

A STRONGER SWIMMER THAN THE DEADLY MALIE.

WHEN BLOND GARTH CAME TO MANHOOD.

HE FELL IN LOVE WITH TARA DAUGHTER OF THE KING.

CIMBARU SENDS A WAR CANOE.

THEY COME FOR THE YEARLY TRIBUTE.

FOR RANGIPU'S TRIBUTE CIMBARU THE MIGHTY ORDERS RAHUI TO SEND TEN PRETTY MAIDENS LED BY PRINCESS TARA.

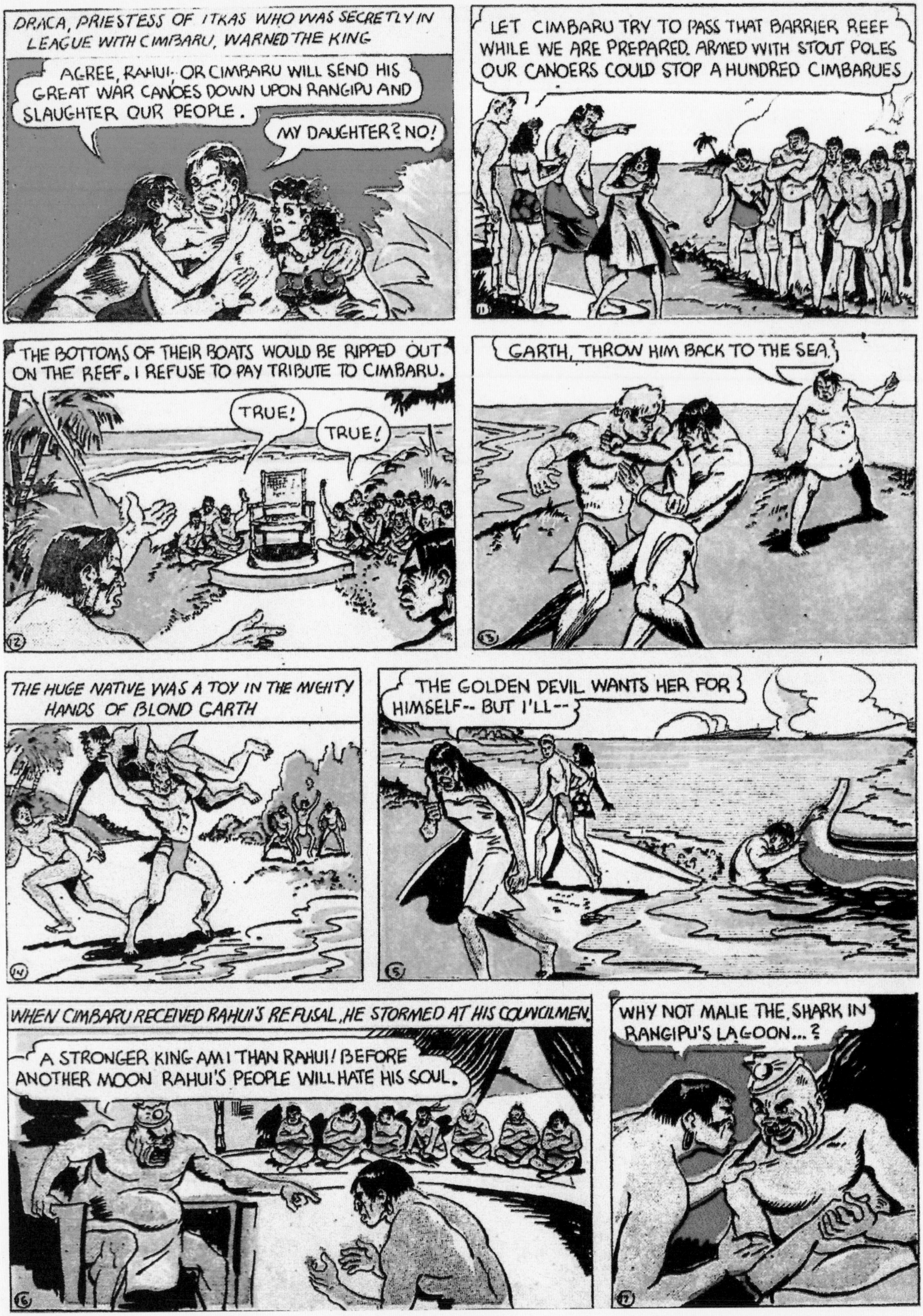

DRACA, PRIESTESS OF ITKAS WHO WAS SECRETLY IN LEAGUE WITH CIMBARU, WARNED THE KING
AGREE, RAHUI-- OR CIMBARU WILL SEND HIS GREAT WAR CANOES DOWN UPON RANGIPU AND SLAUGHTER OUR PEOPLE.
MY DAUGHTER? NO!
LET CIMBARU TRY TO PASS THAT BARRIER REEF WHILE WE ARE PREPARED. ARMED WITH STOUT POLES OUR CANOERS COULD STOP A HUNDRED CIMBARUES
THE BOTTOMS OF THEIR BOATS WOULD BE RIPPED OUT ON THE REEF. I REFUSE TO PAY TRIBUTE TO CIMBARU.
TRUE!
TRUE!
GARTH, THROW HIM BACK TO THE SEA.
THE HUGE NATIVE WAS A TOY IN THE MIGHTY HANDS OF BLOND GARTH
THE GOLDEN DEVIL WANTS HER FOR HIMSELF-- BUT I'LL--
WHEN CIMBARU RECEIVED RAHUI'S REFUSAL, HE STORMED AT HIS COUNCILMEN.
A STRONGER KING AM I THAN RAHUI! BEFORE ANOTHER MOON RAHUI'S PEOPLE WILL HATE HIS SOUL.
WHY NOT MALIE THE SHARK IN RANGIPU'S LAGOON...?

FOR DAYS THE FLATHEAD WOMEN OF CIMBARU WORKED AT TOP SPEED SEWING A GREAT NET OF HEMP.

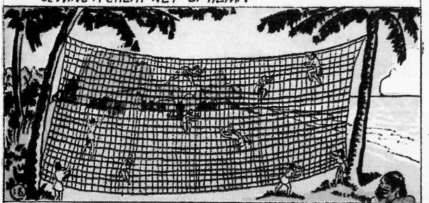

THEN TWO HUGE WAR CANOES SET OUT WITH THE NET SPREAD BETWEEN THEM IN THE SEA...

THIS IS A JOB FOR CIMBARU, HIMSELF.

AFTER DAYS OF SEARCHING DURING WHICH SCORES OF LESSER SHARKS WERE PASSED BY.

THERE HE IS! THE KING OF SHARKS-- MALIE, HIMSELF!

THE NET WAS SPREAD..

HERE, O MALIE, COME GET YOUR SUPPER.

MALIE DARTED IN TO FEAST ON LIVE PIG...

WHEN THE MOON WAS HIDDEN BEHIND THE CLOUDS..

NOW LET RAHUI'S PEOPLE DIVE FOR PEARLS.

NEXT DAY THE PEARL SEASON OPENED, THE PEOPLE OF RANGIPU CAME TO THE LAGOON.

TO AHALA, ONLY SON OF RAHUI, WENT THE HONOR OF THE FIRST DIVE OF THE NEW SEASON.

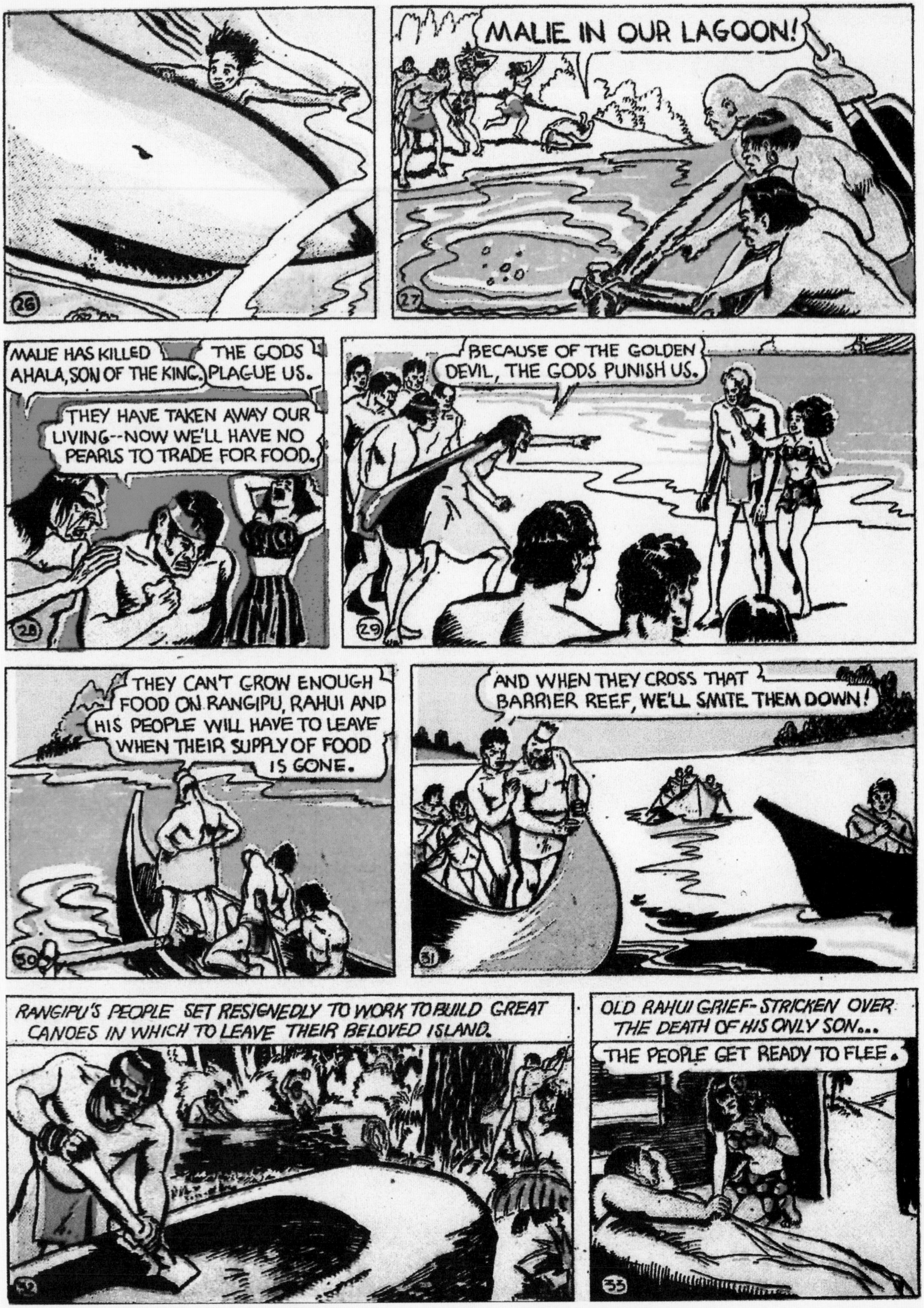
MALIE IN OUR LAGOON!
MALIE HAS KILLED AHALA, SON OF THE KING.
THE GODS PLAGUE US.
THEY HAVE TAKEN AWAY OUR LIVING--NOW WE'LL HAVE NO PEARLS TO TRADE FOR FOOD.
BECAUSE OF THE GOLDEN DEVIL, THE GODS PUNISH US.
THEY CAN'T GROW ENOUGH FOOD ON RANGIPU, RAHUI AND HIS PEOPLE WILL HAVE TO LEAVE WHEN THEIR SUPPLY OF FOOD IS GONE.
AND WHEN THEY CROSS THAT BARRIER REEF, WE'LL SMITE THEM DOWN!
RANGIPU'S PEOPLE SET RESIGNEDLY TO WORK TO BUILD GREAT CANOES IN WHICH TO LEAVE THEIR BELOVED ISLAND.
OLD RAHUI GRIEF-STRICKEN OVER THE DEATH OF HIS ONLY SON...
THE PEOPLE GET READY TO FLEE.

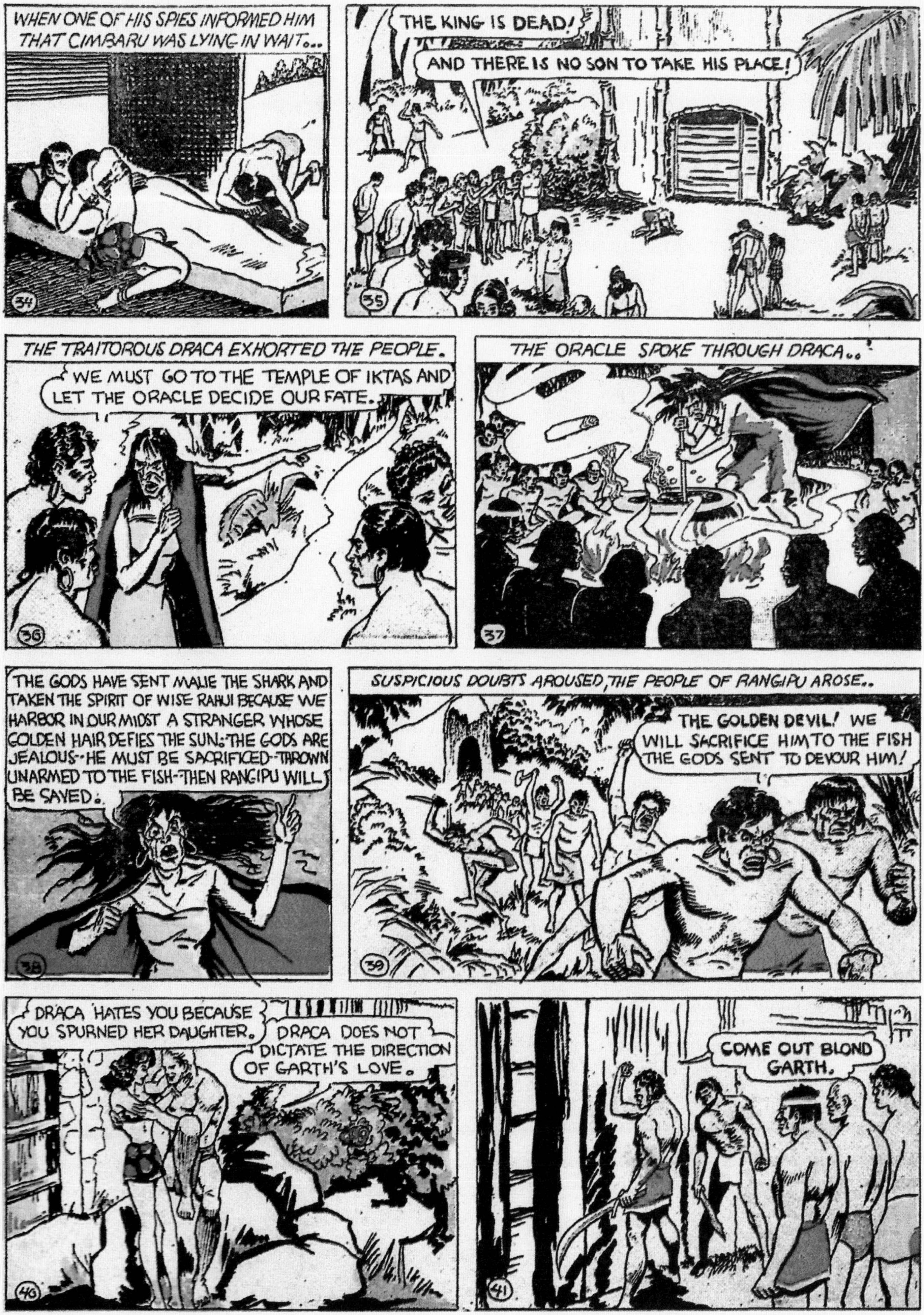
WHEN ONE OF HIS SPIES INFORMED HIM THAT CIMBARU WAS LYING IN WAIT...
34
THE KING IS DEAD!
AND THERE IS NO SON TO TAKE HIS PLACE!
35
THE TRAITOROUS DRACA EXHORTED THE PEOPLE.
WE MUST GO TO THE TEMPLE OF IKTAS AND LET THE ORACLE DECIDE OUR FATE.
36
THE ORACLE SPOKE THROUGH DRACA..
37
THE GODS HAVE SENT MALIE THE SHARK AND TAKEN THE SPIRIT OF WISE RAHUI BECAUSE WE HARBOR IN OUR MIDST A STRANGER WHOSE GOLDEN HAIR DEFIES THE SUN. THE GODS ARE JEALOUS--HE MUST BE SACRIFICED--THROWN UNARMED TO THE FISH--THEN RANGIPU WILL BE SAVED.
38
SUSPICIOUS DOUBTS AROUSED, THE PEOPLE OF RANGIPU AROSE..
THE GOLDEN DEVIL! WE WILL SACRIFICE HIM TO THE FISH THE GODS SENT TO DEVOUR HIM!
39
DRACA HATES YOU BECAUSE YOU SPURNED HER DAUGHTER.
DRACA DOES NOT DICTATE THE DIRECTION OF GARTH'S LOVE.
40
COME OUT BLOND GARTH.
41

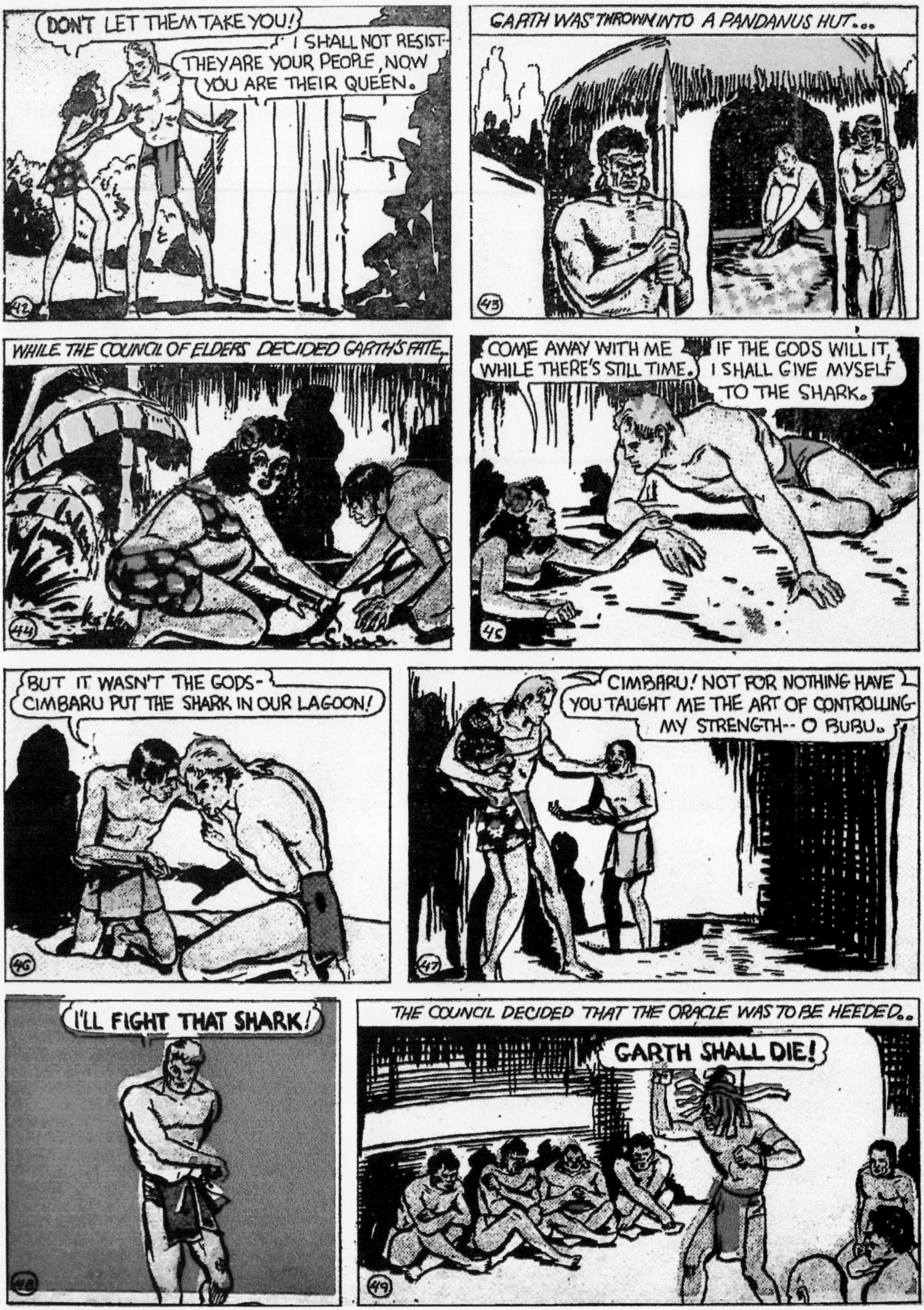
DON'T LET THEM TAKE YOU!
I SHALL NOT RESIST- THEY ARE YOUR PEOPLE, NOW YOU ARE THEIR QUEEN.
GARTH WAS THROWN INTO A PANDANUS HUT...
WHILE THE COUNCIL OF ELDERS DECIDED GARTH'S FATE...
COME AWAY WITH ME WHILE THERE'S STILL TIME.
IF THE GODS WILL IT, I SHALL GIVE MYSELF TO THE SHARK.
BUT IT WASN'T THE GODS- CIMBARU PUT THE SHARK IN OUR LAGOON!
CIMBARU! NOT FOR NOTHING HAVE YOU TAUGHT ME THE ART OF CONTROLLING MY STRENGTH-- O BUBU.
I'LL FIGHT THAT SHARK!
THE COUNCIL DECIDED THAT THE ORACLE WAS TO BE HEEDED..
GARTH SHALL DIE!

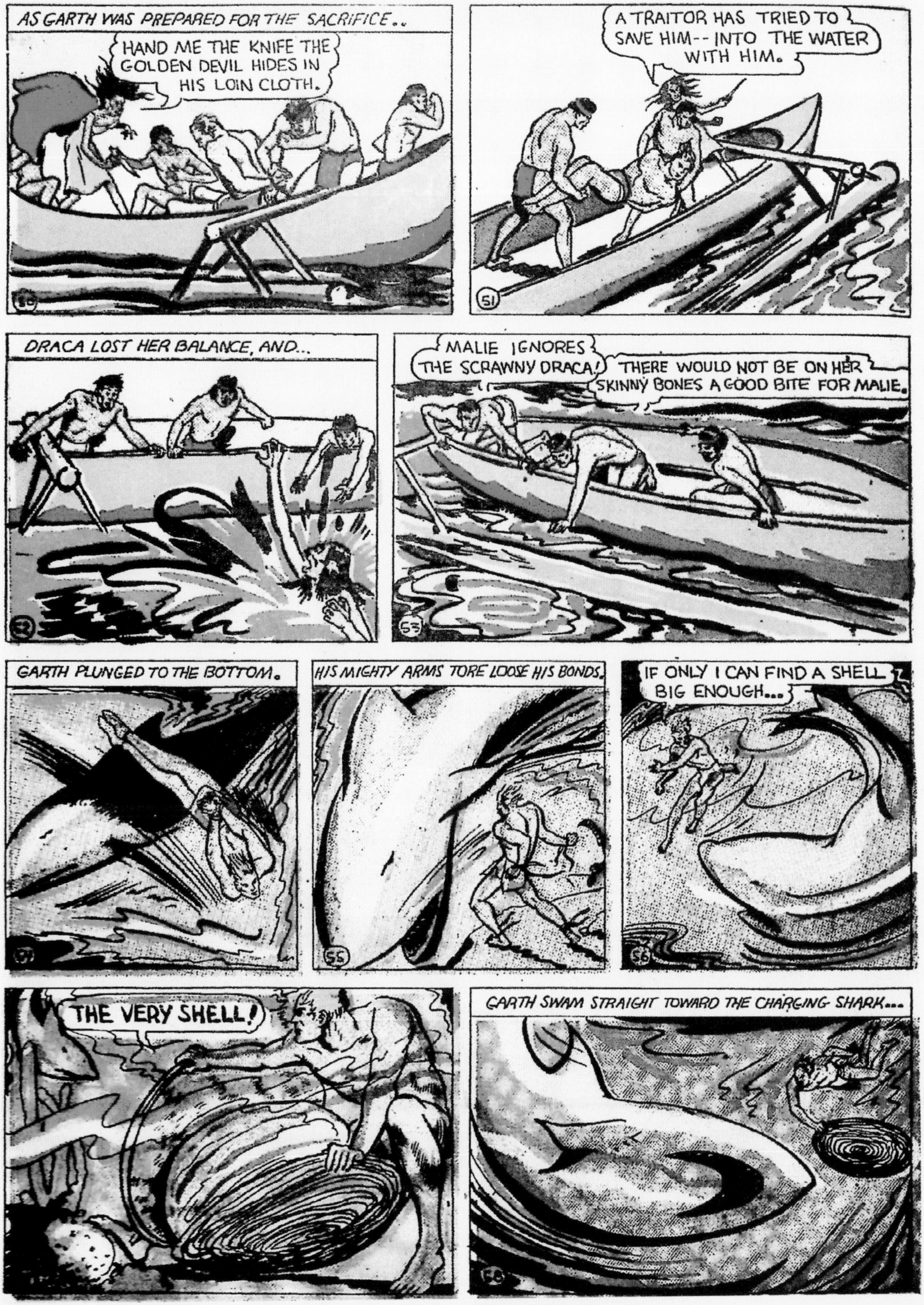

AS GARTH WAS PREPARED FOR THE SACRIFICE..
HAND ME THE KNIFE THE GOLDEN DEVIL HIDES IN HIS LOIN CLOTH.
A TRAITOR HAS TRIED TO SAVE HIM-- INTO THE WATER WITH HIM.
DRACA LOST HER BALANCE, AND...
MALIE IGNORES THE SCRAWNY DRACA!
THERE WOULD NOT BE ON HER SKINNY BONES A GOOD BITE FOR MALIE.
GARTH PLUNGED TO THE BOTTOM.
HIS MIGHTY ARMS TORE LOOSE HIS BONDS.
IF ONLY I CAN FIND A SHELL BIG ENOUGH...
THE VERY SHELL!
GARTH SWAM STRAIGHT TOWARD THE CHARGING SHARK...

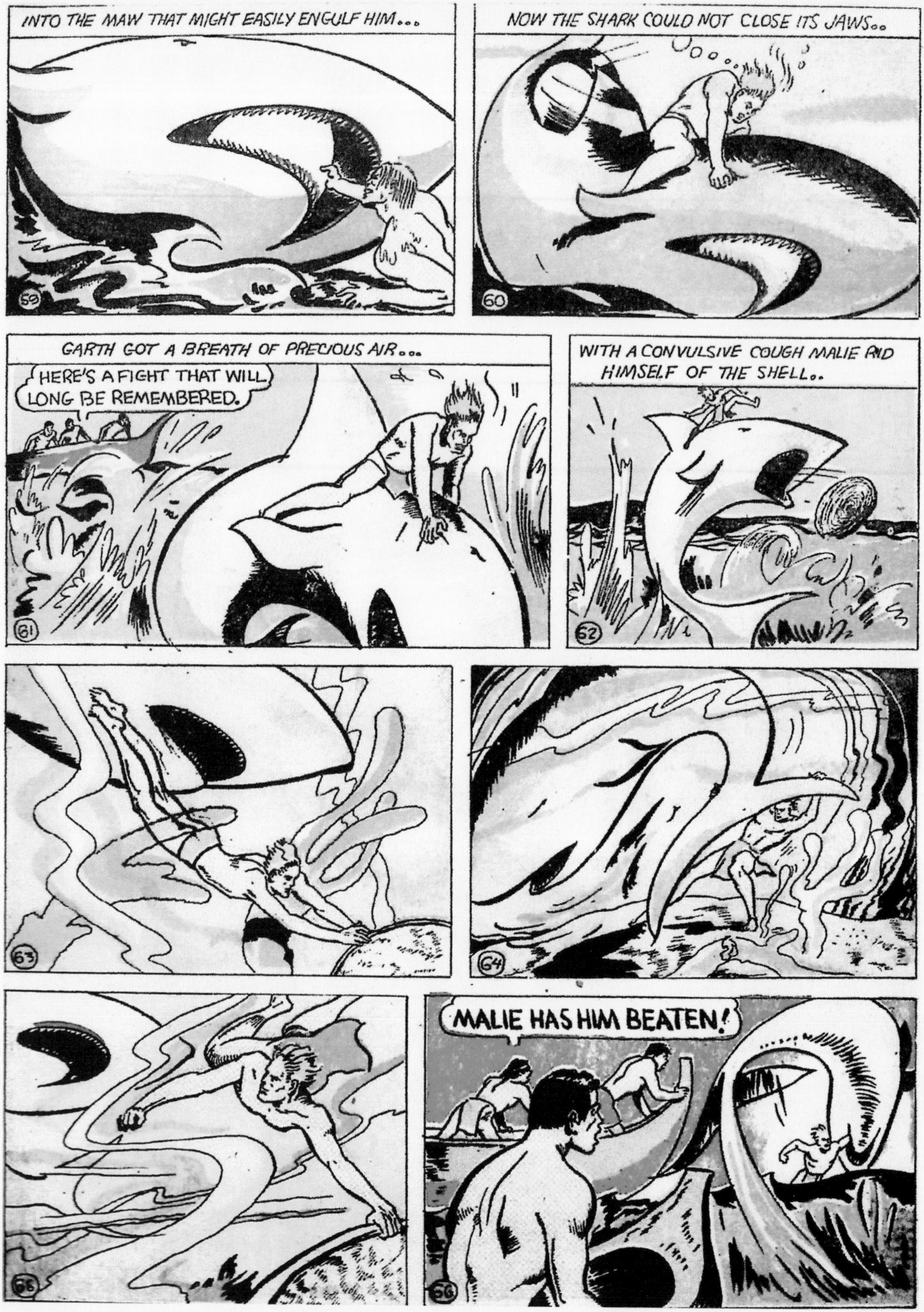
INTO THE MAW THAT MIGHT EASILY ENGULF HIM...
59
NOW THE SHARK COULD NOT CLOSE ITS JAWS..
60
GARTH GOT A BREATH OF PRECIOUS AIR...
HERE'S A FIGHT THAT WILL LONG BE REMEMBERED.
61
WITH A CONVULSIVE COUGH MALIE RID HIMSELF OF THE SHELL..
62
63
64
65
MALIE HAS HIM BEATEN!
66

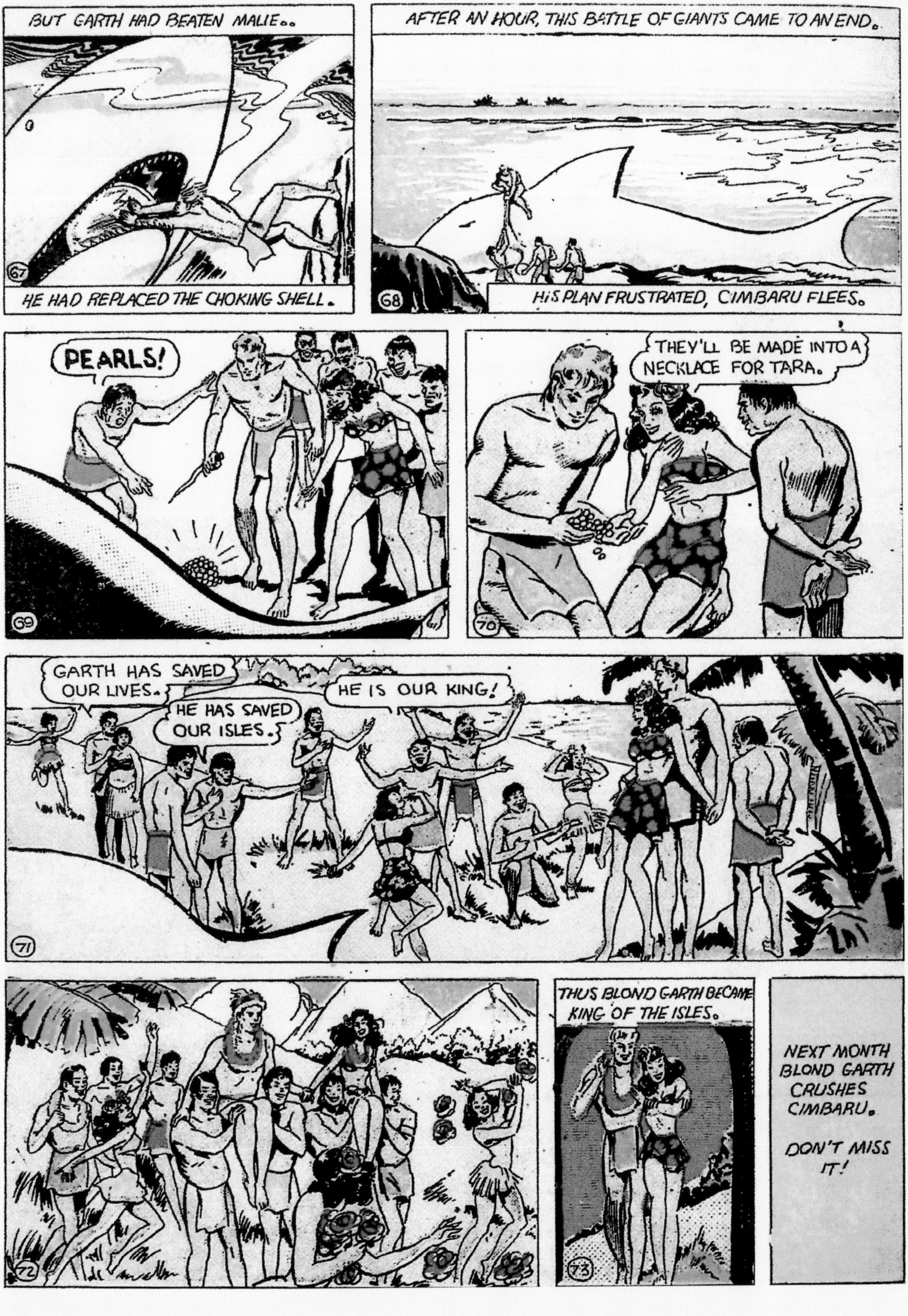

BUT GARTH HAD BEATEN MALIE..
HE HAD REPLACED THE CHOKING SHELL.
AFTER AN HOUR, THIS BATTLE OF GIANTS CAME TO AN END.
HIS PLAN FRUSTRATED, CIMBARU FLEES.
PEARLS!
THEY'LL BE MADE INTO A NECKLACE FOR TARA.
GARTH HAS SAVED OUR LIVES.
HE HAS SAVED OUR ISLES.
HE IS OUR KING!
THUS BLOND GARTH BECAME KING OF THE ISLES.
NEXT MONTH BLOND GARTH CRUSHES CIMBARU.
DON'T MISS IT!

OWEN CHARLES MIDDLETON
Resilient Idealist

T"Truth is not beautiful, neither is it ugly. Why should it be either? Truth is truth…"

Despite his seeming indifference, "Convict 79206" was living an ugly truth when he wrote those words. He was several years into his life sentence being served in Sing Sing prison, in isolation no less. That Owen Middleton could remain so coolly philosophical in view of his current situation was a testament to a man who had often experienced the harsher aspects of truth.

Owen was born in Charleston, South Carolina, on March 2, 1888. His father, Jonas, was born a slave in the uniquely Afrocentric Gullah culture that existed on St. Helena's Island, just months before the first shots of the Civil War were fired up the coast at Fort Sumter. Owen's mother, Elizabeth, originally from the border state of Kentucky, had six children with Jonas, only four of which lived beyond infancy. In 1893, two devastating storms killed many of the Blacks living in the Lowcountry region and destroyed

countless homes: the Sea Islands Hurricane of August, quickly followed by another Category 3 storm in October that hit Charleston directly. This destruction likely led to the Middletons' move to Cleveland, Ohio, where Jonas found work as a plasterer.

Owen Middleton displayed his artistic talents early. In an era when few people of any color attended college, he spent two years at Case Western in Cleveland before attending the prestigious Art Institute of Chicago. Soon after, he was hired by the *Chicago Tribune* as a quick sketch artist, a great achievement. It made him one of the first Blacks ever employed on the reportorial staff of a major American newspaper. These facts would seem to indicate that he was well on the path to a stable career, but other actualities show that Middleton's path wasn't without obstacles.

He [Middleton] was caught in a juvenile escapade with a group of white youths, and sentenced to two years in a Boys Reformatory at Cleveland where he was beaten and otherwise horribly mis-

treated. The white youths went free. [Ford, James, "Letters," *Mainstream*, 1957, pp.57-59]

It was something of which Middleton rarely spoke about in his later years, and only a few people were aware: he had spent nearly 25 years in and out of prison. His first conviction came in 1909, for an unspecified petty crime, likely the incident that his friend (and perennial American Communist Party Vice Presidential candidate) James W. Ford recounted above. He was paroled the next year but was in trouble with the law several more times. This included an arrest in Cleveland in 1916, for altering the amount on a money order he tried to cash in a Chicago saloon (from $1.75 to $91.75). According to Ford, Middleton also refused to participate in the upcoming military draft, claiming "war objector" status. This stand led to his imprisonment in the Leavenworth federal penitentiary on October 13, 1916, before his release with all the other conscientious objectors imprisoned there, in May 1919.

During his incarceration at Leavenworth, Middleton made the acquaintance of William "Big Bill" Haywood, leader and one of the founders of the Industrial Workers of the World (IWW). Middleton was himself a member of the union, a so-called "Wobbly," and had been one since he was assigned to cover their national convention by the *Chicago Tribune*.

After his release from prison, Middleton worked a number of jobs, including a position as a "surgical artist" at a hospital and as the head designer for a furniture company in Michigan. He even spent some time as a seaman, which allowed him to travel the world. Unfortunately, though, he found that racism wasn't limited to the United States. James Ford recalled:

Once he landed at a seaport in Turkey and became associated with Turkish workers, but he became stranded and was without money for food. On a principal thoroughfare of this seaport City, he asked a British official for a few pennies for food, whereupon he was knocked, kicked and called a black N . . . bastard. Owen rose and beat up the official who however had him released. On learning of Owen's talents as an artist, he was employed to draw maps of the surrounding area which were filed away for British military use. When he earned enough money, he returned to America with deep hatred of British racism." [Ibid, p.59.]

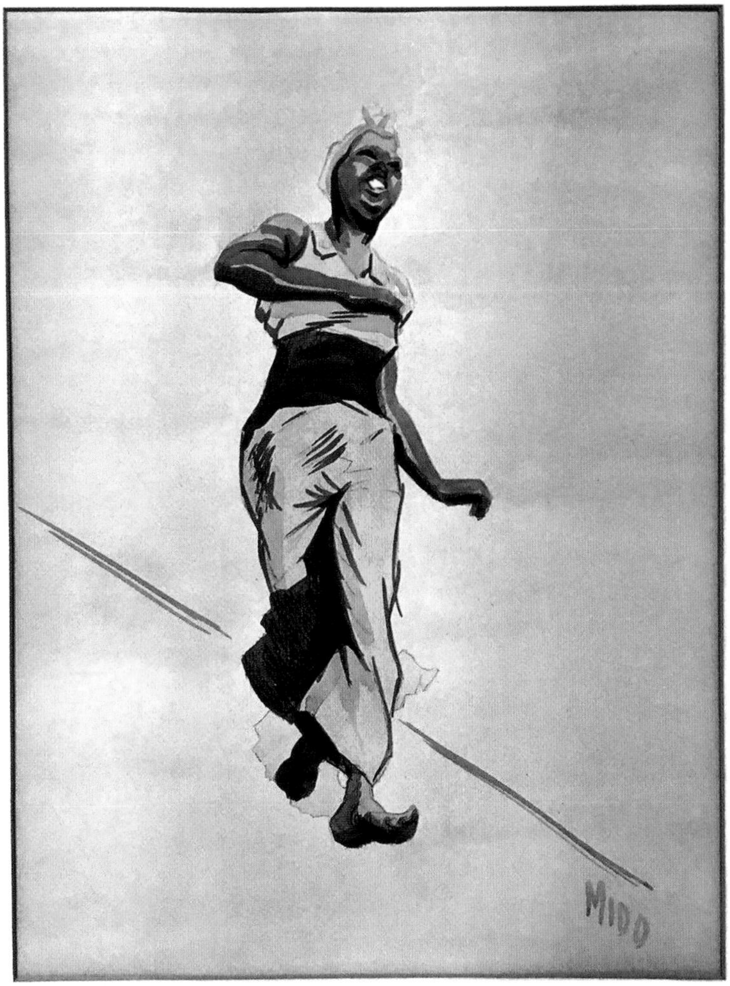

MIDO

Back home and his life seemingly back on track, Middleton married Lillian Forte in July 1922, in Brooklyn, New York, where he had moved.

Any stability Middleton had obtained was upended in 1926, when once again, he was arrested, this time for committing a hold-up while using a gun. He was convicted of third degree robbery on November 18, 1926, a crime he attributed to "worry and sickness." He had reason to be worried. Since this was his fourth conviction, Middleton fell victim to the sentencing rules mandated by the new "Baumes law" that New York state had just enacted. According to that statute, anyone convicted of three separate felonies, no matter the circumstances involved, was sentenced to life imprisonment.

Middleton's experience as a medical illustrator led to his assignment as an assistant to the prison physician, in which capacity he was to illustrate surgeries performed by the doctor. Over time, the two became friends and upon the physician's retirement, he recommended a pardon for Middleton. This was not to be, as Middleton was party to a scandal that played out in the newspapers in July 1928 and was a great embarrassment to warden Lewis E. Lawes.

Middleton's watercolor painting of a woman completed while he was a student at the Art Institute of Chicago studying abroad at the Académie Julian in Paris (c. 1909). Note his usage of the pseudonym "Mido."

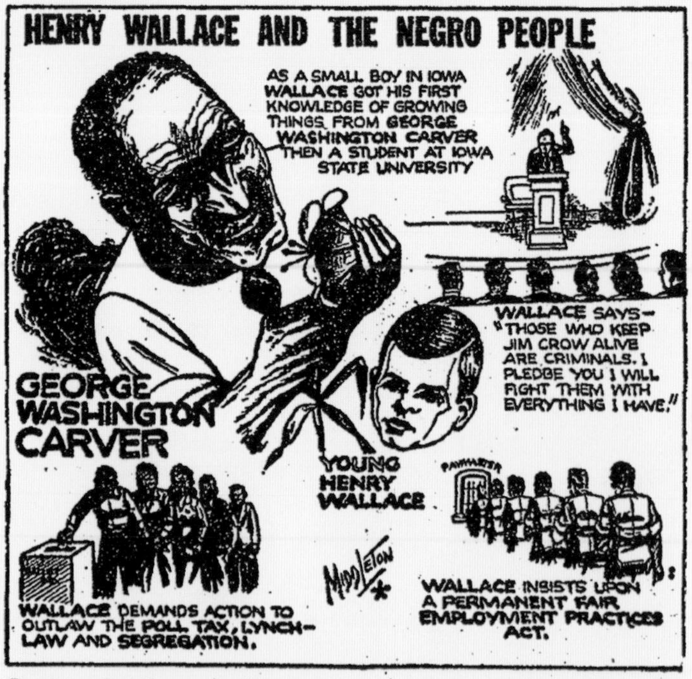
HENRY WALLACE AND THE NEGRO PEOPLE
AS A SMALL BOY IN IOWA WALLACE GOT HIS FIRST KNOWLEDGE OF GROWING THINGS FROM GEORGE WASHINGTON CARVER THEN A STUDENT AT IOWA STATE UNIVERSITY
WALLACE SAYS— "THOSE WHO KEEP JIM CROW ALIVE ARE CRIMINALS. I PLEDGE YOU I WILL FIGHT THEM WITH EVERYTHING I HAVE."
GEORGE WASHINGTON CARVER
YOUNG HENRY WALLACE
MIDDLETON
WALLACE DEMANDS ACTION TO OUTLAW THE POLL TAX, LYNCH-LAW AND SEGREGATION.
WALLACE INSISTS UPON A PERMANENT FAIR EMPLOYMENT PRACTICES ACT.

Getting the drop on the campaigns of the other parties, the National Wallace for President Committee has begun issuing informational material to Negro newspapers from its New York headquarters, where George B. Murphy, formerly with the NAACP, is assistant campaign manager. This cartoon was drawn for the Wallace group by Owen Middleton, well-known Negro cartoonist.

Sing Sing had already received bad press over the recent escape of two prisoners and the arrest of two prison guards for extortion when it was discovered that another guard named Fred Garlick had smuggled out a sketch drawn by Middleton. The drawing violated the censorship rules of the prison and was considered contraband. For his actions, Garlick was fired, but Middleton's punishment wasn't as forgiving. He was placed in solitary confinement.

It was while he was serving time in "the hole" that Middleton penned a letter to philosopher Will Durant.

Durant was a former seminarian and teacher who gained celebrity status with the publication of his first book *The Story of Philosophy*, in 1926. Much of his success came from the readability of his writing style and his personalization of lofty topics. A historian as well as a philosopher, Durant is best remembered for his multi-volume magnum opus, *The Story of Civilization*, written in collaboration with his wife, Ariel. He was already at work on the first book in that series, when a chance interaction with a man contemplating suicide in the fall of 1930 inspired him to put together an anthology comprised of responses to the weighty question: "What is the meaning or worth of human life?"

To provide the text for *On the Meaning of Life*, Durant had sent letters posing his query to "certain famous contemporaries here and abroad for whose intelligence I have high regard." Sinclair Lewis, George Bernard Shaw, Will Rogers, and Mohandas Gandhi were among the recipients of these letters, and they all responded. So, too, did Middleton, incarcerated deep in the bowels of Sing Sing.

Why Middleton was included on the list of such celebrated minds was explained in the Appendix to Durant's book. The Appendix was entitled "Being a Communication from Convict 79206, Sing Sing Prison." Durant wrote:

After the foregoing manuscript had been prepared it occurred to the publishers to send a copy of the initial letter to a man recently sentenced to life imprisonment as a fourth offender, what meaning did life seem to have from the viewpoint of one so unjustly condemned to apparently so empty a future?

The reply was so well thought out, and so well expressed, that it commanded a place in this symposium. It is incredible that we should be unable to find any better use for such intelligence than to lock it up forever. [Durant, Will, "Being a Communication from Convict 79206, Sing Sing Prison," appendix of *On the Meaning of Life*, 1933, p.137]

Middleton's letter has since become an oft-quoted classic. Over its seven-plus pages, he revealed himself to be a man unbowed by his circumstance and remarkably sanguine about the vagaries of happiness:

Confinement in prison doesn't cause unhappiness, else all those who are free would be happy. Poverty doesn't cause it, else the rich all would be happy. Those who live and die in one small town are often as happy, or happier, than many who spend their entire lives in travel. I once knew an aged negro who could not tell the meaning of one letter from that of another, yet he was happier than the college professor for whom he worked.

What then can it be, and from what deep well does it spring?

Reason tells us that it is a form of mental contentment and—if this is true—it's logical abode must be within the mind. The mind, so we are told, is capable of rising above matter. Can we be wrong then in assuming that mental contentment may be achieved under any condition, even in prison? [Ibid, pp.140-141]

Perhaps it was this letter, aided by pushback against the Baumes law's mandatory sentencing by prison reformists, that led to Middleton's pardon and release from Sing Sing in 1935. Even in the wake of his long prison term, Middleton didn't shy away from his Leftist beliefs. He

[Above] "Henry Wallace and The Negro People" (June 5, 1948) drawn by Middleton for the Henry A. Wallace Presidential campaign. Wallace was the nominee of the left-wing Progressive Party.

[Opposite page] Owen Middleton campaign ad (October 30, 1952), *New York Amsterdam News*. Middleton ran as the American Labor Party (ALP) candidate for the New York State Senate in 1952. Two weeks before the election, Middleton died suddenly on October 20th. Despite his death, the ALP ran an ad in the *New York Amsterdam News* encouraging readers to vote for him nonetheless as a symbolic gesture of protest against the major political parties.

Owen Middleton
The American Labor Party's Candidate in the 11th Senatorial District, was the only Negro candidate for State Senator in Brooklyn.
Owen Middleton died last week. He devoted his life to the battle for full equality for the Negro people — for Negro and white unity for a world of peace. By a ruling of the Board of Elections, his name cannot now be withdrawn from the ballot.
What Owen Middleton stood for deserves your vote. His spirit, his program, his ideal is the true expression of the Negro people and their struggles, and the best example of enlightened politics, regardless of political opinion or party affiliation.
On Election Day we respectfully ask you to pull the lever opposite the name of Owen Middleton. That way you will be voting for Negro Representation, Negro rights, Negro equality. That way we honor Owen Middleton,—who fought for all of us. That way we help to insure that NEVER AGAIN will the Republicans or Democrats dare keep a Negro candidate for this high office off their slate in the Bedford-Stuyvesant district.
VOTE
VOTE ROW D
AMERICAN LABOR PARTY
A.L.P.

was soon named to the managing board of *Champion Labor Monthly* as its art editor, a risky undertaking considering it was a Communist Party publication that was under scrutiny by the Federal government.

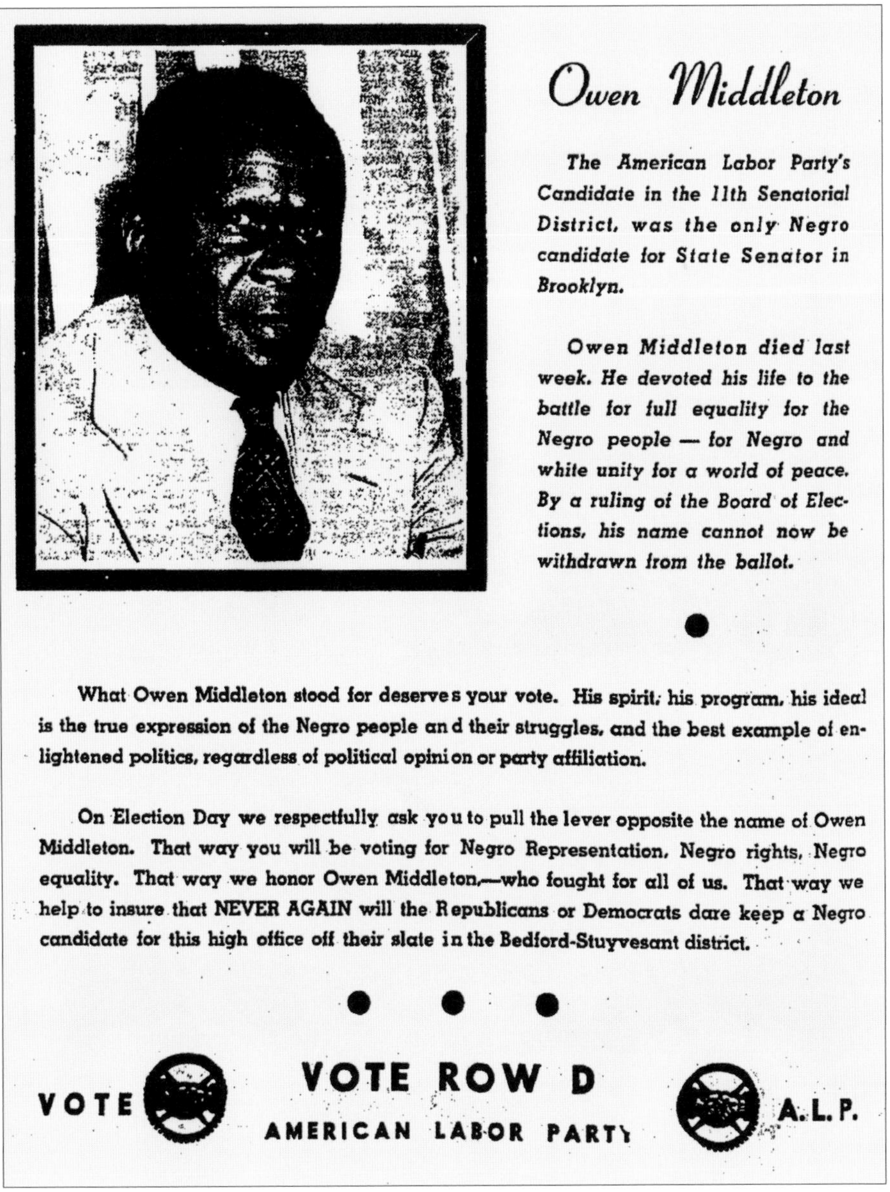

Middleton was one of the organizers of a Brooklyn rally in June 1939 that sought to put pressure on the U.S. Congress and Senate to pass the Federal Anti-Lynching Bill before them. (It failed.) He also added his voice to the condemnation of the 1940 Smith Act, aimed at anyone calling for the violent overthrow of the American government, which he believed unfairly targeted Blacks.

Middleton also resumed editorial cartooning, with one noteworthy series of drawings concerning the Scottsboro Boys running in Black newspapers in 1937. But like many other artists caught up in the Great Depression, Middleton found paying jobs hard to come by, so in the early 1940s he began supplementing his income with work in the burgeoning comic book industry. Middleton told interviewer Augusta Strong:

[Comics are] the only kind of art you can make a living as the idea of an attic studio somewhere and cheese and crackers does not appeal to me, and never did. Besides, there is no color line in this work. [Strong, Augusta, "Comic Artist Is Seasoned Unionist," *People's Voice*, Apr. 15, 1944]

People's Voice was a left-leaning Black newspaper founded and edited by Adam Clayton Powell Jr., the charismatic Harlem activist preacher/politician. Middleton's interview was reflective of its editorial viewpoint, as was his apparent disdain for the stereotypical bourgeois aspects of the artist's lifestyle. Strong wrote:

According to the artist, there are quite a few Negroes now working in the field of comic art, which has mushroomed out in the last decade and a half into one of the most lucrative phases of the publishing houses. [Ibid]

Middleton said:

It used to be a terribly exploited field. Some studios used to pay as low as $3 a page. Now the average comic artist makes from $15 to $50 a page and has all the work he can handle. [Ibid]

Although it helped put food on his table, Middleton had little regard for comic art. Strong wrote:

Middleton's "comics" are simply a routine matter to him, though he draws them exceptionally well, he has no interest in comics, and admits that he never reads them. [Ibid]

To date, only one signed example of Middleton's comic book artwork has been identified: a six-page story entitled "Two Months in the Bush," that appeared in Dell Publishing's *War Heroes* #5 (July-Sept. 1943). The artwork is fairly nondescript and isn't much of an indicator of Middleton's skill as an artist. As with many traditionally-trained fine artists, he had a difficult time "dumbing down" his drawings to comply with his perception of what comic book artwork should look like. Based upon that one example, it would be hard to identify any other comic book work by Middleton. However, the *People's Voice* piece helpfully reprinted several images of his comic artwork from various Fawcett Publications comics.

The two identifiable comic book pages shown are a "Spy Smasher" page from *Whiz Comics* #22 (Oct. 3, 1941), and a "Bulletman" page from *Bulletman* #2 (Fall 1941). The

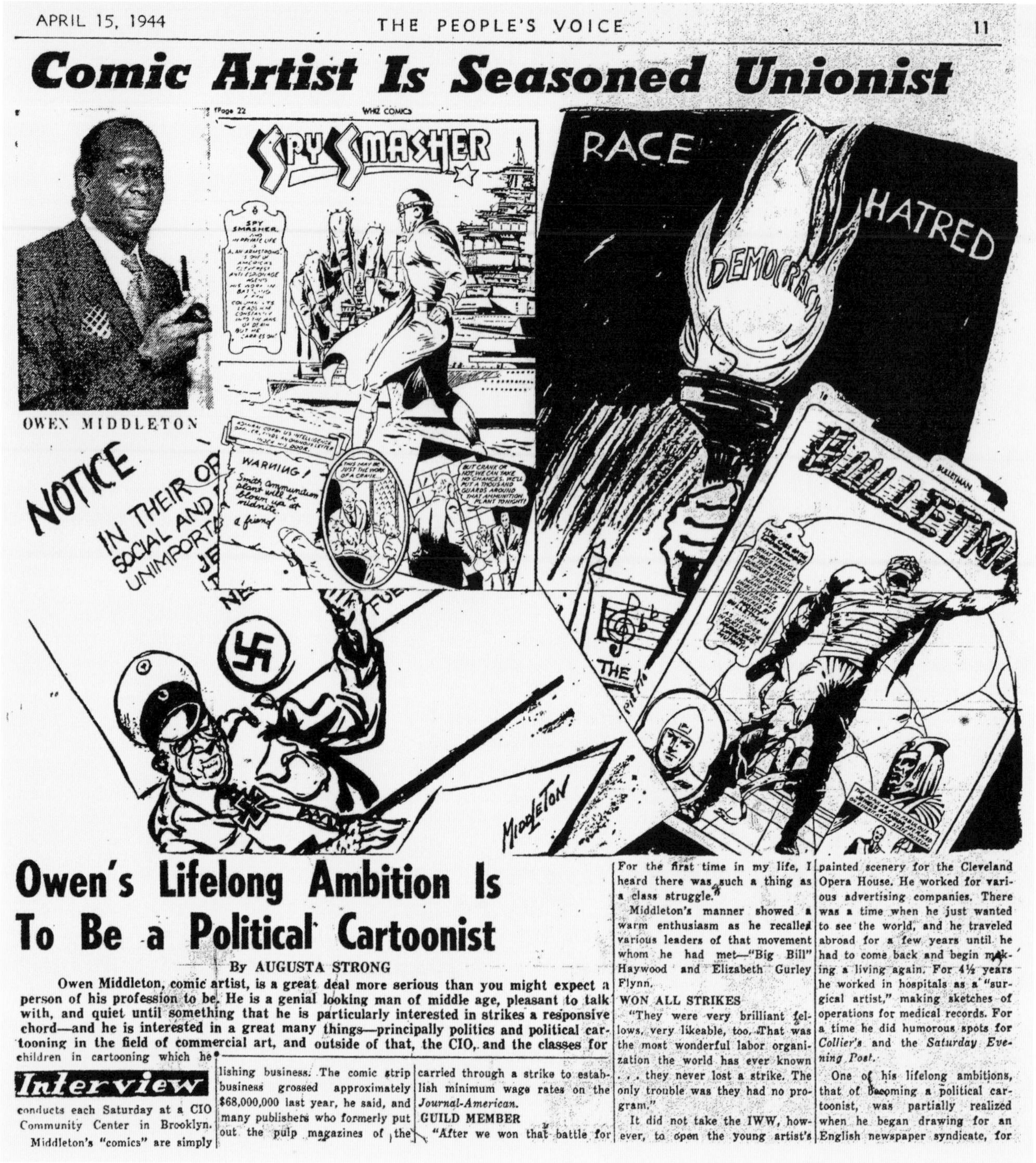

APRIL 15, 1944 THE PEOPLE'S VOICE 11

Comic Artist Is Seasoned Unionist

OWEN MIDDLETON
SPY SMASHER
WARNING! Smith ammunition plant will be blown up at midnite. a friend
RACE
HATRED
DEMOCRACY
NOTICE
MIDDLETON

Owen's Lifelong Ambition Is To Be a Political Cartoonist

By AUGUSTA STRONG

Owen Middleton, comic artist, is a great deal more serious than you might expect a person of his profession to be. He is a genial looking man of middle age, pleasant to talk with, and quiet until something that he is particularly interested in strikes a responsive chord—and he is interested in a great many things—principally politics and political cartooning in the field of commercial art, and outside of that, the CIO, and the classes for children in cartooning which he

Interview

conducts each Saturday at a CIO Community Center in Brooklyn.

Middleton's "comics" are simply

lishing business. The comic strip business grossed approximately $68,000,000 last year, he said, and many publishers who formerly put out the pulp magazines of the

carried through a strike to establish minimum wage rates on the *Journal-American.*

GUILD MEMBER

"After we won that battle for

For the first time in my life, I heard there was such a thing as a class struggle."

Middleton's manner showed a warm enthusiasm as he recalled various leaders of that movement whom he had met—"Big Bill" Haywood and Elizabeth Gurley Flynn.

WON ALL STRIKES

"They were very brilliant fellows, very likeable, too. That was the most wonderful labor organization the world has ever known . . . they never lost a strike. The only trouble was they had no program."

It did not take the IWW, however, to open the young artist's

painted scenery for the Cleveland Opera House. He worked for various advertising companies. There was a time when he just wanted to see the world, and he traveled abroad for a few years until he had to come back and begin making a living again. For 4½ years he worked in hospitals as a "surgical artist," making sketches of operations for medical records. For a time he did humorous spots for *Collier's* and the *Saturday Evening Post.*

One of his lifelong ambitions, that of becoming a political cartoonist, was partially realized when he began drawing for an English newspaper syndicate, for

pencils for both pieces of artwork are credited to Charles Sultan, the art director for the Harry 'A' Chesler comic shop at the time. From this it can be assumed that Middleton worked in the Chesler shop as an inker, specifically over Sultan's pencil work.

It should be noted that such uncredited roles were common among comic artists of the era, and not necessarily a sign of discrimination against a Black artist. It should also be noted that the one signed piece of Middleton comic art appeared in *War Heroes* #5 (July-Sept. 1943), an issue featuring five entire stories drawn by Elmer C. Stoner. Did Stoner, who was working for Dell at the time and one of their primary artists, play a part in Middleton getting the assignment? It's a reasonable assumption that he did.

This scant information provides the barest outline of Middleton's short comic book career, indicating that it lasted from early 1941 to at least 1944, likely ending with the cessation of WWII and the return of the White artists from military service.

The bulk of the *People's Voice* interview was devoted to Middleton's long involvement with labor unions, which

[Above] "Comic Artist is a Seasoned Unionist" was an article profiling Middleton's career as a comic book artist. It ran in Adam Clayton Powell Jr.'s *People's Voice* newspaper on April 15, 1944. Note the splash pages from Fawcett comic book stories.

[Right] This is the printed "Spy Smasher" splash page depicted in the *People's Voice* article. Pencils are credited to Charles Sultan, while Middleton provided the inks. *Whiz Comics* #22, October 3, 1941; Fawcett Publications.

included membership in the seminal Commercial Artists and Designers Union, in its formative years of the 1930s. Interviewer Strong recounted:

Middleton's interest in the organized labor movement dates back to about 35 years ago, when he had just graduated from art school and was holding his first job—that of a staff artist on the Chicago Tribune.

"That was during the witch-hunts of the Wobblies (International Workers of the World), in Chicago," Middleton explained, "and I became acquainted with them through a story on the printer of the Wobbly paper. For the first time in my life, I heard there was such a thing as a class struggle." [Ibid]

Despite his employment as a sketch artist, Middleton stated that because he was a "Negro," the editors at the *Chicago Tribune* denied him the opportunity to follow his greatest desire as an artist: to draw political cartoons. Middleton said:

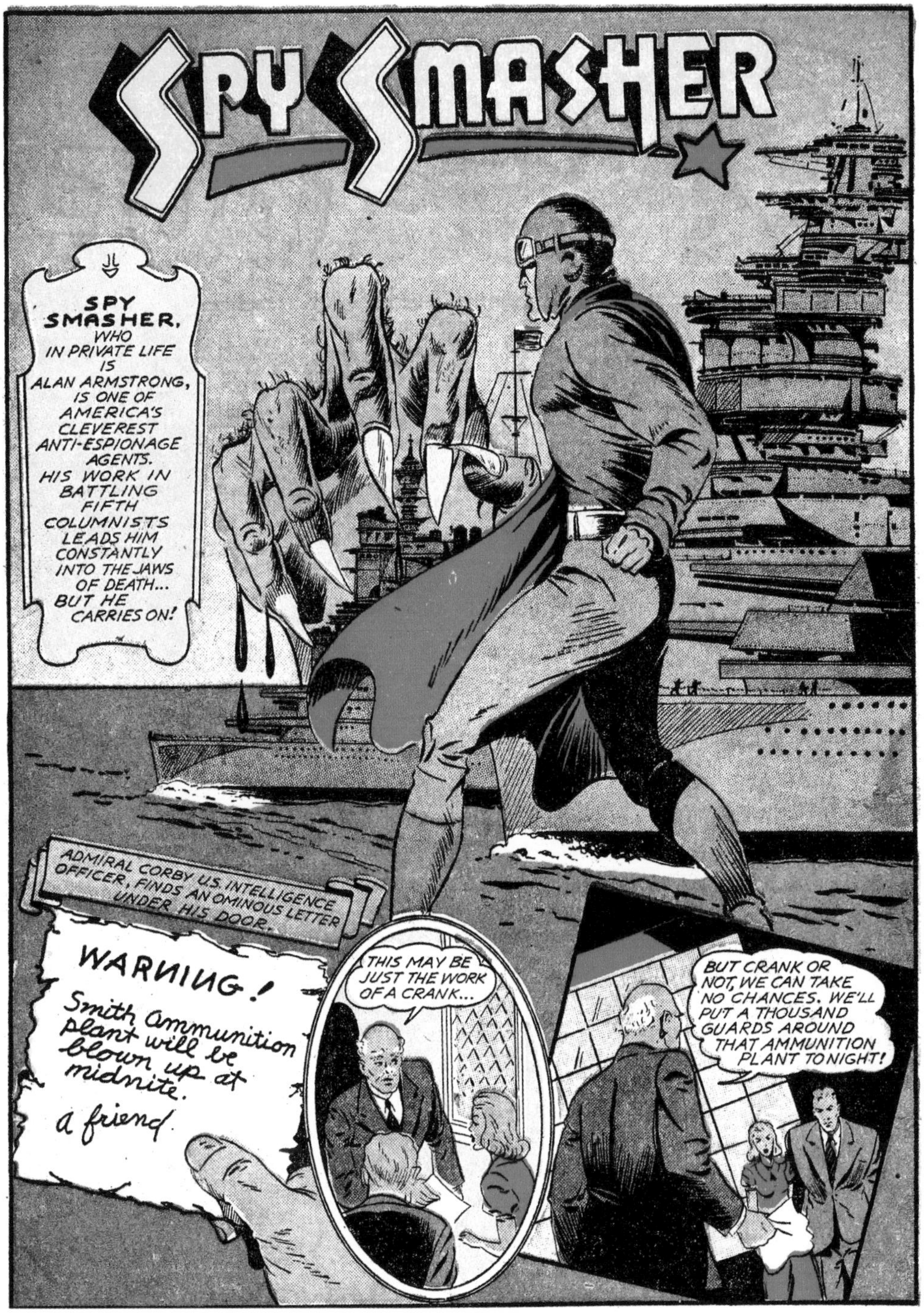

SPY SMASHER
SPY SMASHER, WHO IN PRIVATE LIFE IS ALAN ARMSTRONG, IS ONE OF AMERICA'S CLEVEREST ANTI-ESPIONAGE AGENTS. HIS WORK IN BATTLING FIFTH COLUMNISTS LEADS HIM CONSTANTLY INTO THE JAWS OF DEATH... BUT HE CARRIES ON!
ADMIRAL CORBY U.S. INTELLIGENCE OFFICER, FINDS AN OMINOUS LETTER UNDER HIS DOOR.
WARNING! Smith ammunition plant will be blown up at midnite. a friend
THIS MAY BE JUST THE WORK OF A CRANK...
BUT CRANK OR NOT, WE CAN TAKE NO CHANCES. WE'LL PUT A THOUSAND GUARDS AROUND THAT AMMUNITION PLANT TONIGHT!

One political cartoon is worth one hundred editorials which people do not read...and as long as newspapers have something to fight against and something to fight for, the cartoonist has an irreplaceable role to play. [Ibid]

A rare instance in which his work found a place in a prominent White newspaper was when the *New York Times* published a Middleton cartoon on Sunday, May 6, 1945. Columnist Michael Carter, writing in the *Baltimore Afro-American*, noted that this made Middleton "probably the first colored artist to have a humorous drawing in the Book Review section of the *NY Times*." [Carter, Michael, "New York Diary," *Baltimore Afro-American*, May 5, 1945]

Ironically, Middleton's cartoon was actually a reprinting, having originally appeared in the *Birmingham Gazette*, a British daily. Chances are that the editors at the *Times* were totally unaware of Middleton's skin color or the significance of his work's appearance in their publication.

Middleton spent the post-war years drawing cartoons for Black papers and involving himself in various social causes and politics. In 1948, he worked with the national campaign committee for Henry Wallace, Presidential nominee of the left-wing Progressive Party. Middleton drew informational material about Wallace that was sent out to Black newspapers around the country.

Middleton also served on the National Council of the Arts, Sciences, and Professions (NCASP), a Leftist organization formed primarily in opposition to the actions of the House Committee on Un-American Activities. Under the auspices of the NCASP, Middleton was part of a delega-

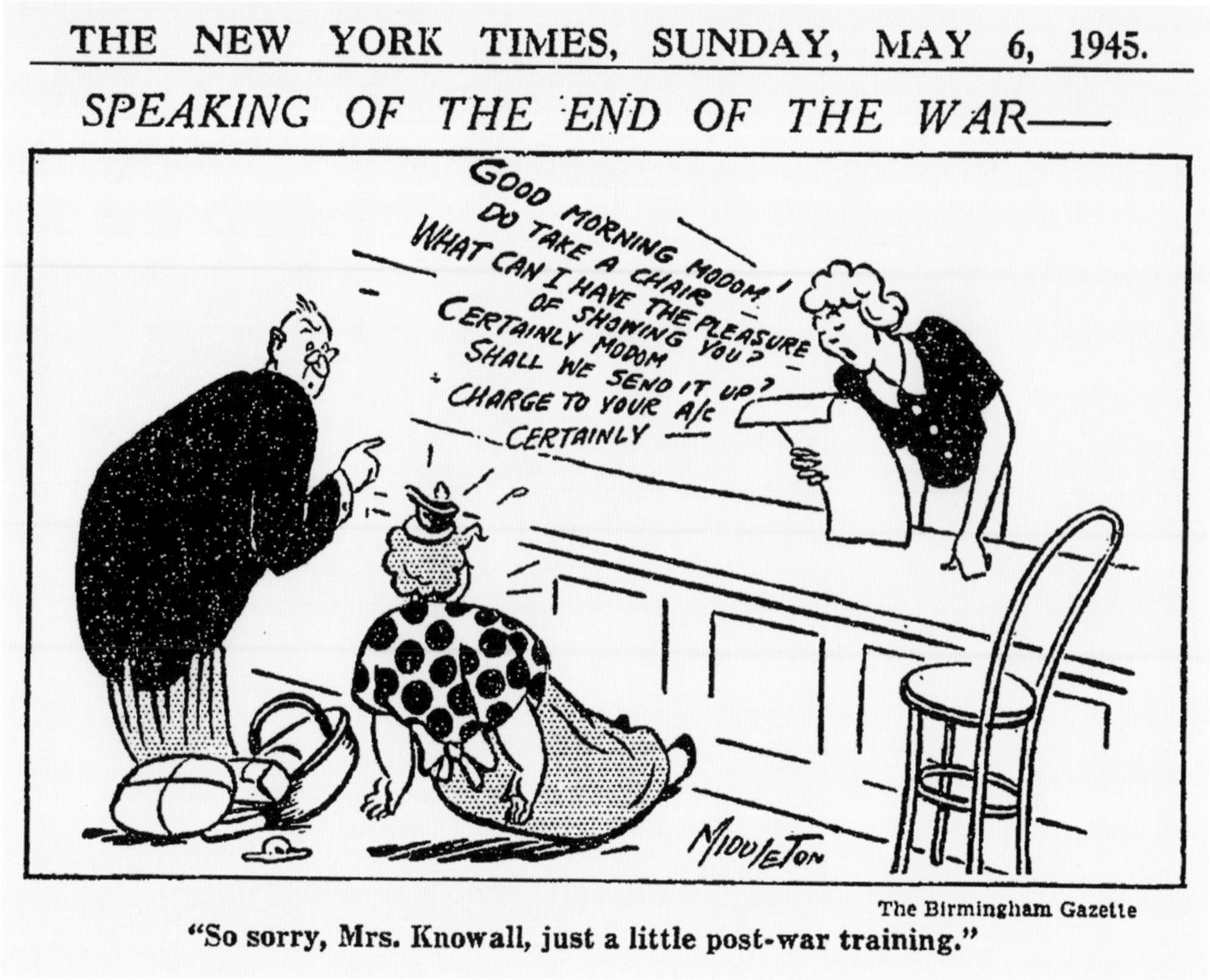
THE NEW YORK TIMES, SUNDAY, MAY 6, 1945.

SPEAKING OF THE END OF THE WAR——

GOOD MORNING MODOM!
DO TAKE A CHAIR
WHAT CAN I HAVE THE PLEASURE OF SHOWING YOU?
CERTAINLY MODOM
SHALL WE SEND IT UP?
CHARGE TO YOUR A/c
CERTAINLY
MIDDLETON

The Birmingham Gazette

"So sorry, Mrs. Knowall, just a little post-war training."

tion that appeared before the United Nations in May 1949, regarding the disposition of the former Italian colonies in Africa. Middleton served, too, as an officer of the National Committee To Defend Negro Leadership, which called for the end to the persecution of Blacks in general and of their leaders specifically.

He became more involved with local politics as well. Middleton was a member of the Bedford-Stuyvesant Action Committee for Fair Employment, which concerned itself with bias in employment within their community. The committee's first project, in January 1951, involved a Black female pharmacist fired by a White-owned drug store. They rallied community support for the dismissed employee, whom they claimed was unfairly let go. An amicable settlement with the store's owners was reached, resulting in the woman's rehiring.

Middleton's activism in his community eventually led to his candidacy in November 1952. He was the only American Labor Party nominee for the New York State Senate seat representing the 11th District of Brooklyn (Bedford-Stuyvesant) and the only Black candidate for state office in that borough. However, on October 20th, two weeks before the election, Middleton died unexpectedly.

The suddenness of his passing so close to election day didn't allow time for another candidate to be named as his replacement. In light of this, the local branch of the American Labor Party ran an ad in the Black-owned *New York Amsterdam News* imploring voters to still vote for Middleton as a symbolic gesture.

That way you will be voting for Negro Representation, Negro rights, Negro equality. That way we honor Owen Middleton—who fought for all of us. That way we help to insure [sic] that NEVER AGAIN will Republicans or Democrats dare keep a Negro candidate for this high office off their slate in the Bedford-Stuyvesant district." [American Labor Party, "Owen Middleton," *New York Amsterdam News*, Oct. 30, 1954]

Knowing full well that he couldn't win and that it was only a symbolic gesture, 967 people agreed—and honored Owen Middleton posthumously with their vote.

[Above] "Speaking of the End of the War" is a Middleton cartoon that first ran in a British newspaper and was reprinted shortly thereafter in the *New York Times*. This made him likely the first Black artist to have a cartoon run in the *Times* Book Review section. May 6, 1945, *Birmingham Gazette*.

[Right] "Two Months in the Bush" is the only comic book story carrying Middleton's signature. It appeared in an issue of *War Heroes* that also featured a cover and four stories drawn by Elmer C. Stoner. *War Heroes* #5, July-September 1943, Dell.

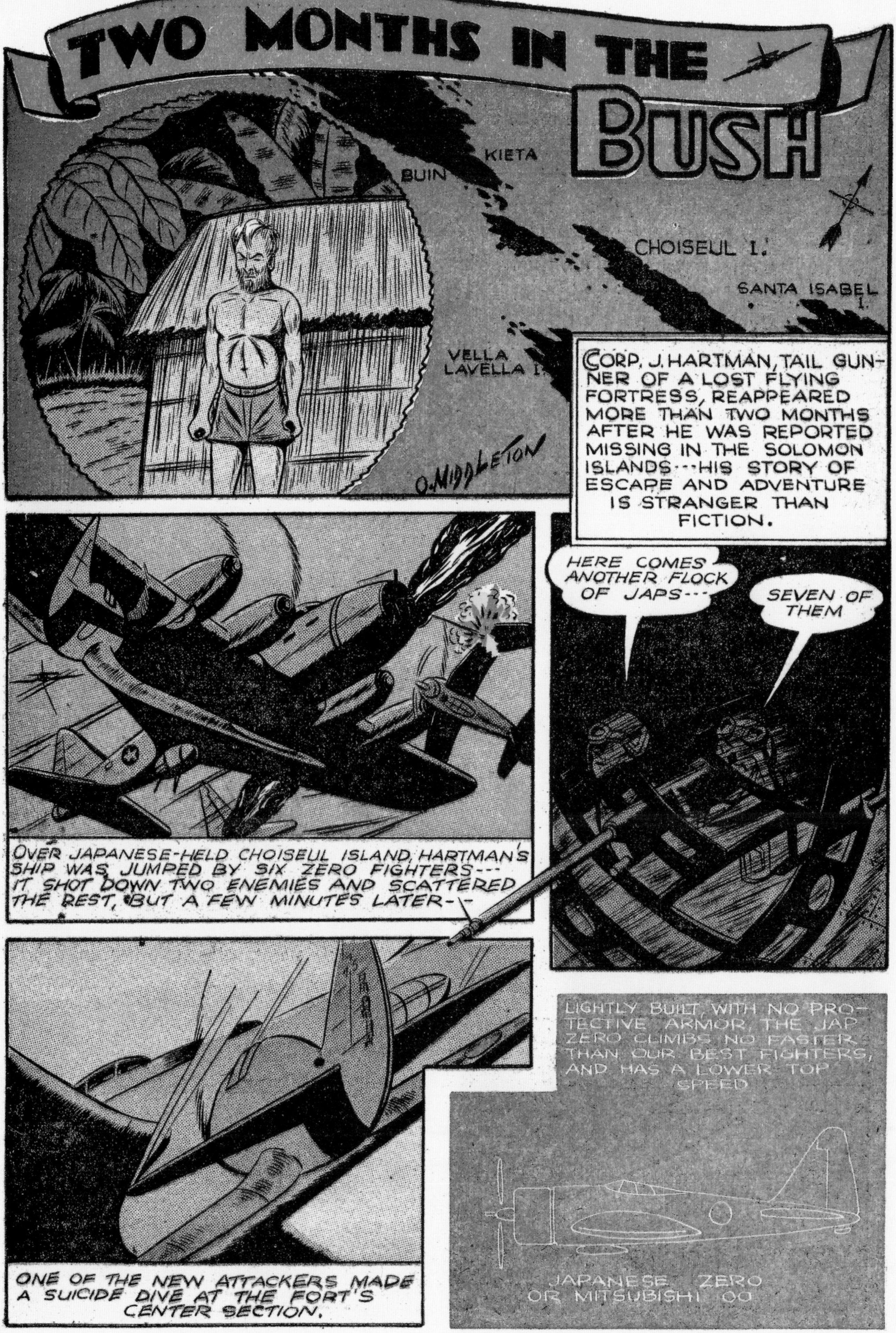

TWO MONTHS IN THE BUSH
BUIN
KIETA
CHOISEUL I.
SANTA ISABEL I.
VELLA LAVELLA I.
O. MIDDLETON
CORP. J. HARTMAN, TAIL GUNNER OF A LOST FLYING FORTRESS, REAPPEARED MORE THAN TWO MONTHS AFTER HE WAS REPORTED MISSING IN THE SOLOMON ISLANDS--HIS STORY OF ESCAPE AND ADVENTURE IS STRANGER THAN FICTION.
OVER JAPANESE-HELD CHOISEUL ISLAND, HARTMAN'S SHIP WAS JUMPED BY SIX ZERO FIGHTERS--- IT SHOT DOWN TWO ENEMIES AND SCATTERED THE REST, BUT A FEW MINUTES LATER--
HERE COMES ANOTHER FLOCK OF JAPS---
SEVEN OF THEM
ONE OF THE NEW ATTACKERS MADE A SUICIDE DIVE AT THE FORT'S CENTER SECTION.
LIGHTLY BUILT, WITH NO PROTECTIVE ARMOR, THE JAP ZERO CLIMBS NO FASTER THAN OUR BEST FIGHTERS, AND HAS A LOWER TOP SPEED
JAPANESE ZERO OR MITSUBISHI OO

THE JAP FIGHTER SLICED CLEAN THROUGH THE FORT'S FUSELAGE, SETTING THE FRONT HALF OF THE GREAT SHIP ABLAZE.

THE TAIL SECTION SPUN SEAWARD WITH HARTMAN IN THE TAIL TURRET "BLACKED-OUT" WITH HEAD INJURIES.

A FEW SECONDS LATER HARTMAN CAME TO.

WHAT---UH--- HAPPENED?

IT'S GONE! THE WHOLE FRONT OF THE SHIP IS GONE--- AND I'M FALLING---

STRUGGLING INTO HIS PARACHUTE HARNESS, HARTMAN DIVED CLEAR.

HERE'S HOPING---

TAIL TURRET B-17

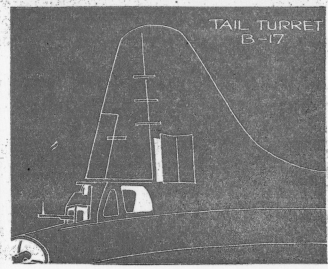

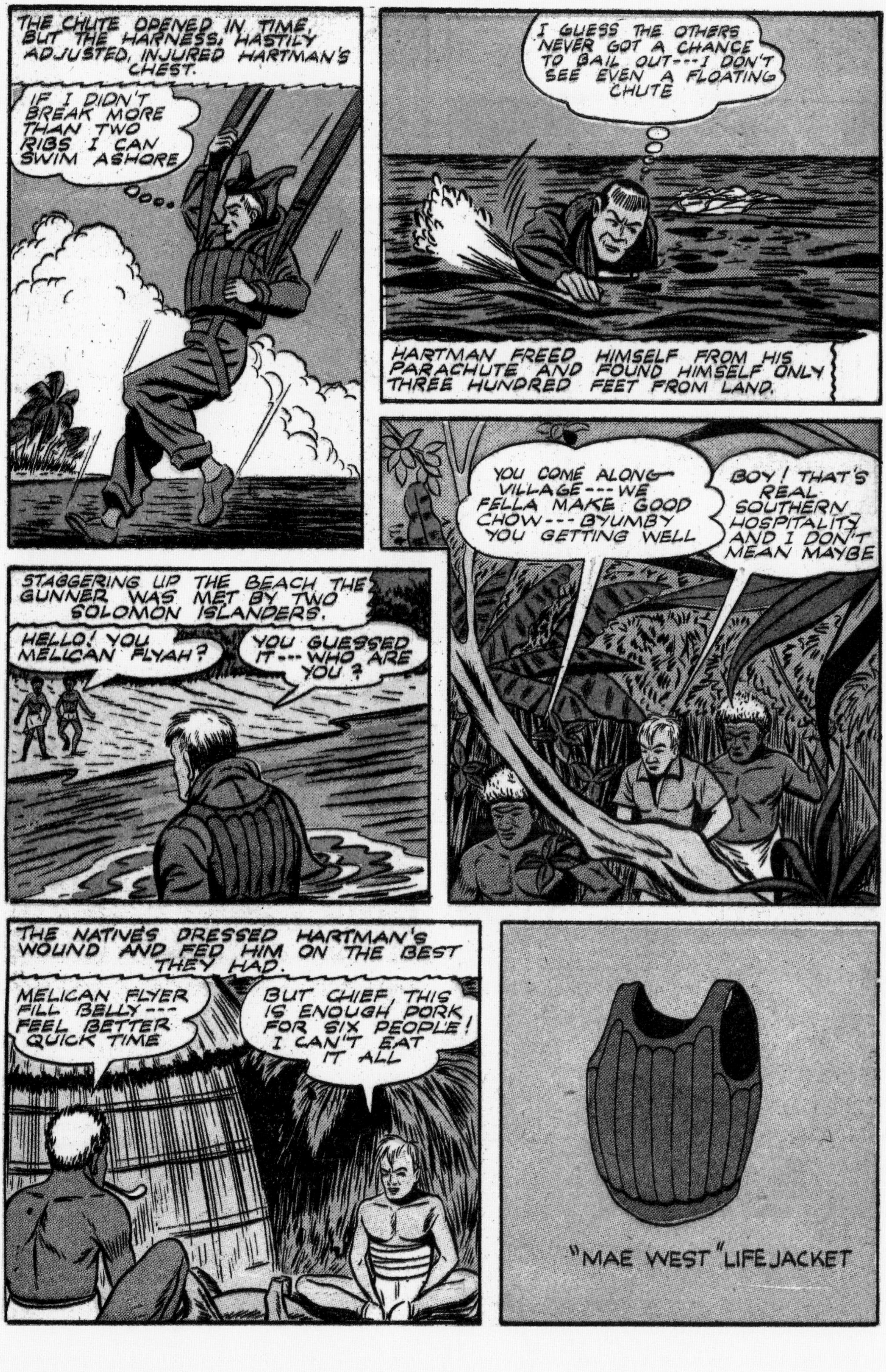
THE CHUTE OPENED IN TIME, BUT THE HARNESS, HASTILY ADJUSTED, INJURED HARTMAN'S CHEST.
IF I DIDN'T BREAK MORE THAN TWO RIBS I CAN SWIM ASHORE
I GUESS THE OTHERS NEVER GOT A CHANCE TO BAIL OUT---I DON'T SEE EVEN A FLOATING CHUTE
HARTMAN FREED HIMSELF FROM HIS PARACHUTE AND FOUND HIMSELF ONLY THREE HUNDRED FEET FROM LAND.
STAGGERING UP THE BEACH THE GUNNER WAS MET BY TWO SOLOMON ISLANDERS.
HELLO! YOU MELICAN FLYAH?
YOU GUESSED IT---WHO ARE YOU?
YOU COME ALONG VILLAGE---WE FELLA MAKE GOOD CHOW---BYUMBY YOU GETTING WELL
BOY! THAT'S REAL SOUTHERN HOSPITALITY AND I DON'T MEAN MAYBE
THE NATIVES DRESSED HARTMAN'S WOUND AND FED HIM ON THE BEST THEY HAD.
MELICAN FLYER FILL BELLY---FEEL BETTER QUICK TIME
BUT CHIEF, THIS IS ENOUGH PORK FOR SIX PEOPLE! I CAN'T EAT IT ALL
"MAE WEST" LIFEJACKET

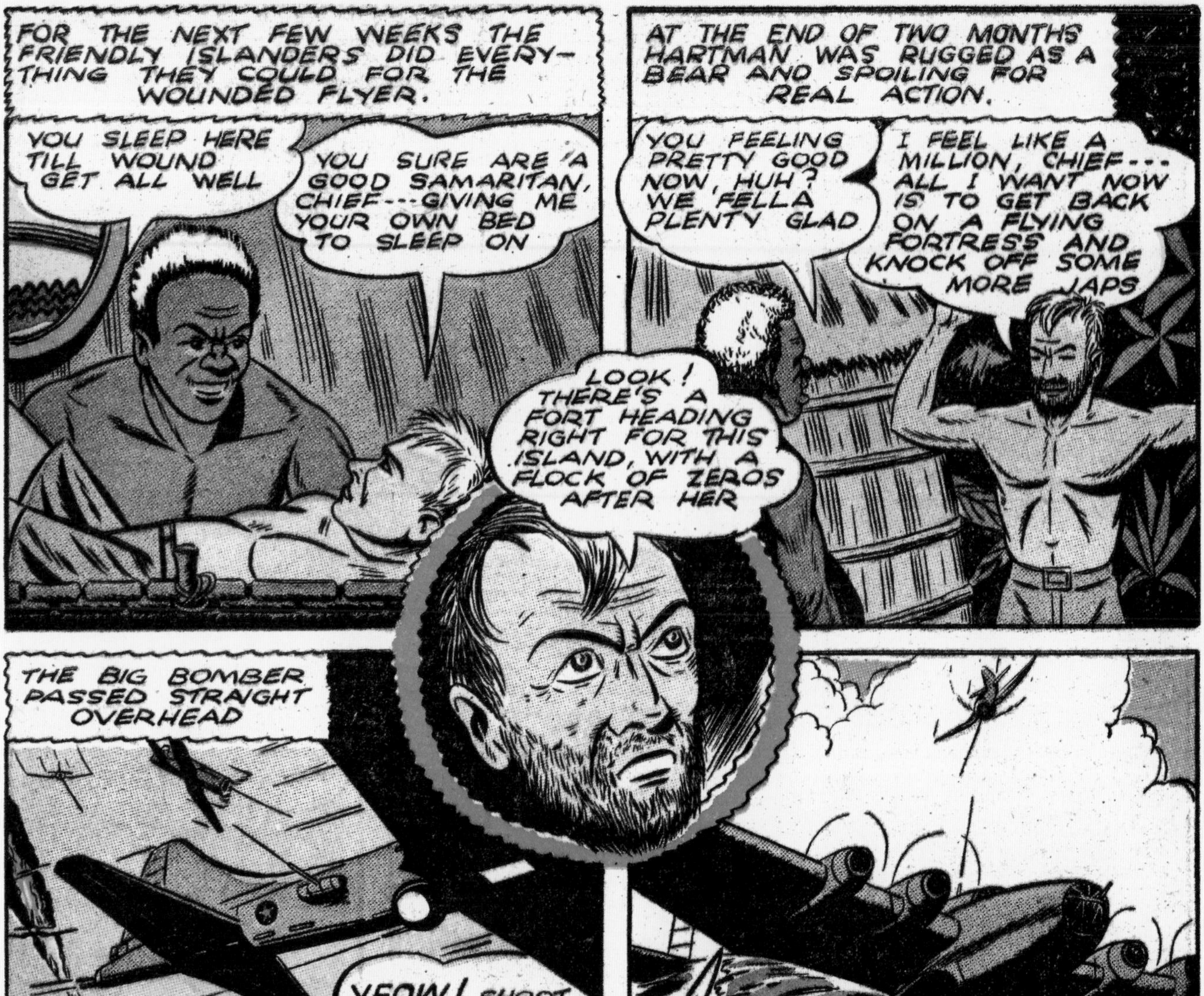
FOR THE NEXT FEW WEEKS THE FRIENDLY ISLANDERS DID EVERYTHING THEY COULD FOR THE WOUNDED FLYER.
YOU SLEEP HERE TILL WOUND GET ALL WELL
YOU SURE ARE A GOOD SAMARITAN, CHIEF---GIVING ME YOUR OWN BED TO SLEEP ON
AT THE END OF TWO MONTHS HARTMAN WAS RUGGED AS A BEAR AND SPOILING FOR REAL ACTION.
YOU FEELING PRETTY GOOD NOW, HUH? WE FELLA PLENTY GLAD
I FEEL LIKE A MILLION, CHIEF... ALL I WANT NOW IS TO GET BACK ON A FLYING FORTRESS AND KNOCK OFF SOME MORE JAPS
LOOK! THERE'S A FORT HEADING RIGHT FOR THIS ISLAND, WITH A FLOCK OF ZEROS AFTER HER
THE BIG BOMBER PASSED STRAIGHT OVERHEAD
YEOW! SHOOT 'EM UP, YOU GUYS! KNOCK THOSE JAPS CLEAN OUT OF THE SKY
CRIPPLED BY ENEMY SHELLFIRE, THE FORTRESS WAS FORCED DOWN. A ZERO FIGHTER ALSO TOOK TO THE WATER.

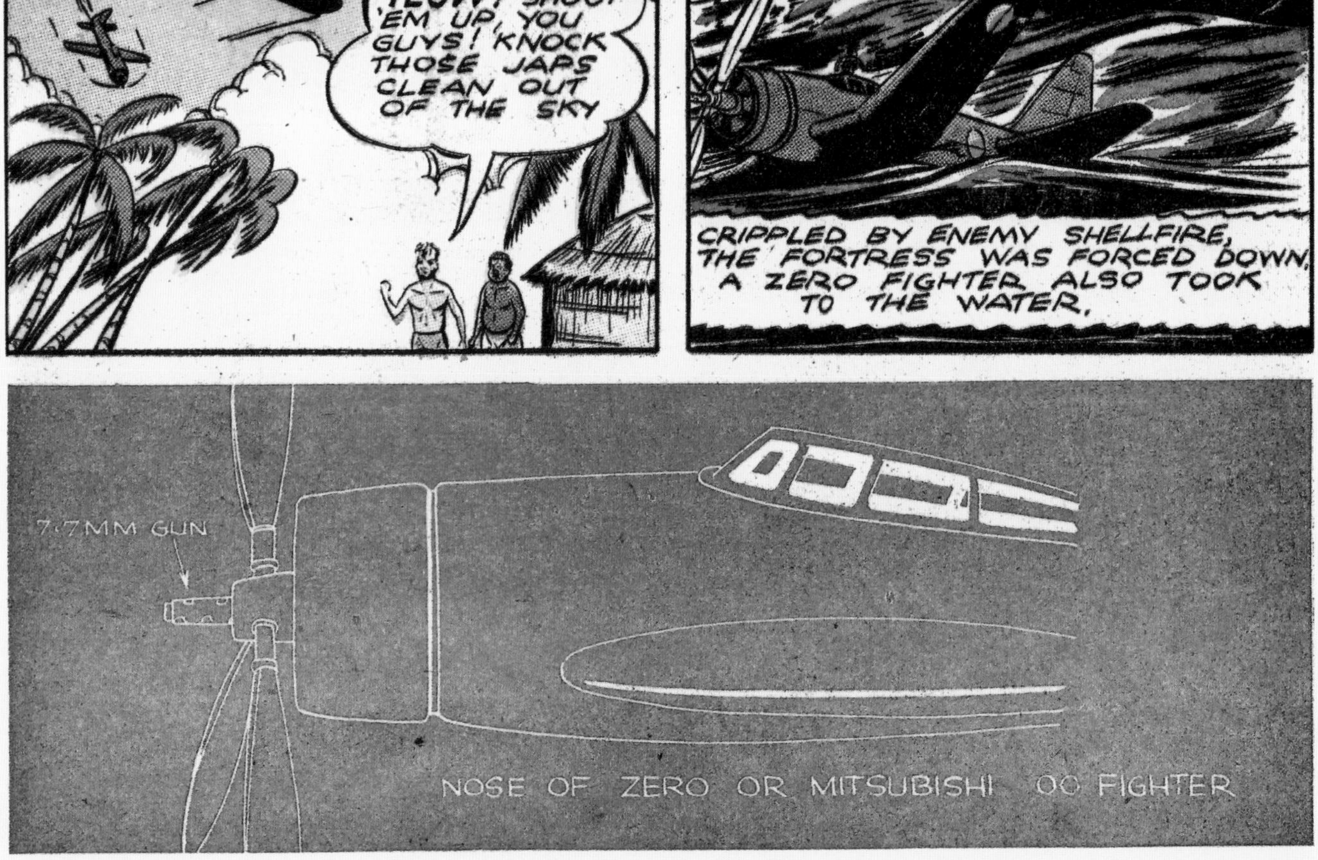
7.7MM GUN
NOSE OF ZERO OR MITSUBISHI 00 FIGHTER

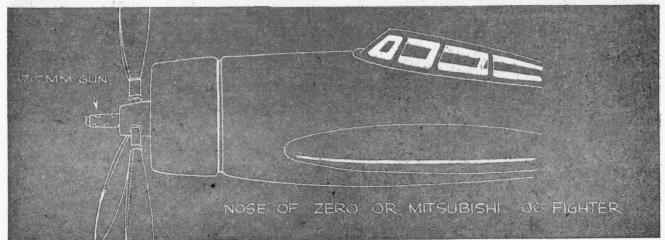

ONLY THE JAP PILOT REACHED SHORE---HIS FRIENDS HAD MACHINE-GUNNED THE AMERICAN FLYERS IN THE WATER.

MELICAN FLYAH, COME QUICK TIME, KETCHUM JAP'NEE FELLA IN BUSH

YOU BET I'LL COME! JUST SHOW ME THE LITTLE SNAKE

SILENT AS A PANTHER--- HARTMAN STALKED HIS ARMED ENEMY---

---AND CAUGHT HIM IN AN IRON GRIP. DROP THAT GUN BEFORE I BREAK YOUR ARM, TOJO

NOW, MARCH! AND IF YOU TRY TO MAKE A BREAK THERE'LL BE ONE LESS JAP IN THESE ISLANDS

BUT THE JAP PREFERRED TO RISK ESCAPE---AND PAID FOR IT WITH HIS LIFE.

YOU ASKED FOR IT FELLA!

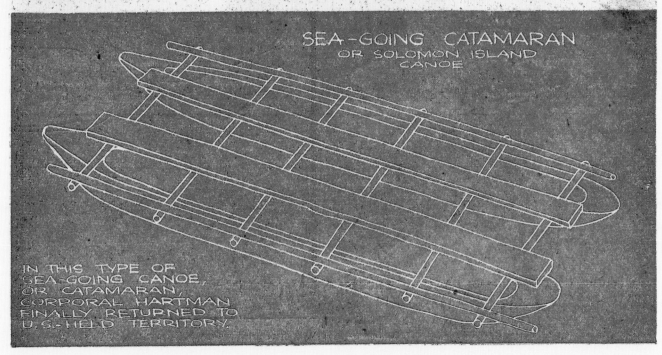

SEA-GOING CATAMARAN
OR SOLOMON ISLAND CANOE

IN THIS TYPE OF SEA-GOING CANOE, OR CATAMARAN, CORPORAL HARTMAN FINALLY RETURNED TO U.S.-HELD TERRITORY.

AT LAST THE CORPORAL PERSUADED HIS FRIENDS TO RISK A LONG SEA VOYAGE.

WE FELLA LIKE YOU STAY LONG US--- BUT WE TAKE YOU WHERE YOU WANTUM GO

YOU BOYS HAVE BEEN SWELL TO ME, CHIEF, BUT I'VE GOT A JOB FIGHTING JAPS, AND IT WON'T WAIT

THE TRIP TOOK SEVEN DAYS, THROUGH DANGEROUS WATERS.

HOW LONG BEFORE WE HIT AN AMERICAN ISLAND, CHIEF?

THREE-FOUR DAYS MORE WE COME SANT ISABEL, FINDUM MELICAN FIGHTING MAN THERE

REACHING SANTA ISABEL, HARTMAN FOUND HIMSELF A CURIOSITY.

HI, YOU LEATHERNECKS! HAVE YOU CLEANED THE JAPS OUT OF GUADALCANAL YET?

A WHITE MAN IN A NATIVE WAR CANOE! WHERE DID HE COME FROM?

SO YOU LEFT A SOUTH SEA ISLAND PARADISE TO GET BACK IN THE SCRAP, HUH?

YOU OUGHT TO BE IN THE MARINES IF YOU LIKE FIGHTING THAT MUCH

NOPE! JUST GIVE ME TWO GUNS IN THE TAIL OF A FLYING FORT--

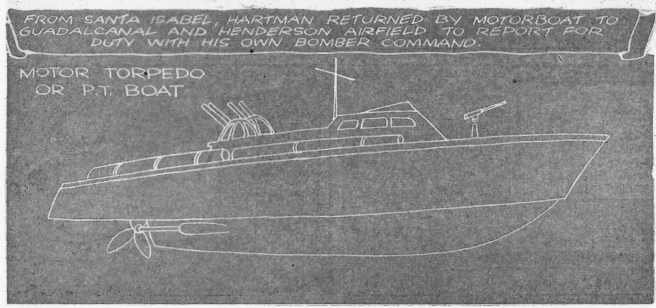

FROM SANTA ISABEL, HARTMAN RETURNED BY MOTORBOAT TO GUADALCANAL AND HENDERSON AIRFIELD TO REPORT FOR DUTY WITH HIS OWN BOMBER COMMAND.

MOTOR TORPEDO OR P.T. BOAT

ELTON CLAY FAX
GEORGE DEWEY LIPSCOMB
The Progressive and The Professor

Sometimes a defining moment is born of trauma, a devastating catastrophe that alters a life. Sometimes it is a transcendent event, uplifting and empowering. But sometimes it is simply a minor occurrence, soon forgotten, its impact only realized from the distance of time. Elton Clay Fax recalled just such a moment:

I clearly recall the incident. I was about seven, and my mother and I had just started out to the market. Several paces ahead, a well-dressed white man had gathered a group of threadbare Black boys. The latter watched with eager tenseness as the man eased his right hand deep into a pocket. With a swift, flinging motion he withdrew and opened his fist, showering the cobblestone street with pennies. As if choreographed to that action, the urchins raced and scrambled toward the scattering coins. One rolled close to us, and at that instant I heard my mother's warning: "Don't you dare touch it!"

The man was now laughing fit to kill. Indeed the spectacle of flailing skinny arms, legs, and bodies wallowing wildly about amid piles of horse manure struck my funny bone too. Again my mother's quiet voice seemed to rise above the screeches and the mocking laughter: *"That's not funny! Besides, don't you ever, no matter how much you need money, lower yourself like that to get it!"* [Fax, Elton, "It's Been a Beautiful But Rugged Journey," *Black American Literature Forum*, 1986, p.273]

Elton, named after his uncle, was born on October 9, 1909, in the Druid Heights section of Baltimore. The year of Fax's birth, Booker T. Washington visited the city and commented that this Black enclave "possibly contains more homes and better homes owned and occupied by colored people than any other similar district in any of the large cities of the country." [Washington, Booker T., "Law and Order and the Negro," *Outlook*, November 6, 1909.]

Washington's comment, though, only applied to the homes along northern Druid Hill Avenue, an area once occupied by wealthy Whites who had since relocated to the suburbs. The southern portion of Druid Heights, where the Faxes rented a rowhouse, had far humbler homes, more in keeping with other Black communities in big cities.

Elton's father, Mark Oakland Fax, was by his son's description a "small and frail" man, who toiled in various jobs—porter, waiter, stevedore—until 1911, when he began

Elton Fax [left], George Lipscomb [right].

"Come, let us take counsel together!"

Attend NAACP

WARTIME CONFERENCE FOR TOTAL PEACE

CHICAGO

JULY 12-16

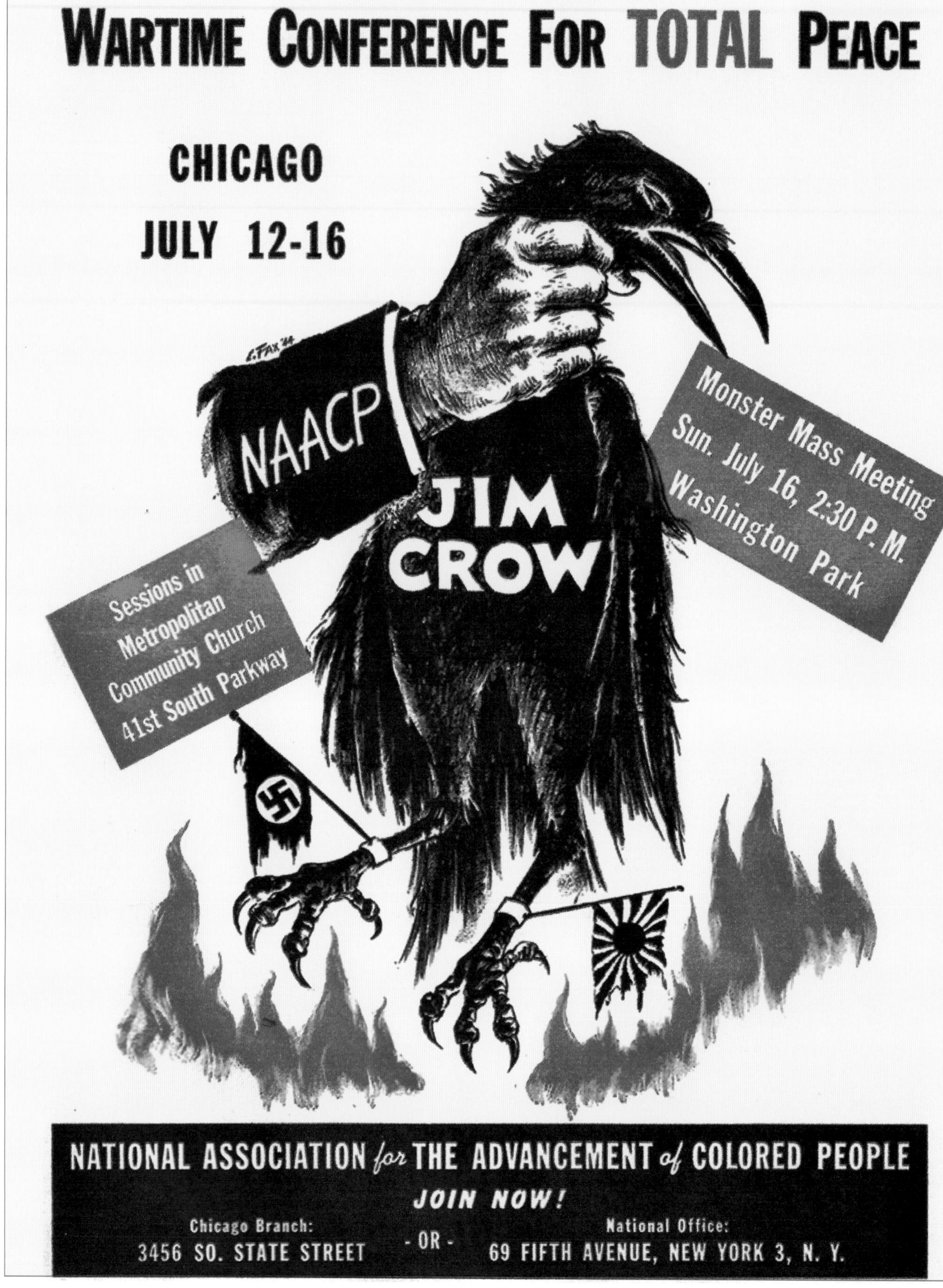

NAACP
JIM CROW
Monster Mass Meeting
Sun. July 16, 2:30 P. M.
Washington Park
Sessions in
Metropolitan
Community Church
41st South Parkway

NATIONAL ASSOCIATION *for* THE ADVANCEMENT *of* COLORED PEOPLE

JOIN NOW!

Chicago Branch: 3456 SO. STATE STREET - OR - National Office: 69 FIFTH AVENUE, NEW YORK 3, N. Y.

attending the newly opened New York School of Chiropody (aka Podiatry). At the time of Mark's attendance, chiropody was still in its early years as a recognized medical profession overseen by state medical boards. Previous to 1895, when the first laws regulating its practice were passed in New York, it suffered the public perception of being a menial service seemingly performed by "every barber, masseur and shoemaker." [Lewi, Maurice, *Text Book of Chiropody*, 1914. p.71]

Upon his graduation and state licensing, Dr. Fax began running ads in the *Baltimore Afro-American* newspaper, offering to see patients in the evening at his home at 1516 Presstman Street. This side-job was a bonus, however; he still couldn't give up his primary source of income as a stevedore.

Willie Estelle Fax (née Smith), Elton's mother, worked out of the home as a dressmaker. One of seven college-educated sisters, Willie was actively involved in her children's education. She taught school at some point and was elected president of the local parent-teachers association. She was strict, loving, and—as was her husband—very religious. Elton recalled:

From both parents as well as from other close family members, I learned early to guard my own dignity carefully and to respect that of others. [Fax 1986, op. cit. p.273]

Willie was protective of both her sons, but especially the youngest, Mark. Named after his father, Mark shared his frailty. Elton, on the other hand, was an extrovert, a jovial, self-described "cutup." He earned the nickname "Humpty Dumpty" from his classmates, based upon his round face. Conversely, young Mark was introverted, quiet, and a child musical prodigy. At age 14, he was playing the organ in large churches and at silent film theaters.

Both boys went to Frederick Douglass High School, the city's first all-Black high school and the country's second. Elton remembered the school with a mixture of emotions. Fax wrote:

Though our segregated schools of Baltimore were unequal to those for whites, we youngsters learned from dedicated Black teachers.

Fax drew two posters for the National Association for the Advancement of Colored People (NAACP). The first proclaimed the group's Wartime Conference for Peace being held in Chicago in July 1944. It featured the striking image of a dead "Jim Crow" strangled by the hand of the NAACP. Hanging from the bird's legs were the flags of Nazi Germany and Japan, a damning connection that would not be lost on anyone viewing it.

They were valiant souls who toiled in overcrowded, rundown buildings. To compound their misery, they were paid less than their white counterparts. [Fax 1986, op. cit. p.273]

For many years, Baltimore had the largest Black population in the country. Even when Maryland was a slave state prior to the Civil War, the city was home to many free Blacks. Still, it was a strained coexistence, fraught with deep-seated distrust, racial tension, and inequity.

To understand better, one has to consider the city's location. Baltimore is situated about 40 miles north of the nation's capital, and about the same distance south of the Mason-Dixon Line.

On one hand, it seemed to be the model of Black opportunity. Two major Black colleges were established within its boundaries: Morgan State, founded in 1867, and Coppin State, a teacher's college. It spawned the *Baltimore Afro-American*, one of the leading Black newspapers boasting a national circulation. Additionally, one of the first chapters of the National Association for the Advancement of Colored People (NAACP) opened in the city in 1912.

At the same time, Baltimore had among its White citizenry many supporters of the "Lost Cause" ideology that arose around 1900. This reinterpretation of the Confederate states' motivations and rationale leading to the Civil War, promulgated by Southern war veterans and their sympathizers, led directly to the construction of monuments memorializing Confederate servicemen and women in the city. Gains made by Blacks during the initial years of Reconstruction were gradually peeled back, and they faced increasing discrimination. This was exemplified in early 1911, when the city passed the West Segregation Ordinance, which confined Blacks and Whites to separate housing blocks—the first segregation law ever enacted in the United States. Segregation, both institutional and de facto, became the norm throughout the city.

Both parents expected much and wanted more for their sons; but at some point in the mid-1920s, the Faxes separated for reasons unknown. Dr. Fax, who likely suffered from tuberculosis, spent time in a Baltimore sanitarium before moving to Los Angeles for his health. In August 1927, he died and was buried there. Meanwhile, Willie Estelle took her sons and moved in with two of her sisters, both of whom were teachers. This arrangement would have a significant impact upon each of the Fax children.

The aunts convinced the boys that a college education was a necessity. Despite his reputation for "foolishness,"

SUMMER 1945   **10¢**

Young **LIFE**

P D C

- COMICS • SWING
- MOVIES • SPORTS
- FICTION • FASHIONS
- TEEN AGERS IN ACTION

SKIPPY HOMEIER
Movie Star At 14
Page 23

By **EILEEN BARTON**
My Boss—Sinatra
Page 10

By **LOUIS PRIMA**
Man With A Horn
Page 32

ACTION!
SUSPENSE!

Crime Crashes The Canteen! Page 12

to help a bit with finances, but much of their money came from odd jobs. Elton spent six months as a pot washer at the Baltimore Country Club earning $22 a week, and subsequently, as a bell-man at the Stafford Hotel. Back at school, he met fellow student Grace Turner, a native Syracusan and his future wife. Elton graduated in June 1931, with a Bachelor of Fine Arts degree and a view of his college experience that was both good and bad.

Splendid school that it is, and solid as the training we received there was, we found Syracuse to be severely infected with racism. [Fax 1986, op. cit. p.274]

Elton returned to Baltimore, where he exhibited his paintings in a series of one-man shows. One of the first was held in the Assembly Hall of the *Afro-American* building. His work received acclaim, but also stirred controversy.

Critics declared that the two paintings violate the rules of classicism in art. They further intimated that they represent a modern touch too shocking for a city as staid and conservative in its estimates of what constitutes good art as Baltimore is. ["Baltimore Painter's Work Shocks Conservative Baltimore Critics," *Baltimore Afro-American*, Apr. 23, 1932]

Such showings quickly led to Elton's reputation as one of the city's leading artists. Along with presentations of his

Elton graduated from Douglass in June 1926, a year behind future Supreme Court Justice Thurgood Marshall, and in the same class as musician Cab Calloway. He entered Syracuse University in 1927 as an engineering student and was paired with a roommate majoring in art. It was a fortuitous match, as Elton soon realized he was more interested in art than his planned career. He flunked his math classes and decided to pursue his true calling as he switched his major to fine art.

Still, Elton's college education had its obstacles. Both he and his brother, who followed him to Syracuse two years later, worked their way through school. Their aunts were able

[Above] Fax provided the cover artwork and a number of stories and illustrations for the interior of this teen-oriented comic. A mix of humor, helpful hints, movie and music star biographies, and inspirational stories, *Young Life* was a creation of New Age Publishers, an arm of the American Communist Party. *Young Life* #1, Summer 1945.

[Right] *Carolina Chain Gang* is a painting by Fax depicting Black prisoners toiling under the watchful eyes of an armed White guard and his dogs. *Baltimore Afro-American* on December 14, 1935.

own work, he juried exhibitions by others and picked up a part-time job at the *Afro-American* as its resident art critic. Then, in late 1933, he was the recipient of a prized commission through the Civil Works Administration (CWA).

The CWA was a New Deal program enacted in November 1933, that was designed to quickly create public works jobs for the unemployed. Elton's commission was to paint murals for Dunbar Junior High School. For this work, he received $42.50 per week. That equates to nearly $800 in today's dollars; not bad pay for a young artist.

Soon after, in early 1935, Elton took a position at Claflin College in Orangeburg, South Carolina, teaching art. A private school for Blacks, Claflin was founded by two local Methodist ministers in the wake of the Civil War. Fax spent part of two years at Claflin, when he received a letter that would change the course of his life. Elton recalled years later:

I was teaching down south when one day a letter came saying that there was a job for me in Harlem. The job was a WPA job, Augusta Savage had at that time established art classes under government sponsorship on 136th Street... [Kisseloff, Jeff, *You Must Remember This*, 1989, p.327]

Fax had actually met Augusta Savage two years previously when he made a brief visit to New York. He found his post at Claflin uninspiring and was intrigued by her letter. The opportunity to work with Savage couldn't be ignored. Her fame as a talented artist extended far beyond Harlem, and she was equally well-known as a forceful advocate for the Black art movement.

Born in Florida in 1892, Savage sought a career as a sculptor over the violent objections of her Methodist minister father, who viewed her sculpting of "graven images" as sacrilege, and subsequently "almost whipped all the art out of me." [Bearden, Romare & Henderson, Harry, *A History of African-American Artists: From 1792 to the Present*, 1993, p.168]

Years of futility followed, until she came to the attention of noted sculptor Solon Borglum. Unable to afford the tuition at the School of American Sculpture where he taught, Savage instead attended the tuition-free Cooper Union. Despite her obvious talent, Savage encountered rejection after rejection, both because of her race and her sex. After her receipt of several Rosenwald Fellowships that allowed her to study in France, Savage returned to New York City and founded her own studio. This studio, as well as her membership in the legendary 306 Group, allowed her to befriend and mentor many in the Harlem art world. Fax's

CAROLINA CHAIN GANG—By Elton Fax, Baltimore artist. Convicts are shown working at top speed between two white guards armed with shot guns and pistols. At the feet of one of the guards are two bloodhounds used to trail escaped prisoners.

invitation to join Savage provided him with immediate access and acceptance into that same world.

Through Savage, Fax met such artists as Romare Bearden, Charles Alston, and E. Simms Campbell, whose success inspired Fax to direct his talents toward commercial art. He likely also met for the first time Robert Pious, another budding commercial artist. Both Fax and Pious would follow Savage as she took on her position as the director of the newly formed Harlem Community Art Center in December 1937.

This center was the outgrowth of Savage's decade-long dream of establishing a "broad base for cultural development among the colored people of Harlem." [Thompson, John, "What Art Study Has Done in Harlem," *Chicago Defender*, May 27, 1939]

Savage eventually secured government funding through the Work Projects Administration (WPA) Federal Art Project to open the center, with Fax and Pious among the staff she hired.

Fax's fame as an artist grew through his participation in the well-received Contemporary Negro Artists exhibition in his hometown of Baltimore in February 1939, and the historic 1940 American Negro Exhibition in Chicago. However, funding for most art projects dried up with the dismantlement of the WPA in 1943. Romare Bearden wrote:

Those cuts were devastating for African-Americans, not only were black artists dependent on the WPA at a crucial phase in their development, but many other African-Americans supported their families with WPA jobs. [Bearden, Romare & Henderson, Harry, *A History of African-American Artists: From 1792 to the Present*, 1993, p.236]

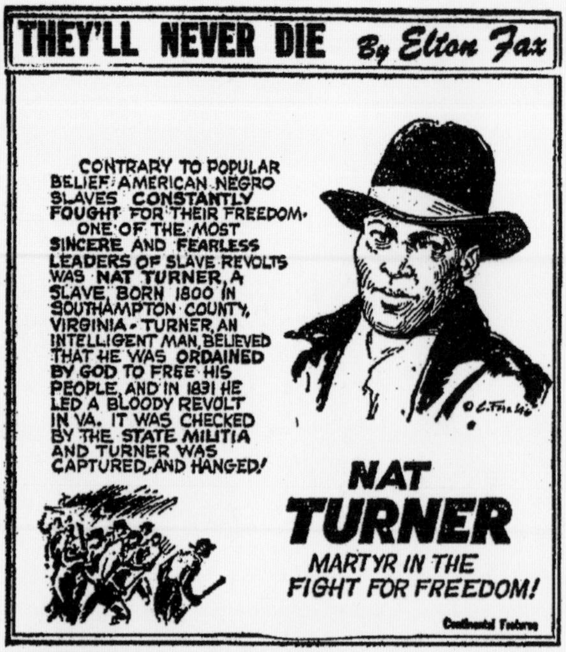
THEY'LL NEVER DIE By Elton Fax
CONTRARY TO POPULAR BELIEF AMERICAN NEGRO SLAVES CONSTANTLY FOUGHT FOR THEIR FREEDOM. ONE OF THE MOST SINCERE AND FEARLESS LEADERS OF SLAVE REVOLTS WAS NAT TURNER, A SLAVE, BORN 1800 IN SOUTHAMPTON COUNTY, VIRGINIA. TURNER, AN INTELLIGENT MAN, BELIEVED THAT HE WAS ORDAINED BY GOD TO FREE HIS PEOPLE, AND IN 1831 HE LED A BLOODY REVOLT IN VA. IT WAS CHECKED BY THE STATE MILITIA AND TURNER WAS CAPTURED, AND HANGED!
NAT TURNER
MARTYR IN THE FIGHT FOR FREEDOM!
Continental Features

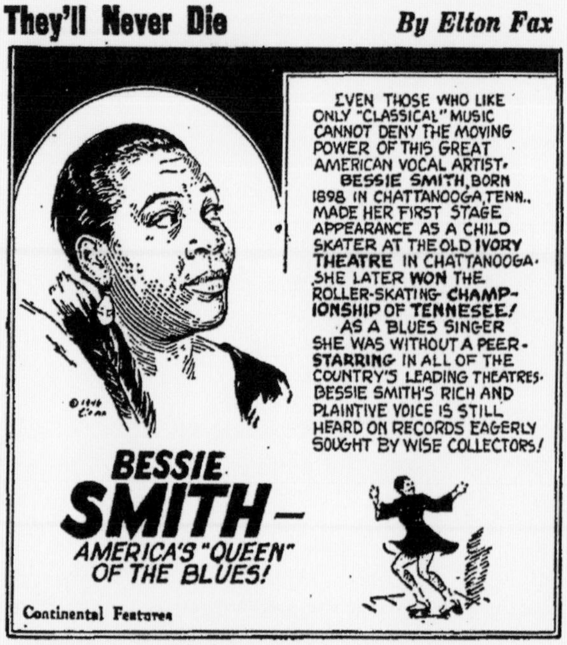
They'll Never Die By Elton Fax
EVEN THOSE WHO LIKE ONLY "CLASSICAL" MUSIC CANNOT DENY THE MOVING POWER OF THIS GREAT AMERICAN VOCAL ARTIST. BESSIE SMITH, BORN 1898 IN CHATTANOOGA, TENN., MADE HER FIRST STAGE APPEARANCE AS A CHILD SKATER AT THE OLD IVORY THEATRE IN CHATTANOOGA. SHE LATER WON THE ROLLER-SKATING CHAMPIONSHIP OF TENNESEE! AS A BLUES SINGER SHE WAS WITHOUT A PEER. STARRING IN ALL OF THE COUNTRY'S LEADING THEATRES. BESSIE SMITH'S RICH AND PLAINTIVE VOICE IS STILL HEARD ON RECORDS EAGERLY SOUGHT BY WISE COLLECTORS!
BESSIE SMITH—
AMERICA'S "QUEEN" OF THE BLUES!
Continental Features

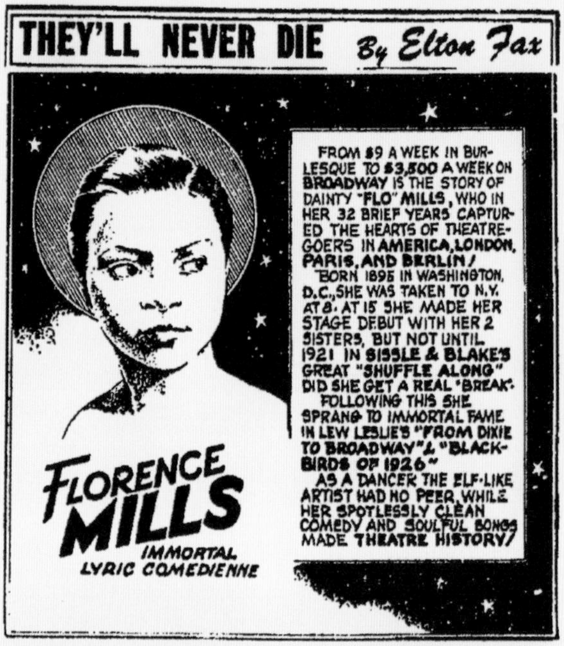
THEY'LL NEVER DIE By Elton Fax
FROM $9 A WEEK IN BURLESQUE TO $3,500 A WEEK ON BROADWAY IS THE STORY OF DAINTY "FLO" MILLS, WHO IN HER 32 BRIEF YEARS CAPTURED THE HEARTS OF THEATREGOERS IN AMERICA, LONDON, PARIS, AND BERLIN! BORN 1895 IN WASHINGTON, D.C., SHE WAS TAKEN TO N.Y. AT 8. AT 15 SHE MADE HER STAGE DEBUT WITH HER 2 SISTERS, BUT NOT UNTIL 1921 IN SISSLE & BLAKE'S GREAT "SHUFFLE ALONG" DID SHE GET A REAL "BREAK". FOLLOWING THIS SHE SPRANG TO IMMORTAL FAME IN LEW LESLIE'S "FROM DIXIE TO BROADWAY" & "BLACKBIRDS OF 1926" AS A DANCER THE ELF-LIKE ARTIST HAD NO PEER, WHILE HER SPOTLESSLY CLEAN COMEDY AND SOULFUL SONGS MADE THEATRE HISTORY!
FLORENCE MILLS
IMMORTAL LYRIC COMEDIENNE

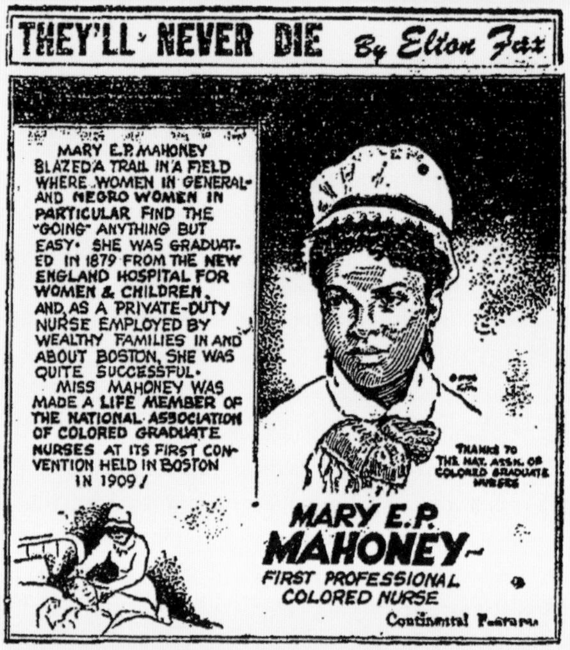
THEY'LL NEVER DIE By Elton Fax
MARY E.P. MAHONEY BLAZED A TRAIL IN A FIELD WHERE WOMEN IN GENERAL AND NEGRO WOMEN IN PARTICULAR FIND THE "GOING" ANYTHING BUT EASY. SHE WAS GRADUATED IN 1879 FROM THE NEW ENGLAND HOSPITAL FOR WOMEN & CHILDREN, AND, AS A PRIVATE-DUTY NURSE EMPLOYED BY WEALTHY FAMILIES IN AND ABOUT BOSTON, SHE WAS QUITE SUCCESSFUL. MISS MAHONEY WAS MADE A LIFE MEMBER OF THE NATIONAL ASSOCIATION OF COLORED GRADUATE NURSES AT ITS FIRST CONVENTION HELD IN BOSTON IN 1909!
THANKS TO THE NAT. ASSN. OF COLORED GRADUATE NURSES
MARY E.P. MAHONEY—
FIRST PROFESSIONAL COLORED NURSE
Continental Features

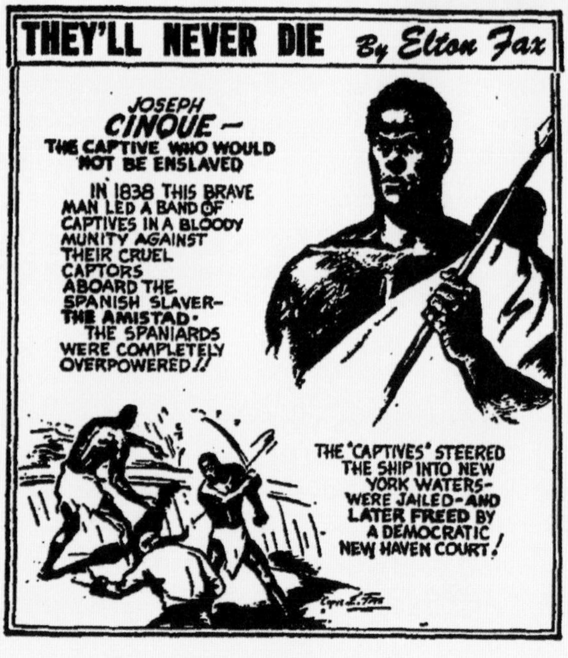
THEY'LL NEVER DIE By Elton Fax
JOSEPH CINQUE—
THE CAPTIVE WHO WOULD NOT BE ENSLAVED
IN 1838 THIS BRAVE MAN LED A BAND OF CAPTIVES IN A BLOODY MUNITY AGAINST THEIR CRUEL CAPTORS ABOARD THE SPANISH SLAVER—THE AMISTAD. THE SPANIARDS WERE COMPLETELY OVERPOWERED!!
THE "CAPTIVES" STEERED THE SHIP INTO NEW YORK WATERS—WERE JAILED—AND LATER FREED BY A DEMOCRATIC NEW HAVEN COURT!

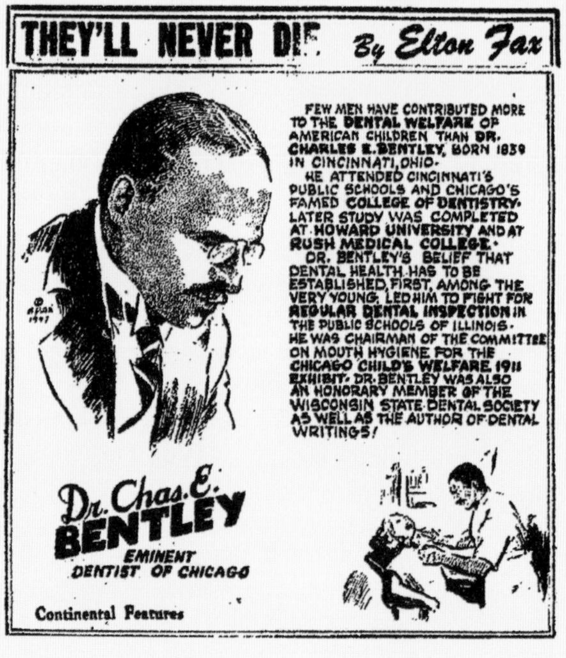
THEY'LL NEVER DIE By Elton Fax
FEW MEN HAVE CONTRIBUTED MORE TO THE DENTAL WELFARE OF AMERICAN CHILDREN THAN DR. CHARLES E. BENTLEY, BORN 1859 IN CINCINNATI, OHIO. HE ATTENDED CINCINNATI'S PUBLIC SCHOOLS AND CHICAGO'S FAMED COLLEGE OF DENTISTRY. LATER STUDY WAS COMPLETED AT HOWARD UNIVERSITY AND AT RUSH MEDICAL COLLEGE. DR. BENTLEY'S BELIEF THAT DENTAL HEALTH HAS TO BE ESTABLISHED, FIRST, AMONG THE VERY YOUNG, LED HIM TO FIGHT FOR REGULAR DENTAL INSPECTION IN THE PUBLIC SCHOOLS OF ILLINOIS. HE WAS CHAIRMAN OF THE COMMITTEE ON MOUTH HYGIENE FOR THE CHICAGO CHILD'S WELFARE 1911 EXHIBIT. DR. BENTLEY WAS ALSO AN HONORARY MEMBER OF THE WISCONSIN STATE DENTAL SOCIETY AS WELL AS THE AUTHOR OF DENTAL WRITINGS!
Dr. Chas. E. BENTLEY
EMINENT DENTIST OF CHICAGO
Continental Features

Well aware that governmental funding was coming to an end, Fax pursued a different path.

With a wife, two children, and a determination to earn a livelihood at art, I directed my energies toward drawing for pulp magazines and children's books. [Fax 1986, op. cit. p.274]

It appears that Fax's first work in that direction came while the WPA was still active. He supplied illustrations for two books produced under the WPA New Reading Materials Program in 1940, under the auspices of the Board of Education of the City of New York. The books, intended to improve the reading skills of the city's children, were Mack Corbert's *War Cloud* and *The Pygmies*, written by George D. Lipscomb, a Black author who would team with Fax again several years hence.

Following the path blazed several years earlier by Elmer Stoner, Fax began illustrating pulp magazines circa 1942. He made the rounds. Fax's drawings appeared in pulps such as *Weird Tales, Real Western,* and *Astounding.* Working for a variety of publishers and a range of genres—from science fiction, to Westerns, to sports—Fax was as versatile as he was prolific. Underscoring those skills was the additional fact that he was at the same time drawing a weekly comic strip for Black newspapers entitled *Susabelle.*

Syndicated through L. H. Stanton's Continental Features, *Susabelle* was a mostly wordless strip about a young, mischievous Black girl, somewhat akin to Marjorie Buell's more famous White tyke, Little Lulu. The strip started appearing in the late summer of 1942, in such papers as the *Philadelphia Tribune.* It ran into 1943, often appearing on the same page as Pious' editorial cartoons.

The comic book industry was booming, but at the same time it was losing many of its artists and writers—mostly White—to military service. The pulp publishers took notice. Many of them looked to cash in on this latest publishing bonanza by expanding into it. So like Stoner and other Black artists, Fax began drawing for comic books.

It is nearly impossible to know how many comic books Fax worked on. Unlike many pulp illustrations, the artwork in comic books of this era was not always signed by the artist. Individual credits didn't matter to most, and that is the way publishers and the comic studios (aka comic shops)

who produced the material preferred it. Freelancing artists, including Fax, would come and go from the shops, which were organized as a production line. Also, it behooved the publishers to maintain their anonymity so they could be replaced without the average reader noticing the change.

However, Fax did sign some of his work. The "Bulls-Eye Bill" stories in *Target Comics* vol. 5 #8 (Feb. 1945) and vol. 6 #3 (May 1945) both carry his signature. Fax's artwork was indicative of his experience as an illustrator. It showed clean, precise line-work, with almost no unnecessary shading or crosshatching. He was a more than competent comics artist.

A brief biographical piece appeared in Ramona Lowe's "New York in Review" column that ran in the *Chicago Defender* on December 2, 1944. It mentioned that Fax had worked for Curtis Publishing. Curtis owned the well-known *Parents' Magazine,* and their comic book division, Novelty Press, produced *Target Comics.* A few months later, in her "Land of the Noble Free" column, Layle Lane expanded upon that by noting that Fax "worked for the *Parents' Magazine* illustrating *True Comics.*" [Lane, Layle, "Land of the Noble Free," *New York Age,* Feb. 2, 1945]

The material that appeared in both *Target Comics* and *True Comics* was produced by Lloyd Jacquet's Funnies, Inc. comic shop. Once again, this follows the path blazed by other Black artists who worked through comic shops to avoid dealing directly with publishers who may balk at hiring a Black.

Unfortunately, none of Fax's work for *True Comics* was signed, but extrapolating from the known information, it is assumed his work appeared in issues published in 1944-1945.

It is noteworthy that Robert Pious, Fax's co-worker from his Harlem Community Art Center days, was also working through Funnies Inc. at the same time. Furthermore, they worked for the same pulp magazine publishers previously; another link. These connections suggest a friendship, or at least a working relationship, between the two artists. Perhaps even to the point that they worked as a team on some assignments.

It appears that Fax's Funnies Inc. assignments ended circa 1945—once again, when most of the White artists returned from the war—but he wasn't done with comics entirely.

Young Life appeared on newsstands in February 1945, with the first issue cover-dated Summer 1945. It was a teen-oriented comic, with a mix of humor, helpful hints, movie and music

Starting in 1945 and running through the late 1940s, Fax drew a biographical panel cartoon entitled *They'll Never Die,* depicting Black notables. These cartoons were syndicated by Continental Features to Black newspapers, and were reprinted numerous times.

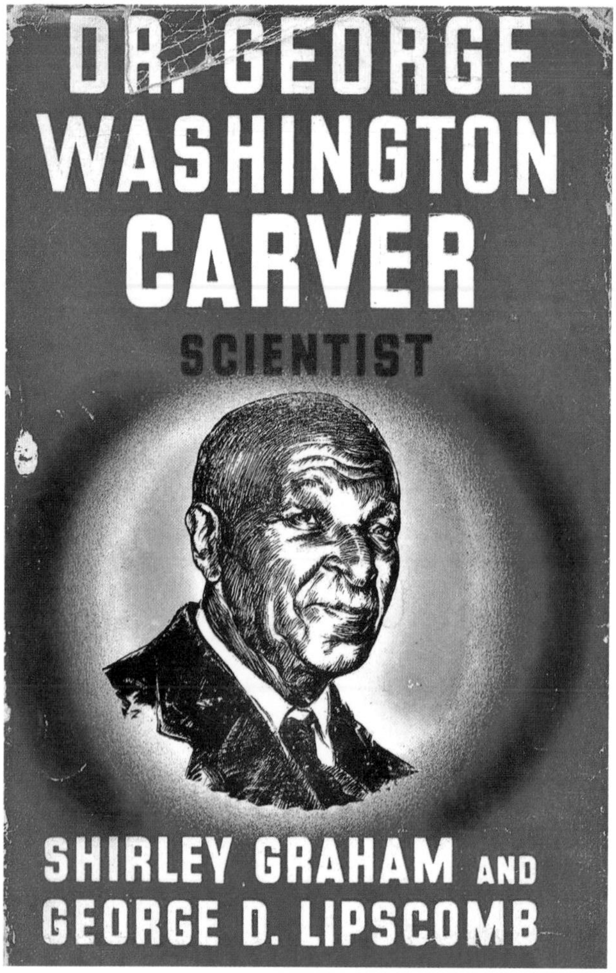
DR. GEORGE
WASHINGTON
CARVER
SCIENTIST
SHIRLEY GRAHAM AND
GEORGE D. LIPSCOMB

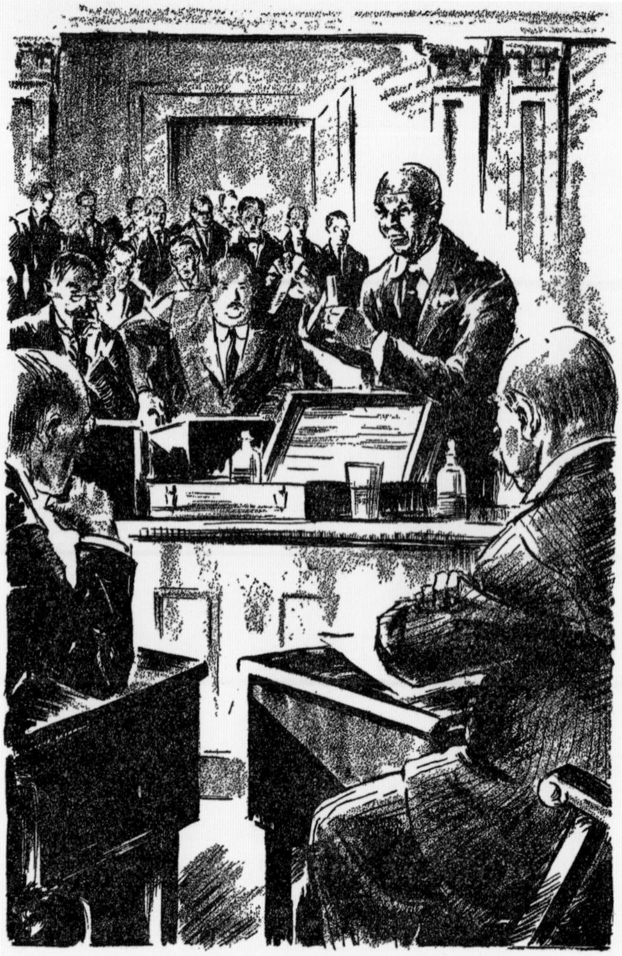

"Gentlemen, I give you the peanut!"

star bios, and inspirational stories. Fax provided the signed cover artwork and a number of stories and illustrations on its interior. He also contributed to the title's second issue and to its final few issues when it was renamed *Teen Life*.

The publisher of these comics was New Age Publishers, which up to that point had only published one other title, *Hollywood Comics*, a funny-animal anthology. The seemingly innocuous output concealed a fact that may have troubled some parents if they knew who actually was behind the publication of these comics. New Age Publishers was the reincarnation of American Youth for Democracy, a publishing arm of the American Communist Party. Furthermore, named as its owner in the owner's statement which appeared in *Teen Life* #4 was Lev Gleason.

Gleason was a well-known comic book publisher. He had been in the business since the 1920s, moving from advertising to owning his own company. While he published a number of comic titles, he was best known for *Crime Does Not Pay* and similarly-themed crime comics. These were notoriously violent, often condemned, and extremely well-selling. They spawned numerous imitators and were an impetus to the growing concern parents and others had about comic books.

Additionally, Lev Gleason was a Communist. He often denied membership, but he had published Party materials for years and had been involved in organizations formed under its auspices. These activities brought him to the attention of the FBI, and in 1947 he was indicted along with 16 others for contempt of Congress based upon his testimony to that body in its investigation of the Joint Anti-Fascist Refugee Committee in 1946. Although he was only fined for his actions, it was front page news and Gleason bore its brand for years.

That Fax was such a significant contributor to the New Age comics seems to indicate that he was at least sympathetic to the group behind them. Even though it was a hazardous connection to have as the Cold War was beginning, it was not an unusual one for Black intellectuals. Paul Robeson, W. E. B. Du Bois, and fellow artist Owen Middleton were among the influential Blacks who openly embraced Communist goals, even though they may have never been official Party members. Fax was subtler, more circumspect. Still, his acceptance of work on the New Age comics, along with work produced for the socialistic Trade Union New Service, revealed Fax's growing admiration for left-wing policies.

There was one other bit of comic book artwork that can likely be attributed to Fax, even if it cannot be absolutely

Dr. George Washington Carver, Scientist was written by Shirley Graham Du Bois and George D. Lipscomb. Fax provided the cover and interior illustrations to this biography of the great scientist. April 1944; Julian Messner, Inc.

proven. It was the artwork to a story written by George D. Lipscomb, Fax's former collaborator at the WPA. Pertinent to the subject at hand, Lipscomb was quite possibly the only Black writer of comics' "Golden Age."

George Dewey Lipscomb was from Freeport, Illinois, born September 7, 1898. He was the son of Alice and John Lipscomb, who was born a slave and worked as a night watchman in George's youth. Early on, George showed his remarkable ability as a debater, winning the statewide debating contest in June 1916, despite being only a junior at Freeport High School. His winning oratory, "The Future of the American Negro," gained him near-unanimous praise from the judges. Lipscomb's success earned him a scholarship to Northwestern University.

Lipscomb's education, though, was interrupted by the entry of the U.S into World War I. While a student at Northwestern, Lipscomb volunteered for the Army and served for two months in late 1918 before peace was declared. He then resumed his studies and, once again, was the stand-out on the school's debate team.

After graduation, Lipscomb held several posts, including working as a teacher of dramatic art at the Chicago University of Music; this was followed by a position at Wiley College in Marshall, Texas, where he was head of the English department. While there, he won first prize in a literary contest sponsored by *Opportunity* magazine, an academic journal published by the National Urban League. When the magazine published his winning one-act play, *Frances*, it gave him national recognition as a respected author.

Lipscomb's reputation took an even greater jump with the April 1944 publication of his latest book, *Dr. George Washington Carver, Scientist*. This biography was co-written with author Shirley Graham, who was reportedly brought in to help after Lipscomb completed the first draft. Graham was a prominent Black writer, playwright, and political activist, whose Leftist beliefs and avowed membership in the American Communist Party made her a longtime target of the FBI. In 1943, she was named Field Secretary of the NAACP, and in 1951 she married W. E. B. Du Bois. Her name recognition would help sell books, which made her the right match for the lesser-known Lipscomb.

Illustrating the Carver book was Elton Fax. It was his first true book illustration job, and the positive reception given the book by critics and readers extended to his drawings.

Lipscomb would continue teaching and writing, but in 1945, he made news when he wrote a letter to U.S. Senator Theodore G. Bilbo of Mississippi, an unabashed White supremacist and a leading advocate for segregation of the races. He agreed, though, with Black separatists such as Marcus Garvey, who called for the repatriation of Blacks back to Africa. Lipscomb referenced this stand in his letter and made Bilbo an interesting offer. He wrote:

"I'll go back to Africa if the Congress will vote me my back pay, I want every cent of the money you stole from my fathers from 1619 to 1863. I mean wages for the work they did in slavery.

"Just sixty-five cents an hour pay us, now that you say you don't need us any more and we're a problem. Figure it on a basis of this 40-hour week to which we've returned after helping to trounce Japan."

Lipscomb calculated that the sum total of money he and his wife were owed came to $1,256,387.20. [Conrad, Earl, "Back to Africa for $1,256,387.20," Chicago Defender, Sept. 8, 1945]

The next year, Lipscomb's *Tales from the Land of Simba* was published. This collection of five adventure stories featured illustrations by Felice Worden. But when one of the stories—"Simba Bwana, Lion Master"—was adapted by Lipscomb for inclusion in the *Jack Armstrong #1* (Nov. 1947) comic book, she wasn't the artist. Instead, the uncredited illustrator was probably Fax. This assumption is based upon the fact that not only had Fax previously worked with Lipscomb, but that he was also an experienced comic artist who had worked for the comic's publisher, Parents Press, in the past.

Although this was likely Fax's final comic book work (if indeed it was his work), it was only the beginning for Lipscomb.

In March 1947, the Gilberton Company began the syndication of a Sunday comic strip version of their *Classics Illustrated* comic book. With art and story provided by the Iger Studio, the strips contained adaptations of such literary masterpieces as *Alice in Wonderland*, *The Man in the Iron Mask*, and *Kidnapped*. In June of that year, an adaptation of Charles Dickens *David Copperfield* began running, with text written by Lipscomb. Curiously, these comic strip versions ran a year before the comic book versions appearing in issues of *Classics Illustrated*. Although the comic strips were all published in the period from March 1947 to March 1948, the comic book versions were spread out over the next three years. *David Copperfield*, for example, appeared in *Classics Illustrated #48* (June 1948).

Over the course of the one-year run of the comic strip, Lipscomb also provided scripts for: James Fenimore Cooper's "The Spy" in *Classics Illustrated #51* (Sept. 1948),

Dickens' *A Christmas Carol* from *Classics Illustrated* #53 (Nov. 1948), Sir Walter Scott's "The Lady of the Lake," which appeared in *Classics Illustrated* #75 (Sept. 1950), and the W.H. Hudson *Green Mansions* adaptation appearing in *Classics Illustrated* #90 (Dec. 1951).

There may have been even more. Lipscomb's obituary from January 26, 1957 mentions that his comic adaptations included work by Shakespeare. This is likely a reference to the *Julius Caesar* adaptation that ran in both the comic strip version and in *Classics Illustrated* #68 (Feb. 1950).

Meanwhile, Elton Fax had moved on. After the success of the George Washington Carver book, he began picking up more illustration assignments. In 1944, he drew both the cover to the November issue of *Story Parade* and interior illustrations for "Forever Christmas Tree" appearing in the December *Child Life* magazine. This led to his career as a children's book illustrator, a high-profile and very profitable direction that carried through the rest of his life.

Fax didn't abandon Black publications, though. Starting in 1945 and running through the late 1940s, he drew a biographical panel cartoon titled *They'll Never Die*, which depicted Black notables. Additionally, he illustrated Lila Marshall's "Viney Taylor" short-story for *Negro Story* magazine. More significantly, Fax provided the artwork for several posters that have since become iconic.

The first of these appeared in the summer of 1943, as a large placard on the side of buses in Gary, Indiana, bearing the stern visage of a helmeted Black soldier. Bearing the words, "500,000 of these lads are fighting for you! Let them and theirs share in our democracy," the poster was drawn by Fax under his role as the art consultant for the Association for Tolerance in America. This organization, under the direction of Black columnist George S. Schuyler, was formed in the attempt to eliminate racial prejudice through "mass education." ["Plan Racial Education for Whites," *Chicago Defender*, Feb. 27, 1943]

Fax also drew two posters for the NAACP. The first, in 1944, proclaimed the group's Wartime Conference for Peace being held in Chicago that July. It featured the striking image of a dead "Jim Crow," strangled by the hand of the NAACP. Hanging from the bird's legs were the flags of Nazi Germany and Japan, a damning connection that would not be lost on anyone viewing it.

[Above] This photograph features the teaching staff of the WPA-funded Harlem Community Art Center. Among the people are Elton C. Fax [far left] and Robert S. Pious, with a straw hat under his arm. C. 1938, © Schomburg Center for Research in Black Culture.

[Right] *David Copperfield* was an adaptation of the Dickens' classic by George D. Lipscomb as it appeared in the *Illustrated Classics* comic strip on June 14, 1947. A year later, Gilberton published it again in *Classics Illustrated* #48, June 1948.

New York Post • Illustrated CLASSIC
SATURDAY, JUNE 14, 1947

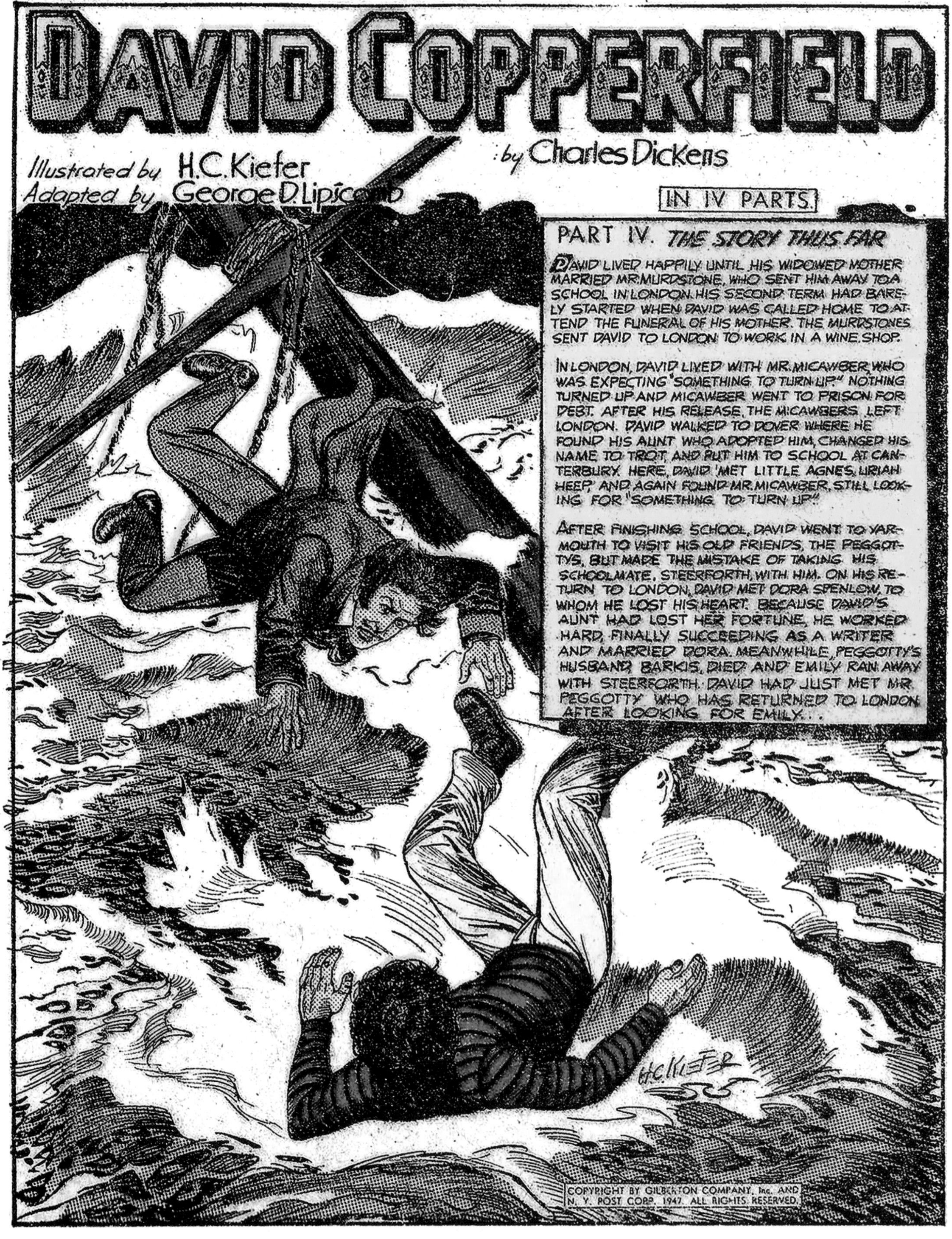
DAVID COPPERFIELD
by Charles Dickens
Illustrated by H.C. Kiefer
Adapted by George D. Lipscomb
IN IV PARTS.
PART IV. THE STORY THUS FAR
DAVID LIVED HAPPILY UNTIL HIS WIDOWED MOTHER MARRIED MR. MURDSTONE, WHO SENT HIM AWAY TO A SCHOOL IN LONDON. HIS SECOND TERM HAD BARELY STARTED WHEN DAVID WAS CALLED HOME TO ATTEND THE FUNERAL OF HIS MOTHER. THE MURDSTONES SENT DAVID TO LONDON TO WORK IN A WINE SHOP.
IN LONDON, DAVID LIVED WITH MR. MICAWBER, WHO WAS EXPECTING "SOMETHING TO TURN UP." NOTHING TURNED UP AND MICAWBER WENT TO PRISON FOR DEBT. AFTER HIS RELEASE, THE MICAWBERS LEFT LONDON. DAVID WALKED TO DOVER WHERE HE FOUND HIS AUNT WHO ADOPTED HIM, CHANGED HIS NAME TO TROT, AND PUT HIM TO SCHOOL AT CANTERBURY. HERE, DAVID MET LITTLE AGNES, URIAH HEEP, AND AGAIN FOUND MR. MICAWBER, STILL LOOKING FOR "SOMETHING TO TURN UP."
AFTER FINISHING SCHOOL, DAVID WENT TO YARMOUTH TO VISIT HIS OLD FRIENDS, THE PEGGOTTYS, BUT MADE THE MISTAKE OF TAKING HIS SCHOOLMATE, STEERFORTH, WITH HIM. ON HIS RETURN TO LONDON, DAVID MET DORA SPENLOW, TO WHOM HE LOST HIS HEART. BECAUSE DAVID'S AUNT HAD LOST HER FORTUNE, HE WORKED HARD, FINALLY SUCCEEDING AS A WRITER AND MARRIED DORA. MEANWHILE, PEGGOTTY'S HUSBAND, BARKIS, DIED AND EMILY RAN AWAY WITH STEERFORTH. DAVID HAD JUST MET MR. PEGGOTTY WHO HAS RETURNED TO LONDON AFTER LOOKING FOR EMILY. .
H.C. KIEFER
COPYRIGHT BY GILBERTON COMPANY, Inc. AND N. Y. POST CORP. 1947. ALL RIGHTS RESERVED.

SUSABELLE
By Elton Fax
IDEA
Copyr. E. FAX 1943
CONTINENTAL FEATURES

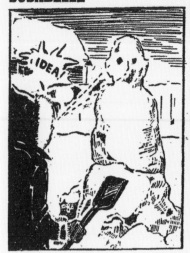

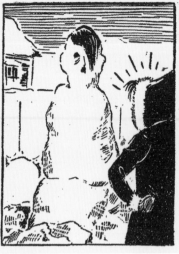

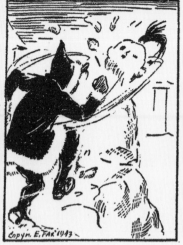

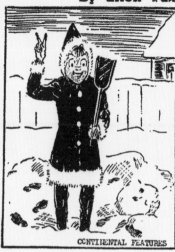

Two years later, the 8th Annual Youth Conference in New Orleans was the poster subject. For this, Fax drew a well-dressed, young Black man holding a scale of justice—a simple image demanding equality. As Fax told interviewer Ramona Lowe:

Art transcends race. I want to command respect on merit and not just because I am a Negro. [Lowe, Ramona, "New York in Review," *Chicago Defender*, Dec. 2, 1944]

In the years that followed, Fax achieved even more success in the commercial art field, as a painter, and as an author—most notably for the book *Seventeen Black Artists* in 1971. He became more outspoken in his views on social justice, and in 1953, he and his family moved to Mexico. He publicly claimed it was a move prompted by his youngest daughter's studies at a university in that country, but years later, he clarified his position, stating that the move owed more to his "seeking a needed respite from social tensions." [Fax 1986, op. cit. p.274]

Fax eventually returned to the United States but continued his criticism of America's racial problems and openly moved further left in his beliefs. After a trip to La Paz, Bolivia, in 1955, he was asked by a U.S. embassy official if he had witnessed any Communist activity during his visit. Fax was taken aback by the question and documented his reaction.

I was offended by the suggestion that I had been expected to eavesdrop, and then report, particularly in the midst of the hunger and misery of the city called "Peace." With a firm grip on my temper I kept my cool knowing full well that I would never have snitched on my hosts even if their "Communism" had paraded itself stark naked before me. [Fax 1986, op. cit. p.277]

Despite his political leanings, Fax was chosen in 1964 by the U.S. State Department to represent the country on a goodwill tour of east Africa. As time went on, he accrued numerous honors—including the Coretta Scott King Award from the American Library Association in 1972—for his art and for his writing. In 1990, he was the recipient of the Chancellor's Award from his alma mater, Syracuse University.

Elton Clay Fax died in Queens, New York on May 13, 1993. He lived as the embodiment of W. E. B. Du Bois' "double consciousness," which the noted Black activist described in his treatise, *The Souls of Black Folk*.

The history of the American Negro is the history of this strife—this longing to attain self-conscious manhood, to merge his double self into a better and truer self. In this merging he wishes neither of the older selves to be lost. He would not Africanize America, for America has too much to teach the world and Africa. He would not bleach his Negro soul in a flood of white Americanism, for he knows that Negro blood has a message for the world. He simply wishes to make it possible for a man to be both a Negro and an American, without being cursed and spit upon by his fellows, without having the doors of Opportunity closed roughly in his face. [Du Bois, W. E. B., *The Souls of Black Folk: Essays and Sketches*, 1903, p.3]

Fax surely wasn't alone in this. His artist peers, other Blacks, lived the same reality. But his success as an artist and author intensified the dichotomy.

[Above] Fax's *Susabelle* was a mostly wordless strip about a young, mischievous Black girl and her older sister. Continental Features syndicated the strip, which started appearing in the late summer of 1942 and ran into 1943. This early example is from September 19, 1942.

[Right] When the *Baltimore Afro-American* debuted their new comics section in early 1948, Fax took over the *Jim Steele* strip from the original artist, Melvin Tapley. At the same time, Robert S. Pious' *Facts On The Negros of World War Two* began appearing in the "Afro Comics" section of the same paper. March 6, 1948; Continental Features.

AFRO COMICS

Four Full Pages of Funnies by Nationally-Known Artists

TED SHEARER
ELTON FAX & C. VAN BUREN
R. S. PIOUS
TAP MELVIN

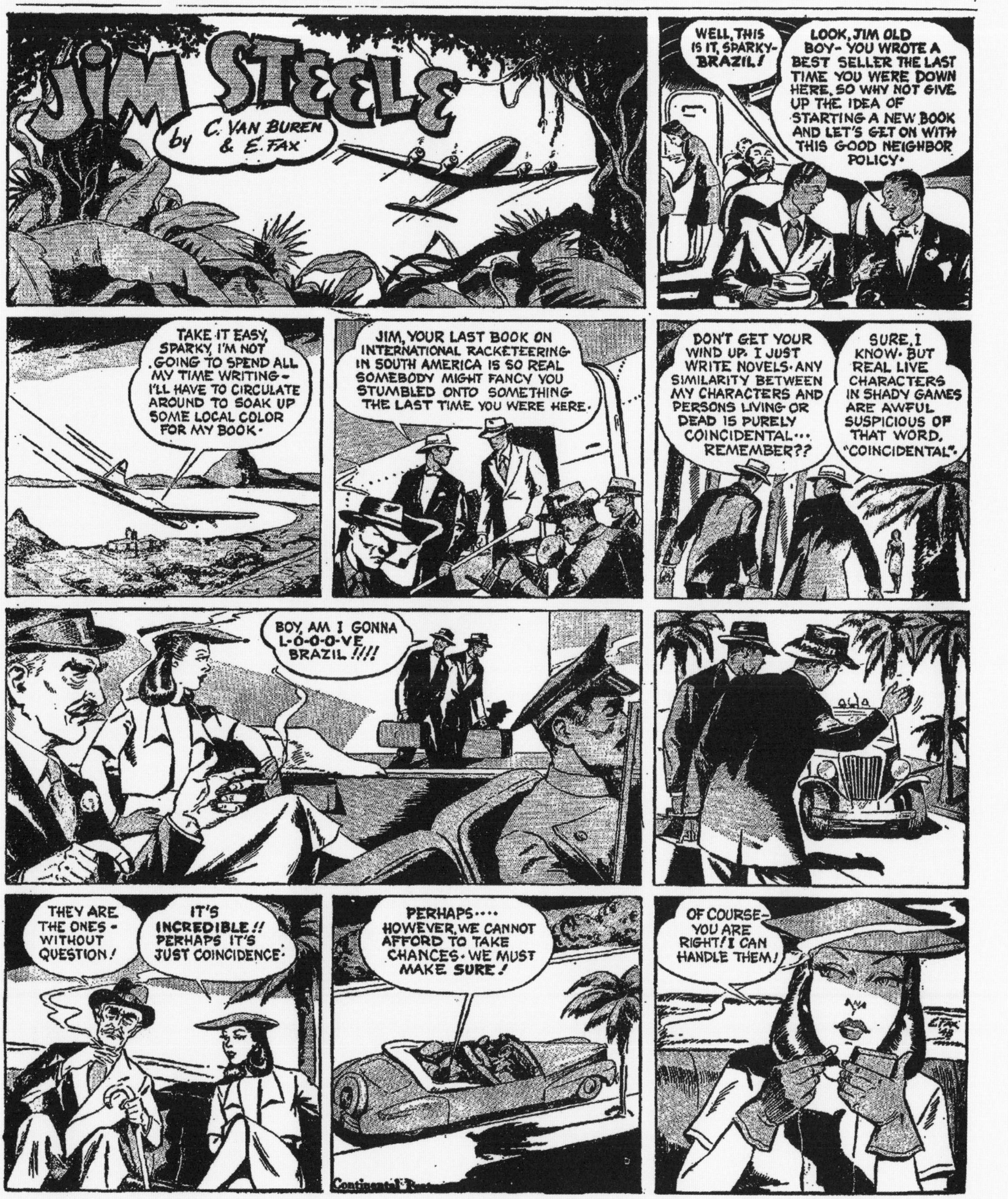

JIM STEELE
by C. VAN BUREN & E. FAX
WELL, THIS IS IT, SPARKY-BRAZIL!
LOOK, JIM OLD BOY- YOU WROTE A BEST SELLER THE LAST TIME YOU WERE DOWN HERE, SO WHY NOT GIVE UP THE IDEA OF STARTING A NEW BOOK AND LET'S GET ON WITH THIS GOOD NEIGHBOR POLICY.
TAKE IT EASY, SPARKY, I'M NOT GOING TO SPEND ALL MY TIME WRITING- I'LL HAVE TO CIRCULATE AROUND TO SOAK UP SOME LOCAL COLOR FOR MY BOOK.
JIM, YOUR LAST BOOK ON INTERNATIONAL RACKETEERING IN SOUTH AMERICA IS SO REAL SOMEBODY MIGHT FANCY YOU STUMBLED ONTO SOMETHING THE LAST TIME YOU WERE HERE.
DON'T GET YOUR WIND UP. I JUST WRITE NOVELS. ANY SIMILARITY BETWEEN MY CHARACTERS AND PERSONS LIVING OR DEAD IS PURELY COINCIDENTAL... REMEMBER??
SURE, I KNOW. BUT REAL LIVE CHARACTERS IN SHADY GAMES ARE AWFUL SUSPICIOUS OF THAT WORD, "COINCIDENTAL".
BOY, AM I GONNA L-O-O-O-VE BRAZIL !!!!
THEY ARE THE ONES - WITHOUT QUESTION!
IT'S INCREDIBLE!! PERHAPS IT'S JUST COINCIDENCE.
PERHAPS.... HOWEVER, WE CANNOT AFFORD TO TAKE CHANCES. WE MUST MAKE SURE!
OF COURSE- YOU ARE RIGHT! I CAN HANDLE THEM!

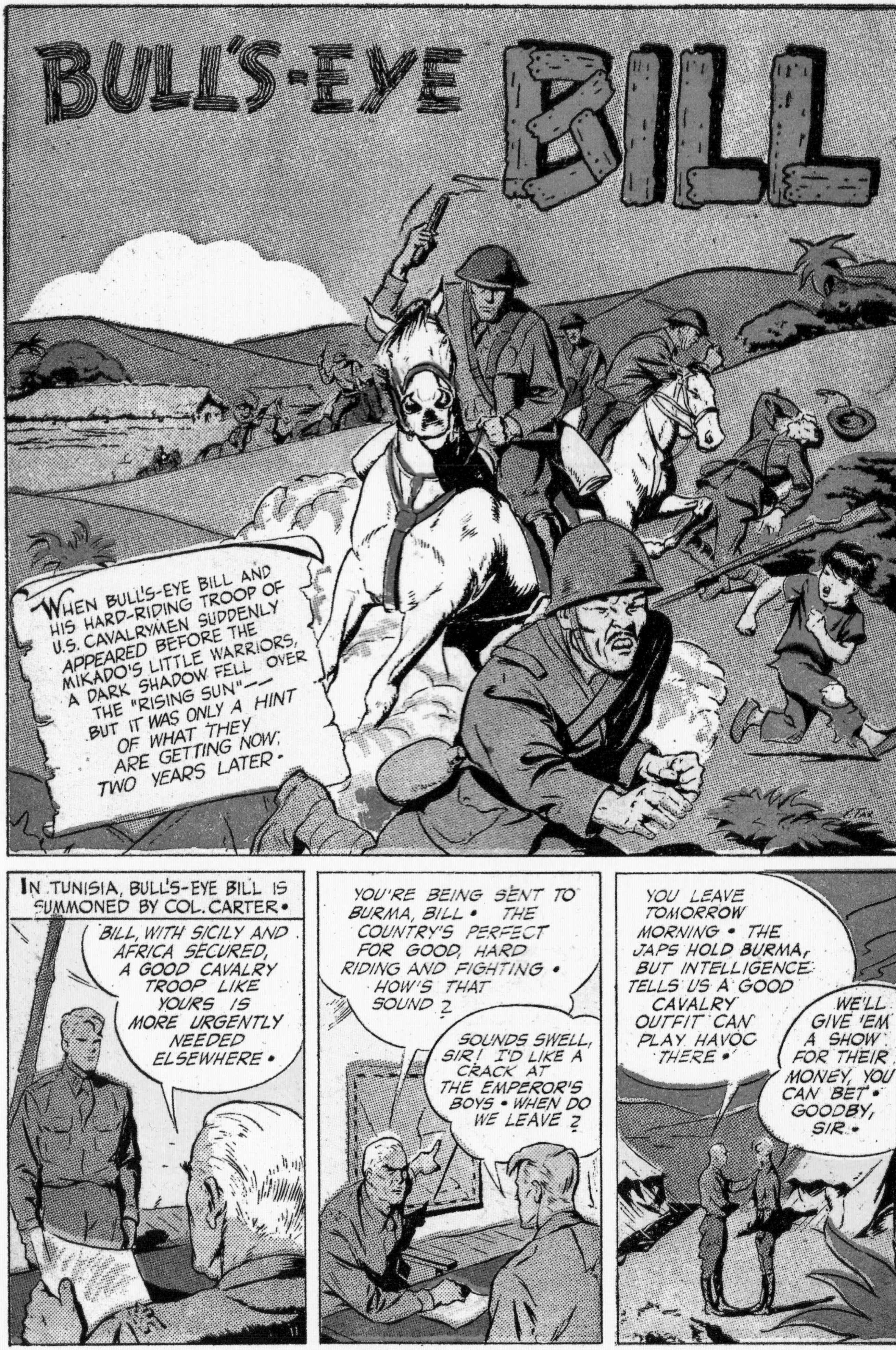
BULL'S-EYE BILL
WHEN BULL'S-EYE BILL AND HIS HARD-RIDING TROOP OF U.S. CAVALRYMEN SUDDENLY APPEARED BEFORE THE MIKADO'S LITTLE WARRIORS, A DARK SHADOW FELL OVER THE "RISING SUN"-- BUT IT WAS ONLY A HINT OF WHAT THEY ARE GETTING NOW, TWO YEARS LATER.
IN TUNISIA, BULL'S-EYE BILL IS SUMMONED BY COL. CARTER.
BILL, WITH SICILY AND AFRICA SECURED, A GOOD CAVALRY TROOP LIKE YOURS IS MORE URGENTLY NEEDED ELSEWHERE.
YOU'RE BEING SENT TO BURMA, BILL. THE COUNTRY'S PERFECT FOR GOOD, HARD RIDING AND FIGHTING. HOW'S THAT SOUND ?
SOUNDS SWELL, SIR! I'D LIKE A CRACK AT THE EMPEROR'S BOYS. WHEN DO WE LEAVE ?
YOU LEAVE TOMORROW MORNING. THE JAPS HOLD BURMA, BUT INTELLIGENCE TELLS US A GOOD CAVALRY OUTFIT CAN PLAY HAVOC THERE.
WE'LL GIVE 'EM A SHOW FOR THEIR MONEY, YOU CAN BET. GOODBY, SIR.

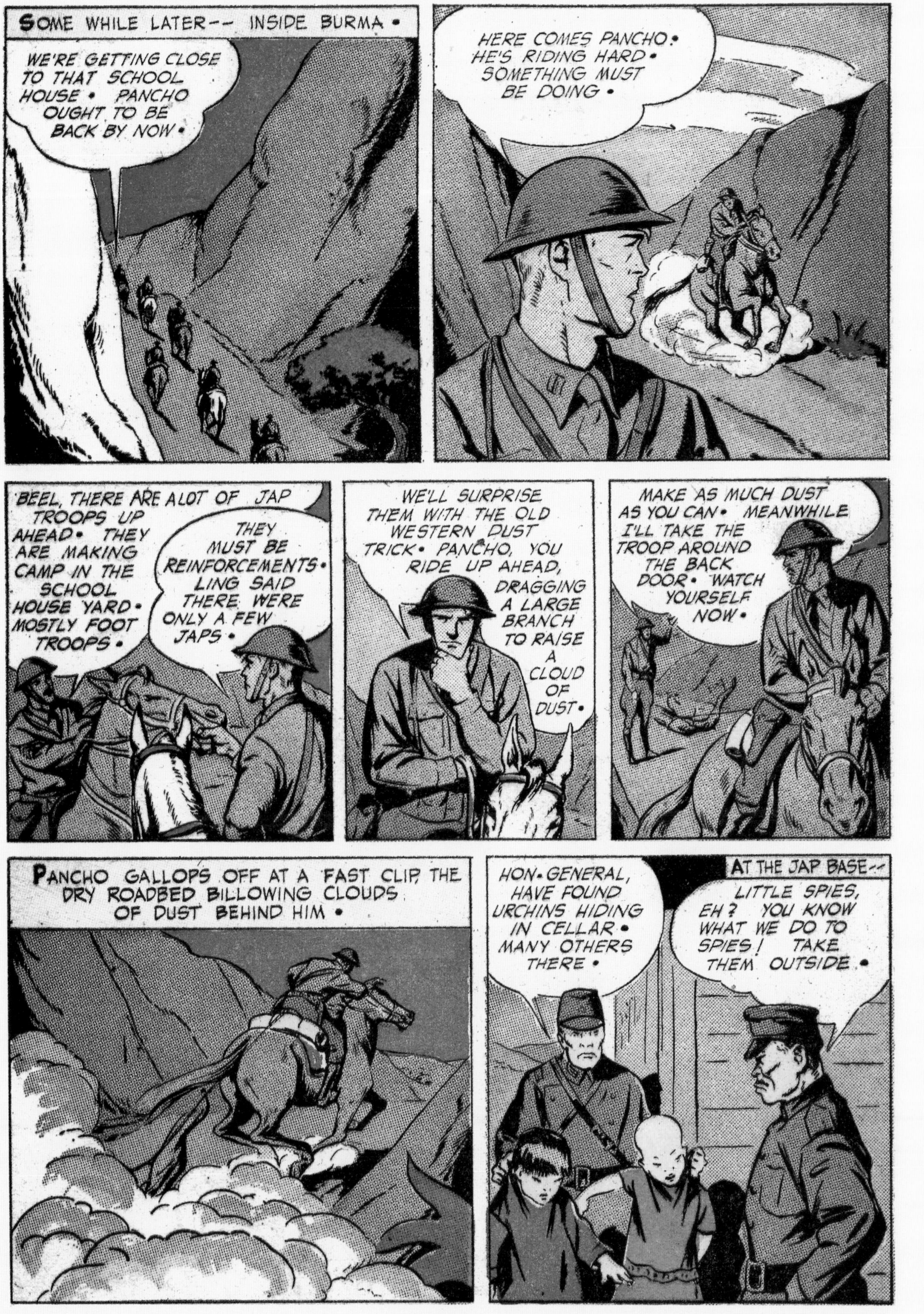
SOME WHILE LATER-- INSIDE BURMA •
WE'RE GETTING CLOSE TO THAT SCHOOL HOUSE • PANCHO OUGHT TO BE BACK BY NOW •
HERE COMES PANCHO • HE'S RIDING HARD • SOMETHING MUST BE DOING •
BEEL, THERE ARE ALOT OF JAP TROOPS UP AHEAD • THEY ARE MAKING CAMP IN THE SCHOOL HOUSE YARD • MOSTLY FOOT TROOPS •
THEY MUST BE REINFORCEMENTS • LING SAID THERE WERE ONLY A FEW JAPS •
WE'LL SURPRISE THEM WITH THE OLD WESTERN DUST TRICK • PANCHO, YOU RIDE UP AHEAD, DRAGGING A LARGE BRANCH TO RAISE A CLOUD OF DUST •
MAKE AS MUCH DUST AS YOU CAN • MEANWHILE I'LL TAKE THE TROOP AROUND THE BACK DOOR • WATCH YOURSELF NOW •
PANCHO GALLOPS OFF AT A FAST CLIP, THE DRY ROADBED BILLOWING CLOUDS OF DUST BEHIND HIM •
AT THE JAP BASE--
HON • GENERAL, HAVE FOUND URCHINS HIDING IN CELLAR • MANY OTHERS THERE •
LITTLE SPIES, EH? YOU KNOW WHAT WE DO TO SPIES! TAKE THEM OUTSIDE •

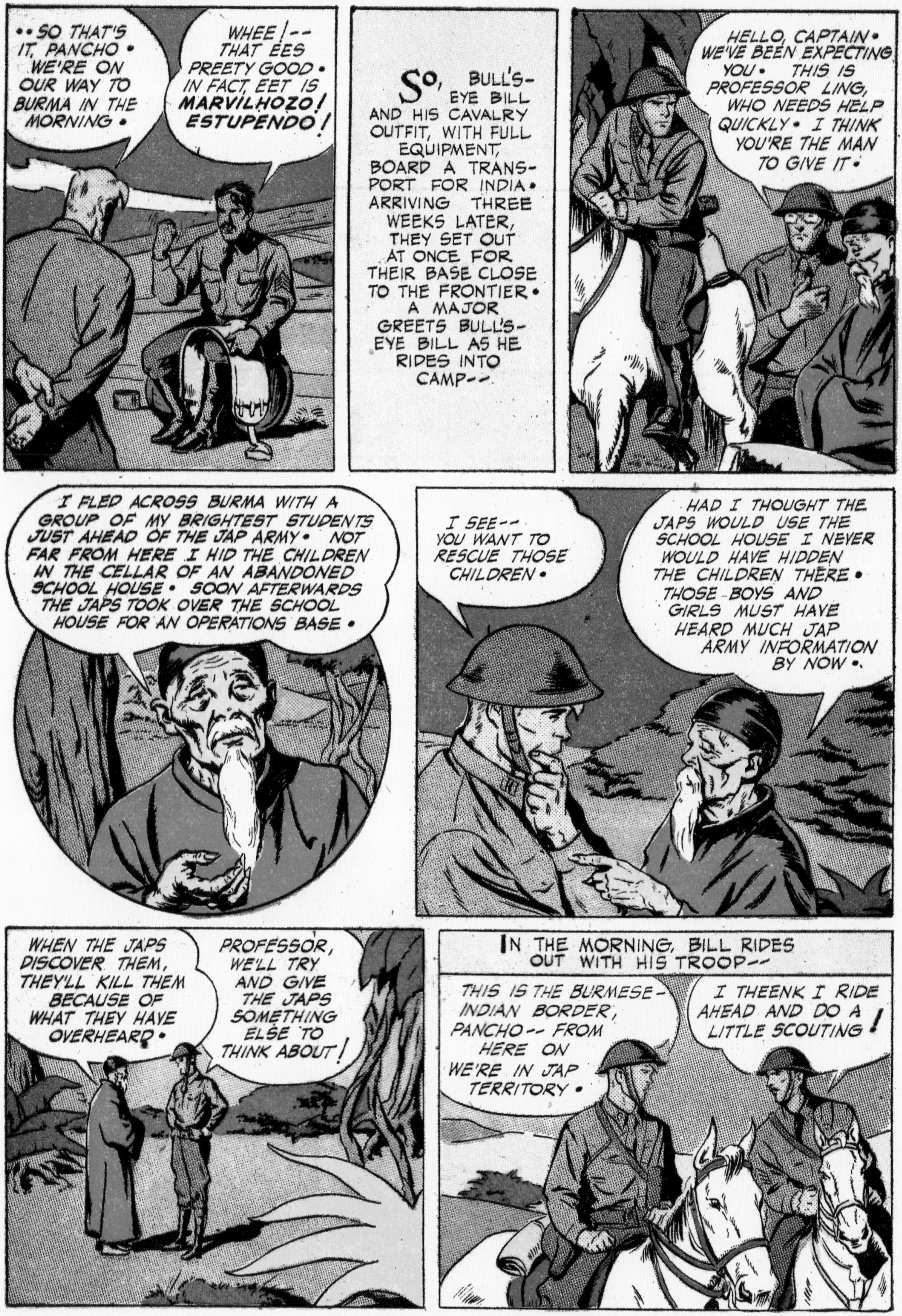
• • SO THAT'S IT, PANCHO • WE'RE ON OUR WAY TO BURMA IN THE MORNING •
WHEE ! - - THAT EES PREETY GOOD • IN FACT, EET IS MARVILHOZO ! ESTUPENDO !
SO, BULL'S-EYE BILL AND HIS CAVALRY OUTFIT, WITH FULL EQUIPMENT, BOARD A TRANSPORT FOR INDIA • ARRIVING THREE WEEKS LATER, THEY SET OUT AT ONCE FOR THEIR BASE CLOSE TO THE FRONTIER • A MAJOR GREETS BULL'S-EYE BILL AS HE RIDES INTO CAMP - -
HELLO, CAPTAIN • WE'VE BEEN EXPECTING YOU • THIS IS PROFESSOR LING, WHO NEEDS HELP QUICKLY • I THINK YOU'RE THE MAN TO GIVE IT •
I FLED ACROSS BURMA WITH A GROUP OF MY BRIGHTEST STUDENTS JUST AHEAD OF THE JAP ARMY • NOT FAR FROM HERE I HID THE CHILDREN IN THE CELLAR OF AN ABANDONED SCHOOL HOUSE • SOON AFTERWARDS THE JAPS TOOK OVER THE SCHOOL HOUSE FOR AN OPERATIONS BASE •
I SEE - - YOU WANT TO RESCUE THOSE CHILDREN •
HAD I THOUGHT THE JAPS WOULD USE THE SCHOOL HOUSE I NEVER WOULD HAVE HIDDEN THE CHILDREN THERE • THOSE BOYS AND GIRLS MUST HAVE HEARD MUCH JAP ARMY INFORMATION BY NOW •
WHEN THE JAPS DISCOVER THEM, THEY'LL KILL THEM BECAUSE OF WHAT THEY HAVE OVERHEARD •
PROFESSOR, WE'LL TRY AND GIVE THE JAPS SOMETHING ELSE TO THINK ABOUT !
IN THE MORNING, BILL RIDES OUT WITH HIS TROOP - -
THIS IS THE BURMESE-INDIAN BORDER, PANCHO - - FROM HERE ON WE'RE IN JAP TERRITORY •
I THEENK I RIDE AHEAD AND DO A LITTLE SCOUTING !

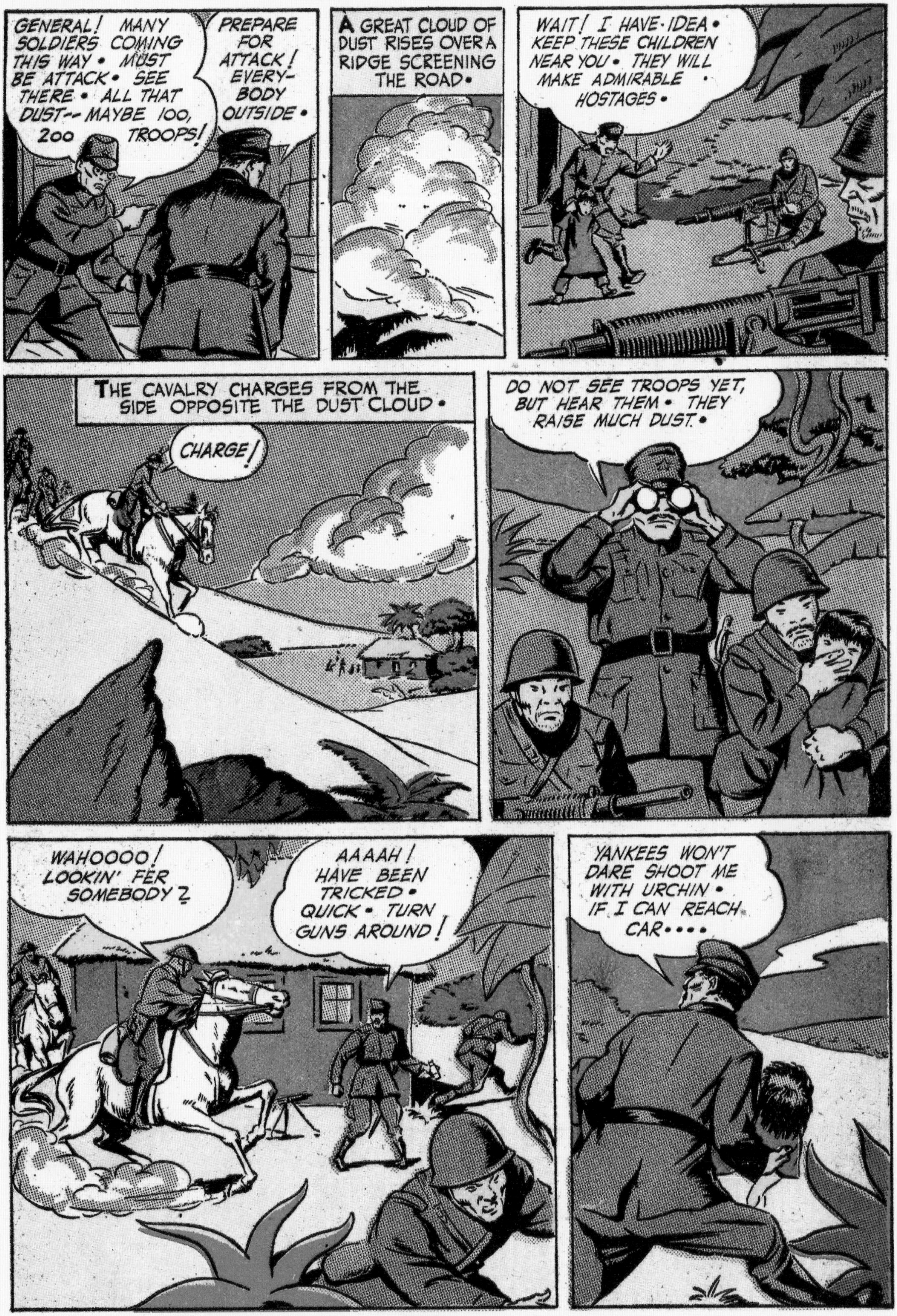

GENERAL! MANY SOLDIERS COMING THIS WAY • MUST BE ATTACK • SEE THERE • ALL THAT DUST-- MAYBE 100, 200 TROOPS!
PREPARE FOR ATTACK! EVERY-BODY OUTSIDE •
A GREAT CLOUD OF DUST RISES OVER A RIDGE SCREENING THE ROAD •
WAIT! I HAVE IDEA • KEEP THESE CHILDREN NEAR YOU • THEY WILL MAKE ADMIRABLE HOSTAGES •
THE CAVALRY CHARGES FROM THE SIDE OPPOSITE THE DUST CLOUD •
CHARGE!
DO NOT SEE TROOPS YET, BUT HEAR THEM • THEY RAISE MUCH DUST •
WAHOOOO! LOOKIN' FER SOMEBODY ?
AAAAH! HAVE BEEN TRICKED • QUICK • TURN GUNS AROUND!
YANKEES WON'T DARE SHOOT ME WITH URCHIN • IF I CAN REACH CAR • • • •

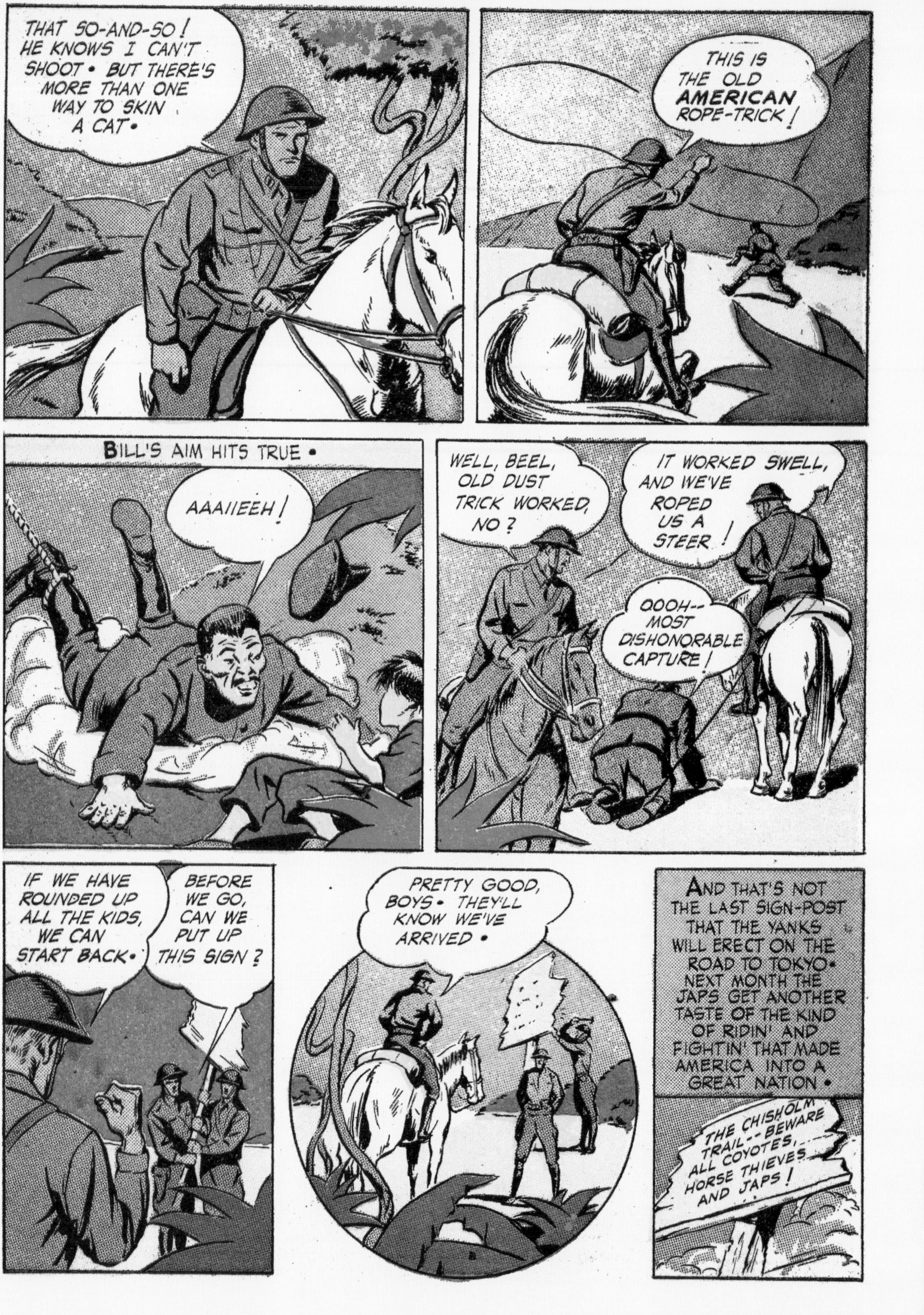

THAT SO-AND-SO! HE KNOWS I CAN'T SHOOT • BUT THERE'S MORE THAN ONE WAY TO SKIN A CAT •
THIS IS THE OLD AMERICAN ROPE-TRICK!
BILL'S AIM HITS TRUE •
AAAIIEEH!
WELL, BEEL, OLD DUST TRICK WORKED, NO?
IT WORKED SWELL, AND WE'VE ROPED US A STEER!
OOOH-- MOST DISHONORABLE CAPTURE!
IF WE HAVE ROUNDED UP ALL THE KIDS, WE CAN START BACK•
BEFORE WE GO, CAN WE PUT UP THIS SIGN?
PRETTY GOOD, BOYS• THEY'LL KNOW WE'VE ARRIVED •
AND THAT'S NOT THE LAST SIGN-POST THAT THE YANKS WILL ERECT ON THE ROAD TO TOKYO• NEXT MONTH THE JAPS GET ANOTHER TASTE OF THE KIND OF RIDIN' AND FIGHTIN' THAT MADE AMERICA INTO A GREAT NATION •
THE CHISHOLM TRAIL--BEWARE ALL COYOTES, HORSE THIEVES AND JAPS!

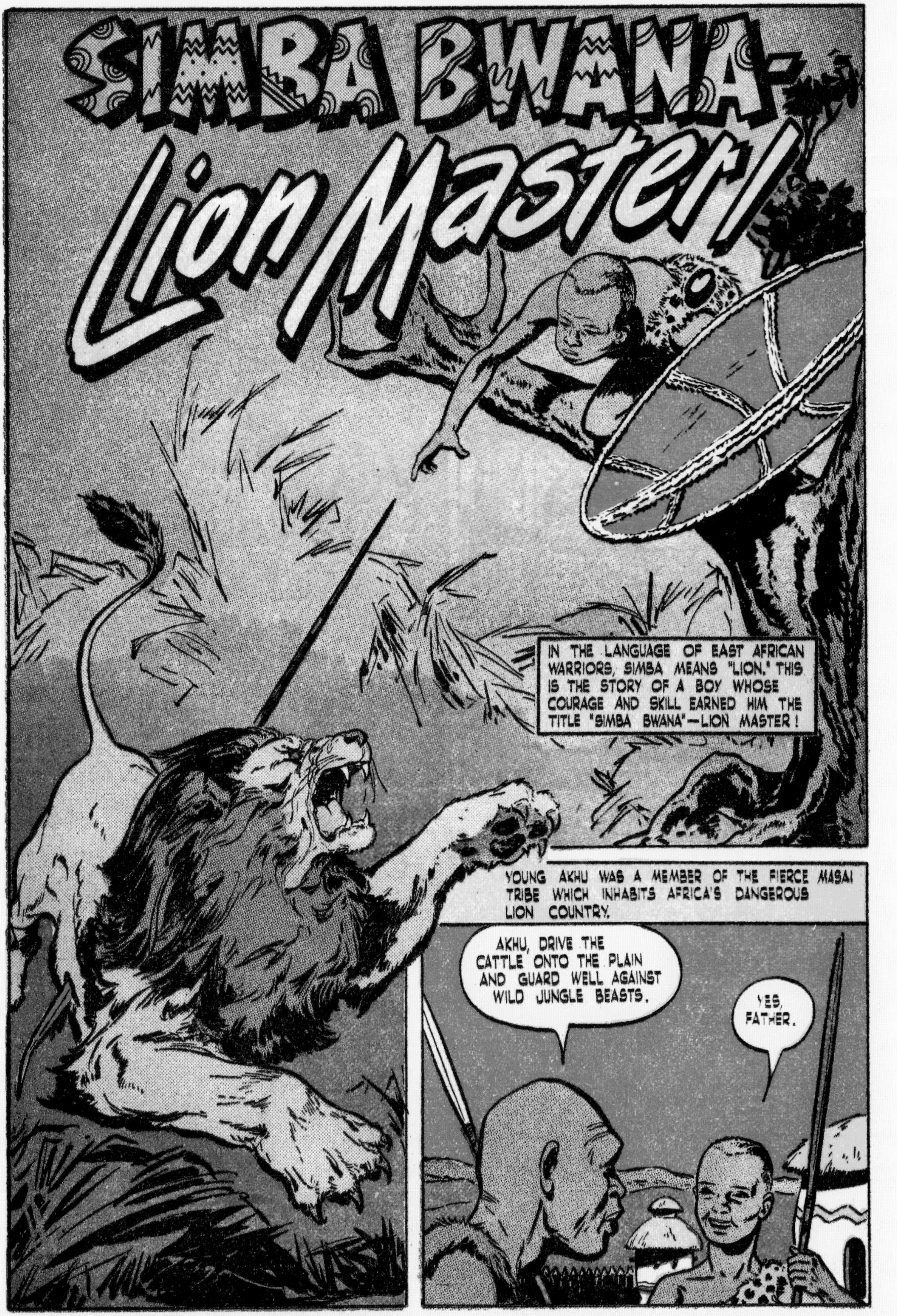
SIMBA BWANA-
Lion Master!
IN THE LANGUAGE OF EAST AFRICAN WARRIORS, SIMBA MEANS "LION." THIS IS THE STORY OF A BOY WHOSE COURAGE AND SKILL EARNED HIM THE TITLE "SIMBA BWANA"—LION MASTER!
YOUNG AKHU WAS A MEMBER OF THE FIERCE MASAI TRIBE WHICH INHABITS AFRICA'S DANGEROUS LION COUNTRY.
AKHU, DRIVE THE CATTLE ONTO THE PLAIN AND GUARD WELL AGAINST WILD JUNGLE BEASTS.
YES, FATHER.

George Lipscomb wrote the book *Tales from the Land of Simba* (1946) and adapted it for this comic. The likely artist was Fax who worked with Lipscomb for this publisher. *Jack Armstrong* #1, November 1947, Parents' Institute.

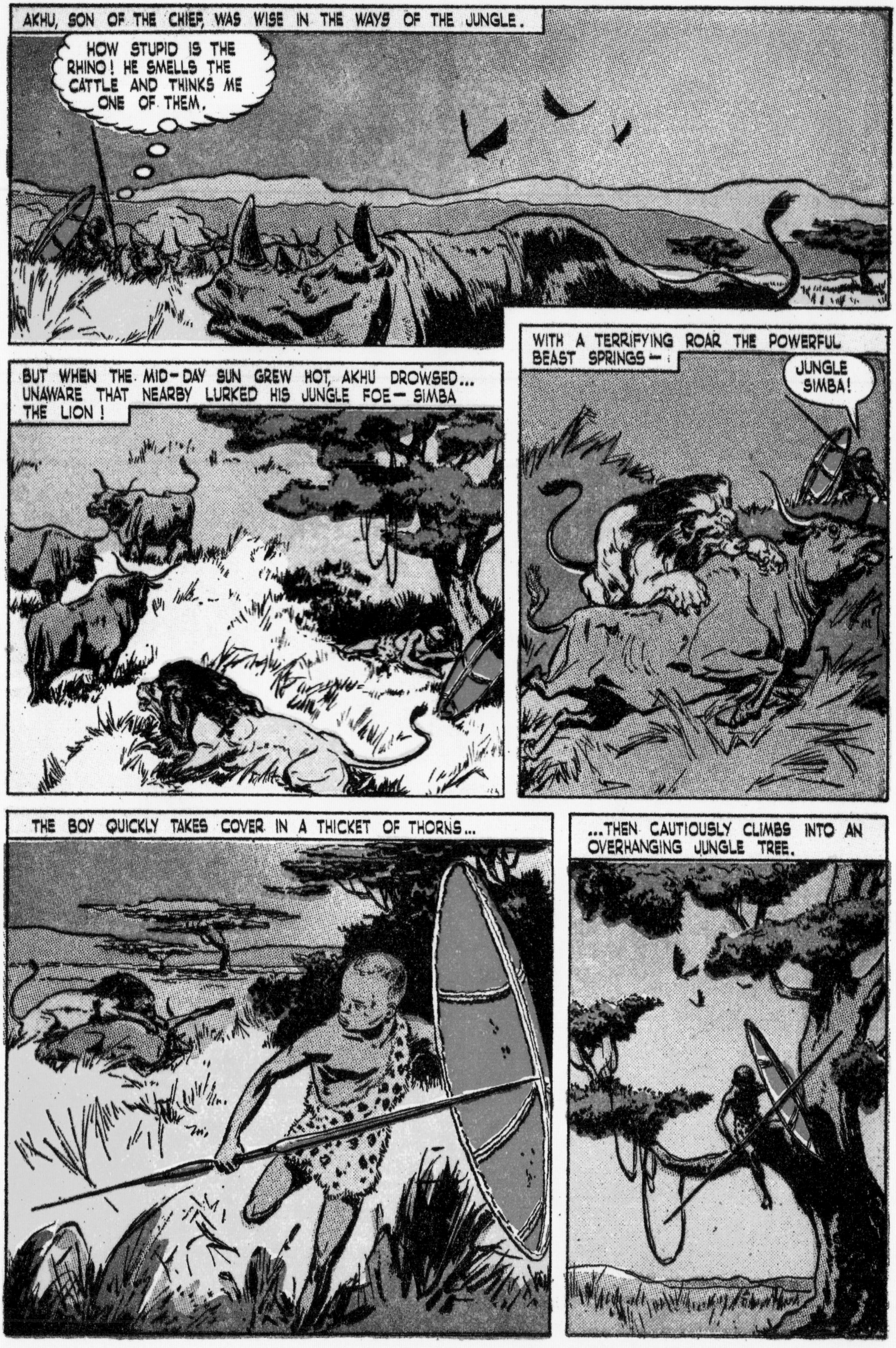
AKHU, SON OF THE CHIEF, WAS WISE IN THE WAYS OF THE JUNGLE.
HOW STUPID IS THE RHINO! HE SMELLS THE CATTLE AND THINKS ME ONE OF THEM.
BUT WHEN THE MID-DAY SUN GREW HOT, AKHU DROWSED... UNAWARE THAT NEARBY LURKED HIS JUNGLE FOE— SIMBA THE LION!
WITH A TERRIFYING ROAR THE POWERFUL BEAST SPRINGS—
JUNGLE SIMBA!
THE BOY QUICKLY TAKES COVER IN A THICKET OF THORNS...
...THEN CAUTIOUSLY CLIMBS INTO AN OVERHANGING JUNGLE TREE.

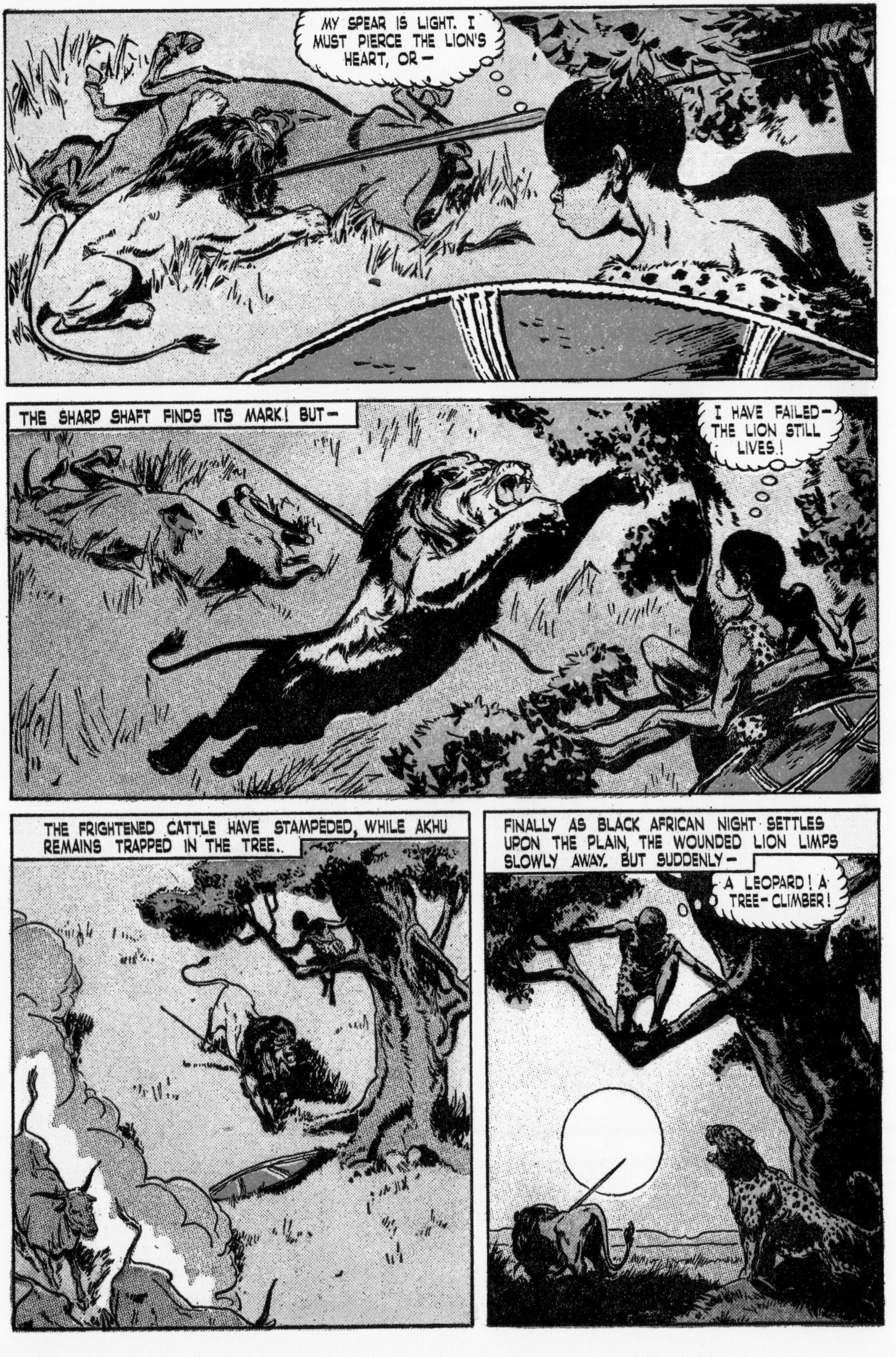
MY SPEAR IS LIGHT. I MUST PIERCE THE LION'S HEART, OR—
THE SHARP SHAFT FINDS ITS MARK! BUT—
I HAVE FAILED—THE LION STILL LIVES!
THE FRIGHTENED CATTLE HAVE STAMPEDED, WHILE AKHU REMAINS TRAPPED IN THE TREE..
FINALLY AS BLACK AFRICAN NIGHT SETTLES UPON THE PLAIN, THE WOUNDED LION LIMPS SLOWLY AWAY. BUT SUDDENLY—
A LEOPARD! A TREE-CLIMBER!

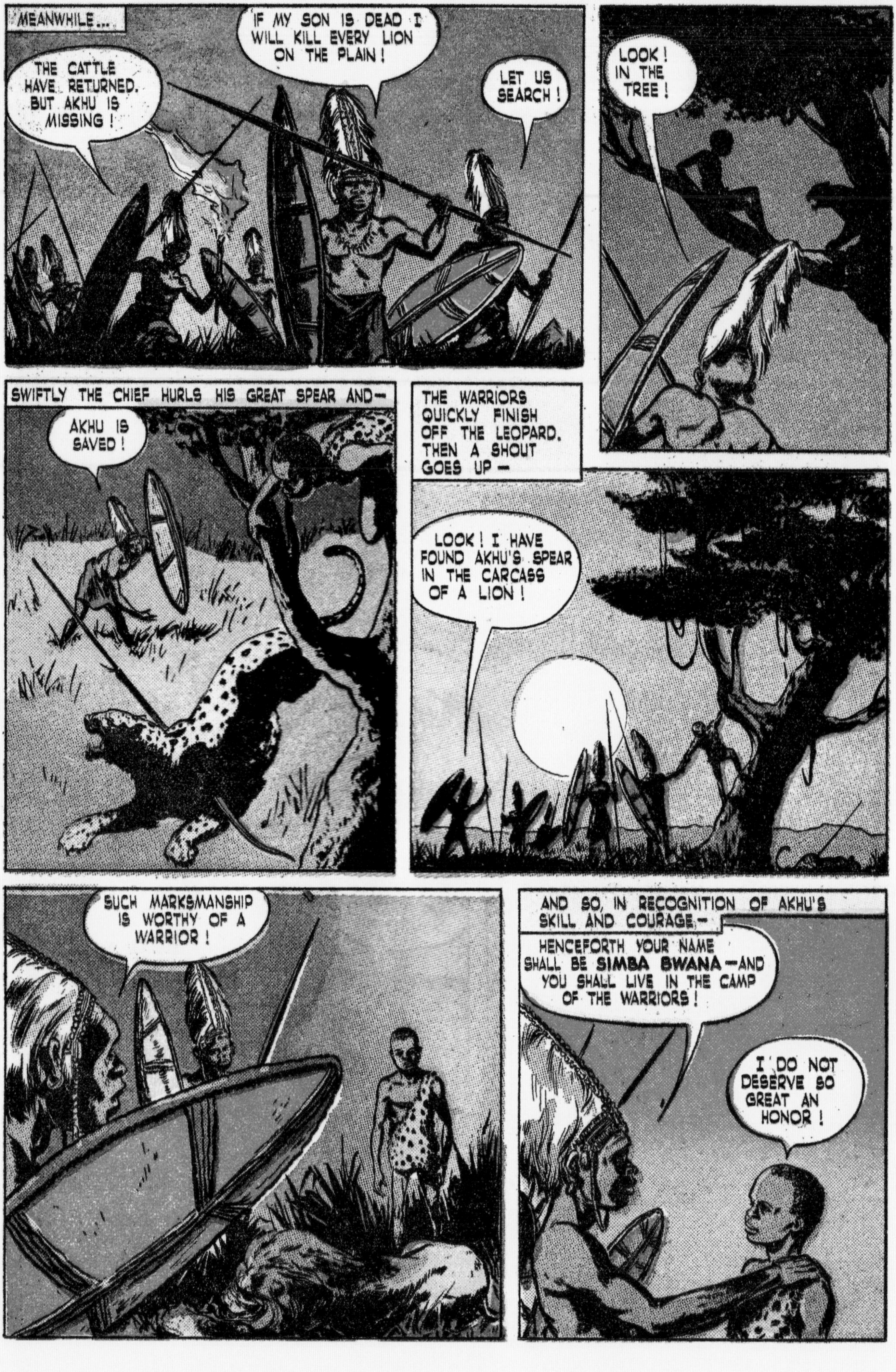
MEANWHILE...
THE CATTLE HAVE RETURNED. BUT AKHU IS MISSING !
IF MY SON IS DEAD I WILL KILL EVERY LION ON THE PLAIN !
LET US SEARCH !
LOOK ! IN THE TREE !
SWIFTLY THE CHIEF HURLS HIS GREAT SPEAR AND—
AKHU IS SAVED !
THE WARRIORS QUICKLY FINISH OFF THE LEOPARD. THEN A SHOUT GOES UP—
LOOK ! I HAVE FOUND AKHU'S SPEAR IN THE CARCASS OF A LION !
SUCH MARKSMANSHIP IS WORTHY OF A WARRIOR !
AND SO, IN RECOGNITION OF AKHU'S SKILL AND COURAGE.—
HENCEFORTH YOUR NAME SHALL BE SIMBA BWANA—AND YOU SHALL LIVE IN THE CAMP OF THE WARRIORS !
I DO NOT DESERVE SO GREAT AN HONOR !

CLARENCE MATTHEW BAKER
The Natural

If you lived in Forsyth County, North Carolina, chances are you knew someone named Lash. The family had deep roots in the area, going back to Jacob Loesch, who came to Forsyth from Pennsylvania in 1753. He moved to the region to run the business affairs of the Moravians who had settled in the area.

The Moravians were a German Protestant sect (the first, even predating the Lutherans) who settled in Bethabara, located in what is now Winston-Salem. Loesch eventually went back north, but his progeny stayed, changed their family name to Lash, then prospered and multiplied. They became bankers, farmers, and the most prominent merchants in the county.

Moravians were pious, hard-working, trusting, and pacifistic, and traditionally opposed to slavery. However, this part of the Piedmont was sparsely populated, and farm help was hard to find. Despite the concept of human chattel being morally reprehensible, they believed it was economically convenient to own slaves.

The conflicted Moravians set rules limiting the number of slaves that could be owned by the community.

They baptized and welcomed the slaves into their church. They debated the ethics and continuance of the institution of slavery, but the practice persisted until the early 1850s.

Franklin W. Lash was born during the Civil War, in 1863, and was considered a mulatto—a vestige of colonialism and a racial designation long used to describe a person of mixed race. Franklin, who went by the name of Frank, wasn't a banker or a merchant; he was a tenant farmer. Frank and his wife, Lucinda (aka Lovie), had several children, including Ethel Viola, who was born March 15, 1896. On July 3, 1916, Ethel married Clarence Matthew Baker, himself the son of a tenant farmer and the eventual father of a son bearing the same name.

Clarence's father John had a vague past. He had once worked for the Fulk family as a farm laborer, but beyond that, little is known. His mother Ella (or Ellen) had a similarly uncertain history, all too common among Southern Blacks. Even Clarence's birth date is open to conjecture, sometimes given as Dec. 5, 1895, sometimes 1896. What is known, though, is that when he filled out his first draft

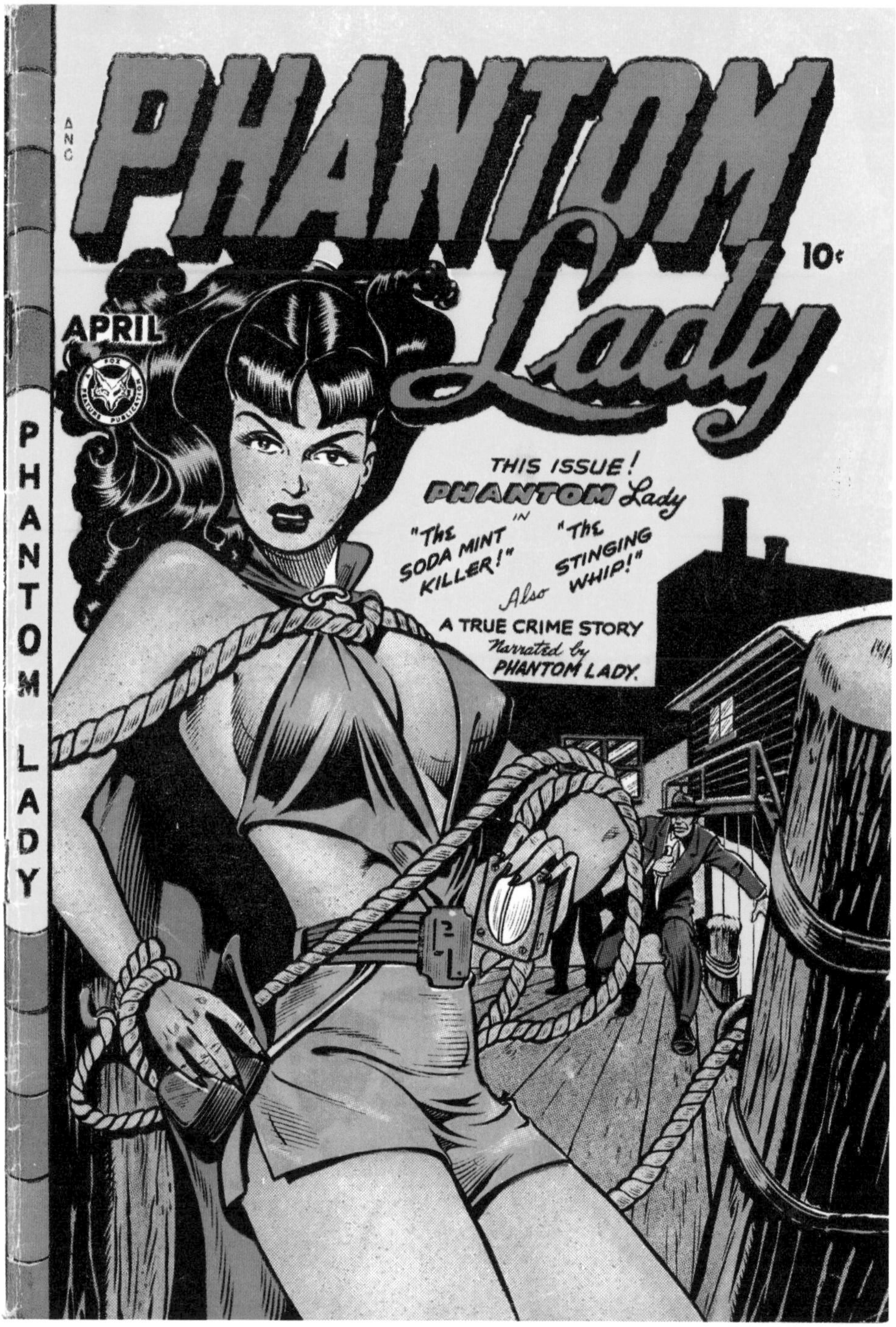
PHANTOM Lady
10¢
APRIL
PHANTOM LADY
THIS ISSUE!
PHANTOM Lady
IN
"THE SODA MINT KILLER!"
"THE STINGING WHIP!"
Also
A TRUE CRIME STORY
Narrated by
PHANTOM LADY.

Sometime after, circa 1924, the family joined the Great Migration north and moved to Pennsylvania, but tragically, Clarence hadn't long to live. Confined to Mayview State Hospital southwest of Pittsburgh, an institution for the poor that was primarily used as an insane asylum, he died on December 15, 1925, just a few days past his 29th birthday. Tuberculosis killed him. His father John had also died at a young age. An ominous heritage.

Now a widow, Ethel continued on as a single mother, working as a maid and raising her three children alone until 1930, when she married Matthew Robinson.

The Homewood-Brushton neighborhood where they lived was in transition. Highly coveted by middle-class Whites in the early part of the 20th century for its location away from the steel mills, by the 1920s it was being settled by Italian immigrants and Blacks. A 1939 study ordered by the mayor of Pittsburgh looked into the reasons for the changing population.

Because of the cultural and social differences between the original settlers and these newcomers, the presence of one Italian family on a street would sometimes cause all other residents to sell and move. Naturally, the most profitable sales could then be made to other Italian or Negro families. Thus, whole streets rather rapidly underwent a change in the color and nationality of their residents. [Bureau of Social Research, Federation of Social Agencies of Pittsburgh and Allegheny, 1939, *Homewood Brushton*, p.11]

The residents of Homewood-Brushton tended to be financially better off than in other working class areas of the city, due to the predominance of workers from nearby Westinghouse Electric and Manufacturing Company.

card in June 1917, he was working for the Huntley-Hill Stockton furniture store in Winston-Salem, most likely as a delivery driver.

Curiously, a year later in June 1918, he filled out yet another draft card, this time while he and Ethel were living in Lakewood, Ohio, where he was employed by a man named James Caldwell. There is an indication that Clarence may have been trying to hide his true identity, as he listed his name as "Clarence Madison Baker" and his wife as "Ethel Lee Baker." Whatever his reasons, by 1920, the family was back in Winston-Salem, where Clarence had a job as a chauffeur at the Brown-Williamson Tobacco Company. At the time, he and his wife had two children. They would soon have another, as son Clarence Matthew Baker was born on December 10, 1921.

[Above] Matt Baker's iconic *Phantom Lady* cover was a prime exhibit pictured in the pages of *Seduction of The Innocent* (1954, Rinehart & Co.), the anti-comics screed by Dr. Fredric Wertham. *Phantom Lady* #17, April 1948, Fox Feature Syndicate.

[Right] "Tiger Girl," *Fight Comics* #42, February 1946. Original artwork from the collection of Craig Yoe.

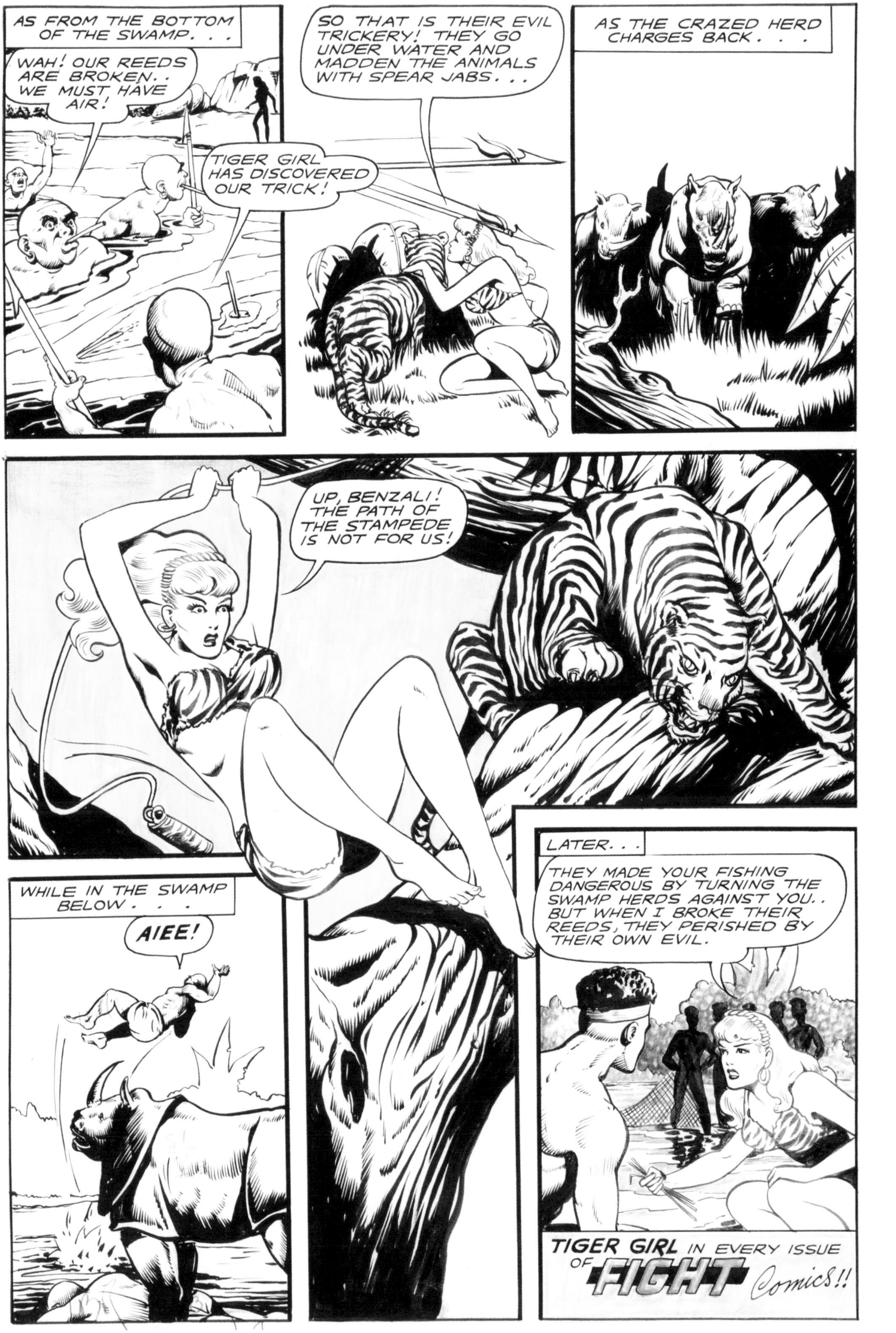
AS FROM THE BOTTOM OF THE SWAMP. . .
WAH! OUR REEDS ARE BROKEN.. WE MUST HAVE AIR!
TIGER GIRL HAS DISCOVERED OUR TRICK!
SO THAT IS THEIR EVIL TRICKERY! THEY GO UNDER WATER AND MADDEN THE ANIMALS WITH SPEAR JABS. . .
AS THE CRAZED HERD CHARGES BACK. . .
UP, BENZALI! THE PATH OF THE STAMPEDE IS NOT FOR US!
WHILE IN THE SWAMP BELOW. . .
AIEE!
LATER. . .
THEY MADE YOUR FISHING DANGEROUS BY TURNING THE SWAMP HERDS AGAINST YOU.. BUT WHEN I BROKE THEIR REEDS, THEY PERISHED BY THEIR OWN EVIL.
TIGER GIRL IN EVERY ISSUE OF FIGHT Comics!!

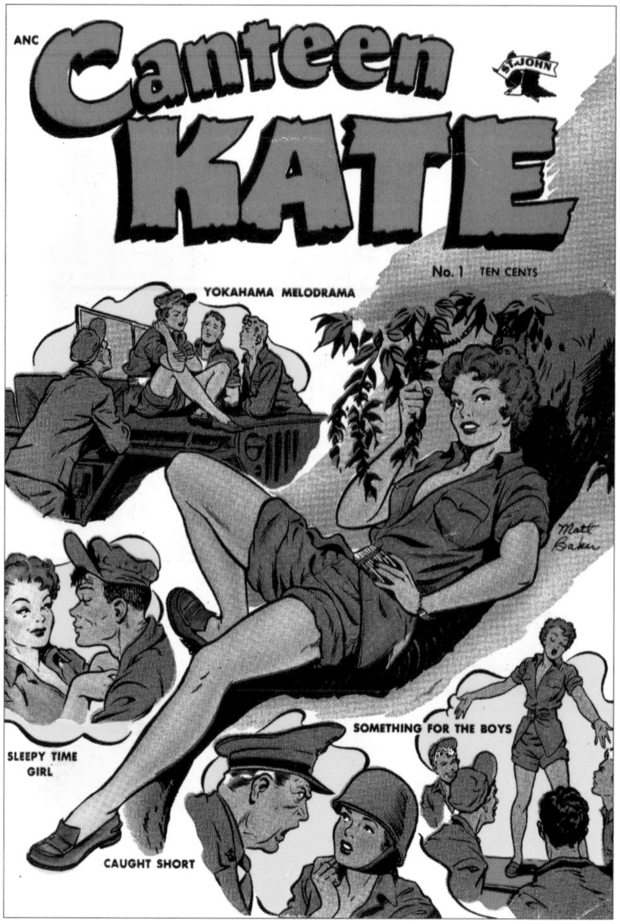
ANC
Canteen
KATE
ST. JOHN
No. 1 TEN CENTS
YOKAHAMA MELODRAMA
Matt Baker
SOMETHING FOR THE BOYS
SLEEPY TIME GIRL
CAUGHT SHORT

Matthew Robinson was one of those workers, listing himself as a coppersmith in the 1930 U.S. census. Still, even within Homewood-Brushton there was a stratification of its residents. Virtually all of the Italians lived south of the Pennsylvania Railroad tracks bisecting the neighborhood, while most of the Blacks lived north of it. The 1939 research study noted that the northern area was far more highly zoned for industrial purposes and that "this land usage would point to the fact that the district north of the tracks is deteriorating as a residential community." [Ibid, p.19]

The Baker-Robinson clan eventually moved a little over a mile away, to a free-standing home at 7614 Susquehanna Street, with four bedrooms and more space for a large family. In the same part of town was George Westinghouse High School, which all of the combined family members attended. That included Clarence, who never used his first name, preferring to go with his middle name, Matt. He so detested his first name that once he was on his own, he forevermore appeared in the telephone directories as "C. Matthew Baker."

In his 1940 senior yearbook, Matt (also known by his nickname "Mac") listed his activities as "camera," his ambition to be a "commercial artist," and his avocation as "drawing." It was a list demonstrating a dedication to, and a remarkably prescient forecast of, his future career.

About two years after graduation, Matt and his older brother John, also an aspiring artist, moved to Washington, D.C. in search of opportunity. America's entry into war after the attack on Pearl Harbor brought with it a boom in government jobs. As much of the able-bodied White male population was caught up in military service, even more opportunities were created for those left behind. Neither Matt nor John were eligible for conscription and therefore couldn't have joined even if they wished to serve. John had a busted eardrum and Matt had heart problems going back to childhood. The belief is that these heart issues were due to a bout of rheumatic fever in his youth.

The brothers took up residence in a home at 1419 Q Street NW, near Logan Circle. Their apartment in the Victorian Era townhouse was a definite step up from their crowded home back in Homewood-Brushton, but still affordable.

Matt got a job at the Navy Department, but exactly what he did there isn't yet clear. What is known is that the two left Washington sometime in 1943 and moved to New York City. Matt took an apartment in a building at 1348 Pacific Street in the mostly White neighborhood of Crown Heights, Brooklyn. There were more job opportunities, perhaps, but Matt still wasn't employed in his preferred career. He found work at the National War Labor Board at 220 E. 42nd Street as a mail clerk.

A newspaper article celebrating this agency's employment of eleven Blacks "on the basis of merit and equality" noted Matt as a beneficiary of its open-mindedness. It added in passing that "Mr. Baker uses his spare time to continue studies in art at Cooper Union." [Malliett, A. M. Wendell, "Race No Barrier—They Made It on Merit," *New York Amsterdam News*, Jan. 29, 1944]

Baker signed up in the Fall 1943 semester at the Cooper Union for one evening art class, but he left the school without taking any more classes. His reason may have been that he had picked up his first art assignments from the Iger Studio.

Samuel "Jerry" Iger was an old-time newspaper cartoonist who worked at the *New York American* among others; never very successful, never making it into the "big time." He knocked around for a bit during the Great Depression before being hired in 1936 by John Henle, a

[Above] Baker's most fully realized creation, Canteen Kate, was a Titian-haired whirlwind, whose well-meaning antics usually courted disaster before being resolved favorably. Kate debuted in *Fightin' Marines* #2 (October 1951) before getting her own title. *Canteen Kate* #1, June 1952, St. John Publishing.

[Right] The covers Baker produced for St. John romance comics set the gold standard for the genre. *Cinderella Love* #25, December 1954, St. John Publishing.

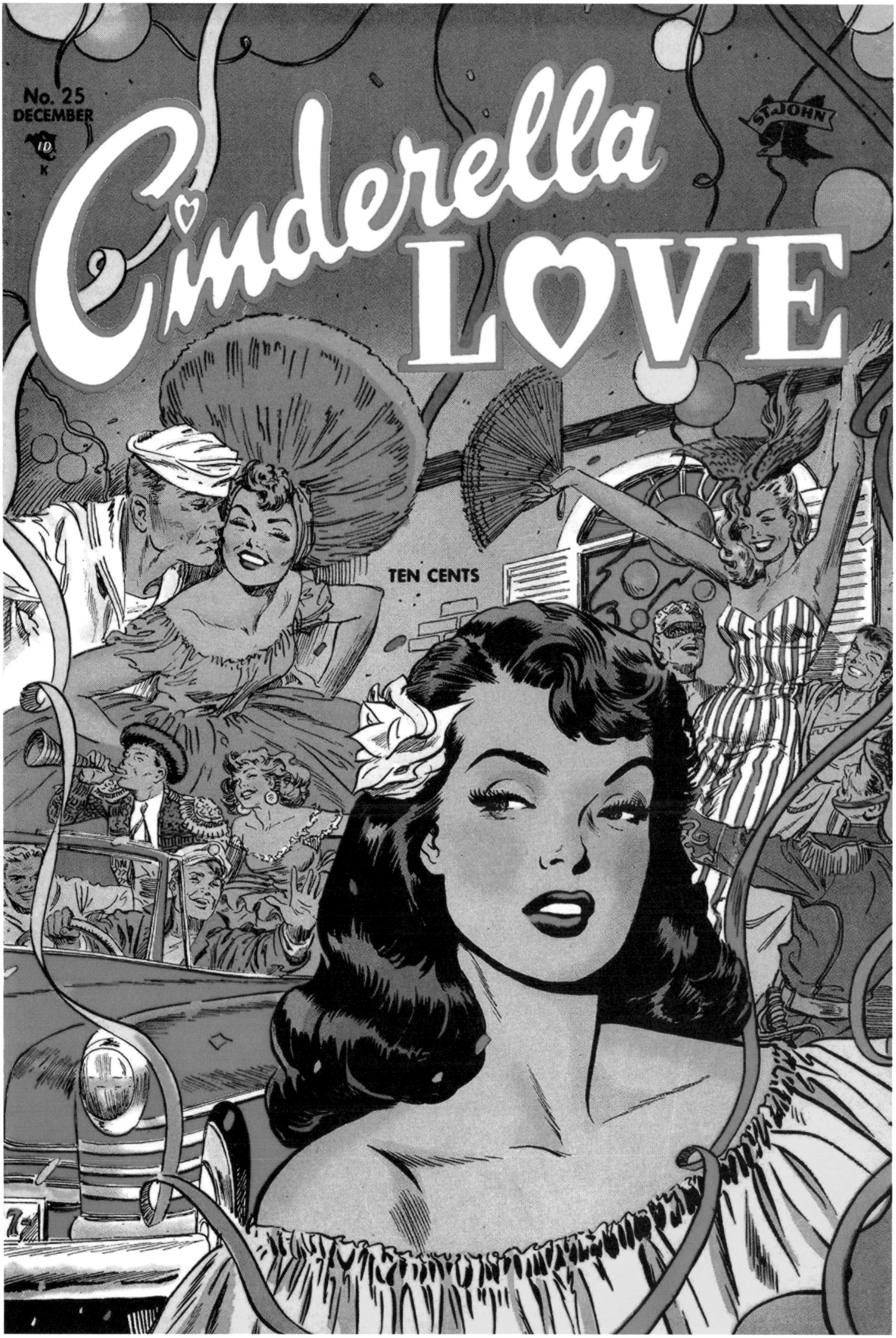
No. 25
DECEMBER
Cinderella
LOVE
ST. JOHN
TEN CENTS

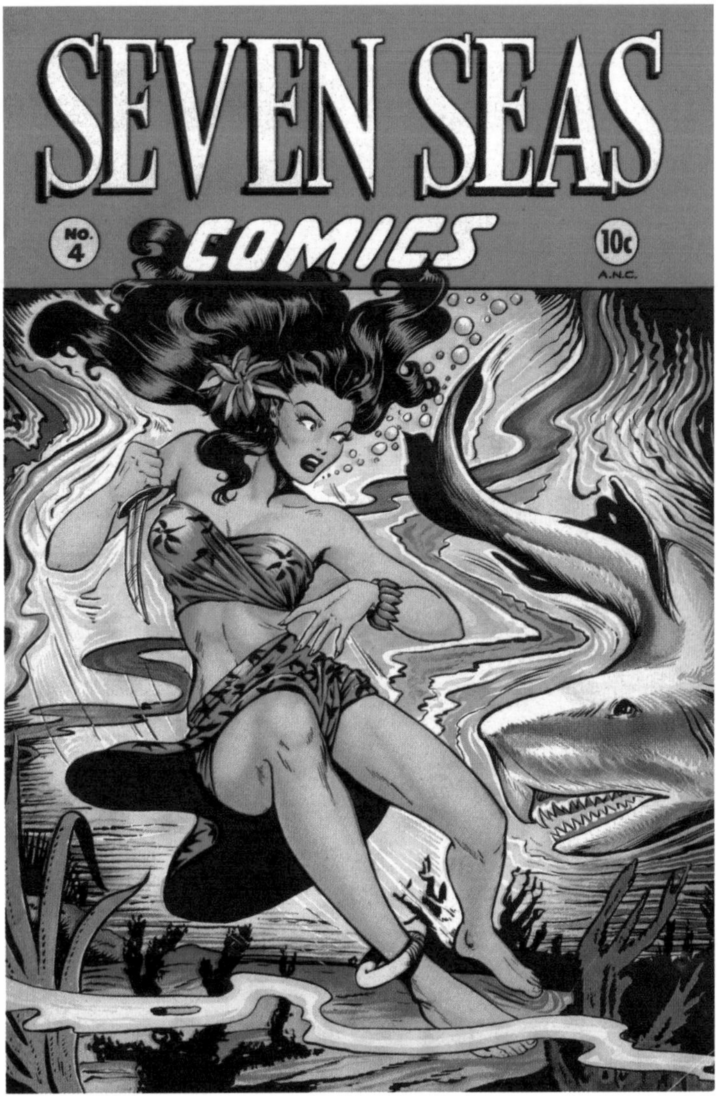
SEVEN SEAS
NO. 4
COMICS
10c
A.N.C.

clothing manufacturer who wanted to cash in on the fledgling comic book industry by starting his own publishing company. Iger was to be his editor for their one and only publication, *Wow, What a Magazine!*

Henle Publications opened shop in a portion of its owner's clothing factory on Fifth Avenue, and Iger set about hiring a staff to produce the comic. The people he hired were a mix of veteran, underemployed artists, and hungry kids trying to break into the field. None of his hires was more important than Will Eisner. Eisner was not only a talented artist and writer, but a creative dynamo with far-reaching ambitions.

Bluntly put, the comic was a flop. It lasted only four issues, leaving its editor and staff back out on the street looking for jobs. Eisner had an idea that he presented as a business proposition to Iger. He proposed that they form a studio which would produce content for comic books. This studio would supply completed art and text for publishers unwilling to cobble together a staff of their own. Iger agreed and the Eisner & Iger Studio was formed.

Eisner terminated the partnership in early 1940 when he was offered his own syndicated comic strip, which took form as *The Spirit*. Iger, embittered by the break-up, continued on with the studio, renaming it after himself. It remained one of the most successful "comic shops," producing material for comics throughout the 1940s and into the '50s. It was near its peak when Baker hired on in 1944. His hiring single-handedly raised the shop's potential to another level.

Whatever personal failings Iger may have had (and stories of these abound), he had an eye for artistic talent. He immediately recognized Baker's skill, particularly his ability for drawing beautiful women. Baker's initial assignments were to draw the women onto the artwork of other artists who lacked his talent. The "Sheena" story in *Jumbo Comics* #69 (Nov. 1944) has been identified as probably his first work for Iger, depicting the feature's star and the other jungle girls running through its pages. For the record, the other artists on this story were Robert Webb and Alex Blum, two very capable and talented professionals.

Iger gave Baker his own feature, "Sky Girl," a back-up in *Jumbo Comics,* depicting the high-flying adventures of a feisty red-head pilot named Ginger Maguire. Though competently drawn by Blum previously, Baker gave "Sky Girl" a new, glamorous look. Under Baker's penciling, Ginger transformed into a Hollywood starlet—slim-lined, long-legged and unabashedly sexy.

Iger wasn't about to limit Baker to just one feature in one comic. Baker's artwork would quickly start showing up everywhere: first, in the line of comics they produced for Fiction House, and then throughout much of their other output for other publishers. He was even utilized on *Classic Comics* #32 (Dec. 1946), lending a bit of sex appeal to the adaptation of Richard D. Blackmore's 19th century romance novel, *Lorna Doone*.

Baker was unique. Unlike most other Black comic book artists of the era, his work was produced in shop, among all the other White artists. He had their respect. He was a star to his peers, who all marveled at his talent and, at least overtly, ignored the color of his skin.

Baker's star had risen so high that he was tapped as the artist for a proposed syndicated comic strip. Written

[Above] Yet another Baker cover while working for the Iger studio. This one features South Sea Girl, the fierce female ruler of an island nation. *Seven Seas* #4, 1947, Leader Enterprises.

[Right] Illustration from the men's pulp, *Mystery Tales* #6, October 1959, Atlas Magazines.

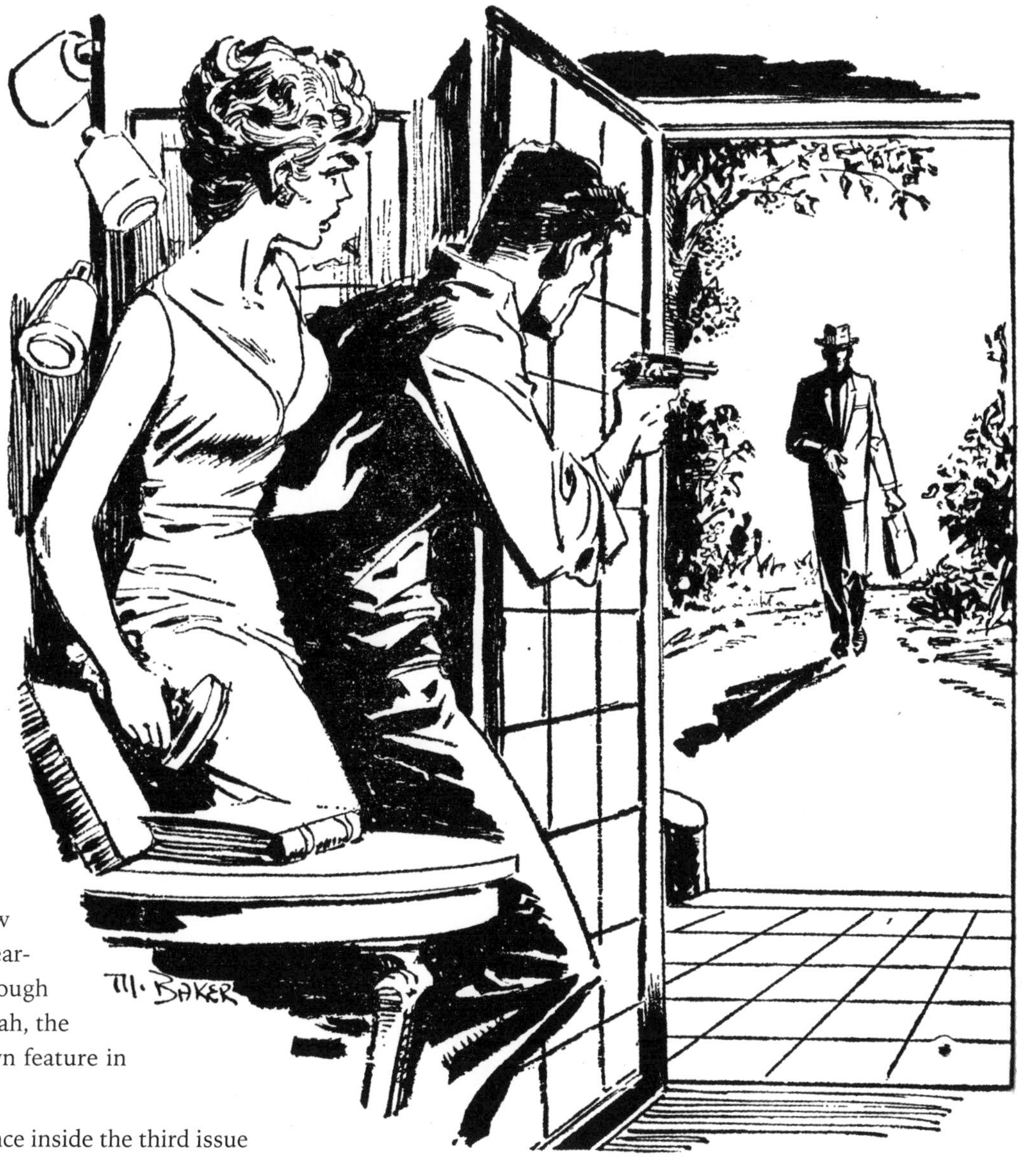
M. BAKER

by Iger's partner Ruth Roche, the process of creating the gypsy dancing girl "Flamingo" was described in a promotional brochure.

Slowly Flamingo began to take her lovely form. But not until endless research for authentic gypsy material was completed, not until she almost breathed from the magic touch of MATT BAKER's brush. [Roche, Ruth, *Flamingo* promotional brochure, c.1940s]

One thing that couldn't be ignored was that just about all the heroes and heroines in the jungle comics were White: Sheena, Rulah, Kaänga. Somehow all of them ended up in Africa wearing animal skins and swinging through the trees. One exception was Voodah, the first Black hero to be given his own feature in a White comic book.

Voodah made his initial appearance inside the third issue of *Crown Comics* (Fall 1945). In a striking dichotomy, the racist cover depicts a smiling young White boy attacking a Black native with a spear, who is also being bitten on the ankle by the boy's dog. However, in the interior, the dark-skinned Voodah debuts, leaping from a tree, knife in hand, to save an equally ebon woman being held captive.

A Black hero in a White comic book—a Black hero in any form of White media—was virtually unheard of in this era. Did the fact that it was drawn by Baker influence the decision to create this feature? The answer is unknown, but any thought that it may have just been a coloring mistake by the printer was dispelled when the next issues of *Crown Comics* hit the newsstand. In #4 and #5, Voodah was Black in the inside story, however he was White on the cover of #5, as the publisher hedged his bets. That was a decision likely made to placate distributors and newsdealers who would be leery of carrying a comic with a Black man on its cover.

Black Voodah didn't last long and his stories ended with issue #5. From issue #6 on, the safer, White Voodah took over the inside stories and continued to appear on many of *Crown Comics* covers.

Before Al Feldstein attained legendary status as an artist, writer, and editor for the Entertaining Comics (EC) line, he was a young artist working for the Iger shop; one with an advantageous vantage point from which to observe Baker. Feldstein wrote:

When I returned from Service in 1945 and took my old job back at the S. M. Iger Studio, Matt Baker was there...and I was assigned a drawing board right next to his. But, although I inked a lot of his pencils and I learned a lot about drawing voluptuous women from him, I never really got to know him that well. Matt was extremely private and withdrawn and rarely communicated with me except on a rather superficial level.

I do not remember Matt ever joining any of us for our short lunch breaks...or socializing with us to any degree. I do not know if Matt saw any of the other Iger artists socially. He kept pretty much to himself.

As I recall, he was treated as an equal by all of us, which his unique, special and outstanding talent demanded. He was well respected for that talent. But this was 1945-6...and the Racial Divide in America was still pretty much with us. Matt, I am sure, was

OHHH... YOU POOR FOOT... YOU'RE BLEEDING... ALL ON ACCOUNT OF A STUPID PIG!
AMBROSIA! SO, YOU GYPSY THIEF! I CAUGHT YOU...
THIEF, HE CALLS ME! BUT FOR YOUR FOOLISH PIG I WOULDN'T HAVE CUT MY FOOT!
Ruth Roche
PHOENIX FEATURES

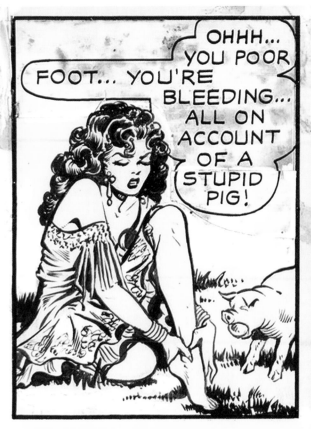

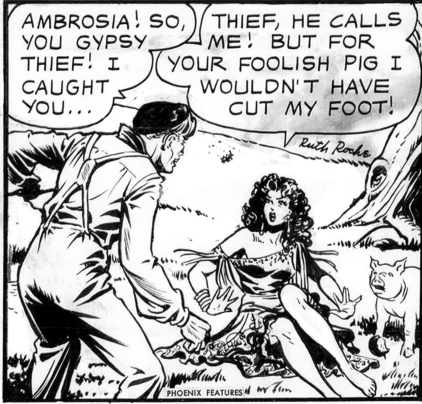

acutely aware of this unwritten abomination...as was [sic] the rest of us...so it kept all of us apart. ["Matt Baker," email from Al Feldstein to the author, Apr. 24, 2006]

Baker did have some friends in the Iger shop, though, one being a teenage artist from Queens named Frank Giusto.

According to Giusto, he and Baker met in the summer of 1944, after he graduated from high school in June and before he entered the Navy in September. Baker was already working for Iger, which places his beginning at that studio sometime in the early part of that year. They struck up a friendship during Giusto's brief time at the shop and kept it up via mail when Giusto was in the service. The envelopes of Baker's letters to Giusto were often adorned with cartoonish drawings of semiclad women.

In 1947, Baker added assignments for the Fox Features comics to his workload, particularly their jungle-themed titles, such as *Zoot Comics,* featuring Rulah, and *Jo-Jo Comics*. Any opportunity to get an animal-skin wearing White jungle princess drawn by Baker onto a cover was taken. His most lasting contribution to Fox, however, was found in his *Phantom Lady* comics.

The character had originally appeared in comics produced by Iger for the Quality Comics group, which stopped running the feature with *Police Comics* #23 (Oct. 1943). It stayed dormant until Iger decided to revive the character for his new client, Fox Features Syndicate, in 1947. The fact that Baker was handed this revival was a calculated risk. While super-hero comics as a genre were on the wane, comics featuring scantily clad women were booming.

It was all part of the ongoing industry-wide change. The generation of kids who had read comics during the war was growing up, and their older brothers had returned from military service. The heroic exploits of super-powered demigods were giving way to comics appealing to the adolescent-to-adult reader's baser cravings for violence and sex. Hence, there was the upsurge in crime, jungle, and romance genres.

Baker's makeover of Phantom Lady gave the alter ego of Sandra Knight a new, more revealing costume. Whereas the previous version fought crime in a yellow one-piece outfit, Baker's was more fashionably contemporary. She now wore a blue two-piece, bearing a likeness to Louis Réard's scandalous new bikini, with a concession to modesty accomplished by the substitution of very short shorts serving as its bottom half.

It's little wonder that Baker was so conscious of Phantom Lady's style choice. He was a fashion plate himself, garnering praise as a natty dresser from all who met him. Relatively tall and lean, Baker had movie star looks, prompting an apt comparison from his half-brother. Fred Robinson told interviewer, Jim Amash:

Matt bore a strong resemblance to Lawrence Olivier when Olivier was young. [Amash, Jim, "'The Matt Baker Woman' Struck a Responsive Chord," *Alter Ego*, Apr. 2005, p.55]

Baker's Flamingo appeared as a newspaper comic strip. This original art is dated August 1 and is circa 1953. It was distributed by Jerry Iger's Phoenix Features Syndicate.

YOU BAITED HER ALONG WITH AN APPLE! I SAW YOU!
I BLEED TO DEATH AND YOU JUST STAND THERE AND SHOUT! GO... GO AND LET ME DIE IN PEACE!
8-1
BAH! A SCRATCH THE GENDARMES WILL HAVE BUSINESS WITH YOU...
WHO DARES TO CALL MY GRANDCHILD A THIEF?
PEPO!

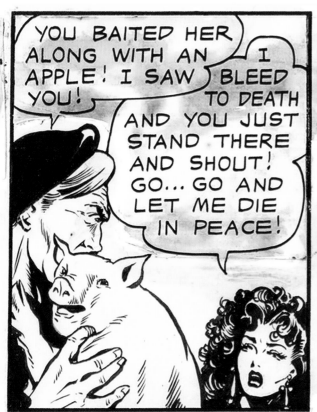

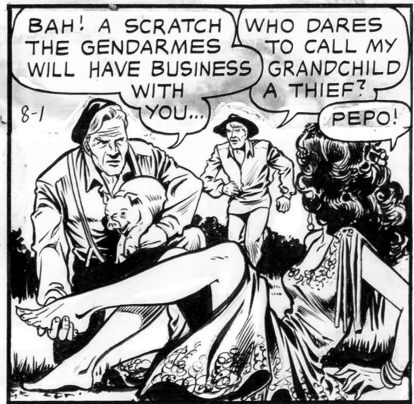

By 1948, Baker was taking jobs outside of the Iger shop. Notably, he was freelancing for a new comic book company named St. John Publishing, owned by Archer St. John.

St. John may have been a newcomer to the comic book industry, but he had a long history of publishing experience. Born in Chicago, Archer and his brother Robert started their own newspaper in nearby Cicero, to publicly combat the influence and criminal activities of the infamous gangster Al Capone. Their reportage and editorializing infuriated Capone, to the point that he had his thugs beat up Robert on a street in broad daylight and take his younger brother Archer "for a ride." Archer was released later in the day, but only after he had been blindfolded and bound, and left miles away from where he had been taken. Capone eventually rid himself of the St. John brothers by buying their paper out from under them. Robert went on to become a famous broadcaster, and Archer went into advertising. After a long stint as advertising manager for Lionel Trains, he went on to form his own publishing company that catered to airplane enthusiasts, and from there to the more profitable business of comic book publishing.

Baker's reputation preceded him. His artwork, particularly on covers, was a game changer for the comic book industry. He was widely copied, both within the Iger shop and beyond. Looking to make a splash, St. John courted the best artists he could find, and Baker was among the first artists he approached.

Baker was assigned to comics almost exclusively edited by Marion McDermott. Although she had several different comic genres under her control, McDermott wisely realized that Baker's talents were best employed in their line of romance comics. These comics were geared toward young girls, on the cusp of puberty, dreaming of love, and eventually marriage. The heroines in their stories were cast as role models; and no matter their emotional state, they were always beautiful. Who better to draw them than Matt Baker?

The result was the perfect marriage of artist and subject. No longer compelled to pose his women improbably in order to expose as much cleavage and leg as possible, Baker's artwork took on a more relaxed, natural look. His covers became increasingly refined; his women more demurely attractive. And no comic book artist ever depicted glamour more confidently.

Fronting such titles as *Teen-Age Romances*, *Cinderella Love*, *Diary Secrets*, and *Going Steady*, these weren't just comic book covers—these were masterpieces.

Of course, Baker also drew assignments in other comic genres. Many issues of *Authentic Police Cases* featured his artwork, both on the inside and on covers generally displaying a gun moll in a no-nonsense power stance, hand on hip, pistol in hand.

Baker was also instrumental in an early attempt at what became known as the graphic novel. In 1949, two young writers named Arnold Drake and Leslie Waller brought Archer St. John an idea they had for a new type of comic book. Their proposal envisioned "a series of Picture Novels that were, essentially, action, mystery, Western, and romance novels" using sequential artwork, to be published as a paperback intended for an adult readership. ["It

Rhymes with Lust," email from Arnold Drake to the author, March 7, 2005]

St. John was sold. He commissioned the duo to write the story, and assigned Baker to illustrate it. The result was entitled *It Rhymes With Lust*, a tale of a scheming widow and the men she used and left in her wake. Drake wrote:

[It Rhymes With] Lust *would have made a good Joan Crawford or Barbara Stanwyck film. Both often played beautiful-but-treacherous women—and* Lust *was about one such.* [Ibid.]

Baker's work on *It Rhymes With Lust* was a departure from everything else he had drawn up to that point. Published in 1950, near the beginning of his tenure at St. John, it had a maturity to it that his Iger Shop work lacked, exhibiting a subtle, cinematic style that leaned more heavily on exposition rather than action. He utilized a specialized type of paper, duotone or something similar, on which to draw the story. This paper, which was actually a sort of Bristol board, revealed a pebbled, gray-tone shading when a special chemical was brushed onto it. Baker had his inker, Ray Osrin, render the foreground images in solid black ink and then complete the background art using the gray tones. This made the black-inked images jump out, and gave the artwork depth, creating a three-dimensional look that was especially effective since it was published in black-and-white.

It is somewhat ironic that the one continuing feature Baker is best known for at St. John came not in a romance comic, but a war title.

Tucked in among stories with titles such as "Yalu Death Squad," tales full of bullets and blood and grace under fire, Canteen Kate debuted in *Fightin' Marines* #2 (Oct. 1951).

Kate was a Titian-haired whirlwind, proclaimed as the "Bombshell from Brooklyn," whose well-meaning antics usually courted disaster before being resolved favorably. Her look and her storylines invite comparisons to *I Love Lucy*, except that "Canteen Kate" appeared on the newsstands several months before *Lucy* premiered on television.

Kate, who ran a canteen on a Marine base in Japan, was basically an updated version of "Sky Girl," Ginger Maguire. In her post-WWII stories, Ginger had gone blond, but she, too, worked in a diner. This was several years on, though, it was now the Korean conflict that was ongoing, and Kate was in uniform. Sort of.

Baker dressed Kate in modified khakis, a bit too form fitting, showing a little too much skin to ever truly pass inspection. Despite her undeniable beauty and frequent flashes of exposed flesh, none of the other Marines ever seemed to notice. It was a wink to the reader, letting them know that they were in on the joke.

This element of unconscious sexiness was perfectly expressed by Baker's approach—low-keyed, deceptively subtle. He didn't force Kate's poses, and the comedic exaggeration was kept to a minimum. This was a military humor strip, but Baker made it look pretty.

Baker's contributions didn't go unrewarded. He was made art director at St. John. Whether this position brought with it more money isn't known, but it does demonstrate the respect that St. John had for the artist.

Archer St. John was a visionary. He saw beyond standard newsstand comics. His company experimented with various comic formats throughout its history, pioneered the detective digest format with *Manhunt*, and in the late summer of 1955, was moving into the thriving men's magazine market with a *Playboy* knock-off entitled *Nugget*. According to Fred Robinson, it was Baker who pitched the idea to St. John.

Baker took his first tentative steps into commercial illustration with *Manhunt*, providing drawings to accompany the hard-boiled words of Mickey Spillane and others of that ilk. *Nugget* Vol.1 #1 (Nov. 1955) went a step further. It featured Baker's first professional nude artwork. He was moving into rarefied company. Only a few top notch "cheesecake" artists existed: Alberto Vargas, Gil Elvgren, George Petty, and a few others. You could just about count them on one hand. Baker had the talent to compete at their level; he just needed the opportunity, and St. John was giving him one.

Everything comes to an end, though, and so did St. John Publishing. The company suffered a tremendous financial setback when the publisher overestimated the staying power of 3-D comics. St. John had invested heavily in a process which was brought to it by brothers Norman and Leonard Maurer and their partner, Joe Kubert. In anticipation of it being a trend rather than a fad, Archer St. John had purchased large quantities of the special paper on which to print the three-dimensional artwork. Unfortunately, it was just a fad and died a quick, very expensive death. Then, about a year later, on August 13, 1955, the publisher was found dead of a drug overdose in the apartment of his mistress. The company fell into the control of Archer's young son Michael, and soon after, he contracted the comic book work to an outside shop and Baker never worked for the company again.

Baker was devastated not just by the untimely death of his friend and benefactor, but by the loss of what might

ALL TRUE LOVE STORIES!
ANC
a TEEN-AGE Temptations
ST. JOHN
WOW! LOOK AT THAT! I NEVER SAW HIM BEFORE. DO YOU THINK SHE KNOWS HIM?
NO, BUT THAT'S LINDA FOR YOU!
YOU'D RATHER GO BACK IN MY CAR, WOULDN'T YOU?
No. 2
TEN CENTS
MY FORBIDDEN KISSES

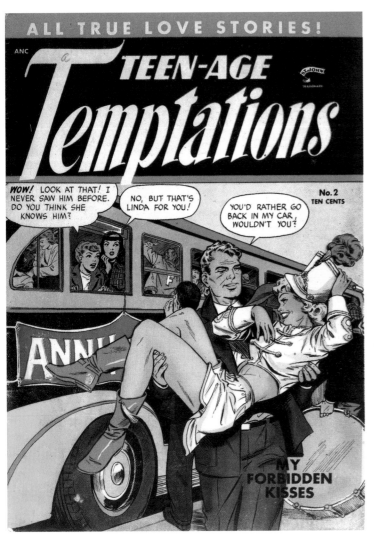

Archer St. John, owner of the company, so appreciated Baker's talent that he made him art director of his romance line. *Teen-Age Temptations* #2, June 1953, St. John Publishing.

have been. Not only had he lost the comic book work, but when the second issue of *Nugget* came out in February 1956, under the aegis of Michael St. John, Baker's artwork was nowhere to be found in it.

He had to start over. Baker had already begun penciling the exploits of "Lassie" for Dell. While it was a relatively well-paying job, his work on it was uninspiring. Like just about every other Black comic book artist still working in the industry, Baker picked up assignments over at Timely/Atlas from editor Stan Lee. But this was a bad time to be looking for work in comics.

The Senate subcommittee hearings looking into the connection between comics and juvenile delinquency were only a year in the past, and still fresh in the minds of many. The outside pressure applied by this governmental scrutiny, concerned parents, and vocal critics such as Dr. Fredric Wertham had compelled the comic book publishers to create their own censoring body, the Comics Code Authority. Even this didn't save everyone, as many publishers either closed up shop or decided that publishing comic books was no longer worth the fight. Then came the collapse of American News Company (ANC), which had been the largest distributor of magazines and comics in the country. When it suddenly went out of business in June 1957, it had catastrophic repercussions for certain publishers, particularly Timely/Atlas, which was nearly dragged down along with the distributor.

By late 1956, Baker had also found an outlet for his illustrative work, albeit appealing to a different demographic than the sophisticated *Playboy* crowd. He began drawing for men's "sweat magazines." These were a popular, and lucrative, new type of periodical, printed on cheap pulp paper behind colorful covers. These covers were generally emblazoned with a man engaged in a death duel with another man, a murderous hoard of men, or a crazed animal, and he was almost always accompanied by a partially clothed woman in need of rescue.

Baker's job was illustrating the interior stories of derring-do, torture, and sadomasochistic sex. The drawings stopped short of complete nudity, but didn't shy away from violence. He worked exclusively for Arnold Magazines, an outfit owned by Everett "Busy" Arnold, a well-established comic book publisher (Quality Comics) who had recently gotten out of the comic book business when things started getting tough. Baker had completed some romance comic jobs for Quality in 1956 just before its demise, which likely led directly to his work on Arnold's "sweats."

His drawings were rendered in ink and gray wash, and lingered in an illustrative purgatory between his comic book and his *Nugget* artwork. The work was solid and professional, despite its cringeworthy subject matter.

Eventually, though, this work too went away, as his last "sweat" illustrations appeared in early 1958. The comic book work was drying up as well. Timely/Atlas barely survived ANC's collapse, and for a time, they weren't buying any more artwork. When they did start handing out assignments again, Baker's art seemed to have lost something. While competent, it was uninspired and oft-times buried beneath the inks of Vince Colletta, not his most complementary inker. Baker's final comic book work seems to have been done for Charlton Comics, a notoriously low-paying company out of Derby, Connecticut. His last published artwork appeared in Charlton's *Strange Suspense Stories* #47 (May 1960), on a story entitled, "Redemption By Robots."

With no apparent work produced for Black publications, and his success tied so tightly to mainstream White comics, it begs the question of whether or not the Black community was even aware that Baker was a Black artist. Indications are that they were. Samuel Joyner wrote:

Around 1950 or 1951, I went to New York City with my portfolio of cartoons and advertising spot drawings. As a beginning cartoonist, I was encouraged to talk to other colored illustrators for information about breaking into this lucrative field.

I was given the names and studio address of a few African-American professionals. Most worked in Manhattan. E.C. Stoner, Matt Baker, Ted Shearer, Chas. Allen, Mel Bolden, etc.

I visited Matt Baker's studio workshop only once, and he too was encouraging. I was with another beginner [Cal Massey], and Matt showed us several pages of comic book art, gave us tips on how to approach assignments. [Samuel Joyner to the author, Apr. 4, 2004]

Cartoonist Ted Shearer mentioned Baker in an article detailing the recent successes of Black commercial artists, rightfully referring to him as "one of the top artists in the comic book field." [Shearer, Teddy, "Artists' Colony Lists Big Names," *New York Age*, Aug. 22, 1953]

Baker moved easily among all cultures and skin hues. When he first came to New York City, he lived at 104 W. 116th Street in East Harlem, an area heavily Hispanic and Italian. When his finances improved at the end of the 1940s, he took an apartment over at 139 E. 45th Street in midtown Manhattan near Grand Central Station and the publishers he worked for.

Stylish and handsome, women were drawn to Baker. Fred said:

He was quite a ladies' man. He was very good-looking, and he had a couple of very close women friends that I knew. I don't know exactly how close they were, but they were obviously very close. [Amash 2005, op. cit. p.51]

Despite his numerous girlfriends, Baker never married—a fact, if taken at face value, which could just mean he enjoyed his bachelorhood. It was, however, an era rife with suspicions and rumor, leading some—including one of his best friends—to question his sexual orientation.

In an interview with comics historian Shaun Clancy, Frank Giusto asked:

You knew Matt was gay, right? He and I were very, very close, but not sexually at all. A lot of times in his apartment house he probably had the hots for me, so to speak, and he would just get up and walk out and come back in an hour or so. ["Frank Giusto Interview," conducted by Shaun Clancy, Feb. 2011]

Yet another close friend, Ray Osrin, primary inker of much of Baker's artwork from 1949 to 1957, had this to say:

There was talk of him being gay. I can't say one way or the other. I never thought so. He had a flare for the dramatic as many New York people do. ["Ray Osrin Interview," conducted by Shaun Clancy, Oct. 27, 1999]

With so much of what is known about the man being anecdotal, it leaves researchers at the mercy of another person's perceptions. Baker never openly came out and that is all that can be stated as fact.

A heavy cigarette smoker—reportedly Camels were his preferred brand—Baker never made concessions to his ongoing heart problems. He defied them and the heritage of early death passed from his father and grandfather. He lived his life, popping a digitalis tablet when necessary, until he couldn't. On August 11, 1959, his half-brother Fred opened the door of Baker's darkened apartment and found him in bed, unresponsive.

Like Raphael, like Van Gogh, and Antoine Watteau—other great artists gone too soon—Matt Baker died at age 37.

Matt Baker drew the historically important Voodah, the first clearly Black hero to have his own feature in a comic book (*Crown Comics* #3). Voodah also appeared in *Crown* #4 and 5 as a Black man, although he was white-skinned on the cover of #5. His skin color remained white, both on covers and in interior stories, from issue #6 onward. *Crown Comics* #3, Fall 1945; Golfing, Inc.

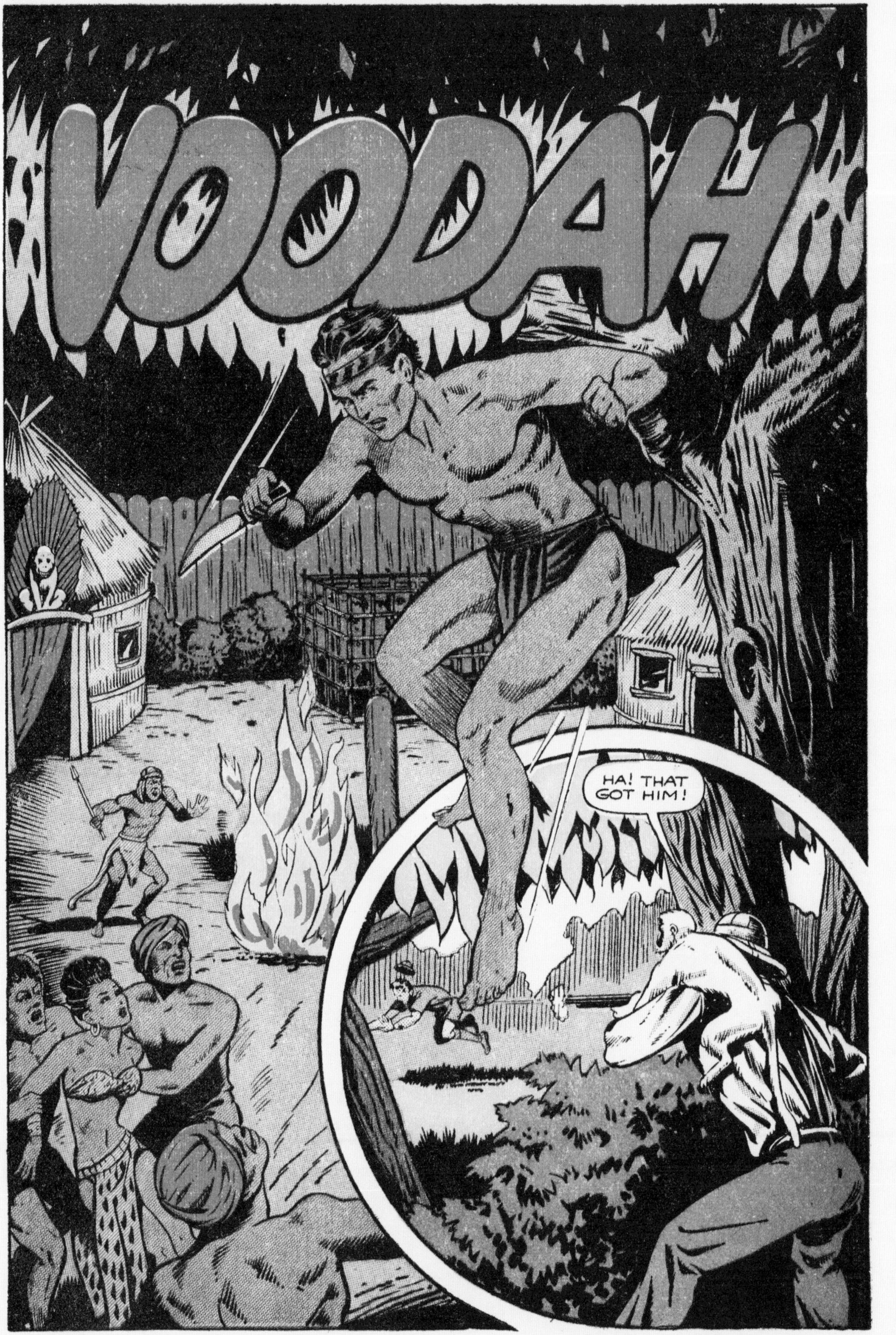
VOODAH
HA! THAT GOT HIM!

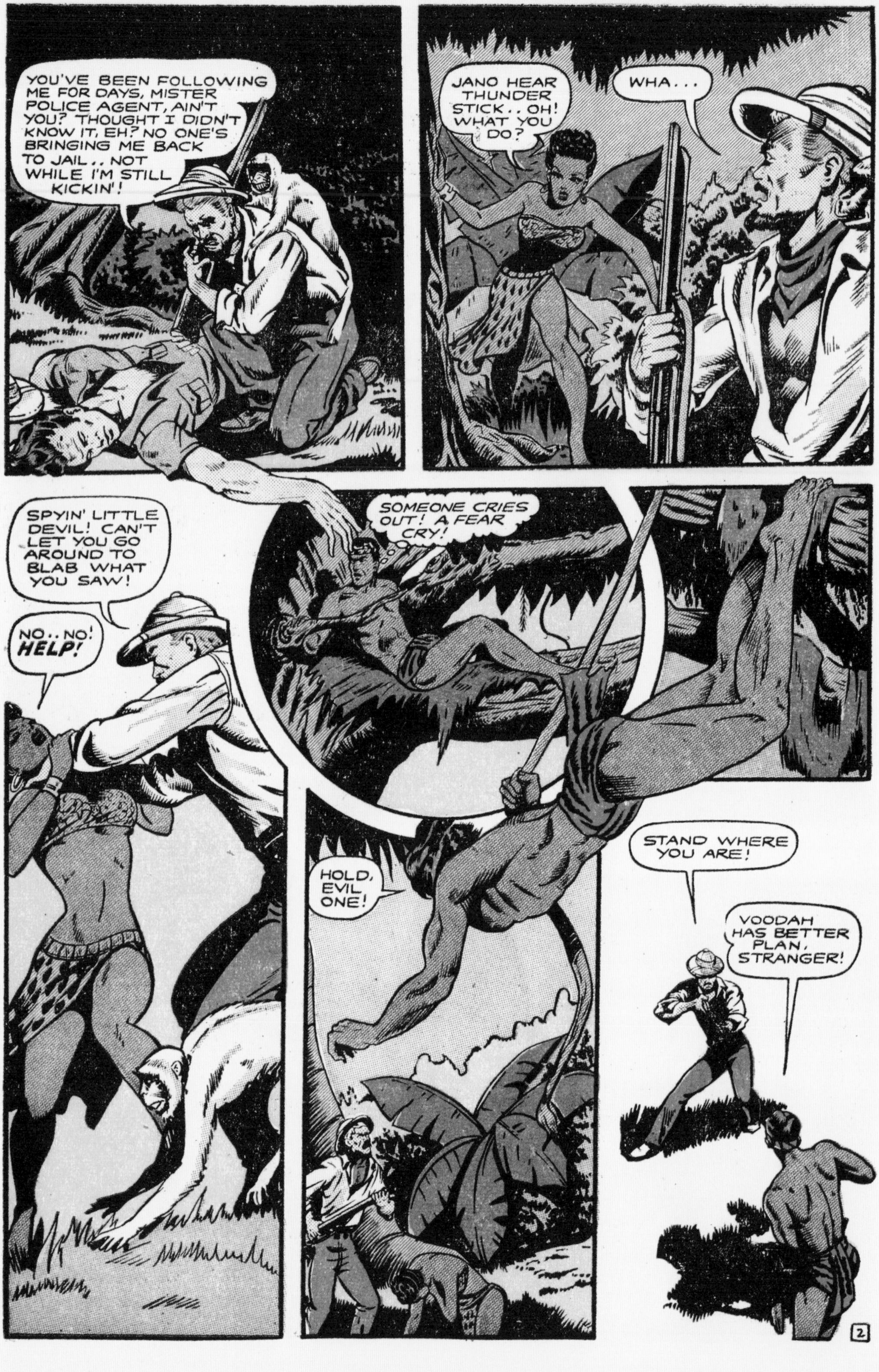
YOU'VE BEEN FOLLOWING ME FOR DAYS, MISTER POLICE AGENT, AIN'T YOU? THOUGHT I DIDN'T KNOW IT, EH? NO ONE'S BRINGING ME BACK TO JAIL.. NOT WHILE I'M STILL KICKIN'!
JANO HEAR THUNDER STICK.. OH! WHAT YOU DO?
WHA...
SPYIN' LITTLE DEVIL! CAN'T LET YOU GO AROUND TO BLAB WHAT YOU SAW!
NO.. NO! HELP!
SOMEONE CRIES OUT! A FEAR CRY!
HOLD, EVIL ONE!
STAND WHERE YOU ARE!
VOODAH HAS BETTER PLAN, STRANGER!
2

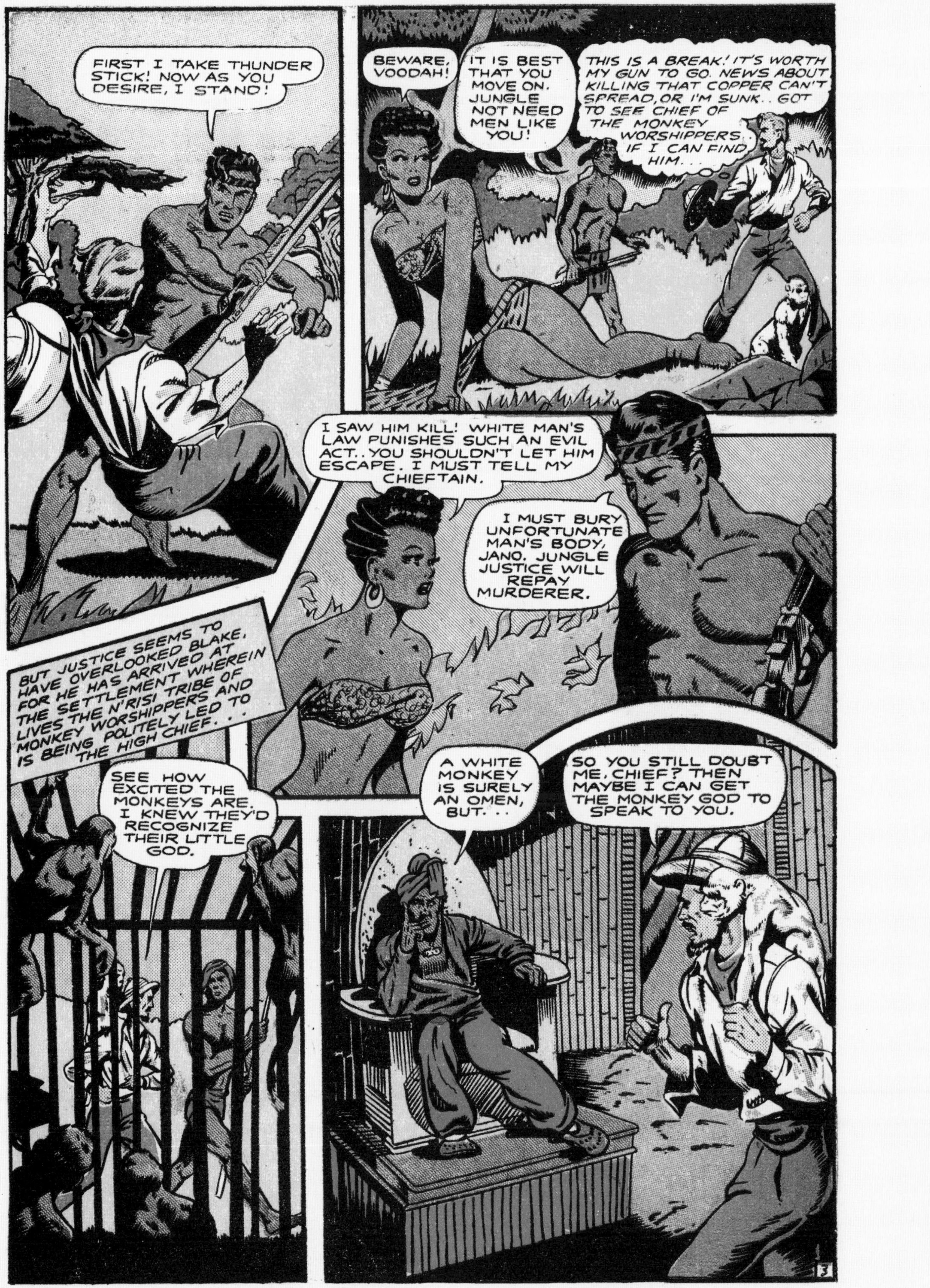

FIRST I TAKE THUNDER STICK! NOW AS YOU DESIRE, I STAND!
BEWARE, VOODAH!
IT IS BEST THAT YOU MOVE ON. JUNGLE NOT NEED MEN LIKE YOU!
THIS IS A BREAK! IT'S WORTH MY GUN TO GO. NEWS ABOUT KILLING THAT COPPER CAN'T SPREAD, OR I'M SUNK.. GOT TO SEE CHIEF OF THE MONKEY WORSHIPPERS. IF I CAN FIND HIM...
I SAW HIM KILL! WHITE MAN'S LAW PUNISHES SUCH AN EVIL ACT.. YOU SHOULDN'T LET HIM ESCAPE. I MUST TELL MY CHIEFTAIN.
I MUST BURY UNFORTUNATE MAN'S BODY, JANO. JUNGLE JUSTICE WILL REPAY MURDERER.
BUT JUSTICE SEEMS TO HAVE OVERLOOKED BLAKE, FOR HE HAS ARRIVED AT THE SETTLEMENT WHEREIN LIVES THE N'RISI TRIBE OF MONKEY WORSHIPPERS AND IS BEING POLITELY LED TO THE HIGH CHIEF...
SEE HOW EXCITED THE MONKEYS ARE. I KNEW THEY'D RECOGNIZE THEIR LITTLE GOD.
A WHITE MONKEY IS SURELY AN OMEN, BUT...
SO YOU STILL DOUBT ME, CHIEF? THEN MAYBE I CAN GET THE MONKEY GOD TO SPEAK TO YOU.
3

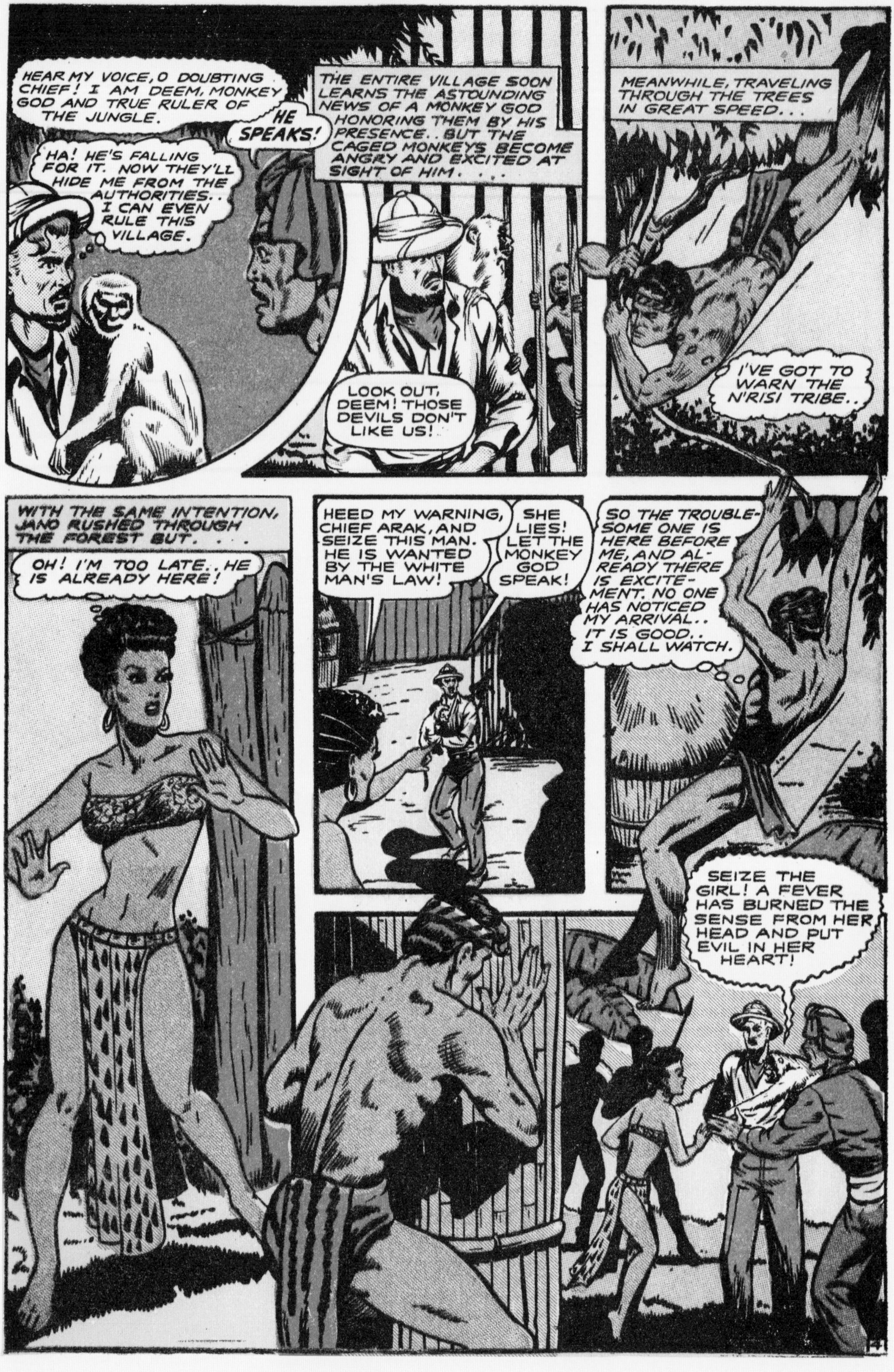

HEAR MY VOICE, O DOUBTING CHIEF! I AM DEEM, MONKEY GOD AND TRUE RULER OF THE JUNGLE.
HE SPEAKS!
HA! HE'S FALLING FOR IT. NOW THEY'LL HIDE ME FROM THE AUTHORITIES.. I CAN EVEN RULE THIS VILLAGE.
THE ENTIRE VILLAGE SOON LEARNS THE ASTOUNDING NEWS OF A MONKEY GOD HONORING THEM BY HIS PRESENCE.. BUT THE CAGED MONKEYS BECOME ANGRY AND EXCITED AT SIGHT OF HIM. . .
LOOK OUT, DEEM! THOSE DEVILS DON'T LIKE US!
MEANWHILE, TRAVELING THROUGH THE TREES IN GREAT SPEED. . .
I'VE GOT TO WARN THE N'RISI TRIBE..
WITH THE SAME INTENTION, JANO RUSHED THROUGH THE FOREST BUT. . .
OH! I'M TOO LATE..HE IS ALREADY HERE!
HEED MY WARNING, CHIEF ARAK, AND SEIZE THIS MAN. HE IS WANTED BY THE WHITE MAN'S LAW!
SHE LIES! LET THE MONKEY GOD SPEAK!
SO THE TROUBLESOME ONE IS HERE BEFORE ME, AND ALREADY THERE IS EXCITEMENT. NO ONE HAS NOTICED MY ARRIVAL.. IT IS GOOD.. I SHALL WATCH.
SEIZE THE GIRL! A FEVER HAS BURNED THE SENSE FROM HER HEAD AND PUT EVIL IN HER HEART!
4

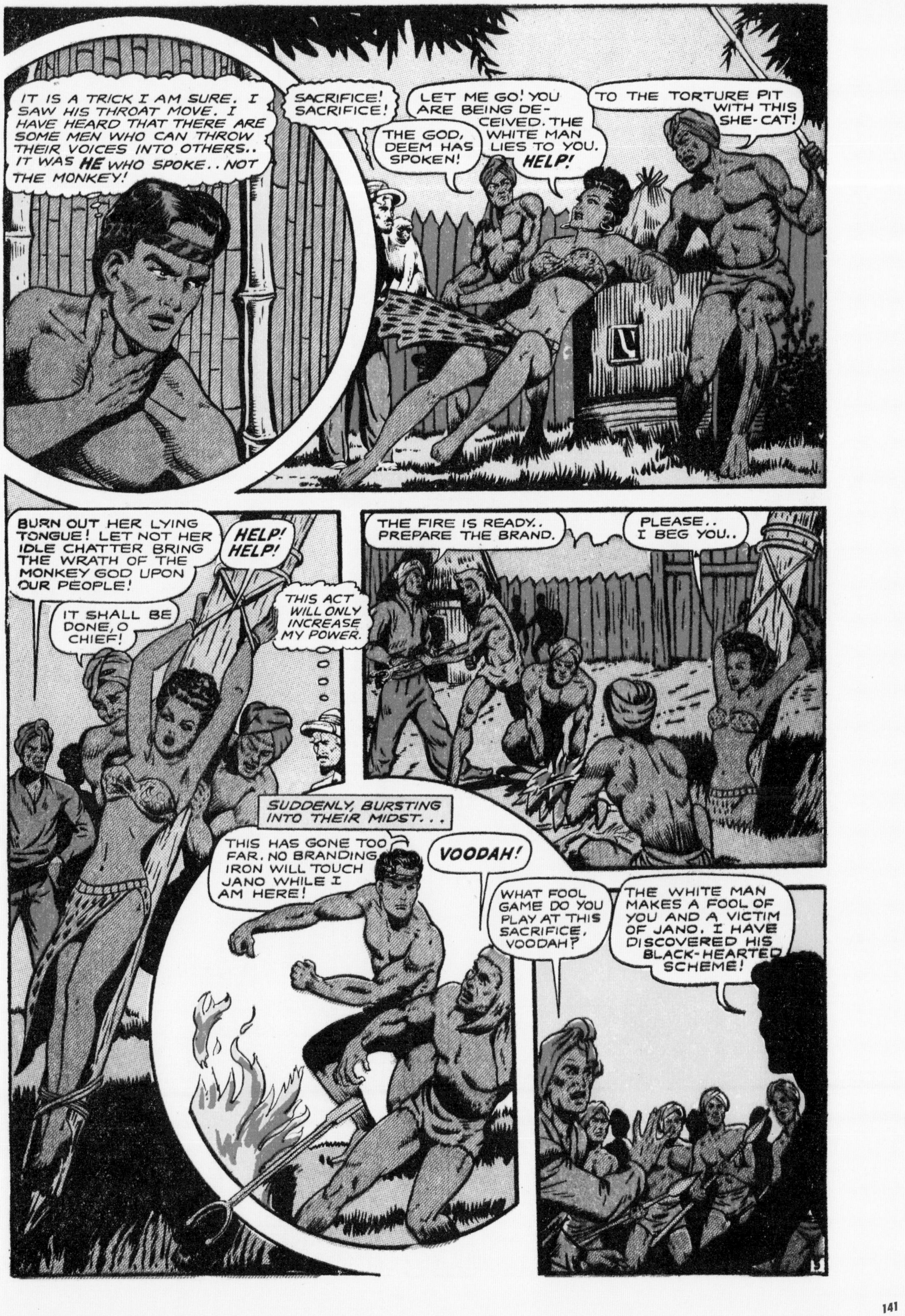
IT IS A TRICK I AM SURE. I SAW HIS THROAT MOVE. I HAVE HEARD THAT THERE ARE SOME MEN WHO CAN THROW THEIR VOICES INTO OTHERS.. IT WAS HE WHO SPOKE.. NOT THE MONKEY!
SACRIFICE! SACRIFICE!
THE GOD, DEEM HAS SPOKEN!
LET ME GO! YOU ARE BEING DE-CEIVED. THE WHITE MAN LIES TO YOU. HELP!
TO THE TORTURE PIT WITH THIS SHE-CAT!
BURN OUT HER LYING TONGUE! LET NOT HER IDLE CHATTER BRING THE WRATH OF THE MONKEY GOD UPON OUR PEOPLE!
HELP! HELP!
IT SHALL BE DONE, O CHIEF!
THIS ACT WILL ONLY INCREASE MY POWER.
THE FIRE IS READY.. PREPARE THE BRAND.
PLEASE.. I BEG YOU..
SUDDENLY, BURSTING INTO THEIR MIDST...
THIS HAS GONE TOO FAR. NO BRANDING IRON WILL TOUCH JANO WHILE I AM HERE!
VOODAH!
WHAT FOOL GAME DO YOU PLAY AT THIS SACRIFICE, VOODAH?
THE WHITE MAN MAKES A FOOL OF YOU AND A VICTIM OF JANO. I HAVE DISCOVERED HIS BLACK-HEARTED SCHEME!

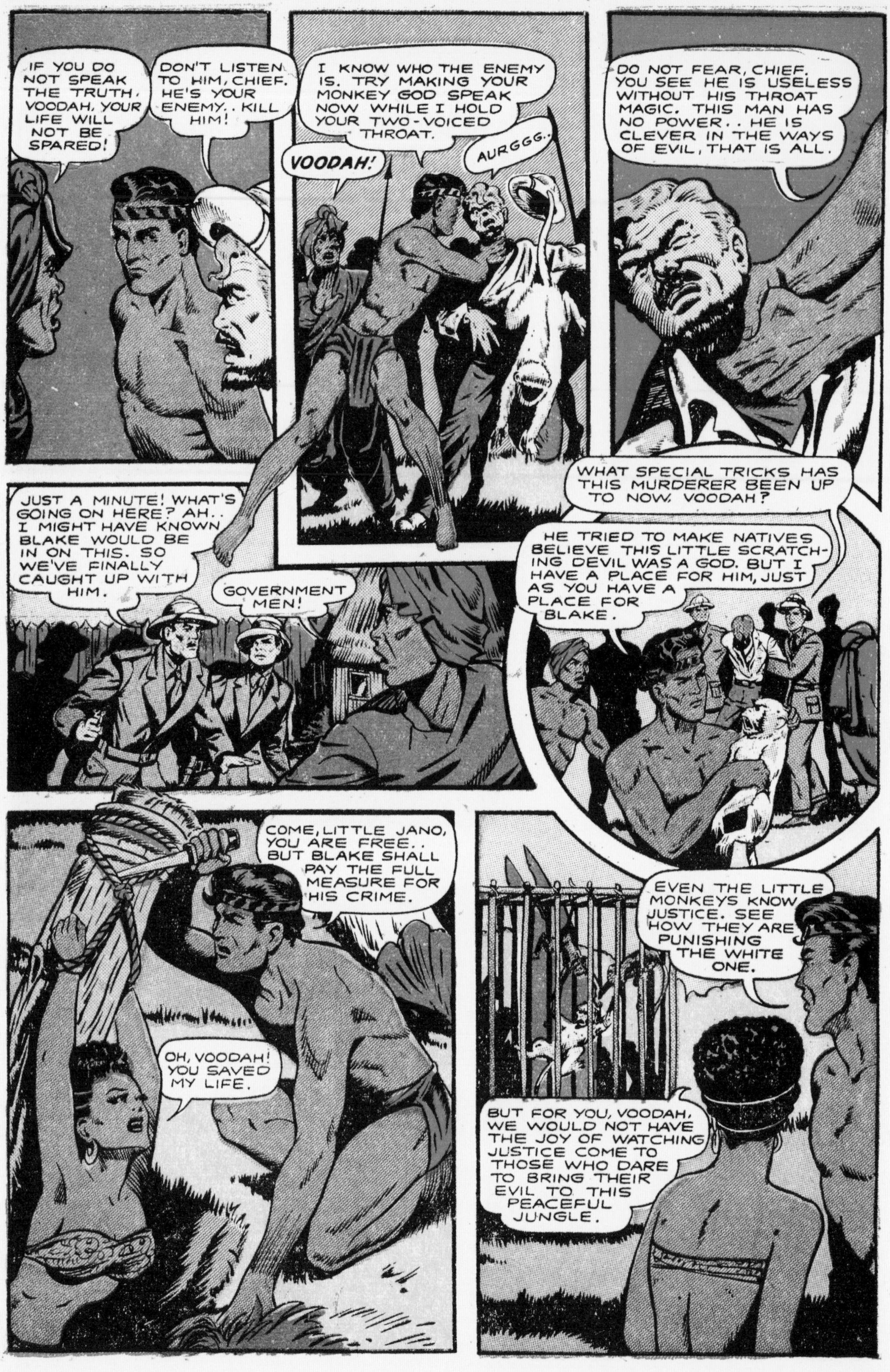

IF YOU DO NOT SPEAK THE TRUTH, VOODAH, YOUR LIFE WILL NOT BE SPARED!
DON'T LISTEN TO HIM, CHIEF. HE'S YOUR ENEMY.. KILL HIM!
I KNOW WHO THE ENEMY IS. TRY MAKING YOUR MONKEY GOD SPEAK NOW WHILE I HOLD YOUR TWO-VOICED THROAT.
VOODAH!
AURGGG..
DO NOT FEAR, CHIEF. YOU SEE HE IS USELESS WITHOUT HIS THROAT MAGIC. THIS MAN HAS NO POWER.. HE IS CLEVER IN THE WAYS OF EVIL, THAT IS ALL.
JUST A MINUTE! WHAT'S GOING ON HERE? AH.. I MIGHT HAVE KNOWN BLAKE WOULD BE IN ON THIS. SO WE'VE FINALLY CAUGHT UP WITH HIM.
GOVERNMENT MEN!
WHAT SPECIAL TRICKS HAS THIS MURDERER BEEN UP TO NOW, VOODAH?
HE TRIED TO MAKE NATIVES BELIEVE THIS LITTLE SCRATCHING DEVIL WAS A GOD. BUT I HAVE A PLACE FOR HIM, JUST AS YOU HAVE A PLACE FOR BLAKE.
COME, LITTLE JANO, YOU ARE FREE.. BUT BLAKE SHALL PAY THE FULL MEASURE FOR HIS CRIME.
OH, VOODAH! YOU SAVED MY LIFE.
EVEN THE LITTLE MONKEYS KNOW JUSTICE. SEE HOW THEY ARE PUNISHING THE WHITE ONE.
BUT FOR YOU, VOODAH, WE WOULD NOT HAVE THE JOY OF WATCHING JUSTICE COME TO THOSE WHO DARE TO BRING THEIR EVIL TO THIS PEACEFUL JUNGLE.

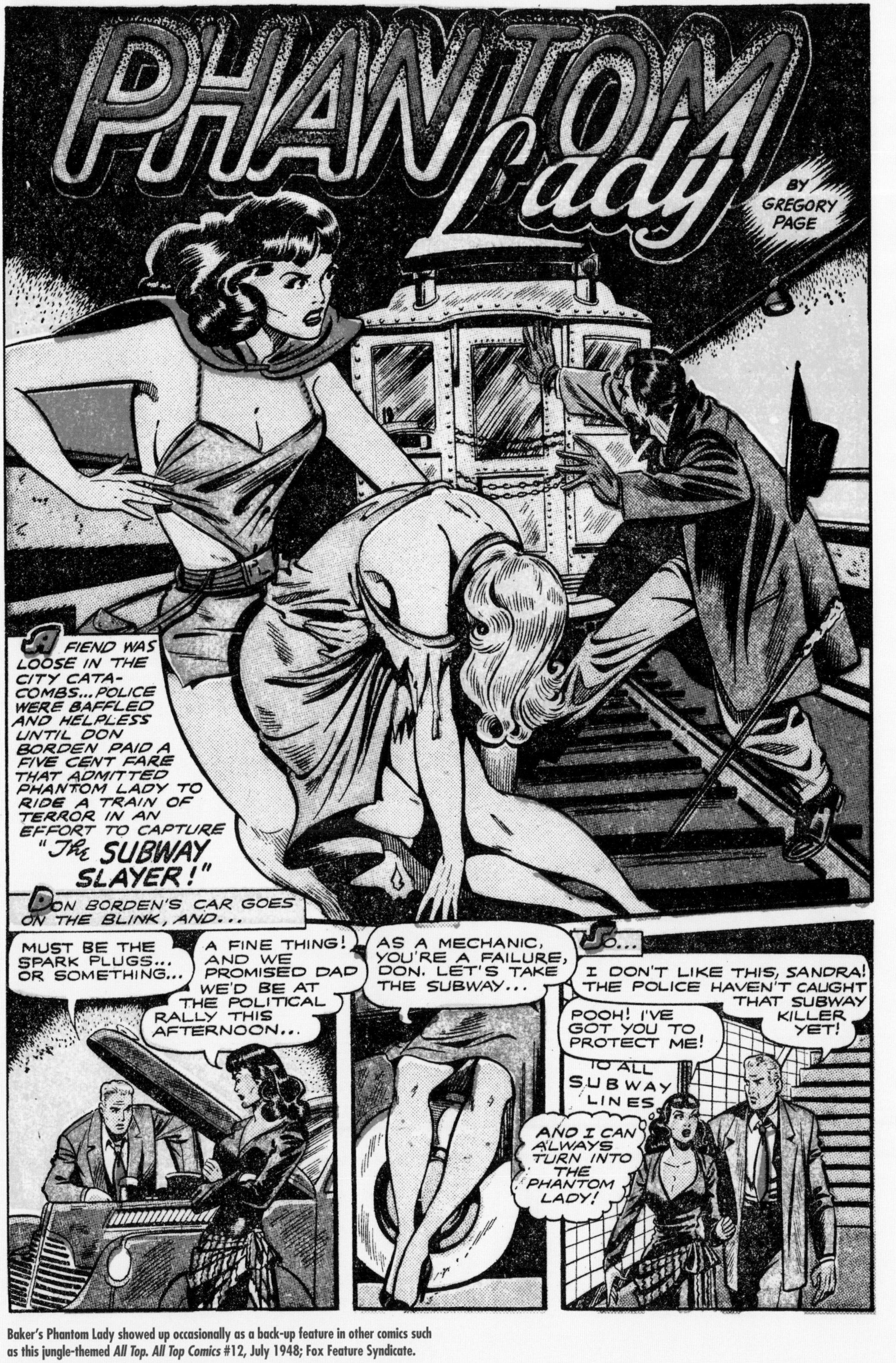
PHANTOM Lady
BY GREGORY PAGE
A FIEND WAS LOOSE IN THE CITY CATA-COMBS...POLICE WERE BAFFLED AND HELPLESS UNTIL DON BORDEN PAID A FIVE CENT FARE THAT ADMITTED PHANTOM LADY TO RIDE A TRAIN OF TERROR IN AN EFFORT TO CAPTURE "The SUBWAY SLAYER!"
DON BORDEN'S CAR GOES ON THE BLINK, AND...
MUST BE THE SPARK PLUGS... OR SOMETHING...
A FINE THING! AND WE PROMISED DAD WE'D BE AT THE POLITICAL RALLY THIS AFTERNOON...
AS A MECHANIC, YOU'RE A FAILURE, DON. LET'S TAKE THE SUBWAY...
SO...
I DON'T LIKE THIS, SANDRA! THE POLICE HAVEN'T CAUGHT THAT SUBWAY KILLER YET!
POOH! I'VE GOT YOU TO PROTECT ME!
TO ALL SUBWAY LINES
AND I CAN ALWAYS TURN INTO THE PHANTOM LADY!

Baker's Phantom Lady showed up occasionally as a back-up feature in other comics such as this jungle-themed *All Top. All Top Comics* #12, July 1948; Fox Feature Syndicate.

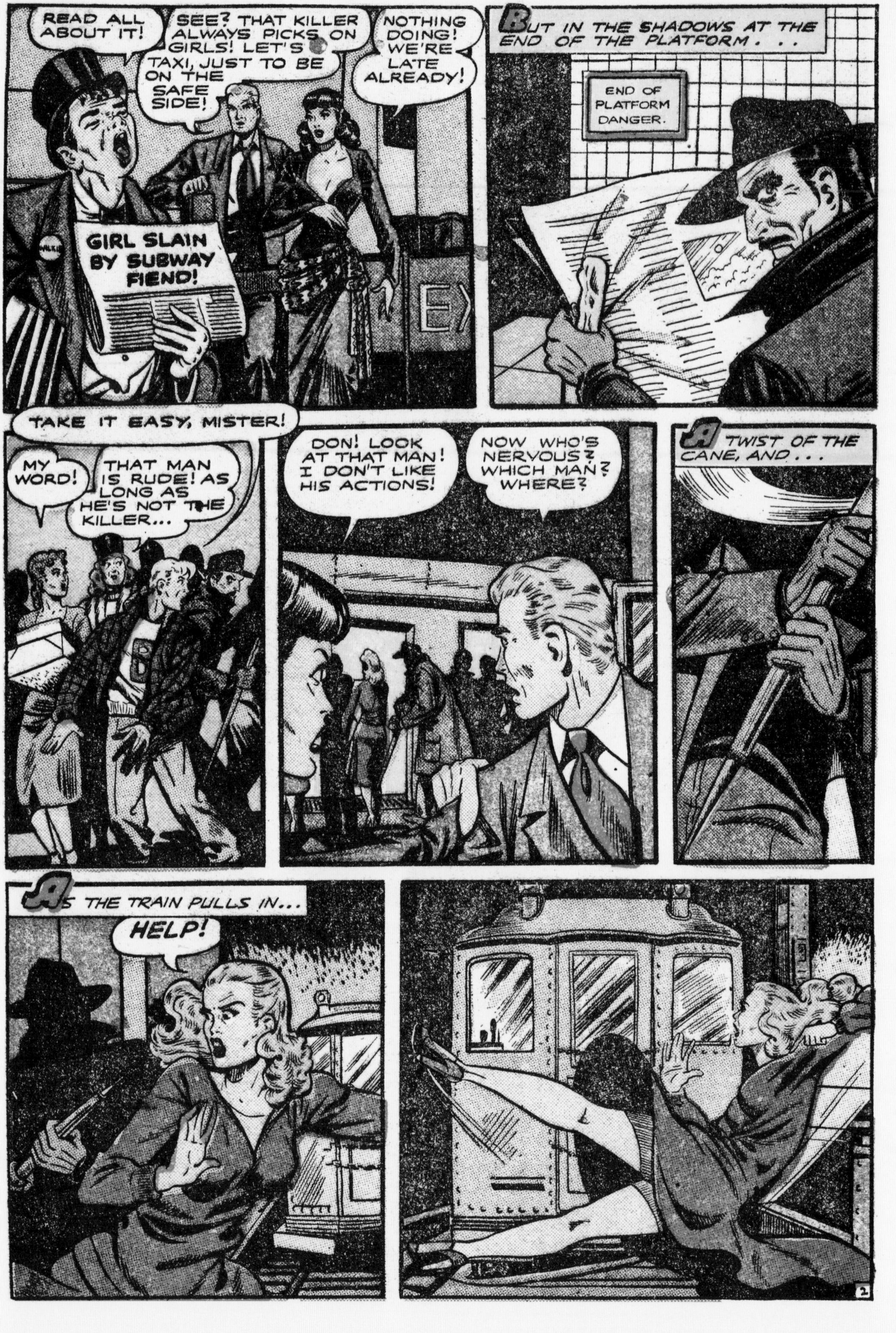
READ ALL ABOUT IT!
SEE? THAT KILLER ALWAYS PICKS ON GIRLS! LET'S TAXI, JUST TO BE ON THE SAFE SIDE!
NOTHING DOING! WE'RE LATE ALREADY!
GIRL SLAIN BY SUBWAY FIEND!
BUT IN THE SHADOWS AT THE END OF THE PLATFORM . . .
END OF PLATFORM DANGER.
TAKE IT EASY, MISTER!
MY WORD!
THAT MAN IS RUDE! AS LONG AS HE'S NOT THE KILLER...
DON! LOOK AT THAT MAN! I DON'T LIKE HIS ACTIONS!
NOW WHO'S NERVOUS? WHICH MAN? WHERE?
A TWIST OF THE CANE, AND . . .
AS THE TRAIN PULLS IN...
HELP!
2

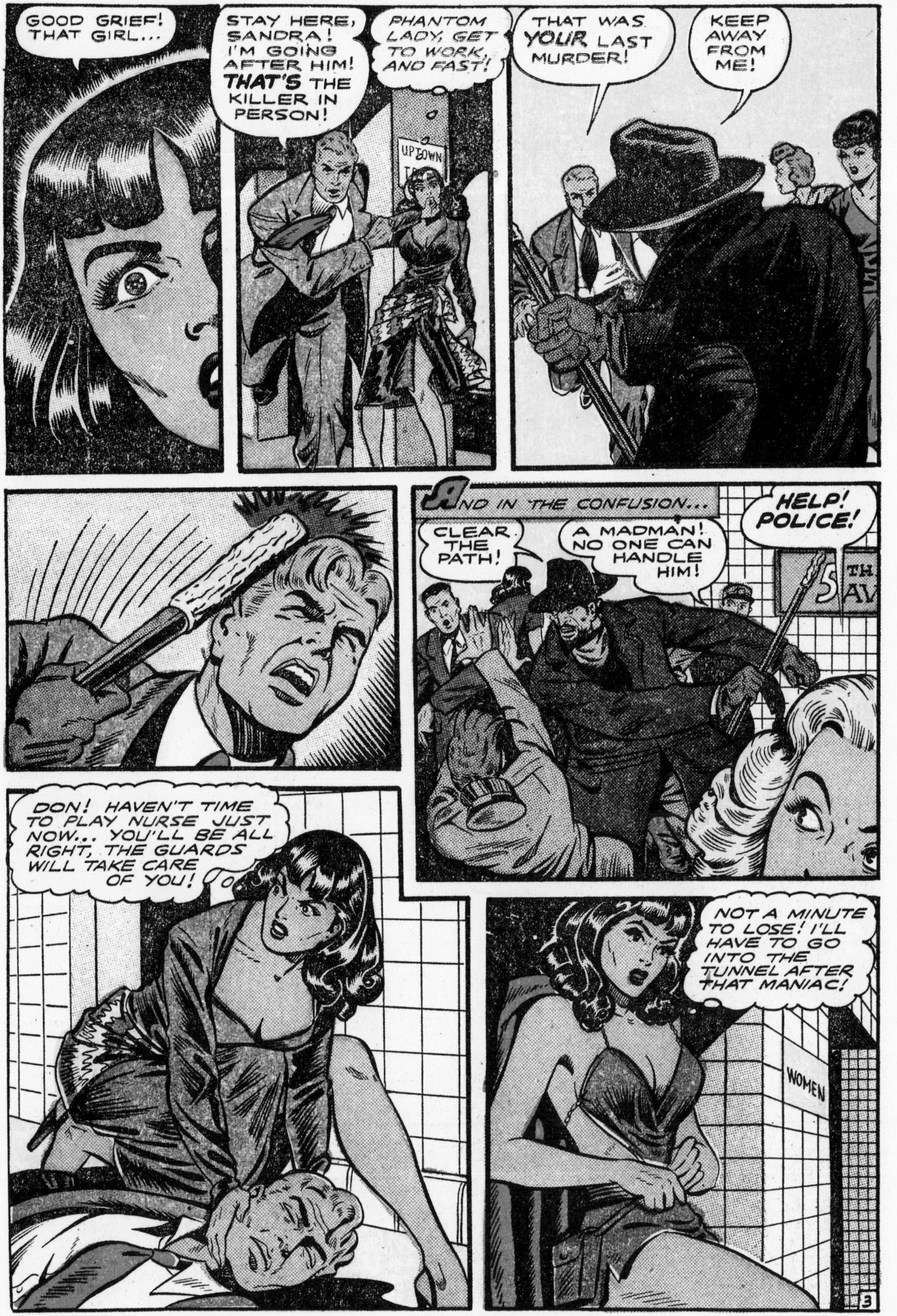
GOOD GRIEF! THAT GIRL...
STAY HERE, SANDRA! I'M GOING AFTER HIM! THAT'S THE KILLER IN PERSON!
PHANTOM LADY, GET TO WORK, AND FAST!
UPTOWN
THAT WAS YOUR LAST MURDER!
KEEP AWAY FROM ME!
AND IN THE CONFUSION...
CLEAR THE PATH!
A MADMAN! NO ONE CAN HANDLE HIM!
HELP! POLICE!
DON! HAVEN'T TIME TO PLAY NURSE JUST NOW... YOU'LL BE ALL RIGHT, THE GUARDS WILL TAKE CARE OF YOU!
NOT A MINUTE TO LOSE! I'LL HAVE TO GO INTO THE TUNNEL AFTER THAT MANIAC!
WOMEN
3

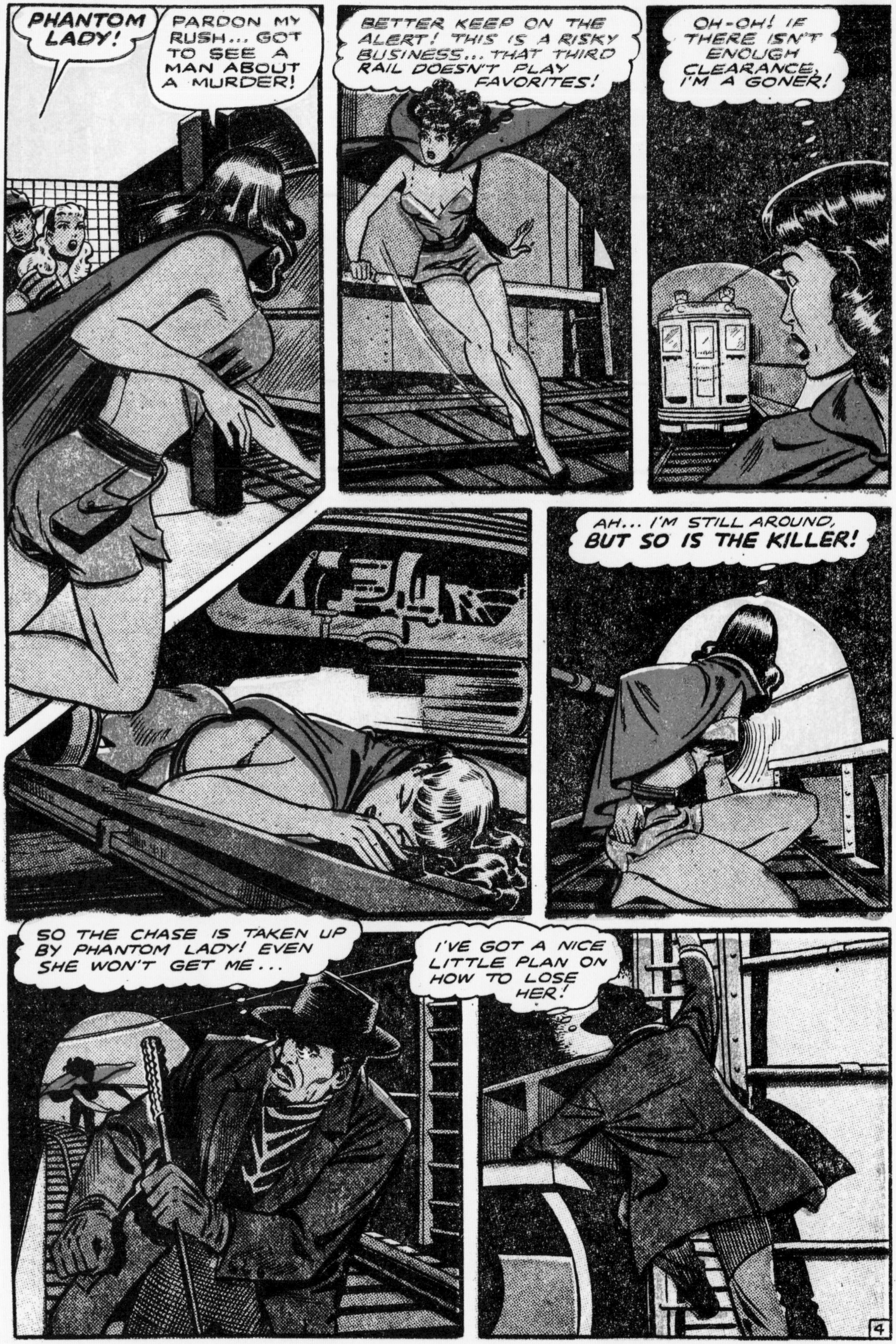
PHANTOM LADY!
PARDON MY RUSH... GOT TO SEE A MAN ABOUT A MURDER!
BETTER KEEP ON THE ALERT! THIS IS A RISKY BUSINESS... THAT THIRD RAIL DOESN'T PLAY FAVORITES!
OH-OH! IF THERE ISN'T ENOUGH CLEARANCE, I'M A GONER!
AH... I'M STILL AROUND, BUT SO IS THE KILLER!
SO THE CHASE IS TAKEN UP BY PHANTOM LADY! EVEN SHE WON'T GET ME...
I'VE GOT A NICE LITTLE PLAN ON HOW TO LOSE HER!
4

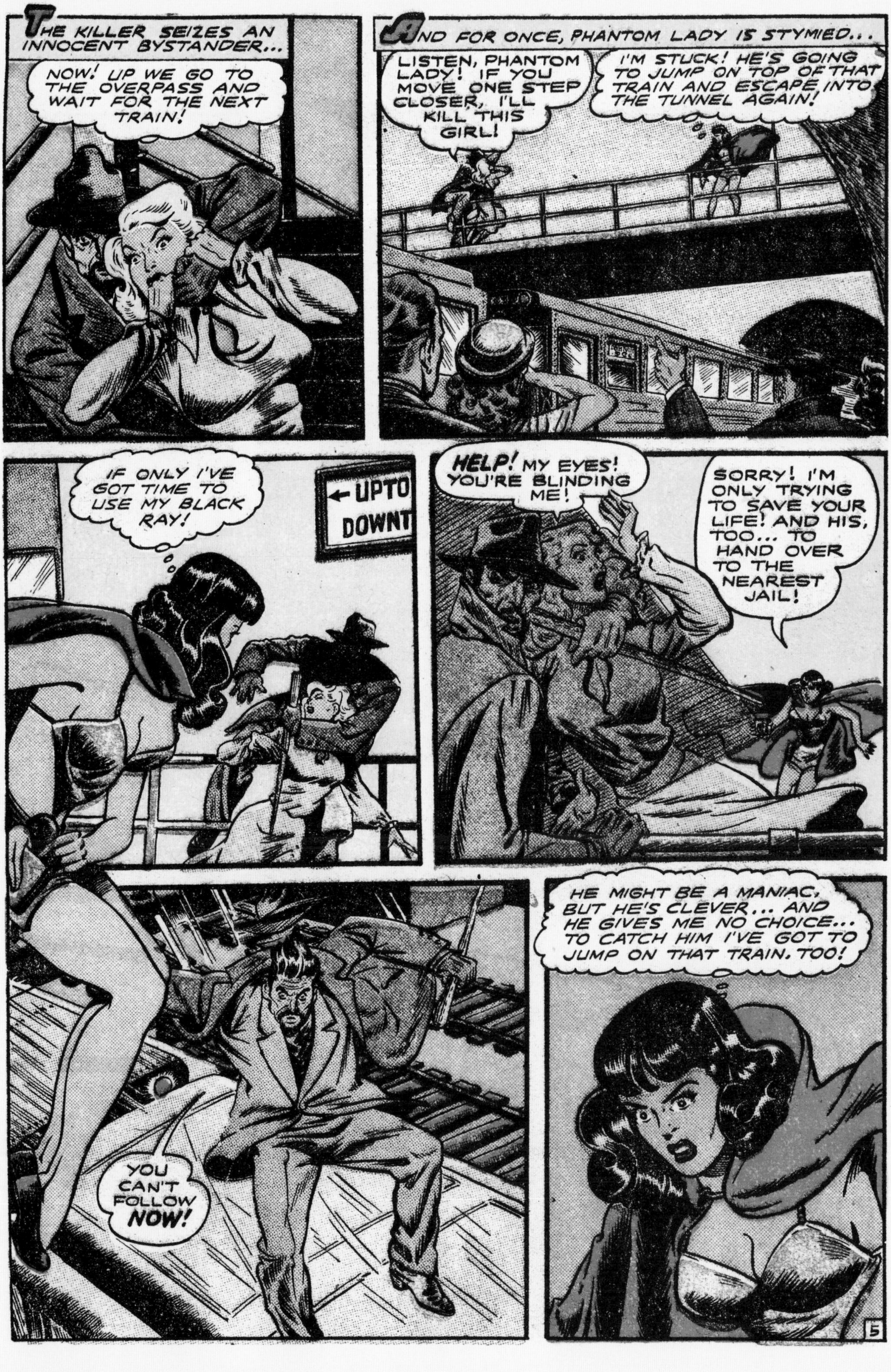
THE KILLER SEIZES AN INNOCENT BYSTANDER...
NOW! UP WE GO TO THE OVERPASS AND WAIT FOR THE NEXT TRAIN!
AND FOR ONCE, PHANTOM LADY IS STYMIED...
LISTEN, PHANTOM LADY! IF YOU MOVE ONE STEP CLOSER, I'LL KILL THIS GIRL!
I'M STUCK! HE'S GOING TO JUMP ON TOP OF THAT TRAIN AND ESCAPE INTO THE TUNNEL AGAIN!
IF ONLY I'VE GOT TIME TO USE MY BLACK RAY!
← UPTO
DOWNT
HELP! MY EYES! YOU'RE BLINDING ME!
SORRY! I'M ONLY TRYING TO SAVE YOUR LIFE! AND HIS, TOO... TO HAND OVER TO THE NEAREST JAIL!
YOU CAN'T FOLLOW NOW!
HE MIGHT BE A MANIAC, BUT HE'S CLEVER... AND HE GIVES ME NO CHOICE... TO CATCH HIM I'VE GOT TO JUMP ON THAT TRAIN, TOO!
5

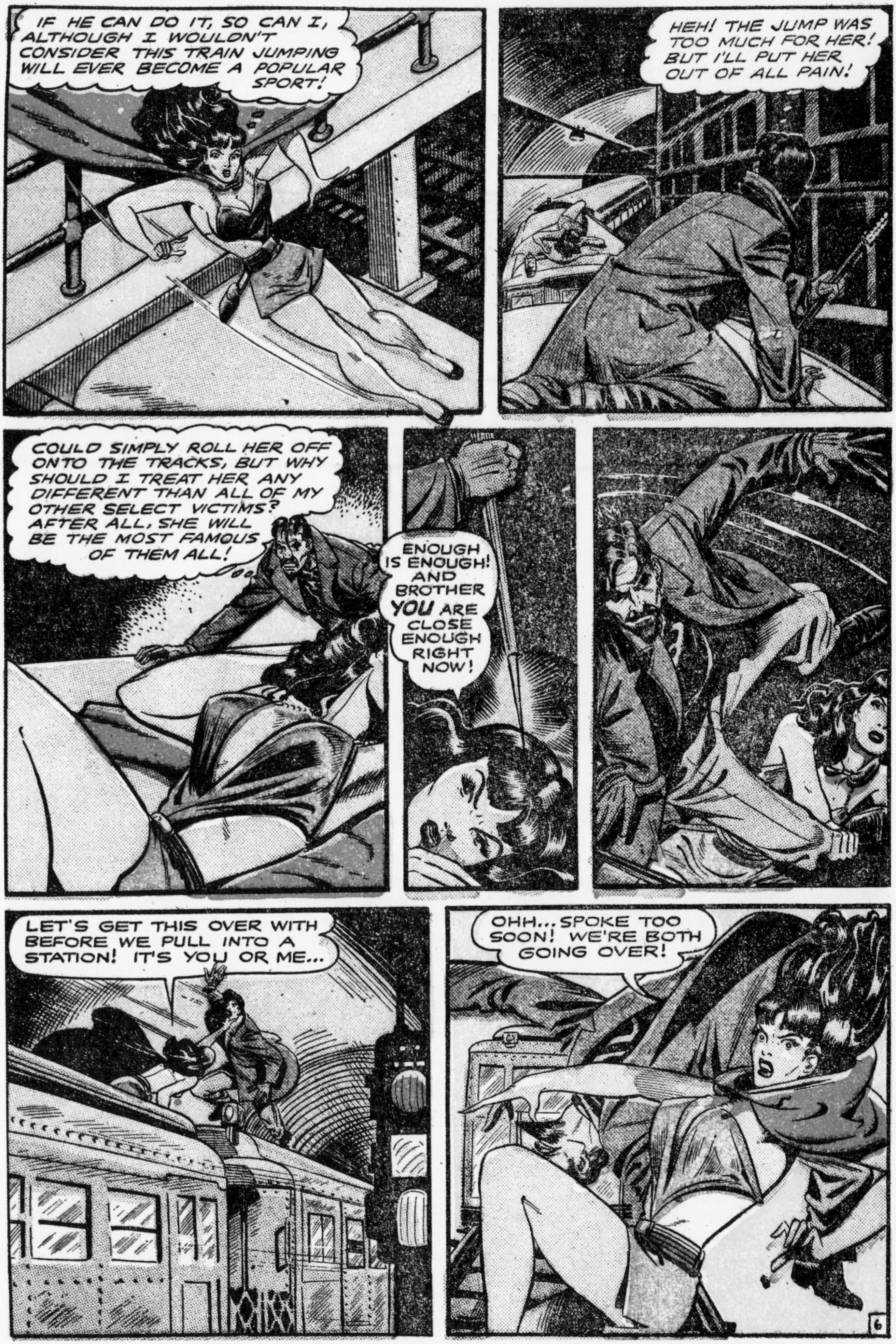
IF HE CAN DO IT, SO CAN I, ALTHOUGH I WOULDN'T CONSIDER THIS TRAIN JUMPING WILL EVER BECOME A POPULAR SPORT!
HEH! THE JUMP WAS TOO MUCH FOR HER! BUT I'LL PUT HER OUT OF ALL PAIN!
COULD SIMPLY ROLL HER OFF ONTO THE TRACKS, BUT WHY SHOULD I TREAT HER ANY DIFFERENT THAN ALL OF MY OTHER SELECT VICTIMS? AFTER ALL, SHE WILL BE THE MOST FAMOUS OF THEM ALL!
ENOUGH IS ENOUGH! AND BROTHER YOU ARE CLOSE ENOUGH RIGHT NOW!
LET'S GET THIS OVER WITH BEFORE WE PULL INTO A STATION! IT'S YOU OR ME...
OHH... SPOKE TOO SOON! WE'RE BOTH GOING OVER!
6

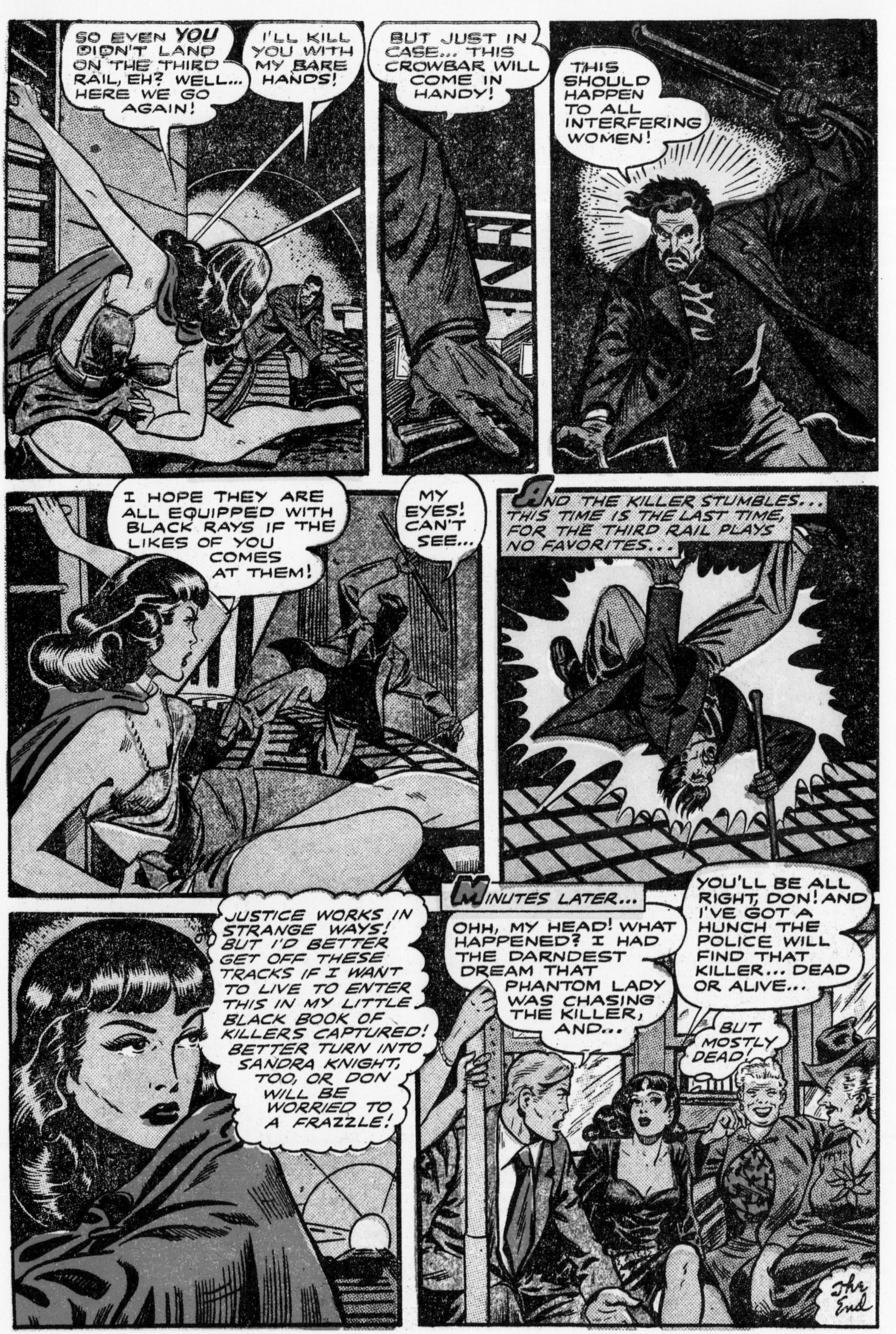
SO EVEN YOU DIDN'T LAND ON THE THIRD RAIL, EH? WELL... HERE WE GO AGAIN!
I'LL KILL YOU WITH MY BARE HANDS!
BUT JUST IN CASE... THIS CROWBAR WILL COME IN HANDY!
THIS SHOULD HAPPEN TO ALL INTERFERING WOMEN!
I HOPE THEY ARE ALL EQUIPPED WITH BLACK RAYS IF THE LIKES OF YOU COMES AT THEM!
MY EYES! CAN'T SEE...
AND THE KILLER STUMBLES... THIS TIME IS THE LAST TIME, FOR THE THIRD RAIL PLAYS NO FAVORITES...
JUSTICE WORKS IN STRANGE WAYS! BUT I'D BETTER GET OFF THESE TRACKS IF I WANT TO LIVE TO ENTER THIS IN MY LITTLE BLACK BOOK OF KILLERS CAPTURED! BETTER TURN INTO SANDRA KNIGHT, TOO, OR DON WILL BE WORRIED TO A FRAZZLE!
MINUTES LATER...
OHH, MY HEAD! WHAT HAPPENED? I HAD THE DARNDEST DREAM THAT PHANTOM LADY WAS CHASING THE KILLER, AND...
YOU'LL BE ALL RIGHT, DON! AND I'VE GOT A HUNCH THE POLICE WILL FIND THAT KILLER... DEAD OR ALIVE...
BUT MOSTLY DEAD!
The End

ALVIN CARL HOLLINGSWORTH
The Young Professional

Young, aspiring artists living in New York City had opportunities of which their counterparts growing up elsewhere in the country could only dream. A large artist community supported by seemingly limitless wealthy benefactors, access to a number of world-class museums, and the sheer number of potential employers were just some of the benefits enjoyed by Gothamites. Another was the city's educational system.

In the depths of the Great Depression, New York was graced with two new high schools with similar purpose: the High School of Music and Art, and the School of Industrial Art.

Both schools were the beneficiaries of Mayor Fiorello LaGuardia's administrative plans to provide "recognition of municipal responsibility in providing opportunities for music, art, and higher education." [Merriam, Charles, "Fusion's Interim Report," *Saturday Review*, Nov. 7, 1936, p.22]

The Music and Art school opened first, with students attending inaugural classes in February 1936. It was LaGuardia's pet project, a school devoted to educating the best students in music and fine art. He got the New York City Board of Education to agree and in it welcomed its first students in February 1936.

What was unique about both schools was that admission was offered to any student from any of the five boroughs who could pass their rigorous tests, no matter the color of their skin. An article touting the virtues of the Industrial Art school read:

They take an intelligence test and a general knowledge test. Then they make a quick drawing on an assigned subject. No one expects

[Right] This Hollingsworth horror cover depicts a scene from the two-page text story appearing in the comics' interior. *Diary of Horror!* #1, 1952, Avon Periodical.

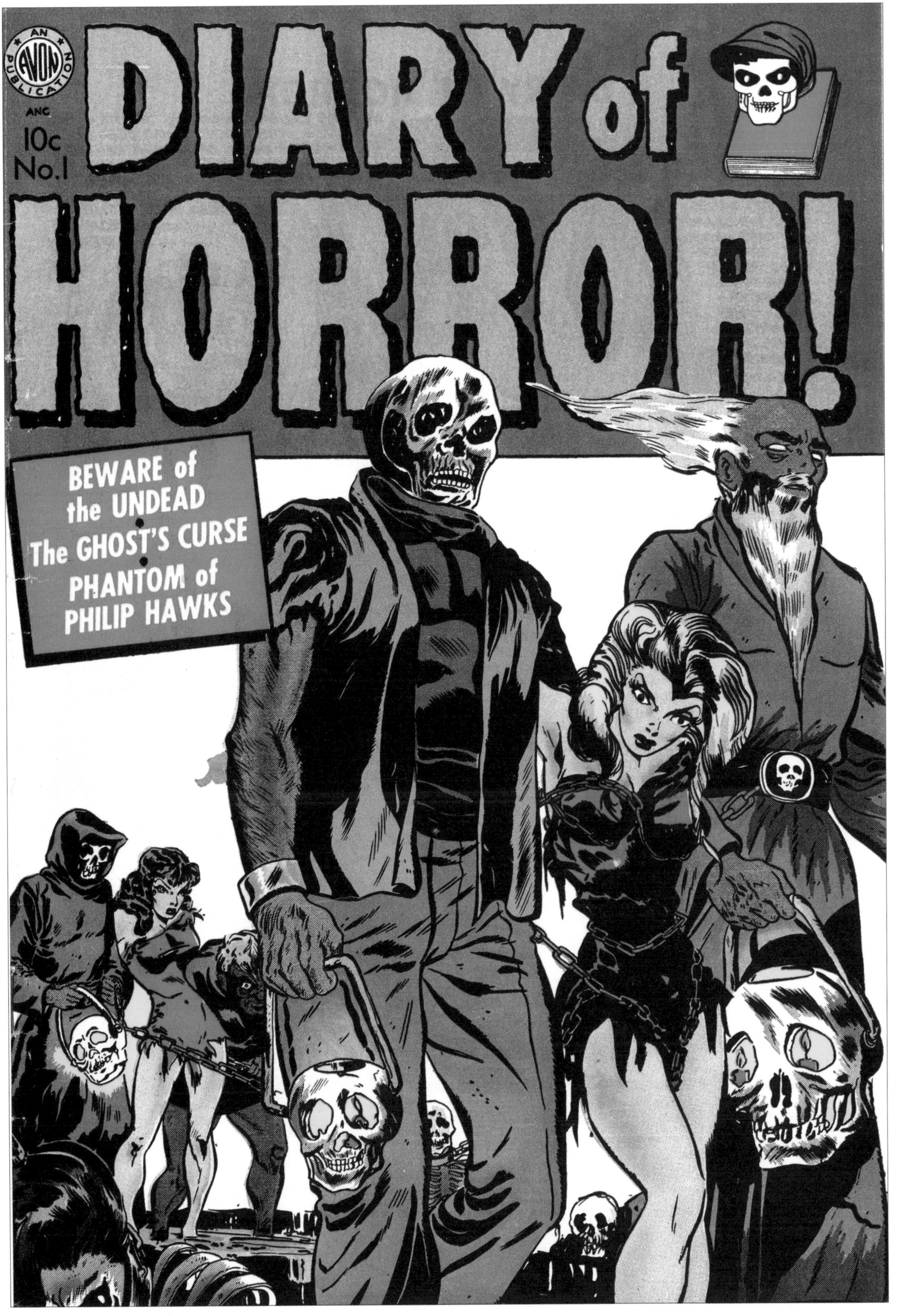
AN AVON PUBLICATION
ANC
10c
No.1
DIARY of HORROR!
BEWARE of the UNDEAD
The GHOST'S CURSE
PHANTOM of PHILIP HAWKS

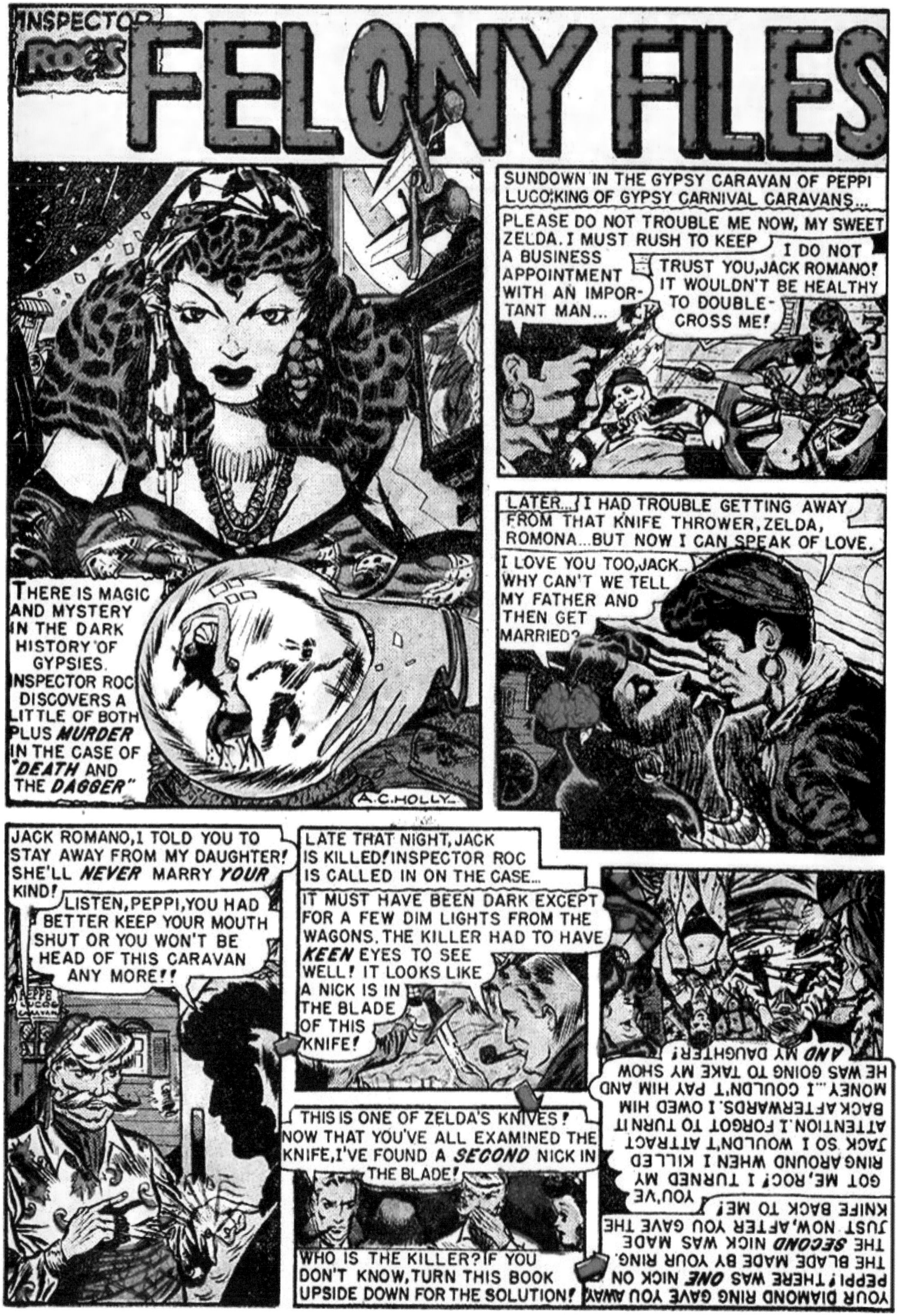
INSPECTOR ROC'S FELONY FILES
THERE IS MAGIC AND MYSTERY IN THE DARK HISTORY OF GYPSIES. INSPECTOR ROC DISCOVERS A LITTLE OF BOTH PLUS MURDER IN THE CASE OF "DEATH AND THE DAGGER"
A.C. HOLLY
SUNDOWN IN THE GYPSY CARAVAN OF PEPPI LUCO, KING OF GYPSY CARNIVAL CARAVANS...
PLEASE DO NOT TROUBLE ME NOW, MY SWEET ZELDA. I MUST RUSH TO KEEP A BUSINESS APPOINTMENT WITH AN IMPORTANT MAN...
I DO NOT TRUST YOU, JACK ROMANO! IT WOULDN'T BE HEALTHY TO DOUBLE-CROSS ME!
LATER... I HAD TROUBLE GETTING AWAY FROM THAT KNIFE THROWER, ZELDA, ROMONA...BUT NOW I CAN SPEAK OF LOVE.
I LOVE YOU TOO, JACK... WHY CAN'T WE TELL MY FATHER AND THEN GET MARRIED?
JACK ROMANO, I TOLD YOU TO STAY AWAY FROM MY DAUGHTER! SHE'LL NEVER MARRY YOUR KIND!
LISTEN, PEPPI, YOU HAD BETTER KEEP YOUR MOUTH SHUT OR YOU WON'T BE HEAD OF THIS CARAVAN ANY MORE!!
PEPPI LUCO CARAVAN
LATE THAT NIGHT, JACK IS KILLED! INSPECTOR ROC IS CALLED IN ON THE CASE...
IT MUST HAVE BEEN DARK EXCEPT FOR A FEW DIM LIGHTS FROM THE WAGONS. THE KILLER HAD TO HAVE KEEN EYES TO SEE WELL! IT LOOKS LIKE A NICK IS IN THE BLADE OF THIS KNIFE!
THIS IS ONE OF ZELDA'S KNIVES! NOW THAT YOU'VE ALL EXAMINED THE KNIFE, I'VE FOUND A SECOND NICK IN THE BLADE!
WHO IS THE KILLER? IF YOU DON'T KNOW, TURN THIS BOOK UPSIDE DOWN FOR THE SOLUTION!
YOUR DIAMOND RING GAVE YOU AWAY, PEPPI! THERE WAS ONE NICK ON THE BLADE MADE BY YOUR RING. THE SECOND NICK WAS MADE JUST NOW, AFTER YOU GAVE THE KNIFE BACK TO ME!
YOU'VE GOT ME, ROC! I TURNED MY RING AROUND WHEN I KILLED JACK SO I WOULDN'T ATTRACT ATTENTION. I FORGOT TO TURN IT BACK AFTERWARDS. I OWED HIM MONEY... I COULDN'T PAY HIM AND HE WAS GOING TO TAKE MY SHOW AND MY DAUGHTER!

She loved him and she did not care that she had no right to. Not until she had to say---

Farewell to Love

BONNIE, I LOVE YOU! YOU'VE GOT TO SEE IT MY WAY! I CAN'T GIVE YOU UP! I SIMPLY CAN'T!

WE'VE BEEN OVER ALL THIS BEFORE, LARRY. IT'S NO USE. I SIMPLY REFUSE TO GIVE UP MODELING AND LIVE ON THE INCOME A STRUGGLING YOUNG DOCTOR COULD MAKE! AND UNLESS YOU DECIDE TO BE SENSIBLE ABOUT THIS THING, WE'RE THROUGH!

ART BY A.C. HOLLINGSWORTH

those drawings to look like the work of finished artists (most entrants haven't had any previous art training at all) but they are expected to show innate talent. ["High School for Bread and Butter Artists," *Seventeen*, March 1946, pp.138-139]

Alvin Hollingsworth was already a working artist at Holyoke Publications when his co-worker and friend, Joe Kubert, suggested he apply at the same high school he was going to attend, the School of Music and Art. Kubert told an interviewer:

The question of race never ever entered into the equation with my friendship with Alvin or for my parents. He came into the house as my friend. When we were 13 or 14, we would be wrestling together or just palling around so what I would try and do...I would try and help [him] as much as I could just as I was helped getting in as well. ["Joe Kubert Interview," conducted by Shaun Clancy, May 13, 2011]

Thanks to a drought of artists due to their being lost to military service, both boys—barely in their teens—had gotten jobs assisting older artists with their comic book assignments. Doing anything that was asked of them, they even-

tually were allowed to draw pages themselves.

It was a curious friendship. Kubert was a Polish-born Jew, while Hollingsworth was a Black whose roots led back to the Caribbean.

Charles Haynes came to the U.S. with his mother, sister, and uncle aboard the S.S. *Panama* on July 3, 1917, just weeks before that ship ignominiously rammed the troopship *Saratoga* in a collision off Staten Island. The young family was emigrating from Cristóbal in the Panama Canal Zone. They were all natives of Barbados, a small island that was part of the larger collective island group forming the British West Indies.

Whenever the past is recalled, bits are missing, forgotten, misremembered. Much is lost to the "mists of time." When and how Charles and his relatives came to America is provable via official documentation. The identity of his father, though, is less certain. Charles' mother is listed as "Mrs. Gordon Haynes" on the manifest of the S.S. *Panama* and she is noted to be a married woman. Yet, a handwritten notation indicates that she was a "widow." Curiously, a man named Gordon Haynes, also a Barbadian, had emigrated from the same port in Panama in March 1917, several months earlier. The ship he sailed on listed him as married and that his "wife and family [were still] in Panama." All indications are that he was probably the right Gordon Haynes.

But why was Charles' mother listed as a widow? And even stranger, years later when Gordon applied for U.S. citizenship, he stated that he had five children, none of whom were Charles or his sister, Amy. Did Gordon have two families? Did he remarry? Was there another Gordon Haynes? These are questions that as yet have no answer.

In any case, Mrs. Haynes and her children found a welcoming West Indian community upon their arrival. It was a close-knit, homogeneous one within the larger Black community of Harlem. Like many immigrants new to America, they mostly lived among and associated with people from their same place of origin. It was in this environment that

[Left] Hollingsworth teamed with his childhood friend, legendary comic artist Joe Kubert. Kubert anonymously helped with this "Inspector Roc's Felony Files" page. Hollingsworth inked Kubert's penciled art and signed it as "A.C. Holly." *Blue Beetle* #51, December 1947, Fox Feature Syndicate.

[Above] First panel of the Hollingsworth-drawn romance story, "Farewell To Love." *True-to-Life Romances* #9, January – February 1950, Star Publications.

I GUESS TERRY DIDN'T HEAR ME!
COMFORTABLE, TERRY?
UH-HUH!
OKAY, ADAM, STEP ON IT!

Charles met, and eventually married, Cynthia Jones.

West Indians had a long history in America, albeit not a voluntary one. European traders had developed a triangular trade route that began with them bringing manufactured goods to Africa, which were then traded to locals for slaves, who were then shipped to the West Indies in exchange for raw materials to be sent back to Europe. The second leg of this forced journey is referred to as the Middle Passage. These were voyages of intolerable suffering that first brought Africans to the Americas. From the West Indies, the slaves were then sold to plantation owners, including those in the southern United States.

Although they shared similar histories, Blacks in the U.S. and those in the West Indies developed different racial identities. These differences came to the fore with the increased immigration of West Indians in the early part of the 20th century. These islanders joined the huge influx of immigrants from every nation streaming into America in search of new opportunities. Many had worked the huge sugar plantations that dominated the economies of their homelands. But like many immigrants of other nationalities and race, West Indians found assimilation into established native American Black communities difficult. It was a relationship shaped by differing racial identities. This created distrust and friction between the two populations and was a subject of concern for many Black commentators.

The consummation of union between West Indians and Americans of African descent could only come about by the West Indians first dropping their own prejudices against the different islanders other than their own island, the abolition of color prejudice, and readiness to get rid of any thought of superiority over the American Negro. [Miller, Clifford, "West Indian-American Negro Problem Cure Is Suggested," *New York Amsterdam News*, Aug. 24, 1927]

He is accustomed to class distinction with himself frequently well above the lower class; he is not unaccustomed to a racial intermarriage; and he is not a minority group. Consequently, he has none of that, which for lack of a better name, we call inferiority complex in the average American Negro." [Smith, Alfred Edgar, "West Indian on the Campus," *Opportunity*, Aug. 1933, p.238]

Black historian Carter G. Woodson postulated that these differing racial personalities were historically derived.

In 1931, he wrote:

The native West Indian is almost two generations farther removed from slavery than the native Negro of the United States. Being in a country where the blacks decidedly outnumber the whites, the Negroes on those islands have figured more conspicuously in the social, economic and political life than members of this race have been able to do in the United States. [Woodson, Carter, "Tells of Contributions of the 'West Indian Negro' to the U.S.," *Pittsburgh Courier*, Oct. 31, 1931]

So, it was unsurprising that Cynthia, too, was from Barbados, having come to the U.S. by way of Chile in May 1920, apparently unaccompanied even though she was just 16 years old. She was headed to Brooklyn, the borough so populated with her countrymen that one newspaper reported:

Because of the large number of West Indian natives here who have come to the United States in search of employment, Brooklyn is practically a Barbadian city. ["Brooklyn Is Another Barbados," *Baltimore Afro-American*, Sept. 1, 1920]

Cynthia and Charles married on February 17, 1923, and they had a son the next year, whom they named Roy. Four years after that, on February 25, 1928, Alvin Carl was born. At some point, presumably prior to Alvin's birth, the Haynes changed their last name to Hollingsworth. Why this change was made is unknown. One possibility is that Charles was trying to distance himself from an absentee father.

Charles worked as both a porter and a shipping clerk at a dress factory. This was a common circumstance as many

Unpublished original artwork for a Hollingsworth comic strip about a Black school teacher. Around the same time, the artist was also trying to sell a similar strip titled *Bob Mentor* to newspaper syndicates. *Dorothy Tutor*, c. early 1950s.

I DON'T LIKE THE LOOKS OF THAT CROWD. I THINK I'LL CHECK WITH TERRY'S PARENTS!
WHERE ARE WE GOING, JOE??

West Indians took on several jobs at once. Alvin once told an interviewer:

I grew up on 115th Street, between Seventh and Eighth Avenues. My parents were from Barbados and they were strict and unbending. I had to do well. I had to succeed. When I was about ten, all my friends were making money shining shoes. My father said to me, "The day I catch you with a shoe-shine box in your hand is the day your ass will sing with pain." [Coombs, Orde, "People: Al Hollingsworth: Portrait of the Artist as a Believer," *Essence*, Feb. 1971, p.50]

The Hollingsworths were together into the 1930s, when Cynthia apparently either left Charles or she passed away. According to the 1940 U.S. census, she was no longer living with the family. However, Charles continued to list himself as "married." His mother and sister lived with him, though, and presumably helped raise the boys.

It was not long after, in the early 1940s, that Joe Kubert met Alvin and their friendship developed; but while Kubert may have inspired him to attend the same high school, Hollingsworth credited someone else for making it happen. Hollingsworth said:

While I was in junior high, a Mr. Johnson, a white teacher, thought I should be thinking more about my art. He insisted that I get a portfolio together, and then helped me get into the High School of Music and Art. I don't think I would have made it without his help. [Ibid, p.50]

Hollingsworth was a husky six-footer, much bigger than his father, who was a thin, small man, the same height as his wife. Alvin boxed when he went to high school and was a weight lifter most of his life, none of which made much difference when he faced the realities of growing up in Harlem. Hollingsworth told his interviewer:

I grew up in the age of gangs. In the heyday of the Turf Gang and the Socialistics. I was sure that my ass would be in heat. I just knew that I would have to join them or face punishment every day. They didn't like my brother and me anyway. We weren't mixers. What saved me was that I started working at 13. I started making money, and so I had their respect.

Even at Music and Art I was lucky. The place was highly competitive, but there was less bigotry there than at the other high schools. Even so, when I got there, I was wondering whom I would have to fight. One week passed. Two weeks. Three weeks. No bullies. No fights. I couldn't believe it.

At 13, I was already bold. I went downtown to get an original drawing from a guy named Charles Quinlan who was doing "Catman," a cartoon series. Now I could see what was going through his mind. 'Why the hell would this black boy want my drawing?' Well, for the things I'm interested in, I have an almost photographic memory, and so I told him what I liked and didn't like about cartoons he had done years ago. He was flabbergasted. And I became his prodigy. [Ibid, p.70]

Charles M. Quinlan Sr. was a veteran comic book artist, a one-time rodeo star, and the de facto art director for Holyoke Publishing Company.

At 14, I had my own feature. I worked after school from 3:30 to 8:30 and then went home to do my homework. When I wanted to skip these lessons, my father would say no deal. He was, as I mentioned, from the West Indies and he had begun to work when he was eight as a tailor's apprentice, so what I was doing didn't impress him too much. [Ibid, p.70]

Hollingsworth's earliest comic book work is virtually impossible to identify, unsigned and lost among all the other anonymously created artwork churned out for a few dollars a page. What is identifiable begins appearing in late 1943. Although it wasn't drawn for Holyoke, an example can be found in *Crime Does Not Pay* #31 (Jan. 1944), on a story entitled, "Million Dollar Bank Robbery," which bears Hollingsworth's nom de plume, "Holly."

Over the next several years, Hollingsworth freelanced and found work through the Bernard Baily Studio, yet another so-called "comic shop," used by publishers in lieu of hiring their own stable of artists and writers. And as evidenced by the stories of Stoner, Pious, Fax, and others, such shops were also the frequent employers of Black comic artists who were unwilling to personally chance encounters with White editors and publishers.

Baily was himself a respected comic book artist by the time he started his own studio in late 1942. Most of his clients were smaller publishers, many existing only as frontmen. They were surrogates for larger publishers and printers who were unable to acquire the necessary paper to publish comics under their own name. Wartime restrictions limited each publisher to a predetermined quota, and exceeding that amount resulted in huge fines and imprisonment. Baily's comic book shop supplied content to these surrogate publishers and to a few of the established ones. Since his was a smaller shop, and paid commensurately, Baily usually employed older artists nearing the end of their careers, or younger ones, too young for military service, including Hollingsworth.

Once again, much of the work done at the Baily shop was unsigned. One likely bit of his work, though, can be seen in *Navy Heroes* #1 (1945). In this patriotically-themed comic, Hollingsworth has been identified as the artist for the page devoted to Captain S. G. Fuqua, who was bestowed the Medal of Honor for his actions aboard the U.S.S. *Arizona* during the attack on Pearl Harbor.

A mainstay of the Baily shop was Elmer C. Stoner. Although Stoner freelanced as well, his work on *Blue Beetle* and his other artwork published by the Fox Feature Syndicate was probably done through Baily. Hollingsworth, too, drew several stories for the *Blue Beetle* comic book series while working for Baily. Knowing that he was often the conduit for Black artists hoping to enter the comic book business, perhaps Stoner was instrumental in getting the young artist a job at the studio.

Hollingsworth's first positively identifiable artwork for Baily comes in the first appearance of the super-hero named Bronze Man in *Blue Beetle* #42 (July-Aug. 1946). Using the pseudonym of "Alec Hope," Hollingsworth is credited as both the artist and writer. It tells the tale of a disfigured WWII hero who dons a bronze mask. He puts on a costume to "challenge any force threatening the peace he sacrificed so much to help win." ["The Liberty Bell," *Blue Beetle* #42, July-Aug. 1946, p.1]

This is a reasonable assumption given that the word "bronze" was, at the time, a frequently used and more genteel alternative when referring to "Negroes" or "black skin." Despite his intention, and the very brief life of Matt

Baker's Voodah as a Black man, it is unlikely either Baily or publisher Victor Fox would have approved a Black comic book hero.

Along with Bronze Man, Hollingsworth drew a few installments of "Minit Mystery" and "Inspector Roc's Felony Files" for Fox. Appearing late in 1947, these probably came when Hollingsworth returned to freelancing after the demise of the Baily shop earlier that year. Supporting that conclusion is the fact that at least two of the "Inspector Roc Felony Files" one-page mysteries were penciled by his friend Joe Kubert and inked by Hollingsworth.

Working under yet another pseudonym, "A.C. Holly," Hollingsworth and Kubert collaborated on "The Bloodless Corpse" page in *Blue Beetle* #50 (Nov. 1947) and "Death and the Dagger" appearing in *Blue Beetle* #51 (Dec. 1947).

Beginning in the mid-1940s, Hollingsworth worked wherever he could pick up an assignment, both freelancing and working through various comic shops, sometimes several at one time—wherever he could pick up an assignment. He even did a few illustrations for *Planet Stories*, a science fiction pulp. Having graduated from Music and Art in June 1946, he had more time to devote to pursuing his career.

Through the Leonard B. Cole comic shop, he produced a few stories for *Contact Comics* and *Captain Aero* comics published by Frank Z. Temerson, who was also owner of Holyoke Publishing. There were two signed jobs for Lloyd Jacquet's Funnies, Inc.—a couple of text story illustrations for *Future World* #1 (Summer 1946) and a short three-page effort titled, "The Wonders of Sea Life" for *Catholic Comics* vol. 1 #12 (June 1947). It was over at Jerry Iger's studio, though, that Hollingsworth's career began taking off.

Generally, Hollingsworth was relegated to drawing back-up stories, often in comics bearing covers of scantily-clad

[Above] Hollingsworth created both "girlie" cartoons (for men's magazines) and erotic art after leaving the comic book industry. Along with two other Black artists, Al Sargent and Charles Ferguson, Hollingsworth was also listed as the Art Editor for *Relax* magazine, a short-lived *Playboy* imitation. *Relax* vol. 1 #1, May 1957, Finesse Publishing. From the collection of Ger Apeldoorn.

[Right] Hollingsworth's first identifiable comic book work was on "Bronze Man," a feature which he is believed to have both written and drawn. Hollingsworth signed the story "Alec Hope," possibly using the first two letters of his first and last name to make up the pseudonym.

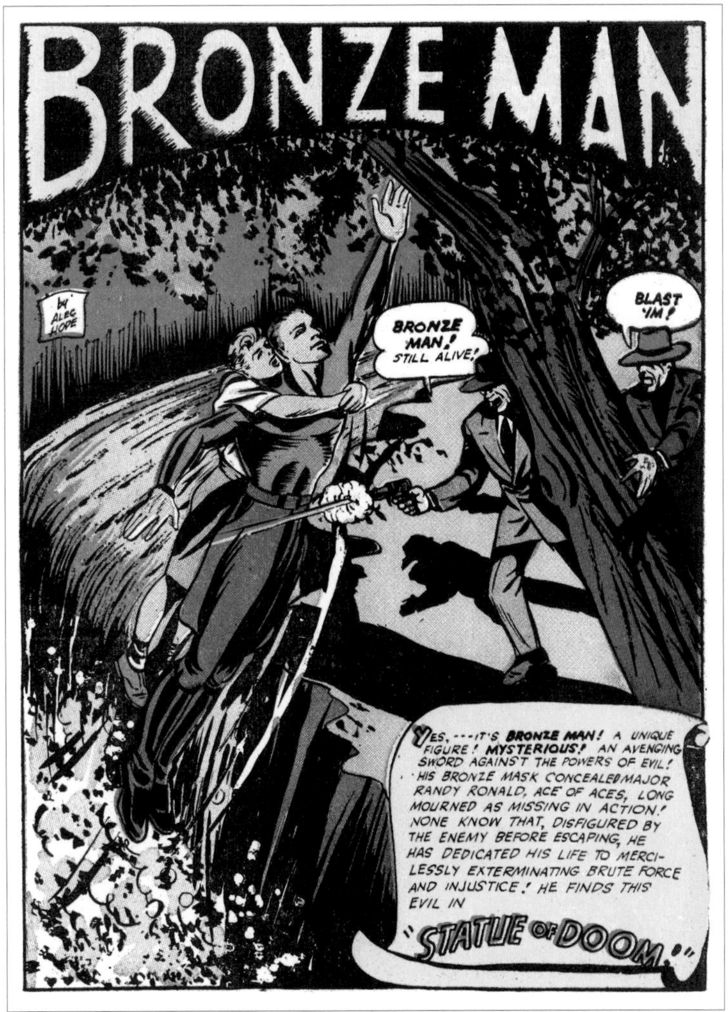
BRONZE MAN
by ALEC HOPE
BRONZE MAN! STILL ALIVE!
BLAST 'IM!
YES,---IT'S BRONZE MAN! A UNIQUE FIGURE! MYSTERIOUS! AN AVENGING SWORD AGAINST THE POWERS OF EVIL! HIS BRONZE MASK CONCEALED MAJOR RANDY RONALD, ACE OF ACES, LONG MOURNED AS MISSING IN ACTION! NONE KNOW THAT, DISFIGURED BY THE ENEMY BEFORE ESCAPING, HE HAS DEDICATED HIS LIFE TO MERCILESSLY EXTERMINATING BRUTE FORCE AND INJUSTICE! HE FINDS THIS EVIL IN
"STATUE OF DOOM!"

women drawn by Iger's star artist, Matt Baker. Unlike Baker, who worked in the offices occupied by the Iger Studio, Hollingsworth worked outside the shop. Al Feldstein, later famous as an editor and writer for E.C. comics, was an artist for Iger in the same time period. He never recalled seeing any other Black artist in the studio other than Baker, likely confirming Hollingsworth's free-lance status.

Some of Hollingsworth's earliest Iger jobs were on stories starring White jungle goddesses bearing names such as Numa and Juanda, and whose African co-stars were either bit players or villains. There were also a few miscellaneous Western and crime comics Hollingsworth contributed to for Iger. The closest he came to a steady job was on the "Suicide Smith" feature which appeared in issues of Fiction House's *Wings Comics*.

Suicide Smith had been appearing in *Wings* since its first issue in 1940. He was one of its heroic flyboys, fighting the Axis in the skies over Europe during WWII and continuing to take on dangerous missions after the war. Hollingsworth's tenure on the feature ran from *Wings Comics* #105 (May 1949) to #111 (Spring 1950), with the exception of issue #110 in which the strip didn't appear.

Hollingsworth's personal style developed over the months. His characters, men and women both, were routinely lean and serious and his panels were crammed with action and detail, as if he feared leaving an empty space.

Two standout efforts from this period appear in the first couple of issues of *Juke Box Comics*. Published by Eastern Color Printing, the comic presented exactly what its title suggested: profiles of popular singers of the day. In *Juke Box* #1 (March 1948), Duke Ellington was the subject, and Hollingsworth showed a different side of his art style. The panels were no less cluttered, but he gave more effort to depicting his characters realistically, in keeping with the purpose of portraying actual people. In *Juke Box* #2 (May 1948), Lena Horne was the assignment, and Hollingsworth's attempt at "realism" continued.

From 1949 on, Hollingsworth's comic book career was in high gear, as he churned out artwork at the frenzied pace demanded of the industry. He quickly became one of the most notable artists in the crime and horror genres, working on titles such as *Dark Mysteries*, *Beware*, *Fight Against Crime*, and *Eerie*.

Eerie was published by Avon Periodicals, a paperback publisher owned by the huge magazine distributor American News Company. Avon had expanded into comic books and became an early entrant in the horror comic market. Hollingsworth worked on a handful of Avon comics from 1951-1953. Most of his work during the early 1950s, though, was for the lines of comics linked by their ownership.

Formed in 1934, Trojan Publishing Corporation was primarily a publisher of the thick, cheaply-printed pulp magazines that crowded the newsstands in the years preceding the comic book boom. Not wanting to miss out on the hot, new thing, they began publishing comics, too.

Operating under various names, such as Ribage, Master, and Story as well as Trojan, they published the aforementioned titles along with several others, generally violent, grisly crime and horror comics. Hollingsworth's art appeared in many of them. While the income earned from drawing comics was steady, it wasn't particularly good, so Hollingsworth looked for other avenues by which to monetize his talents. He was disappointed by the results.

In 1953 I got hungry and went to work as a syndicated cartoonist for Associated Press. I had had ten years in the business although I was only 23 [note: actually, 25]. My character was Scorchy Smith, a kind of Steve Canyon in space.

Well, I wrote and illustrated the cartoon. I had 110 million readers, but I was making very little money, and there was no food in

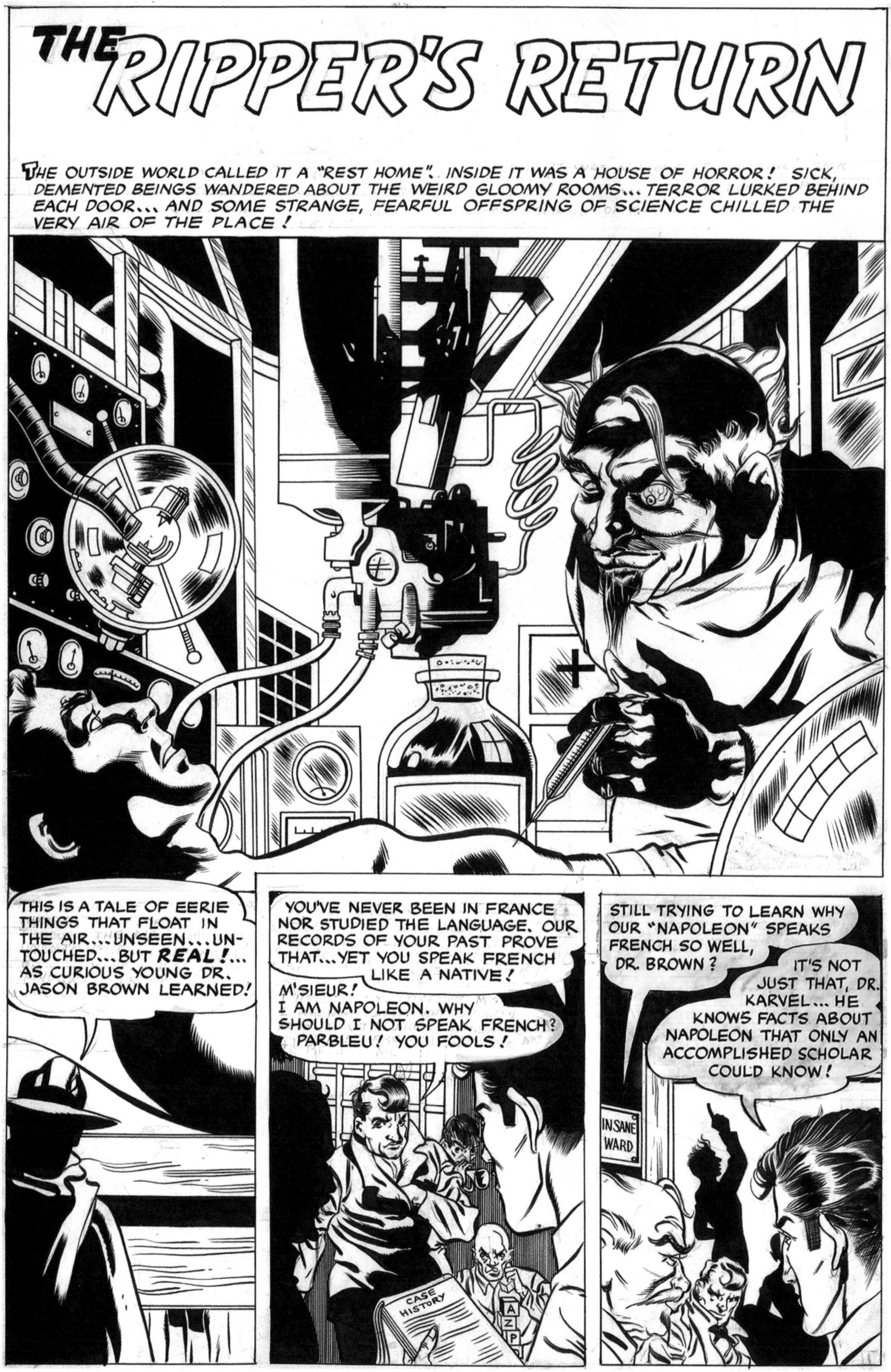
THE RIPPER'S RETURN
THE OUTSIDE WORLD CALLED IT A "REST HOME". INSIDE IT WAS A HOUSE OF HORROR! SICK, DEMENTED BEINGS WANDERED ABOUT THE WEIRD GLOOMY ROOMS... TERROR LURKED BEHIND EACH DOOR... AND SOME STRANGE, FEARFUL OFFSPRING OF SCIENCE CHILLED THE VERY AIR OF THE PLACE!
THIS IS A TALE OF EERIE THINGS THAT FLOAT IN THE AIR... UNSEEN... UNTOUCHED... BUT REAL!... AS CURIOUS YOUNG DR. JASON BROWN LEARNED!
YOU'VE NEVER BEEN IN FRANCE NOR STUDIED THE LANGUAGE. OUR RECORDS OF YOUR PAST PROVE THAT... YET YOU SPEAK FRENCH LIKE A NATIVE!
M'SIEUR! I AM NAPOLEON. WHY SHOULD I NOT SPEAK FRENCH? PARBLEU! YOU FOOLS!
CASE HISTORY
STILL TRYING TO LEARN WHY OUR "NAPOLEON" SPEAKS FRENCH SO WELL, DR. BROWN?
IT'S NOT JUST THAT, DR. KARVEL... HE KNOWS FACTS ABOUT NAPOLEON THAT ONLY AN ACCOMPLISHED SCHOLAR COULD KNOW!
INSANE WARD

my house. I went to [Mister] Charlie and told him I wanted a raise. He looked at me. His mouth fell open and he said: "Do you know you are the only Negro on the front page of 140 newspapers?" I was supposed to eat that! I said screw you and I quit. [Coombs 1971, op. cit. p.70]

Hollingsworth's words here convey more than just the memory of a recalled event. Note his usage of the pejorative expression, "Mister Charlie," in talking about his White syndicate editor. This was contemporaneous slang within the Black community for an imperious White man and was indicative of the relationship as perceived by both races.

A different memory of Hollingsworth's exit from *Scorchy Smith* was given by Charles Ferguson in an unpublished February 2013 interview with historian Shaun Clancy. Ferguson, another Black artist who had known Hollingsworth since junior high, assisted on the strip, as inker of Hollingsworth's penciled artwork and as its writer. According to Ferguson, he used specific information in his writing that he copied from research done by a professor in Florida. When the strip was published, it was seen by this professor who then threatened *Scorchy Smith*'s syndicate with legal action. This threat directly led to Hollingsworth and Ferguson being fired by the syndicate.

For a brief time, in 1951, Hollingsworth attended the Art Students League before enrolling at the City College of New York (CCNY) for its Fall semester in 1952.

After I quit that job, I went back to school. But when I got out of school, necessity forced me to do buckeye painting...painting for the buck. For six months, I did nothing but ballet dancers, clowns, waterfalls, and I must have painted the Manhattan skyline ten different ways. [Coombs 1971, op. cit. p.70]

Unmentioned by Hollingsworth were his several other forays into the comic strip field.

Comic strip historian Alberto Becattini has attributed a number of *The Spirit* Sunday strips from the period of August 5, 1951, to June 1, 1952, to being a collaboration between penciler Jerry Grandenetti and Hollingsworth as his inker.

There were failures as well. Prior to getting the *Scorchy Smith* job in late 1953, Hollingsworth apparently tried out as the assistant to George Shedd on his *Marlin Keel* seafaring

Original Hollingsworth splash page artwork for "The Ripper's Return" horror story that appeared in *Tales of Horror* #2, September 1952, Minoan Publishing. From the collection of George Hagenauer.

feature. A page of original artwork bearing both Shedd and Hollingsworth signatures exists, likely drawn sometime before the strip's debut on September 14, 1953. It's not clear, however, if the page was intended as a Sunday strip tryout or a proposal for a comic book.

Around the same time, Hollingsworth had several strip proposals under his own name. Apparently intended for the Black newspaper market, *Bob Mentor* and *Dorothy Tutor* were similarly themed: serial stories starring the eponymous Black teachers. Neither strip sold.

However, another strip did. *Kandy* revolved around the adventures of the beautiful Black daughter of race car owner Bill Mackay. The strip began appearing in the *Pittsburgh Courier* on December 4, 1954, under Hollingsworth's byline. Like his work on *Scorchy Smith*, the art on *Kandy* was more sophisticated, cleaner, and less hurried-looking, than his contemporaneous comic book style. The strip, which was syndicated to other Black newspapers by the Smith-Mann Syndicate, ran less than a year. It ended unceremoniously in mid-story on October 22, 1955. For the most part, his comic book career ended at nearly the same time, but with some noticeable changes.

He was beginning to show signs of his art school training. Whereas he had for years reflected the mentorship of Joe Kubert, with bits of the latter's style creeping into his own, Hollingsworth's artwork began taking on an impressionistic look. The panels of his comic book pages lost much of the clutter of which he was so previously fond. He introduced a more judicious, sparer use of lines, and an increase in the use of patterns—sometimes hand-drawn, other times by use of zip-a-tone sheets. All contributed to a purposeful flattening of the imagery, a painterly approach popular at the time. While Hollingsworth was still contributing to the Grand Guignol demanded by the comic book publishers, he was evolving into a fine artist.

Hollingsworth finally obtained his Bachelor of Fine Arts degree from CCNY in 1956, graduating Phi Beta Kappa and winning its Alumni Award the following year. He was on his way to beginning his teaching career and establishing his credentials as a painter. Still, he wasn't entirely done with commercial art, or even comic books for that matter.

Owned by Martin Goodman, the same man who owned Timely/Atlas comics located in the same building, Magazine Management published material that appealed to the parts of the male psyche that Eisenhower-era prudery tried to ignore. Their books featured ripping yarns of sadistic Nazis,

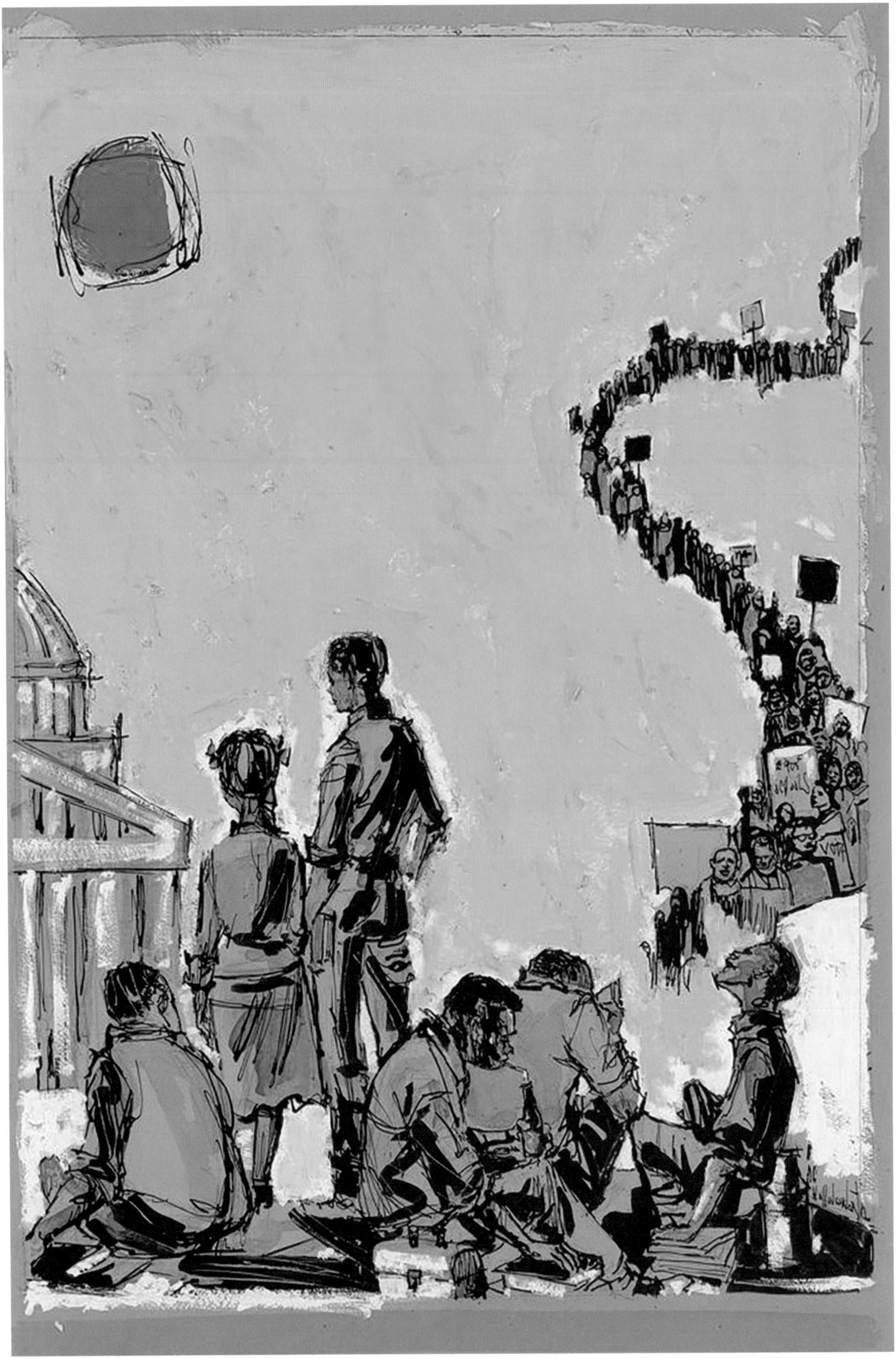

scheming Commies, bloodthirsty savages, he-man hero-ism, and sex. Polite company referred to them as "men's adventure magazines;" industry insiders referred to them as "sweat mags." Bruce Jay Friedman was the editor who pumped them out for Goodman.

The "sweats" were printed on the same cheap pulp paper used in the comics, and bore such testosterone-oozing titles as *Male* and *Stag*, with action-packed covers that often featured a buxom young woman in some state of désha-billé and in danger of ravagement, displayed sexily in the foreground. Inside, the illustrations accompanying the stories were like-minded. Friedman hired some of the top illustrators in the business for these magazines—respected professionals like Mort Kunstler and James Bama—but he went out on the limb a bit with his hiring of Hollingsworth in 1955. Hollingsworth was known as a comic book artist to everyone in the building, but Friedman saw something more in the young Black artist.

Hollingsworth's risqué-themed drawings for Friedman were essentially a tryout, and he swiftly moved on to the publisher's top-of-the-line *Playboy* imitators, *Bachelor* and *Swank*. These were the "class" of the magazine line; publications printed on higher quality glossy paper, with posed color photographs and the occasional name writer augmenting the in-house staff writers who normally ground out the material in the "sweats."

[Left] This gouache painting by Hollingsworth symbolically depicts the 1963 March on Washington. It was likely produced while he was part of the historic Spiral Group, an artist's collective formed in the wake of the march. The group sought to define the role of Black artists in the civil rights movement.

[Above] *Trapped*, a painting and mixed media collage, was part of Hollingsworth's "Cry City" series. The piece was created while working with the Spiral Group. Representative of Hollingsworth's growing activism in the civil rights movement, this work evokes the haunting isolation and desperation of a faceless figure in a stark, urban landscape. National Museum of African American Culture and History, 1965.

Hollingsworth's illustrations began popping up in *Bachelor* soon after his graduation from CCNY in 1956. In fact, it was a Hollingsworth illustration that appears on the first page of *Bachelor* #1 (Jan. 1957). He provided the illustration for that issue's installment of "Notes from a Gay Dog," a monthly column anonymously written by "the sly bachelor on the loose."

These illustrations were another step in Hollingsworth's evolution. Gone was all the detail of his earlier comic book work, and what remained were sparse, loosely-drawn lines, with swatches of gray wash or color overlays. It was hard to tell that it was even the same artist.

While Hollingsworth continued contributing to the Goodman magazines right into 1958, he also produced similar work for others. As with his transition from Timely/Atlas comics over to Magazine Management, Hollingsworth made use of other contacts from his comic book tenure to further his career as an illustrator.

Some of his earliest assignments came from Leonard B. Cole, through whose comic shop Hollingsworth's artwork appeared in such mid-1940s comics as *Contact* and *Captain Aero*. Hollingsworth illustrations appeared in several early issues of the Cole-published *Man's Daring Adventures* in late 1955.

Even while he was getting work from Magazine Management, Hollingsworth accepted the position of Art Editor for a competing new men's publication with the comforting title of *Relax*.

Yet another cheaply-produced *Playboy* imitator, *Relax* was unique for the number of Black artists on its masthead. Along with Hollingsworth, there was Charles Ferguson, his *Scorchy Smith* collaborator, and Albert E. Sargent, a painter and longtime Hollingsworth's friend. Their artwork was sprinkled throughout the two issues of the magazine's short 1957 run.

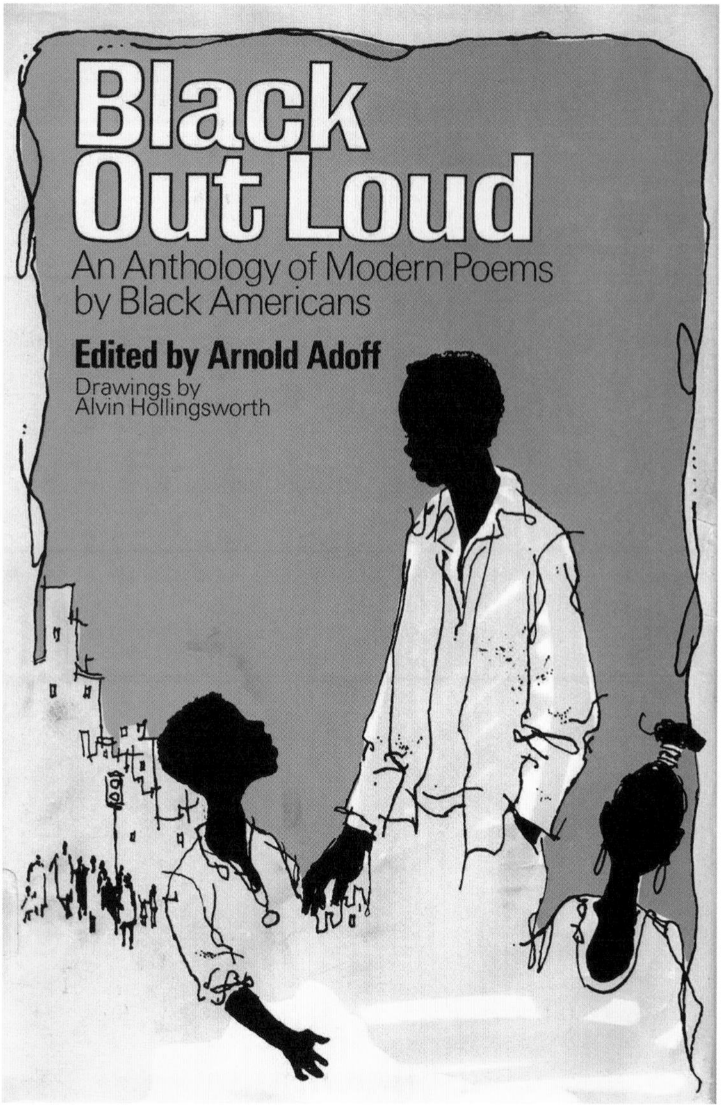
Black
Out Loud
An Anthology of Modern Poems
by Black Americans
Edited by Arnold Adoff
Drawings by
Alvin Hollingsworth

Bernard Baily had given Hollingsworth some of his earliest comic book assignments, and now he was editor and art director of several men's magazines for Periodical House. These were truly odd publications. The first was *Hi*, debuting in May 1957. To begin with, it measured 11 inches high and only a shade over four inches wide. Fully embracing its oddness, *Hi* sub-titled itself, *The TALL Magazine For Men*. A short introduction inside gave a bit of a clue as to why they chose this unusual format.

You're going to have a good time when you turn the pages of this tall, breast-pocket magazine for men. Our first issue is filled with stories, pictures, cartoons and articles that will Hi-light your lonely evenings. So, go ahead, dig in, and have yourself a Hi old time. ["Hi," *Hi*, May 1957, p.3]

Baily utilized Hollingsworth in much the same way Friedman had on *Bachelor* and *Swank*. His illustrations accompanied the text stories and usually spread over two of the narrow pages. Hollingsworth was still transforming. The looseness of his line-work was wandering further into abstraction, with blotches of ink and indefinite representational imagery.

Baily chose to honor Hollingsworth's progression as an artist in the December 1957 issue of the re-named *High*, with a six-page layout of pen sketches he had made of his native Harlem. The sketches were closely akin to his illustrations, quick life studies acting as snapshots, capturing moments in time on the city's streets. It was probably the first public recognition given Hollingsworth in the White media.

Hollingsworth's illustrations reached full abstraction with the now-standard-sized January 1959 issue of *High*. Spilling over the first two pages of an article titled "The Battle of the Exes," Hollingsworth was in a full-on Picasso mode. These drawings were representational in the barest sense, almost childlike in their perceived simplicity.

Hollingsworth and Al Sargent teamed up to work on *Thimk*, a *Mad* magazine imitator from Counterpoint Publishing that premiered in May 1958. Under the pseudonyms of "Holly and Sarge," they contributed a large amount of the material used in the magazine. The satire was weak, and their collaborative artwork tried desperately to mimic *Mad*'s, with mixed results. The magazine died a quick and unmourned death in early 1959.

Hollingsworth's final work for a comic book publisher was found in a men's cartoon magazine, *Cartoon Spice*. It was produced by Charlton Publications, a low-end operation that survived the mid-1950s decimation of the comic book industry. *Cartoon Spice* collected standalone risqué panel cartoons into a standard-size comic book format. This title had a limited run of five issues, from Spring of 1957 to Spring 1958. Hollingsworth's cartoons were very much in keeping with his illustration work in the same period, employing a modernistic, two-dimensional style. Several years later, starting in 1962, Charlton used the same concept for the similar *Cartoon Carnival*, which also contained Hollingsworth's cartoons, scattered about random issues over its long run.

Hollingsworth obtained his master's degree from CCNY in 1959, and as if emerging from a chrysalis, he had transformed. The constraints and demands of a commercial art career fell away, replaced by the freedom of expression allowed to a fine artist. He took his first job teaching art at Hoffman Junior High School in The Bronx, had his first gal-

[Above] Hollingsworth drew the cover and interior illustrations for *Black Out Loud* (1970, Arnold Adoff and The Macmillan Co.), an anthology of modern Black poetry.

[Right] "Harlem," a series of sketches that appeared in the Bernard Baily-edited *High* men's magazine. Hollingsworth had worked for Baily's comic shop during the 1940s and he often contributed to magazines edited by his old employer during the 1950s. *High* vol. 1 #4, December 1957, Periodical House.

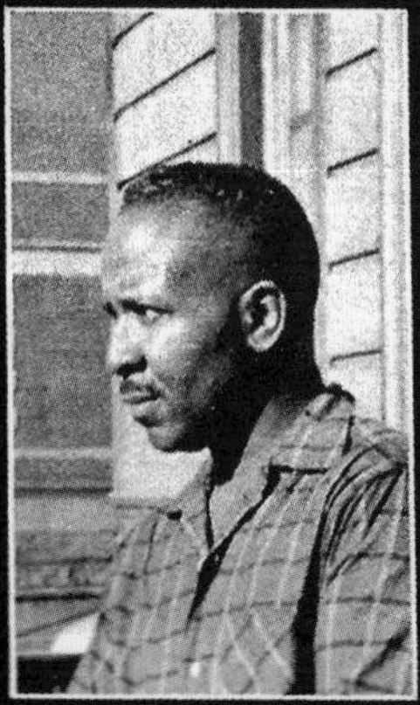

Alvin Hollingsworth

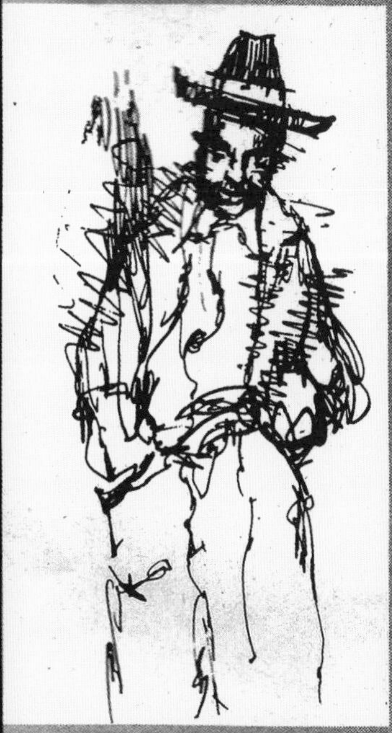

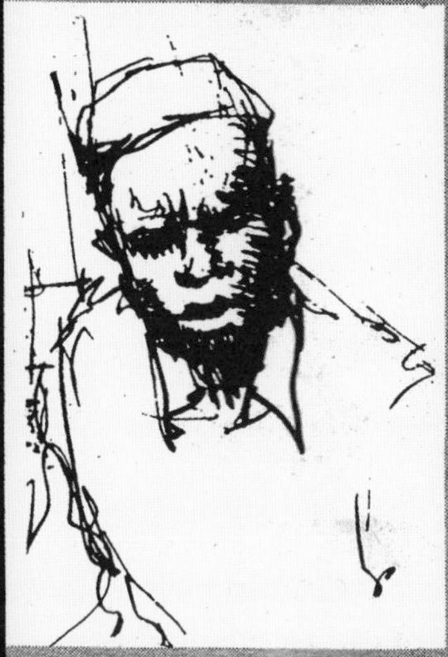

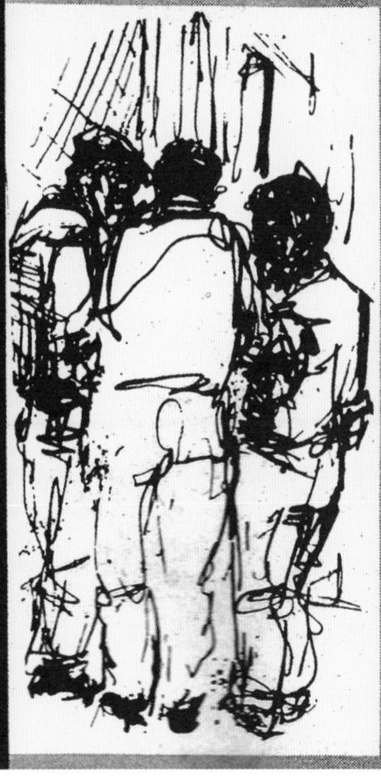

SOMETIME ago, when Alvin Hollingsworth brought his art portfolio in to us, we took the liberty, (while his back was turned) to glance through it to see the work he didn't show us. What we discovered pleased us considerably. His artistic hand didn't just dabble in magazine illustration. We learned that he'd recently won the "Achievement Medal of the Art Alumni" presented by the College of the City of New York. Checking further, we discovered that for the past few years he has received many such prizes and awards for his art work. His ability to capture studies of people and places is amazing, and his dramatic rendering is equally outstanding. Alvin Hollingsworth stands as one of the upcoming greats in the art world. HIGH is pleased to present this series of his pen-and-ink sketches of Harlem.

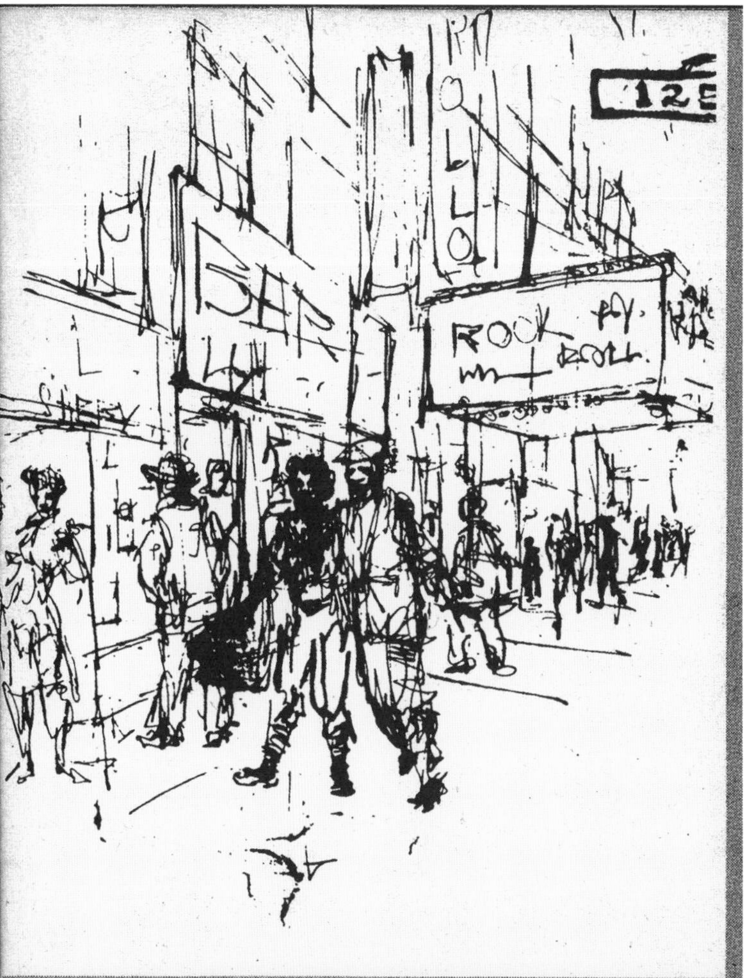

HARLEM

Say the name and it conjures up the vision of Hi-De-Ho! and red hot *Sneaky Pete* and searing Jazz. Of blues-singin' ladies and high-livin' men. Of all-night gin parties and razz-a-ma-tazz!

Yes, that's Harlem. But not all of it. Not the real place. Harlem is also where people live—and people die. Where folks go to Sunday meetin'—and work—and cry!
Harlem's a big city—within the biggest city in the world. A place to itself. A place just like any other place. With the same problems, the same fears, the same yearnings.

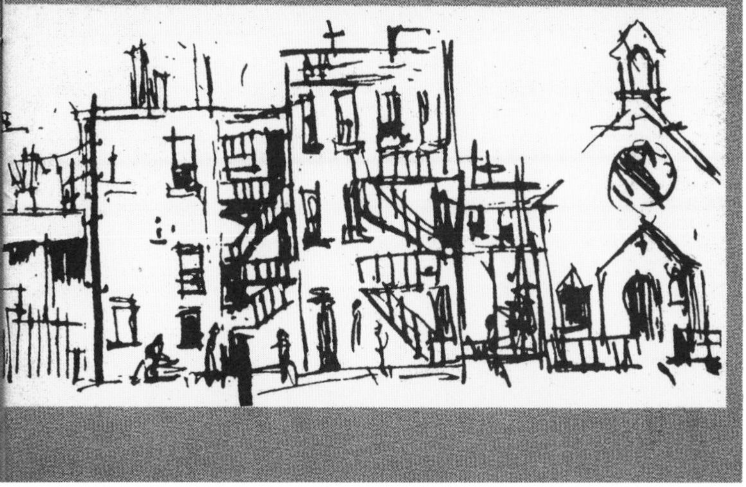

lery showings, and began receiving recognition outside the Black community.

The cover of the October 13, 1960 issue of highly regarded newsmagazine *The Reporter* featured a Hollingsworth illustration of an African market scene. In a profile that appeared in *Cavalcade*, a men's magazine, Hollingsworth explained his unique approach to painting. He told the writer:

First, I recognized I should take advantage of themes close to me. Secondly, I felt there should be some fusion of my figurative experience with my abstract experiences with color. [Waldo, A. E., "Return of the Classical Nude," *Cavalcade*, Aug. 1962, p.48]

By now, Hollingsworth received an appointment teaching at the newly rechristened High School of Art and Design (formerly the School of Industrial Art), the other arts high school created along with his alma mater, Music and Art. There, he taught alongside his old friend, Charles Ferguson, as well as Charles Allen, another veteran Black cartoonist who had created *Tan Topics* for Continental Features back in the 1940s.

It was 1963, in the wake of the March on Washington, when Hollingsworth joined a collective of Black artists—which included Romare Bearden, Charles Alston, and Norman Lewis—that coalesced as the Spiral Group. Growing out of discussions among the artists to consider "the commitment of the Negro artist in the present struggle for civil liberties...and common aesthetic problems," the group became pivotal toward the development of a Black art identity and its role in society. [Bearden, Romare, and Harry Henderson. *A History of African-American Artists : From 1792 to the Present*. 1993. p.400.]

Hollingsworth's response took form in his famed "Cry City" series of mixed media paintings. The artworks, crafted from various paints, charcoal, and found objects merged together on Masonite, were highly personal, emotive reflections upon the urban landscape he witnessed daily.

He seemed boundless and ubiquitous, everywhere and involved in everything at once. Even as his notoriety and acclaim went up, Hollingsworth stayed true to his commitment to his students, teaching painting. He participated in numerous exhibitions, many with old friends such as Al Sargent, Charles Allen, and Tom Feelings, yet another Black comic book artist who had moved on to fine art. In the June 1964 issue of *American Artist*, he penned an article about "Teaching Art to the Gifted in a New York High School." The year 1970 was a particularly hectic one, as Hollingsworth was chosen to write and host a ten-part television series entitled *You're Part of Art*; he produced a children's book, *I'd Like the Goo-Gen-Heim*, as a kid's level guidebook through the Guggenheim Museum; and he illustrated *Black Out Loud: An Anthology of Modern Poems by Black Americans*.

A one-man show of Hollingsworth's series of paintings devoted to the subject of author Kahlil Gibran opened on October 4, 1970, at the Studio Museum in Harlem. The paintings were displayed with quotations from Gibran's book *The Prophet*, invoking the artist's personal philosophic evolution.

We have neglected our human relations. The prophets are people who have given us warnings. They say you have to work with what you have—with nature and human relations—or there won't be any tomorrow. ["Hollingsworth Art in Harlem Exhibit," *New York Amsterdam News*, Oct. 3, 1970]

The expansiveness of Hollingsworth's intellectual curiosity never ceased. He continued to write, teach, and paint, and even learned to arrange electronic music. All the while he worked to obtain his PhD.

After a long, lingering illness, Hollingsworth passed away on July 14, 2000, leaving behind not only grieving family and friends, but the legacy of a creative genius who never forgot his roots.

We are left with this thought from Hollingsworth:

An artist is the sum total of all his experiences. [Hollingsworth, Alvin, *Eyes of the City Exhibition Catalog*, 1974]

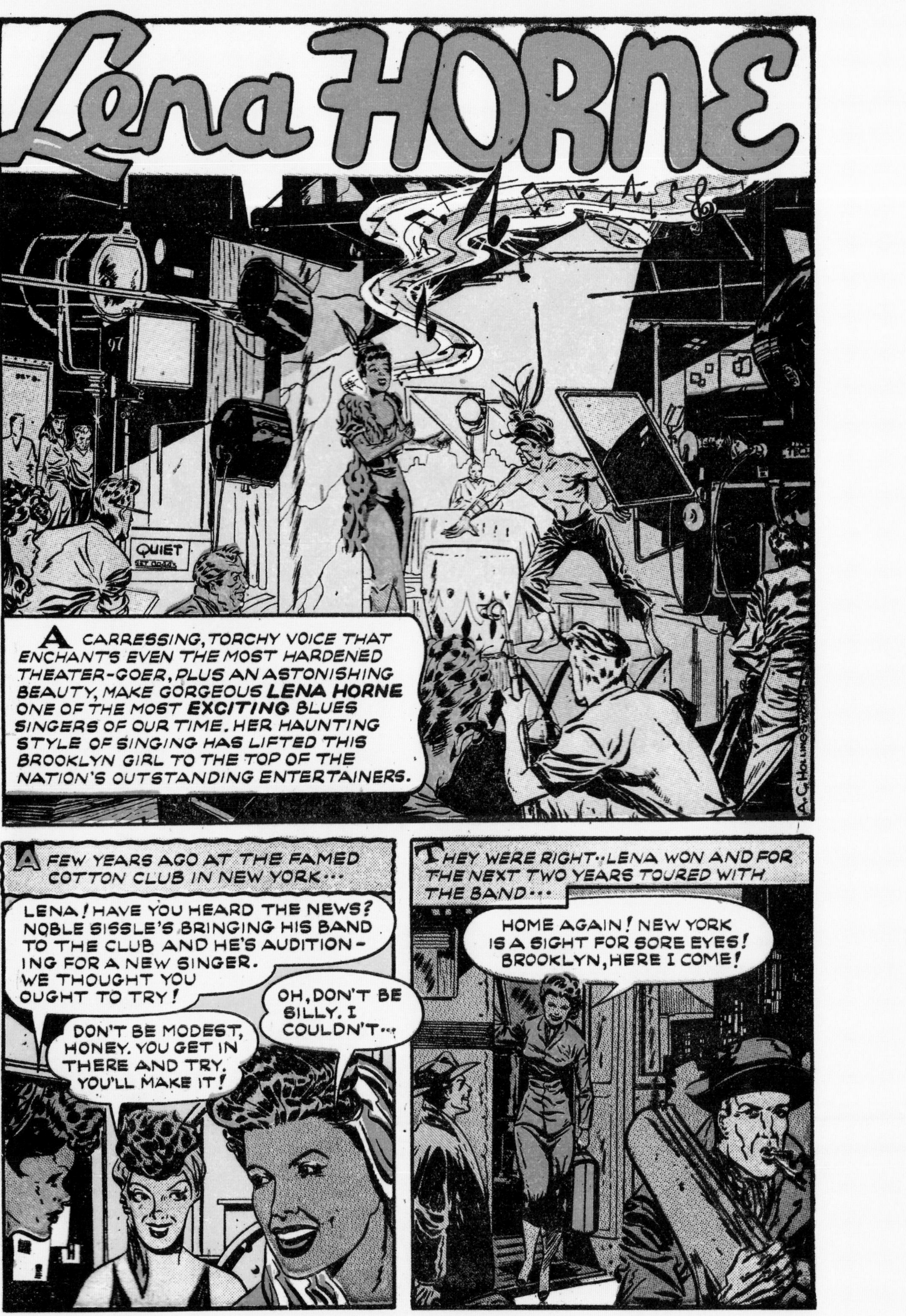
Lena HORNE
QUIET
A CARRESSING, TORCHY VOICE THAT ENCHANTS EVEN THE MOST HARDENED THEATER-GOER, PLUS AN ASTONISHING BEAUTY, MAKE GORGEOUS LENA HORNE ONE OF THE MOST EXCITING BLUES SINGERS OF OUR TIME. HER HAUNTING STYLE OF SINGING HAS LIFTED THIS BROOKLYN GIRL TO THE TOP OF THE NATION'S OUTSTANDING ENTERTAINERS.
A FEW YEARS AGO AT THE FAMED COTTON CLUB IN NEW YORK...
LENA! HAVE YOU HEARD THE NEWS? NOBLE SISSLE'S BRINGING HIS BAND TO THE CLUB AND HE'S AUDITION-ING FOR A NEW SINGER. WE THOUGHT YOU OUGHT TO TRY!
OH, DON'T BE SILLY. I COULDN'T...
DON'T BE MODEST, HONEY. YOU GET IN THERE AND TRY. YOU'LL MAKE IT!
THEY WERE RIGHT.. LENA WON AND FOR THE NEXT TWO YEARS TOURED WITH THE BAND...
HOME AGAIN! NEW YORK IS A SIGHT FOR SORE EYES! BROOKLYN, HERE I COME!

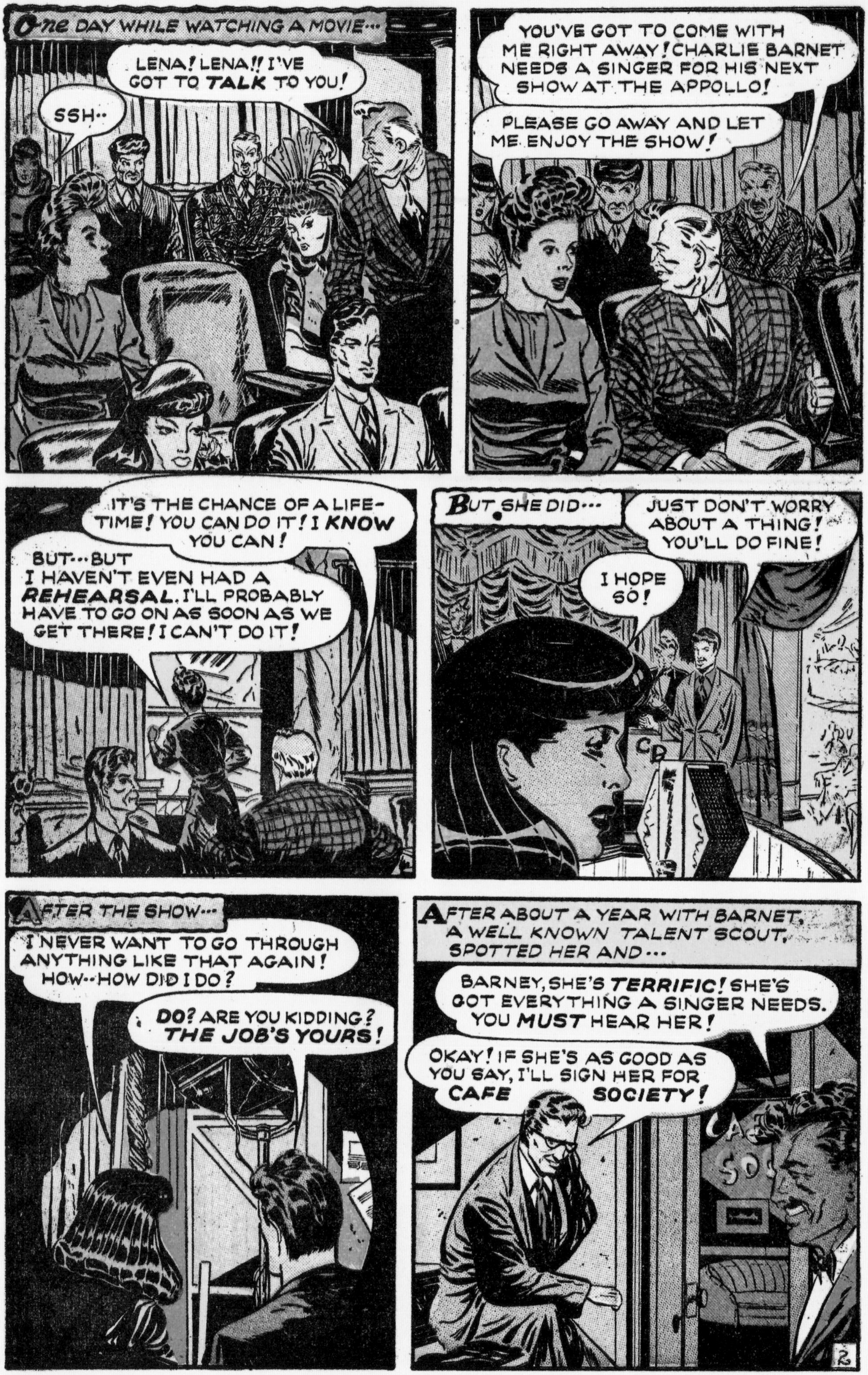
ONE DAY WHILE WATCHING A MOVIE...
LENA! LENA!! I'VE GOT TO TALK TO YOU!
SSH..
YOU'VE GOT TO COME WITH ME RIGHT AWAY! CHARLIE BARNET NEEDS A SINGER FOR HIS NEXT SHOW AT THE APPOLLO!
PLEASE GO AWAY AND LET ME ENJOY THE SHOW!
IT'S THE CHANCE OF A LIFE-TIME! YOU CAN DO IT! I KNOW YOU CAN!
BUT...BUT I HAVEN'T EVEN HAD A REHEARSAL. I'LL PROBABLY HAVE TO GO ON AS SOON AS WE GET THERE! I CAN'T DO IT!
BUT SHE DID...
JUST DON'T WORRY ABOUT A THING! YOU'LL DO FINE!
I HOPE SO!
AFTER THE SHOW...
I NEVER WANT TO GO THROUGH ANYTHING LIKE THAT AGAIN! HOW--HOW DID I DO?
DO? ARE YOU KIDDING? THE JOB'S YOURS!
AFTER ABOUT A YEAR WITH BARNET, A WELL KNOWN TALENT SCOUT, SPOTTED HER AND...
BARNEY, SHE'S TERRIFIC! SHE'S GOT EVERYTHING A SINGER NEEDS. YOU MUST HEAR HER!
OKAY! IF SHE'S AS GOOD AS YOU SAY, I'LL SIGN HER FOR CAFE SOCIETY!
2

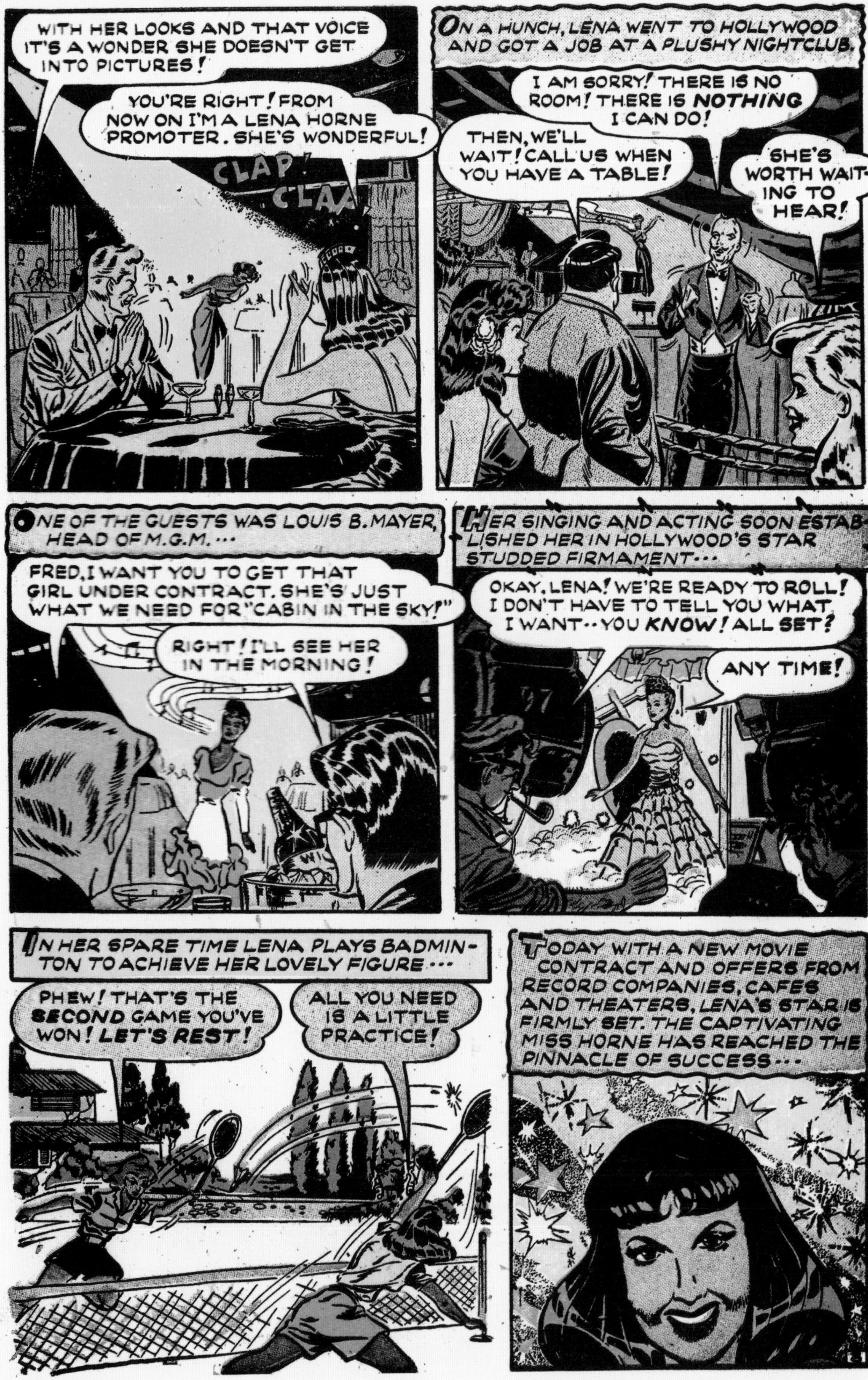
WITH HER LOOKS AND THAT VOICE IT'S A WONDER SHE DOESN'T GET INTO PICTURES!
YOU'RE RIGHT! FROM NOW ON I'M A LENA HORNE PROMOTER. SHE'S WONDERFUL!
CLAP! CLAA
ON A HUNCH, LENA WENT TO HOLLYWOOD AND GOT A JOB AT A PLUSHY NIGHTCLUB.
I AM SORRY! THERE IS NO ROOM! THERE IS NOTHING I CAN DO!
THEN, WE'LL WAIT! CALL US WHEN YOU HAVE A TABLE!
SHE'S WORTH WAITING TO HEAR!
ONE OF THE GUESTS WAS LOUIS B. MAYER, HEAD OF M.G.M. ...
FRED, I WANT YOU TO GET THAT GIRL UNDER CONTRACT. SHE'S JUST WHAT WE NEED FOR "CABIN IN THE SKY!"
RIGHT! I'LL SEE HER IN THE MORNING!
HER SINGING AND ACTING SOON ESTABLISHED HER IN HOLLYWOOD'S STAR STUDDED FIRMAMENT...
OKAY, LENA! WE'RE READY TO ROLL! I DON'T HAVE TO TELL YOU WHAT I WANT.. YOU KNOW! ALL SET?
ANY TIME!
IN HER SPARE TIME LENA PLAYS BADMINTON TO ACHIEVE HER LOVELY FIGURE...
PHEW! THAT'S THE SECOND GAME YOU'VE WON! LET'S REST!
ALL YOU NEED IS A LITTLE PRACTICE!
TODAY WITH A NEW MOVIE CONTRACT AND OFFERS FROM RECORD COMPANIES, CAFES AND THEATERS, LENA'S STAR IS FIRMLY SET. THE CAPTIVATING MISS HORNE HAS REACHED THE PINNACLE OF SUCCESS...

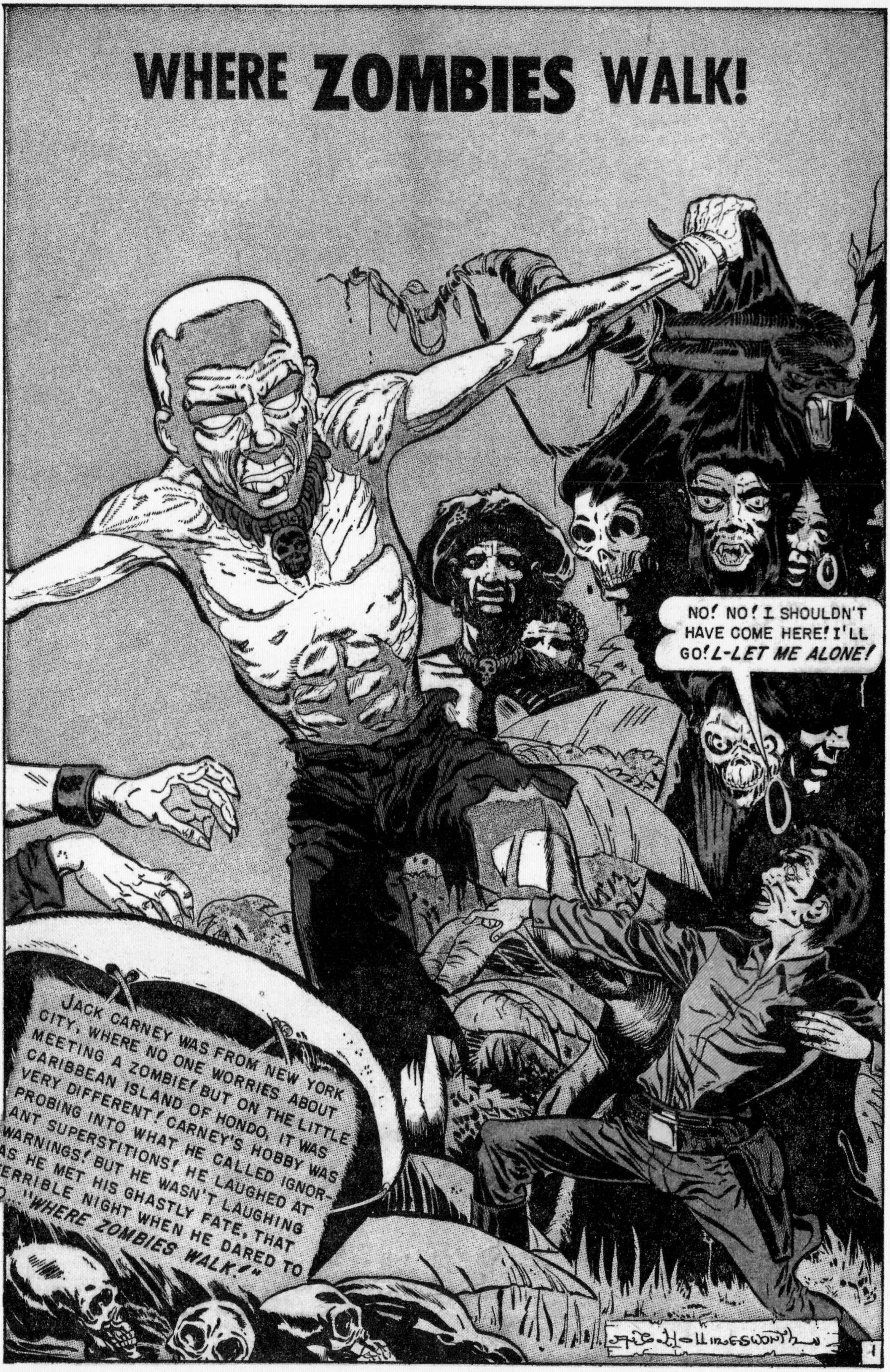
WHERE ZOMBIES WALK!
NO! NO! I SHOULDN'T HAVE COME HERE! I'LL GO! L-LET ME ALONE!
JACK CARNEY WAS FROM NEW YORK CITY, WHERE NO ONE WORRIES ABOUT MEETING A ZOMBIE! BUT ON THE LITTLE CARIBBEAN ISLAND OF HONDO, IT WAS VERY DIFFERENT! CARNEY'S HOBBY WAS PROBING INTO WHAT HE CALLED IGNORANT SUPERSTITIONS! HE LAUGHED AT WARNINGS! BUT HE WASN'T LAUGHING AS HE MET HIS GHASTLY FATE, THAT TERRIBLE NIGHT WHEN HE DARED TO GO... "WHERE ZOMBIES WALK!"
1

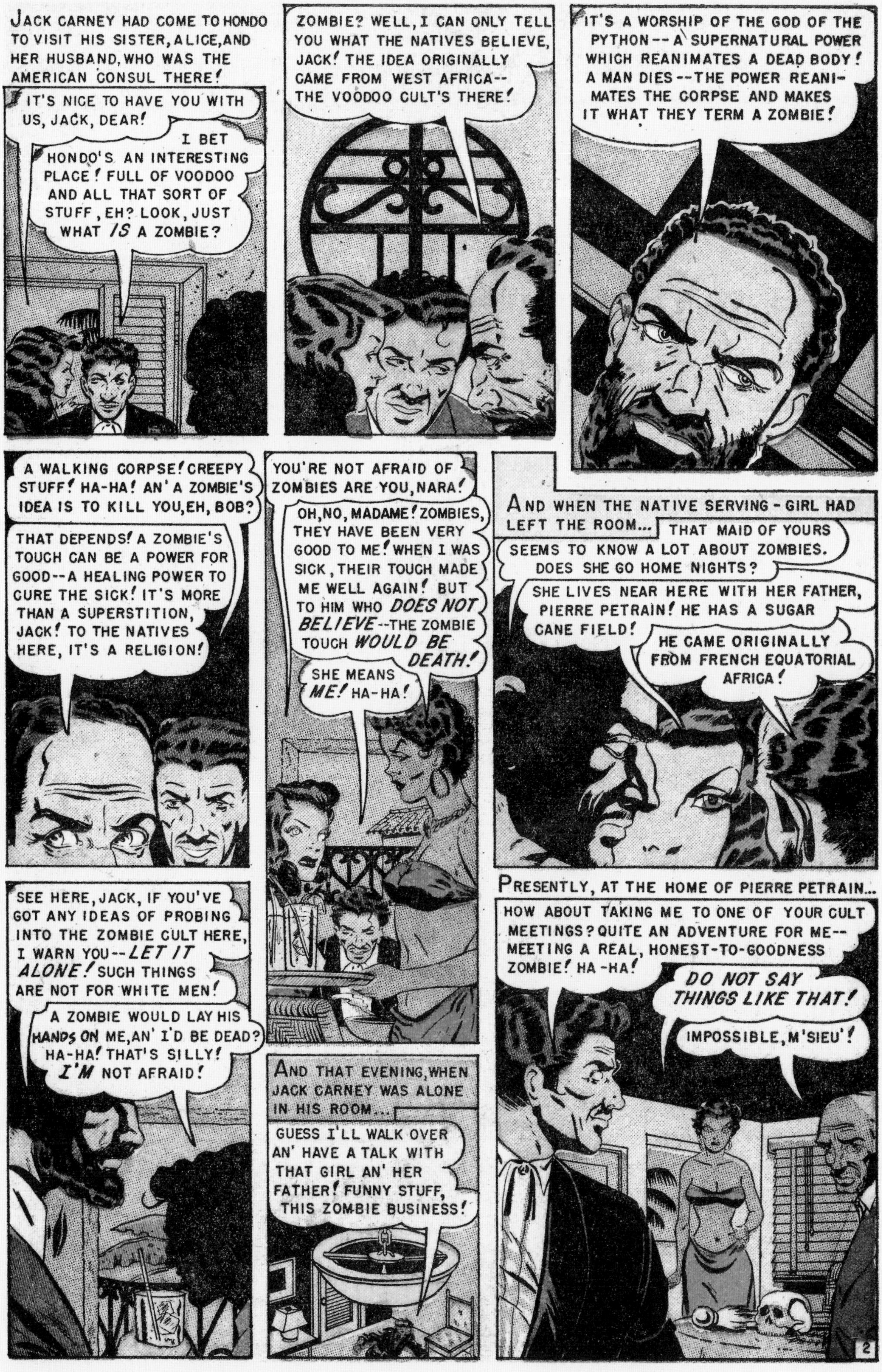
JACK CARNEY HAD COME TO HONDO TO VISIT HIS SISTER, ALICE, AND HER HUSBAND, WHO WAS THE AMERICAN CONSUL THERE!
IT'S NICE TO HAVE YOU WITH US, JACK, DEAR!
I BET HONDO'S AN INTERESTING PLACE! FULL OF VOODOO AND ALL THAT SORT OF STUFF, EH? LOOK, JUST WHAT *IS* A ZOMBIE?
ZOMBIE? WELL, I CAN ONLY TELL YOU WHAT THE NATIVES BELIEVE, JACK! THE IDEA ORIGINALLY CAME FROM WEST AFRICA-- THE VOODOO CULT'S THERE!
IT'S A WORSHIP OF THE GOD OF THE PYTHON -- A SUPERNATURAL POWER WHICH REANIMATES A DEAD BODY! A MAN DIES -- THE POWER REANIMATES THE CORPSE AND MAKES IT WHAT THEY TERM A ZOMBIE!
A WALKING CORPSE! CREEPY STUFF! HA-HA! AN' A ZOMBIE'S IDEA IS TO KILL YOU, EH, BOB?
THAT DEPENDS! A ZOMBIE'S TOUCH CAN BE A POWER FOR GOOD--A HEALING POWER TO CURE THE SICK! IT'S MORE THAN A SUPERSTITION, JACK! TO THE NATIVES HERE, IT'S A RELIGION!
YOU'RE NOT AFRAID OF ZOMBIES ARE YOU, NARA!
OH, NO, MADAME! ZOMBIES, THEY HAVE BEEN VERY GOOD TO ME! WHEN I WAS SICK, THEIR TOUCH MADE ME WELL AGAIN! BUT TO HIM WHO *DOES NOT BELIEVE*--THE ZOMBIE TOUCH *WOULD BE DEATH!*
SHE MEANS *ME!* HA-HA!
AND WHEN THE NATIVE SERVING-GIRL HAD LEFT THE ROOM...
THAT MAID OF YOURS SEEMS TO KNOW A LOT ABOUT ZOMBIES. DOES SHE GO HOME NIGHTS?
SHE LIVES NEAR HERE WITH HER FATHER, PIERRE PETRAIN! HE HAS A SUGAR CANE FIELD!
HE CAME ORIGINALLY FROM FRENCH EQUATORIAL AFRICA!
SEE HERE, JACK, IF YOU'VE GOT ANY IDEAS OF PROBING INTO THE ZOMBIE CULT HERE, I WARN YOU--*LET IT ALONE!* SUCH THINGS ARE NOT FOR WHITE MEN!
A ZOMBIE WOULD LAY HIS HANDS ON ME, AN' I'D BE DEAD? HA-HA! THAT'S SILLY! *I'M* NOT AFRAID!
AND THAT EVENING, WHEN JACK CARNEY WAS ALONE IN HIS ROOM...
GUESS I'LL WALK OVER AN' HAVE A TALK WITH THAT GIRL AN' HER FATHER! FUNNY STUFF, THIS ZOMBIE BUSINESS!
PRESENTLY, AT THE HOME OF PIERRE PETRAIN...
HOW ABOUT TAKING ME TO ONE OF YOUR CULT MEETINGS? QUITE AN ADVENTURE FOR ME-- MEETING A REAL, HONEST-TO-GOODNESS ZOMBIE! HA-HA!
DO NOT SAY THINGS LIKE THAT!
IMPOSSIBLE, M'SIEU'!
2

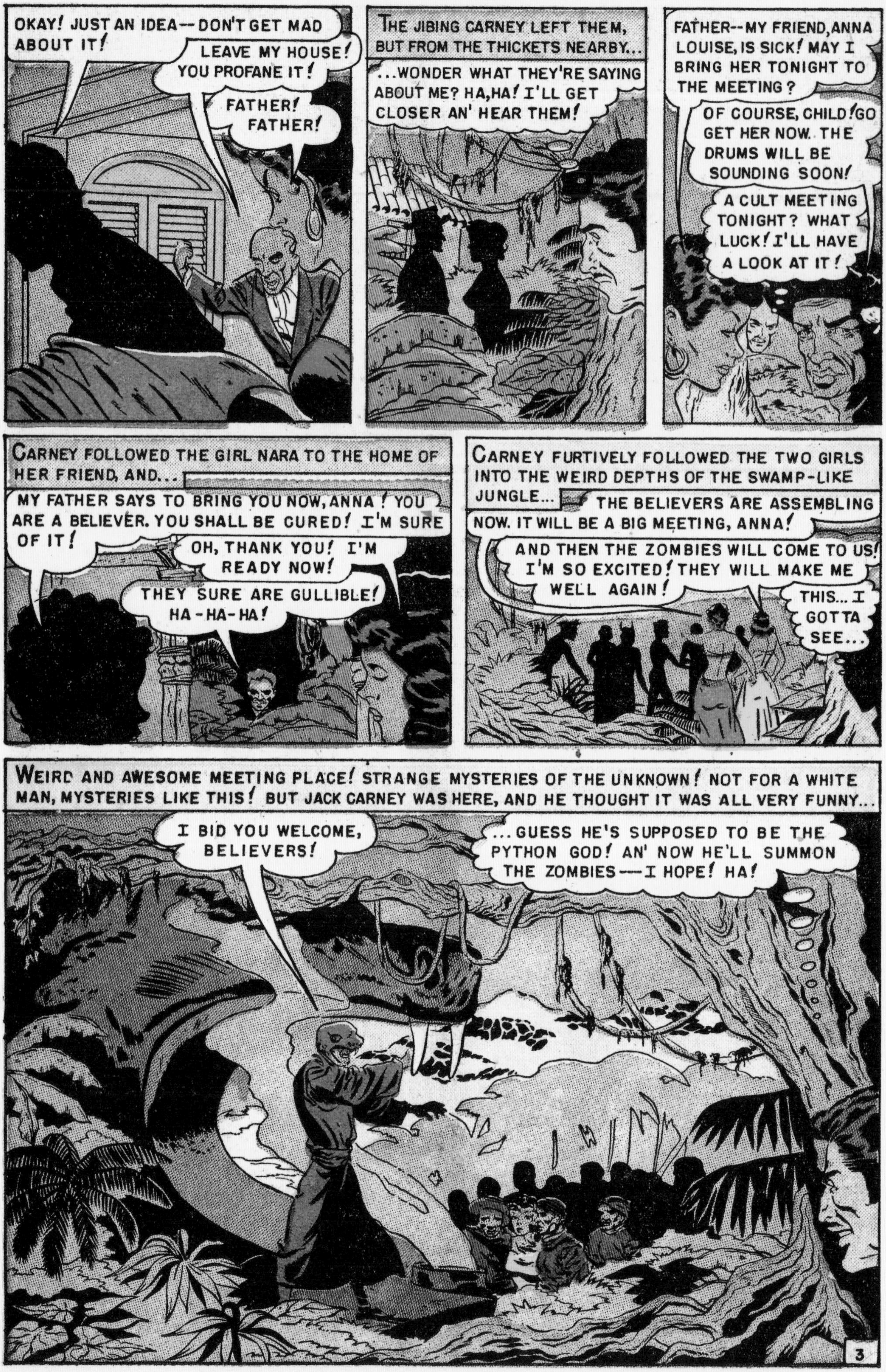
OKAY! JUST AN IDEA--DON'T GET MAD ABOUT IT!
LEAVE MY HOUSE! YOU PROFANE IT!
FATHER! FATHER!
THE JIBING CARNEY LEFT THEM, BUT FROM THE THICKETS NEARBY...
...WONDER WHAT THEY'RE SAYING ABOUT ME? HA,HA! I'LL GET CLOSER AN' HEAR THEM!
FATHER--MY FRIEND, ANNA LOUISE, IS SICK! MAY I BRING HER TONIGHT TO THE MEETING?
OF COURSE, CHILD! GO GET HER NOW. THE DRUMS WILL BE SOUNDING SOON!
A CULT MEETING TONIGHT? WHAT LUCK! I'LL HAVE A LOOK AT IT!
CARNEY FOLLOWED THE GIRL NARA TO THE HOME OF HER FRIEND, AND...
MY FATHER SAYS TO BRING YOU NOW, ANNA! YOU ARE A BELIEVER. YOU SHALL BE CURED! I'M SURE OF IT!
OH, THANK YOU! I'M READY NOW!
THEY SURE ARE GULLIBLE! HA-HA-HA!
CARNEY FURTIVELY FOLLOWED THE TWO GIRLS INTO THE WEIRD DEPTHS OF THE SWAMP-LIKE JUNGLE...
THE BELIEVERS ARE ASSEMBLING NOW. IT WILL BE A BIG MEETING, ANNA!
AND THEN THE ZOMBIES WILL COME TO US! I'M SO EXCITED! THEY WILL MAKE ME WELL AGAIN!
THIS... I GOTTA SEE...
WEIRD AND AWESOME MEETING PLACE! STRANGE MYSTERIES OF THE UNKNOWN! NOT FOR A WHITE MAN, MYSTERIES LIKE THIS! BUT JACK CARNEY WAS HERE, AND HE THOUGHT IT WAS ALL VERY FUNNY...
I BID YOU WELCOME, BELIEVERS!
...GUESS HE'S SUPPOSED TO BE THE PYTHON GOD! AN' NOW HE'LL SUMMON THE ZOMBIES---I HOPE! HA!
3

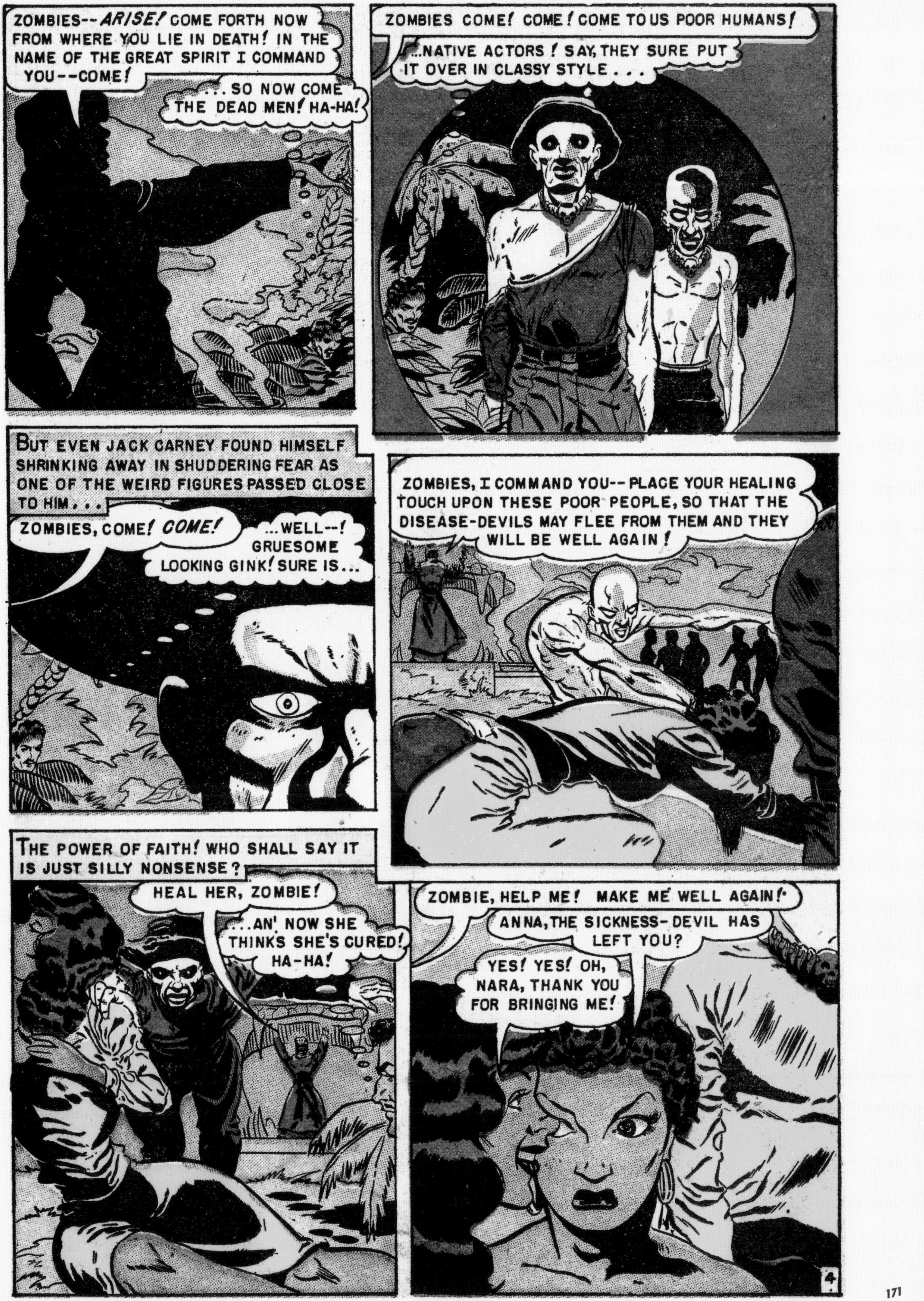

ZOMBIES--ARISE! COME FORTH NOW FROM WHERE YOU LIE IN DEATH! IN THE NAME OF THE GREAT SPIRIT I COMMAND YOU--COME!
...SO NOW COME THE DEAD MEN! HA-HA!
ZOMBIES COME! COME! COME TO US POOR HUMANS!
...NATIVE ACTORS! SAY, THEY SURE PUT IT OVER IN CLASSY STYLE...
BUT EVEN JACK CARNEY FOUND HIMSELF SHRINKING AWAY IN SHUDDERING FEAR AS ONE OF THE WEIRD FIGURES PASSED CLOSE TO HIM...
ZOMBIES, COME! COME!
...WELL--! GRUESOME LOOKING GINK! SURE IS...
ZOMBIES, I COMMAND YOU--PLACE YOUR HEALING TOUCH UPON THESE POOR PEOPLE, SO THAT THE DISEASE-DEVILS MAY FLEE FROM THEM AND THEY WILL BE WELL AGAIN!
THE POWER OF FAITH! WHO SHALL SAY IT IS JUST SILLY NONSENSE?
HEAL HER, ZOMBIE!
...AN' NOW SHE THINKS SHE'S CURED! HA-HA!
ZOMBIE, HELP ME! MAKE ME WELL AGAIN!
ANNA, THE SICKNESS-DEVIL HAS LEFT YOU?
YES! YES! OH, NARA, THANK YOU FOR BRINGING ME!
4

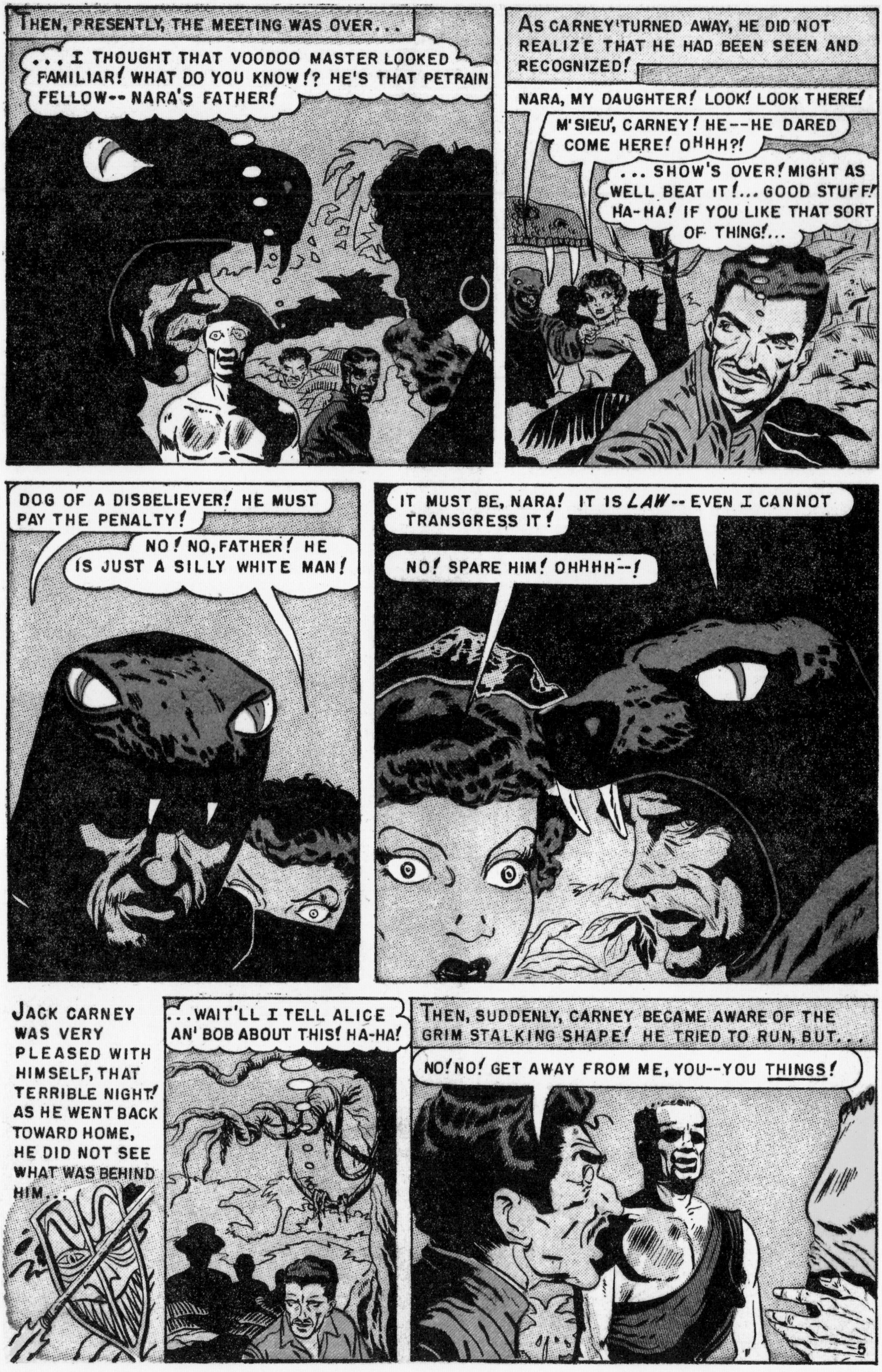
THEN, PRESENTLY, THE MEETING WAS OVER...
... I THOUGHT THAT VOODOO MASTER LOOKED FAMILIAR! WHAT DO YOU KNOW!? HE'S THAT PETRAIN FELLOW-- NARA'S FATHER!
AS CARNEY TURNED AWAY, HE DID NOT REALIZE THAT HE HAD BEEN SEEN AND RECOGNIZED!
NARA, MY DAUGHTER! LOOK! LOOK THERE!
M'SIEU', CARNEY! HE--HE DARED COME HERE! OHHH?!
... SHOW'S OVER! MIGHT AS WELL BEAT IT!... GOOD STUFF! HA-HA! IF YOU LIKE THAT SORT OF THING!...
DOG OF A DISBELIEVER! HE MUST PAY THE PENALTY!
NO! NO, FATHER! HE IS JUST A SILLY WHITE MAN!
IT MUST BE, NARA! IT IS LAW-- EVEN I CANNOT TRANSGRESS IT!
NO! SPARE HIM! OHHHH--!
JACK CARNEY WAS VERY PLEASED WITH HIMSELF, THAT TERRIBLE NIGHT! AS HE WENT BACK TOWARD HOME, HE DID NOT SEE WHAT WAS BEHIND HIM...
...WAIT'LL I TELL ALICE AN' BOB ABOUT THIS! HA-HA!
THEN, SUDDENLY, CARNEY BECAME AWARE OF THE GRIM STALKING SHAPE! HE TRIED TO RUN, BUT...
NO! NO! GET AWAY FROM ME, YOU--YOU THINGS!
5

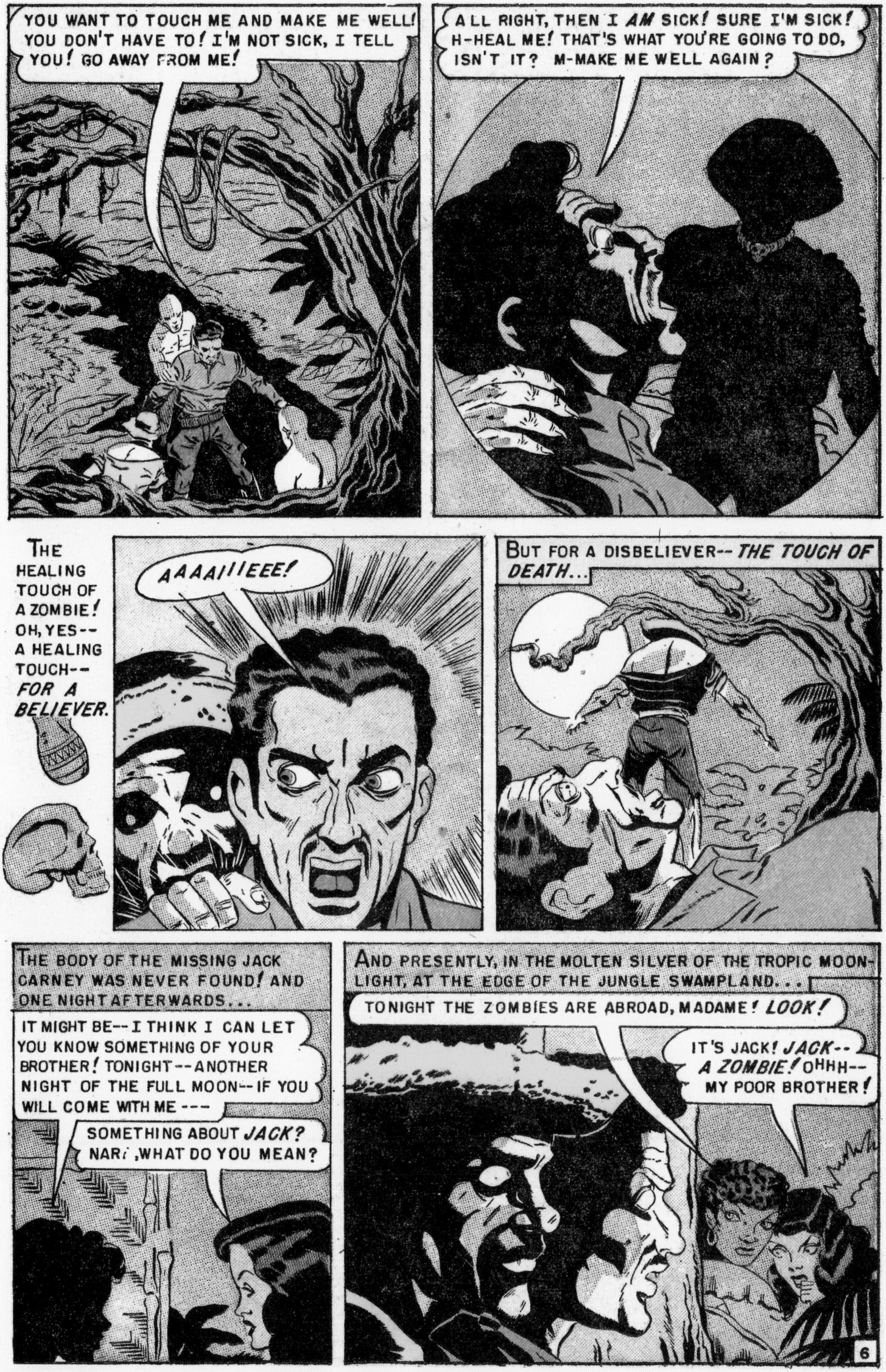
YOU WANT TO TOUCH ME AND MAKE ME WELL! YOU DON'T HAVE TO! I'M NOT SICK, I TELL YOU! GO AWAY FROM ME!
ALL RIGHT, THEN I AM SICK! SURE I'M SICK! H-HEAL ME! THAT'S WHAT YOU'RE GOING TO DO, ISN'T IT? M-MAKE ME WELL AGAIN?
THE HEALING TOUCH OF A ZOMBIE! OH, YES-- A HEALING TOUCH-- FOR A BELIEVER.
AAAAIIIEEE!
BUT FOR A DISBELIEVER-- THE TOUCH OF DEATH...
THE BODY OF THE MISSING JACK CARNEY WAS NEVER FOUND! AND ONE NIGHT AFTERWARDS...
IT MIGHT BE-- I THINK I CAN LET YOU KNOW SOMETHING OF YOUR BROTHER! TONIGHT-- ANOTHER NIGHT OF THE FULL MOON-- IF YOU WILL COME WITH ME ---
SOMETHING ABOUT JACK? NAR; ,WHAT DO YOU MEAN?
AND PRESENTLY, IN THE MOLTEN SILVER OF THE TROPIC MOONLIGHT, AT THE EDGE OF THE JUNGLE SWAMPLAND...
TONIGHT THE ZOMBIES ARE ABROAD, MADAME! LOOK!
IT'S JACK! JACK-- A ZOMBIE! OHHH-- MY POOR BROTHER!
6

EZRA CLYDE JACKSON
ALFONSO GREENE
A Tale of Two Students

They were schoolmates with seemingly much in common. Both were artists with enough skill and intelligence to pass the tough examinations required to get into the School of Industrial Art and both wanted to draw comic books. More significantly, both were Black and had that extra burden to bear in a predominately White school. Ezra Jackson rose to the challenges presented him and excelled. Alfonso Greene, however, followed another path.

The School of Industrial Art opened in November 1936 on the Upper East Side of Manhattan. It was a vocational high school for the artistically inclined, teaching its students commercial art. This included illustration and cartooning, but also photography, clothing, and architectural design.

This high school didn't open without controversy. There was already an ongoing industrial art program housed within the same building at 257 W. 40th Street, but that one was aimed at adults and sponsored by the WPA, outside the New York school system. When the high school students started moving in, it forced the adult students' classes to move to the evening. This promoted sit-in protests by many of the adult students and their WPA union teachers, who lost their fight and were forced out of the building. A few years later, the high school relocated to 211 E. 79th Street.

This was a magnet school that drew students from all over the city regardless of where they lived—from Astoria to Bulls Head, from Harlem to Bedford-Stuyvesant. If you could pass the entrance exam, you could get in and have an opportunity to receive its specialized curriculum.

Black families faced significant challenges in moving into the historic district. Many white residents saw their presence as a "threat to their neighborhood and reacted with fear, anger, hostility, and discrimination." Groups like the Gates Avenue Association, founded in 1922, were dedicated to excluding African-Americans from Bedford-Stuyvesant, urging white homeowners not to sell to black purchasers or to deal with unfamiliar agents who might represent them.

[Above, left] High School of Industrial Art yearbook photo of Ezra Jackson, 1944.

[Above, right] Alfonso Greene during his arrest in 1964.

[Right] High School of Industrial Art, c. 1955, at 211 E. 79th Street in Manhattan. The school was attended by Ezra Jackson and Alfonso Greene, as well as a number of future White comic book professionals.

[NYC Landmarks Designation Commission [NYC Landmarks Preservation Commission, "Later History of the Bedford Historic District," *Bedford Historic Designation Report*, Dec. 8, 2015, p.31]

When Albert and Olive Jackson first moved to Bedford-Stuyvesant, they did so because that was one of the better Black neighborhoods in New York City. The route they had taken there was anything but direct.

Both of them were born in Jamaica, where Albert learned the carpenter's trade, where they married, and where their first two children were born. Daughter Edna died young, but son Eric survived. The Jacksons then moved to Panama, a good place for a man with Albert's skills, as the canal was being built and jobs were plentiful. Another son, Allan, was born there. Then, in 1918, Albert took a boat out of Havana to Tampa, Florida, with Olive and the two boys following a year behind him. They briefly lived in Charleston, South Carolina, in the era and the setting of *Porgy and Bess*, where Olive gave birth to yet another son, Samuel, in 1920.

The Jacksons became part of the Great Migration, heading north soon after, which ended with them finding a home at 461 Gates Avenue in Bedford-Stuyvesant, Brooklyn. It was while living there that their youngest son, Ezra Clyde Jackson, was born on August 15, 1926.

Like the Jacksons, many of the new Black families in the neighborhood came from the British West Indies, and had worked hard to make enough money to move into homes nicer than the ones they left behind or could find in Harlem.

They worked two and three jobs at a time, the women as well as the men; they scrimped and saved their few "raw-mout pennies;" they borrowed from the loan shark when the banks refused them credit because they were black—and they bought house. They played the numbers and hoped for a big hit—and bought house. To economize, they ate the tough, 5-cents-a-pound, blue-back chickens that were sold live in the Moore Street market—and bought house. [Marshall, Paule, "Rising Islanders of Bed-Stuy," *New York Times Magazine*, Nov. 3, 1985]

So, Albert plied his trade, and Olive worked as a scrub-woman and raised their four children. What they hadn't planned on when they moved from the Jim Crow South was what would greet them in the great northern metropolis.

Blacks continued to move in. The neighborhood was pretty much defined by Fulton Street. The majority of Blacks lived south of it; the remaining Whites lived north. Eventually, though, Blacks began moving into homes north of Fulton and that's when the Whites got concerned, and they got organized. The group leading the push to keep any more Blacks from moving into Bedford-Stuyvesant had the benign name of the Midtown Civic League, whose president was Sumner A. Sirtl.

Sirtl was a successful attorney who lived in Bedford-Stuyvesant and who tapped into the growing resentment of not only the White homeowners, but the businessmen in the area who believed that the increasing Black population was driving away business. In 1937, one of the League's first actions was to contest the selling of a White Grace Presbyterian Church to the Bethel African Methodist Episcopal Church, on the grounds that it would lower the area's property values and status.

The head of the organization, Sumner Sirtl, advocated relocating Bedford-Stuyvesant's black families to empty city-owned land on Jamaica Bay. [NYC Landmarks Preservation Commission 2015, op. cit. p.31]

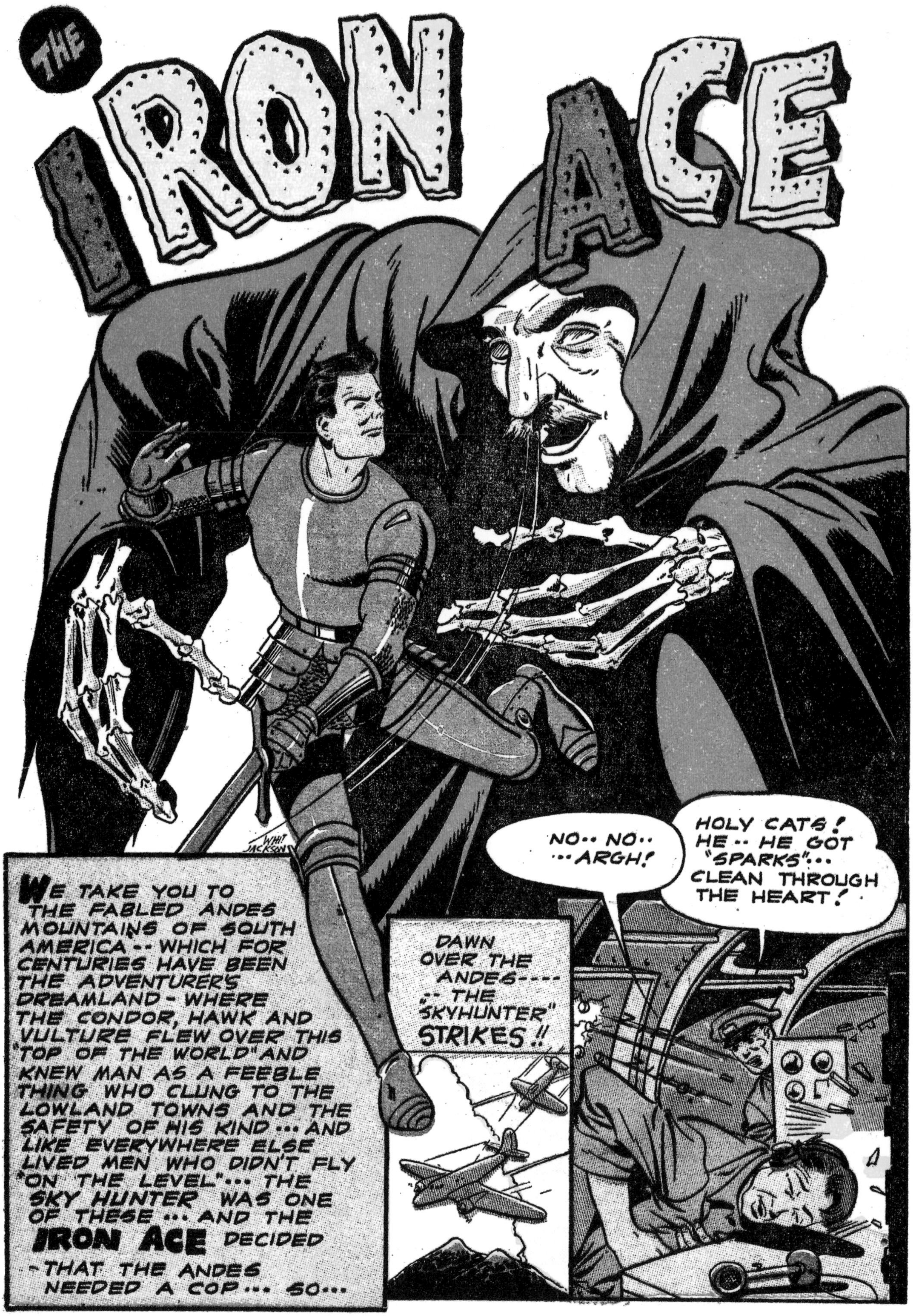
THE IRON ACE
WHIT JACKSON
WE TAKE YOU TO THE FABLED ANDES MOUNTAINS OF SOUTH AMERICA -- WHICH FOR CENTURIES HAVE BEEN THE ADVENTURER'S DREAMLAND - WHERE THE CONDOR, HAWK AND VULTURE FLEW OVER THIS "TOP OF THE WORLD" AND KNEW MAN AS A FEEBLE THING WHO CLUNG TO THE LOWLAND TOWNS AND THE SAFETY OF HIS KIND ... AND LIKE EVERYWHERE ELSE LIVED MEN WHO DIDN'T FLY "ON THE LEVEL"... THE SKY HUNTER WAS ONE OF THESE ... AND THE IRON ACE DECIDED - THAT THE ANDES NEEDED A COP ... SO...
DAWN OVER THE ANDES---- -- THE "SKYHUNTER" STRIKES!!
NO.. NO.. ...ARGH!
HOLY CATS! HE -- HE GOT "SPARKS"... CLEAN THROUGH THE HEART!

The League also claimed that the crime rate was going up and that Mayor LaGuardia hadn't assigned enough police to the neighborhood to keep the peace. Sirtl and the League had a forceful solution. An Associated Press wire story reported:

Businessmen sought to arm themselves and organize a "vigilante committee." 1,000 strong, to end a series of street assaults and robberies. "Thirty-eight persons already have applied for pistol permits," said Sumner A. Sirtl, president of the Midtown Civic League. "We have had to take this matter into our own hands—to protect our wives, our families, and our businesses." [Associated Press, "Vigilante Days Now Ahead for Brooklyn," Nov. 15, 1937]

Understandably, Blacks throughout New York City were outraged and angry. The Black newspapers lambasted Sirtl and the League, and compared them to the Ku Klux Klan and the fascists. The local Communists, seeking inroads into the Black community, spurred them on, calling for protests and boycotts of White businesses. It was a dangerous environment, primed for explosion, but it never came. Black and White neighbors who sought less-confrontational solutions organized into block associations. These associations tried to find mutual points of agreement and to address similar concerns, such as garbage pick-up and the unwanted proliferation of bars. Eventually, as more and more Blacks moved into Bedford-Stuyvesant, the League lost influence.

Albert Jackson didn't live to see peace come to his neighborhood. He died on January 4, 1937. Olive was a widow with her two youngest boys still living at home in 1940,

the same year Ezra began attending the prestigious High School of Industrial Art.

Ezra Jackson's first comic book artwork appeared late in 1944. He graduated from Industrial Art in June of that year and, as with most other Black comic artists, he was getting assignments through the buffer of a comic art shop. In his case, it was Leonard B. Cole's operation.

Jackson was paired with Maurice Whitman, an older White artist who had been discharged from the military because of his flat feet. After his discharge, Whitman freelanced and bounced around from comic shop to comic shop. One of his stops was Cole's studio. Why the two teamed up is a mystery; but over the next couple of years, they produced artwork for various comics under a variety of pseudonyms.

It was common practice for such art teams to sign their names with that of the penciler first, followed by the name of the inker. The majority of their collaborations were signed traditionally, "Whitman—Jackson," particularly their earliest work for Cole. Jackson inked over Whitman's pencils with a heavy line and generous amounts of ink for the solid black background areas that made the artwork stand out from the page. A good example is found in *Contact Comics #5* (March 1945), in which the opening air battle is dramatically depicted against a dark sky for optimal effect.

This team's tour de force was *Patches Comics #1* (March-April 1945). Except for the cover, which was drawn by studio owner Cole, the issue was entirely the work of Whitman and Jackson. The comic centered around a young White boy named "Patches," his grandmother, and his group of friends who had a club called "The Secret Seven." While the stories themselves were standard kid-gang fare, one aspect was not. One of the seven was a Black boy named "Jimmie." Not only was Jimmie treated as an equal member of the gang, his race was never mentioned and never a factor in any of

[Left] Splash page to an "Iron Ace" story, a collaboration of the art team of Maurice Whitman and Ezra Jackson. Usually signing their work with a pseudonym, this is signed as "Whit Jackson." *Airboy Comics* vol. 3 #2, March 1946, Hillman Periodicals.

[Above] Photograph of cartooning teacher Charles Allen (1955), in his classroom at the High School of Industrial Art. Allen was a well-known gag cartoonist who during his tenure had renowned comic book artist Neal Adams as one of his students.

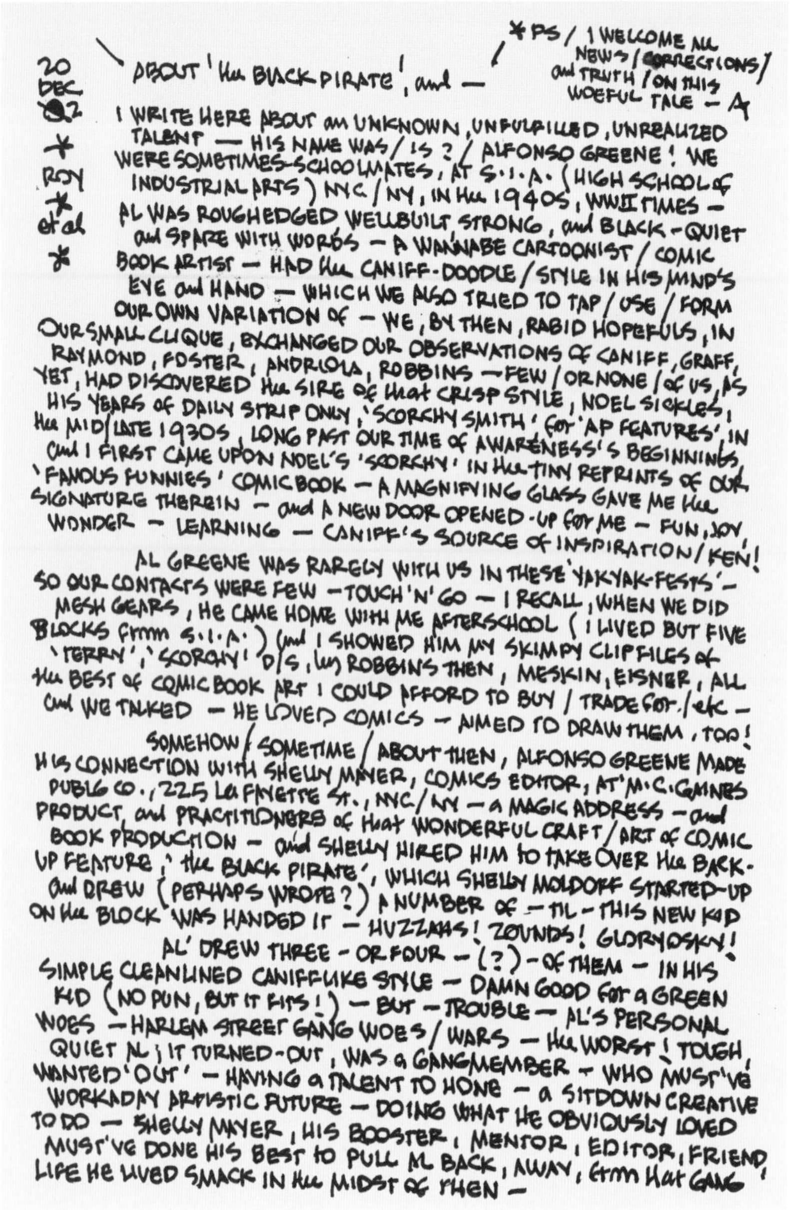
20 DEC 02 * ROY * et al *
ABOUT 'the BLACK PIRATE', and —
*PS / I WELCOME ALL NEWS / CORRECTIONS / and TRUTH / ON THIS WOEFUL TALE — A
I WRITE HERE ABOUT an UNKNOWN, UNFULFILLED, UNREALIZED
TALENT — HIS NAME WAS / IS ? / ALFONSO GREENE ! WE
WERE SOMETIMES-SCHOOLMATES, AT S.I.A. (HIGH SCHOOL of
INDUSTRIAL ARTS) NYC / NY, IN the 1940S, WWII TIMES —
AL WAS ROUGHEDGED WELLBUILT STRONG, and BLACK — QUIET
and SPARE WITH WORDS — A WANNABE CARTOONIST / COMIC
BOOK ARTIST — HAD the CANIFF-DOODLE / STYLE IN HIS MIND'S
EYE and HAND — WHICH WE ALSO TRIED TO TAP / USE / FORM
OUR OWN VARIATION OF — WE, BY THEN, RABID HOPEFULS, IN
OUR SMALL CLIQUE, EXCHANGED OUR OBSERVATIONS OF CANIFF, GRAFF,
RAYMOND, FOSTER, ANDRIOLA, ROBBINS — FEW / OR NONE / of US, AS
YET, HAD DISCOVERED the SIRE of that CRISP STYLE, NOEL SICKLES,
HIS YEARS OF DAILY STRIP ONLY, 'SCORCHY SMITH' for 'AP FEATURES', IN
the MID / LATE 1930S, LONG PAST OUR TIME OF AWARENESS'S BEGINNINGS,
and I FIRST CAME UPON NOEL'S 'SCORCHY' IN the TINY REPRINTS OF OUR
'FAMOUS FUNNIES' COMICBOOK — A MAGNIFYING GLASS GAVE ME the
SIGNATURE THEREIN — and A NEW DOOR OPENED-UP for ME — FUN, JOY,
WONDER — LEARNING — CANIFF'S SOURCE OF INSPIRATION / KEN!
AL GREENE WAS RARELY WITH US IN THESE 'YAKYAK-FESTS' —
SO OUR CONTACTS WERE FEW — TOUCH 'N' GO — I RECALL, WHEN WE DID
MESH GEARS, HE CAME HOME WITH ME AFTERSCHOOL (I LIVED BUT FIVE
BLOCKS from S.I.A.) and I SHOWED HIM MY SKIMPY CLIPFILES of
'TERRY', 'SCORCHY' D/S, Wy ROBBINS THEN, MESKIN, EISNER, ALL
the BEST of COMICBOOK ART I COULD AFFORD TO BUY / TRADE for / etc —
and WE TALKED — HE LOVED COMICS — AIMED TO DRAW THEM, TOO!
SOMEHOW / SOMETIME / ABOUT THEN, ALFONSO GREENE MADE
HIS CONNECTION WITH SHELLY MAYER, COMICS EDITOR, AT 'M.C. GAINES
PUBLG CO., 225 LaFAYETTE ST., NYC / NY — A MAGIC ADDRESS — and
PRODUCT, and PRACTITIONERS of that WONDERFUL CRAFT / ART of COMIC
BOOK PRODUCTION — and SHELLY HIRED HIM to TAKE OVER the BACK-
UP FEATURE, 'the BLACK PIRATE', WHICH SHELLY MOLDOFF STARTED-UP
and DREW (PERHAPS WROTE?) A NUMBER OF — TIL — THIS NEW KID
ON the BLOCK WAS HANDED IT — HUZZAHS! ZOUNDS! GLORYOSKY!
AL' DREW THREE - OR FOUR - (?) - OF THEM - IN HIS
SIMPLE CLEANLINED CANIFFLIKE STYLE — DAMN GOOD for a GREEN
KID (NO PUN, BUT IT FITS!) — BUT — TROUBLE — AL'S PERSONAL
WOES — HARLEM STREET GANG WOES / WARS — the WORST! TOUGH,
QUIET AL; IT TURNED-OUT, WAS a GANGMEMBER — WHO MUST'VE
WANTED 'OUT' — HAVING a TALENT TO HONE — a SITDOWN CREATIVE
WORKADAY ARTISTIC FUTURE — DOING WHAT HE OBVIOUSLY LOVED
TO DO — SHELLY MAYER, HIS BOOSTER, MENTOR, EDITOR, FRIEND
MUST'VE DONE HIS BEST to PULL AL BACK, AWAY, from that GANG
LIFE HE LIVED SMACK IN the MIDST OF THEN —

the stories.

While most of Jackson's work was done in collaboration with Whitman, there was one assignment he signed alone. It appeared in *Suspense Comics* #9 (Aug. 1945), in a story titled, "Sentence of Death." The splash page catches the eye immediately with the image of a skeleton judge passing sentence upon a tough gun moll before him. Though Jackson's figures are a bit stiff and lack the facile flow of Whitman's, they are solidly drawn. Here too, he favored a liberal amount of black ink to limn his images.

Whitman and Jackson apparently worked together throughout 1945 and into 1946, with several back-up features in *Airboy Comics* among the last collaborations. They simply signed their "Sky Wolf" story in *Airboy Comics* vol. 2 #12 (Jan. 1946) as "W.I.J." Two issues later, in *Airboy Comics* vol. 3 #2 (April 1946), they were "Whit Jackson." Their final work published was also their single longest story. It was *Classics Illustrated* #36 (April 1947), an adaptation of Herman Melville's *Typee*.

The story of *Typee* was based upon Melville's personal experiences as a castaway on Nuku Hiva in the South Pacific, living with a tribe that practiced cannibalism. The artwork by Whitman and Jackson on this story is a departure from their previous work, perhaps an indication that Jackson was the pencil artist this time and Whitman the inker. It has a simplistic, almost humorous look to it—an odd stylistic choice given the subject. Also unusual was the way the two artists signed this story: "Ezra Whiteman," a play upon both of their names and interracial partnership.

When asked years later, Whitman's son said his father had never mentioned having a partner or the name of Ezra Jackson.

Jackson left comics around this time. The industry was changing, as the war had ended and the White artists were returning to reclaim jobs.

In 2007, Jackson's daughter, Congresswoman Sheila Jackson Lee wrote in the Congressional Record:

I pay tribute to my father, my late father, a man who worked hard for his family, who believed that no job was beneath him to support his family, a man who was a brilliant artist. But because of segregation, the work that he had, he was, if you will, replaced when men came back who happened to be white, from World War II. [Jackson Lee, Sheila, Congressional Record, vol. 153 Pt. 7, Apr. 23, 2007, p.9686]

After Ezra moved into a flat above a restaurant at 1732 Amsterdam Avenue in the Bronx, he met Ivalita Bennett who, like him, was a Seventh-day Adventist.

Along with her younger sister, Ivalita moved from St. Petersburg, Florida, to New York City in the early 1940s, when she was only 16 years old. Like so many others, they came looking for opportunities. Her church was very important to her and so, too, it was for Ezra. They married in 1949 and had two children, Sheila and Michael.

Ezra had become an Elder, first at the Jamaica church and then in Linden. Ivalita served both churches as well. She graduated from Oakwood College and became a nurse at Salvation Army Booth Memorial Hospital in 1957.

[Above] Toth was a friend and classmate of Alfonso, and wrote this poignant tribute years later for Roy Thomas's *Alter Ego* magazine. *Alter Ego* #27, August 2003, TwoMorrows Publishing.

[Right] Alphonso Greene's arrest with three associates made the New York City newspapers. *Daily News*, January 21, 1964.

Years later, Jackson received an opportunity to get back to comics by Bertram Fitzgerald, an enterprising new Black publisher. Fitzgerald's idea was to tell Black history through the use of the comic book medium. His brainchild saw light as the *Golden Legacy* line and Jackson was among the first artists he recruited.

Jackson's art appeared in *Golden Legacy* #3 (1968). Along with Black artists Tom Feelings and Joan Bacchus, Jackson illustrated "Crispus Attucks," the main story. Ezra also worked on the subsequent issue's feature: a biography of Benjamin Banneker.

In this period, Ezra also found employment with Myron Fass. Like Jackson, Fass was a former comic book artist with the majority of his work published in the late 1940s and 1950s. In the 1960s, Fass became a publisher, with financial backing, of several scandal tabloids. He also drifted back into comics with a short-lived series of titles published under his M. F. Enterprises imprint. Later in the decade, he started a line of black-and-white horror magazines, which used material from grizzly 1950s comics. Jackson's job was to redraw these stories to be even gorier and more horrific.

Eventually, Ezra provided illustrations for other Fass productions, such as *Great West* magazine, a slightly more respectable publication.

His later years were devoted to his family and church activities. On June 2, 1996, surrounded by his family, Ezra Jackson died from prostate cancer.

***

Across town in Harlem, Alfonso Greene took a far different path to arrive at the same school.

Alphonso and Melanie [Warren] Greene married in Cleveland, Ohio, on March 23, 1926. Both had made the trek north in the Great Migration of Blacks during the early years of the century; she from Alabama, he from South Carolina. They settled where most other Blacks had settled in Cleveland: the neighborhood of Central. As the Jews and Italians who had been there previously moved on to better housing in other parts of the city, the Blacks continued to move in. Their son Alfonso was born here, on December 6, 1927. The elder Alphonso (who sometimes spelled his name the same way as his son) toiled at odd jobs, most often as a laborer in garages. In the depths of the Depression, the family moved to Harlem.

NEWS, TUESDAY, JANUARY 21, 1964 C5

4 With Guns, Ether Seized In a Waldorf Kidnap Scheme

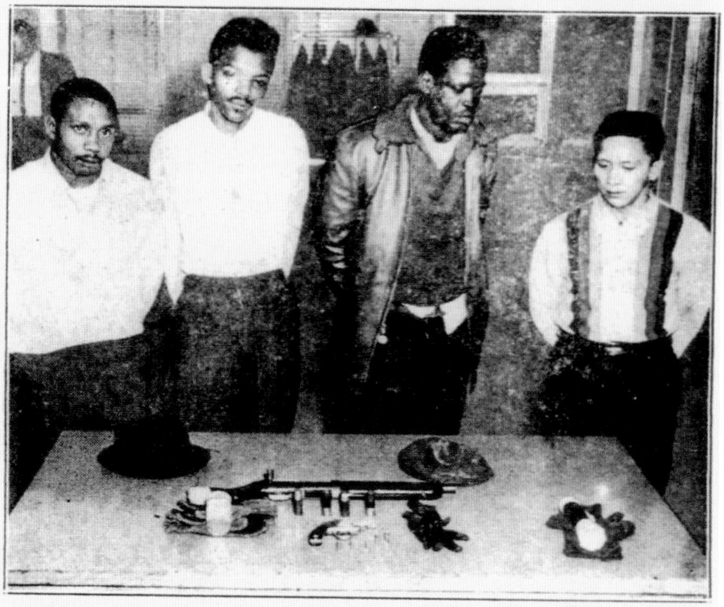

(NEWS foto by George Lockhart)

Prisoners Charles Downs, Samuel Rhone, Alfonso Greene and Manuel Bacolod (l. to r.) stand before table with confiscated weapons at police station.

By WILLIAM NEUGEBAUER

Four men, accused of lying in wait in a car outside the Waldorf-Astoria to kidnap and rob any wealthy guest who happened by, were arraigned yesterday on

Not every life is easy to document, with tracing made difficult by the commonality of names, or the lack of newspaper-worthy achievements. Poverty enhances the chance of anonymity. Many are doomed to obscurity without someone to tell their story. Alfonso Greene lived such a life and may have stayed unknown if not for remembrances of his White classmate Alex Toth.

Toth would eventually become a legendary comic book artist, a stylistic master of design who would influence generations of artists that came after him. His talents extended to the animation industry, for which he either created or designed numerous cartoon characters throughout the 1960s and '70s. He was also a keen-eyed critic and comics historian whose famously stream-of-consciousness writings offered unsparing critiques along with historical insights. It was in such writing that Toth recounted his memories of Alfonso Greene:

Al was roughedged, wellbuilt, strong, and black—quiet and spare with words—a wannabe cartoonist/comic book artist—had the [Milton] Caniff-doodle/style in his mind's eye and hand...We, by then, rabid hopefuls, in our small clique, exchanged our observations ... Al Greene was rarely with us in these "yak yak fests"—so our contacts were few...when we did mesh gears, he came home with me after school...and we talked—he loved comics—aimed to draw them, too! [Toth, Alex, "About 'The Black Pirate'—And Alfonso Greene!" *Alter Ego* #27, Aug. 2003, pp.28-29]

Greene and Toth were both students at the Industrial Art high school. While both desired to be comic book artists,

"THE SECRET SEVEN"

SECRET SEVEN.

AN IMORTANT MEETING IS CALLED IN THE HIDDEN HEAD-QUARTERS OF THE "SECRET SEVEN"—

they certainly weren't unique among their schoolmates. Through those halls walked dozens of other future comic creators. Greene, though, was special. He got his first professional art assignments while still a student. Toth recalled:

Alfonso Greene made his connection with Shelly Mayer, comics editor, at M. C. Gaines Pub. Co., 225 Lafayette St...and Shelly hired him to take over the backup feature, "The Black Pirate." [Ibid.]

Sheldon "Shelly" Mayer wasn't much older than Greene when he began working in the comic book industry in 1935. Only 18 years old at the time, Mayer already had professional experience in the field of animation via Fleischer Studios when he was hired as M.C. "Max" Gaines' assistant at the McClure Syndicate. In his self-described "minor editorial capacity," Mayer was tasked with finding and developing material for publication. His greatest coup, a property that had been offered to just about every other editor in town, was a creation by two teenagers from Cleveland. While all other editors had passed on *Superman*, Mayer saw its potential and brought the feature to the attention of his boss Max Gaines, who sold DC on the feature.

Mayer spent the rest of his long comics career as both an editor and an artist for DC Comics. His most personal creation was "Scribbly," a comic about a young cartoonist who was a thinly-disguised version of himself. Beginning in the latter part of the 1940s, likely with Mayer's instigation, a "Scribbly Award" was given annually to the most promising cartoonist at the High School of Industrial Art, the same school at which he found Greene.

[Above] In this early collaboration, Maurice Whitman (penciler) and Ezra Jackson (inker) provided all the interior artwork for the first issue of *Patches Comics*. One of its stories, "The Secret Seven," relates the adventures of a boys' club in their only appearance. The club includes Jimmie, a Black boy respectfully presented as an equal to his peers and realistically drawn as opposed to the depiction of many Black characters of this time. *Patches Comics* #1, March – April 1945, Rural Home Publishing.

[Right] Cover to an adaptation of Herman Melville's *Typee*. This collaboration between Maurice Whitman and Ezra Jackson was signed under the pen name "Ezra Whiteman," likely an in-joke between the two artists. *Classics Illustrated* #36, April 1947, Gilberton.

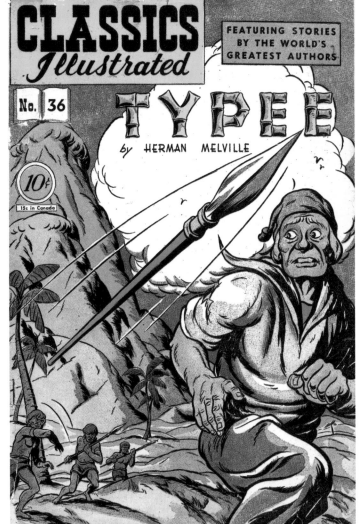

Greene's work on "The Black Pirate" saw publication from late 1944 to early 1946, as did the *Wonder Woman* comics backup feature, "Wonder Women of History." One of the women profiled in this feature was Sojourner Truth, the former slave who became an abolitionist and civil rights icon. Appearing in *Wonder Woman* #13 (Summer 1945), this was the first comic book story to be both devoted to a Black person and also drawn by one. It was a landmark achievement not touted at the time.

CLASSICS Illustrated
FEATURING STORIES BY THE WORLD'S GREATEST AUTHORS
No. 36
TYPEE
by HERMAN MELVILLE
10¢
15¢ in Canada

Perhaps tellingly, Greene's senior photo never appeared in his high school yearbook in 1946, the year he should have graduated. At this same point, his career stops suddenly.

Toth revealed a darker side to Greene's story:

> *Al drew three or four [stories]...in his simple clean-lined Canifflike style...Al's personal woes—Harlem street gang woes/wars—the worst! Tough, quiet Al; turned-out, was a gangmember.*
>
> *Shelly Mayer, his booster, mentor, editor, friend, must've done his best to pull Al back, away, from that gang life he lived smack in the midst of...Al was in a knife fight/gunfight/was wounded/wounded others/had a trial/served time in prison.* [Ibid.]

The Turks, the Slicksters, the Sabers, the Imperials—stories of the ongoing turf wars between these gangs and others filled both the Black and White newspapers throughout 1945.

It wasn't just Black gangs fighting each other. Race relations were a concern in New York City at the time, particularly among high school-aged boys. On September 27 and 28, 1945, a large scale fight between White and Black students at Benjamin Franklin High School in East Harlem broke out. Despite the best efforts of the mayor's Committee on Unity to downplay the incident, it was acknowledged by most to be an outgrowth of simmering resentments between the races.

This timing, along with the Harlem location of this gang warfare, lends credence to Toth's recollection that Greene was involved in gang activity.

> *Al served time—was out again—and Shelly put him back on "Black Pirate"—but yet again—gang war—Al shot and, I think, shot to death...someone from the rival gang and subsequently ended up in prison.* [Ibid.]

Indeed, the *New York Times* reported fights between rival black gangs in The Bronx and Harlem on the nights of August 20, 21, and September 1, 1945. Several gang members were shot and at least one died.

Toth's memory was fuzzy on the details, but he seemed to remember that Eleanor Roosevelt testified on Greene's behalf, "citing his talent, proven and prior attempts to cut loose of his gang life." [Ibid.]

Memories are often imperfect and Toth's claim that Eleanor Roosevelt was a character witness on Greene's behalf is unproven. Such a magnanimous act by the most famous woman in America at that time would warrant mention in newspapers of the day, but no corroboration has been found.

However, Theodore Roosevelt's daughter-in-law, Eleanor Butler Roosevelt, was involved with many charitable organizations such as the Girl Scouts and the Red Cross and, significantly, served on Fawcett Comics' editorial advisory board. It seems likely that she would have been aware of Greene and his legal problems more so than the First Lady.

Several years passed before any more art bearing Greene's name was published. He then contributed to *Heroic Comics*, published by Eastern Color Printing. This tenure was also brief, lasting from 1949 to late 1950. The reason for the cessation was tragically familiar. News accounts told a story that could have come right out of a *Crime Does Not Pay* comic book. Alfonso and his three partners "employed the novel

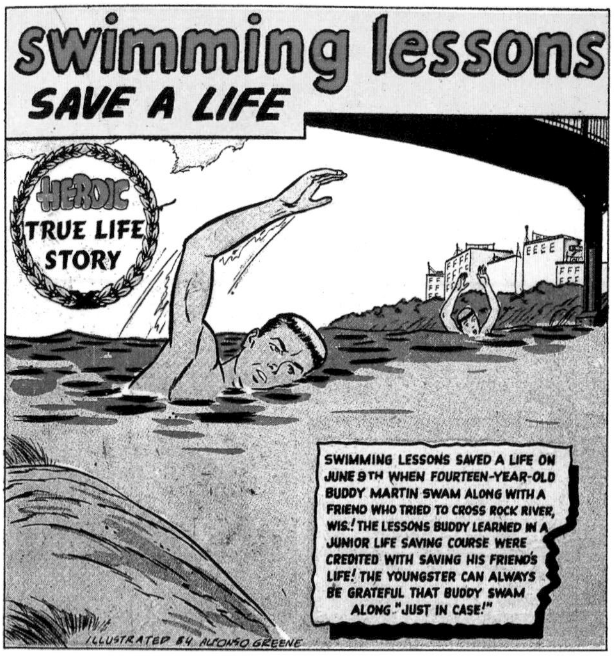
swimming lessons
SAVE A LIFE
HEROIC
TRUE LIFE STORY
SWIMMING LESSONS SAVED A LIFE ON JUNE 9TH WHEN FOURTEEN-YEAR-OLD BUDDY MARTIN SWAM ALONG WITH A FRIEND WHO TRIED TO CROSS ROCK RIVER, WIS.! THE LESSONS BUDDY LEARNED IN A JUNIOR LIFE SAVING COURSE WERE CREDITED WITH SAVING HIS FRIEND'S LIFE! THE YOUNGSTER CAN ALWAYS BE GRATEFUL THAT BUDDY SWAM ALONG "JUST IN CASE!"
ILLUSTRATED BY ALFONSO GREENE

idea of putting half a lemon into a robbery victim's mouth before taping it. Then, if the tape worked loose, the puckered condition of his mouth would keep him from yelling for help right away." ["Cops Put Squeeze on 'Lemon Gang,' Nab 4 Harlemites," *New York Age*, Aug. 12, 1950]

Despite making off with the $1,023 payroll they stole, the Lemon Gang didn't get far. Their victim was able to wriggle the tape off and get the attention of several policemen in the area. All members of the gang were convicted of the crime. Greene's three partners were juveniles and were sent to a reformatory. Greene was 22 years old and received a sentence of five to five and a half years in prison.

After serving his time, Alfonso Greene started working for Timely (commonly referred to as Timely/Atlas, later called Marvel Comics) circa 1956.

Timely's managing editor Stan Lee employed many Black freelance artists working in comics during the 1950s. Cal Massey was the most consistently used, with job assignments spread fairly evenly throughout the decade. The majority of Warren Broderick's identifiable work was for the same company in a brief tenure. Most notably, the great Matt Baker, seeking work in the wake of St. John Publishing's demise, finished out his comic book career at Timely/Atlas.

In a short period, Greene turned in at least 16 jobs to Lee. Whatever dubious past he had, Greene now was gainfully employed and, since he was still young, probably looking at a long career in the comic book industry.

Then came "The Atlas Implosion." By the mid-'50s, comic books were undergoing a major upheaval. Governmental scrutiny, public condemnation, the popularity of television, and various economic factors placed terrific pressure on the industry, resulting in the collapse of many publishers. The final straw came in April 1957 with the failure of the American News Company (ANC), the largest distributor of comics in the country. One of the companies most affected was Timely/Atlas. Within weeks of ANC's demise, the comic book company stopped assigning work to artists and writers.

Greene was working at Timely/Atlas consistently until the work stoppage. The company used an in-house coding system that combined letters and digits to designate the story work assignments. These job numbers ended abruptly with O-403 pre-Implosion. Greene's last assignment was O-370. Although his art appeared in *Strange Tales* #66 (Dec. 1958), he actually completed the artwork in early 1957.

Except for one story published in *Classics Illustrated—World Around Us* #2 ["Indians"] (Oct. 1958), Greene's promising art career was yet again thwarted, ironically this time not by his actions, but by the wane of the industry. Where he went and what he did thereafter has yet to be fully determined.

A possible postscript to Greene's story may be found in the pages of the *New York Times* dated January 31, 1964. Unfortunately, the article is not about a gallery showing of a rising artist. It recounts the release from police custody of four men being held on weapons charges. They had been found lingering suspiciously outside the Waldorf-Astoria Hotel in Manhattan with guns and a bottle of ether. A judge determined that there was insufficient evidence linking them to a crime. One of the four was named Alfonso Greene.

Consistent with other mysteries surrounding Greene's life were the circumstances of his death. All that can be said with certainty is that a man bearing his name, born on December 6, 1927, died in the Bronx in October 1977.

Toth concluded:

I'll never forget Alfonso Greene—and what might have been, for him, as a pro, a rough, tough, but good guy—amen! [Toth 2003, op. cit.]

Jackson and Greene shared a school, but their choices and circumstance brought them down different paths. While their fates may have differed, they are both deserving of notice as significant pioneers among the invisible men.

[Above] The splash panel for "Swimming Lessons Save a Life" signed by Alfonso Greene (*New Heroic Comics* #64, January 1951, Eastern Color).

[Right] This story is the only one yet found signed by Ezra Jackson alone. *Suspense Comics* #9, August 1945, Continental Magazines.

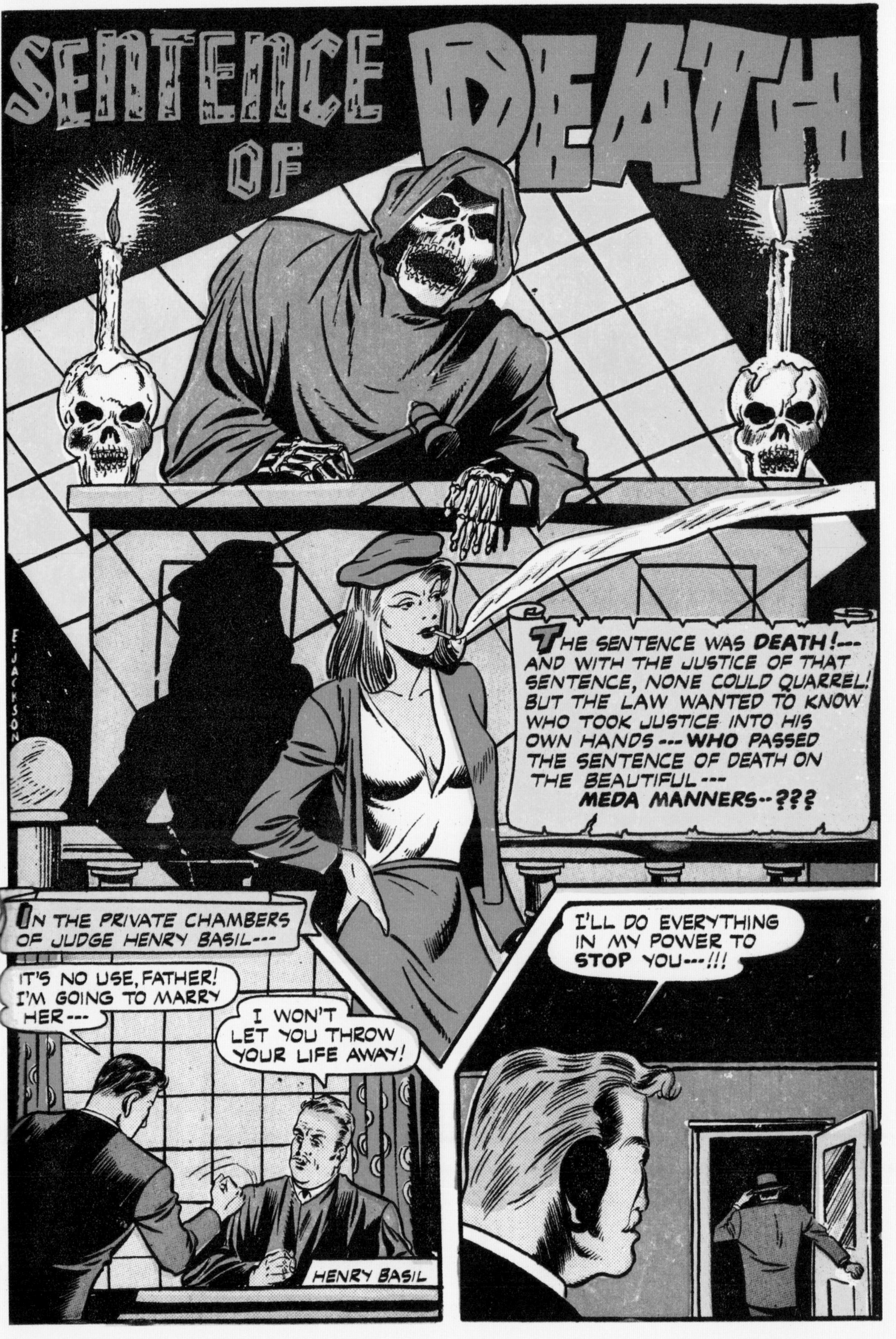
SENTENCE OF DEATH
E. JACKSON
THE SENTENCE WAS DEATH!--- AND WITH THE JUSTICE OF THAT SENTENCE, NONE COULD QUARREL! BUT THE LAW WANTED TO KNOW WHO TOOK JUSTICE INTO HIS OWN HANDS --- WHO PASSED THE SENTENCE OF DEATH ON THE BEAUTIFUL --- MEDA MANNERS--???
IN THE PRIVATE CHAMBERS OF JUDGE HENRY BASIL---
IT'S NO USE, FATHER! I'M GOING TO MARRY HER---
I WON'T LET YOU THROW YOUR LIFE AWAY!
HENRY BASIL
I'LL DO EVERYTHING IN MY POWER TO STOP YOU---!!!

MEDA MANNERS, EH? I'LL GO TO SEE HER AT ONCE--!!

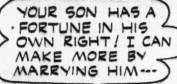

LATER--

WHY JUDGE BASIL! I NEVER THOUGHT I'D SEE YOU HERE!

YOU LITTLE SHE-DEVIL! YOU KNEW I'D COME!

I'LL PAY YOU WHATEVER YOU ASK! ONLY KEEP AWAY FROM MY SON--!

THE ANSWER IS NO!

YOUR SON HAS A FORTUNE IN HIS OWN RIGHT! I CAN MAKE MORE BY MARRYING HIM---

I'LL KILL YOU FIRST!

SHOW THE JUDGE THE WAY OUT, ERIC--!

YES, MISS MANNERS!

I'LL GO--! BUT I WARN YOU! IF YOU MARRY MY SON, YOU'LL NEVER LIVE TO REGRET IT--!

I'LL SEND HIM AWAY! HE'S TOO YOUNG TO REALIZE WHAT MARRIAGE TO A WOMAN LIKE THAT WILL DO TO HIS LIFE---

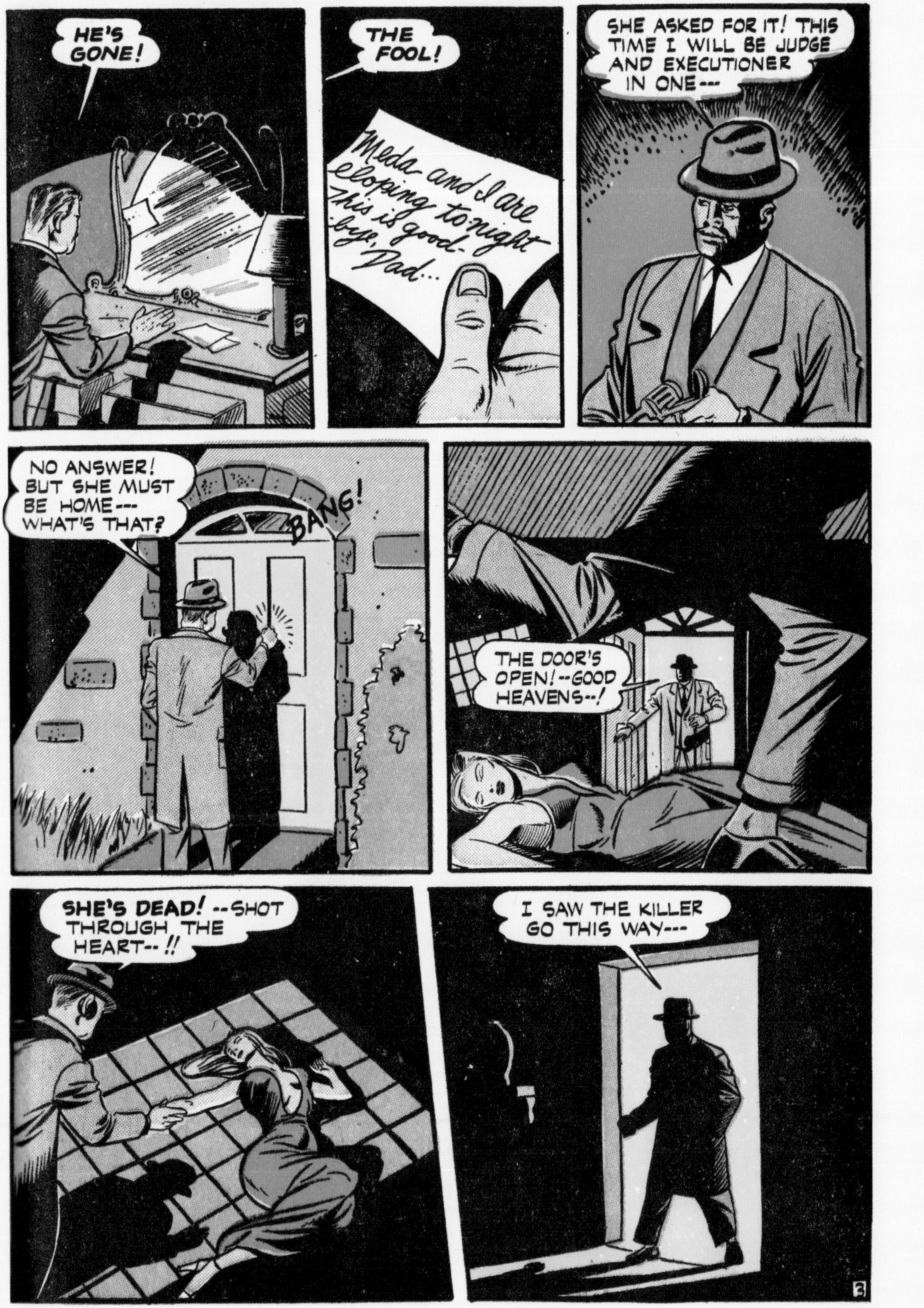
HE'S GONE!
THE FOOL!
Meda and I are eloping to-night This is good-bye, Dad...
SHE ASKED FOR IT! THIS TIME I WILL BE JUDGE AND EXECUTIONER IN ONE---
NO ANSWER! BUT SHE MUST BE HOME--- WHAT'S THAT?
BANG!
THE DOOR'S OPEN!--GOOD HEAVENS--!
SHE'S DEAD! --SHOT THROUGH THE HEART-- !!
I SAW THE KILLER GO THIS WAY---
3

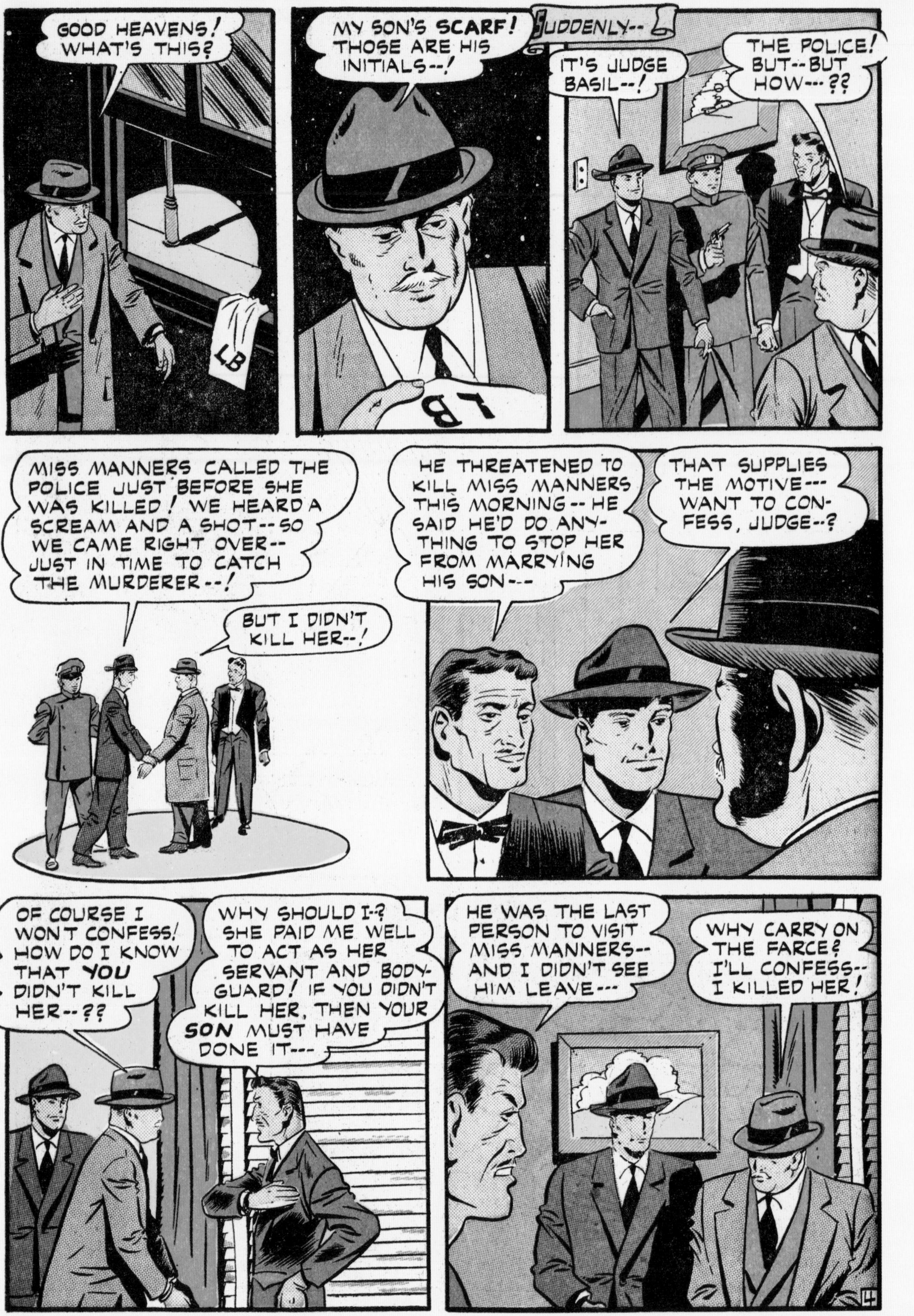
GOOD HEAVENS! WHAT'S THIS?
LB
MY SON'S SCARF! THOSE ARE HIS INITIALS--!
LB
SUDDENLY--
IT'S JUDGE BASIL--!
THE POLICE! BUT--BUT HOW---??
MISS MANNERS CALLED THE POLICE JUST BEFORE SHE WAS KILLED! WE HEARD A SCREAM AND A SHOT--SO WE CAME RIGHT OVER--JUST IN TIME TO CATCH THE MURDERER--!
BUT I DIDN'T KILL HER--!
HE THREATENED TO KILL MISS MANNERS THIS MORNING--HE SAID HE'D DO ANYTHING TO STOP HER FROM MARRYING HIS SON---
THAT SUPPLIES THE MOTIVE---WANT TO CONFESS, JUDGE--?
OF COURSE I WON'T CONFESS! HOW DO I KNOW THAT YOU DIDN'T KILL HER--??
WHY SHOULD I-? SHE PAID ME WELL TO ACT AS HER SERVANT AND BODYGUARD! IF YOU DIDN'T KILL HER, THEN YOUR SON MUST HAVE DONE IT---
HE WAS THE LAST PERSON TO VISIT MISS MANNERS--AND I DIDN'T SEE HIM LEAVE---
WHY CARRY ON THE FARCE? I'LL CONFESS--I KILLED HER!
4

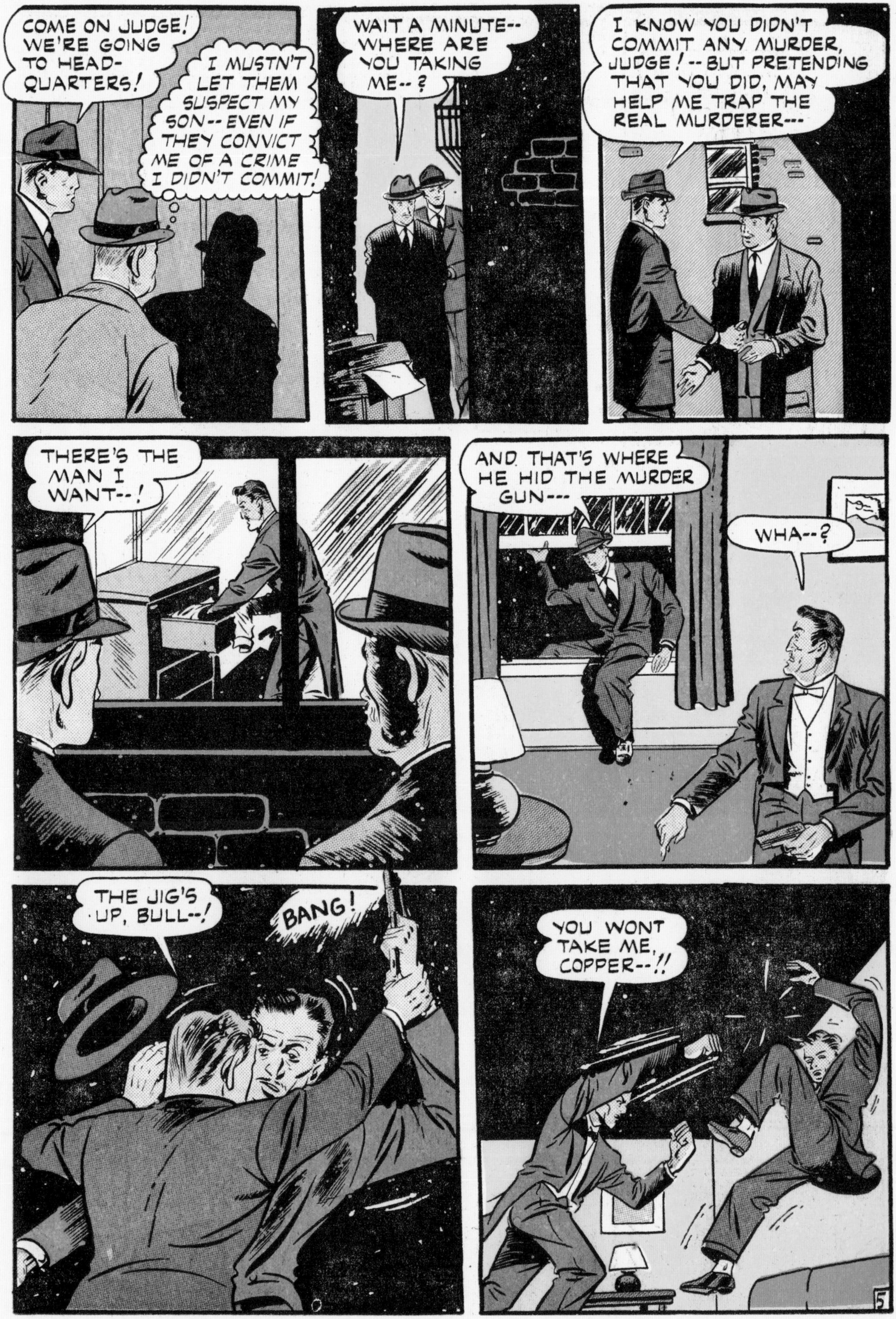
COME ON JUDGE! WE'RE GOING TO HEAD-QUARTERS!
I MUSTN'T LET THEM SUSPECT MY SON-- EVEN IF THEY CONVICT ME OF A CRIME I DIDN'T COMMIT!
WAIT A MINUTE-- WHERE ARE YOU TAKING ME--?
I KNOW YOU DIDN'T COMMIT ANY MURDER, JUDGE! -- BUT PRETENDING THAT YOU DID, MAY HELP ME TRAP THE REAL MURDERER---
THERE'S THE MAN I WANT--!
AND THAT'S WHERE HE HID THE MURDER GUN---
WHA--?
THE JIG'S UP, BULL--!
BANG!
YOU WONT TAKE ME, COPPER--!!
5

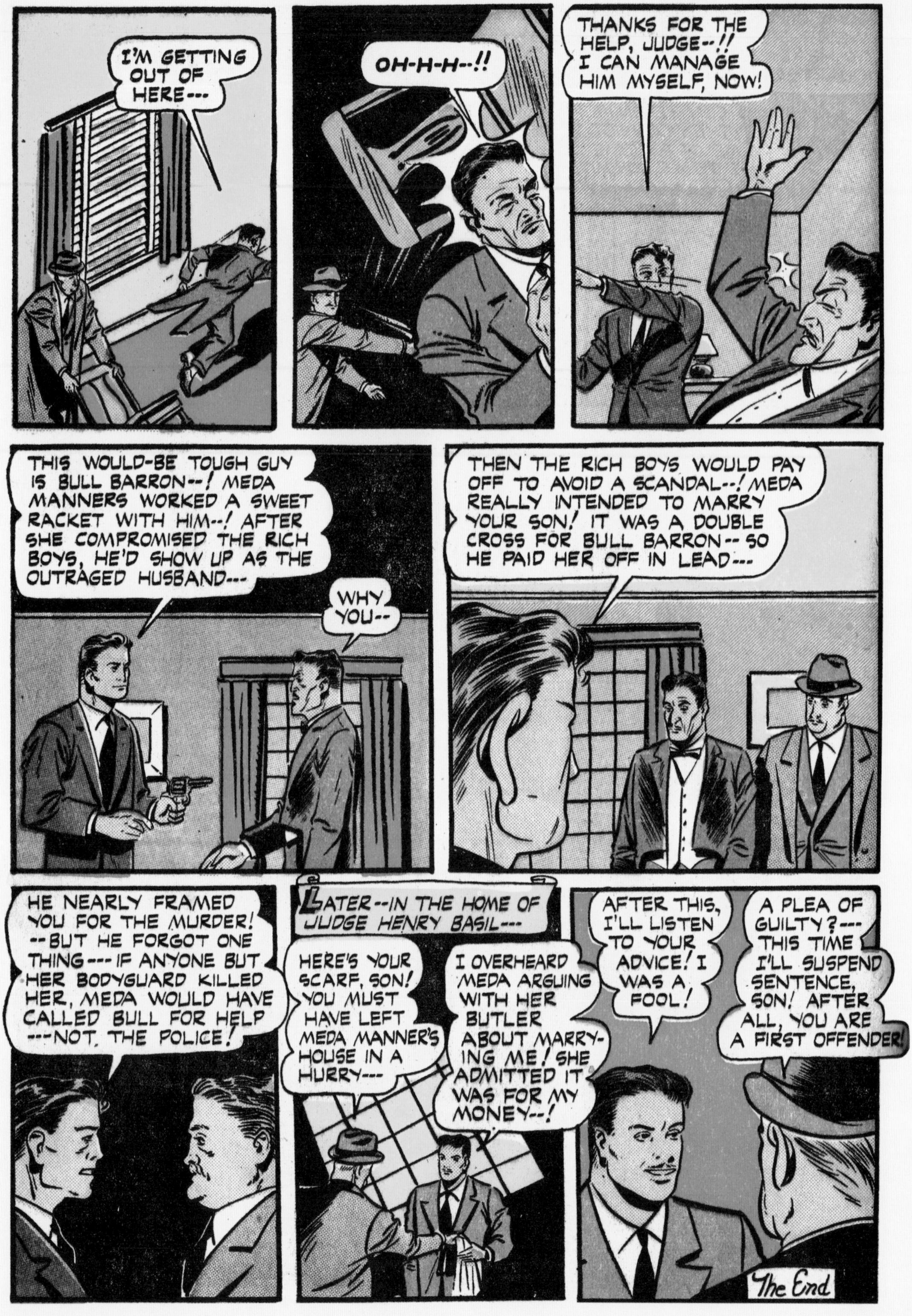
I'M GETTING OUT OF HERE---
OH-H-H--!!
THANKS FOR THE HELP, JUDGE--!! I CAN MANAGE HIM MYSELF, NOW!
THIS WOULD-BE TOUGH GUY IS BULL BARRON--! MEDA MANNERS WORKED A SWEET RACKET WITH HIM--! AFTER SHE COMPROMISED THE RICH BOYS, HE'D SHOW UP AS THE OUTRAGED HUSBAND---
WHY YOU--
THEN THE RICH BOYS WOULD PAY OFF TO AVOID A SCANDAL--! MEDA REALLY INTENDED TO MARRY YOUR SON! IT WAS A DOUBLE CROSS FOR BULL BARRON-- SO HE PAID HER OFF IN LEAD---
HE NEARLY FRAMED YOU FOR THE MURDER! --BUT HE FORGOT ONE THING---IF ANYONE BUT HER BODYGUARD KILLED HER, MEDA WOULD HAVE CALLED BULL FOR HELP ---NOT THE POLICE!
LATER--IN THE HOME OF JUDGE HENRY BASIL---
HERE'S YOUR SCARF, SON! YOU MUST HAVE LEFT MEDA MANNER'S HOUSE IN A HURRY---
I OVERHEARD MEDA ARGUING WITH HER BUTLER ABOUT MARRYING ME! SHE ADMITTED IT WAS FOR MY MONEY--!
AFTER THIS, I'LL LISTEN TO YOUR ADVICE! I WAS A FOOL!
A PLEA OF GUILTY?--- THIS TIME I'LL SUSPEND SENTENCE, SON! AFTER ALL, YOU ARE A FIRST OFFENDER!
The End

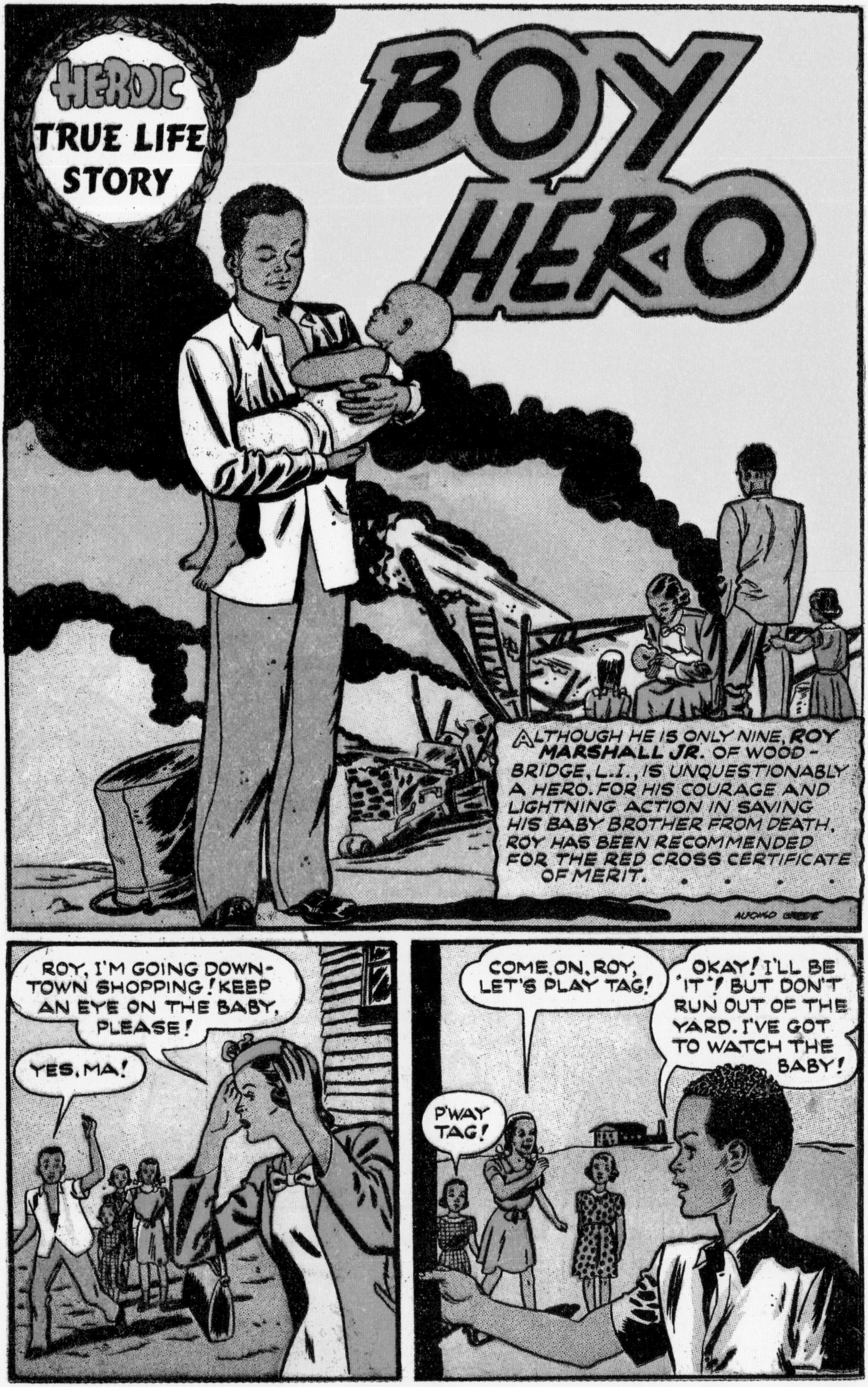
HEROIC
TRUE LIFE STORY
BOY HERO
ALTHOUGH HE IS ONLY NINE, ROY MARSHALL JR. OF WOOD-BRIDGE, L.I., IS UNQUESTIONABLY A HERO. FOR HIS COURAGE AND LIGHTNING ACTION IN SAVING HIS BABY BROTHER FROM DEATH, ROY HAS BEEN RECOMMENDED FOR THE RED CROSS CERTIFICATE OF MERIT. . . . .
ROY, I'M GOING DOWN-TOWN SHOPPING! KEEP AN EYE ON THE BABY, PLEASE!
YES, MA!
COME ON, ROY, LET'S PLAY TAG!
OKAY! I'LL BE 'IT'! BUT DON'T RUN OUT OF THE YARD. I'VE GOT TO WATCH THE BABY!
P'WAY TAG!

This Greene-drawn two-page story appearing in the aptly named *New Heroic Comics* featured the true story of Roy Marshall, a young Black child who risked his life to save his baby brother from a fire. *New Heroic Comics* #53, March 1949, Famous Funnies.

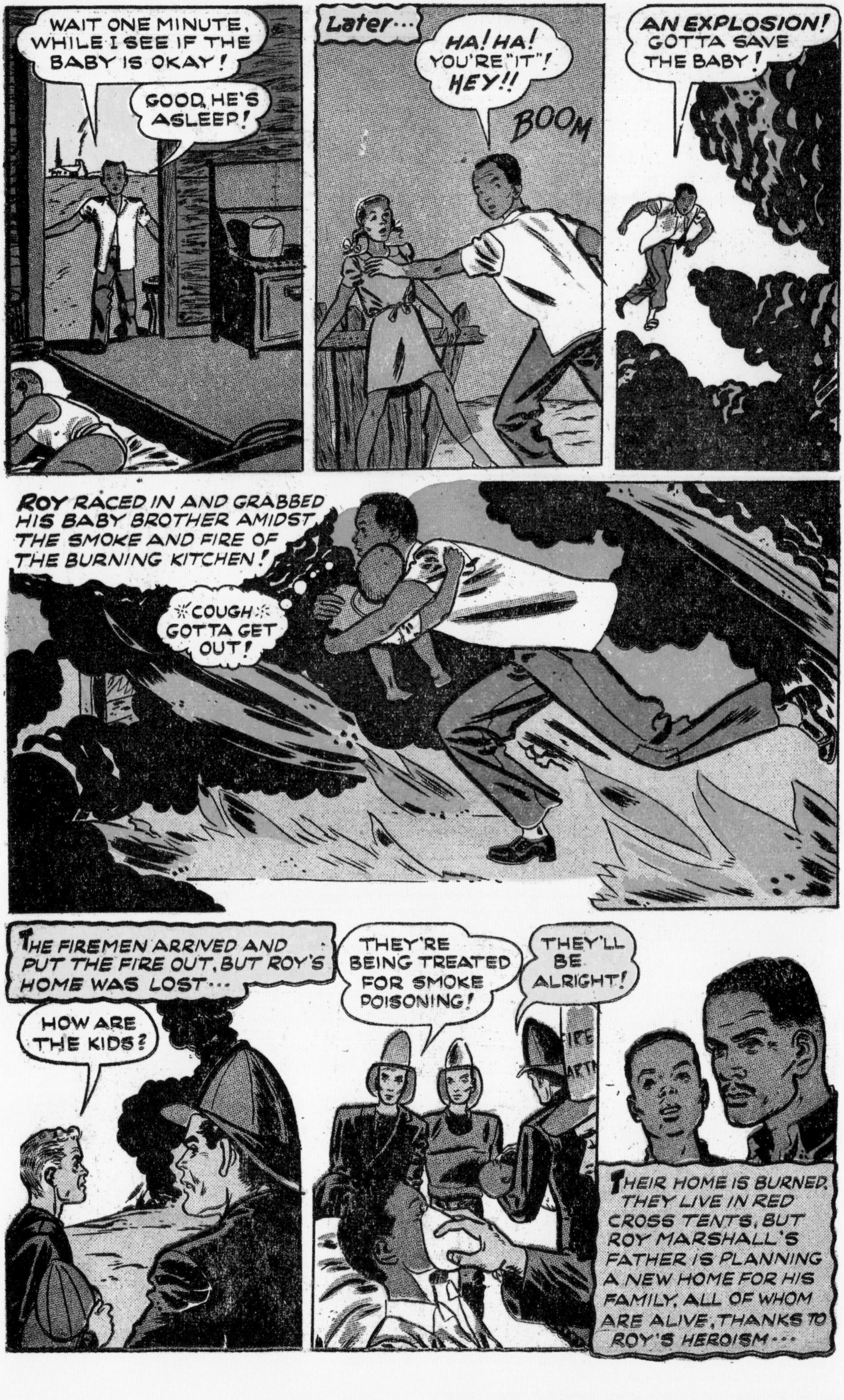
WAIT ONE MINUTE, WHILE I SEE IF THE BABY IS OKAY!
GOOD, HE'S ASLEEP!
Later...
HA! HA! YOU'RE "IT"! HEY!!
BOOM
AN EXPLOSION! GOTTA SAVE THE BABY!
ROY RACED IN AND GRABBED HIS BABY BROTHER AMIDST THE SMOKE AND FIRE OF THE BURNING KITCHEN!
COUGH GOTTA GET OUT!
THE FIREMEN ARRIVED AND PUT THE FIRE OUT, BUT ROY'S HOME WAS LOST...
HOW ARE THE KIDS?
THEY'RE BEING TREATED FOR SMOKE POISONING!
THEY'LL BE ALRIGHT!
THEIR HOME IS BURNED, THEY LIVE IN RED CROSS TENTS, BUT ROY MARSHALL'S FATHER IS PLANNING A NEW HOME FOR HIS FAMILY, ALL OF WHOM ARE ALIVE, THANKS TO ROY'S HEROISM...

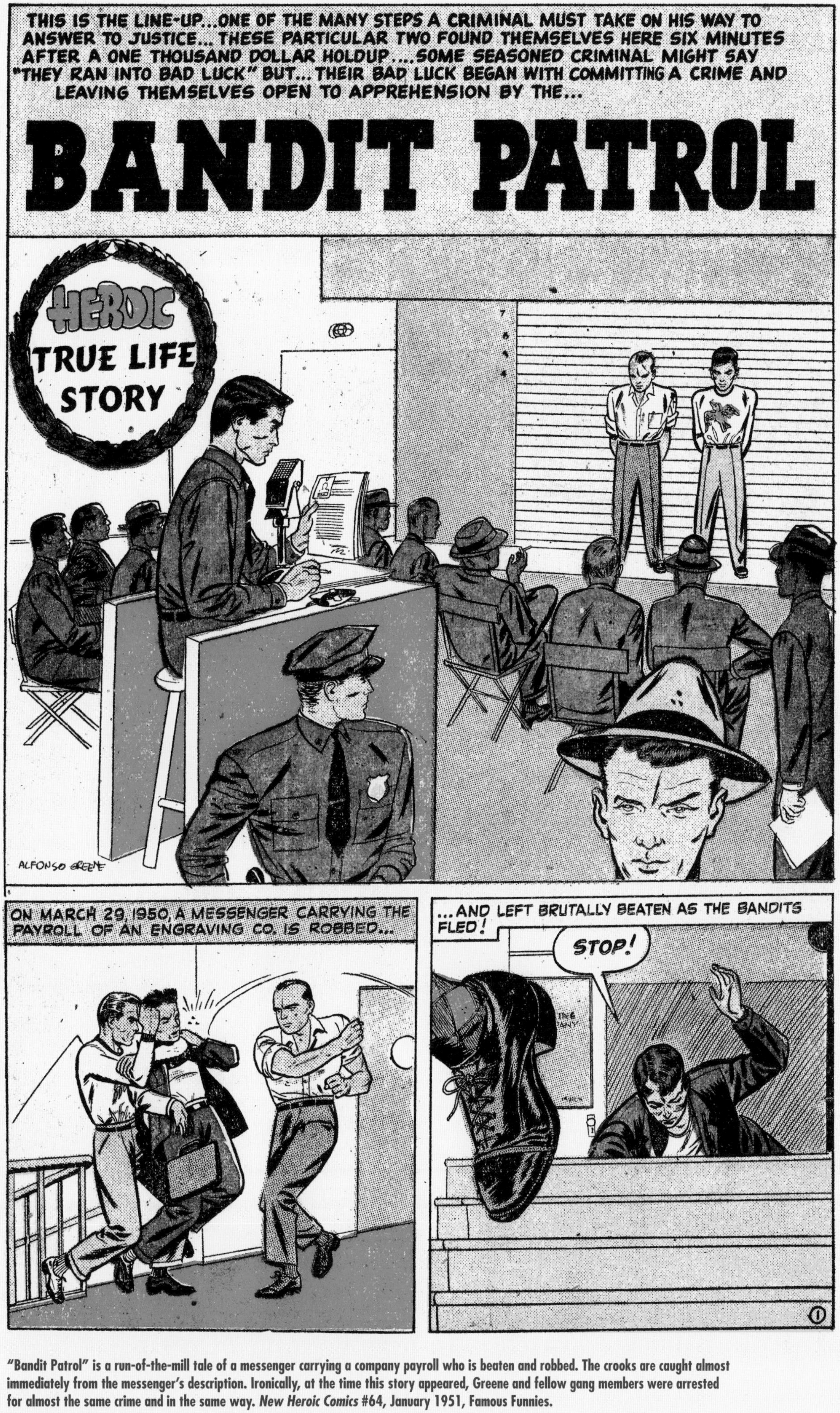
THIS IS THE LINE-UP...ONE OF THE MANY STEPS A CRIMINAL MUST TAKE ON HIS WAY TO ANSWER TO JUSTICE... THESE PARTICULAR TWO FOUND THEMSELVES HERE SIX MINUTES AFTER A ONE THOUSAND DOLLAR HOLDUP....SOME SEASONED CRIMINAL MIGHT SAY "THEY RAN INTO BAD LUCK" BUT... THEIR BAD LUCK BEGAN WITH COMMITTING A CRIME AND LEAVING THEMSELVES OPEN TO APPREHENSION BY THE...
BANDIT PATROL
HEROIC
TRUE LIFE STORY
ALFONSO GREENE
ON MARCH 29, 1950, A MESSENGER CARRYING THE PAYROLL OF AN ENGRAVING CO. IS ROBBED...
...AND LEFT BRUTALLY BEATEN AS THE BANDITS FLED!
STOP!
1

"Bandit Patrol" is a run-of-the-mill tale of a messenger carrying a company payroll who is beaten and robbed. The crooks are caught almost immediately from the messenger's description. Ironically, at the time this story appeared, Greene and fellow gang members were arrested for almost the same crime and in the same way. *New Heroic Comics* #64, January 1951, Famous Funnies.

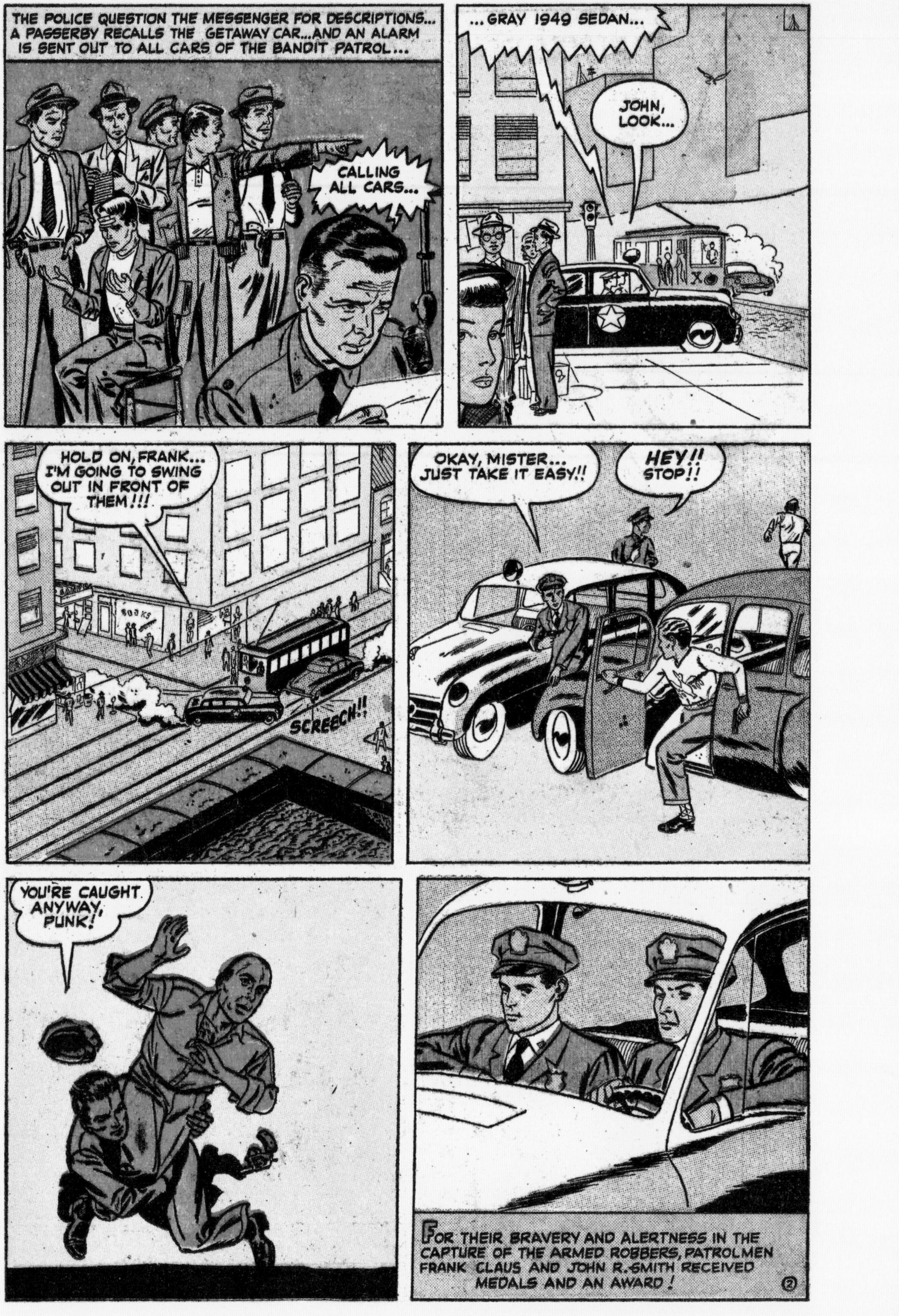
THE POLICE QUESTION THE MESSENGER FOR DESCRIPTIONS... A PASSERBY RECALLS THE GETAWAY CAR...AND AN ALARM IS SENT OUT TO ALL CARS OF THE BANDIT PATROL...
CALLING ALL CARS...
...GRAY 1949 SEDAN...
JOHN, LOOK...
HOLD ON, FRANK... I'M GOING TO SWING OUT IN FRONT OF THEM!!!
BOOKS
SCREECH!!
OKAY, MISTER... JUST TAKE IT EASY!!
HEY!! STOP!!
YOU'RE CAUGHT ANYWAY, PUNK!
FOR THEIR BRAVERY AND ALERTNESS IN THE CAPTURE OF THE ARMED ROBBERS, PATROLMEN FRANK CLAUS AND JOHN R. SMITH RECEIVED MEDALS AND AN AWARD!
2

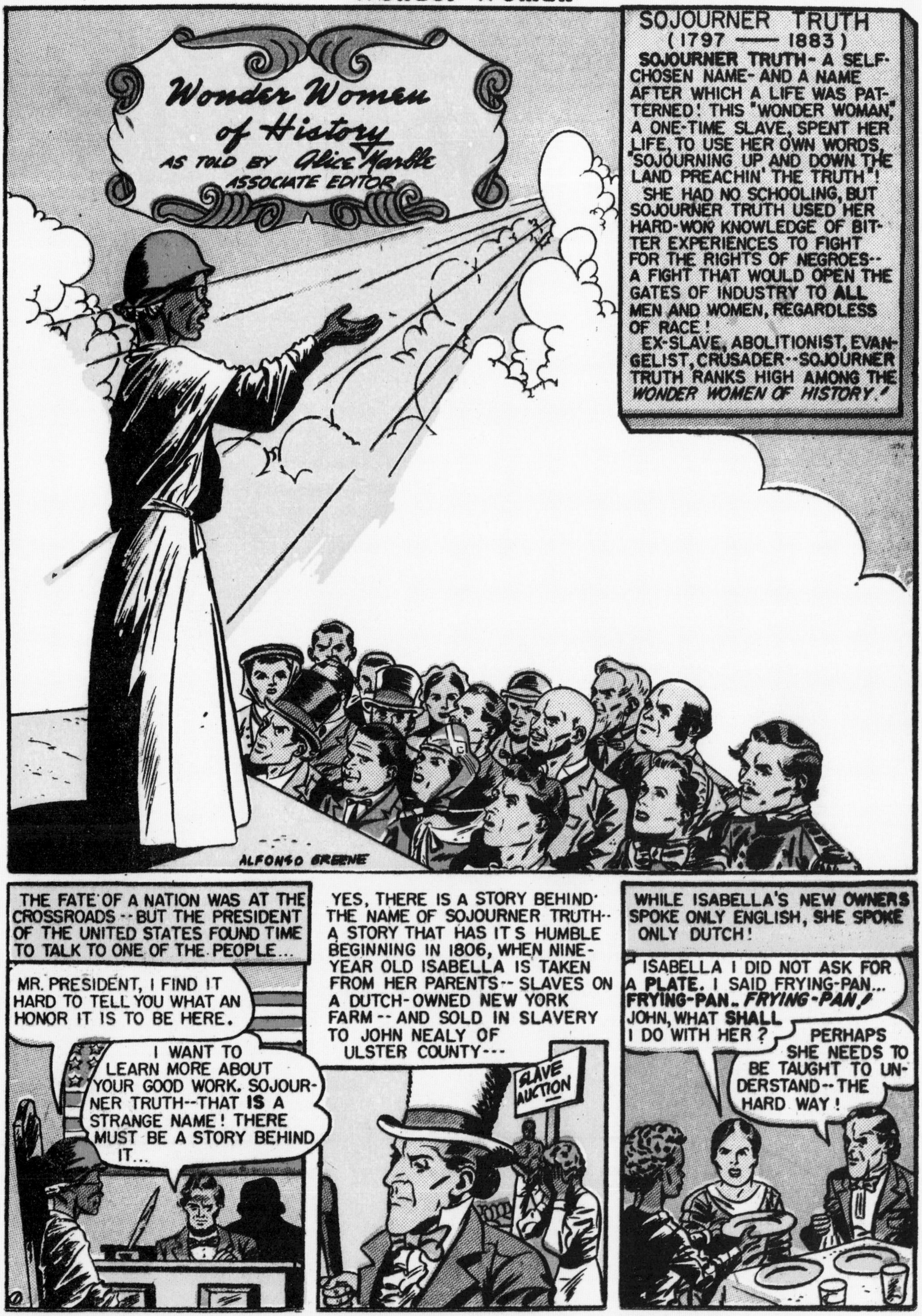
Wonder Women of History
AS TOLD BY Alice Marble
ASSOCIATE EDITOR
SOJOURNER TRUTH
(1797 —— 1883)
SOJOURNER TRUTH- A SELF-CHOSEN NAME- AND A NAME AFTER WHICH A LIFE WAS PATTERNED! THIS "WONDER WOMAN", A ONE-TIME SLAVE, SPENT HER LIFE, TO USE HER OWN WORDS, "SOJOURNING UP AND DOWN THE LAND PREACHIN' THE TRUTH"!
SHE HAD NO SCHOOLING, BUT SOJOURNER TRUTH USED HER HARD-WON KNOWLEDGE OF BITTER EXPERIENCES TO FIGHT FOR THE RIGHTS OF NEGROES-- A FIGHT THAT WOULD OPEN THE GATES OF INDUSTRY TO ALL MEN AND WOMEN, REGARDLESS OF RACE!
EX-SLAVE, ABOLITIONIST, EVANGELIST, CRUSADER--SOJOURNER TRUTH RANKS HIGH AMONG THE WONDER WOMEN OF HISTORY!
ALFONSO GREENE
THE FATE OF A NATION WAS AT THE CROSSROADS--BUT THE PRESIDENT OF THE UNITED STATES FOUND TIME TO TALK TO ONE OF THE PEOPLE...
MR. PRESIDENT, I FIND IT HARD TO TELL YOU WHAT AN HONOR IT IS TO BE HERE.
I WANT TO LEARN MORE ABOUT YOUR GOOD WORK. SOJOURNER TRUTH--THAT IS A STRANGE NAME! THERE MUST BE A STORY BEHIND IT...
YES, THERE IS A STORY BEHIND THE NAME OF SOJOURNER TRUTH-- A STORY THAT HAS ITS HUMBLE BEGINNING IN 1806, WHEN NINE-YEAR OLD ISABELLA IS TAKEN FROM HER PARENTS-- SLAVES ON A DUTCH-OWNED NEW YORK FARM--AND SOLD IN SLAVERY TO JOHN NEALY OF ULSTER COUNTY---
SLAVE AUCTION
WHILE ISABELLA'S NEW OWNERS SPOKE ONLY ENGLISH, SHE SPOKE ONLY DUTCH!
ISABELLA I DID NOT ASK FOR A PLATE. I SAID FRYING-PAN... FRYING-PAN.. FRYING-PAN! JOHN, WHAT SHALL I DO WITH HER?
PERHAPS SHE NEEDS TO BE TAUGHT TO UNDERSTAND--THE HARD WAY!

Appearing in the feature "Wonder Women of History," this is the biography of civil rights pioneer Sojourner Truth. It is likely the first positive depiction of a Black historical figure drawn by a Black artist, Alfonso Greene, to appear in a comic book. *Wonder Woman* #13 © DC Comics (Summer 1945).

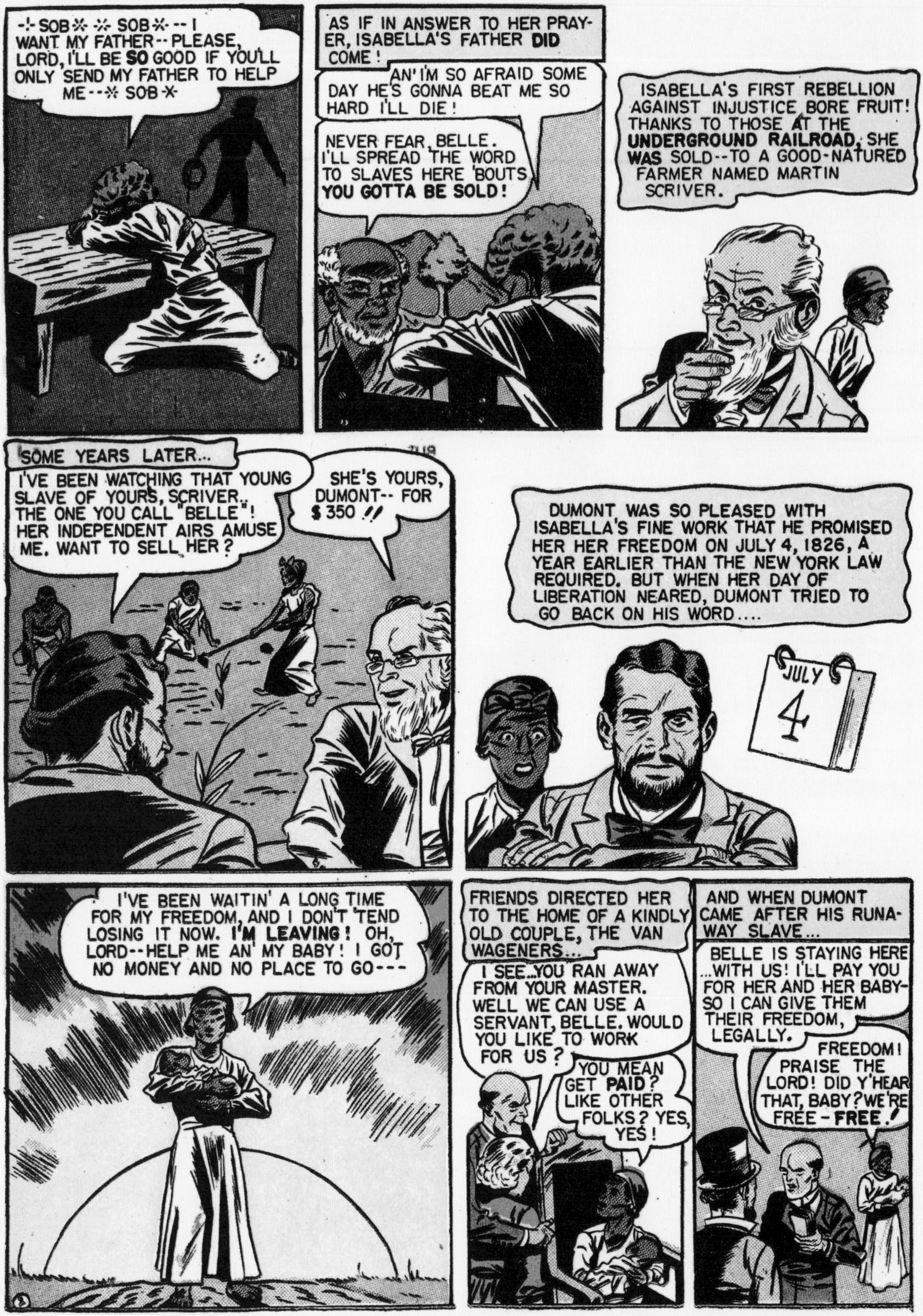
-:- SOB -:- -:- SOB -:- -- I WANT MY FATHER -- PLEASE, LORD, I'LL BE SO GOOD IF YOU'LL ONLY SEND MY FATHER TO HELP ME -- -:- SOB -:-
AS IF IN ANSWER TO HER PRAYER, ISABELLA'S FATHER DID COME!
AN' I'M SO AFRAID SOME DAY HE'S GONNA BEAT ME SO HARD I'LL DIE!
NEVER FEAR, BELLE. I'LL SPREAD THE WORD TO SLAVES HERE 'BOUTS YOU GOTTA BE SOLD!
ISABELLA'S FIRST REBELLION AGAINST INJUSTICE BORE FRUIT! THANKS TO THOSE AT THE UNDERGROUND RAILROAD, SHE WAS SOLD -- TO A GOOD-NATURED FARMER NAMED MARTIN SCRIVER.
SOME YEARS LATER...
I'VE BEEN WATCHING THAT YOUNG SLAVE OF YOURS, SCRIVER.. THE ONE YOU CALL "BELLE"! HER INDEPENDENT AIRS AMUSE ME. WANT TO SELL HER?
SHE'S YOURS, DUMONT -- FOR $350!!
DUMONT WAS SO PLEASED WITH ISABELLA'S FINE WORK THAT HE PROMISED HER HER FREEDOM ON JULY 4, 1826, A YEAR EARLIER THAN THE NEW YORK LAW REQUIRED. BUT WHEN HER DAY OF LIBERATION NEARED, DUMONT TRIED TO GO BACK ON HIS WORD....
JULY 4
I'VE BEEN WAITIN' A LONG TIME FOR MY FREEDOM, AND I DON'T 'TEND LOSING IT NOW. I'M LEAVING! OH, LORD -- HELP ME AN' MY BABY! I GOT NO MONEY AND NO PLACE TO GO---
FRIENDS DIRECTED HER TO THE HOME OF A KINDLY OLD COUPLE, THE VAN WAGENERS...
I SEE... YOU RAN AWAY FROM YOUR MASTER. WELL WE CAN USE A SERVANT, BELLE. WOULD YOU LIKE TO WORK FOR US?
YOU MEAN GET PAID? LIKE OTHER FOLKS? YES, YES!
AND WHEN DUMONT CAME AFTER HIS RUNAWAY SLAVE...
BELLE IS STAYING HERE ...WITH US! I'LL PAY YOU FOR HER AND HER BABY - SO I CAN GIVE THEM THEIR FREEDOM, LEGALLY.
FREEDOM! PRAISE THE LORD! DID Y'HEAR THAT, BABY? WE'RE FREE - FREE!

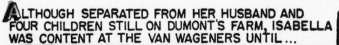

ALTHOUGH SEPARATED FROM HER HUSBAND AND FOUR CHILDREN STILL ON DUMONT'S FARM, ISABELLA WAS CONTENT AT THE VAN WAGENERS UNTIL...

BELLE! YOUR BOY, PETER-- DUMONT'S SOLD HIM-- AN' **OUT OF THE STATE!**

BUT- IT'S AGAINST THE LAW!.. I MUST FIGHT TO SAVE HIM!

WHERE YOU GOIN' BELLE? EVEN IF IT IS AGAINST THE LAW-THERE AIN'T NOTHIN' **YOU** CAN DO!

I DON'T KNOW ABOUT THAT. BUT I DO KNOW I WANT MY CHILD, SAME'S ANY WHITE WOM- AN. AN' I'M GOING T'GET HIM BACK IF I HAVE TO KEEP TALKIN' THE REST OF MY LIFE!

THE COURAGEOUS WOMAN WENT STRAIGHT TO THE GRAND JURY, THEN IN SESSION AT KINGSTON, NEW YORK!...

AN' I ASK YOU GENTLEMEN, YOU UPHOLDERS OF THE LAW, TO PLEASE GET BACK MY SON... WHO'S BEEN SOLD OUTSIDE THE STATE AGAINST THE LAW!

GOOD HEAVENS! WHO LET **HER** IN?

RIDICULOUS!

BUT ONE MAN DID **NOT** THINK ISABELLA'S CASE RIDICULOUS--A YOUNG LAWYER---

HMMM.... A COLORED WOMAN BRINGING A WHITE MAN TO COURT--THIS HAS NEVER HAPPENED BEFORE! AND YET--LEGALLY, YOU'RE RIGHT, ISABELLA, I'M GOING TO HELP YOU!

BLESS YOU, MR. LAWYER!

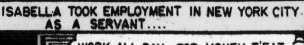

AT LAST, AFTER WEEKS OF LEGAL ACTION...

MOMMY!

MY POOR BOY! YOU'RE BACK WITH MOMMY AGAIN. I KNOW WHAT IT MEANS TO BE TAKEN AWAY FROM YOUR FOLKS AND MADE TO WORK AS A SLAVE. IT WON'T HAPPEN TO YOU!

ISABELLA TOOK EMPLOYMENT IN NEW YORK CITY AS A SERVANT....

WORK ALL DAY--FOR MONEY T'EAT SO'S I CAN WORK THE NEXT DAY! THE LORD MEANT ME TO DO SOMETHING MORE IMPORTANT THAN THIS--I FEEL IT!...I KNOW IT!...

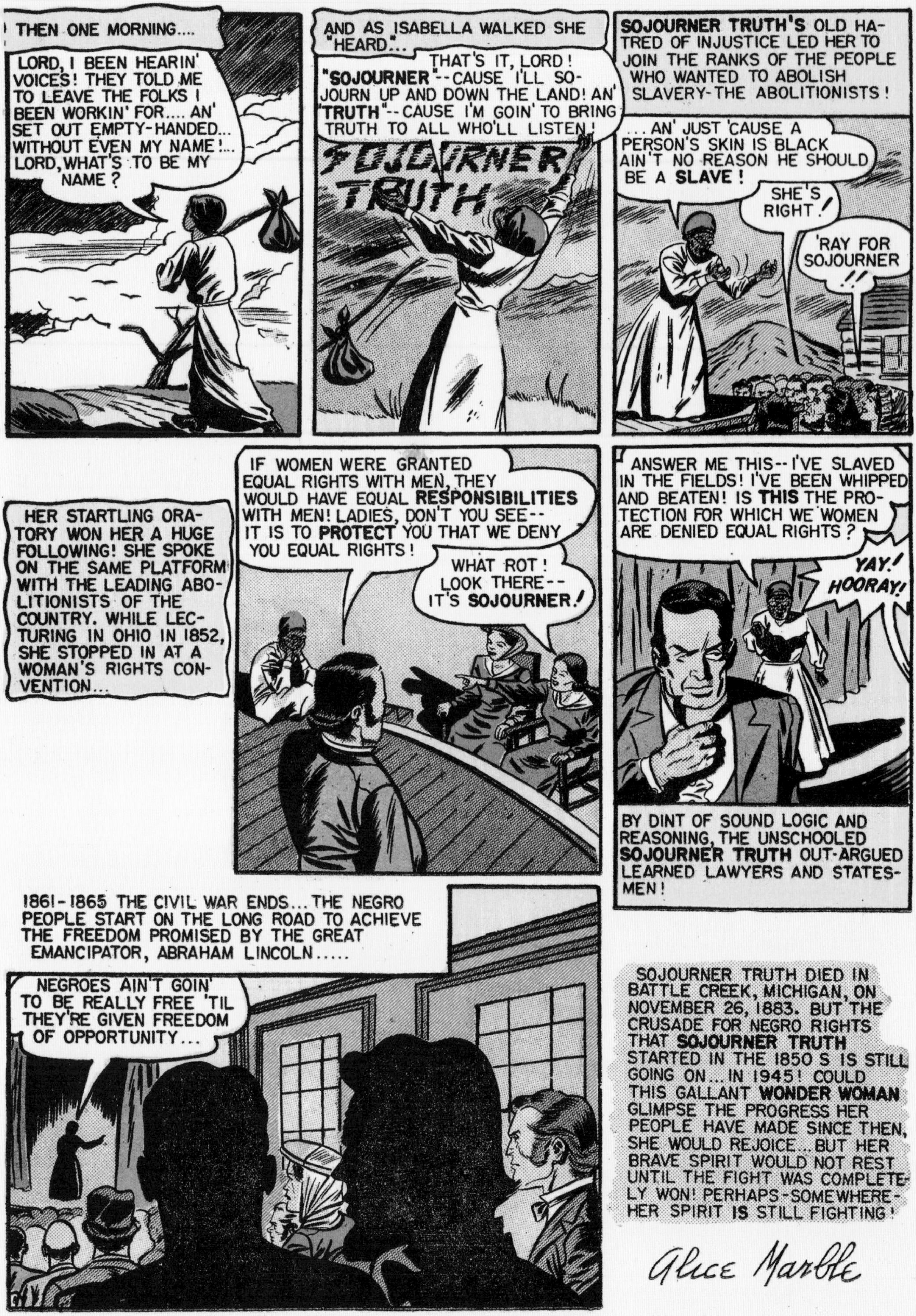
THEN ONE MORNING....
LORD, I BEEN HEARIN' VOICES! THEY TOLD ME TO LEAVE THE FOLKS I BEEN WORKIN' FOR.... AN' SET OUT EMPTY-HANDED... WITHOUT EVEN MY NAME!... LORD, WHAT'S TO BE MY NAME?
AND AS ISABELLA WALKED SHE "HEARD"...
THAT'S IT, LORD! "SOJOURNER"--CAUSE I'LL SOJOURN UP AND DOWN THE LAND! AN' "TRUTH"--CAUSE I'M GOIN' TO BRING TRUTH TO ALL WHO'LL LISTEN!
SOJOURNER TRUTH
SOJOURNER TRUTH'S OLD HATRED OF INJUSTICE LED HER TO JOIN THE RANKS OF THE PEOPLE WHO WANTED TO ABOLISH SLAVERY-THE ABOLITIONISTS!
...AN' JUST 'CAUSE A PERSON'S SKIN IS BLACK AIN'T NO REASON HE SHOULD BE A SLAVE!
SHE'S RIGHT!
'RAY FOR SOJOURNER!!
HER STARTLING ORATORY WON HER A HUGE FOLLOWING! SHE SPOKE ON THE SAME PLATFORM WITH THE LEADING ABOLITIONISTS OF THE COUNTRY. WHILE LECTURING IN OHIO IN 1852, SHE STOPPED IN AT A WOMAN'S RIGHTS CONVENTION...
IF WOMEN WERE GRANTED EQUAL RIGHTS WITH MEN, THEY WOULD HAVE EQUAL RESPONSIBILITIES WITH MEN! LADIES, DON'T YOU SEE-- IT IS TO PROTECT YOU THAT WE DENY YOU EQUAL RIGHTS!
WHAT ROT! LOOK THERE-- IT'S SOJOURNER!
ANSWER ME THIS--I'VE SLAVED IN THE FIELDS! I'VE BEEN WHIPPED AND BEATEN! IS THIS THE PROTECTION FOR WHICH WE WOMEN ARE DENIED EQUAL RIGHTS?
YAY! HOORAY!
BY DINT OF SOUND LOGIC AND REASONING, THE UNSCHOOLED SOJOURNER TRUTH OUT-ARGUED LEARNED LAWYERS AND STATESMEN!
1861-1865 THE CIVIL WAR ENDS...THE NEGRO PEOPLE START ON THE LONG ROAD TO ACHIEVE THE FREEDOM PROMISED BY THE GREAT EMANCIPATOR, ABRAHAM LINCOLN.....
NEGROES AIN'T GOIN' TO BE REALLY FREE 'TIL THEY'RE GIVEN FREEDOM OF OPPORTUNITY...
SOJOURNER TRUTH DIED IN BATTLE CREEK, MICHIGAN, ON NOVEMBER 26, 1883. BUT THE CRUSADE FOR NEGRO RIGHTS THAT SOJOURNER TRUTH STARTED IN THE 1850 S IS STILL GOING ON...IN 1945! COULD THIS GALLANT WONDER WOMAN GLIMPSE THE PROGRESS HER PEOPLE HAVE MADE SINCE THEN, SHE WOULD REJOICE...BUT HER BRAVE SPIRIT WOULD NOT REST UNTIL THE FIGHT WAS COMPLETELY WON! PERHAPS-SOMEWHERE-HER SPIRIT IS STILL FIGHTING!
Alice Marble

EUGENE BILBREW
A Different Talent

Not every life, not every career, fits the same mold. That logical statement applies to comic book artists as well. While many of the Black artists took similar paths, one stands out as particularly circuitous.

Though of the same generation as the others previously profiled, the majority of this artist's career occurred years after World War II ended. He was their peer, though, and for that reason, Gene Bilbrew deserves mention.

Eugene W. Bilbrew was born on June 29, 1923, and spent the early part of his life in Los Angeles, the son of Omri (aka Watson) and Carrie Bilbrew.

Although Blacks were routinely passed over by local draft boards during WWII, Bilbrew enlisted in the U.S. Army on May 18, 1943. For some reason, his military service didn't last long, and he was out by summer. While he had been a waiter before joining the army, it seems that Bilbrew was also a singer, a good one, who made a name for himself in his hometown with a quartet called the Mellow Tones. A reviewer enthused:

May I take time here and space here to give credit to this aggregation of scintillating rhythm whose talent speaks for itself. Ranging in ages between nineteen and twenty, these five young fellows Hal McEwen, Ruben Saunders, Gene Bilbrew, Walter Johnson and accompanist Evon Morgan have definitely come a long way in the two short months they have been organized. [Warren, Althea, "What's Doing in the Younger Set," *California Eagle*, Sept. 30, 1943]

Eugene certainly wasn't the only popular singer in the family. His uncle Ralph was also a singer, a baritone, married to the former Alice C. Harris, who sang professionally under the name A. C. Bilbrew. Madame Bilbrew, as she became known, made her first impact singing and acting in 1929's *Hearts in Dixie*, the first Black "talkie" motion picture. Performing as "Hoodoo Woman," she appeared alongside a young comedian also making his debut named Stepin Fetchit. As time went on, her eponymously named A.C. Bilbrew Choir toured the country and became one of the leading gospel choirs in America. Madame Bilbrew was a civic leader and a staunch NAACP supporter. In 1955, she wrote "The Death of Emmett Till," a two-part protest song recorded by the Ramparts, memorializing the horrific lynching of the 14 year-old teenager in Mississippi.

"ASTRO-GAL"
WELL, HERE I AM--- THE FIRST GIRL ON THE MOON!
YI-IIK! LOOKS LIKE I SPOKE TO SOON! THEY MUST BE MOON-MEN! GOSH, THEY'RE GRUESOME AND HERE THEY COME!
SUFFERIN' SANDS

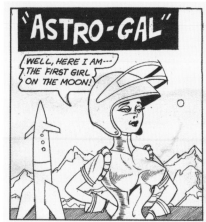

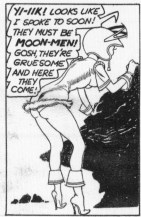

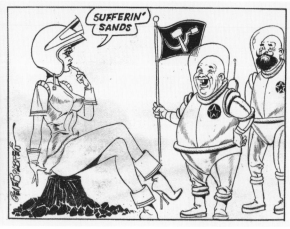

The prominence of Eugene's aunt may well have played a part in the Mellow Tones' ascendance in the local music scene. They came under the management of actor Mantan Moreland and his partner, Ben Carter, and began touring with Earl "Fatha" Hines and Duke Ellington. Eventually, they came to the attention of a Black entertainer and entrepreneur named Leon Rene, owner of Exclusive Records, who signed them to a recording contract. Ormand Wilson, founder of the group, changed their name to the Basin Street Boys, reviving the name of a group from the 1930s. They cut two records for Exclusive before they finally hit it big with their third single, "I Sold My Heart to the Junk Man," in the summer of 1946. It was a huge hit.

While it was still hot, the group appeared on Dick Lane's local Los Angeles television variety program, and the group went on a countrywide tour throughout 1947. Affirming their success was a publicity photo which appeared in the February 2nd issue of *Cash Box*, which pictured the smiling group bracketing their boss Rene and crowded around a copy of that magazine.

Soon after, a couple of the group members began using stage names including Bilbrew, who started going by the name "Gene Price." They recorded five more records that year, but by 1948, their popularity dwindled. The group split up in 1951, but it isn't clear whether Bilbrew was still with them at that time.

Bilbrew was fortunate, though. He had another talent beyond singing. He could draw. According to various sources, he met another Black artist named William (Bill) Alexander, who was the illustrator of the clever record label drawings on Roy Milton's Miltone Records circa 1946-'47.

According to various sources, Bilbrew and Alexander co-created "the first" Black super-hero, "The Bronze Bomber," which allegedly appeared in the Black newspaper the *Los Angles Sentinel*. However, that tantalizing bit of information has yet to be corroborated.

debut records
PRESENTS THE
CHARLES MINGUS
OCTET
PLAYING
miss bliss
eclipse
pink topsy
blue tide
GENE BILBREW

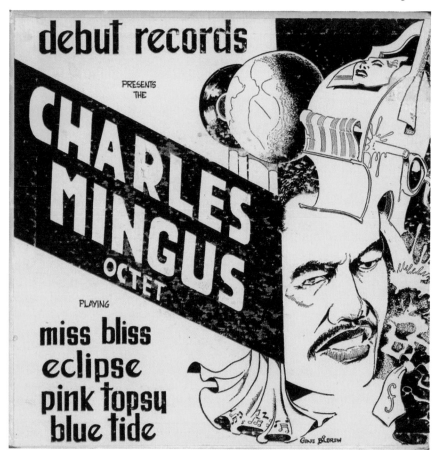

What can be confirmed, though, is that Bilbrew did some work for *Let's Live* magazine, a pioneering health food monthly that extolled the virtues of raw vegetables and soy. It was published in Hollywood by Clarke Irvine, a sandal-wearing, long-haired nonconformist, who preached in his editorials that the evils of "modern civilization—wheels, drugs, food refining, is killing man." ["Clarke Irvine With A Haircut," *Honolulu Advertiser*, July 5, 1948]

A seemingly incongruous display ad for the magazine running in the *Sentinel* advised readers: "Don't miss the chuckles created by Gene Bilbrew, talented Los Angeles Negro Cartoonist." ["Have You Read Let's Live Magazine?" *Los Angeles Sentinel*, June 23, 1949]

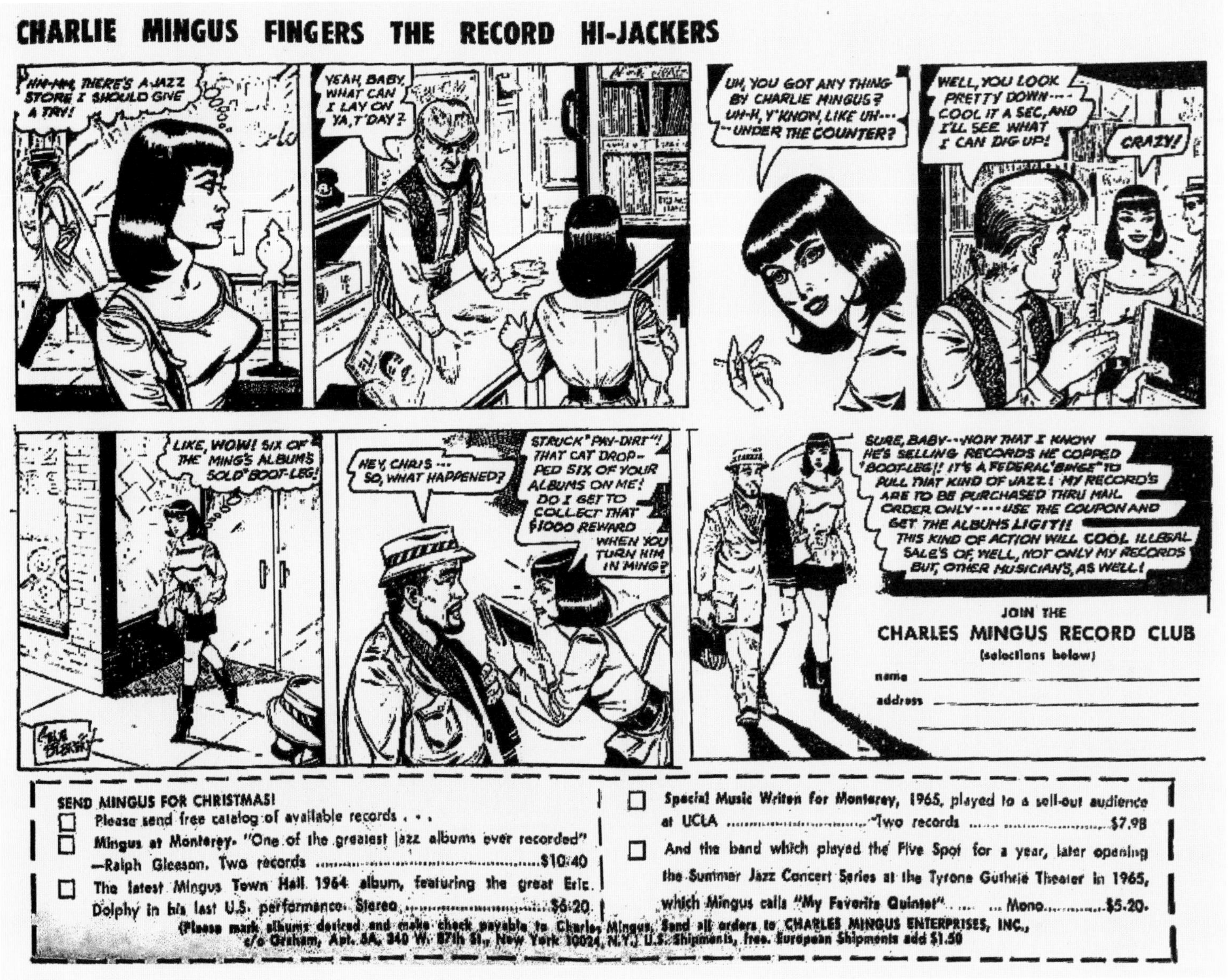

CHARLIE MINGUS FINGERS THE RECORD HI-JACKERS
HM-HM, THERE'S A JAZZ STORE I SHOULD GIVE A TRY!
YEAH, BABY, WHAT CAN I LAY ON YA, T'DAY?
UH, YOU GOT ANY THING BY CHARLIE MINGUS? UH-H, Y'KNOW, LIKE UH--- UNDER THE COUNTER?
WELL, YOU LOOK PRETTY DOWN--- COOL IT A SEC, AND I'LL SEE WHAT I CAN DIG UP!
CRAZY!
LIKE, WOW! SIX OF THE MING'S ALBUMS SOLD "BOOT-LEG!
HEY, CHRIS --- SO, WHAT HAPPENED?
STRUCK "PAY-DIRT"! THAT CAT DROPPED SIX OF YOUR ALBUMS ON ME! DO I GET TO COLLECT THAT $1000 REWARD WHEN YOU TURN HIM IN MING?
SURE, BABY---NOW THAT I KNOW HE'S SELLING RECORDS HE COPPED "BOOT-LEG!! IT'S A FEDERAL "BINGE" TO PULL THAT KIND OF JAZZ! MY RECORD'S ARE TO BE PURCHASED THRU MAIL ORDER ONLY----USE THE COUPON AND GET THE ALBUMS LIGIT!!
THIS KIND OF ACTION WILL COOL ILLEGAL SALE'S OF, WELL, NOT ONLY MY RECORDS BUT, OTHER MUSICIAN'S, AS WELL!
JOIN THE
CHARLES MINGUS RECORD CLUB
(selections below)
name
address
SEND MINGUS FOR CHRISTMAS!
Please send free catalog of available records . . .
Mingus at Monterey. "One of the greatest jazz albums ever recorded" —Ralph Gleason. Two records $10.40
The latest Mingus Town Hall 1964 album, featuring the great Eric Dolphy in his last U.S. performance. Stereo $6.20
Special Music Writen for Monterey, 1965, played to a sell-out audience at UCLA ....Two records $7.98
And the band which played the Five Spot for a year, later opening the Summer Jazz Concert Series at the Tyrone Guthrie Theater in 1965, which Mingus calls "My Favorite Quintet" .... Mono........$5.20.
(Please mark albums desired and make check payable to Charles Mingus. Send all orders to CHARLES MINGUS ENTERPRISES, INC., c/o Graham, Apt. 6A, 340 W. 87th St., New York 10024, N.Y.) U.S. Shipments, free. European Shipments add $1.50

It is possible that this was the actual publication containing the *Bronze Bomber* strip, as a super-hero character in a healthy-living venue seems a comfortable fit.

In any case, by 1951, Bilbrew ended up across the country in New York City. There, he worked for a little over a year for Will Eisner on a back-up feature appearing in the Sunday *The Spirit* comic book section. The strip was entitled, "Clifford," and Bilbrew took it over from its previous artist, the legendary Jules Feiffer, in the spring of 1951.

The strip was entirely Feiffer's creative brainchild, the young artist both writing and drawing the ongoing adventures of a boy wise beyond his years. While, in the years since, the child-speaking-as-an-adult has become an established comic strip trope, at the time the concept was fresh and uniquely reflected its creator's philosophic bent.

The fact that Bilbrew was tapped to carry on Feiffer's creation when the latter was drafted cannot be overstated. This was a tremendous coup. Here he was, an unknown Black cartoonist from the West Coast, being assigned a nationally syndicated feature, working in the studio of Will Eisner, one of the most respected creators in the comics field. From any perspective, Bilbrew's prospects for success were great. Fate had other plans.

It wasn't Bilbrew's fault. His artwork on "Clifford" was fine: solid, pleasingly cherubic depictions of White children. The strip missed Feiffer's introspective observations, but that would have been difficult for anyone to duplicate. The problem was that Eisner was losing interest. The weekly obligation of producing a Sunday comic book section was taking away from his other business interest—creating promotional comic books. Besides, *The Spirit* comic book section was losing readership. So, in late 1952, Eisner ended it, presumably leaving Bilbrew without a steady job.

[Top, left] *Astro-Gal* was a rather tame comic strip drawn by Bilbrew that appeared in the first issue of *Orbit*, a soft-core magazine that had him listed as its art director. *Orbit* #1, 1961, Selbee Associates.

[Bottom, left] A rare record sleeve drawn by Bilbrew for the Charlie Mingus Octet, (1954, Debut Records).

[Above] Comic strip-style ad for the "Charlie Mingus Record Club," calling out shady record dealers who sold illegal bootleg copies of Mingus' recordings. *Village Voice*, December 1, 1966; The Village Voice.

THE BASIN STREET BOYS—with the assistance of pretty doctor's assistant, Ophelia Bradford, ganged up on Ormonde Wilson of the Exclusive recording quartet to see what makes him tick, since the lyrics of their best hit insist: "I Sold My Heart to the Junk Man." Pictured are Gene Price, Reuben Saunders, Miss Bradford, Ormonde and Artie Waters. The boys are appearing in Detroit on the first leg of a cross-country tour. (Adrian photo).

What happened next is open to speculation. Did Bilbrew continue on for a while, employed by Eisner's studio, working on promotional comics? Was he even offered a position? Reportedly, he attended the Cartoonists and Illustrators School in New York City, where he probably first caught Eisner's eye. At that school, so the story goes, he also met Eric Stanton, another aspiring artist who was just beginning his professional career. Whatever the circumstances, the two artists, along with Bill Alexander, Bilbrew's collaborator back in Los Angeles, began working for a soon-to-be notorious publisher named Irving Klaw.

Originally, Klaw and his sister were the owners of a business called Movie Star News, which sold still photos of actors through his storefront in the East Village of Manhattan and through the mail around the country. Toward the end of the 1940s, the Klaws also began selling fetish magazines aimed at the secretive market of bondage enthusiasts who were ignored by proper newsdealers and bookstores. In time, Klaw began commissioning material for his own publications to service this specialized clientele. Enter Bilbrew, Stanton, and Alexander.

This became Bilbrew's world and his legacy. Under both his given name and the pseudonym, "Eneg," he would produce artwork appealing to virtually every sexual proclivity, orientation and fantasy—subjects most other artists wouldn't even consider depicting.

Even so, Bilbrew brought a comic book artist's training to his fetish work. Many times, his work looked like any other comic story, except for its sordid subject matter. In some respects, his work anticipated the underground comix that would evolve throughout the 1960s. The difference was that Bilbrew's readership took his work far more seriously.

Bilbrew's career choice necessarily brought him into the company of mobsters and pornographers—people with rap sheets and sketchy lifestyles. Despite this, there are indications that Bilbrew aspired to something more. In 1961, he was the art director of a fairly traditional men's magazine for Selbee Associates, entitled *Orbit*. Bilbrew provided full-page illustrations for the magazine; and, somewhat surprisingly, rather tame cartoons—including one titled *Astro-Gal*.

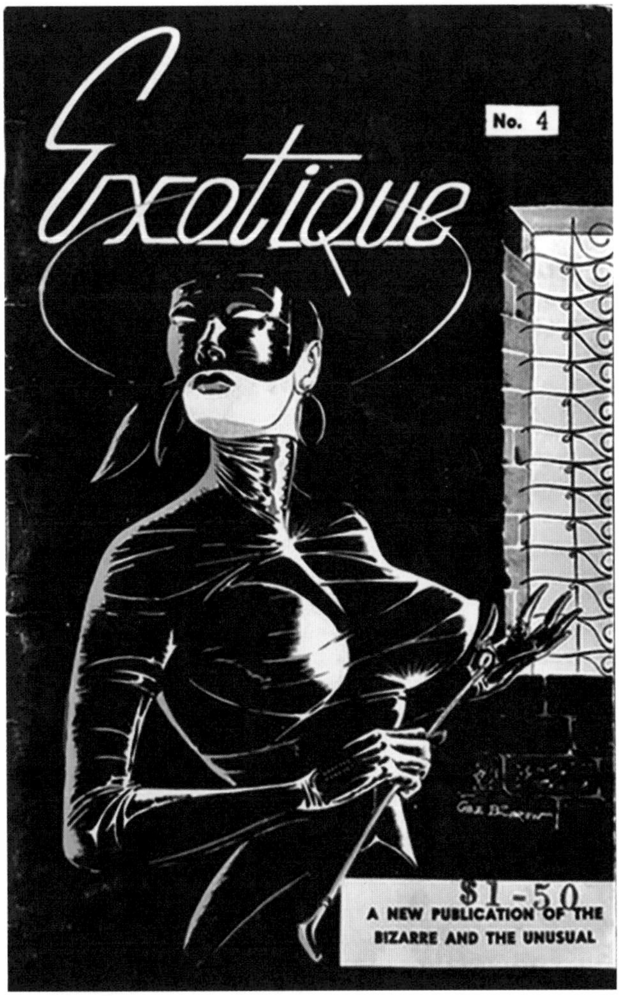
Exotique
No. 4
$1-50
A NEW PUBLICATION OF THE
BIZARRE AND THE UNUSUAL

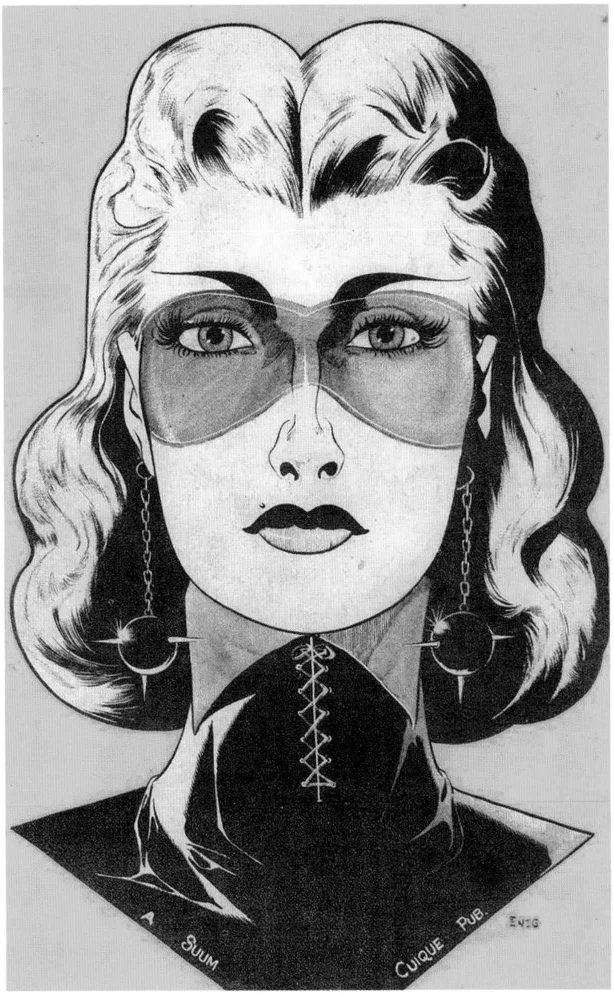
A SUUM CUIQUE PUB.

Bilbrew did make other forays into mainstream illustration, such as the record sleeve he drew for jazz great Charles Mingus. Mingus was a contemporary of Bilbrew and grew up in the same Watts neighborhood of Los Angeles. If they didn't already know one another, it's highly likely the two crossed paths as they played the local music circuit in the late 1940s. In any case, Bilbrew provided the artwork for the "Charles Mingus Octet" extended play 45, released in 1953 by Debut Records. As late as 1965, Bilbrew provided the artwork for a "Charles Mingus Record Club" ad that ran in the *Village Voice*.

Then there were the covers he drew for Wholesale Book Group in the early 1970s. This was a publisher of niche softcover books such as *Ahmed's Dream Book & Numbers* and a simplified Spanish-English dictionary. Somewhat esoteric, it was nevertheless straightforward, run-of-the-mill, commercial art.

Any respectability Bilbrew sought, though, was undermined by the preponderance of his published work. In 1966, one of the publishers he drew for, named Edward Mishkin, was convicted of preparing, possessing and distributing obscene material. Books bearing Bilbrew's artwork were prominent among the offending publications.

Given his unconventional career, it's probably no surprise that Bilbrew's later life has long been the object of rumors, innuendos and unsubstantiated speculation. Some claim that he was a crossdresser and a heroin addict and that he died of an overdose in the backroom of a 42nd Street porn bookstore. The veracity of all of those claims is disputable, a point made by noting that the official Social Security Death Index lists his place of demise as California, a continent away from Times Square, in May 1974.

[Left] Photo of The Basin Street Boys, with Bilbrew using the stage name of "Gene Price." *Cashbox,* August 16, 1947; The Cashbox.

[Above] In the last part of his career, Bilbrew drew fetish artwork, like the cover of *Exotique* #4, 1957, Burmel Publishing, and the image on the right.

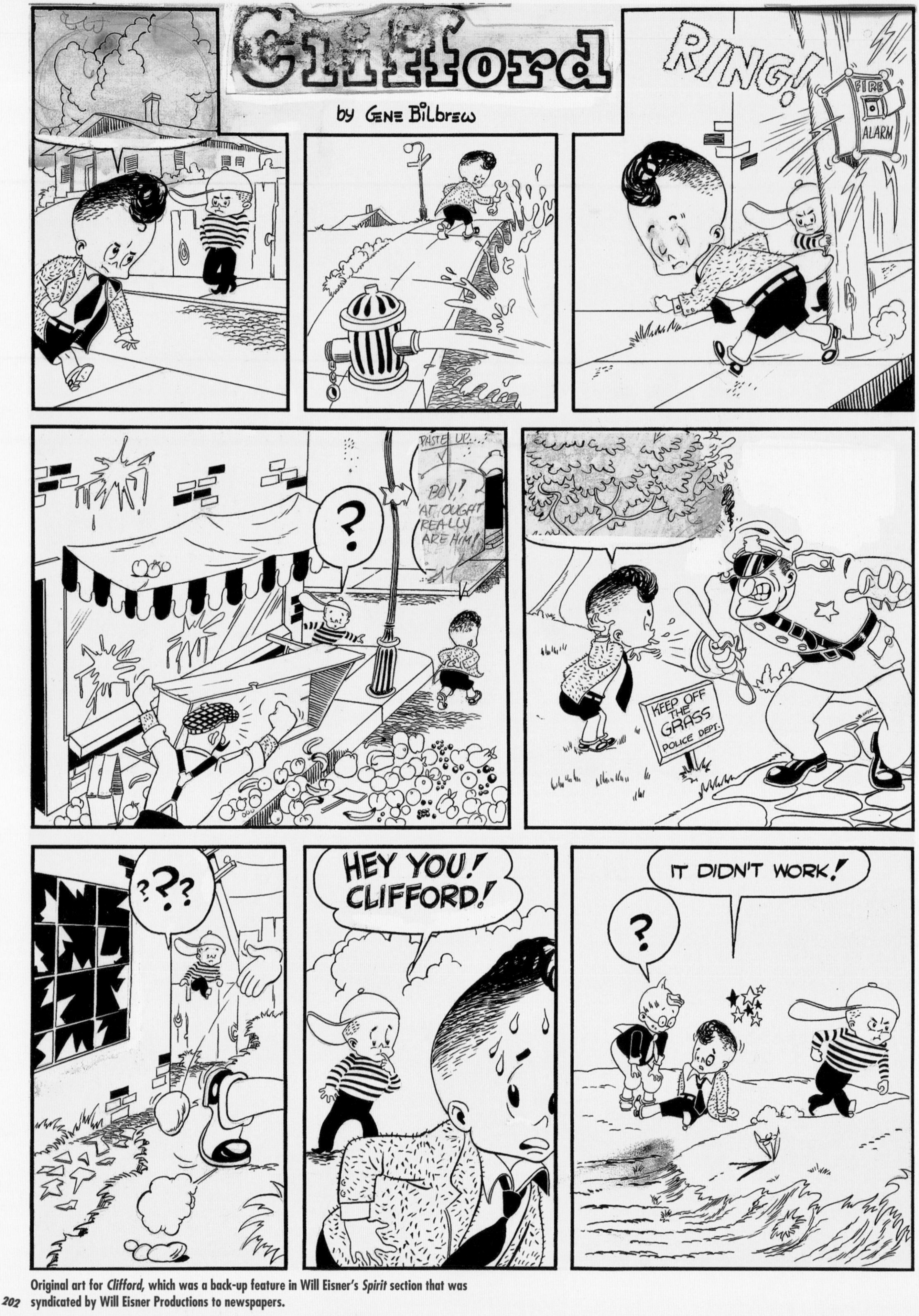
Clifford
by Gene Bilbrew
RING!
FIRE ALARM
?
KEEP OFF THE GRASS POLICE DEPT.
???
HEY YOU! CLIFFORD!
?
IT DIDN'T WORK!

Original art for *Clifford,* which was a back-up feature in Will Eisner's *Spirit* section that was syndicated by Will Eisner Productions to newspapers.

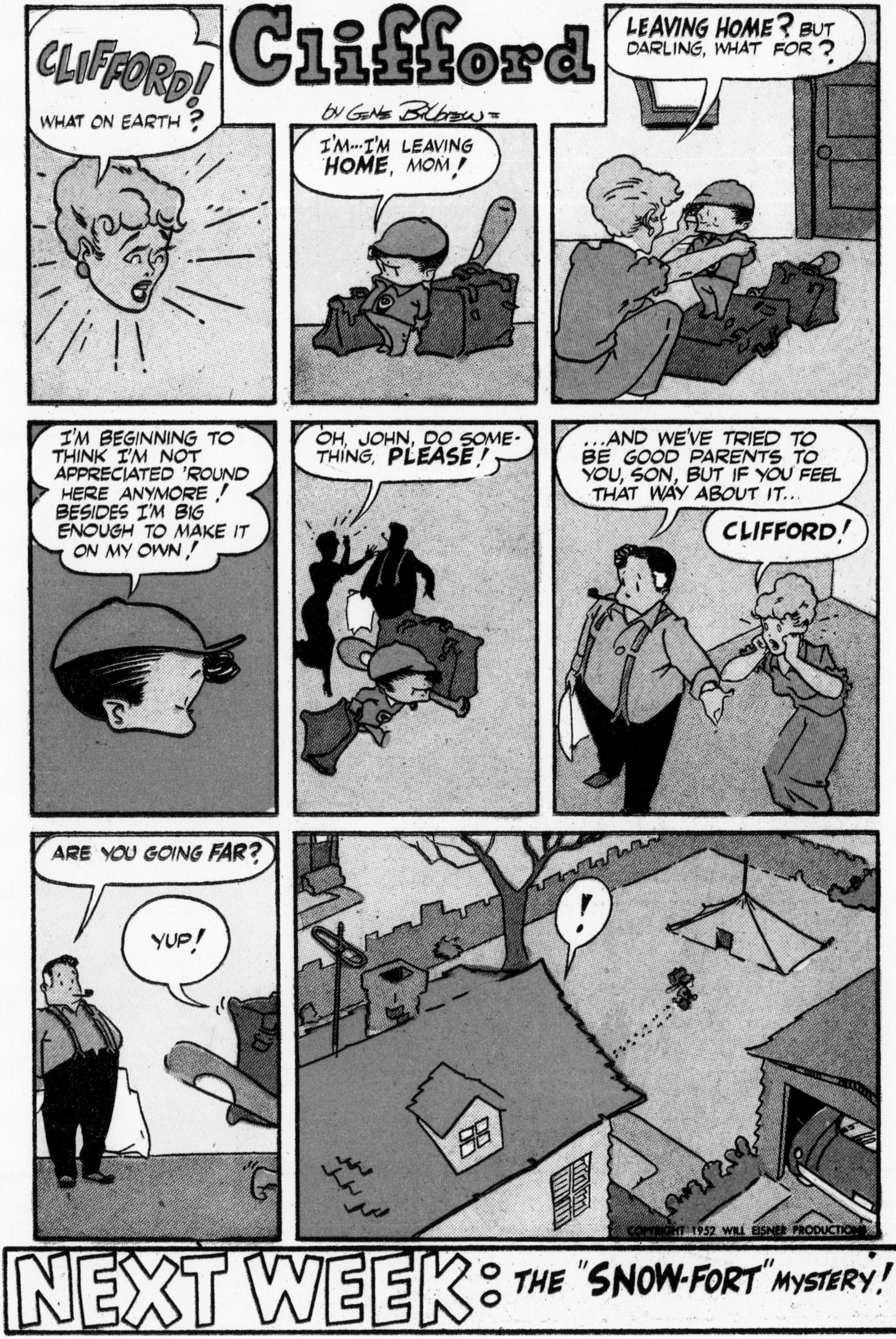
Clifford
by Gene Bilbrew
CLIFFORD! WHAT ON EARTH?
I'M...I'M LEAVING HOME, MOM!
LEAVING HOME? BUT DARLING, WHAT FOR?
I'M BEGINNING TO THINK I'M NOT APPRECIATED 'ROUND HERE ANYMORE! BESIDES I'M BIG ENOUGH TO MAKE IT ON MY OWN!
OH, JOHN, DO SOMETHING, PLEASE!
...AND WE'VE TRIED TO BE GOOD PARENTS TO YOU, SON, BUT IF YOU FEEL THAT WAY ABOUT IT...
CLIFFORD!
ARE YOU GOING FAR?
YUP!
!
COPYRIGHT 1952 WILL EISNER PRODUCTIONS
NEXT WEEK: THE "SNOW-FORT" MYSTERY!

Clifford, February 3, 1952; Will Eisner Productions.

ORRIN C. EVANS, GEORGE J. EVANS JR. JOHN H. TERRELL, WILLIAM H. SMITH LEONARD COOPER

At Last, The First

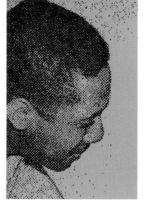

The reaction to adversity defines a person. It can destroy them, or it can be seen as an opportunity. It's often said that the successful pick up the lemons that Fate tosses their way and start a lemonade stand.

The closing of the *Philadelphia Record* was viewed as a tragedy by its ardent readership. Its publisher, J. David Stern, was a rarity—an important newspaper owner admired and respected by his employees. He was known for taking progressive stances, such as the hiring of Orrin Evans, a Black newspaperman, as a general news reporter, making him one of the first to hold such a position on a White newspaper. Stern also invited unions to represent his employees when other publishers fought them vehemently. That is why he was shocked and hurt when the American Newspaper Guild called a strike against the *Record* in November 1946.

The Guild was demanding more money for its membership, more than Stern thought fair.

During the three months of negotiations, he kept his paper going with the help of nonunion editorial staff. This included managing editor Harry T. Saylor, sports editor Bill Driscoll, and two advertising men who weren't represented by the union—Joe McGoldrick and Maury Mustin—who were teasingly referred to as the "Gold Dust Twins" because of their close friendship.

Toward the end of January 1947, the *Record* made its final offer to the Guild, which was approved by its leadership, but voted down by its members. Stern determined that he couldn't remain financially solvent if he gave into the Guild's demands, so he made the decision to close the *Record* on February 1, 1947.

Everyone was out on the street, including the editors and Orrin Evans. That's when they decided to make lemonade.

[Above] The staff of All-Negro Comics: Orrin Evans [top row, left], George Evans [top, right], John Terrell [bottom row, left], Leonard Cooper [bottom, right].

[Right] The cover of *All-Negro Comics* #1, June 1947; All-Negro Comics, Inc.

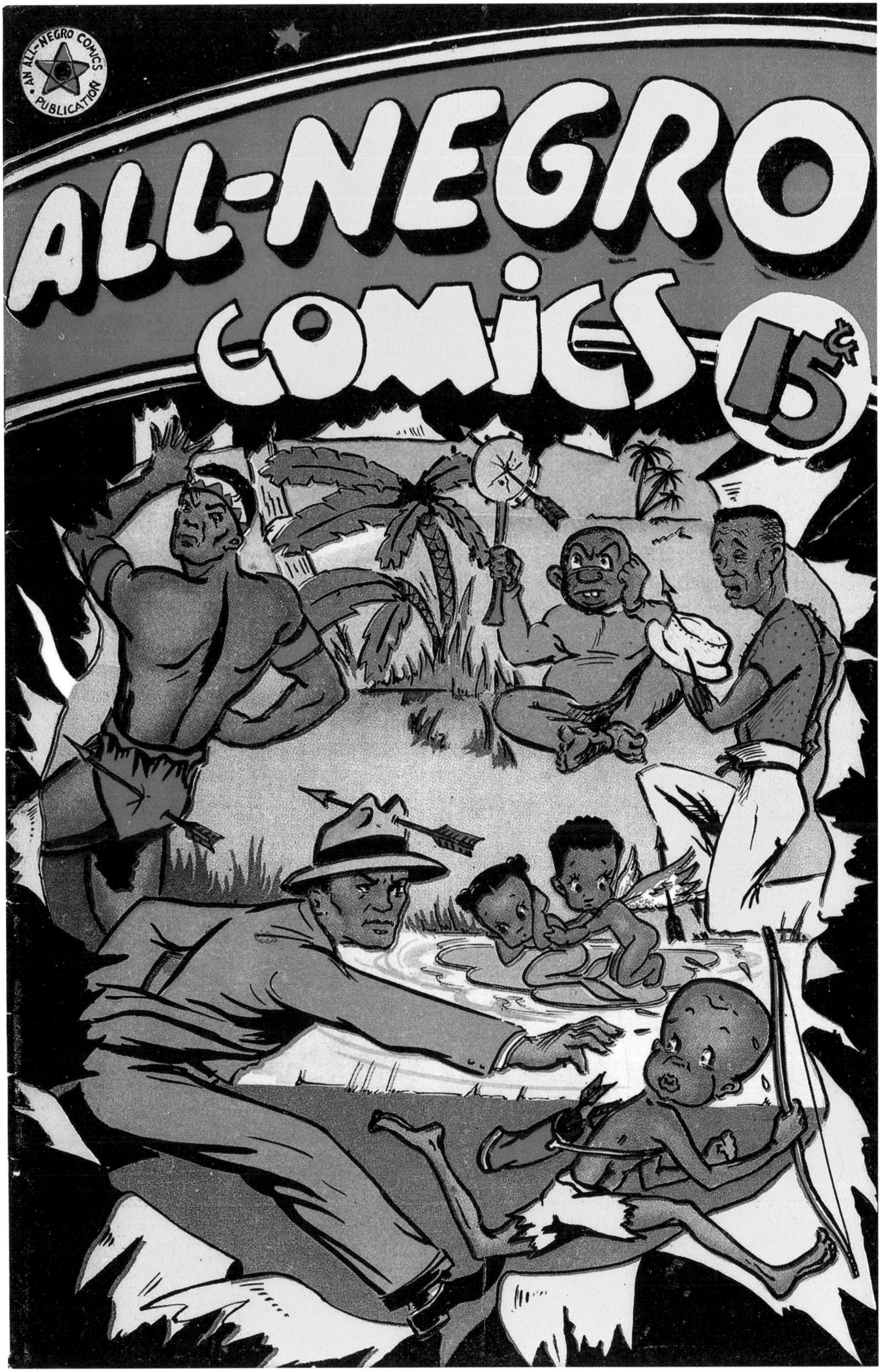
AN ALL-NEGRO COMICS PUBLICATION
ALL-NEGRO COMICS
15¢

ON SALE
here
10¢
NEGRO
NEGRO HEROES

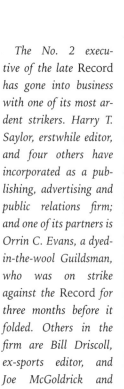

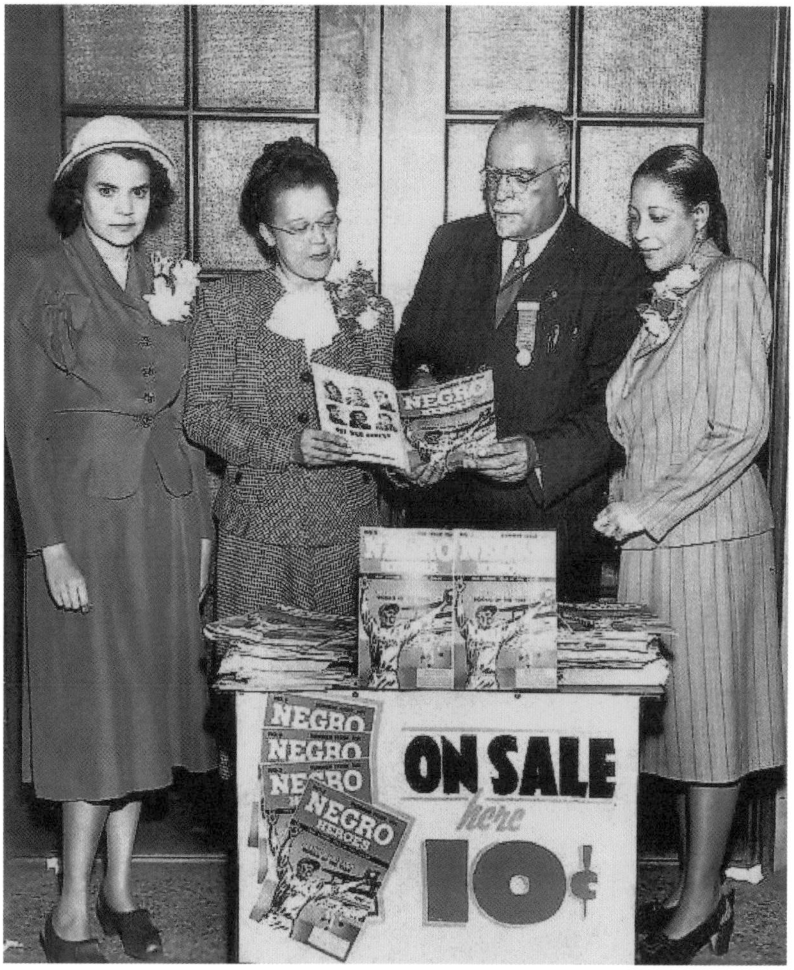

The No. 2 executive of the late Record *has gone into business with one of its most ardent strikers. Harry T. Saylor, erstwhile editor, and four others have incorporated as a publishing, advertising and public relations firm; and one of its partners is Orrin C. Evans, a dyed-in-the-wool Guildsman, who was on strike against the* Record *for three months before it folded. Others in the firm are Bill Driscoll, ex-sports editor, and Joe McGoldrick and Maury Mustin, advertising men.* [Brookhouser, Frank, "It's Happening Here," *Philadelphia Inquirer*, Apr. 23, 1947]

The company they formed was named Record Associates, Inc., and its stated goal was to provide writing, editing, publicity, advertising, and publishing services to prospective clients. One of their first actions was to act as the holding company for All-Negro Comics, Inc., a newly-created firm under the guidance of Record Associates' vice-president, Orrin Cromwell Evans.

Evans was more than qualified for the role. He was born September 5, 1902, in Steelton, Pennsylvania, a town whose lifeblood was reflected in its name. His father, George, was a butler at the time, likely for one of the executives of the Pennsylvania Steel Company that virtually owned the town. Orrin's mother, Maud, was a music teacher, a rare position for a woman at the time, not to mention for her race.

By 1920, the Evanses had moved to Philadelphia, where George was now owner of a garage and Orrin attended West Philadelphia High School. When he was only 17 years old, Orrin had gotten a job on a local sports publication. After graduation, he went to Drexel Institute in the city, leading to jobs at the *Philadelphia Tribune*, the *Philadelphia Afro-American*, and the *Philadelphia Independent*, all Black newspapers. His next position, though, was groundbreaking, when he was hired by David Stern as a reporter for the heretofore totally White *Philadelphia Record*.

Evans was usually assigned to cover stories of interest to the Black community. In 1944, he wrote a series of articles exposing the problems Black soldiers stationed in the southern states had with getting transportation to and from their posts. The exposé was an embarrassment to President Harry Truman's administration and the War Department in particular. Orders were immediately issued to the offending base commanders to rectify the situation and

...to provide decent, adequate and non-Jim Crow bus transportation for Negro troops between camp and town.

[John J.] McCloy, chairman of the departmental racial relations committee, gave full credit for this important reform to a series of articles written by Orrin Evans for the Philadelphia Record. [Durhan, Richard, "Gibson Denies Army 'Jim Crow' Orders," *Chicago Defender*, June 10, 1944]

Herman P. Eberharter, a U.S. House Representative from Pennsylvania, was inspired to enter Evans' articles into the Congressional Record. The following year, the series garnered Evans runner-up position for the prestigious Heywood Broun Award from the American Newspaper Guild.

None of which was of much help when Evans and everyone else on the *Philadelphia Record* found themselves unemployed. The resourceful Evans soon moved on to a thought he had had previously, about using comic books as a means of communicating. He didn't go far to begin assembling his staff.

[Above] Members of the National Urban League posing with copy of *Negro Heroes* #2 (Summer 1948, Parents' Magazine Press). The woman holding the comic is Sadie T. M. Alexander, first President of the Delta Sigma Theta, a prestigious Black sorority and sponsor of the comic.

[Right] Illustration by William H. Smith depicting Black sailors and Marines under attack on a naval ship. *Baltimore Afro-American,* May 9, 1942.

Can This Happen in Mr. Knox's Navy?

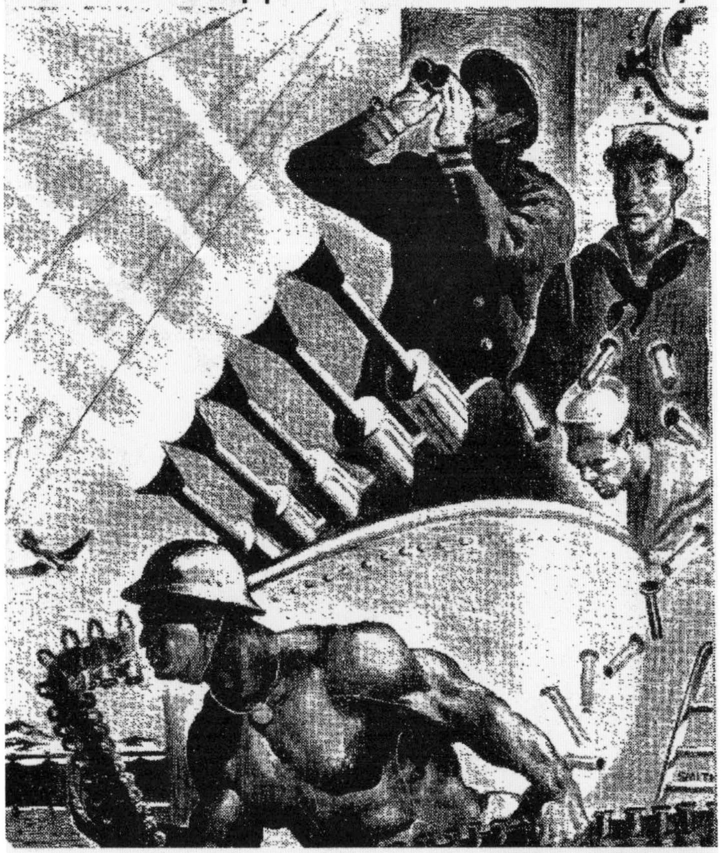

In the above drawing by William H. Smith, student at the Pennsylvania Museum of Art, Philadelphia, colored marines and officers are shown on the bridge of a fast destroyer engaged in the grim business of fending off at-tacking dive bombers.

George J. Evans Jr. was Orrin's younger brother by eight years. He had taken a different path than his older brother, spending a year in college before accepting a job in "hotel and restaurant management." On August 9, 1943, he enlisted in the U.S. Army for the duration of the war. After finishing that obligation, he attended the Philadelphia Museum of Art school, working toward a career in commercial art.

The Philadelphia Museum was only a few blocks away from All-Negro Comics' office at 1318 Spruce Street, an advantageous location from which to recruit artists, as two more students of that school came on board.

William H. Smith was originally from Baltimore. He placed first in an art competition at the New York World's Fair, contributed illustrations to the *Baltimore Afro-American,* and won a scholarship to the Philadelphia Academy of the Fine Arts. He was asked to leave that school by a dean due to ongoing "animosity between Blacks and Whites," leading him to transfer to the Museum of Art school. It wouldn't be the only time Smith would confront racism in pursuit of his commercial art career. Smith recalled:

Little companies were terrified to hire Blacks. One young art director, who had admired my stuff, held my portfolio for a week, came back crestfallen. He would use me—if I were white. [Tapley, Mel, "Three Outstanding Artists in Lambertville Gallery Show," *New York Amsterdam News,* March 25, 1989]

Leonard Cooper was the other Museum of Art student hired by Evans. He had attended the school prior to joining the Army in WWII. While he was still in service, stationed at Fort Ord in Salinas, California, he competed in several art exhibitions around the country. Back at home in Philadelphia, he was once again back in school.

The last artist Evans hired was by far the most experienced. John H. Terrell was from Williamsport, Pennsylvania. He was on the staff of a weekly local newspaper, but he quit in 1934 to become a full-time freelance cartoonist. Subsequently, his first professional cartooning job was at *Judge,* a national humor magazine. Terrell desired to be a syndicated cartoonist and to that end, in 1940, he created *Adventures of Tiger Ragg* for the *New York Amsterdam News.*

Tiger Ragg only ran a few months, and even then, its publication was sporadic. He found a stabler job the next year at the Philadelphia Naval Yard. He began there as a laborer, but within two years, he was given the job as safety officer. Terrell took that position and ran with it, combining his cartooning skills with the duties of his office. He drew posters featuring characters he created: Paul N. Yankee, Dora Droop, Yappy, and Lester Lukewarm. People noticed, and he started contributing cartoons to the Navy Department Safety Office monthly, *Safety Review,* and also the *Safety Bulletin* for the U.S. Compensation Commission. He even drew war bond posters during the war. Somewhere in all that, Terrell had squeezed in a period where he, too, attended the School of Industrial Art, which was also run by the Museum of Art. ["Cartoonist Saves Lives, Sells Bonds with Comics," *Baltimore Afro-American,* Apr. 27, 1946]

A much-quoted press release, apparently sent to much of the media, outlined Evans' hopes and aspirations for *All-Negro Comics*:

I feel this book will serve a genuine need. It's not slapstick, nor is it propaganda. My associates and I, and a good cross section of Negroes, who have seen color proofs of the book, feel it is an intelligent, interesting, well-conceived mixture of good comics, artistry and clean humor. Nothing like it, I am sure, ever has been done before. ["*All-Negro Comics* Magazine Makes Its Advent on News[s] tands," *Atlanta Daily World,* Aug. 7, 1947]

With an office, a staff, and a vision, Evans was ready to begin production of *All-Negro Comics.* It was going to be the first comic book ever created entirely by Black creators, but it wasn't the first aimed specifically for the Black readership. That distinction fell to another comic that was published earlier in 1947.

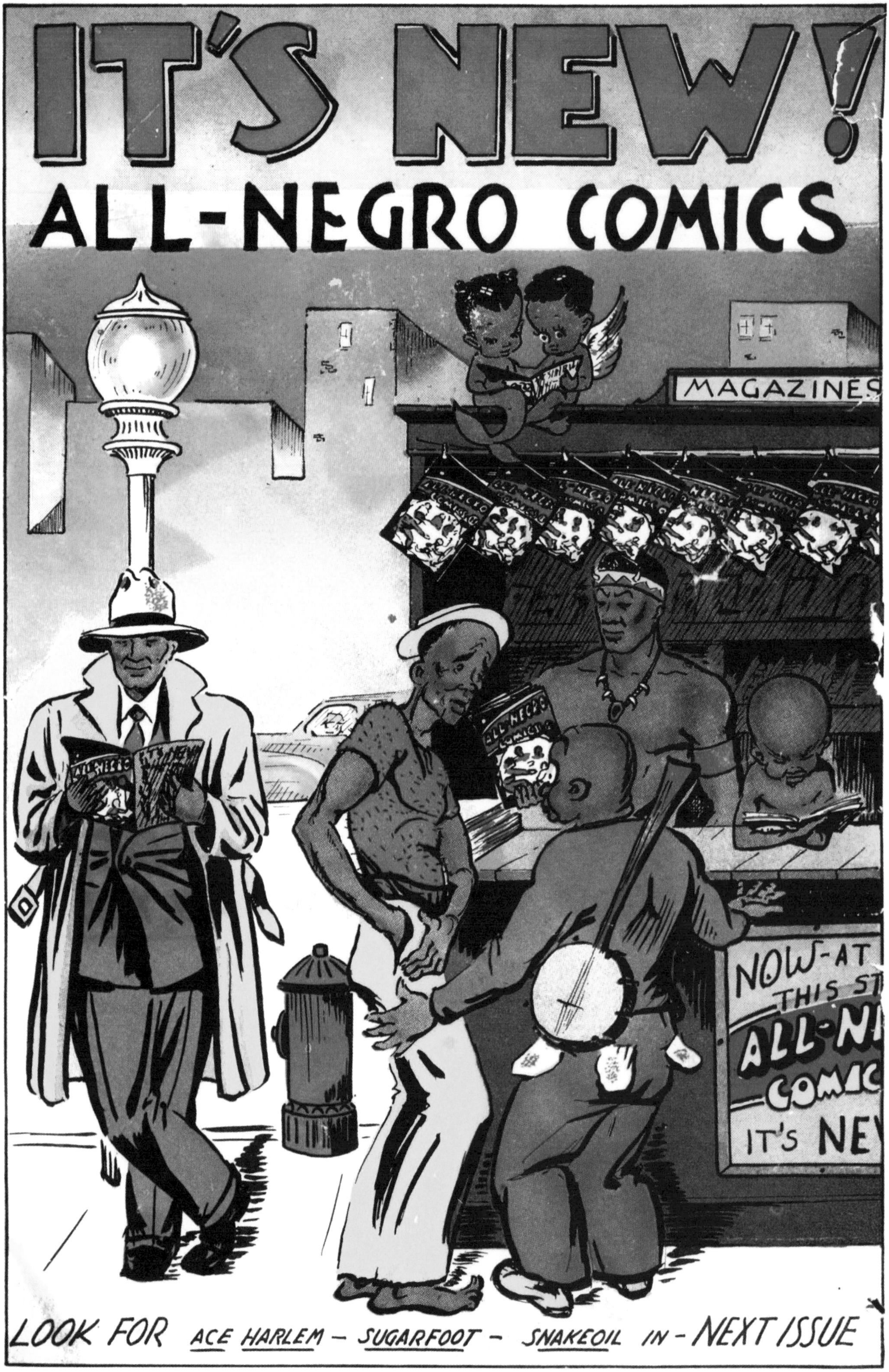
IT'S NEW!
ALL-NEGRO COMICS
MAGAZINES
ALL-NEGRO COMICS
NOW-AT THIS ST
ALL-N
COMIC
IT'S NE
LOOK FOR ACE HARLEM – SUGARFOOT – SNAKEOIL IN – NEXT ISSUE

ADVENTURES OF TIGER RAGG
By Terrell
TIGER RAGG
TOMMY (TIGER) RAGG HOME FROM SCHOOL TO HELP HIS FATHER A FORMER CAPT OF POLICE..."BUSTED" BY "AL" JUDD GANG CHIEF..."TIGER" GETS A JOB AS SPARRING TO "AL JUDD'S" FIGHTER "KILLER" MILLER.........SHOWING THE "KILLER" AS COWARDLY BULLY..THE "KILLER" TRIES TO GET THE "TIGER" BUT "CURLEY" A TRAINER HELPS "TIGER" ROUT THE "KILLER'S" THUGS.."CURLEY" AND "TIGER" STOP IN A RESTAURANT
UNNOTICED BY "CURLEY" AND "TIGER"..."BAT" (ONE OF AL'S BOYS)–SLIPS IN THE NEXT BOOTH AND OVERHEARS "CURLEY."
AND WHEN I HEARD ABOUT YOUR FATHER BEING IN TROUBLE I ASKED LEAVE OF ABSENCE AND GOT A JOB WITH "JUDD" I FOUND HE KEEPS A LITTLE BOOK, WITH ALL THE RECORDS OF HIS BRIBE MONEY AND CROOKED DEALS IN!..NOW IF WE COULD GET HOLD OF THAT...WE COULD NOT ONLY CLEAR YOUR DAD...WE COULD SEND JUDD UP FOR LIFE!..JUDD'S OUT.. SO WE'LL SEARCH HIS ROOM!
"BAT," SLIPS OUT AND PHONES "AL" JUDD!!
SO CURLEY IS A COP, EH! AN' THE KID IS CAP' RAGG SON–NOW "BAT" YOU TAIL 'EM. I'LL PICK UP THE BOYS.. AN' MEET YA' AT MY PLACE!
UNAWARE THAT "JUDD" HAS BEEN TIPPED OFF...."CURLEY" AND "TIGER" GO TO "JUDD'S" PLACE!
WE'VE TURNED THE PLACE INSIDE OUT,.. AND STILL NO TRACE OF IT!!
I HATE TO GIVE UP...BUT HE MUST HAVE IT IN HIS OFFICE, OR WITH HIM!
"CURLEY" AND THE "TIGER" ARE SURPRISED BY "JUDD" AND HIS GANG!!
KEEP 'EM UP!..YOU MUGGS HAD ME FOOLED FOR AWHILE...YOU'RE BOTH GOING ON A ONE WAY RIDE FOR BEING TOO SMART...

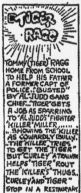

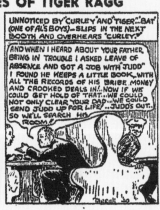

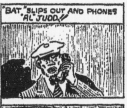

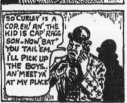

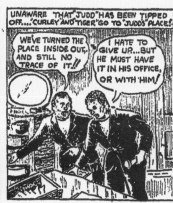

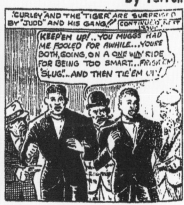

George J. Hecht had a problem with comic books. As President of the Parents' Institute and publisher of *Parents' Magazine*, he was an early and outspoken critic of the emerging medium. He considered comics a "threat to character development" and loathed the hold they had upon children. Hecht was probably the unlikeliest person to become a comic book publisher, but he did, albeit reluctantly and with the hope that "all comics, including my own, were put out of business." ["Comics' Effects on Youth Scored," *New York Times*, Nov. 6, 1941]

Despite his misgivings about comics, Hecht realized they weren't going away, so he resolved that through "substitution rather than prohibition," comics could be a positive influence. To that end, The Parents' Institute (aka Parents' Magazine Press) published *True Comics* #1 (April 1941), followed several months later by *Real Heroes* #1 (Sept. 1941). Their success spawned other titles—*Calling All Girls* and *True Aviation* among them—and even a one-shot intended to rally kids to the war effort entitled, *How Boys and Girls Can Help Win the War* (1942). It was a similar planned one-shot that gave Hecht the idea that comics could be utilized to reach a generally under-served Black American population.

Hecht broached the subject in a letter to Dr. Wilbur Schramm, an expert in the field of mass communication and propaganda working for the Office of War Information (OWI). Hecht's letter of January 20, 1943, began:

I have given further thought to the subject you brought up during my visit; namely, how to reach negroes, many of whom do not read fluently. I think the comic technique would be a most effective one in bringing a message to colored people.

May I suggest that you authorize our Company to get out a 16 page booklet the size of Extra, *copies of which I enclose*. [George J. Hecht letter to Dr. Wilbur Schramm, Jan. 20, 1943]

A copy of *Extra*, the aforementioned comic, was found along with this letter in the files at the National Archives by archivist and historian Ray Bottorff. It was a typically-sized promotional comic made up of previously published stories from Parents' Magazine Press comics.

Hecht's letter continued:

All 16 pages would be in the comic technique. We are ready to write the script and do the art work for the OWI at cost and you could then have any quantity you wanted printed. I suggest that a publication like this might have one of the following names: Negro Heroes, Colored Heroes, Picture Stories for Colored People. [Ibid.]

Hecht's letter went on to tout stories that his company had already published regarding Blacks, offering to re-use this material if Schramm wished, or to have more drawn. While Hecht was well-intentioned, it is also obvious that parts of his letter were very problematic:

I suggest that features be drawn about extraordinary work that negroes have done in war industries and then there could be included several pages as to why we are fighting, all told in the comic technique. Everybody reads the comics, but they are exceptionally good means of reaching people of low intelligence to whom reading solid text is somewhat difficult. [Ibid.]

Apparently, Hecht's sales pitch didn't work on Schramm. The OWI didn't buy his idea for a comic aimed at Blacks. However, about a year after the war's end and the dissolution of the OWI, the National Urban League apparently was convinced and so partnered with the Parents' Institute on *Negro Heroes*.

Published without a cover date, *Negro Heroes* #1 (copyrighted on February 4, 1947) was well-covered by Black newspapers when it was launched in a program at the McAlpin Hotel on February 28th.

The executive secretary of the National Urban League presided over the program. Along with the usual remarks by chosen dignitaries, it featured the appearance of Matthew Henson, the Black polar explorer and the subject of one of the stories in *Negro Heroes*.

Some of the information regarding the comic was misconstrued, such as an assumption by *New York Age* editorial writer Ludlow W. Werner. He doled out compliments to "Guichard Parris, consulting editor of *Negro Heroes*, who has gathered around him a top-flight staff of advisers, writers

[Left] The back cover of *All-Negro Comics* #1 June 1947; All-Negro Comics, Inc.

[Above] *Adventures of Tiger Ragg* was a comic strip by John Terrell that appeared briefly. *New York Amsterdam News*, April 27, 1940.

and cartoonists, who have in the first issue done a bang-up job." [Werner, Ludlow, "Across the Desk," *New York Age*, March 15, 1947]

Parris was director of publicity for the National Urban League, and in truth his "consulting editor" position was largely ceremonial, as the majority of the material used in *Negro Heroes* #1 was reprinted from various Parents' Magazine Press comics. In fact, the only new material in the entire comic was the two-page story, "Sacrifice at Sea."

No matter, the plaudits were deserved and extensive—at least, in the Black publications. To this point, no mention of *Negro Heroes* has been found in any mainstream White newspaper.

The Spring 1947 issue of the National Urban League journal, *Opportunity*, featured a young boy reading *Negro Heroes* on its cover. Inside, it carried an ad telling readers how to obtain copies of the comic and a letter from Ambrose Caliver, Senior Specialist in the Education of Negroes in the Department of Education. As one of the most influential voices in America regarding Black education, Caliver's approval of *Negro Heroes* was a coup. It also had another influential fan of literary fame. In his weekly column "Here to Yonder," Langston Hughes wrote:

I have started reading comic books, and the comic book that started me reading comic books is a comic book published by the National Urban League in full colors. It is called Negro Heroes *and it is all about that wizard of science Dr. Carver, and Lt. Charles Thomas, and the stirring story of Mary McLeod Bethune all in wonderful pictures with the words coming right out of the characters' mouths. Paul Robeson is in there, too, so I reckon the book will be banned in Peoria.*

The Urban League tells me they have published a hundred and seventy-five thousand copies, but the demand for this swell comic book has been so great that they wish they had published five hundred thousand copies. [Hughes, Langston, "Here to Yonder," *Chicago Defender*, May 3, 1947]

As noted by Hughes, the sales for *Negro Heroes* were successful enough to justify the publication of *Negro Heroes* #2 the following year.

Hitting the newsstands in June 1948, this issue received a larger printing of 300,000 copies. Along with the sponsorship of the National Urban League, *Negro Heroes* #2 also had the backing of the Delta's Sigma Theta Sorority.

This sorority was founded in 1913 at Howard University and was specifically dedicated to public service activities.

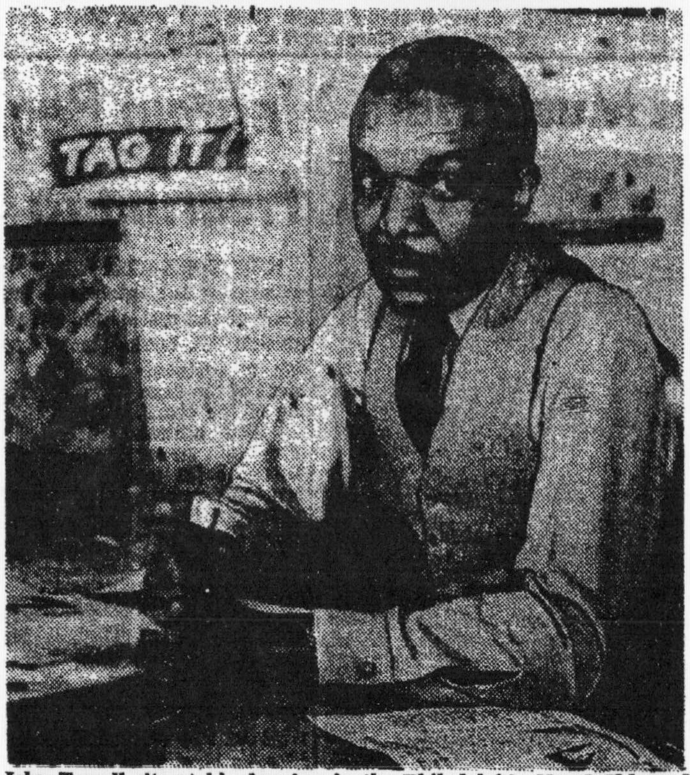

Saves Lives with Comics

TAG IT

John Terrell sits at his drawing in the Philadelphia Naval Shipyard, where he is a safety officer, with the special title of illustrator. Beginning at the "yard" in 1941 as a laborer, he was placed in his present job after a naval officer noticed his skill in transcribing ideas on safety to the graphic medium of hard-hitting posters.

The Deltas first national president was Sadie Tanner Mossell Alexander, who was serving on President Harry Truman's Committee on Civil Rights in 1948 when *Negro Heroes* #2 was released. She was also the subject of one of that comic's stories, "Woman of the Year."

The other persons honored in *Negro Heroes* #2 included baseball legend Jackie Robinson, Russian poet Alexander Pushkin, and Frank "Sugar Chile" Robinson, a child prodigy pianist. Unlike the first issue of *Negro Heroes*, this one contained a greater mix of new and previously published material.

It's unclear how well this last issue of *Negro Heroes* sold, but despite its short life, this comic book was the first attempt by any publisher to address the Black readership. Coming soon after in its wake, *All-Negro Comics* would take Blacks a step beyond being the subjects of a comic book by involving them in the actual creation of one.

Evans wasted no time in getting the comic into production. Even though the company had only been formed in April, the comic came out with a cover date of June, and was copyrighted on July 15th. *All-Negro Comics* actually hit the newsstands on July 18, 1947. Still a fast start, but

[Above] John Terrell at his job as safety officer at the Philadelphia Shipyard. *Baltimore Afro-American*, April 27, 1946.

[Right] A panel from "Sugarfoot" by William H. Smith, *All-Negro Comics* #1 (June 1947; All-Negro Comics, Inc.).

possible indications of either production or distribution problems.

Orrin edited *All-Negro* and had a hand in the creation of most of the features. Terrell, being the most experienced cartoonist, drew the cover depicting characters from the strips. On the interior, his "Ace Harlem" was a Chester Gould-like, gritty detective story, with a couple of menacing hoodlums and several shocking stranglings. Terrell showed his humorous side with "Lil' Eggie," a one-page take on the time-honored "hen-pecked husband" trope. He was probably the artist for the illustration accompanying the text story, "Ezekiel's Manhunt," as well.

Leonard Cooper drew the sweet "Dew Dillies" tale of Black fairies and its thematic opposite, "Hep Chicks on Parade," a page containing four individual cartoons of stylish Black women, a nod in the direction of E. Simms Campbell.

William H. Smith's "Sugarfoot," signed mysteriously as "Cravat," was his only contribution, revealing an art style reminiscent of the great comic creator Harvey Kurtzman. Smith was a novice and less accomplished than Kurtzman, but it is apparent that he was aware of his White contemporary.

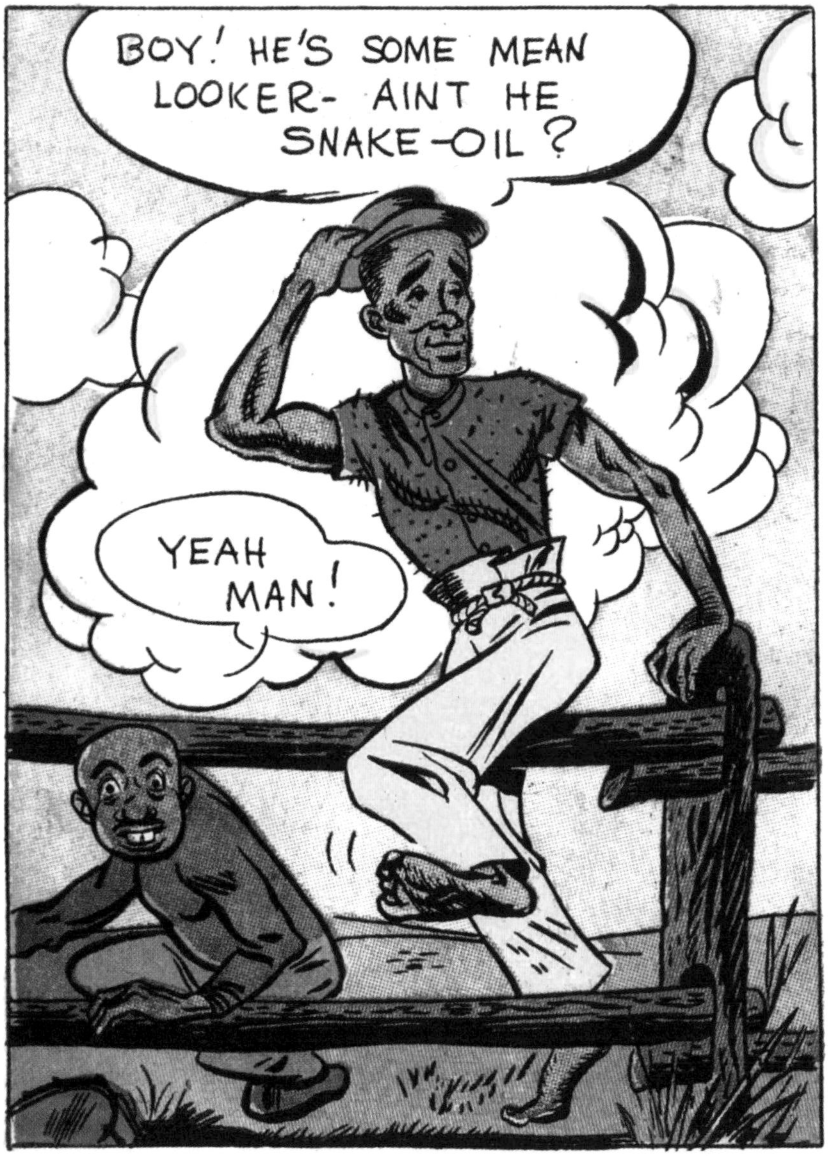
BOY! HE'S SOME MEAN LOOKER- AINT HE SNAKE-OIL?
YEAH MAN!

George Evans' contribution to the comic was "Lion Man," who had a most fully-realized backstory:

American-born, college educated, Lion Man is a young scientist, sent by the United Nations to watch over the fearsome "Magic Mountain" of the African Gold Coast.

In this adventure, Lion Man was pitted against two deceitful White men, who trick and capture him, only to have the tables turned when he escapes with the help of his young companion, Bubba. The story ends with the death of one villain and the escape of the other, setting up a sequel to come in the next issue.

The irony exuded by this feature had to be intentional. This was the story of a Black hero adventuring in Africa. After years of Tarzan and a legion of similarly-toned White jungle men, Lion Man only had Matt Baker's short-lived Voodah as a predecessor.

Orrin Evans was challenging a reality that was unspoken, but inherently understood, within the publishing industry.

Widely read and of great influence are the comic-books. Here, research has shown, the sin is of omission. Few characters are Negro or indeed anything but pure Anglo-Saxon with unmistakable names. Liberal as they are by comparison to the magazine manufacturers, comic-book publishers laugh to scorn any idea of casting a Negro in a hero's role, or even a Jew. "We are interested in circulation primarily," one comic book expert told an interviewer. "Can you imagine a hero named Cohen?" [Winter, Frederick & Fuller, Edmund, "Jim Crow: Editor and Publisher," *New Masses*, Apr. 1, 1947, p.11]

When news of the new comic was released, it was no surprise that White columnists had a different reaction to it than did Black ones. A short clip in *Collier's* seemed almost incredulous at what had been accomplished:

America's new All-Negro Comics *is the first publication of its kind drawn by Negroes and containing only Negro characters.* [Foster, Freling, "Keeping Up with the World," *Collier's*, Nov. 1, 1947, p.6]

Nationally syndicated White columnist Leonard Lyons gave more details on the comic itself and noted the same prejudicial representations of Blacks as had the *New Masses* writers:

LION MAN HAS BEEN WARNED AGAINST AGENTS OF A CERTAIN WARLIKE NATION WHO MIGHT TRY TO SMUGGLE SOME OF THE MOUNTAIN'S TREASURE OUT OF AFRICA. HIS SCIENTIFIC INSTRUMENTS INDICATE A SHIP HAS MOVED UP A NEARBY RIVER.

WORN OUT BY LACK OF SLEEP, LION MAN LIES DOWN FOR A SNOOZE. BUBBA, A LOST ORPHAN WHOM LION MAN HAS ADOPTED IS BORED. ~~~~ THIS IS A *ZULU* HOTFOOT.

In Kingsblood Royal *Sinclair Lewis denounces the comic strips and comic books which make Negro characters "clownish and vile," citing the recent controversial novel about a middle-class White man who discovers he is part Black.*

Orrin Evans, the Negro newspaperman, has started an All Negro Comic Book, *the first ever published, edited and drawn by Negroes. All the heroes and villains in it will be Negroes. The first printing, 300,000 copies, will be on U.S. and West Indies newsstands next week.* [Lyons, Leonard, "The Lyons Den," July 14, 1947]

A column with the telling dateline of "Campobello Island" carried the measured, but ultimately complimentary, comments of a very well-known reviewer, none other than Eleanor Roosevelt:

As my readers already know, I am not very fond of comic books but, having children and grandchildren, I recognize that these books are very widely read and have a tremendous influence. I have just been sent a newcomer in the field, All Negro Comics. *The publisher is Orrin C. Evans, formerly a reporter and editor in the Negro newspaper field. I must say that, as I glanced through the pages of this newcomer, I felt that it compared very favorably with the best of the comic books. In some features it is really better.* [Roosevelt, Eleanor, "My Day," Aug. 2, 1947]

The Black media came at *All-Negro Comics* from a different perspective. It was more personal, more meaningful to them than their White counterparts:

My friend Orrin C. Evans of Philadelphia has launched with appropriate fanfare a journalistic venture that should prove very lucrative and which at the same time, offers a good opportunity to curb juvenile delinquency by showing graphically that crime does not pay, and that there is fun, beauty and adventure in Negro life.

I refer to All-Negro Comics, *a 52-page book of well-drawn cartoons in many colors which hit the stands last week, and which should prove immediately popular with the small fry.*

Comics no longer "lift" me and when I picked up this book, I had not read through one in years. However, I found All-Negro Comics *truly interesting and amusing, and in every way equal to similar comics on the market except that it is better than most of them I have seen. Everything in it is done by colored artists, and the publisher has not found it necessary to charge an exorbitant price simply because he is serving a special field.* [Schuyler, George, "Views and Reviews," *Pittsburgh Courier*, July 26, 1947]

Charley Cherokee, sardonic columnist of the *Chicago Defender*, made just a quick mention of the comic, but was quite clear about what he thought was behind its publication.

[Above] A panel from "Lion Man" by George J. Evans Jr.

[Right] House ad for *All-Negro Comics* by John H. Terrell.

The images on these two pages are from *All-Negro Comics* #1, June 1947; All-Negro Comics, Inc.

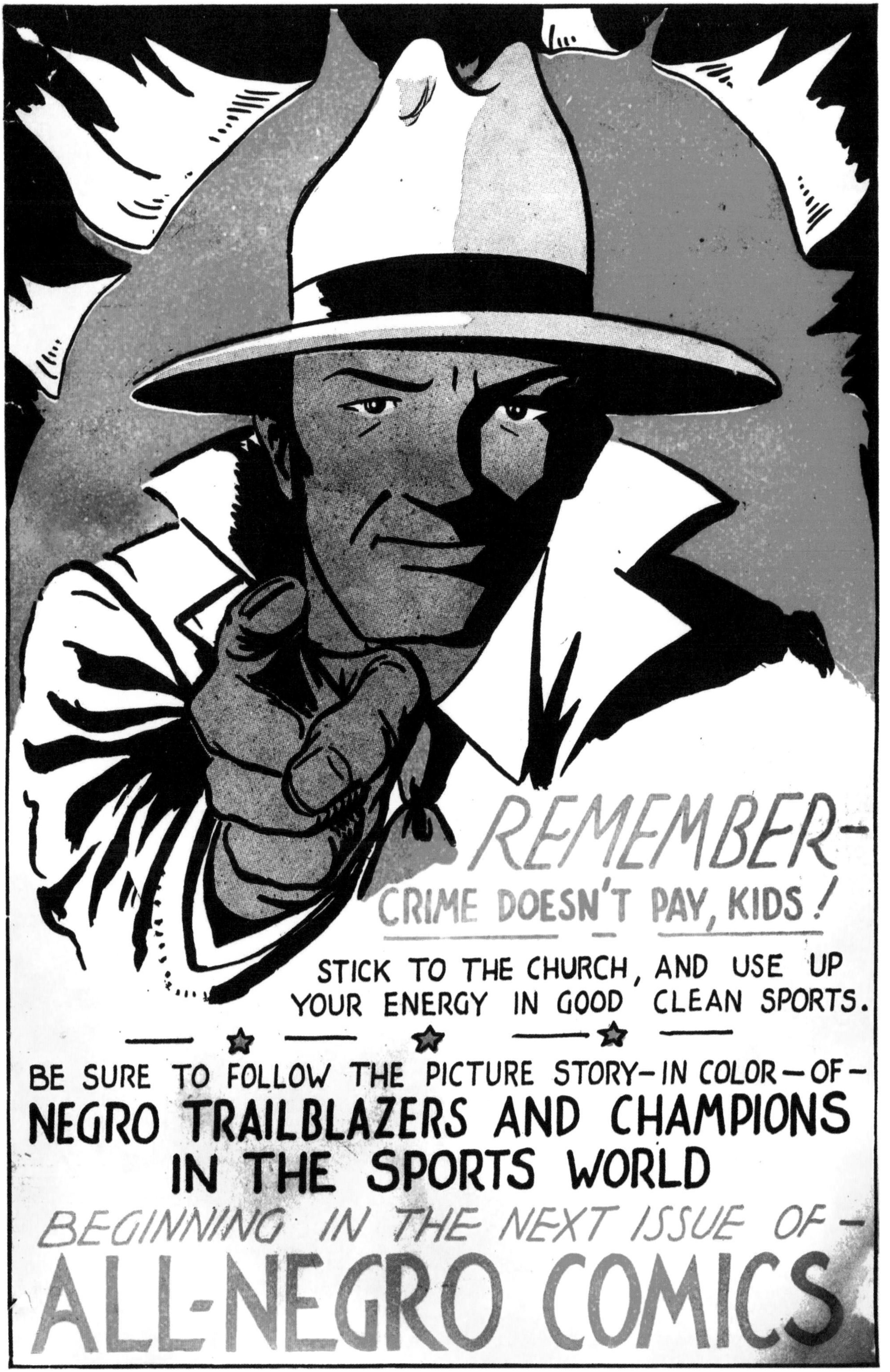
REMEMBER-
CRIME DOESN'T PAY, KIDS!
STICK TO THE CHURCH, AND USE UP YOUR ENERGY IN GOOD CLEAN SPORTS.
BE SURE TO FOLLOW THE PICTURE STORY—IN COLOR—OF—
NEGRO TRAILBLAZERS AND CHAMPIONS IN THE SPORTS WORLD
BEGINNING IN THE NEXT ISSUE OF—
ALL-NEGRO COMICS

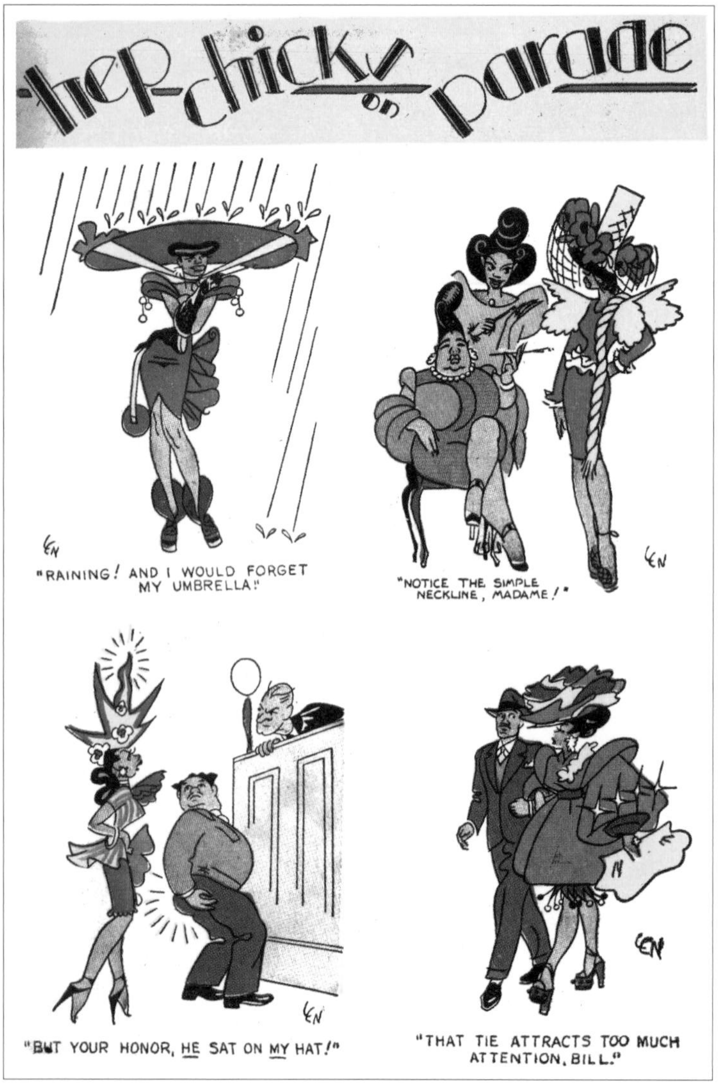
hep-chicks on parade
"RAINING! AND I WOULD FORGET MY UMBRELLA!"
"NOTICE THE SIMPLE NECKLINE, MADAME!"
"BUT YOUR HONOR, HE SAT ON MY HAT!"
"THAT TIE ATTRACTS TOO MUCH ATTENTION, BILL."

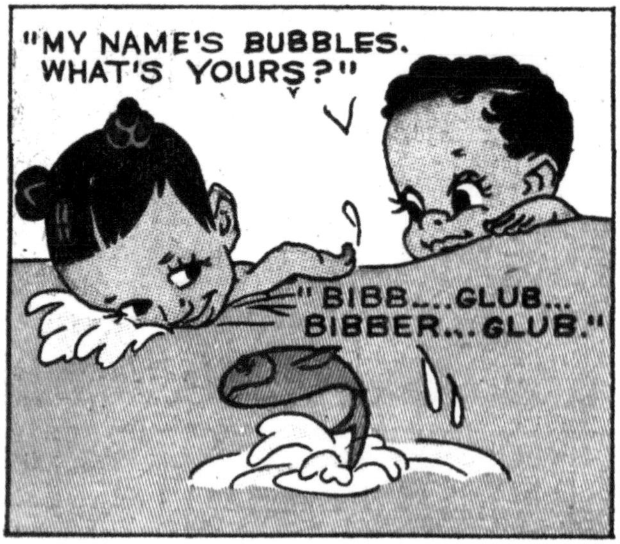
"MY NAME'S BUBBLES. WHAT'S YOURS?"
"BIBB....GLUB... BIBBER...GLUB."

Orrin Evans, veteran newsman in Phila., is heading organization putting out new All-Negro Comics *booklets. This is a commercial venture with no social story to tell like Urban League's* Negro Heroes *or Worker's Defense League's* Joe Worker. [Cherokee, Charley, "National Grapevine," *Chicago Defender*, October 4, 1947.]

Months after its publication, a writer for the *Baltimore Afro-American* was more reflective in his thoughts on the long-term effect of *All-Negro Comics:*

Since the advent of All-Negro Comics, Inc., our funnies have been coming more and more to the foreground. With the untold wealth of esoteric humor at the colored artist's disposal, and the pathos and poignant beauty of oppressed minority life, he should raise this medium of expression to new heights.

Though I pass over the great majority of them, I happen to be a comics addict for some few that I would not miss. These favorites are Barnaby, Blondie and Dagwood, Mr. and Mrs., The Berries, *and the cartoons of J.R. Williams.*

To be an artistic and human success, these colored comics cannot depict people like the above, merely with browned faces. Nor can they preach! But they must have the casual viewpoint of the average Afro-American.

They could bring out daily situations arising from open or latent Jim Crow, and the biting esoteric are met.

By virtue of our history and heritage, Afro-Americans are more sensitive human beings than most white Americans. And they have the greater ability of laughing, even while they weep. This tearful, dark laughter should be the essence of all worthwhile colored comics! [Keelan, Harry, "Voice in the Wilderness," *Baltimore Afro-American*, March 20, 1948]

Although the material for a second issue of *All-Negro Comics* was completed, it was never published. Reportedly, Evans was unable to procure paper from suppliers for printing the comic. As a result, each of the comic's creators went their separate ways. Several found success in their commercial art careers, others became painters. Orrin went back to newspaper reporting at the *Chester Times* [Pennsylvania] until 1962, when he started working for the *Philadelphia Bulletin*.

A publishing visionary and a legendary newsman lauded and hailed by his peers and those who followed him, Orrin C. Evans suffered a burst blood vessel and lingered in critical condition before dying on August 6, 1971.

[Above, left] "Hep Chicks On Parade" page by Leonard Cooper.

[Above, right] A panel from "Dew Dillies" by Leonard Cooper.

[Right] Both the front and back covers and the "Ace Harlem" story within were drawn by John H. Terrell, the most experienced artist working on this comic. The script was probably the work of publisher Orrin C. Evans.

The art on this page and the following story are from *All-Negro Comics* #1, June 1947; All-Negro Comics, Inc.

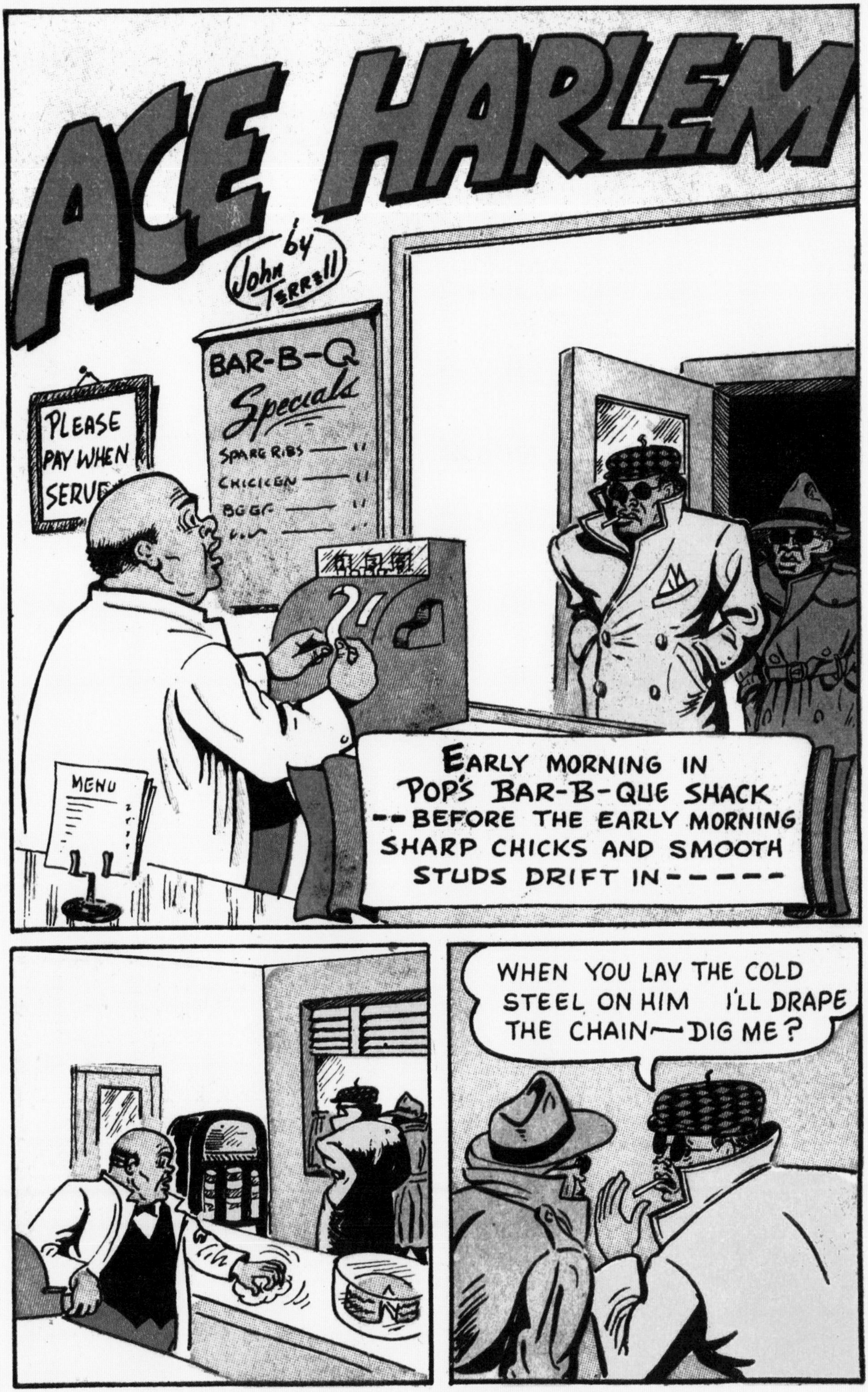
ACE HARLEM
by John Terrell
PLEASE PAY WHEN
BAR-B-Q Specials
SPARE RIBS
CHICKEN
MENU
EARLY MORNING IN POP'S BAR-B-QUE SHACK --BEFORE THE EARLY MORNING SHARP CHICKS AND SMOOTH STUDS DRIFT IN-----
WHEN YOU LAY THE COLD STEEL ON HIM I'LL DRAPE THE CHAIN—DIG ME?

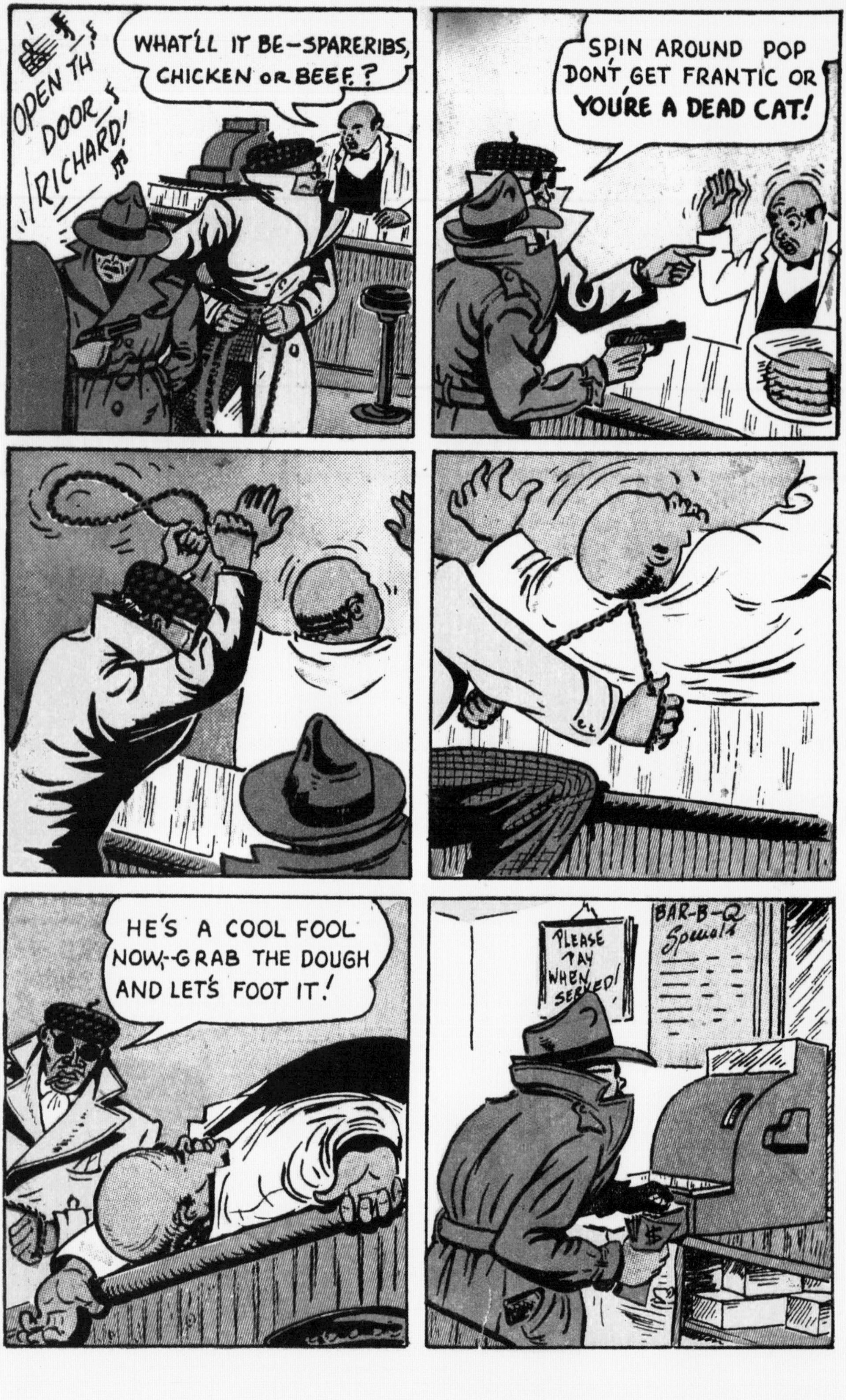
OPEN TH' DOOR RICHARD!
WHAT'LL IT BE—SPARERIBS, CHICKEN OR BEEF ?
SPIN AROUND POP DON'T GET FRANTIC OR YOU'RE A DEAD CAT!
HE'S A COOL FOOL NOW,-GRAB THE DOUGH AND LET'S FOOT IT!
PLEASE PAY WHEN SERVED!
BAR-B-Q Specials

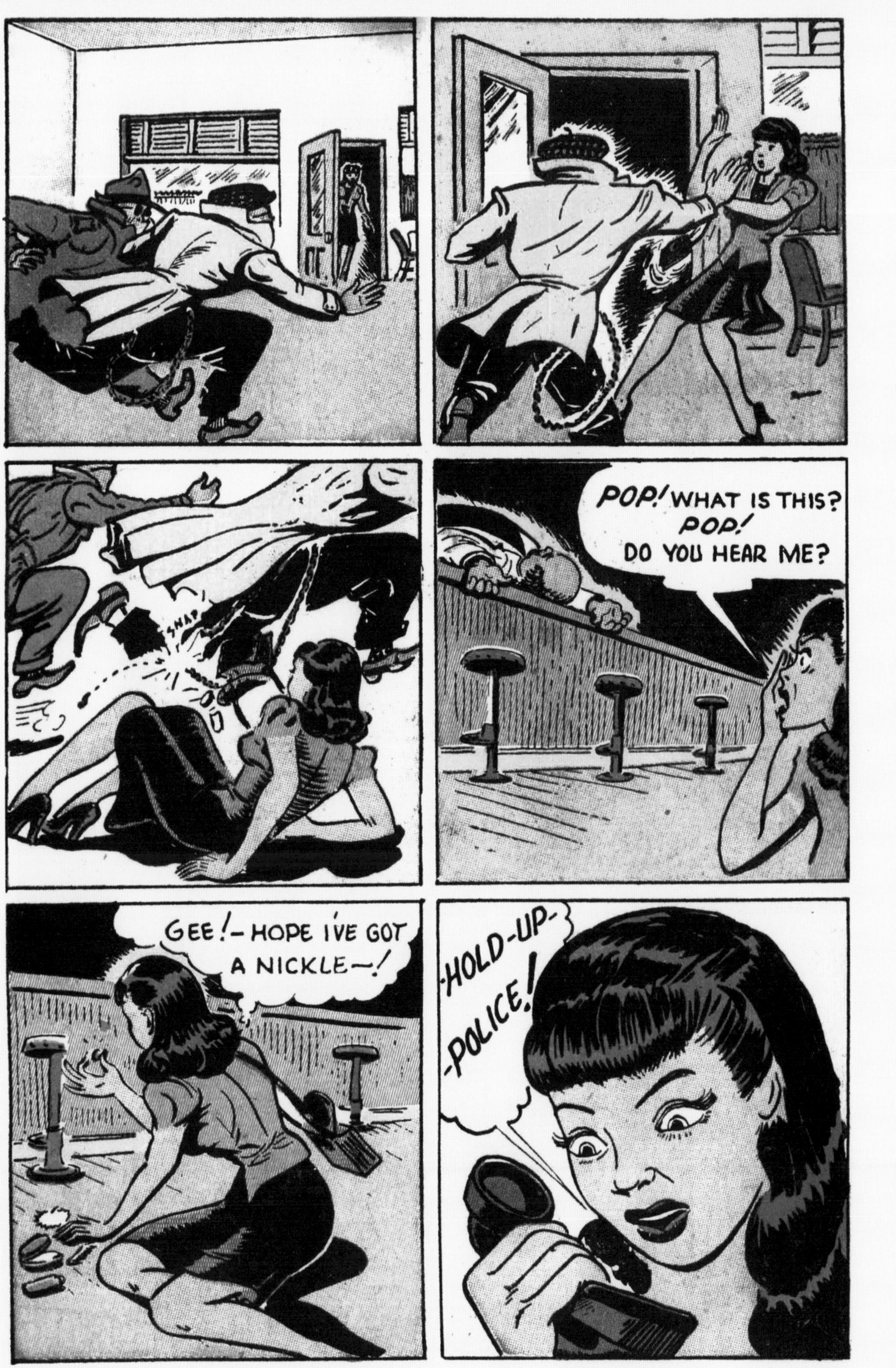
SNAP
POP! WHAT IS THIS? POP! DO YOU HEAR ME?
GEE!– HOPE I'VE GOT A NICKLE–!
-HOLD-UP- -POLICE!

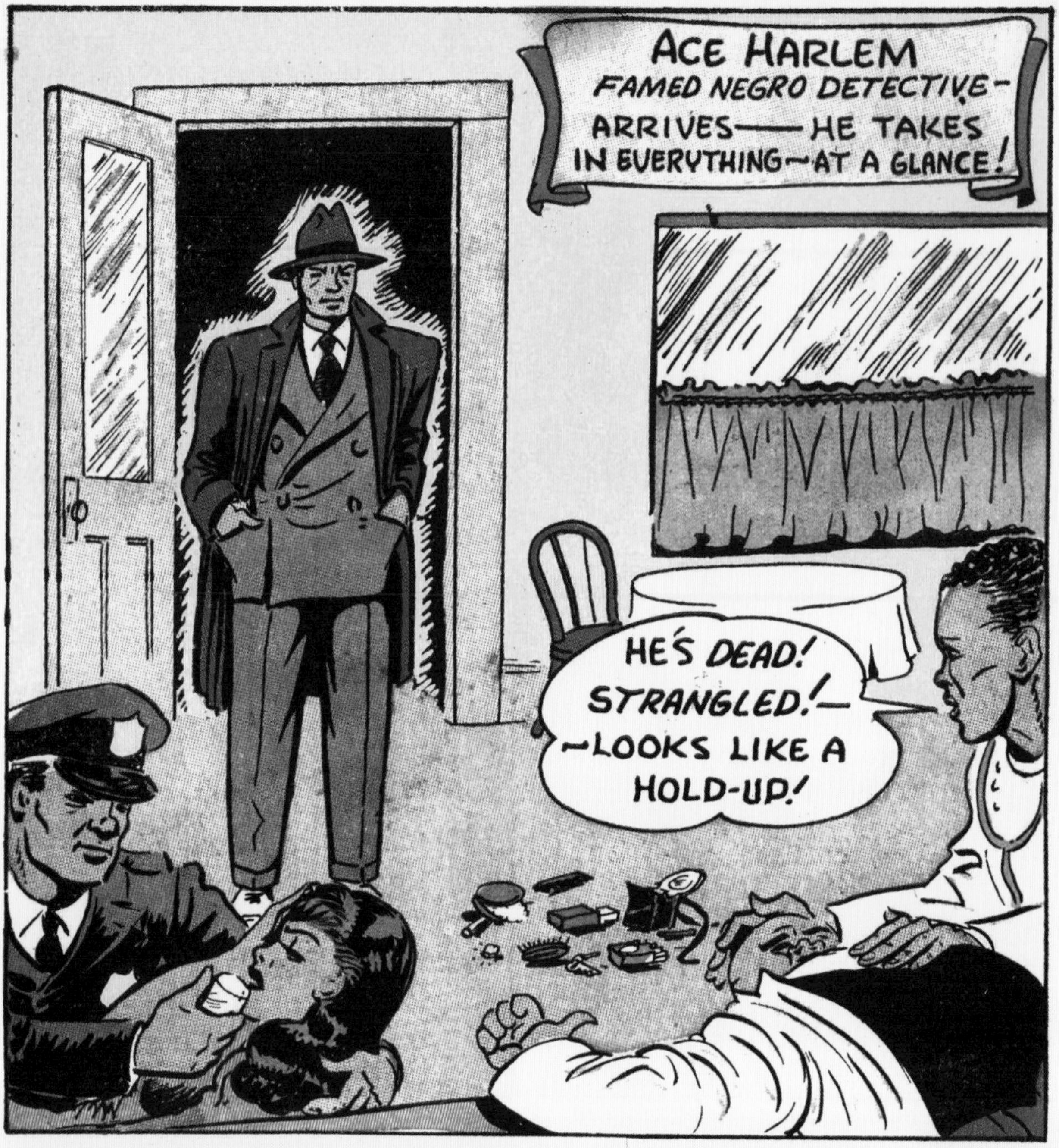
ACE HARLEM
FAMED NEGRO DETECTIVE—
ARRIVES—HE TAKES
IN EVERYTHING—AT A GLANCE!
HE'S DEAD! STRANGLED!— —LOOKS LIKE A HOLD-UP!

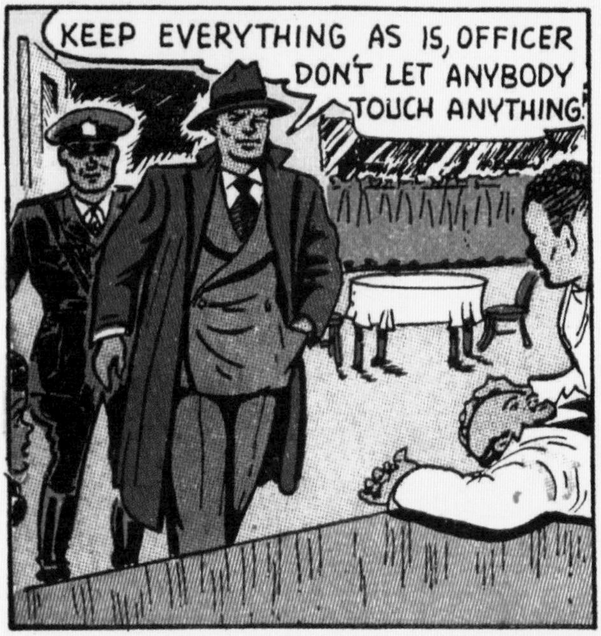
KEEP EVERYTHING AS IS, OFFICER DON'T LET ANYBODY TOUCH ANYTHING!

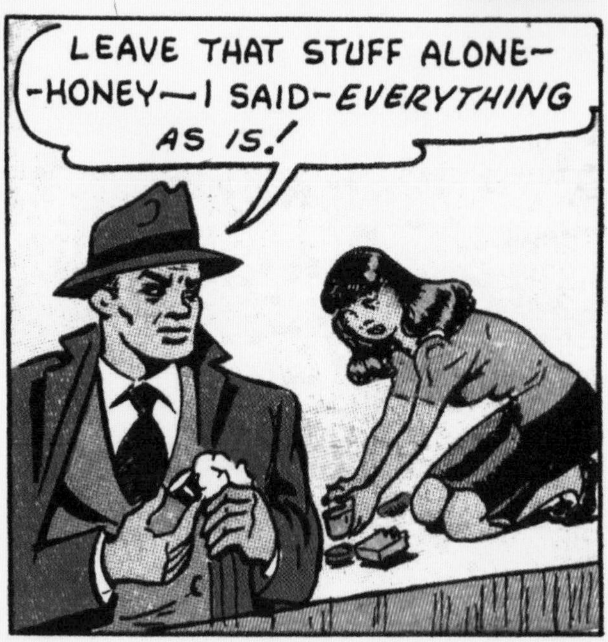
LEAVE THAT STUFF ALONE— —HONEY—I SAID—EVERYTHING AS IS!

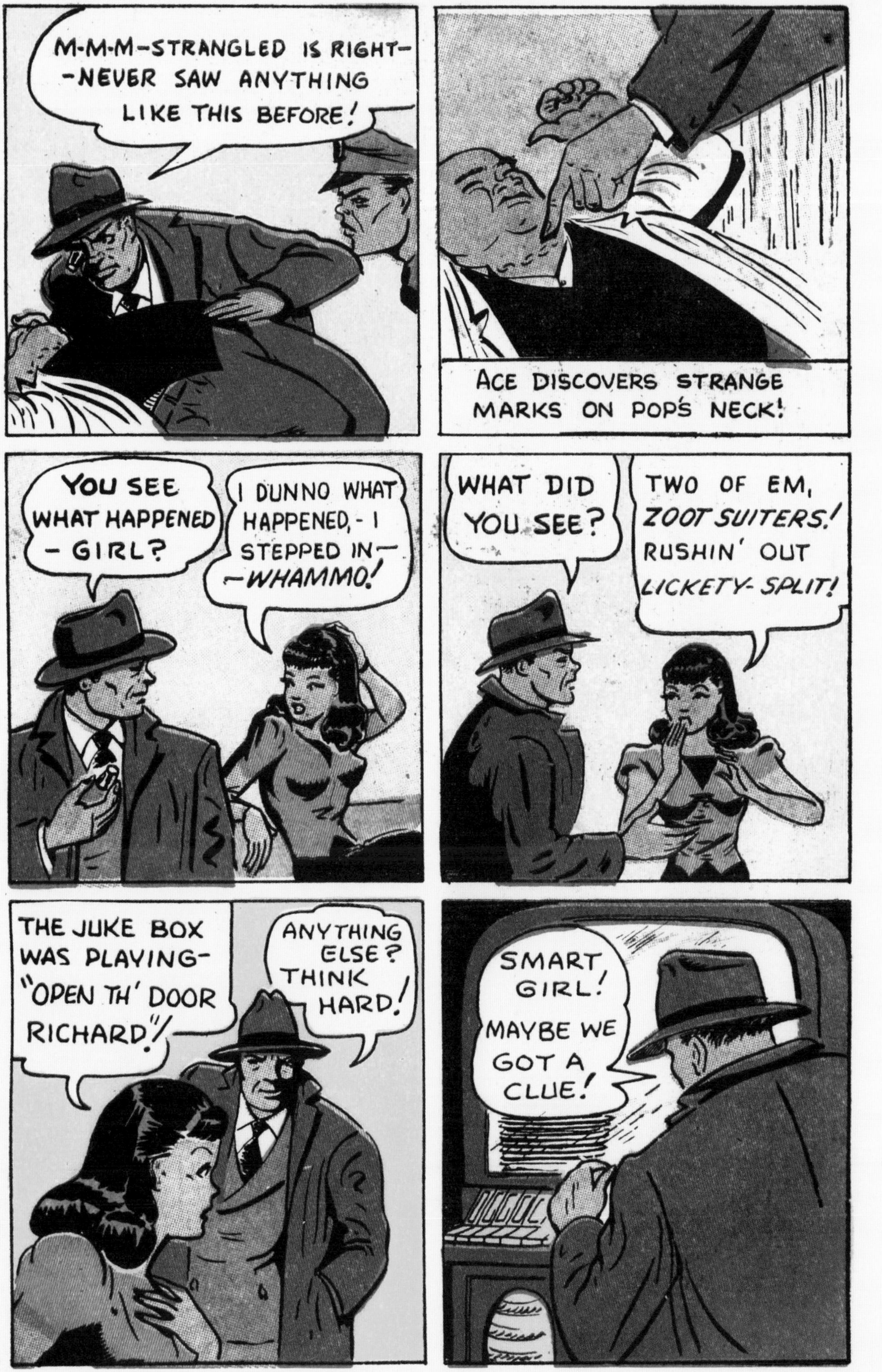
M-M-M–STRANGLED IS RIGHT– –NEVER SAW ANYTHING LIKE THIS BEFORE!
ACE DISCOVERS STRANGE MARKS ON POP'S NECK!
YOU SEE WHAT HAPPENED – GIRL?
I DUNNO WHAT HAPPENED, – I STEPPED IN– –WHAMMO!
WHAT DID YOU SEE?
TWO OF EM, ZOOT SUITERS! RUSHIN' OUT LICKETY-SPLIT!
THE JUKE BOX WAS PLAYING– "OPEN TH' DOOR RICHARD"!
ANYTHING ELSE? THINK HARD!
SMART GIRL!
MAYBE WE GOT A CLUE!

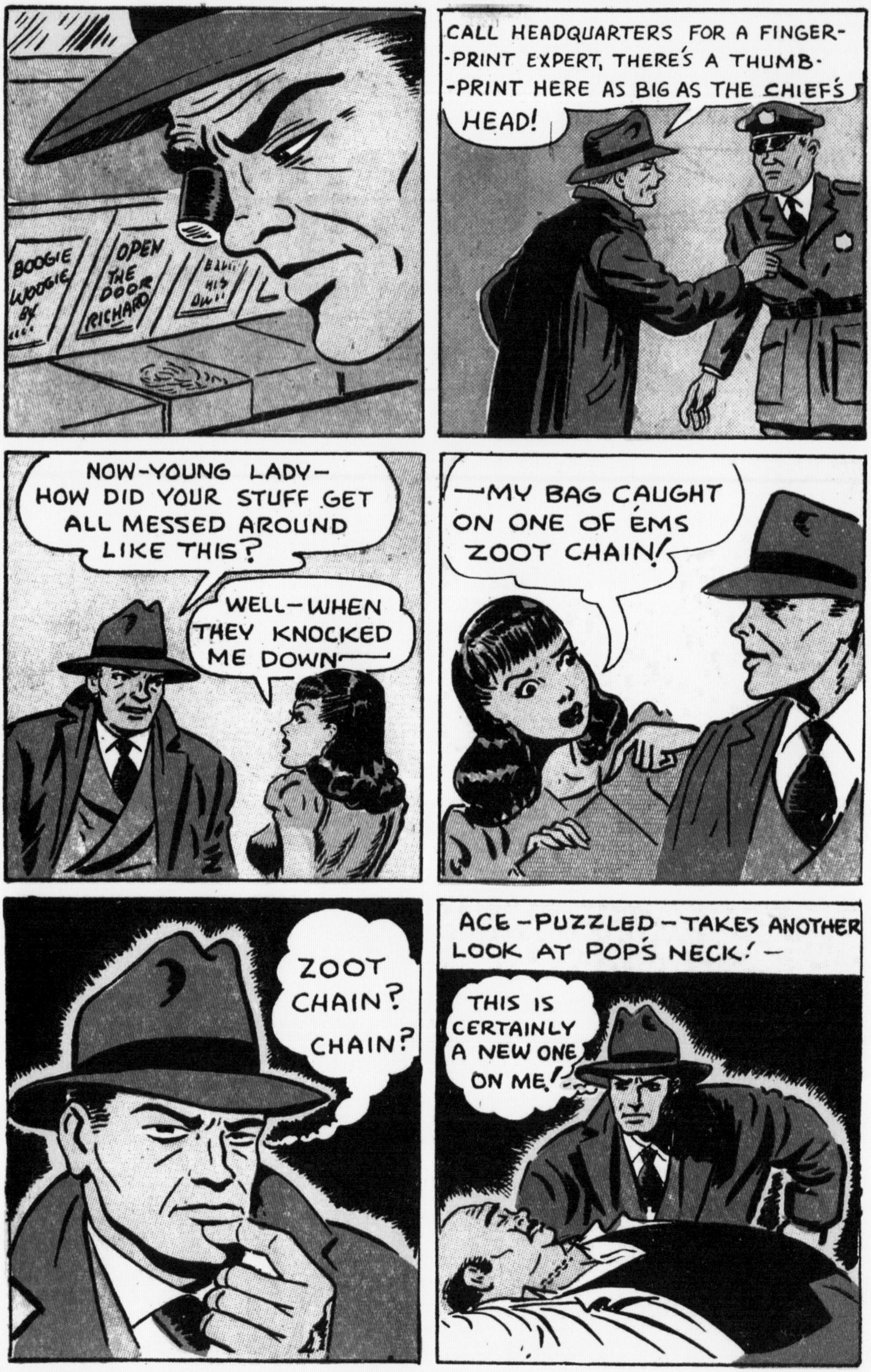
BOOGIE WOOGIE
OPEN THE DOOR RICHARD
CALL HEADQUARTERS FOR A FINGER-PRINT EXPERT, THERE'S A THUMB-PRINT HERE AS BIG AS THE CHIEF'S HEAD!
NOW-YOUNG LADY-HOW DID YOUR STUFF GET ALL MESSED AROUND LIKE THIS?
WELL-WHEN THEY KNOCKED ME DOWN—
—MY BAG CAUGHT ON ONE OF EMS ZOOT CHAIN!
ZOOT CHAIN? CHAIN?
ACE-PUZZLED-TAKES ANOTHER LOOK AT POP'S NECK!—
THIS IS CERTAINLY A NEW ONE ON ME!

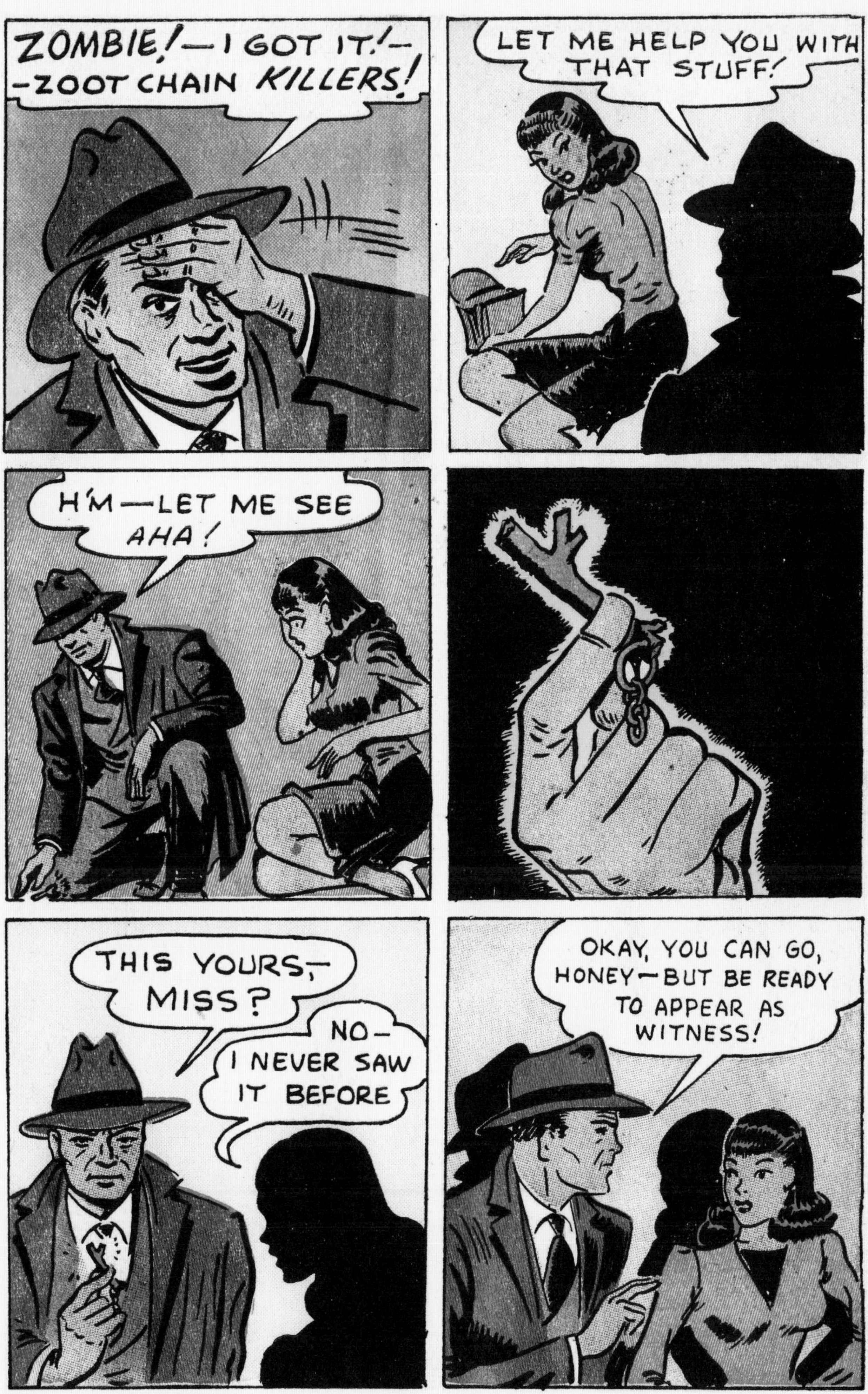
ZOMBIE!—I GOT IT!— —ZOOT CHAIN KILLERS!
LET ME HELP YOU WITH THAT STUFF!
H'M—LET ME SEE AHA!
THIS YOURS,— MISS?
NO— I NEVER SAW IT BEFORE
OKAY, YOU CAN GO, HONEY—BUT BE READY TO APPEAR AS WITNESS!

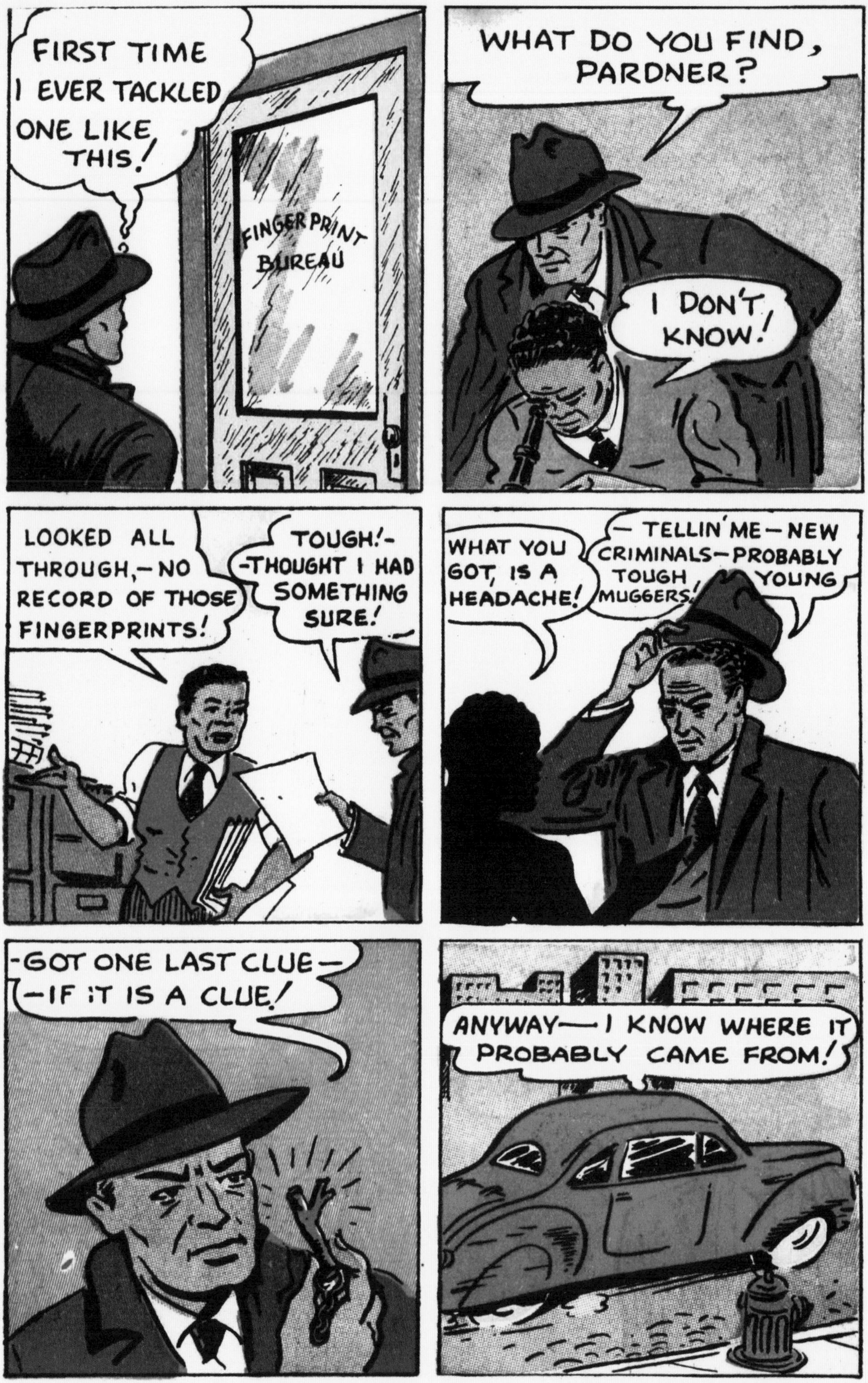

FIRST TIME I EVER TACKLED ONE LIKE THIS!
FINGERPRINT BUREAU
WHAT DO YOU FIND, PARDNER?
I DON'T KNOW!
LOOKED ALL THROUGH,—NO RECORD OF THOSE FINGERPRINTS!
TOUGH!- -THOUGHT I HAD SOMETHING SURE!
WHAT YOU GOT, IS A HEADACHE!
— TELLIN' ME — NEW CRIMINALS — PROBABLY TOUGH YOUNG MUGGERS!
-GOT ONE LAST CLUE— —IF IT IS A CLUE!
ANYWAY— I KNOW WHERE IT PROBABLY CAME FROM!

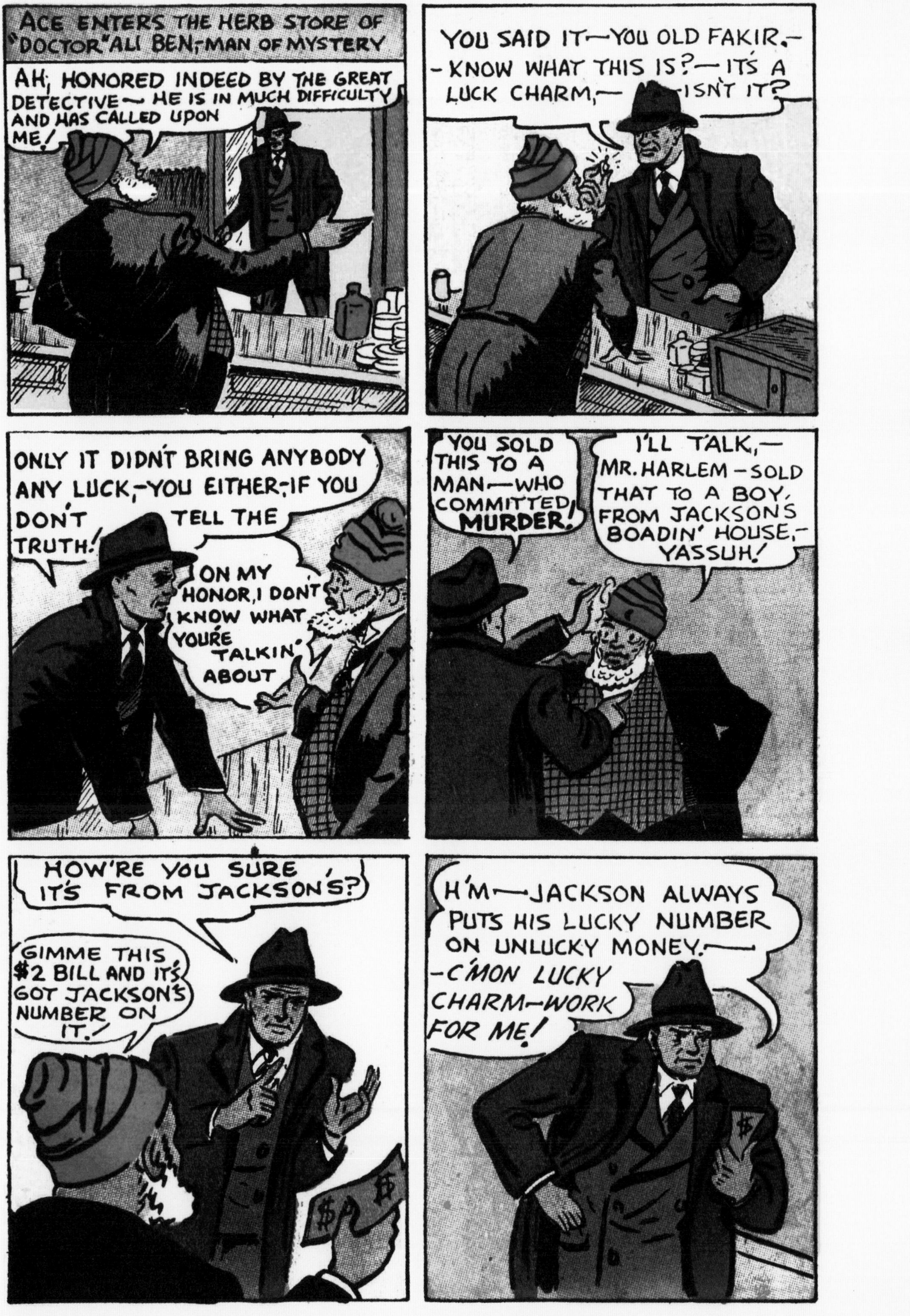

ACE ENTERS THE HERB STORE OF "DOCTOR" ALI BEN,—MAN OF MYSTERY
AH, HONORED INDEED BY THE GREAT DETECTIVE— HE IS IN MUCH DIFFICULTY AND HAS CALLED UPON ME!
YOU SAID IT—YOU OLD FAKIR.— -KNOW WHAT THIS IS?—IT'S A LUCK CHARM,— —ISN'T IT?
ONLY IT DIDN'T BRING ANYBODY ANY LUCK,—YOU EITHER,—IF YOU DON'T TELL THE TRUTH!
ON MY HONOR, I DON'T KNOW WHAT YOU'RE TALKIN' ABOUT
YOU SOLD THIS TO A MAN—WHO COMMITTED MURDER!
I'LL TALK,— MR. HARLEM—SOLD THAT TO A BOY, FROM JACKSON'S BOADIN' HOUSE,— YASSUH!
HOW'RE YOU SURE IT'S FROM JACKSON'S?
GIMME THIS $2 BILL AND IT'S GOT JACKSON'S NUMBER ON IT.!
H'M—JACKSON ALWAYS PUTS HIS LUCKY NUMBER ON UNLUCKY MONEY.—
-C'MON LUCKY CHARM—WORK FOR ME!

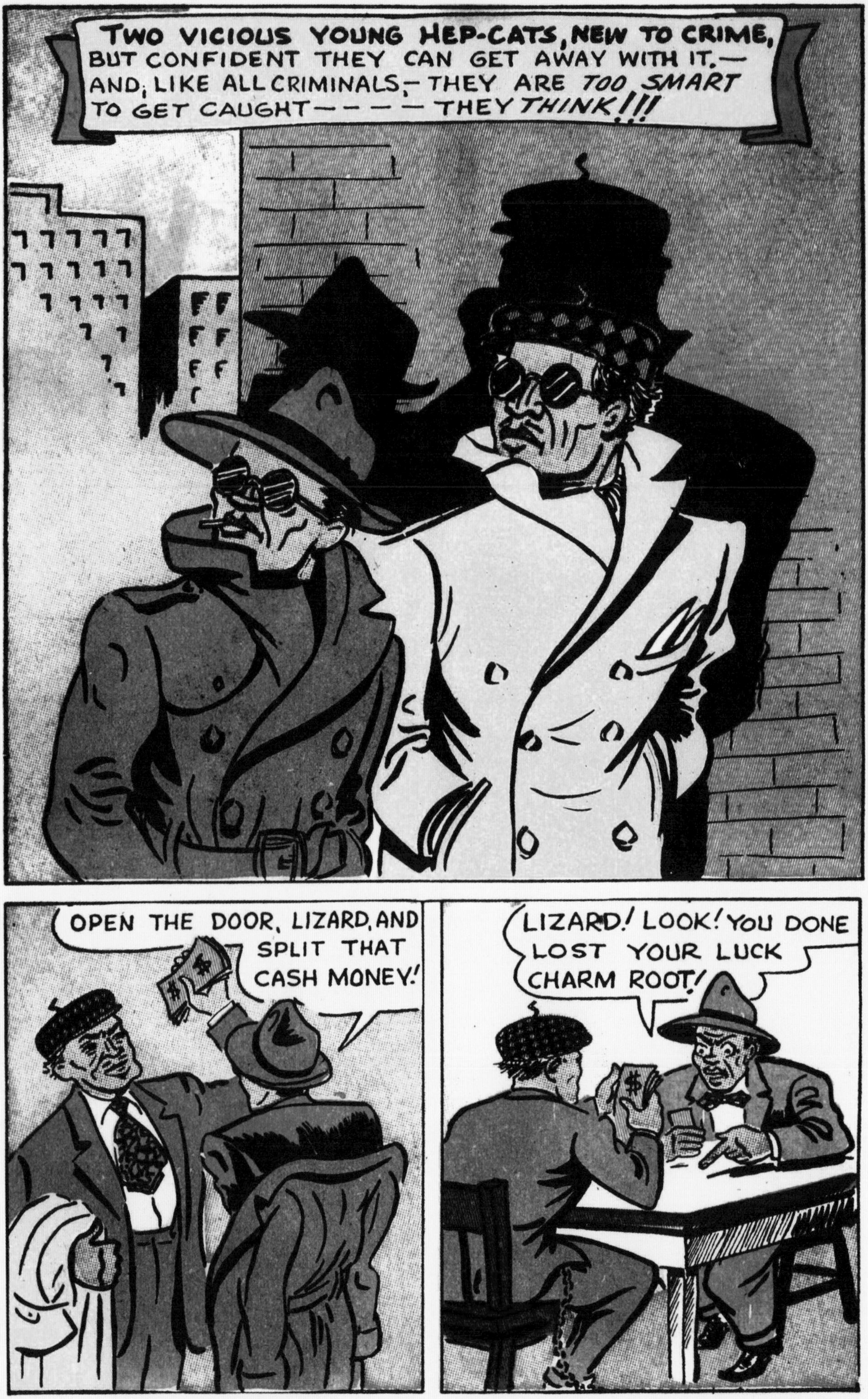
TWO VICIOUS YOUNG HEP-CATS, NEW TO CRIME, BUT CONFIDENT THEY CAN GET AWAY WITH IT.— AND, LIKE ALL CRIMINALS,— THEY ARE TOO SMART TO GET CAUGHT———— THEY THINK!!!
OPEN THE DOOR, LIZARD, AND SPLIT THAT CASH MONEY!
LIZARD! LOOK! YOU DONE LOST YOUR LUCK CHARM ROOT!

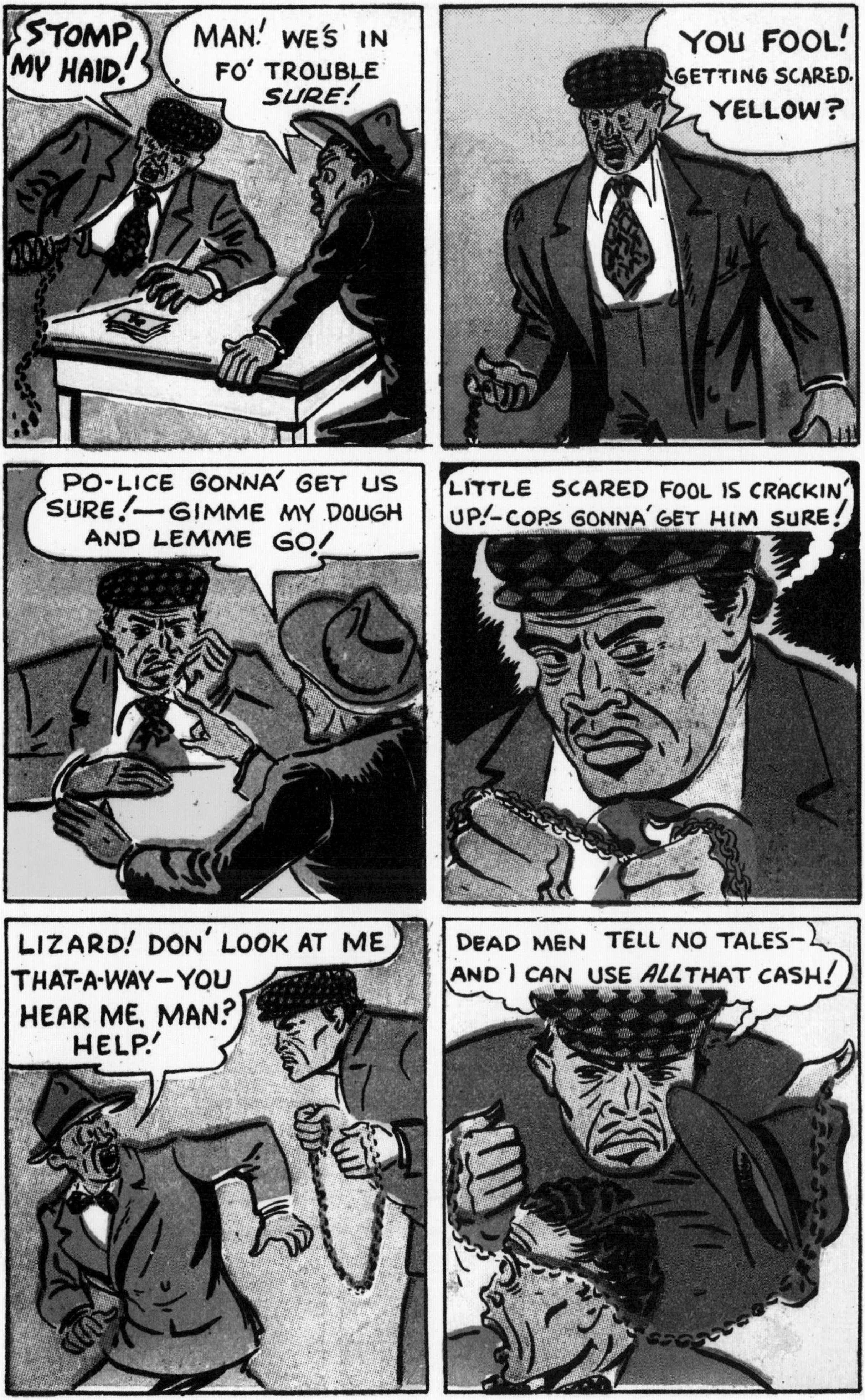
STOMP, MY HAID!
MAN! WE'S IN FO' TROUBLE SURE!
YOU FOOL! GETTING SCARED. YELLOW?
PO-LICE GONNA' GET US SURE!—GIMME MY DOUGH AND LEMME GO!
LITTLE SCARED FOOL IS CRACKIN' UP!—COPS GONNA' GET HIM SURE!
LIZARD! DON' LOOK AT ME THAT-A-WAY—YOU HEAR ME, MAN? HELP!
DEAD MEN TELL NO TALES—AND I CAN USE ALL THAT CASH!

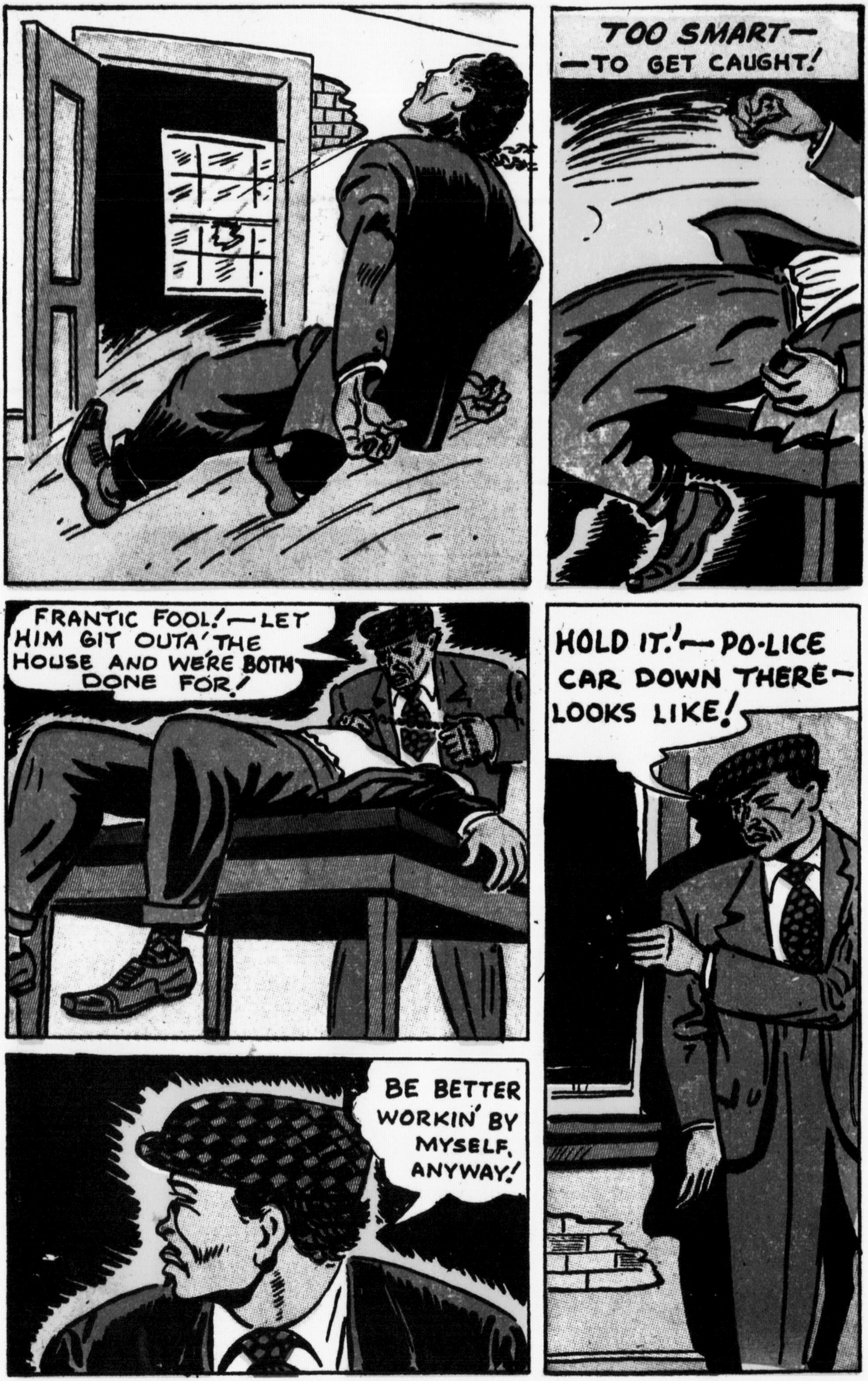

TOO SMART—
—TO GET CAUGHT!
FRANTIC FOOL!—LET HIM GIT OUTA' THE HOUSE AND WE'RE BOTH DONE FOR!
HOLD IT!—PO-LICE CAR DOWN THERE—LOOKS LIKE!
BE BETTER WORKIN' BY MYSELF, ANYWAY!

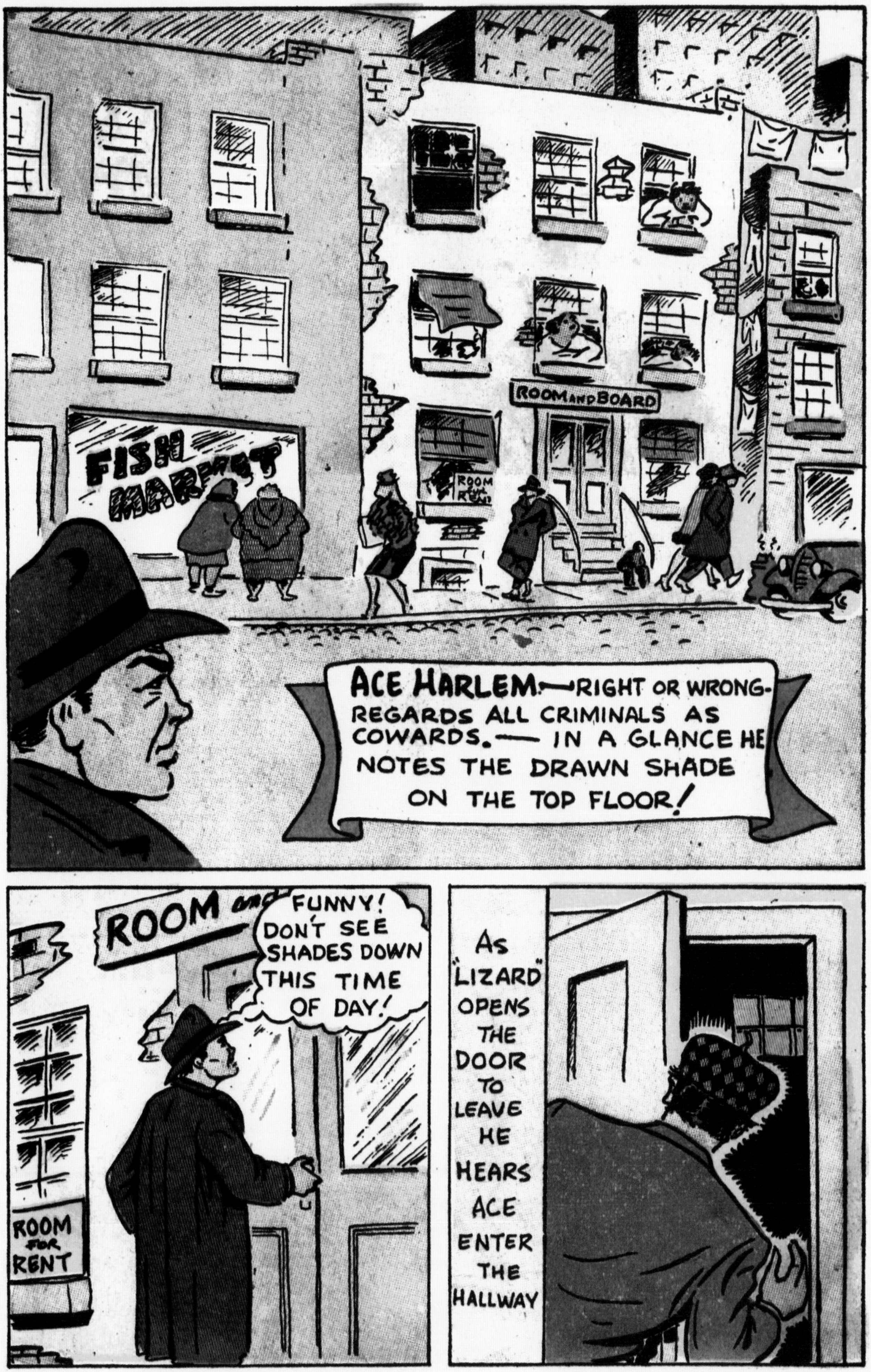
ROOM AND BOARD
FISH MARKET
ROOM FOR RENT
ACE HARLEM—RIGHT OR WRONG-REGARDS ALL CRIMINALS AS COWARDS.— IN A GLANCE HE NOTES THE DRAWN SHADE ON THE TOP FLOOR!
ROOM
FUNNY! DON'T SEE SHADES DOWN THIS TIME OF DAY!
ROOM FOR RENT
AS "LIZARD" OPENS THE DOOR TO LEAVE HE HEARS ACE ENTER THE HALLWAY

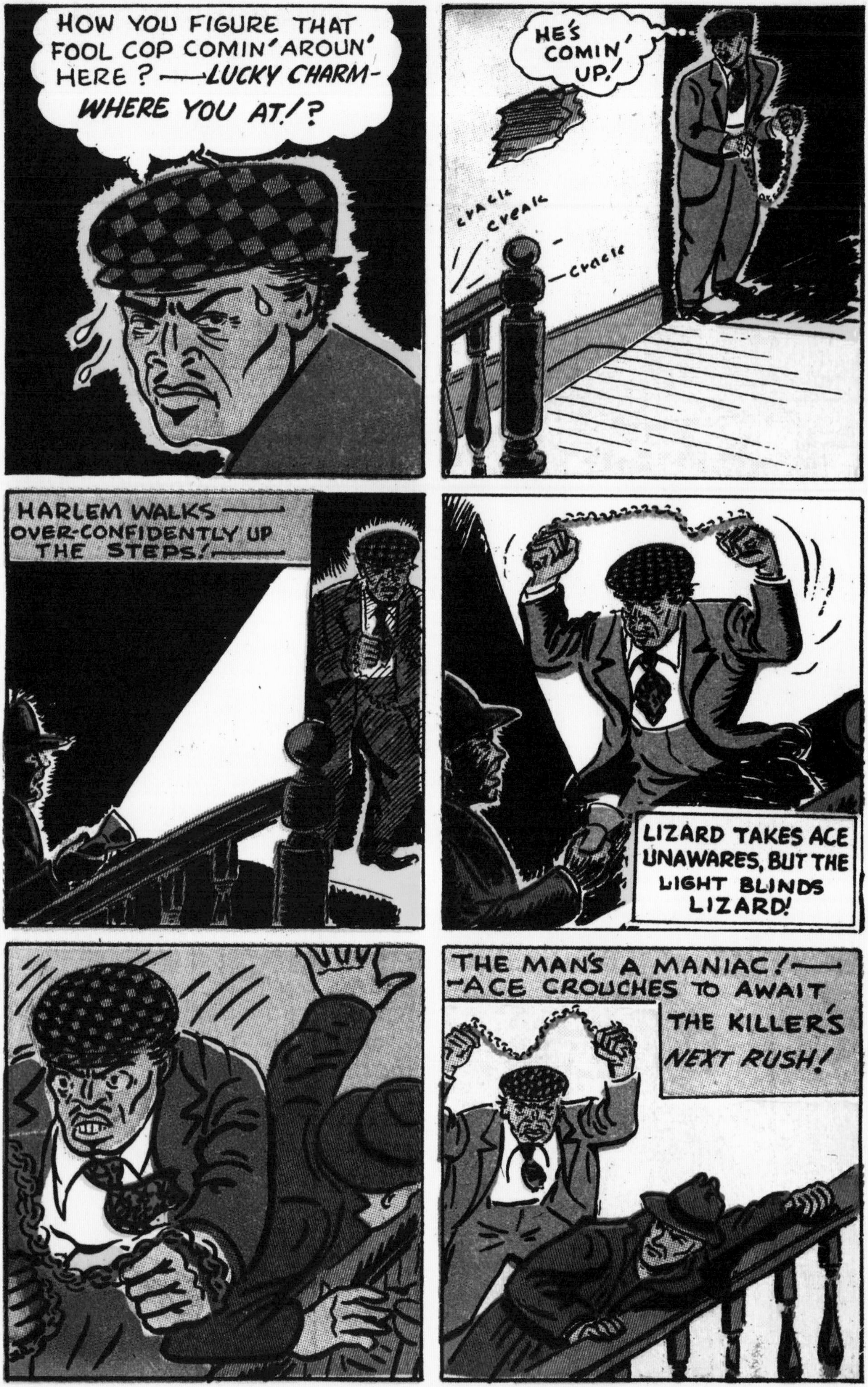
HOW YOU FIGURE THAT FOOL COP COMIN' AROUN' HERE? —LUCKY CHARM- WHERE YOU AT/?
HE'S COMIN' UP!
creak
creak
creak
HARLEM WALKS— OVER-CONFIDENTLY UP THE STEPS!—
LIZARD TAKES ACE UNAWARES, BUT THE LIGHT BLINDS LIZARD!
THE MAN'S A MANIAC!— —ACE CROUCHES TO AWAIT THE KILLER'S NEXT RUSH!

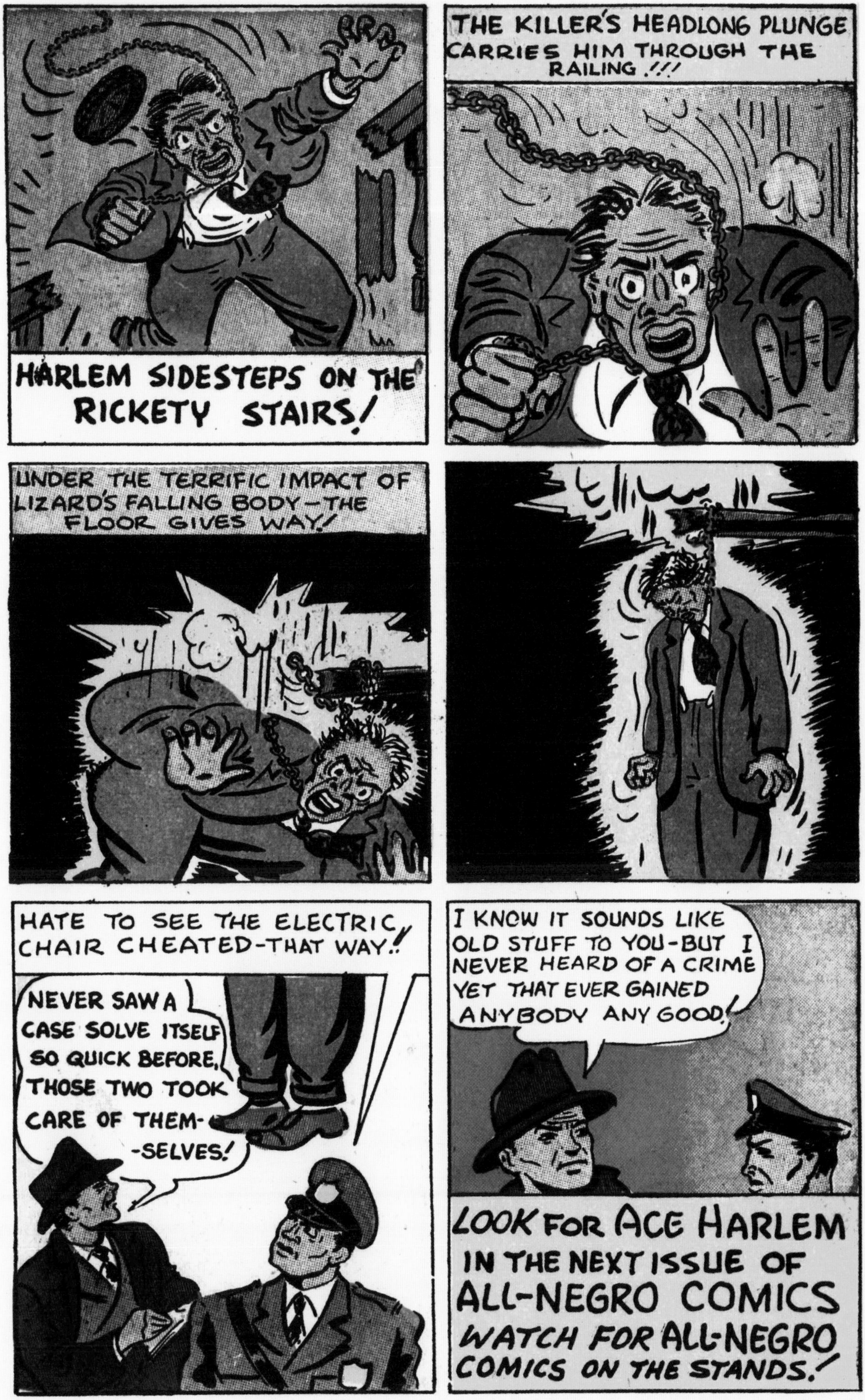
HARLEM SIDESTEPS ON THE RICKETY STAIRS!
THE KILLER'S HEADLONG PLUNGE CARRIES HIM THROUGH THE RAILING!!!
UNDER THE TERRIFIC IMPACT OF LIZARD'S FALLING BODY—THE FLOOR GIVES WAY!
HATE TO SEE THE ELECTRIC CHAIR CHEATED-THAT WAY!
NEVER SAW A CASE SOLVE ITSELF SO QUICK BEFORE, THOSE TWO TOOK CARE OF THEM--SELVES!
I KNOW IT SOUNDS LIKE OLD STUFF TO YOU-BUT I NEVER HEARD OF A CRIME YET THAT EVER GAINED ANYBODY ANY GOOD!
LOOK FOR ACE HARLEM IN THE NEXT ISSUE OF ALL-NEGRO COMICS
WATCH FOR ALL-NEGRO COMICS ON THE STANDS!

CALVIN LEVI MASSEY
Vanguard of the Next Generation

A mere five minute walk separated the offices where Orrin Evans was making his bold venture into comic book publishing, from 34 S. 17th Street—the site of a newly formed art school that was offering returning war veterans an opportunity to learn commercial art skills. Army Air Force veteran Calvin Levi Massey had just turned 20 years old in early 1946, when he was discharged. He was hoping to take advantage of the G.I. Bill's educational allowance in order to pursue his dream of becoming a comic book artist.

John Hussian was a local Philadelphia painter of national renown, who got the idea to open a vocational art school aimed at serviceman looking to utilize the benefits offered by the G.I. Bill. The Hussian School of Art was open to all races, just like the benefits of the G.I. Bill. As was often the case, those benefits were interpreted differently for Blacks than they were for Whites.

One does not require a particularly acute historical sense to surmise that the GI Bill was built on the premise of both legal and de facto inequality; the certainty that blacks would encounter racial restrictions in moving to claim their benefits was surely understood by the political architects of the measure. [Herbold, Hilary, "Never a Level Playing Field: Blacks and the GI Bill," *Journal of Blacks in Higher Education* No. 6, Winter 1994-1995, pp.104-105]

Though Congress granted all soldiers the same benefits theoretically, the segregationist principles of almost every institution of higher learning effectively disbarred a huge proportion of black veterans from earning a college degree. This was particularly true in the northern states where few historically black institutions existed. [Ibid, p.107]

Strict grade requirements, which were often used as a barrier to Black enrollment at many colleges, were not a concern for the vocational program offered at the Hussian School, but for many years, the same couldn't be said for the college where Massey's father worked.

As had many southern Blacks, William N. Massey moved north during the Great Migration of the early 1900s. In his case, this was his childhood home in Maryland. He found work as an elevator operator in Philadelphia before meeting, and eventually marrying, Mildred Bessie Mayo. Bessie, as she preferred to be called, lived with her parents at their home in suburban Morton. This was the same home the newlywed Masseys moved into and where they were living when son Calvin was born on February 10, 1926.

William got a job working in the kitchen at nearby Swarthmore College, a private, co-educational liberal arts school founded by the Quakers and one of the so-called "Little Ivies."

Blacks who had come north did so to flee the Jim Crow laws and lynchings that plagued their lives in the South. They were drawn to the Philadelphia area by the hope of attaining jobs in the booming munitions factories and the newly expanded naval yard. The area in and around Morton was working class and racially integrated, but the continuing influx of Blacks from the South led to increasing tensions with the majority White immigrant population, with whom they competed for jobs and housing. While Morton itself escaped any outbursts of violence, neighboring Chester and nearby Philadelphia weren't as fortunate.

On July 24, 1917, a controversial street confrontation resulted in the death of a White man, William McKinney, and four Blacks being arrested. Friends of McKinney decided to get revenge for his killing and organized a mob that attacked random Blacks with cries of "kill the black snakes!" ["Grim Particulars of Disorderly Street Scene," *Chester Times*, July 26, 1917]. A battle raged for days. Various numbers were reported, but around 360 arrests were made, at least four men were killed, and dozens more were wounded.

Philadelphia would also suffer racial rioting in July of the next year, when a Black woman who had purchased a home in a predominantly White neighborhood shot and wounded a White man who was part of a crowd gathered outside her house demanding that she move. This shooting quickly escalated into roaming mobs of Whites attacking Blacks around the city. But unlike in Chester, where the police responded equally against both races, in Philadelphia they let the Whites attack freely and even joined in. A Black man named Riley Bullock, who had been

arrested, was shot and killed by an officer on the steps of the police station. An outraged delegation of Black clergymen went to the city hall and presented the Mayor of the city with a letter detailing their complaints and accusations:

We desire you to understand that we put the whole blame upon your incompetent police force. But for the sympathy of the police, their hobnobbing with the mob, what has now become the disgrace of Philadelphia would have been nothing more than a petty row. Your police have for a long time winked at disorder. ["Race Riot Area Dry; Detain Policeman in Shooting Probe," *Philadelphia Inquirer*, July 31, 1918]

The rioting subsided after four days. In the end, four people had died, three Whites and one Black. A total of 60 Blacks had been arrested, while only three Whites were jailed. The two police officers charged with the killing of Riley Bullock were tried and found "not guilty" by the jury after a 30 minute deliberation.

At Swarthmore, where William Massey was employed, the school had steadfastly adhered to its tradition of denying Blacks admission. When a highly qualified young Black man applied in 1932, Dean Everett Lee Hunt later stated that "it was decided by a large majority [of the Admissions Committee] that Negro students could not yet be admitted to a coeducational college like Swarthmore. Their admission would raise too many problems and create too many difficulties." [Hunt, Everett Lee, *The Revolt of the Intellectual*, 1963, pp.101-102]

Even though William had risen to the position of assistant chef, as sometimes happens, the Masseys split up in the

"Angel Heart" is Massey's popular depiction of a Black angel. Massey created several versions of the Angel in various media, including this 1987 painting.

mid-1930s. William apparently kept a home at Swarthmore for a while before moving to Detroit.

Meanwhile, Bessie and the four children moved in with a man named Raymond Harris at his small row house at 16 N. MacDade Blvd. in nearby Darby. Even though she and Harris lived as husband and wife, and the children went by the last name of "Harris" for a time, it's not clear whether Bessie and William ever divorced, as she continued to present herself as "Mrs. Bessie Massey."

Bessie took a job as a private maid, as now the family unit had grown to eight people. Although money was tight, her children were encouraged to pursue their interests. Calvin and his siblings all learned to play musical instruments, but it was Calvin's obvious love of drawing that caught his mother's attention. When he was just four years old, she noticed he would hold the Sunday comics section up to the window and try to trace them. Massey would recall years later:

I was fascinated by the figures and the action. My mother told me that they were drawn and she showed me how they were drawn. She provided me with a big sketch pad and I started drawing, copying photographs and making up my own comic strips. [Stanton, Junious, "Cal Massey: Born to be an Artist," *Philadelphia Tribune*, Jan. 2, 1996]

Music was nearly as close to his heart as was art. When he was in his teens, Calvin and his three brothers formed a singing group: The Darby Four Jr. Quartet.

…the Massey boys, a wonderful musical group, ages 10 to 16, Eugene, William, Calvin, and Bernard, under the training of Mr. Wm. McClain, 18 McDade [sic] Boulevard, have shown great ability and will be heard in many future engagements. [Underwood, Jerome, "Darby News," *Philadelphia Tribune*, Feb. 13, 1941]

The brothers sang at the First Baptist Church where their grandfather Edward Mayo was a deacon, while their younger sister Bessie Elinor played the piano. Later on, Massey became a jazz pianist and, at a Philadelphia show, his trio accompanied Aretha Franklin. Once, during a rehearsal, while his brother Bill lead the group, Cal sketched John Coltrane. Musical talent ran in the family: Cal's homonymous cousin was an estimable band leader and jazz trumpet player.

While attending Darby High School, Massey met identical twins who were both artists and both ambidextrous. Calvin was greatly impressed by their talent, and he challenged himself to be as good at drawing as they were.

After completing three years of high school, when Massey turned 18 he joined the Army Air Force Reserves and reported for duty on April 3, 1944. He was first assigned to Kessler Field in Biloxi, Mississippi, where he was trained to be an airplane mechanic. When he was reassigned to the Victorville Army Air Force Base in California, it was dutifully reported in his hometown newspaper. So, too, was his move to Truitt Field in Madison, Wisconsin, where he received additional training as a radio technician. By the time he was discharged in March 1946, Massey had attained the rank of corporal. Soon after, he enrolled at the Hussian School of Art.

At Hussian, Massey's innate talent caught the eye of his instructors immediately. Years later, in an interview for *Alter Ego*, Massey said:

I met a wonderful teacher, Leonard Nelson. He separated me from the rest of the students and gave me split-hair criticism. It got to a point where I was kind of sick of it.

I asked him why he stayed on me and not anybody else. Mr. Nelson said, "You've got a rare gift. So rare, I don't want to see you lose it." [Amash, Jim, "You Have to Earn Your Talent Through Discipline," *Alter Ego* #105, Oct. 2011, pp.55-56]

Nelson knew of what he spoke. He had studied at the Pennsylvania Academy of the Fine Arts, worked on WPA mural projects and, like Massey, served in WWII before he wound up back in Philadelphia teaching art. During the same period he was teaching, Nelson was developing a form of Abstract Expressionist painting that was unique to him. He would become recognized as the leader of the Philadelphia School of artists.

According to Massey, Nelson and school founder John Hussian created a special program for him only, focusing his training on learning life drawing, composition, and illustration. The specialized training paid off. Each year he was at Hussian, Massey was honored with an award as the best draughtsman at the school.

Along with his art studies, Massey also met a kindred spirit at Hussian who played a role in starting him on his career path. Like Massey, Joe Maneely was born and raised in Philadelphia; and like Massey, he dropped out of high school to enlist during WWII. He served in the Navy for three years before returning and enrolling at Hussian. Maneely maintained a studio in the same Middle City Building that housed the school, and worked for the *Philadelphia Bulletin* in their advertising department while taking classes. He made his entry into comic book illustration as a freelancer

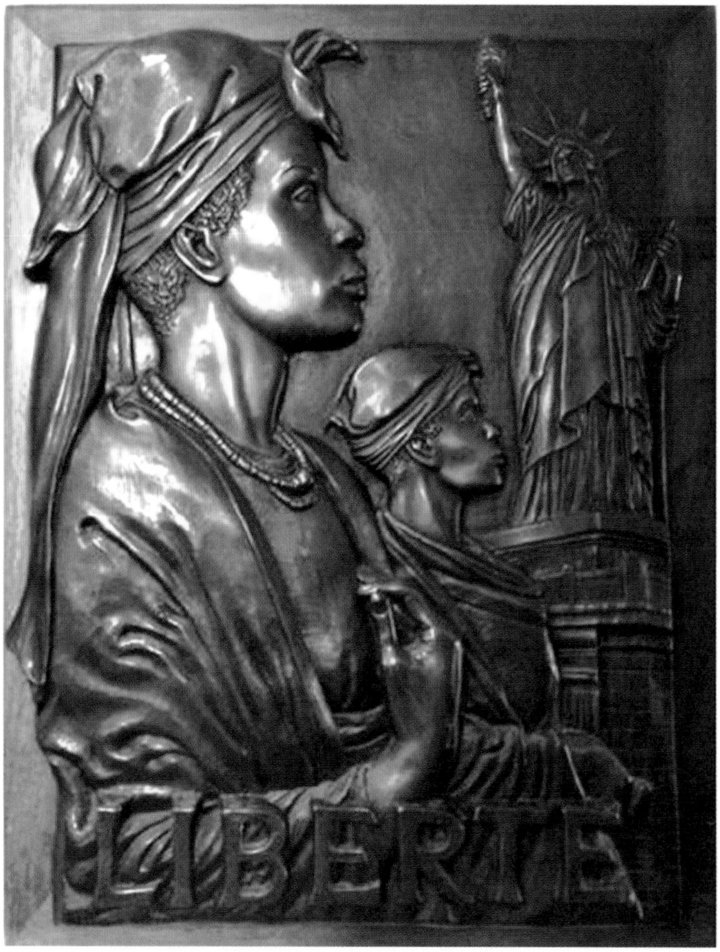
LIBERTE

"French West Indian" is a bas-relief Massey sculpted in 1986. It represents West Indian immigrants arriving at Ellis Island. Fine Arts, Ltd. commissioned 16 distinguished sculptors to create a limited edition series depicting the fourteen major ethnic groups that immigrated into the United States.

in 1948. Having so much in common with Massey and being a step ahead of him by already having entered the comics industry, Maneely became a crucial sounding board for the aspiring professional artist.

While still in school, Massey actually began his career through the chance meeting of an accountant in 1949, who saw examples of his artwork and offered to be his agent. Massey agreed, and the agent made the artist's first sales to Cross Publications.

Cross was a small outfit owned by partners Harold L. Crossman and Edward Bobley. Crossman was a lawyer and a well-connected, very active Democrat Party insider. Bobley was a New York City radio personality, and editor of the company's flagship publication, *Radio Best* magazine. Massey's agent had a connection to the duo and used it to get him drawing assignments.

The timing was perfect. Cross had just decided to enter comic book publishing starting with *Perfect Crime*. Massey was on hand to contribute two stories to the second issue of the title. His solid, polished style fit in nicely alongside the work of seasoned pro Bob Powell. Massey quickly became Cross's most reliable artist, churning out artwork for all three comics in their line, which included *Super Circus* and the humorous *Uncle Milty*, featuring the fictionalized adventures of comedian Milton Berle.

Massey fired his agent when he found out that he was being cheated out of his full pay. Furthermore, he had never had direct contact with Cross, as all of his completed assignments were sent through the mail. So, as Massey was nearing graduation from Hussian in 1950, he and Maneely had a discussion.

We talked off and on about the comic book business, and it was Joe who recommended that I talk to Stan Lee at Timely. [Ibid, p.56]

Massey took Maneely's advice, and with another friend, Samuel R. Joyner, he made a visit to New York City, the center of the comic book industry.

Joyner was yet another young Black artist from Philadelphia hoping to make it in the comic industry. After serving in the Navy during WWII, he studied at the Philadelphia Museum School of Industrial Art. He had made a few sales to local newspapers when he and Massey decided to make their trip. Joyner wrote to the author:

I went to New York City with my portfolio of cartoons and advertising spot drawings. As a beginning cartoonist, I was encouraged to talk to other colored illustrators for information about breaking into this lucrative field.

I was given the names and studio address[es] of a few African-American professionals. Most worked in Manhattan. E.C. Stoner, Matt Baker, Ted Shearer, Chas. Allen, Mel Bolden...etc.

Cal [Massey] and I visited Matt Baker in his New York studio... Matt showed us several pages of comic book art, gave us tips on how to approach assignments. [Samuel Joyner letter to the author, Apr. 21, 2004]

Massey recalled this same meeting with Baker in a bit more detail:

I asked the editor [St. John editor, Marion McDermott] *if there were other black artists in the business, and she told me about Matt Baker. She called him at home and asked if he would see me.* [Amash 2011, op. cit. p.57]

It was, in fact, St. John Publishing and McDermott that published Massey's very first comic book artwork. It appeared in a story entitled "Hijacker of Hearts," in *Teen-Age Diary Secrets* #8 (Feb. 1950). That issue, as with many other St. John romance comics, contained artwork by Baker. He was already an established star in the comic book industry, and Massey jumped at the opportunity to meet him.

Matt lived in a nice section of Brooklyn. Matt and [his brother] *John were both working, and since John was closest to the door when I knocked, he answered.*

Matt was penciling a story, and I was amazed at his ability. He spent quite a bit of time with me that day, discussing brushes, pens, how to put together reference files, other companies I could get work from, and basically talking to me about the pros and cons of the business.

He asked about my work, and I told him I had drawn 'Steve Duncan' for Cross, and that I had just done my first job for St. John, which was a romance story. I told Matt I was having trouble drawing pretty women, and he gave me pointers on how to do that. [Ibid.]

Massey completed several assignments for St. John, but most of his work would come from another publisher, the one Maneely had suggested to him back at Hussian. Speaking about Timely Comics, Massey said:

I knew it as Magazine Management. I walked into the room and Stan Lee said, "Massey's in the cold, cold ground." I sat down, and he said, "Messy Massey." Then I got up and started to leave, when Stan asked me where I was going. I said, "I thought New York had grown past this sort of thing. Have a nice day." Then Stan said, "Massey, get your ass back here. How many stories can you turn out a month?" Of course, after that, he could say anything to me. [Amash 2011, op. cit. p.58]

Massey had immediately recognized Lee's reference to the old Stephen Foster song, "Massa's in de Cold Ground." Foster's lyrics for this minstrel tune were written in 1852, and were unapologetically racist:

Down in de cornfield
Hear dat mournful sound
All de darkeys am a-weeping
Massa's in de cold, cold ground

That Lee felt comfortable saying it to Massey, and that Massey was so willing to forgive this White stranger's insensitivity, is testament to the prevailing interpersonal racial dynamics of the era. That said, it should also be noted that Lee and Timely employed not only Massey, but other Black artists, such as Baker, Warren Broderick, and Alfonso Greene. That was more than any other publisher. In addition, Stan Lee was a fierce advocate against bigotry and racism both in the comic books and public pronouncements.

Despite the fact that the artist continued living in Philadelphia and had to send his completed assignments back via bonded messenger, Lee kept Massey busy at Timely on such titles as *Spellbound, Marines In War,* and *Navy Tales*. Massey once told an interviewer that "he drew everything from science fiction tales to so many war stories 'that I got battle-fatigued.'" [Pompilio, Natalie, "Artist Leaping into Olympic Spotlight," *Philadelphia Inquirer,* Feb.

12, 1996, p.61]

Though the work was welcome, there were always deadlines to meet, which necessitated Massey getting an assist now and then. Samuel Joyner wrote:

Massey and I worked in the same downtown art/illustration studio in the 1950s. When Cal was struggling to meet deadlines on some of his comic book pages, he would slip me a few greenbacks to ink in some of the backgrounds and balloon lettering. [Joyner 2004, op. cit.]

Despite his personal success in the comics field, Massey was prone to the same criticism that was being leveled at all in the industry by outsiders. He had begun his career in the late 1940s, just about the time that Dr. Fredric Wertham was gaining publicity for his virulent opposition to crime and horror comics. His crusade against such comics was followed widely in the news, and the public took notice. Concerned citizens of every race took Wertham's charges seriously. Blacks in particular had reason to respect his words, as Wertham had founded the Lafargue Clinic in Harlem. The clinic worked with troubled youths in the neighborhood who otherwise had no access to mental health facilities. As one of Wertham's strongest complaints was that comics bred racial prejudice, Black comic book artists such as Massey, Hollingsworth, Broderick, and others were especially burdened by the criticism. This led one Black artist, Bill Curry, to address his situation in a newspaper editorial:

The entire comic book industry has but one thought at all times, "Give the public what it wants." Remember it sets the trend. Being a comic book cartoonist for more than four years, I have heard those words a countless number of times. The writers for the comics are, I believe, mostly to blame for any racial hatred that comics may incite, or any story that leads to a child becoming maladjusted. The artist is hired, paid, and wins recognition according to the realistic quality of his illustrations.

Editors sometimes destroy good drawing with these words, "Put more sex appeal into that girl." At this point the artist comes up with a drawing that the pubic calls "vulgar."

So, when a child has a dime to spend for a comic book, and he is faced with a thousand of them, he is going to buy the book that yells, "Hey kid, look at me!" It's the picture that conveys the message. The artist must draw or starve.

The artist all to[o] often is the victim of the public for whom he draws. His dilemma is sacrifice art with integrity for money's sake or refuse to bow to the pressure outlined above and starve. [Curry, Bill, "An Artist's Dilemma," *New York Amsterdam News,* May 1, 1954]

Massey's thoughts reflected those of Curry in this interview:

As a comic book illustrator, I drew blood and guts all the time, but you got to do what you got to do. [Pompilio 1996, op. cit. p.61]

Massey's comic book career ended circa late 1956, as the cumulative effect of waning sales and the collapse of a large magazine distributor led Timely to stop contracting new artwork for their comics. He moved on.

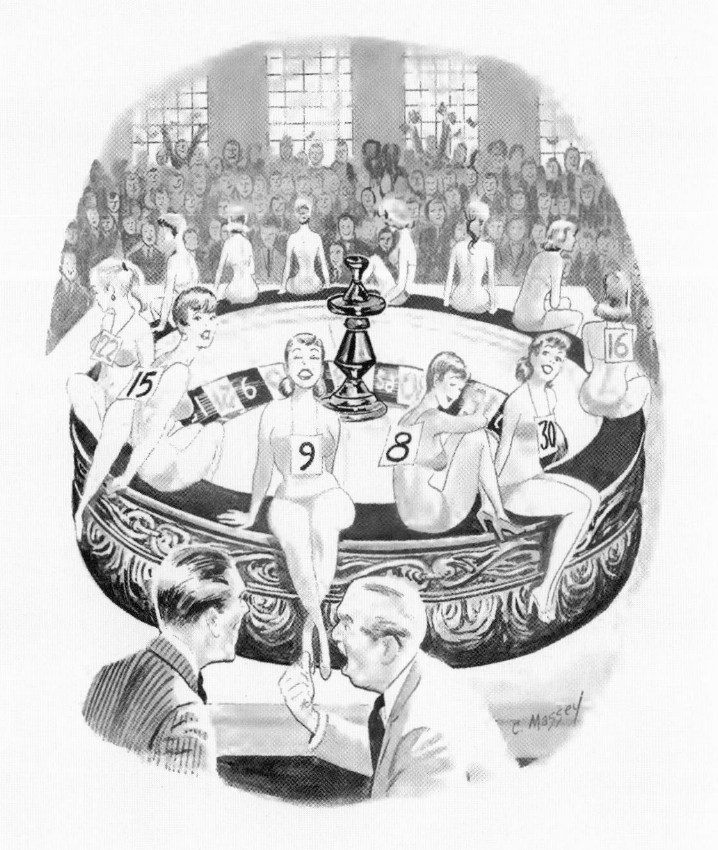
15
9
8
30
16
C. Massey
"Sure it's packing them in—But is it legal?"

Full-page cartoon by Massey drawn for James Warren's first publishing effort, a Philadelphia-based men's magazine. *After Hours* vol. 1 #3, 1957.

Soon after, Massey found a local outlet for his artwork. It was a small Philadelphia publisher named Jay Publishing Co., run by a young advertising man who sought to enter the industry via the path blazed by Hugh Hefner and his wildly successful *Playboy*.

James Warren Taubman borrowed $9,000 to put together and publish his version of *Playboy* which he titled *After Hours*. Its first issue hit the stands in February 1957 and was not a very good imitation. Massey sold the magazine a number of risqué cartoons, revealing a side of his work previously unseen. The magazine only lasted three issues before local authorities deemed it obscene and took Taubman, now simply going by the name "James Warren," to court. The charges were ultimately dropped, and Warren went on to form another publishing company bearing his name that would find success in the 1960s by publishing magazine-sized, adult-oriented horror comics.

Massey had begun developing his fine art skills simultaneous to pursuing his comics career, and was showing his work in local exhibitions. In early 1949, he had also become a member of Les Beaux Arts Club, a cultural society. This group of writers, musicians, artists, poets, and dancers afforded Massey access to White Philadelphians who otherwise may never have known the range of his talents.

Massey befriended, and would often find himself presenting his work alongside another young Black artist named Benjamin Britt, who attended Hussian at the same time and would go on to be an internationally renowned Surrealist painter. Coverage of one of the club's activities in October 1949 noted the completion of Massey's first comic book assignment. At another gathering, compliments were made about a showing of his original comic book artwork and piano playing.

During the program intermissions, Calvin Massey, who exhibited his first edition of cartoons accepted by a New York concern, played popular music… ["Les Beaux Arts Entertain as Quarterly Open House," *Philadelphia Tribune*, Jan. 10, 1950]

It was the income earned from commercial work, though, that allowed Massey the freedom to pursue fine art interests. In the early 1960s, one of his clients was the Philadelphia-based car parts firm Pep Boys. Massey supplied the artwork for their colorful catalogs.

In 1964, Massey provided the drawings for the *LBJ Coloring Book*, an election year novelty hoping to cash in on the short-lived political coloring book fad of the early 1960s. Written by Norman Miller and a product of Philadelphia's Gem Publishing Co., the book's satirical humor got low marks from some, with one reviewer commenting that the book was "about as welcome as a bastard at a family reunion." [Petersen, Clarence, "Hatchets with Soft Cover Sheaths," *Chicago Tribune*, Oct. 4, 1964]

Thankfully for Massey, his career wasn't dependent upon the success of that book. That same year, a Philadelphia entrepreneur named Joseph M. Segel founded a company he dubbed The National Commemorative Society. The company, concerned with the minting of coin-like medals to memorialize historic American events and people, hired Massey as a designer. As such, he was tasked with designing their first medallion honoring the recently deceased war hero, General of the Army Douglas McArthur.

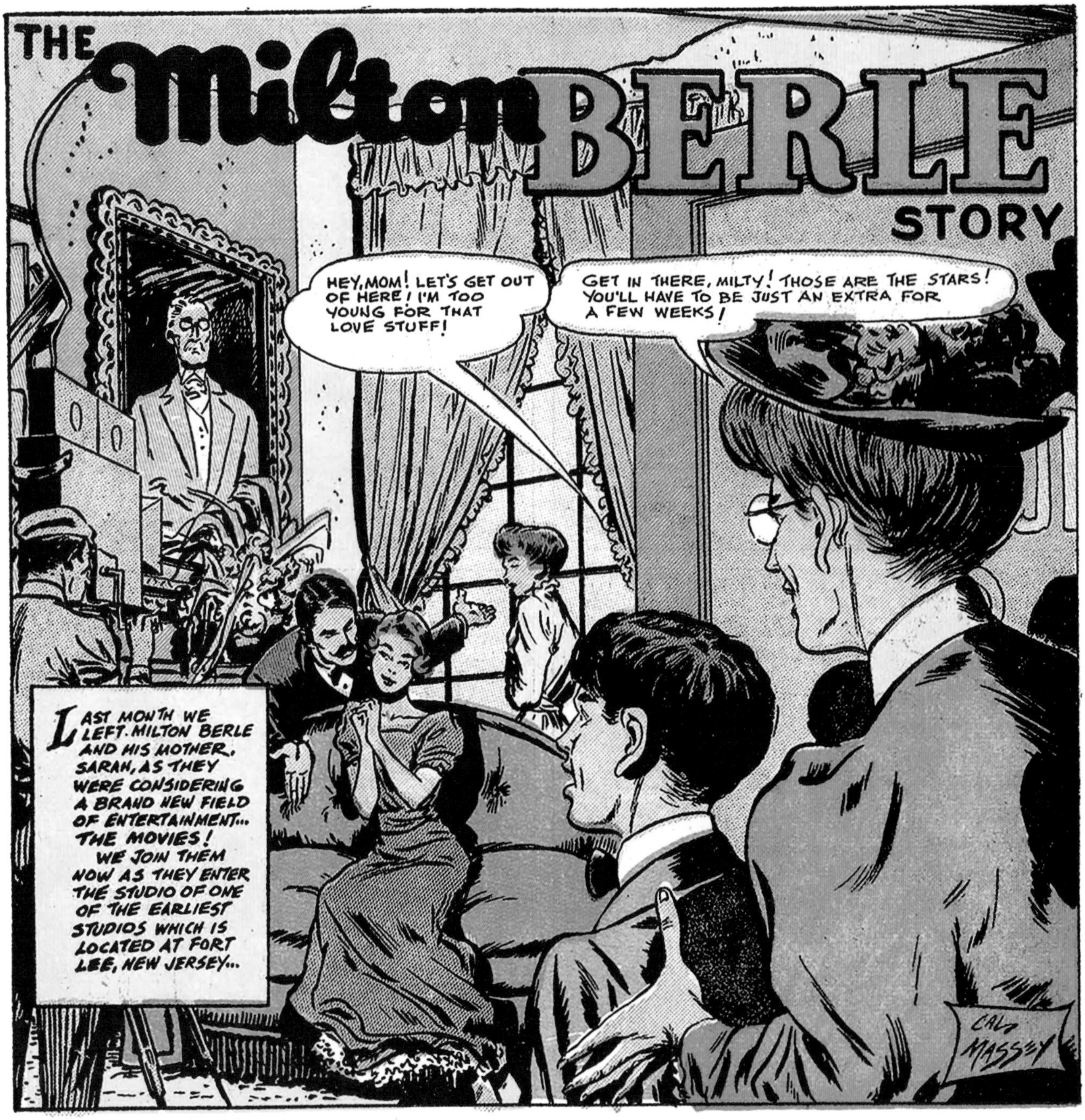
THE Milton BERLE STORY
HEY, MOM! LET'S GET OUT OF HERE! I'M TOO YOUNG FOR THAT LOVE STUFF!
GET IN THERE, MILTY! THOSE ARE THE STARS! YOU'LL HAVE TO BE JUST AN EXTRA FOR A FEW WEEKS!
LAST MONTH WE LEFT MILTON BERLE AND HIS MOTHER, SARAH, AS THEY WERE CONSIDERING A BRAND NEW FIELD OF ENTERTAINMENT... THE MOVIES! WE JOIN THEM NOW AS THEY ENTER THE STUDIO OF ONE OF THE EARLIEST STUDIOS WHICH IS LOCATED AT FORT LEE, NEW JERSEY...
CAL MASSEY

After some time, Massey learned how to sculpt, increasing his value to the newly rechristened Franklin Mint, but not without some resistance from his co-workers.

Being the only African-American sculptor and designer, there was some prejudice there when I went on staff, because the rumor had spread that I designed the very first coin for the Franklin Mint. They didn't want to believe that.

I got pretty mad about it. We had this big room, 30 artists in a booth. I stood up and said, "Go to the library and take [out] the first annual report and turn to page ten." Then it got dead quiet. [Amash 2011, op. cit. p.63]

The Franklin Mint job would last until 1976, during which time Massey designed over 200 commemorative medals. All the while, Massey was taking on freelance work. In the mid-1960s, he illustrated several Christian faith-based children's books for local publishers. By 1970, he provided the drawings for several more young adult books, such as *What Harry Found When He Lost Archie*, featuring Blacks as the main characters. At the same time, appreciation for Massey's skills as a painter and sculptor was growing.

A series of prints, under the collective title "African Women in Perspective," was issued in 1983, using images from three Massey paintings. The most famous of these, "The Ashanti Woman," featured a proud Black woman in profile. Massey used his wife, Iris, as his model. Massey said:

I paint because I have to; it's my way of communicating with the world around me. [Russ, Valerie, "Cal Massey, Prolific Artist, Sculptor, Designer of Valley Forge Monument and

[Above] The opening panel of "The Milton Berle Story." *Uncle Milty* #2, February 1951, Victoria Publications.

[Right] A print from the series "African Women in Prospective," 1983. Massey's model for this figure was his wife, Iris.

Comic Book Illustrator, Dies at 93," *Philadelphia Enquirer*, June 18, 2019]

Years later, Iris Massey [née Williams] recounted meeting her future husband, whom she wed in 1960, at a party and in an unexpected way:

My date told me he had just met the most interesting person who was playing music. So, I went over to talk to him and that's how we met. [Ibid.]

Some of Massey's best-known work came from a series of calendars that featured historical Black figures. He illustrated these for Beach Advertising, and they were published throughout the 1970s.

His sculpting talent came to the fore with his enduring "French West Indian" bas-relief completed in 1986 and the "Patriots of African Descent Monument" at Valley Forge, dedicated on June 19, 1993.

Exhibitions of Massey's work became a common occurrence as his fame grew. Perhaps one of his most satisfying moments came with the showings he gave in the mid-1980s at Swarthmore College, the same school where his father worked in the kitchens and which denied Blacks admission until 1943.

The Philadelphia Enquirer reported in his obituary that Massey was hired by the Olympic Committee:

...the Olympic Committee hired him to be one of 13 artists to design commemorative medals for the 1996 Summer Games. His high jump design, featuring a young black woman with knees bent, was the only commemorative medal for that Olympics to depict a black person. [Ibid.]

Massey's long life allowed him to not only enjoy the fruits of his labor, but to be recognized for the wide range of his talents. Alone among the Black comic artists to begin their careers in the 1940s, he lived long enough to be able to relate his journey out of obscurity, out of invisibility, to become a guiding light to those who would follow. In his obituary, Iris, Massey's wife of 56 years, said:

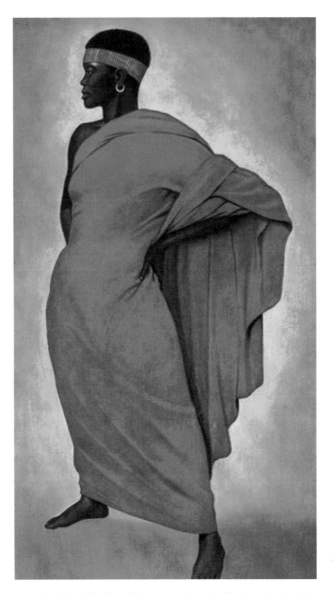

Calvin led a fabulous life. He was the only black artist that has both a statue that he designed in Valley Forge Park and at Ellis Island, at the Statue of Liberty. He designed Olympic medals. There were just so many fabulous things he did. It would have been unusual for anybody to have done in a lifetime. [Ibid.]

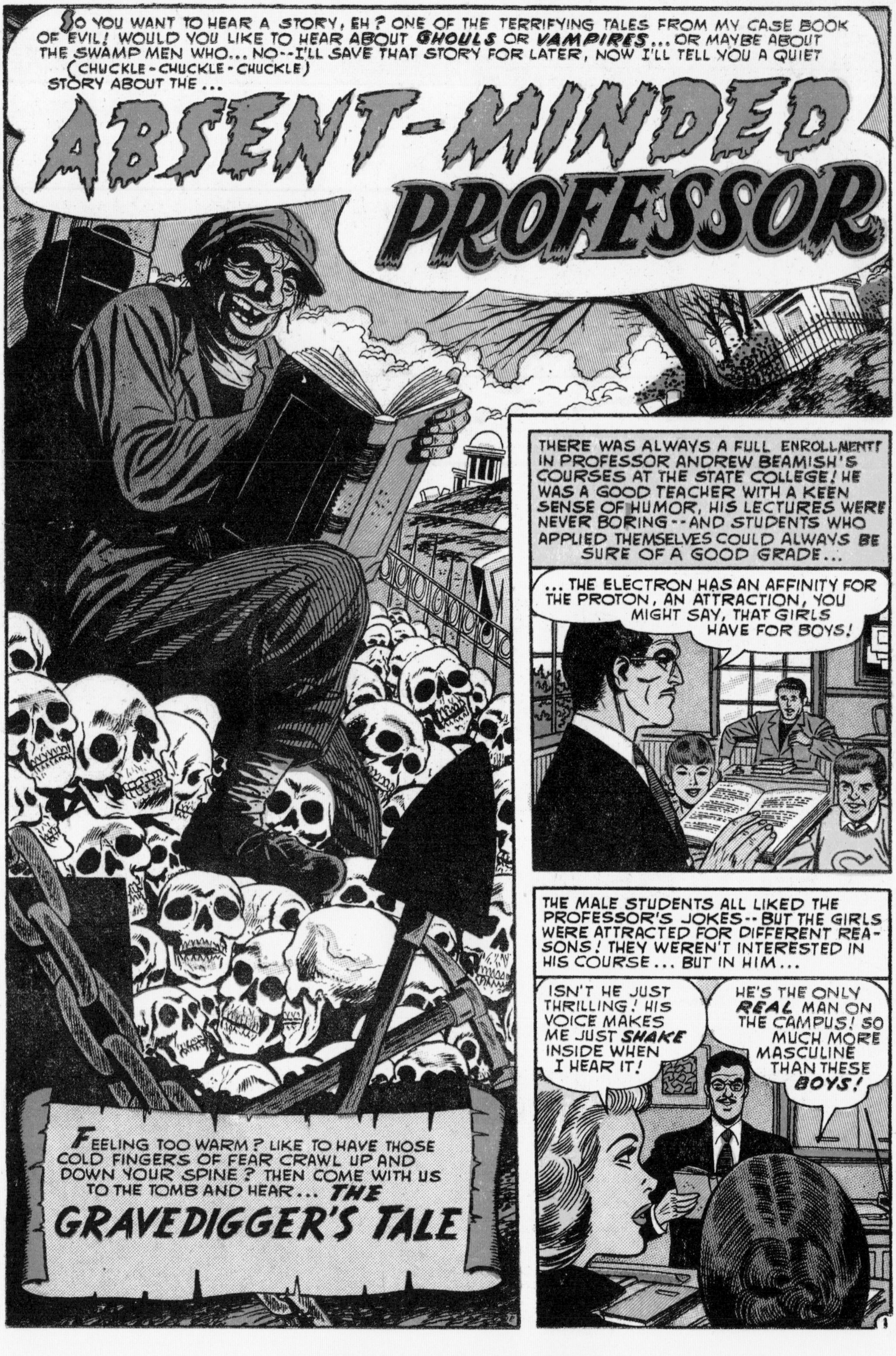
SO YOU WANT TO HEAR A STORY, EH? ONE OF THE TERRIFYING TALES FROM MY CASE BOOK OF EVIL! WOULD YOU LIKE TO HEAR ABOUT GHOULS OR VAMPIRES... OR MAYBE ABOUT THE SWAMP MEN WHO... NO--I'LL SAVE THAT STORY FOR LATER, NOW I'LL TELL YOU A QUIET (CHUCKLE-CHUCKLE-CHUCKLE) STORY ABOUT THE...
ABSENT-MINDED PROFESSOR
FEELING TOO WARM? LIKE TO HAVE THOSE COLD FINGERS OF FEAR CRAWL UP AND DOWN YOUR SPINE? THEN COME WITH US TO THE TOMB AND HEAR... THE GRAVEDIGGER'S TALE
THERE WAS ALWAYS A FULL ENROLLMENT IN PROFESSOR ANDREW BEAMISH'S COURSES AT THE STATE COLLEGE! HE WAS A GOOD TEACHER WITH A KEEN SENSE OF HUMOR, HIS LECTURES WERE NEVER BORING--AND STUDENTS WHO APPLIED THEMSELVES COULD ALWAYS BE SURE OF A GOOD GRADE...
...THE ELECTRON HAS AN AFFINITY FOR THE PROTON, AN ATTRACTION, YOU MIGHT SAY, THAT GIRLS HAVE FOR BOYS!
THE MALE STUDENTS ALL LIKED THE PROFESSOR'S JOKES--BUT THE GIRLS WERE ATTRACTED FOR DIFFERENT REASONS! THEY WEREN'T INTERESTED IN HIS COURSE... BUT IN HIM...
ISN'T HE JUST THRILLING! HIS VOICE MAKES ME JUST SHAKE INSIDE WHEN I HEAR IT!
HE'S THE ONLY REAL MAN ON THE CAMPUS! SO MUCH MORE MASCULINE THAN THESE BOYS!

Horror from The Tomb #1, September 1954; Premiere Magazines.

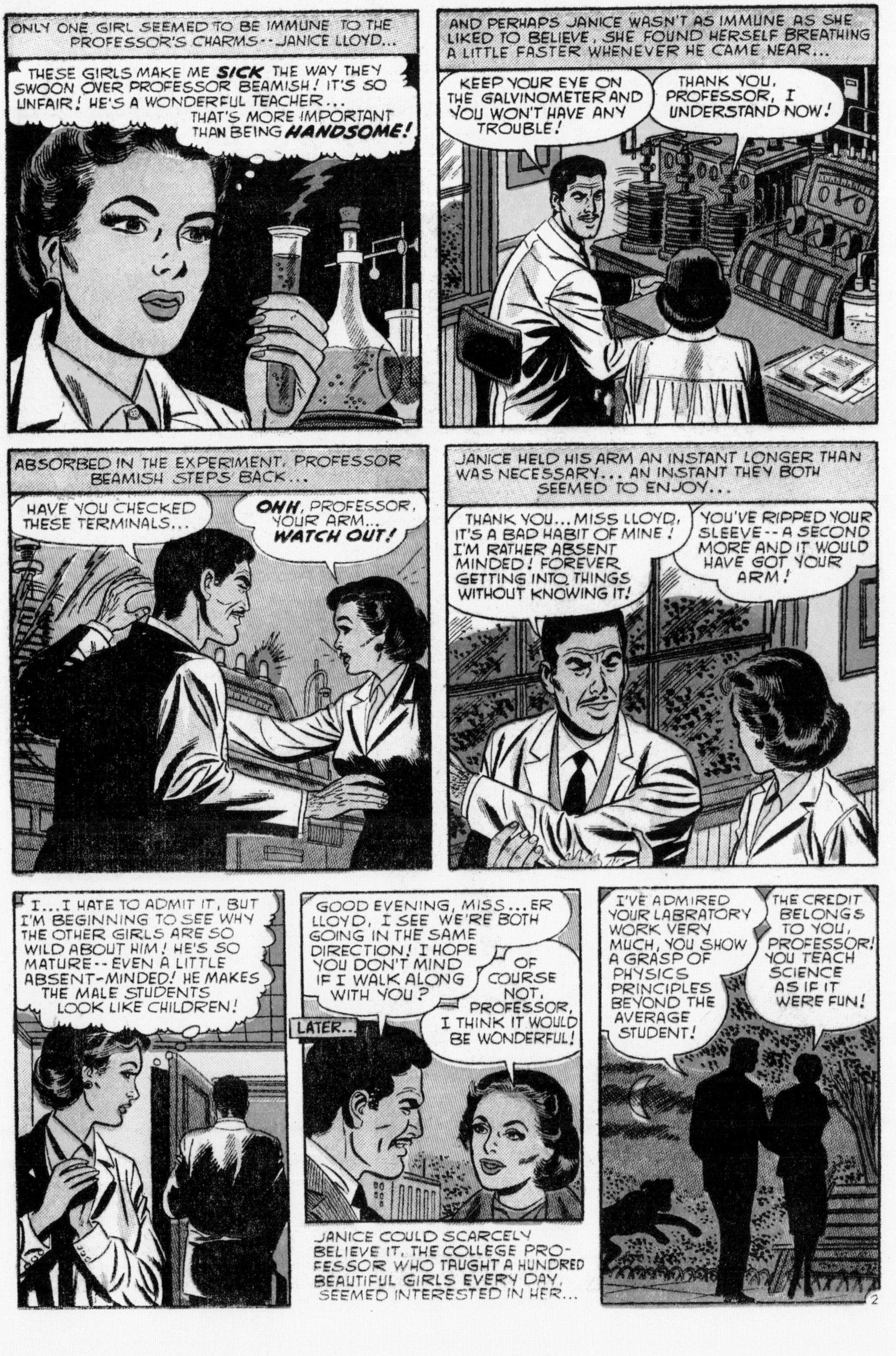
ONLY ONE GIRL SEEMED TO BE IMMUNE TO THE PROFESSOR'S CHARMS--JANICE LLOYD...
THESE GIRLS MAKE ME SICK THE WAY THEY SWOON OVER PROFESSOR BEAMISH! IT'S SO UNFAIR! HE'S A WONDERFUL TEACHER... THAT'S MORE IMPORTANT THAN BEING HANDSOME!
AND PERHAPS JANICE WASN'T AS IMMUNE AS SHE LIKED TO BELIEVE. SHE FOUND HERSELF BREATHING A LITTLE FASTER WHENEVER HE CAME NEAR...
KEEP YOUR EYE ON THE GALVINOMETER AND YOU WON'T HAVE ANY TROUBLE!
THANK YOU, PROFESSOR, I UNDERSTAND NOW!
ABSORBED IN THE EXPERIMENT, PROFESSOR BEAMISH STEPS BACK...
HAVE YOU CHECKED THESE TERMINALS...
OHH, PROFESSOR, YOUR ARM... WATCH OUT!
JANICE HELD HIS ARM AN INSTANT LONGER THAN WAS NECESSARY... AN INSTANT THEY BOTH SEEMED TO ENJOY...
THANK YOU... MISS LLOYD, IT'S A BAD HABIT OF MINE! I'M RATHER ABSENT MINDED! FOREVER GETTING INTO THINGS WITHOUT KNOWING IT!
YOU'VE RIPPED YOUR SLEEVE--A SECOND MORE AND IT WOULD HAVE GOT YOUR ARM!
I... I HATE TO ADMIT IT, BUT I'M BEGINNING TO SEE WHY THE OTHER GIRLS ARE SO WILD ABOUT HIM! HE'S SO MATURE--EVEN A LITTLE ABSENT-MINDED! HE MAKES THE MALE STUDENTS LOOK LIKE CHILDREN!
LATER...
GOOD EVENING, MISS... ER LLOYD, I SEE WE'RE BOTH GOING IN THE SAME DIRECTION! I HOPE YOU DON'T MIND IF I WALK ALONG WITH YOU?
OF COURSE NOT, PROFESSOR, I THINK IT WOULD BE WONDERFUL!
JANICE COULD SCARCELY BELIEVE IT. THE COLLEGE PROFESSOR WHO TAUGHT A HUNDRED BEAUTIFUL GIRLS EVERY DAY, SEEMED INTERESTED IN HER...
I'VE ADMIRED YOUR LABRATORY WORK VERY MUCH, YOU SHOW A GRASP OF PHYSICS PRINCIPLES BEYOND THE AVERAGE STUDENT!
THE CREDIT BELONGS TO YOU, PROFESSOR! YOU TEACH SCIENCE AS IF IT WERE FUN!
2

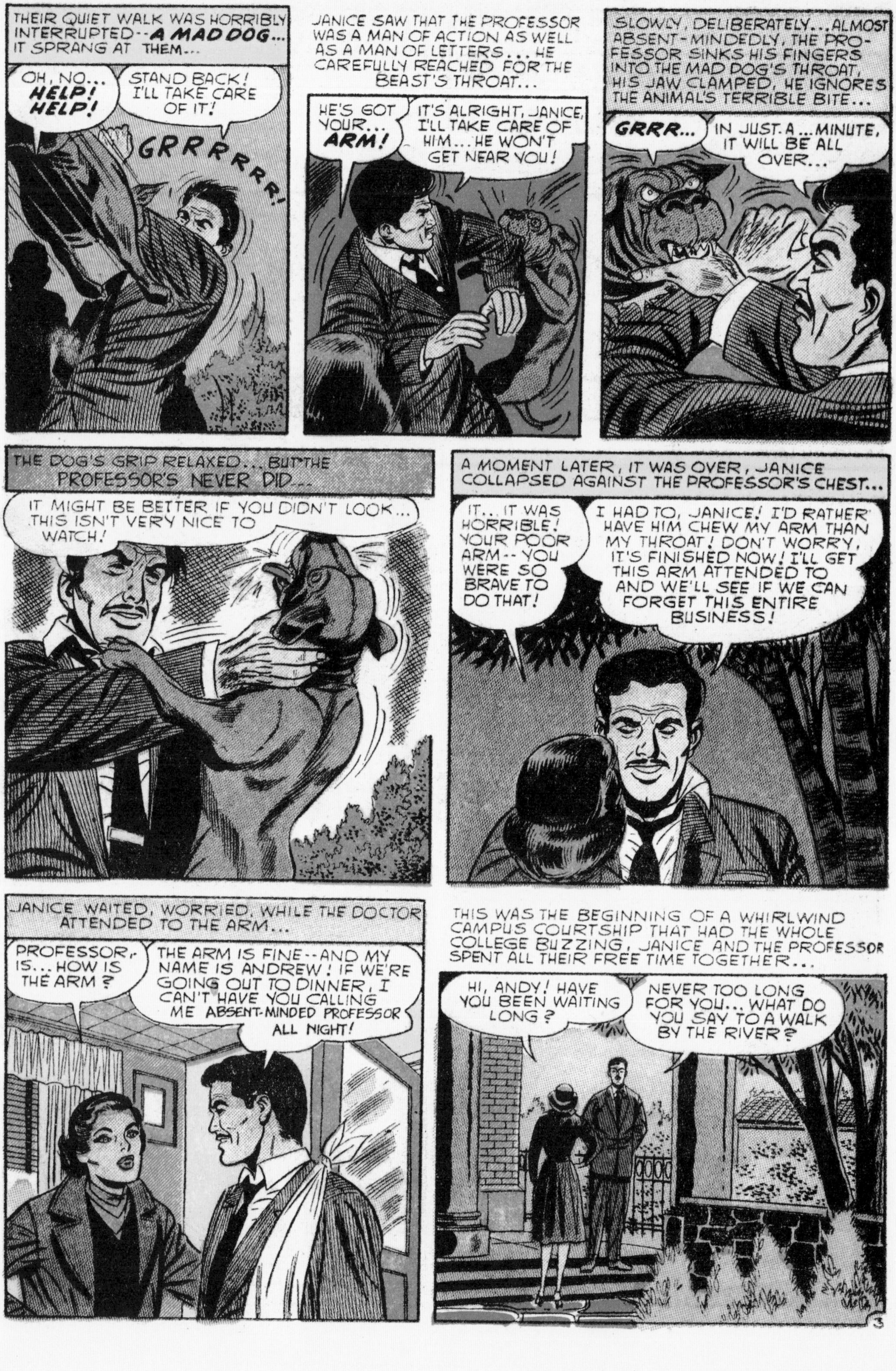
THEIR QUIET WALK WAS HORRIBLY INTERRUPTED--A MAD DOG... IT SPRANG AT THEM...
OH, NO... HELP! HELP!
STAND BACK! I'LL TAKE CARE OF IT!
GRRRRRRR!
JANICE SAW THAT THE PROFESSOR WAS A MAN OF ACTION AS WELL AS A MAN OF LETTERS... HE CAREFULLY REACHED FOR THE BEAST'S THROAT...
HE'S GOT YOUR... ARM!
IT'S ALRIGHT, JANICE, I'LL TAKE CARE OF HIM... HE WON'T GET NEAR YOU!
SLOWLY, DELIBERATELY... ALMOST ABSENT-MINDEDLY, THE PROFESSOR SINKS HIS FINGERS INTO THE MAD DOG'S THROAT, HIS JAW CLAMPED, HE IGNORES THE ANIMAL'S TERRIBLE BITE...
GRRR...
IN JUST A ... MINUTE, IT WILL BE ALL OVER...
THE DOG'S GRIP RELAXED... BUT THE PROFESSOR'S NEVER DID...
IT MIGHT BE BETTER IF YOU DIDN'T LOOK... THIS ISN'T VERY NICE TO WATCH!
A MOMENT LATER, IT WAS OVER, JANICE COLLAPSED AGAINST THE PROFESSOR'S CHEST...
IT... IT WAS HORRIBLE! YOUR POOR ARM--YOU WERE SO BRAVE TO DO THAT!
I HAD TO, JANICE! I'D RATHER HAVE HIM CHEW MY ARM THAN MY THROAT! DON'T WORRY, IT'S FINISHED NOW! I'LL GET THIS ARM ATTENDED TO AND WE'LL SEE IF WE CAN FORGET THIS ENTIRE BUSINESS!
JANICE WAITED, WORRIED, WHILE THE DOCTOR ATTENDED TO THE ARM...
PROFESSOR, IS... HOW IS THE ARM?
THE ARM IS FINE--AND MY NAME IS ANDREW! IF WE'RE GOING OUT TO DINNER, I CAN'T HAVE YOU CALLING ME ABSENT-MINDED PROFESSOR ALL NIGHT!
THIS WAS THE BEGINNING OF A WHIRLWIND CAMPUS COURTSHIP THAT HAD THE WHOLE COLLEGE BUZZING, JANICE AND THE PROFESSOR SPENT ALL THEIR FREE TIME TOGETHER...
HI, ANDY! HAVE YOU BEEN WAITING LONG?
NEVER TOO LONG FOR YOU... WHAT DO YOU SAY TO A WALK BY THE RIVER?
3

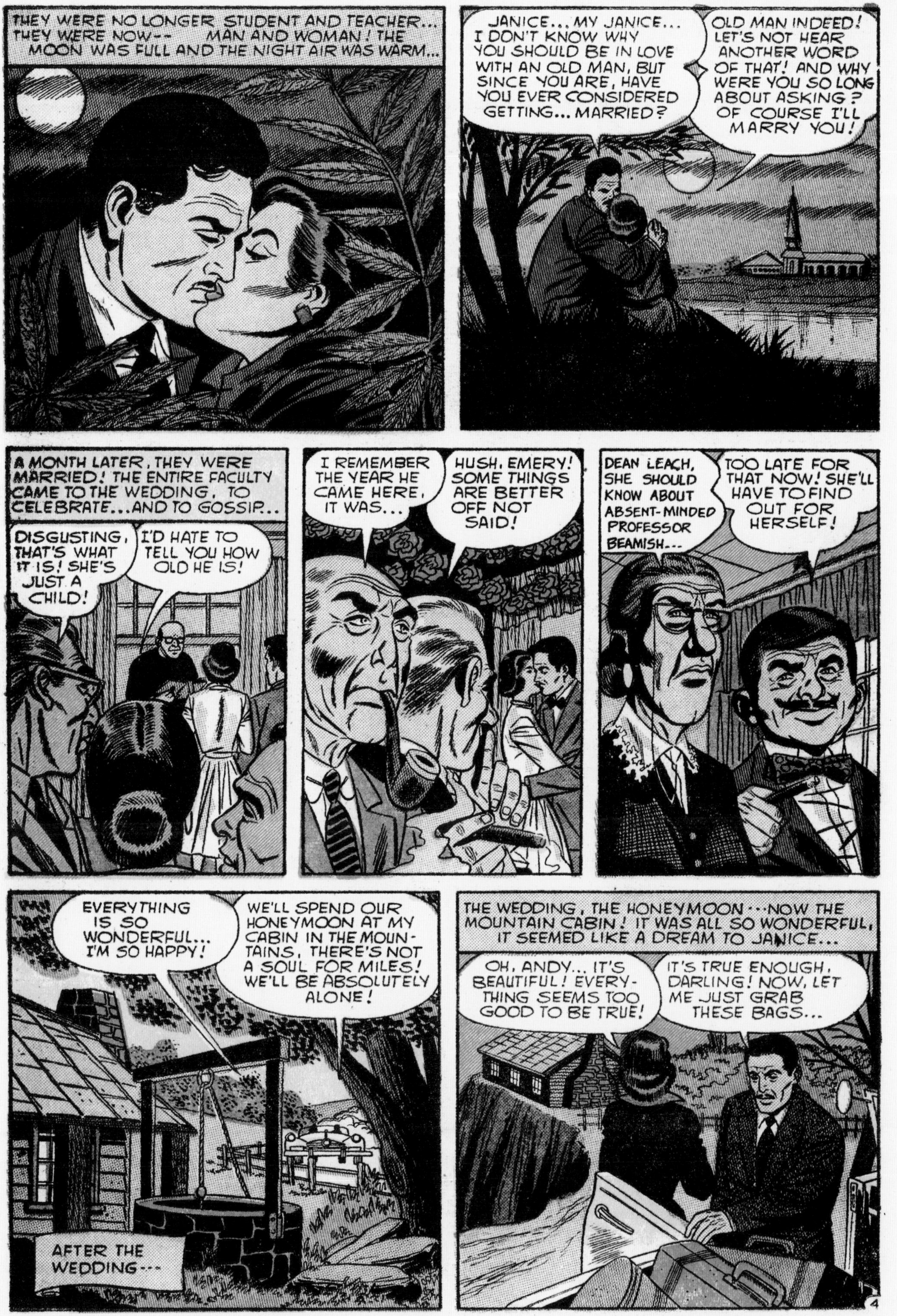

THEY WERE NO LONGER STUDENT AND TEACHER... THEY WERE NOW-- MAN AND WOMAN! THE MOON WAS FULL AND THE NIGHT AIR WAS WARM...
JANICE... MY JANICE... I DON'T KNOW WHY YOU SHOULD BE IN LOVE WITH AN OLD MAN, BUT SINCE YOU ARE, HAVE YOU EVER CONSIDERED GETTING... MARRIED?
OLD MAN INDEED! LET'S NOT HEAR ANOTHER WORD OF THAT! AND WHY WERE YOU SO LONG ABOUT ASKING? OF COURSE I'LL MARRY YOU!
A MONTH LATER, THEY WERE MARRIED! THE ENTIRE FACULTY CAME TO THE WEDDING, TO CELEBRATE...AND TO GOSSIP...
DISGUSTING, THAT'S WHAT IT IS! SHE'S JUST A CHILD!
I'D HATE TO TELL YOU HOW OLD HE IS!
I REMEMBER THE YEAR HE CAME HERE. IT WAS...
HUSH, EMERY! SOME THINGS ARE BETTER OFF NOT SAID!
DEAN LEACH, SHE SHOULD KNOW ABOUT ABSENT-MINDED PROFESSOR BEAMISH...
TOO LATE FOR THAT NOW! SHE'LL HAVE TO FIND OUT FOR HERSELF!
EVERYTHING IS SO WONDERFUL... I'M SO HAPPY!
WE'LL SPEND OUR HONEYMOON AT MY CABIN IN THE MOUNTAINS, THERE'S NOT A SOUL FOR MILES! WE'LL BE ABSOLUTELY ALONE!
AFTER THE WEDDING---
THE WEDDING, THE HONEYMOON ---NOW THE MOUNTAIN CABIN! IT WAS ALL SO WONDERFUL, IT SEEMED LIKE A DREAM TO JANICE...
OH, ANDY... IT'S BEAUTIFUL! EVERYTHING SEEMS TOO GOOD TO BE TRUE!
IT'S TRUE ENOUGH, DARLING! NOW, LET ME JUST GRAB THESE BAGS...
4

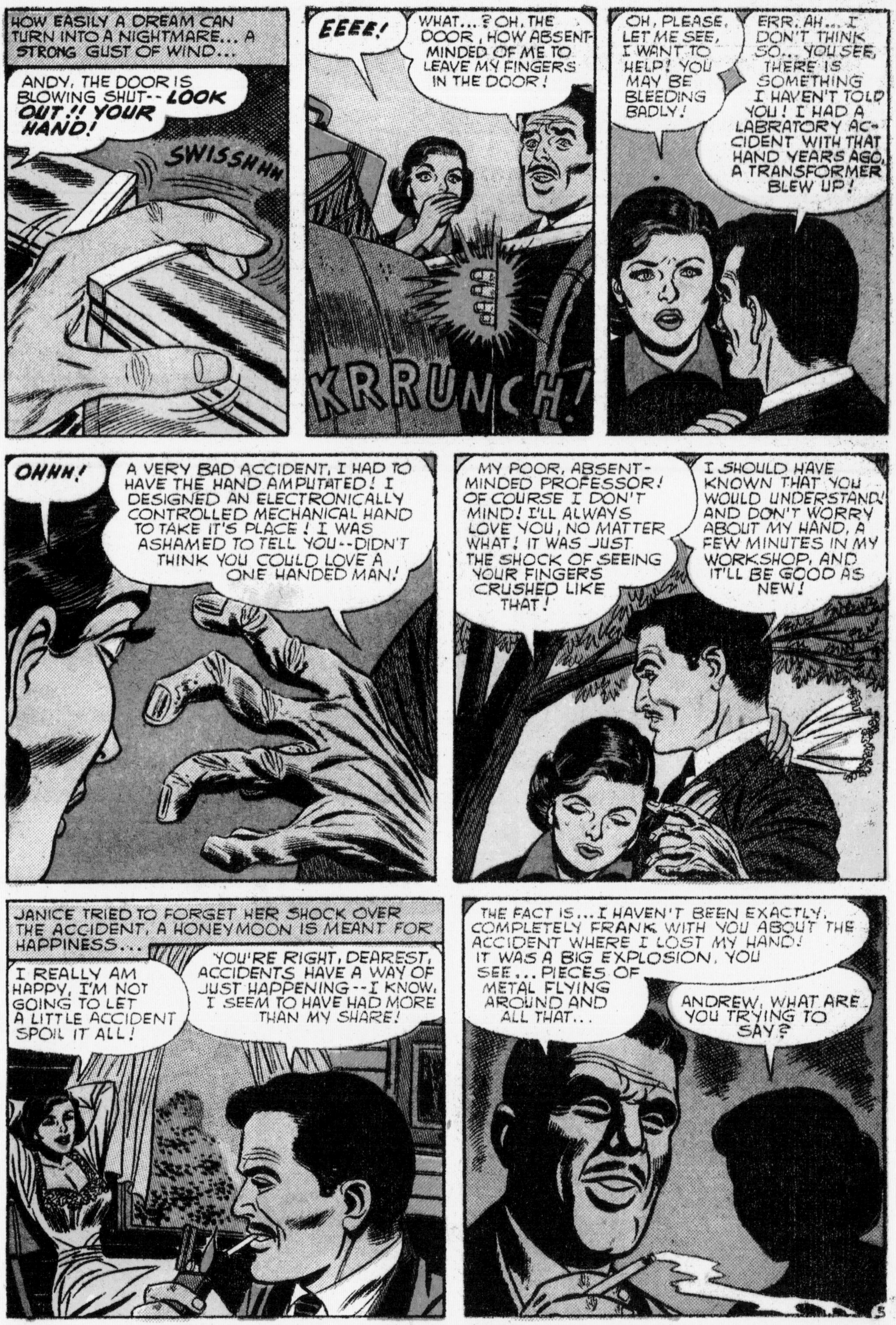
HOW EASILY A DREAM CAN TURN INTO A NIGHTMARE... A STRONG GUST OF WIND...
ANDY, THE DOOR IS BLOWING SHUT-- LOOK OUT!! YOUR HAND!
SWISSHHH
EEEE!
WHAT...? OH, THE DOOR, HOW ABSENT-MINDED OF ME TO LEAVE MY FINGERS IN THE DOOR!
KRRUNCH!
OH, PLEASE, LET ME SEE, I WANT TO HELP! YOU MAY BE BLEEDING BADLY!
ERR, AH... I DON'T THINK SO... YOU SEE, THERE IS SOMETHING I HAVEN'T TOLD YOU! I HAD A LABRATORY ACCIDENT WITH THAT HAND YEARS AGO, A TRANSFORMER BLEW UP!
OHHH!
A VERY BAD ACCIDENT, I HAD TO HAVE THE HAND AMPUTATED! I DESIGNED AN ELECTRONICALLY CONTROLLED MECHANICAL HAND TO TAKE IT'S PLACE! I WAS ASHAMED TO TELL YOU--DIDN'T THINK YOU COULD LOVE A ONE HANDED MAN!
MY POOR, ABSENT-MINDED PROFESSOR! OF COURSE I DON'T MIND! I'LL ALWAYS LOVE YOU, NO MATTER WHAT! IT WAS JUST THE SHOCK OF SEEING YOUR FINGERS CRUSHED LIKE THAT!
I SHOULD HAVE KNOWN THAT YOU WOULD UNDERSTAND! AND DON'T WORRY ABOUT MY HAND, A FEW MINUTES IN MY WORKSHOP, AND IT'LL BE GOOD AS NEW!
JANICE TRIED TO FORGET HER SHOCK OVER THE ACCIDENT, A HONEYMOON IS MEANT FOR HAPPINESS...
I REALLY AM HAPPY, I'M NOT GOING TO LET A LITTLE ACCIDENT SPOIL IT ALL!
YOU'RE RIGHT, DEAREST, ACCIDENTS HAVE A WAY OF JUST HAPPENING--I KNOW, I SEEM TO HAVE HAD MORE THAN MY SHARE!
THE FACT IS... I HAVEN'T BEEN EXACTLY, COMPLETELY FRANK WITH YOU ABOUT THE ACCIDENT WHERE I LOST MY HAND! IT WAS A BIG EXPLOSION, YOU SEE... PIECES OF METAL FLYING AROUND AND ALL THAT...
ANDREW, WHAT ARE YOU TRYING TO SAY?
5

PIECES OF METAL HIT MY ANKLE, JUST ABOUT TOOK IT OFF! I MADE THIS FOOT--YOU CAN'T REALLY TELL IT FROM THE ORIGINAL!

DID... DID *ANYTHING* ELSE HAPPEN THEN--TELL ME!

WELL, NO, NOTHING HAPPENED THEN! BUT ABOUT A YEAR LATER YOU KNOW, I REALLY AM ABSENT MINDED, I FORGOT A CARBON-ARC WAS ON! TURNED AROUND TOO FAST AND LOST THIS EYE-- BUT THIS GLASS EYE IS JUST AS GOOD AS REAL!

NO... NO...

VERY HOT FLAME HIT THIS SIDE OF MY FACE, BURNED MY HAIR AND SCALP OFF IN A INSTANT! THIS EAR IS QUITE A GOOD JOB, DON'T YOU THINK? I WASN'T OUT OF THE HOSPITAL A WEEK WHEN A POWER RACK COLLAPSED...

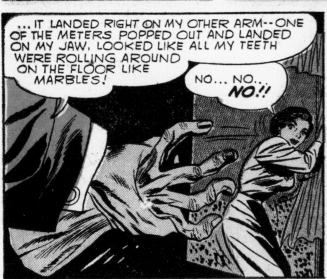

...IT LANDED RIGHT ON MY OTHER ARM--ONE OF THE METERS POPPED OUT AND LANDED ON MY JAW, LOOKED LIKE ALL MY TEETH WERE ROLLING AROUND ON THE FLOOR LIKE MARBLES!

NO... NO.. *NO!!*

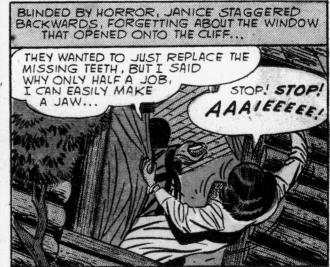

BLINDED BY HORROR, JANICE STAGGERED BACKWARDS, FORGETTING ABOUT THE WINDOW THAT OPENED ONTO THE CLIFF...

THEY WANTED TO JUST REPLACE THE MISSING TEETH, BUT I SAID WHY ONLY HALF A JOB, I CAN EASILY MAKE A JAW...

STOP! *STOP! AAAIEEEEE!*

THE WINDOW FRAME GAVE AND THE TERROR STRIKEN BRIDE PLUNGED TOWARDS THE VALLEY FLOOR...

IT DOESN'T REALLY MATTER WHAT YOU LOSE, WITH A LITTLE IMAGINATION YOU CAN EASILY MAKE A PART THAT WILL DO JUST AS WELL, DID YOU SAY SOMETHING, DEAR?

EEEEEE!

JANICE LAY CRUSHED AND DEAD IN THE VALLEY BELOW, WHILE THE REVOLTING LUMP OF SCARRED FLESH THAT WAS THE ABSENT-MINDED PROFESSOR BEAMISH, SAT ALONE IN THE HONEYMOON CABIN...

DID YOU SAY SOMETHING? OH DEAR, WHERE DID I PUT THAT EAR... I CAN'T SEE IT! I KNEW I SHOULDN'T HAVE TAKEN BOTH MY EYES OUT AT THE SAME TIME, THAT ALWAYS CAUSES ME SO MUCH TROUBLE!

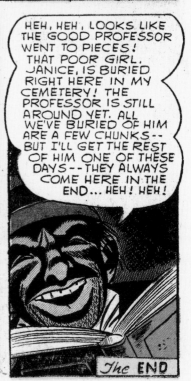

HEH, HEH, LOOKS LIKE THE GOOD PROFESSOR WENT TO PIECES! THAT POOR GIRL, JANICE, IS BURIED RIGHT HERE IN MY CEMETERY! THE PROFESSOR IS STILL AROUND YET. ALL WE'VE BURIED OF HIM ARE A FEW CHUNKS-- BUT I'LL GET THE REST OF HIM ONE OF THESE DAYS-- THEY ALWAYS COME HERE IN THE END... HEH! HEH!

The END

AFTERWORD

Of course, the stories of Black comic creators don't end here. These chosen few were among the first, but not the only. There were certainly others, less prominent or more transient, who had only a glancing impact upon the comic book industry. Sadly, some of them will never be known, a fate shared with many other comic book veterans of any complexion.

Four years of war had altered America. The images of what hatred had wrought were too vivid to overlook. Tattooed numbers on bony arms, gas chambers, charnel house horrors. Daily reminders of man's inhumanity to man.

The hoped-for result of the Double V campaign—victory over the Axis and victory at home over racism—was only half-realized. Racism still existed, but there was more awareness of its poisonous consequences. Changes came, incrementally and often grudgingly, or as a single act of courage. President Truman desegregated the armed forces, Jackie Robinson was called up by the Brooklyn Dodgers, and a group of schoolchildren shamed Fawcett Comics into getting rid of an insulting stereotype.

Thick-lipped, kinky-haired, with ape-like stance and moronic drawl, Steamboat roamed the pages of Captain Marvel *comic books. "Roamed"—past tense—because a group of youngsters representing one of the 157 chapters of Youthbuilders, Inc., persuaded Fawcett Publications to drop the character.*

...a committee called upon William Lieberson, Fawcett Publications' executive editor of comic books. After announcing they liked Captain Marvel, they went on to explain that Steamboat was a Negro stereotype tending to magnify race prejudice.

One boy drew an enlarged portrait of Steamboat and added, "This is not the Negro race, but your one-and-a-half million readers will think it is." That clinched it. Lieberson felt the same way. [Marja, Fern, "Youthbuilders Win an Anti-Bias Victory," *New York Post*, Apr. 24, 1945]

Conscious efforts were made, ever so slowly, to integrate, assimilate, Black America. The Black comic book artists coming into the industry after World War II were finding a nation that no longer could ignore them.

This generation spawned not only Cal Massey, but artists such as Tom Feelings and Warren Broderick, all making contributions to comics of the very late 1940s and well into the 1950s. E. Harper Johnson should be on that list, too, even though there is only one signed, known comic book credit on his résumé. Most definitely there were others. Every one of these artists deserve a further recounting of their lives and work. But not here; this book belongs to the men who came first.

Those men had no clear path before them. As a group, they comprised the first generation of Black creators to work in a new medium. As individuals, they separately broke fresh ground in an industry that, as a consequence of war, had no choice but to employ them. They were, for the most part, working on borrowed time. They knew that their jobs would go back to the White artists who had gone off to war. While a few managed to hang on after the war's end, the majority had to find other means to pay the bills.

Each story was unique: sad, joyful, defeated, triumphant, tragic, blessed, exuberant, reviled, honored, hated, and loved. One thing they shared was that for too long they lingered, out of mind and out of sight of their lighter-skinned peers, evading the scrutiny of historians and the eyes that looked past them, to everyone who saw only their skin color and then saw nothing more. Without body or substance. As if they were invisible.

—Ken Quattro

I hadn't worried too much about whites as people. Some were friendly and some were not, and you tried not to offend either. But here they all seemed impersonal; and yet when most impersonal they startled me by being polite, by begging my pardon after brushing against me in a crowd. Still I felt that even when they were polite they hardly saw me...
—Ralph Ellison, prologue to *Invisible Man*

INDEX

E

F

G

H

I